A History of Advertising from the Earliest Times: Illustrated by Anecdotes, Curious Specimens and Biographical Notes

Henry Sampson

A

HISTORY OF ADVERTISING

From the Earliest Times.

ILLUSTRATED BY ANECDOTES, CURIOUS SPECIMENS, AND BIOGRAPHICAL NOTES.

BY HENRY SAMPSON.

WITH ILLUSTRATIONS AND FACSIMILES.

London:
CHATTO AND WINDUS, PICCADILLY.
1875.

PRINTED BY BALLANTYNE AND COMPANY
EDINBURGH AND LONDON

TO

THE RIGHT HONOURABLE

THOMAS MILNER GIBSON,

IN HUMBLE RECOGNITION OF THE IMPORTANT SERVICES

HE HAS RENDERED TO THE CAUSE OF

ADVERTISING,

AS WELL AS TO JOURNALISM GENERALLY,

This Book

IS RESPECTFULLY DEDICATED,

BY

HIS OBEDIENT SERVANT,

THE AUTHOR.

PREFACE.

IN presenting the following humble attempt at history-writing to the reader, I am selfish enough to admit a preference for his tender mercy rather than for his critical judgment. I would ask him to remember that there are many almost insurmountable difficulties to be faced in the accomplishment of a work like this, and a narrowed space adds to rather than diminishes from their antagonistic power.

When the work was first proposed to me, it was imagined that the subject could be fully disposed of in less than five hundred pages. I have already gone considerably over that number, and feel that the charge of incompleteness may still be brought against the book. But I also feel that if I had extended it to five thousand pages, the charge could still have been made, for with such a subject actual exhaustion cannot be expected; and so, despite the great quantity of unused material I have yet by me, I must rest satisfied with what I have done. I trust the reader will be satisfied also.

Almost everybody has in the course of his lifetime discovered some sort of a pet advertisement without which he considers no collection can be complete. During the progress of this "history" I have received many hundreds such—have received sufficient, with accompanying notes, to fill a bigger volume than this—and I can therefore imagine every fresh reader turning to look for his favourite, and, in the event of his finding it not, condemning the book unconditionally. I hope that in the event of a reconsideration some worthy representative will be found occupying the missing one's place. In like manner, and judging by my own friends' observations, I have found that almost every one would have treated the "history" differently, not only from my way but from each other's. Every one would have done something wonderful with such a wonderful subject. It will not be out of place perhaps, therefore, to ask the reader to think, that because the system adopted has not been that which would have suggested itself to him, it is not necessarily the wrong one after all.

I have received much assistance during the time I have been at work, in the way of hints and observations. For those which I have accepted, as well as for those I have been compelled to reject, I hereby tender my heartfelt thanks. Little in the way of so-called statistics of modern advertisers will be found in the book, as I fancy it is better to be silent than to make untrustworthy statements; and this remark will particularly apply to the amounts of annual outlay generally published in connection with the names of large advertising firms. My own experience is that the firms or their managers are not aware of the exact sums expended by them, or, if they are, do not feel inclined to tell in anything but the vaguest manner. Another observation I have made is, that extensive advertising is likely to result in a desire for the exaggeration of facts—at all events, so far as the individual advertisers themselves are concerned. That any firm, tradesmen, manufacturers, agents, quacks, perfumers, patentees, or whatever they may be, pay a settled annual sum, no more and no less, for advertising, I do not believe now, whatever I may have done before commencing my inquiries.

I have endeavoured as much as possible, and wherever practicable, to make the advertisements tell their own story. At the same time I have tried hard to prevent waste of space, and so far have, if in no other way, succeeded. This is but little merit to claim, and if I am allowed that, I shall be satisfied. Also, if my endeavour should lead to a development of that laudable spirit of emulation so apparent nowadays after the ice has been once broken, I shall be happy to supply any fresh adventurer with copious material which has grown up during the progress of this "history," and which has been omitted only through lack of room. As far as my judgment has allowed me, I have selected what appeared best; other tastes might lead to other results. With this I will take leave of a somewhat unpleasant and apparently egotistical task; and in doing so beg to say that I trust to the reader's kindness, and hope he will overlook the blemishes of a hurried and certainly an unpretentious work, which may, however, be found to contain a little amusement and some amount of information.

H. S.

LONDON, *September* 1874.

CONTENTS.

CHAP.		PAGE
I.	INTRODUCTORY — NEWSPAPERS AND NEWSPAPER ADVERTISING	1
II.	INTRODUCTORY—STREET AND GENERAL ADVERTISING	19
III.	ANCIENT FORMS OF ADVERTISING	33
IV.	MEDIÆVAL AND OTHER VARIETIES OF ADVERTISING	43
V.	NEWSPAPER ADVERTISING FORESHADOWED—ITS EARLIEST USE—HOUGHTON'S LESSONS	61
VI.	DEVELOPMENT OF ADVERTISING	94
VII.	CONCLUSION OF SEVENTEENTH CENTURY	120
VIII.	EARLY PART OF EIGHTEENTH CENTURY	142
IX.	MIDDLE OF EIGHTEENTH CENTURY	176
X.	THE EDUCATION COMPLETED	205
XI.	CURIOUS AND ECCENTRIC ADVERTISEMENTS	240
XII.	SWINDLES AND HOAXES	304
XIII.	THE GREAT BOTTLE-TRICK SWINDLE	365
XIV.	QUACKS AND IMPOSTORS	373

CHAP.		PAGE
XV.	GRAHAM AND HIS CELESTIAL BED . . .	411
XVI.	LOTTERIES AND LOTTERY INSURANCE . . .	422
XVII.	MATRIMONIAL ADVERTISEMENTS AND AGENCIES .	475
XVIII.	HANDBILLS, INSCRIPTIONS, ETC. . . .	510
XIX.	AMERICAN AND COLONIAL ADVERTISEMENTS . .	556
XX.	ADVERSARIA	597

LIST OF FACSIMILES, ETC.

MODERN ADVERTISING: A RAILWAY STATION IN 1874 . . . *Frontispiece*

WEEKELY NEWES FROM ITALY, MAY 23, 1622 . . . *to face page* 4

WALL INSCRIPTIONS IN POMPEII. I. . . . . . ,, 22

AN OLD BILL-STATION . . . . ,, 26

WALL INSCRIPTIONS IN POMPEII. II. . . . . . ,, 38

WALL INSCRIPTIONS IN POMPEII. III. . . . . . ,, 40

"THE BELMAN OF LONDON" . . . . ,, 58

HOLLANDSCHE MERCURIUS, *circa* 1653 . . . . . ,, 64

THE WEEKLY ACCOUNT, JAN. 13, 1646 . . . . . ,, 96

DOMESTICK INTELLIGENCE, OR, NEWS BOTH FROM CITY AND COUNTRY, DEC. 23, 1679 . . . . . . ,, 124

THE TIMES, JAN. 1, 1788—*reduced facsimile of the First Number* . . . . ,, 234

ADVERTISING THE LAST STATE LOTTERY DRAWN IN ENGLAND, 1826 . . . . ,, 464

ONE OF BISH'S LOTTERY ADVERTISEMENTS . . . . ,, 465

THE LAST OF THE LOTTERIES . . . . ,, 470

A

HISTORY OF ADVERTISING.

CHAPTER I.

INTRODUCTORY—NEWSPAPERS AND NEWSPAPER ADVERTISING.

IT must be patent to every one who takes the least interest in the subject, that the study of so important a branch of our present system of commerce as advertising, with its rise and growth, cannot fail to be full of interest. Indeed it is highly suggestive of amusement, as a reference to any of our old newspapers, full as they are of quaint announcements, untrammelled by the squeamishness of the present age, will show. Advertising has, of course, within the last fifty years, developed entirely new courses, and has become an institution differing much from the arrangement in which, so far as our references show, it first appeared in this country; its growth has been attended by an almost entire revulsion of mode, and where we now get long or short announcements by the hundred, dictated by a spirit of business, our fathers received statements couched in a style of pure romance, which fully compensated for their comparatively meagre proportions. Of course, even in the present day, and in the most pure-minded papers, ignorance, intolerance, and cupidity exhibit themselves frequently, often to amusement, but still more often to the annoyance and gust, of thinkers; but in the good old days, when a sp was a spade, and when people did not seek to gloss their weaknesses and frivolities, as they do now, by a tence of virtue and coldness, which, after all, imposes on the weak and credulous, advertisements gave a insight into the life of the people; and so, in the hope our researches will tend to dispel some of the mists w still hang over the sayings and doings of folk who lived to comparatively modern days, we present this work to curious reader.

It is generally assumed—though the assumption has no ground for existence beyond that so common amongst us, that nothing exists of which we are ignorant—that advertisements are of comparatively modern origin. This idea has probably been fostered in the public mind by the fact that so little trouble has ever been taken by encyclopædists to discover anything about them; and as time begets difficulties in research, we are almost driven to regard the first advertisement with which we are acquainted as the actual inaugurator of a system which now has hardly any bounds. That this is wrong will be shown most conclusively, and even so far evidence is given by the statement, made by Smith and others, that advertisements were published in Greece and Rome in reference to the gladiatorial exhibitions, so important a feature of the ancient days of these once great countries. That these advertisements took the form of what is now generally known as "billing," seems most probable, and Rome must have often looked like a modern country town when the advent of a circus or other travelling company is first made known.

The first newspaper supposed to have been published in England appeared in the reign of Queen Elizabeth during the Spanish Armada panic. This journal was called the *English Mercurie*, and was by authority "imprinted at London by

Christopher Barker, Her Highnesses printer, 1583." This paper was said to be started for the prevention of the fulmination of false reports, but it was more like a succession of extraordinary gazettes, and had by no means the appearance of a regular journal, as we understand the term. It was promoted by Burleigh, and used by him to soothe, inform, or exasperate the people as occasion required.* Periodicals and papers really first came into general use during the civil wars in the reign of Charles I., and in the time of the Commonwealth; in fact, each party had its organs, to disseminate sentiments of loyalty, or to foster a spirit of resistance against the inroads of power.† The country was

* This paper seems to have been an imposture, which, believed in at the time, has been comparatively recently detected. A writer in the *Quarterly Review*, June 1855, says, "The *English Mercurie* of 1588 [Qy. 1583], which professes to have been published during those momentous days when the Spanish Armada was hovering and waiting to pounce upon our southern shores, contains amongst its items of news three or four book advertisements, and these would undoubtedly have been the first put forth in England, were that newspaper genuine. Mr Watts, of the British Museum, has, however, proved that the several numbers of this journal to be found in our national library are gross forgeries; and, indeed, the most inexperienced eye in such matters can easily see that neither their type, paper, spelling, nor composition are much more than one instead of upwards of two centuries and a half old." Haydn also says, "Some copies of a publication are in existence called the *English Mercury*, professing to come out under the authority of Queen Elizabeth in 1588, the period of the Spanish Armada. The researches of Mr J. Watts, of the British Museum, have proved these to be forgeries, executed about 1766. The full title of No. 50 is '*The English Mercurie*, published by authoritie, for the prevention of false reports, imprinted by Christopher Barker, Her Highnesses printer, No. 50.' It describes the Spanish Armada, giving 'A journal of what passed since the 21st of this month, between Her Majestie's fleet and that of Spayne, transmitted by the Lord Highe Admiral to the Lordes of Council.'"

† The *Quarterly* mentions a paper which appeared late in the reign of James I.: "The *Weekly News*, published in London in 1622, was the first publication which answered to this description; it contained,

accordingly overflowed with tracts of every size and of various denominations, many of them displaying great courage, and being written with uncommon ability. *Mercury* was the prevailing title, generally qualified with some epithet; and the quaintness peculiar to the age is curiously exemplified in the names of some of the news-books, as they were called: the *Dutch Spye*, the *Scots Dove*, the *Parliament Kite*, the *Screech Owle*, and the *Parliamentary Screech Owle*, being instances in point. The list of *Mercuries* is almost too full for publication. There was *Mercurius Acheronticus*, which brought tidings weekly from the infernal regions; there was *Mercurius Democritus*, whose information was supposed to be derived from the moon; and among other *Mercuries* there was the *Mercurius Mastix*, whose mission was to criticise all its namesakes. It was not, however, until the reign of Queen Anne that a daily paper existed in London—this was the *Daily Courant*, which occupied the field alone for a long period, but which ultimately found two rivals in the *Daily Post* and the *Daily Journal*, the three being simultaneously published in 1724. This state of things continued with very little change during the reign of George I., but publications of every kind increased abundantly during the reign of his successor. The number of newspapers annually sold in England, according to an average of three years ending with 1753, was 7,411,757; in 1760 it amounted to 9,464,790; in 1767 it rose to 11,300,980; in 1790 it was as high as 14,035,636; and in 1792 it amounted to 15,005,760. All this time advertising was a growing art, and advertisements were beginning to make themselves manifest as the main

---

however, only a few scraps of foreign intelligence, and was quite destitute of advertisements." And then, as if to prove what has been already stated by the *Encyclopædia Britannica*, the writer goes on to say, "The terrible contest of the succeeding reign was the hotbed which forced the press of this country into sudden life and extraordinary vigour."

The 23. of May.

VVEEKELY Nevves from Italy, GERMANIE, HVNGARIA, BOHEMIA, the PALATINATE, France, and the Low Countries.

Translated out of the Low Dutch Copie.

LONDON,
Printed by *I. D.* for *Nicholas Bourne* and *Thomas Archer*, and are to be sold at their shops at the *Exchange*, and in *Popes-head Pallace*.
1622.

support and chief source of profit of newspapers, as well as the most natural channel of communication between the buyers and sellers, the needing and supplying members of a vast community.

The victories of Cromwell gave Scotland her first newspaper. This was called the *Mercurius Politicus*, and appeared at Leith in October 1653; but it was in November 1654 transferred to Edinburgh, where it was continued until the 11th April 1660, when it was rechristened, and appeared as the *Mercurius Publicus.* This paper was but a reprint, for the information of the English soldiers, of a London publication. But a newspaper of native manufacture, we are told by a contemporary writer, soon made its appearance under the title of *Mercurius Caledonius.* The first number of this was published at Edinburgh on the 31st December 1660, and comprised, as its title sets forth, "the affairs in agitation in Scotland, with a summary of foreign intelligence." The publication, however, extended to no more than ten numbers, which, it is said by Chambers, "were very loyal, very illiterate, and very affected." After the Revolution the custom was still to reprint in Scotland the papers published in London, an economic way of doing business, which savours much of the proverbial thrift peculiar to the Land o' Cakes. In February 1699 the *Edinburgh Gazette*, the first original Scotch newspaper or periodical, was published by James Watson, author of a "History of Printing;" but he, after producing forty numbers, transferred it to a Mr John Reid, whose son continued to print the paper till even after the Union. In February 1705, Watson, who seems to have been what would now be called a promoter of newspapers, established the *Edinburgh Courant*, but relinquished it after the publication of fifty-five numbers, and in September 1706 commenced the *Scots Courant*, with which he remained connected until about 1718. To these papers were added in October 1708 the *Edinburgh Flying Post;* in

August 1709 the *Scots Postman*, "printed by David Fearne for John Moncur;" and in March 1710 the *North Tatler*, "printed by John Reid for Samuel Colvil." In 1715 the foundation was laid of the present splendid Glasgow press by the establishment of the *Courant*, but this did not in any way affect the publications in the then far more important town of Edinburgh. In March 1714 Robert Brown commenced the *Edinburgh Gazette* or *Scots Postman*, which was published twice a week; and in December 1718 the Town Council gave an exclusive privilege to James M'Ewen to publish three times a week the *Edinburgh Evening Courant*, upon condition, however, that before publication "the said James should give ane coppie of his print to the magistrates." This journal is still published, and it is but fair to assume that the original stipulation is yet complied with. The *Caledonian Mercury* followed the *Courant* on the 28th of April 1720, and was, like its forerunner, a tri-weekly organ. In these, as well as in those we have mentioned, advertisements slowly but gradually and surely began to make their appearance, and, as the sequel proves, to show their value.

It is stated by several writers that the earliest English provincial newspaper is believed to be the *Norwich Postman*, which was published in 1706 at the price of a penny, and which bore the quaint statement, that a halfpenny would not be refused. Newspaper proprietors, publishers, and editors were then evidently, so far as Norwich is concerned, less strong than they are now in their own conceit, and in their belief in the press as an organ of great power This *Postman* was followed in 1714 by the *Norwich Courant* or *Weekly Packet*. York and Leeds followed in 1720, Manchester in 1730, and Oxford in 1740. It was not, however, until advertising became an important branch of commercial speculation that the provincial press began in any way to flourish. Now the journals published in our largest country towns command extensive circulations, and are regarded by many advertising agents, whose opinions are fairly worth taking, as being much more remunerative media than our best London papers. For certain purposes, and under certain circumstances, the same may be said of colonial newspapers, which have, of course, grown up with the colonies in which they are published; for it must be always borne in mind that the essence of advertising is to place your statement where it is most likely to be seen by those most interested in it, and so a newspaper with a very limited supply of readers indeed is often more valuable to the advertiser of peculiar wares or wants than one with "the largest circulation in the world," if that circulation does not reach the class of readers most affected by those who pay for publicity. It would seem, however, that the largest class of advertisers, the general public, who employ no agents, and who consider a large sale everything that is necessary, ignore the argument of the true expert, and lose sight of the fact that, no matter how extensive a circulation may be, it is intrinsically useless unless flowing through the channel which is fairly likely to effect the purpose for which the advertisement is inserted. It is customary to see a sheet, detached from the paper with which it is issued, full of advertisements, which are, of course, unread by all but those who are professedly readers of public announcements, and who are also, of course, not only in a decided minority, but not at all the people to whom the notices are generally directed. The smallest modicum of thought will show how grievous is the error which leads to such a result, and how much better it is to regard actual circulation but as so much evidence as to the value of an advertisement only, and not as a whole, sole, and complete qualification. Not in any incautious way do those who are most qualified to judge of value for money act. Turn to any paper of repute, and it will be seen that the professional advertiser, the theatrical manager, the publisher, the auctioneer, and the others whom constant practice has made wary, lay out their money on quite a different principle from that of the casual advertiser. They have learned their lesson, and if they pay extra for position or insertion, they know that their outlay is remunerative; whereas, if it were not governed by caution and system, it would be simply ruinous. In fact, advertising is a most expensive luxury if not properly regulated, and a most valuable adjunct when coolness and calculation are brought to bear upon it as accessories.

The heavy duties originally imposed upon newspapers, both on them and their advertisements, were at first a considerable check to the number of notices appearing in them. For, in the first place, the high price of the papers narrowed the limits of their application; and, in the second, the extra charge on the advertisements made them above the reach of almost all but those who were themselves possessed of means, or whose business it was to pander to the unholy and libidinous desires of the wealthy. This, we fancy, will be extensively proved by a reference to the following pages; for while it is our endeavour to keep from this book all really objectionable items, we are desirous that it shall place before the reader a true picture of the times in which the advertisements appeared; and we are not to be checked in our duty by any false delicacy, or turned from the true course by any squeamishness, which, unfortunately for us in these days, but encourages the vices it attempts to ignore.

The stamp duty on newspapers was first imposed in 1713, and was one halfpenny for half a sheet or less, and one penny "if larger than half a sheet and not exceeding a whole sheet." This duty was increased a halfpenny by an Act of Parliament, 30 Geo. II. c. 19; and by another Act, 16 Geo. III. c. 34, another halfpenny was added to the tax. This not being considered sufficient, a further addition of a halfpenny was made (29 Geo. III. c. 50), and in the thirty-seventh year of the same wise monarch's reign (c. 90) three-halfpence more was all at once placed to the debit of newspaper readers, which brought the sum total of the duty up to fourpence. An Act of 6 & 7 Will. IV. c. 76 reduced this duty to one penny, with the proviso, however, that when the sheet contained 1550 superficial inches on either side, an extra halfpenny was to be paid, and when it contained 2295, an extra penny. An additional halfpenny was also charged on a supplement, which may be regarded, when the use of supplements in the present day is taken into consideration, as an indirect tax on advertisements. In 1855, by an Act 18 & 19 Vict. c. 27, this stamp duty was abolished, and immediately an immense number of newspapers started into existence, most of which, however, obtained but a most ephemeral being, and died away, leaving no sign. There are, however, a large number of good and useful papers still flourishing, which would never have been published but for the repeal of the newspaper stamp duty. To such repeal many rich men owe their prosperity, while to the same source may now be ascribed the poverty of numbers who were once affluent. At this time, of course, the old papers also reduced their rates, and from thence has grown a system of newspaper reading and advertising which twenty years ago could hardly have been imagined. Up to the repeal of the stamp duty few people bought newspapers for themselves, and many newsvendors' chief duty was to lend the *Times* out for a penny per hour, while a second or third day's newspaper was considered quite a luxury by those whom business or habit compelled to stay at home, and therefore who were unable to glance over the news—generally while some impatient person was scowlingly waiting his turn—at the tavern bar or the coffee-house. Now almost every one buys a penny paper for himself, and with the increase in the circulation of newspapers has, in proportionate ratio, gone on the increase in the demand for advertisements. The supply has, as every one knows, been in no way short of the demand. The repeal of the paper duty in 1861 also affected newspapers much, though naturally in a smaller degree than the abolition of the compulsory stamp. Still the effect on both the papers and their advertisements—especially as concerns those journals which were enabled to still farther reduce their rates—was considerable, and deserves to be noted. In September 1870 the compulsory stamp, which had been retained for postal purposes, was abolished, and on the 1st of October papers were first sent by post with a halfpenny stamp affixed on the wrappers, and not on the journals themselves.

But it was to the abolition of the impost upon advertisements that their present great demand and importance can be most directly traced. For many years a very heavy tax was charged upon every notice published in a paper and paid for, until 1833 no less than 3s. 6d. being chargeable upon each advertisement inserted, no matter what its length or subject-matter. People then, we should imagine—in fact, as application to the papers of that time proves—were not so fond of cutting a long advertisement into short and separate pieces as they are now, for every cut-off rule then meant a charge of 3s. 6d. In 1832, the last year of this charge, the produce of this branch of the revenue in Great Britain and Ireland amounted to £170,649. Fancy what the returns would be if 3s. 6d. were charged on every advertisement published throughout the United Kingdom for the year ending December 31, 1873! It seems almost too great a sum for calculation. There is no doubt, however, that many people would be very glad to do the figures for a very slight percentage on the returns, which would be fabulous, and which would, if properly calculated, amaze many of those *laudatores temporis acti* who, without reason or provocation, are always deploring the decay of everything, and who would unhesitatingly affirm in their ignorance that even newspapers and newspaper advertisements have deteriorated in tone and quantity since the good old times, of which they prove they know nothing by their persistent praises. Certainly if they did say this, they would not be much more wrong than they are generally when lamenting over a period which, could it but return, they would be, as a rule, the very first to object to. Of the sum of £170,649 just referred to, about £127,986, or three-fourths of the whole, may be regarded as being drawn from newspapers, and the other fourth from periodical publications. In 1837, four years after the reduced charge of 1s. 6d. for each advertisement had become law, a table was compiled from the detailed returns of the first six months. As it will doubtless prove interesting to those who take an interest in the growth and increase of newspapers, as well as in those of advertisements, we append it:—

	No. of Papers.	No. of Stamps.	No. of Advertisements.	Amount of Advertisement Duty.		
London Papers, ...	93	15,100,197	292,033	£21,902	9	6
English Provincial Papers,	217	7,290,452	317,474	23,810	11	0
Welsh Papers, ...	10	190,955	6,499	487	6	6
Edinburgh Papers,.........	13	768,071	20,579	1,543	9	6
Scotch Provincial Papers,	46	1,121,658	45,371	3,402	16	8
Dublin Papers, ...	21	1,493,838	45,848	2,292	8	0
Irish Provincial Papers,...	60	1,049,358	41,284	2,064	4	0
Total in Great Britain and Ireland, ...	460	27,014,529	769,088	£55,503	5	2

The reduction to which we have alluded was followed in 1853 by the total abolition of the advertisement duty, the effect of which can be best appreciated by a glance at the columns of any daily or weekly paper, class or general, which possesses a good circulation.

The first paper published in Ireland was a sheet called *Warranted Tidings from Ireland*, and this appeared during the rebellion of 1641; but the first Irish newspaper worthy of the name was the *Dublin Newsletter*, commenced in 1685. *Pue's Occurrences*, a Dublin daily paper, originated in 1700, was continued for half a century, and was followed in 1728 by another daily paper, *Faulkner's Journal*, established by one George Faulkner, "a man celebrated for the goodness of his heart and the weakness of his head." The oldest existing Dublin papers are *Saunders's* (originally *Esdaile's*) *Newsletter*, begun in 1744, and the *Freeman's Journal*, instituted under the title of the *Public Register*, by Dr Lucas in 1755. The *Limerick Chronicle*, the oldest Irish provincial newspaper, dates from 1768. Ireland has now nearly 150 newspapers, most of them celebrated for the energy of their language and the extreme fervour of their political opinions. Their Conservatism and Liberalism are nearly equally divided; about a score take independent views, and nearly fifty completely eschew politics. Irish newspapers flourish as vehicles for advertisement, and their tariffs are about on a par with those of our leading provincial journals.

Colonial newspapers are plentiful and good, and the best of them filled with advertisements of a general character at fairly high rates. Those papers published in Melbourne are perhaps the best specimens of colonial journalism, and best among these are the *Argus* and *Age* (daily), and the *Australasian* and *Leader* (weekly). In fact, we have hardly a weekly paper in London that is fit to compare on all-round merits with the last-named, which is a complete representative of the best class of Australian life, and contains a great show of advertisements, which do much to enlighten the reader as to Antipodean manners and customs.

American newspapers are of course plentiful, and their advertisements, as will be shown during the progress of this volume, are often of an almost unique character. Throughout the United States, newspapers start up like rockets, to fall like sticks; but now and then a success is made, and if once Fortune is secured by an adventurous speculator, she is rarely indeed allowed to escape. The system of work on American (U.S.) journals is very different from that pursued here, everything on such establishments as those of the *New York Herald*, the *Tribune*, and the *Times*, being sacrificed to news. This is more particularly the case with regard to the *Herald*, which has an immense circulation and great numbers of highly-priced advertisements, most of which are unfortunately regarded more in connection with the amount of money they produce to the proprietor than in reference to any effect, moral or otherwise, they may have on the community. It is the boast of American journalists that they have papers in obscure towns many hundreds of miles inland, any one of which contains in a single issue as much news—news in the strictest meaning of the word—as the London *Times* does in six. And, singular as it may at first sight seem, there is a great element of truth about the statement, the telegraph being used in the States with a liberality which would drive an English proprietor to the depths of black despair. The Associated Telegraph Company seem to enjoy a monopoly, and to exercise almost unlimited powers; and not long ago they almost completely ruined a journal of standing in California by refusing to transmit intelligence to it because its editor and proprietor had taken exception to the acts of some members of the Associated Telegraph Company's staff, and it was only on receipt of a most abject apology from the delinquents that the most autocratic power in the States decided to reinstate the paper on its list. This Telegraph Company charges very high rates, and the only visible means by which this system of journalism is successfully carried out is that of advertisements, which are comparatively more plentiful in these papers than in the English, and are charged for at considerably higher rates. Some of these newspapers, notably a small hebdomadal called the *San Francisco Newsletter*, go in for a deliberate system of blackmailing, and have no hesitation in acknowledging that their pages, not the advertisement portions, but their editorial columns, are to be bought for any purpose—for the promotion of blasphemy, obscenity, atheism, or any other "notion"—at a price which is regulated according to the editor's opinion of the former's value, or the amount of money he may have in his pocket at the time. This is a system of advertising little known, happily, in this "effete old country," where we have not yet learned to sacrifice all that should be dear and honourable to humanity—openly, at all events—for a money consideration. It is almost impossible to tell the number of papers published throughout the United States of America, each individual State being hardly aware of the quantity it contains, or how many have been born and died within the current twelvemonths. The Americans are a truly great people, but they have not yet settled down into a regular system, so far, at all events, as newspapers and advertisements are concerned.*

The first paper published in America is said to have been the *Boston Newsletter*, which made its appearance in 1704. The inhabitants of the United States have ever been wide-awake to the advantages of advertising, but it would seem that the Empire City is not, as is generally supposed here, first in rank, so far as the speculative powers of its denizens go, if we are to believe the New Orleans correspondent of the *New York Tribune*, who says in one of his letters:—

* In 1830 America (U.S.), whose population was 23,500,000, supported 800 newspapers, 50 of these being daily; and the conjoined annual circulation was 64,000,000. Fifteen years later these figures were considerably increased—nearly doubled; but since the development of the Pacific States it has been almost impossible to tell the number of papers which have sprung into existence, every mining camp and every village being possessed of its organ, some of which have died, and some of which are still flourishing. A professed and apparently competent critic assures us that there are quite 3000 newspapers now in the States, and that at least a tithe of them are dailies.

"The merchants of New Orleans are far more liberal in advertising than those of your city, and it is they alone which support most of our papers. One firm in this city, in the drug business, expends 20,000 dollars a year in job printing, and 30,000 dollars in advertising. A clothing firm has expended 50,000 dollars in advertising in six months. Both establishments are now enjoying the lion's share of patronage, and are determined to continue such profits and investments. A corn doctor is advertising at over 10,000 dollars a month, and the proprietor of a 'corner grocery' on the outskirts of the city has found it advantageous to advertise to the extent of 7000 dollars during the past winter."

In London the *Times* and *Telegraph* absorb the lion's share of the advertiser's money. The former, the leading journal of the day, of independent politics and magnificent proportions, stands forth first, and, to use a sporting phrase, has no second, so far is it in front of all others as regards advertisements, as well as on other grounds. An average number of the *Times* contains about 2500 advertisements, counting between every cut-off rule; and the receipts in the advertisement department are said to be about £1000 a day, or 8s. each. A number of the *Daily Telegraph* in December 1873 contains 1444 advertisements (also counting between every cut-off rule), and these may fairly be calculated to produce £500 or thereabouts, the tariff being throughout little less than that of the *Times;* for what it lacks in power and influence the *Telegraph* is supposed to make up in circulation. This is rather a change for the organ of Peterborough Court, which little more than eighteen years ago was started with good advertisements to the extent of *seven shillings and sixpence.* The *Telegraph* proprietors do not, however, get all the profit out of the advertisements, for in its early and struggling days they were glad, naturally, to close with advertisement agents, who agreed to take so many columns a day at the then trade price, and who now have a vast deal the best of the bargain. To such lucky accidents, which occur often in the newspaper world, are due the happy positions of some men, who live upon the profits accruing from their columns, and ride in neat broughams, oblivious of the days when they went canvassing afoot, and have almost brought themselves to the belief that they are gentlemen, and always were such. This must be the only bitter drop in the cup of the otherwise happy possessors of the *Telegraph*, which is at once a mine of wealth to them, and an instrument by which they become quite a power in the state. They can, however, well afford the lucky advertisement-agents their profits, and, looking back, may rest satisfied that things are as they are.

But there are many daily papers in London besides the *Times* and *Telegraph*, and all these receive a plentiful share of advertisements. The *Standard* has, within the past few years, developed its resources wonderfully, and may be now considered a good fair third in the race for wealth, and not by any means a distant third, so far as the *Telegraph* is concerned. This paper has a most extensive circulation, being the only cheap Conservative organ in London, if we may except the *Hour*, and as it offers to advertisers a repetition of their notices in the *Evening Standard*, it is not surprising that, spacious as are its advertisement columns, it manages to fill them constantly, and at a rate which would have considerably astonished its old proprietors. The *Daily News*, which a few years back reduced its price to one penny, has, since the Franco-Prussian war, been picking up wonderfully, and with its increased health as a paper its outer columns have proportionally improved in appearance; many experienced advertisers have a great regard for the *News*, which they look upon as offering a good return for investments. The *Morning Advertiser*, as the organ of the licensed victuallers, is of course an invaluable medium of inter-communication among members of "the trade," and in it are to be found advertisements of everything to be obtained in connection with the distillery, the brewery, and the tavern. Publicans who want potboys, and potboys who want employers, barmaids, barmen, and people in want of "snug" businesses, or with "good family trades" to dispose of, all consult the '*Tiser*, which is under the special supervision of a committee of licensed victuallers, who act as stewards, and annually hand over the profits to the Licensed Victuallers' School. An important body is this committee, a body which feels that the eye of Europe is upon it, and which therefore takes copious notes of everything; is broad wideawake, and is not to be imposed on. But it is a kindly and beneficent body, as its purpose shows; and a little licence can well be afforded to a committee which gives its time and trouble, to say nothing of voting its money, in the interest of the widow and the fatherless. A few years back great fun used to be got out of the '*Tiser*, or the "Gin and Gospel Gazette," as it was called, on account of its peculiar views on current questions; but all that is altered now, and since the advent of the present régime the *Advertiser* has improved sufficiently to be regarded as a general paper, and therefore as a general advertising medium. The *Hour* is a new journal, started in opposition to the *Standard*, and professing the same politics. It is hardly within our ken so far, and the same may be said of the *Morning Post*, which has its own exclusive *clientèle*. In referring to the foregoing journals, we have made no remarks beyond those to which we are guided by their own published statements, and we have intended nothing invidious in the order of selection. For obvious reasons we shall say nothing of the evening papers, beyond that all seem to fill their advertisement columns with ease, and to be excellent mediums of publicity.

The weekly press and the provincial press can tell their own story without assistance. In the former the advertisements are fairly classed, according to the pretensions of the papers or the cause they adopt, while with the provincials it is the story of the London dailies told over again. Manchester and Liverpool possess magnificent journals, full of advertisements and of large circulation, and so do all other large towns in the country; but we doubt much if, out of London, Glasgow is to be beaten on the score of its papers or the energy of its advertisers.

CHAPTER II.

INTRODUCTORY—STREET AND GENERAL ADVERTISING.

IT seems indeed singular that we are obliged to regard advertising as a comparatively modern institution; for, as will be shown in the progress of this work, the first advertisement which can be depended upon as being what it appears to be was, so far as can be discovered, published not much more than two hundred years ago. But though we cannot find any instances of business notices appearing in papers before the middle of the seventeenth century, mainly because there were not, so far as our knowledge goes, papers in which to advertise, there is little doubt that the desire among tradesmen and merchants to make good their wares has had an existence almost as long as the customs of buying and selling, and it is but natural to suppose that advertisements in some shape or form have existed not only from time immemorial, but almost for all time. Signs over shops and stalls seem naturally to have been the first efforts in the direction of advertisements, and they go back to the remotest portions of the world's history. Public notices also were posted about in the first days of the children of Israel, the utterances of the kings and prophets being inscribed on parchments and exposed in the high places of the cities. It was also customary, early in the Christian era, for a scroll to be exhibited when any of the Passion or other sacred plays were about to be performed, and comparatively recently we have received positive intelligence that in Pompeii and similar places advertising by means of signs and inscriptions was quite common. The "History of Signboards," a very exhaustive and valuable book, quotes Aristotle, and refers to Lucian, Aristophanes, and others, in proof of the fact that signboard advertisements were used in ancient Greece, but the information is extremely vague. Of the Romans, however, more is known. Some streets were with them known by means of signs. The book referred to tells us that the bush, the Romans' tavern sign, gave rise to the proverb, "Vino vendibili suspensa hedera non opus est;" and hence we derive our own sign of the bush, and our proverb, "Good wine needs no bush." An *ansa* or handle of a pitcher was then the sign of a pothouse, and hence establishments of this kind were afterwards denominated *ansæ*.

A correspondent writing to *Notes and Queries*, in answer to a question in reference to early advertising, says that the mode adopted by the Hebrews appears to have been chiefly by word of mouth, not by writing. Hence the Hebrew word *kara* signifies to cry aloud, and to announce or make known publicly (κηρύσσειν); and the announcement or proclamation, as a matter of course, was usually made in the streets and chief places of concourse. The matters thus proclaimed were chiefly of a sacred kind, as might be expected under a theocracy; and we have no evidence that secular affairs were made the subject of similar announcements. In one instance, indeed (Isa. xiii. 3), *kara* has been supposed to signify the calling out of troops; but this may be doubted. The Greeks came a step nearer to our idea of advertising, for they made their public announcements by writing as well as orally. For announcement by word of mouth they had their κήρυξ, who, with various offices besides, combined that of public crier. His duties as crier appear to have been restricted, with few exceptions, to state announcements and to great occasions. He gave notice, however, of sales. For the publication of their laws the Greeks employed various kinds of tablets, πίνακες, ἄξονες, κύρβεις. On these the laws were written, to be displayed for public inspection. The Romans largely advertised private as well as public matters, and by writing as well as by word of mouth. They had their *præcones*, or criers, who not only had their public duties, but announced the times, places, and conditions of sales, and cried things lost. Hawkers cried their own goods. Thus Cicero speaks of one who cried figs, *Cauneas clamitabat* (De Divin. ii. 40). But the Romans also advertised, in a stricter sense of the term, by writing. The bills were called *libelli*, and were used for advertising sales of estates, for absconded debtors, and for things lost or found. The advertisements were often written on tablets (*tabellæ*), which were affixed to pillars (*pilæ columnæ*). On the walls of Pompeii have been discovered various advertisements. There will be a dedication or formal opening of certain baths. The company attending are promised slaughter of wild beasts, athletic games, perfumed sprinkling, and awnings to keep off the sun (*venatia, athletæ, sparsiones, vela*).* One other mode of public announcement employed by the Romans should be mentioned, and that was by signs suspended or painted on the wall. Thus a suspended shield served as the sign of a tavern (Quintil. vi. 3), and nuisances were prohibited by the painting of two sacred serpents. Among the French, advertising appears to have become very general towards the close of the sixteenth century. In particular, placards attacking private character had, in consequence of the religious wars, become so numerous and outrageous, that subsequently, in 1652, the Government found it necessary to interpose for their repression.†

Speaking of the signs of Herculaneum and Pompeii, the

* The opening notice of the baths at Pompeii was almost perfect when discovered, and originally read thus:—"Dedicatone . Thermarum . Muneris . Cnæi . Allei . Nigidii . Maii . Venalio . Athelæ . Sparsiones . Vela . Erunt . Maio . Principi . Coloniæ . Feliciter."

† *Notes and Queries*, vol. xi., 3d series.

"History of Signboards" says that a few were painted, but, as a rule, they appear to have been made of stone, or terra cotta relievo, and set into the pilasters at the sides of the open shop fronts. Thus there have been found a goat, the sign of a dairy, and a mule driving a mill, the sign of a baker. At the door of a school was the highly suggestive and not particularly pleasant sign to pupils of a boy being birched. Like to our own signs of two brewers carrying a tun slung on a pole, a Pompeian publican had two slaves represented above his door carrying an amphora, and another dispenser of drink had a painting of Bacchus pressing a bunch of grapes. At a perfumer's shop in the street of Mercury were represented various items of that profession, notably four men carrying a box with vases of perfume, and men laying out and perfuming a corpse. There was also a sign of the Two Gladiators, under which, in the usual Pompeian cacography, was the following:—"Abiam venerem Pompeiianama iradam qui hoc læserit." Besides these were the signs of the Anchor, the Ship (possibly a ship-chandler's), a sort of a Cross, the Chequers, the Phallus on a baker's shop, with the words, "Hic habitat felicitas;" whilst in Herculaneum there was a very cleverly painted Amorino, or Cupid, carrying a pair of lady's shoes, one on his head and the other in his hand. It is also probable that the various artificers of Rome used their tools as signs over their workshops and residences, as it is found that they were sculptured on their tombs in the catacombs. On the tombstone of Diogenes, the grave-digger, there is a pickaxe and a lamp; Banto and Maxima have the tools of carpenters, a saw, an adze, and a chisel; Veneria, a tire-woman, has a mirror and a comb. There are others with wool-combers' implements; a physician has a cupping-glass; a poulterer, a case of fowls; a surveyor, a measuring rule; a baker, a bushel measure, a millstone, and some ears of corn; and other signs are numerous on the graves of the departed. Even the modern custom of

1\. LISTACIDIATOVEM NON CENO BARBARVS ILLE MIHI EST — IVSIVS

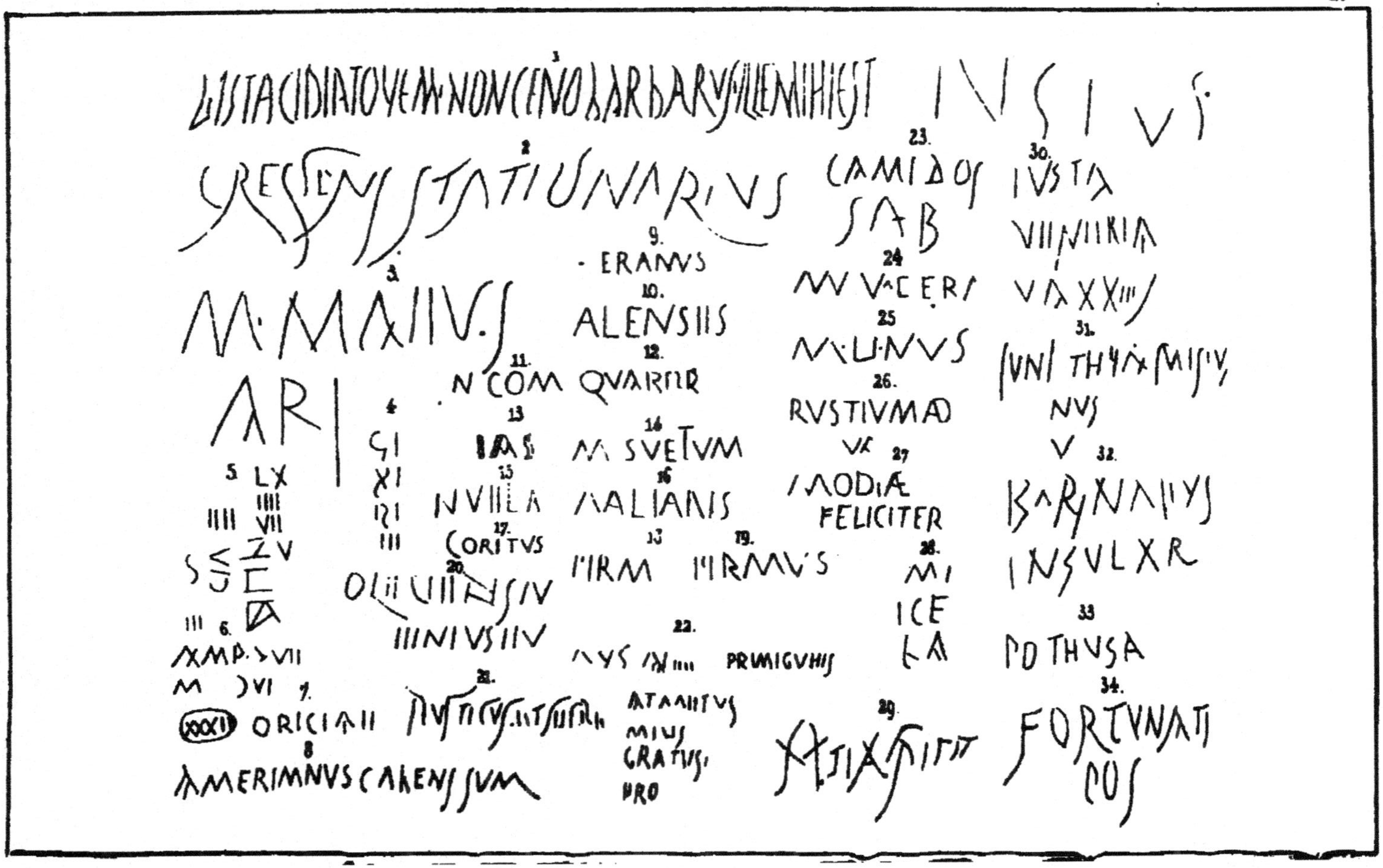

2\. CRESCENS STATIONARIVS

3\. M·MAIIVS

ARI

4\. GI XI RI III

5\. LX IIII VII IIII SIV

6\. III XMP·SVII M DVI

7\. XXXII ORICIAII

8\. AMERIMNVS CARENS SVM

9\. ·ERANVS

10\. ALENSIIS

11\. N COM

12\. QVARTIR

13\. BAS

14\. M SVETVM

15\. NVIILA

16\. MALIANIS

17\. CORITVS

18\. FIRM

19\. FIRMVS

20\. OLIIVIIINSIV IIINIVSIIV

21\. RVSTICVS

22\. NVS IN IIII PRIMIGVHIS ATANIITVS MIVS GRATVS PRO

23\. CAMIDOS SAB

24\. M VACERI

25\. M·LINVS

26\. RVSTIVMAD VX

27\. MODIAE FELICITER

28\. MI ICE LA

29\. ASIASIIII

30\. IVSTA VIINIIRIA VAXXIII

31\. IVNI THYAMISIV NVS V

32\. BARNAIIVS INSVLXR

33\. POTHVSA

34\. FORTVNATI POS

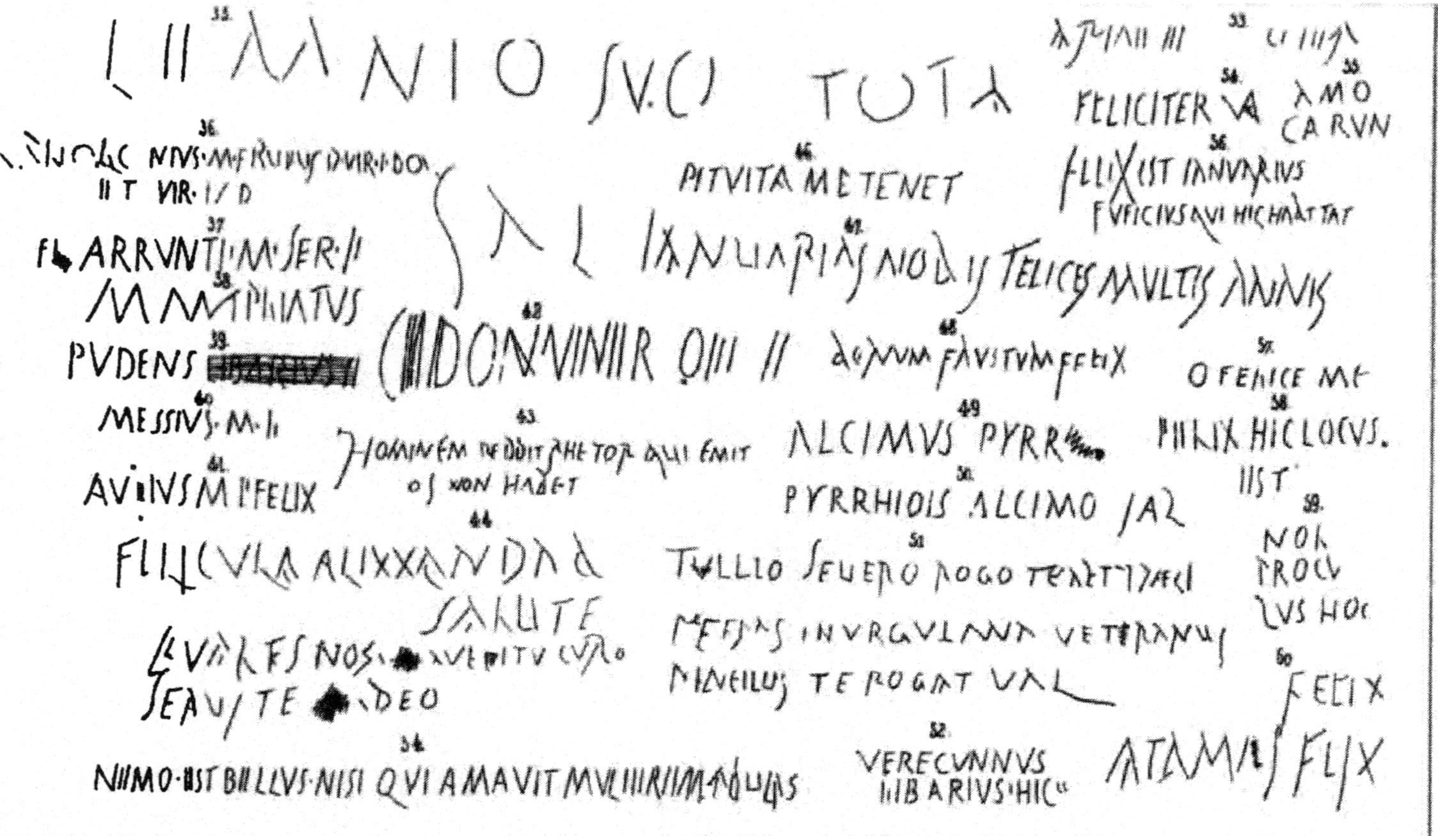

WALL INSCRIPTIONS IN POMPEII.—*Signor Raphael Garrucci, to whom we are indebted for these Plates, in commenting upon Group 5 (LX., IIII., IIII., VI., ZV., E., ΓΑ., III., S., CIA.), says, "I will now give my opinion upon this strange combination of Greek and Roman signs—it seems to me a custom introduced even at Rome since the epoch of Augustus, to mingle the Greek numeral elements with Latin signs."*

punning on the name, so common on signboards, finds its precedent on these stones. The grave of Dracontius was embellished with a dragon, that of Onager with a wild ass, and that of Umbricius with a shady tree. Leo's grave received a lion; Doleus, father and son, two casks; Herbacia, two baskets of herbs; and Porcula, a pig. It requires, therefore, but the least possible imagination to see that all these symbols and advertisements were by no means confined to the use of the dead, but were extensively used in the interests of the living.

Street advertising, in its most original form among us, was therefore without doubt derived from the Romans; and this system gradually grew, until, in the Middle Ages, there was hardly a house of business without its distinctive sign or advertisement; which was the more necessary, as in those days numbers to houses were unknown. "In the Middle Ages the houses of the nobility, both in town and country, when the family was absent, were used as hostelries for travellers. The family arms always hung in front of the house, and the most conspicuous object in those arms gave a name to the establishment amongst travellers, who, unacquainted with the mysteries of heraldry, called a lion gules or azure by the vernacular name of the Red or Blue Lion. Such coats of arms gradually became a very popular intimation that there was—

> Good entertainment for all that passes—
> Horses, mares, men, and asses.

And innkeepers began to adopt them, hanging out red lions and green dragons as the best way to acquaint the public that they offered food and shelter. Still, as long as civilisation was only at a low ebb, the so-called open houses few, and competition trifling, signs were of but little use. A few objects, typical of the trade carried on, would suffice; a knife for the cutler, a stocking for the hosier, a hand for the glover, a pair of scissors for the tailor, a bunch of grapes for the vintner, fully answered public requirements.

But as luxury increased, and the number of houses or shops dealing in the same article multiplied, something more was wanted. Particular trades continued to be confined to particular streets; the desideratum then was to give to each shop a name or token by which it might be mentioned in conversation, so that it could be recommended and customers sent to it. Reading was still a scarce acquirement, consequently to write up the owner's name would have been of little use. Those that could advertised their name by a rebus—thus, a hare and a bottle stood for Harebottle, and two cocks for Cox. Others, whose names could represent, adopted pictorial objects; and as the quantity of these augmented, new subjects were continually required. The animal kingdom was ransacked, from the mighty elephant to the humble bee, from the eagle to the sparrow; the vegetable kingdom, from the palm-tree and cedar to the marigold and daisy; everything on the earth and in the firmament above it was put under contribution. Portraits of the great men of all ages, and views of towns, both painted with a great deal more of fancy than of truth; articles of dress, implements of trades, domestic utensils, things visible and invisible, 'Ea quæ sunt tanquam ea quæ non sunt,' everything was attempted in order to attract attention and to obtain publicity. Finally, as all signs in a town were painted by the same small number of individuals, whose talents and imagination were limited, it followed that the same subjects were often repeated, introducing only a change in the colour for a difference." *

From the foregoing can be traced the gradual growth of street advertising until it has reached its present extensive pitch; and though the process may be characterised as slow, no one who looks around at the well-covered hoardings and the be-plastered signs on detached and prominent

* "History of Signboards."

houses can doubt that it is sure. Proclamations, and suchlike official announcements, were probably the first specimens of street advertising, as we now understand the term; but it was not until printing became general, and until the people became conversant with the mysteries of reading and writing, that posters and handbills were to any extent used. Mention is made in 1679 of a tradesman named Jonathan Holder, haberdasher, of the city of London, who gave to every purchaser to the extent of a guinea a printed list of the articles kept in stock by him, with the prices affixed. The paper in which this item of news was recorded seems to have regarded Mr Holder's practice as a dangerous innovation, and remarks that it would be quite destructive to trade if shopkeepers lavished so much of their capital in printing useless bills. This utterance now seems ridiculous; but in the course of another two centuries many orthodox opinions of the present day will receive as complete a downfall as that just recorded.

Within the recollections of men who are still young street advertising has considerably changed. Twenty years ago the billsticker was a nuisance of the most intolerable kind, and though we can hardly now consider him a blessing, his habits have changed very much for the better. Never heeding the constant announcement to him to beware, the billsticker cared nothing for the privacy of dead walls, or, for the matter of that, of dwelling-houses and street doors; and though he was hardly ever himself to be seen, his disfigurative work was a prominent feature of the metropolis. It was also considered by him a point of honour—if the term may be used in connection with billstickers—to paste over the work of a rival; and so the hoardings used to present the most heterogeneous possible appearance, and though bills were plentiful, their intelligibility was of a very limited description. Sunday morning early used to be a busy time with the wandering billsticker. Provided with a light cart and an assistant, he would make a raid on a whole district, sticking his notices and disappearing with marvellous rapidity. And how he would chuckle as he drove away, more especially if, in addition to disfiguring a private wall, he had succeeded in covering over the handiwork of a rival! For this reason the artful billsticker used to select a time when it was still early enough to evade detection, and yet late enough to deface the work of those who had gone before him. Billsticking was thus an art attended with some difficulties; and it was not until the advent of contractors, like Willing, Partington, and others, that any positive publicity could be depended upon in connection with posting.

Yet, in the days of which we have just been speaking, the man of paste considered himself a very important personage; and it is not so very long since one individual published himself under the style and title of "Champion Billposter," and as such defied all comers. It was for some time doubtful whether his claims depended upon his ability to beat and thrash all rivals at fisticuffs, whether he was able to stick more bills in a given time than any other man, or whether he had a larger and more important connection than usually fell to the poster's lot; in fact, the question has never been settled, for exception having been taken to his assumption of the title of champion from any point of view, and reference having been made to the editors of sporting papers, the ambitious one gracefully withdrew his pretensions, and the matter subsided. A generation ago one of the most popular songs of the day commenced something like this—

"I'm Sammy Slap the billsticker, and you must all agree, sirs,
I sticks to business like a trump while business sticks to me, sirs.
There's some folks calls me plasterer, but they deserve a banging,
Cause yer see, genteelly speaking, that my trade is paperhanging.
With my paste, paste, paste!
All the world is puffing,
So I'll paste, paste, paste!"

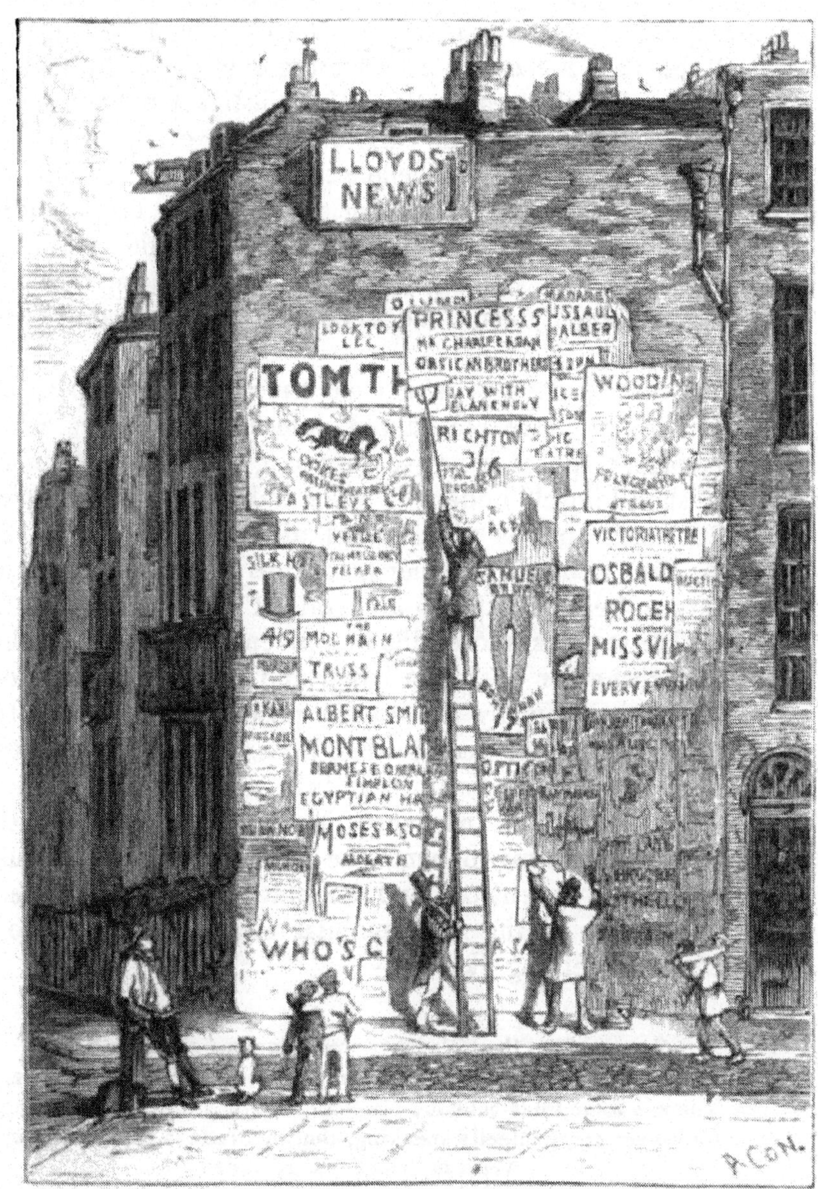

AN OLD BILL-STATION.

The advent of advertisement contractors, who purchased the right, exclusive and absolute, to stick bills on a hoarding, considerably narrowed the avocations of what might almost have been called the predatory billsticker. For a long time the fight was fierce and often; as soon as an "advertisement station" had been finished off, its bills and announcements being all regulated with mathematical precision, a cloud of skirmishers, armed to the teeth with bills, pots, and brushes, would convert, in a few minutes, the orderly arrangements of the contractor to a perfect chaos. But time, which rights all things, aided in the present instance by a few magisterial decisions, and by an unlooked-for and unaccountable alacrity on the part of the police, set these matters straight; and now it is hard to find an enclosure in London the hoarding of which is not notified as being the "advertisement station" of some contractor or other who would blush to be called billsticker. In the suburbs the flying brigade is still to be found hard at work, but daily its campaigning ground becomes more limited, and gradually these Bashi-Bazouks of billsticking are becoming absorbed into the regular ranks of the agents' standing corps.

Placard advertising, of an orderly, and even ornamental, character, has assumed extensive proportions at most of the metropolitan railway stations, the agents to whom we have just referred having extended their operations in the direction of blank spaces on the walls, which they sublet to the general advertising public. Often firms which advertise on an extensive scale themselves contract with the railway companies, and not a few have extended their announcements from the stations to the sides of the line, little enamelled plates being used for this purpose. Any one having a vacant space at the side of his house, or a blank wall to the same, may, provided he live in anything like a business thoroughfare, and that the vantage place is free from obstruction, do advantageous business with an advertisement contractor; and, as matters are progressing, we may some day expect to see not only the private walls of the houses in Belgrave Square and suchlike fashionable localities well papered, but the outsides and insides of our public buildings utilised as well by the hand of the advertiser. One thing is certain, no one could say that many of the latter would be spoiled, no matter what the innovation to which they were subjected.

The most recent novelty in advertising has been the introduction of a cabinet, surmounted by a clock face, into public-house bars and luncheon rooms. These cabinets are divided into spaces of say a superficial foot each, which are to be let off at a set price. So far as we have yet seen, these squares have been filled for the most part with the promoters' advertisements only; and it is admitted by all who know most about advertising that the very worst sign one can have as to the success of a medium is that of an advertisement emanating from the promoters or proprietors of anything in which such advertisement appears. Why this should be we are not prepared to say. We are more able to show why it should not be; for no man, advertisement contractor or otherwise, should, under fair commercial conditions, ask another to do what he would not do himself. So we are satisfied to rest content with the knowledge that what we have stated is fact, however incongruous it may seem, which any one can endorse by applying himself to the ethics of advertising. Certainly, in the instance quoted, the matter looks very suggestive; perhaps it depends on the paradox, that he who is most anxious that others should advertise is least inclined to do so himself.

Not long ago the promoters of a patent umbrella, which seems to have gone the mysterious way of all umbrellas, patent or otherwise, and to have disappeared, availed themselves of a great boat-race to attract public attention to their wares. Skiffs fitted with sails, on each of which were painted the patent parapluie, and a recommendation to buy it, dotted the river, and continually evaded the efforts of the Conservancy Police, who were endeavouring to marshal all the small craft together, so as to leave a clear course for the competitors. Every time one of these advertising boats broke out into mid-stream, carrying its eternal umbrella between the dense lines of spectators, the advertisement was extremely valuable, for straying boats of any kind are on such occasions very noticeable, and these were of course much more so. Still it would seem from the sequel that this bold innovation had been better applied to something more likely to hit the public taste; for whether it was that people, knowing how fleeting a joy is a good umbrella, were determined not to put temptation in the way of their friends, or whether the experiment absorbed all the spare capital of the inventor and patentees, we know not; but this we do know, that since the time of which we speak little or nothing has been heard of the novel "gingham."

Another innovation in the way of advertisements was that, common a few years back, of stencilling the flagstones. At first this system assumed very small proportions, a parallelogram, looking like an envelope with a black border that had been dropped, and containing the address of the advertiser, being the object of the artist entrusted with the mission. Gradually, however, the inscriptions grew, until they became a perfect nuisance, and were put down—if the term applies to anything on such a low level—by the intervention of the police and the magistrates. The undertakers were the greatest sinners in this respect, the invitations to be buried being most numerous and varied. These "black workers" or "death-hunters," as they are often called, are in London most persistent advertisers. They can hardly think that people will die to oblige them and do good for trade, yet in some districts they will, with the most undeviating persistency, drop their little books, informing you how, when, where, and at what rates you may be buried with economy or despatch, or both, as the case may be, down your area, or poke them under your door, or into the letter-box. More, it is stated on good authority, than one pushing contractor, living in a poor neighbourhood, obtains a list of all the folk attended by the parish doctor, and at each of the houses leaves his little pamphlet, let us hope with the desire of cheering and comforting the sick and ailing. To such a man Death must come indeed as a friend, so long, of course, as the grim king comes to the customers only.

A few years back, when hoardings were common property, the undertakers had a knack of posting their dismal little price-lists in the centre of great broadsheets likely to attract any unusual share of attention. They were not particular, however, and any vantage space, from a door-post to a dead wall, came within their comprehension. Another ingenious, and, from its colour, somewhat suggestive, plan was about this time brought into requisition by an undertaker for the destruction of a successful rival's advertisements. He armed one of his assistants with a great can of blacking and a brush, and instructed him to go by secret ways and deface the opposition placards. Of course the other man followed suit, and for a time an undertaker's bill was known best by its illegibility. But ultimately these two men of colour met and fought with the instruments provided by their employers. They did not look lovely when charged before a magistrate next morning, and being bound over to keep the peace, departed to worry each other, or each other's bills, no more. There is another small bill feature of advertising London which is so objectionable that we will pass it by with a simple thankful notice that its promoters are sometimes overtaken by tardy but ironhanded justice.

Most people can recollect the hideous glass pillars or "indicators" which, for advertising purposes, were stuck about London. The first one made its appearance at Hyde Park Corner, and though, in deference to public opinion, it did not remain there very long, less aristocratic neighbourhoods had to bear their adornments until the complete failure of the attempt to obtain advertisements to fill the vacant spaces showed how fatuous was the project. The last of these posts, we remember, was opposite the Angel at Islington, and there, assisted by local faith and indolence, it remained until a short time back. But it too has gone now, and with it has almost faded the recollection of these hideous nightmares of advertising.

The huge vans, plastered all over with bills, which used to traverse London, to the terror of the horses and wonder of the yokels, were improved off the face of the earth a quarter of a century ago; and now the only perambulating advertisement we have is the melancholy sandwich-man and the dispenser of handbills, gentlemen who sometimes "double their parts," to use a theatrical expression. To a playhouse manager we owe the biggest thing in street and general advertising—that in connection with the "Dead Heart"—that has yet been recorded. Mr Smith, who had charge of this department of the Adelphi, has published a statement which gives the totals as follows:—10,000,000 adhesive labels (which, by the way, were an intolerable nuisance), 30,000 small cuts of the guillotine scene, 5000 reams of note-paper, 110,000 business envelopes, 60,000 stamped envelopes, 2000 six-sheet cuts of Bastile scene, 5,000,000 handbills, 1000 six-sheet posters, 500 slips, 1,000,000 cards heartshaped, 100 twenty-eight sheet posters, and 20,000 folio cards for shop windows. This was quite exclusive of newspaper wrappers and various other ingenious means of attracting attention to the play throughout the United Kingdom.

Among other forms of advertising, that on the copper coinage must not be forgotten. The extensive defacement of the pence and halfpence of the realm in the interests of a well-known weekly paper ultimately led to the interference of Parliament, and may fairly be regarded as the cause, or at all events as one of the principal causes, of the sum of £10,000 being voted in July 1855 for the replacement of the old, worn, battered, and mixed coppers by our present bronze coinage.

And now, having given a hurried and summarised glance at the growth and progress of advertising of all kinds and descriptions, from the earliest periods till the present time, we will begin at the beginning, and tell the story with all its ramifications, mainly according to those best possible authorities, the advertisements themselves.

CHAPTER III.

ANCIENT FORMS OF ADVERTISING.

THOUGH it would be quite impossible to give any exact idea as to the period when the identical first advertisement of any kind made its appearance, or what particular clime has the honour of introducing a system which now plays so important a part in all civilised countries, there need be no hesitation in ascribing the origin of advertising to the remotest possible times—to the earliest times when competition, caused by an increasing population, led each man to make efforts in that race for prominence which has in one way or other gone on ever since. As soon as the progress of events or the development of civilisation had cast communities together, each individual member naturally tried to do the best he could for himself, and as he, in the course of events, had naturally to encounter rivals in his way of life, it is not hard to understand that some means of preventing a particular light being hid under a bushel soon presented itself. That this means was an advertisement is almost certain; and so almost as long as there has been a world—or quite as long, using the term as it is best understood now—there have been advertisements. At this early stage of history, almost every trade and profession was still exercised by itinerants, who proclaimed their wares or their qualifications with more or less flowery encomiums, with, in fact, the advertisement verbal, which, under some circumstances, is still very useful. But the time came when the tradesman or professor settled down, and opened what, for argument's sake, we will call a shop. Then another method of obtaining publicity became requisite, and the crier stepped forward to act as a medium between the provider and the consumer. This is, however, but another form of the same system, and, like its simpler congener, has still an existence, though not an ostentatious one. When the art of writing was invented, the means of extending the knowledge which had heretofore been simply cried, was greatly extended, and advertising gradually became an art to be cultivated.

Very soon after the invention of writing in its rudest form, it was turned to account in the way of giving publicity to events in the way of advertisement; for rewards for and descriptions of runaway slaves, written on papyri more than three thousand years ago, have been exhumed from the ruins of Thebes. An early but mythical instance of a reward being offered in an advertisement is related by Pausanias,* who, speaking of the art of working metals, says that the people of Phineum, in Arcadia, pretended that Ulysses dedicated a statue of bronze to Neptune, in the hope that by that deity's intervention he might recover the horses he had lost; and, he adds, "they showed me an inscription on the pedestal of the statue offering a reward to any person who should find and take care of the animals."

The Greeks used another mode of giving publicity which is worthy of remark here. They used to affix to the statues of the infernal deities, in the *temenos* of their temples, curses inscribed on sheets of lead, by which they devoted to the vengeance of those gods the persons who had found or stolen certain things, or injured the advertisers in any other way. As the names of the offenders were given in full in these singular inscriptions, they had the effect of making the grievances known to mortals as well

* Pausanias Græc., lib. viii. c. 14, Arcadia.

as immortals, and thus the advertisement was attained. The only difference between these and ordinary public notices was that the threat of punishment was held out instead of the offer of reward. A compromise was endeavoured generally at the same time, the evil invoked being deprecated in case of restitution of the property. A most interesting collection of such imprecations (*diræ defixiones*, or καταδέσμοι) was found in 1858 in the *temenos* of the infernal deities attached to the temple of Demeter at Cnidus. It is at present deposited in the British Museum, where the curious reader may inspect it in the second vase-room.

A common mode of advertising, about the same time, was by means of the public crier, κήρυξ. In comparatively modern times our town-criers have been proverbial for murdering the king's English, or, at all events, of robbing it of all elecutionary beauties. Not so among the Greeks, who were so nice in point of oratorical power, and so offended by a vicious pronunciation, that they would not suffer even the public crier to proclaim their laws unless he was accompanied by a musician, who, in case of an inexact tone, might be ready to give him the proper pitch and expression. But this would hardly be the case when the public crier was employed by private individuals. In Apuleius ("Golden Ass") we are brought face to face with one of these characters, a cunning rogue, full of low humour, who appears to have combined the duties of crier and auctioneer. Thus, when the slave and the ass are led out for sale, the crier proclaims the price of each with a loud voice, joking at the same time to the best of his abilities, in order to keep the audience in good humour. This latter idea has not been lost sight of in more modern days. "The crier, bawling till his throat was almost split, cracked all sorts of ridiculous jokes upon me [the ass]. 'What is the use,' said he, 'of offering for sale this old screw of a jackass, with his foundered hoofs, his ugly colour, his sluggishness in everything but vice, and a hide that is nothing but a ready-made sieve? Let us even make a present of him, if we can find any one who will not be loth to throw away hay on the brute.' In this way the crier kept the bystanders in roars of laughter." *

The same story furnishes further particulars regarding the ancient mode of crying. When Psyche has absconded, Venus requests Mercury "to proclaim her in public, and announce a reward to him who shall find her." She further enjoins the divine crier to "clearly describe the marks by which Psyche may be recognised, that no one may excuse himself on the plea of ignorance, if he incurs the crime of unlawfully concealing her." So saying, she gives him a little book, in which is written Psyche's name and sundry particulars. Mercury thereupon descends to the earth, and goes about among all nations, where he thus proclaims the loss of Psyche, and the reward for her return :—"If any one can seize her in her flight, and bring back a fugitive daughter of a king, a handmaid of Venus, by name Psyche, or discover where she has concealed herself, let such person repair to Mercury, the crier, behind the boundaries of Murtia,† and receive by way of reward for the discovery seven sweet kisses from Venus herself, and one exquisitely delicious touch of her charming tongue." A somewhat similar reward is offered by Venus in the hue and cry she raises after her fugitive son in the first idyl of Moschus, a Syracusan poet who flourished about 250 years before the Christian era: "If any one has seen my son Eros straying in the cross roads, [know ye] he is a runaway. The informer shall have a reward. The kiss of Venus shall be your pay; and if you bring him, not the bare kiss only, but, stranger, you shall have something

---

* Apuleius, Golden Ass, Book viii., Episode 8.

† The spot here mentioned was at the back of the Temple of Venus Myrtia (the myrtle Venus), on Mount Aventine in Rome.

more." * This something more is probably the "quidquid post oscula dulce" of Secundus, but is sufficiently vague to be anything else, and certainly promises much more than the "will be rewarded" of our own time.

So far with the Greeks and their advertisements. Details grow more abundant when we enter upon the subject of advertising in Rome. The cities of Herculaneum and Pompeii, buried in the midst of their sorrows and pleasures, their joys and cares, in the very midst of the turmoil of life and commerce, and discovered ages after exactly as they were on the morning of that ominous 24th of August A.D. 79, show us that the benefit to be derived from publicity was well understood in those luxurious and highly-cultivated cities. The walls in the most frequented parts are covered with notices of a different kind, painted in black or red. Their spelling is very indifferent, and the painters who busied themselves with this branch of the profession do not appear to have aimed at anything like artistic uniformity or high finish. Still these advertisements, hasty and transitory as they are, bear voluminous testimony as to the state of society, the wants and requirements, and the actual standard of public taste of the Romans in that age. As might be expected, advertisements of plays and gladiators are common. Of these the public were acquainted in the following forms,—

AEDILIS . FAMILIA . GLADIATORIA . PUGNABIT
POMPEIS . PR . K . JUNIAS . VENATIO ET VELA
ERUNT.

or,

N . FESTI AMPLIATI
FAMILIA GLADIATORIA . PUGNA ITERUM
PUGNA . XVI . K . JVN . VENAT . VELA.†

---

* Apuleius, Book vi.

† That is, "The troop of gladiators of the ædil will fight on the 31st of May. There will be fights with wild animals, and an awning

Such inscriptions occur in various parts of Pompeii, sometimes written on smooth surfaces between pilasters (denominated *albua*), at other times painted on the walls. Places of great resort were selected for preference, and thus it is that numerous advertisements are found under the portico of the baths at Pompeii, where persons waited for admission, and where notices of shows, exhibitions, or sales would be sure to attract the attention of the weary lounger.

Baths we find advertised in the following terms,—

THERMAE
M . CRASSI FRUGII
AQUA . MARINA . ET . BALN.
AQUA . DULCI . JANUARIUS . L.

which of course means "warm, sea, and fresh water baths." As provincials add to their notices "as in London," or "à la mode de Paris," so Pompeians and others not unfrequently proclaimed that they followed the customs of Rome at their several establishments. Thus the keeper of a bathing-house near Bologna acquainted the public that—

IN . PRAEDIS
C . LEGIANNI VERI
BALNEUM . MORE . URBICO . LAVAT.
OMNIA COMMODA . PRAESTANTUR.

---

to keep off the sun." Wind and weather permitting, there were awnings over the heads of the spectators; but, generally, there appears to have been too much wind in this breezy summer retreat to admit of this luxury. "Nam ventus populo vela negare solet," says Martial, and the same idea occurs in three other places in this poet's works (vi. 9; xi. 21; xiv. 29). Sometimes, also, the bills of gladiators promise *sparsiones*, which consisted in certain sprinklings of water perfumed with saffron or other odours; and, as they produced what was called a nimbus, or cloud, the perfumes were probably dispersed over the audience in drops by means of pipes or spouts, or, perhaps, by some kind of rude engine.

II.

WALL INSCRIPTIONS IN POMPEII.*—*Antigonus, the hero of 2112 victories. Superbus, a comparatively unknown man. Casuntius, the master of the latter, is supposed to be in the act of advising him to yield to the invincible retiarius. The other figure represents Aniketos Achilles, a great Samnite gladiator, who merited the title of invincible.

At his establishments there were baths according to the fashion of "the town," besides "every convenience." And a similar inscription occurred by the Via Nomentana, eight miles from Rome—

IN . PRAEDIS . AURE
LIAE . FAUSTINIANAE
BALINEUS . LAVAT . MO
RE . URBICO . ET OMNIS.
HUMANITAS . PRAESTA
TUR.

Those who had premises to let or sell affixed a short notice to the house itself, and more detailed bills were posted at the "advertising stations." Thus in Plautus's "Trinummus," Act v., the indignant Callicles says to his spendthrift son, "You have dared to put up in my absence, and unknown to me, that this house is to be sold"—("Ædes venales hasce inscribit literis"). Sometimes, also, the inscription, "Illico ædes venales" ("here is a house for sale") appears to have been painted on the door, or on the *album*. An auctioneer would describe a house as "Villa bona beneque edificata" (a good and well-built house), and full details of the premises were given in the larger placards painted on walls. In the street of the Fullers in Pompeii occurs the following inscription, painted in red, over another which had been painted in black and white-washed over,—

IN . PRAEDIS . JULIAE . S . P . F . FELICIS
LOCANTUR
BALNEUM . VENEREUM . ET . NONGENTUM . PERGULAE
CENACULA . EX . IDIBUS . AUG . PRIORIS . IN . IDUS . AUG .
SEXTAS . ANNOS . CONTINUOS . QUINQUE.
S . Q . D . L . E . N . C.

Which has been translated, "On the estate of Julia Felix, daughter of Spurius Felix, are to let from the 1st to the

6th of the ides of August (*i.e.*, between August 6th and 8th), on a lease of five years, a bath, a venereum, and nine hundred shops, bowers, and upper apartments." * The seven final initials, antiquaries, who profess to read what to others is unreadable, explain, "They are not to let to any person exercising an infamous profession." But as this seems a singular clause where there is a *venereum* to be let, other erudites have seen in it, "Si quis dominam loci eius non cognoverit," and fancy that they read underneath, "Adeat Suettum Verum," in which case the whole should mean, "If anybody should not know the lady of the house, let him go to Suettus Verus." The following is another example of the way in which Roman landlords advertised "desirable residences," and "commodious business premises"—

INSULA ARRIANA
POLLIANA . GN . ALIF I . NIGID I MAI
LOCANTUR . EX . I . JULIS . PRIMIS . TABERNAE
CUM . PERGULIS . SUIS . ET COENACULA
EQUESTRIA . ET . DOMUS . CONDUCTOR
CONVENITO . PRIMUM GN . ALIF I
NIGID I . MAI SER.

Said to mean, "In the Arrian Pollian block of houses, the property of Cn. Alifius Nigidius, senior, are to let from the first of the ides of July, shops with their

* Nine hundred shops in a town which would hardly contain more than about twelve hundred is rather incredible—perhaps it should be ninety. *Pergulæ* were either porticos shaded with verdure, lattices with creeping plants, or small rooms above the shops, bedrooms for the shopkeepers. *Cœnacula* were rooms under the terraces. When they were good enough to let to the higher classes they were called *equestria* (as in the following advertisement). Plutarch informs us that Sylla, in his younger days, lived in one of them, where he paid a rent of £8 a year.

III.

N·KAINS·S·A F
HADRIMTINVS

LVCIVS

h reference to their fancies and favourites, in the

bowers, and gentlemen's apartments. The hirer must apply to the slave of Cn. Alifius Nigidius, senior."

Both the Greeks and the Romans had on their houses a piece of the wall whitened to receive inscriptions relative to their affairs. The first called this λεύκωμα, the latter *album*. Many examples of them are found in Pompeii, generally in very inferior writing and spelling. Even the schoolmaster Valentinus, who on his album, as was the constant practice, invoked the patronage of some high personages, was very loose in his grammar, and the untoward outbreak of Vesuvius has perpetuated his blundering use of an accusative instead of an ablative: "Cum discentes suos." All the Pompeian inscriptions mentioned above were painted, but a few instances also occur of notices being merely scratched on the wall. Thus we find in one place, "Damas audi," and on a pier at the angle of the house of the tragic poet is an Etruscan inscription scratched in the wall with a nail, which has been translated by a learned Neapolitan, "You shall hear a poem of Numerius." But these so-called Etruscan inscriptions are by no means so well understood as we could wish, and their interpretation is far from incontestable. There is another on a house of Pompeii, which has been Latinised into, "Ex hinc viatoriens ante turri xii inibi. Sarinus Publii cauponatur. Ut adires. Vale." That is, "Traveller, going from here to the twelfth tower, there Sarinus keeps a tavern. This is to request you to enter. Farewell." This inscription, however, is so obscure that another *savant* has read in it a notification that a certain magistrate, Adirens Caius, had brought the waters of the Sarno to Pompeii—a most material difference certainly.

We are made acquainted with other Roman bills and advertisements by the works of the poets and dramatists. Thus at Trimalchion's banquet, in the "Satyricon," Pliny mentions that a poet hired a house, built an oratory, hired forms, and dispersed prospectuses. They also read their works publicly,* an occupation in which they were much interrupted and annoyed by idlers and impertinent boys. Another mode of advertising new works more resembled that of our own country. The Roman booksellers used to placard their shops with the titles of the new books they had for sale. Such was the shop of Atrectus, described by Martial—

> Contra Cæsaris est forum taberna
> Scriptis postibus hinc et inde totis
> Omnes ut cito perlegas poetas
> Illinc me pete.

* A. L. Millin, Description d'un Mosaique antique du Musée Pio. Clementin, à Rome, 1819, p. 9.

CHAPTER IV.

MEDIÆVAL AND OTHER VARIETIES OF ADVERTISING.

IN the ages which immediately succeeded the fall of the Roman Empire, and the western migration of the barbarian hordes, darkness and ignorance held paramount sway, education was at a terrible discount, and the arts of reading and writing were confined almost entirely to the monks and the superior clergy. In fact, it was regarded as evidence of effeminacy for any knight or noble to be able to make marks on parchment or vellum, or to be able to decipher them when made. Newspapers were, of course, things undreamt of, but newsmen—itinerants who collected scraps of information and retailed them in the towns and market-places—were now and again to be found. The travelling packman or pedlar was, however, the chief medium of intercommunication in the Middle Ages, and it is not hard to imagine how welcome his appearance must have been in those days, when a hundred miles constituted an immense and almost interminable journey. We know how bad the roads were, and how difficult travelling was in comparatively modern days, but we can form very little idea of the obstacles which beset all attempts at the communication of one commercial centre with another in the early Middle Ages. Everybody being alike shrouded in the darkness of ignorance, it is safe to assume, therefore, that written advertisements were quite unknown, as few beyond those who had written them would have been able to understand them. Nearly the whole of the laity, from the king to the villain or thrall, were equally illiterate, and once more the public crier became the only medium for obtaining publicity; but from the simple mode in which all business was conducted his position was probably a sinecure. An occasional proclamation of peace or war, or a sale of slaves or plunder, was probably the only topic which gave him the opportunity of exercising his eloquence. But with the increase of civilisation, and consequent wealth and competition, the crier's labours assumed a wider field.

The mediæval crier used to carry a horn, by means of which he attracted the people's attention when about to make a proclamation or publication. Public criers appear to have formed a well-organised body in France as early as the twelfth century; for by a charter of Louis VII., granted in the year 1141 to the inhabitants of the province of Berry, the old custom of the country was confirmed, according to which there were to be only twelve criers, five of which should go about the taverns crying with their usual cry, and carrying with them samples of the wine they cried, in order that the people might taste. For the first time they blew the horn they were entitled to a penny, and the same for every time after, according to custom. These criers of wine were a French peculiarity, of which we find no parallel in the history of England. They perambulated the streets of Paris in troops, each with a large wooden measure of wine in his hand, from which to make the passers-by taste the wine they proclaimed, a mode of advertising which would be very agreeable in the present day, but which would, we fancy, be rather too successful for the advertiser. These wine-criers are mentioned by John de Garlando, a Norman writer, who was probably a contemporary of William the Conqueror. "Præcones vini," says he, "clamant hiante gula, vinum venumdandum in tabernis ad quatuor denarios."* A quaint and signifi-

* Glossary, cap. xxvii. "Wine-criers cry with open mouth the wine which is for sale in the taverns at four farthings."

cant story is told in an old chronicle in connection with this system of advertising. An old woman, named Adelheid, was possessed of a strong desire to proclaim the Word of God, but not having lungs sufficiently powerful for the noisy propagation contemplated by her, she paid a wine-crier to go about the town, and, instead of proclaiming the prices of the wine, to proclaim these sacred words: "God is righteous! God is merciful! God is good and excellent!" And as the man went about shouting these words she followed him, exclaiming, "He speaks well! he says truly!" The poor old body hardly succeeded according to her pious desire, for she was arrested and tried, and as it was thought she had done this out of vanity (*causa laudis humanæ*), she was burned alive.* From this it would seem that there was as much protection for the monks in their profession as for the criers, who were very proud of their special prerogatives.

The public criers in France, at an early period, were formed into a corporation, and in 1258 obtained various statutes from Philip Augustus, some of which, relating to the criers of wine, are excessively curious. Thus it was ordained that—

"Whosoever is a crier in Paris may go to any tavern he likes and cry its wine, provided they sell wine from the wood, and that there is no other crier employed for that tavern; and the tavern-keeper cannot prohibit him.

"If a crier finds people drinking in a tavern, he may ask what they pay for the wine they drink; and he may go out and cry the wine at the prices they pay, whether the tavern-keeper wishes it or not, provided always that there be no other crier employed for that tavern.

"If a tavern-keeper sells wine in Paris and employs no crier, and closes his door against the criers, the crier may

* Chronicles of the Monk Alberic des Trois Fontaines, under the year 1235.

proclaim that tavern-keeper's wine at the same price as the king's wine (the current price), that is to say, if it be a good wine year, at seven denarii, and if it be a bad wine year, at twelve denarii.

"Each crier to receive daily from the tavern for which he cries at least four denarii, and he is bound on his oath not to claim more.

"The crier shall go about crying twice a day, except in Lent, on Sundays and Fridays, the eight days of Christmas, and the Vigils, when they shall only cry once. On the Friday of the Adoration of the Cross they shall cry not at all. Neither are they to cry on the day on which the king, the queen, or any of the children of the royal family happens to die."

This crying of wines is frequently alluded to in those French ballads of street-criers known as "Les crieries de Paris." One of them has—

Si crie l'on en plusors leus
Li bon vin fort a trente deux,
A seize, a douze, a six, a huict.*

And another—

D'autres cris on faict plusieurs,
Qui long seroient à reciter,
L'on crie vin nouveau et vieu,
Duquel on donne à tatter.†

Early in the Middle Ages the public crier was still called *Præco*, as among the Romans; and an edict of the town of Tournay, dated 1368, describes him as "the sergeant of the rod (*sergent à verge*), who makes publications (*crie les bans*), and cries whatever else there is to be made known to the town." The Assizes of Jerusalem, which contained

* All around here they cry wine at the rate
Of thirty-two, sixteen, twelve, six, and eight.

† To name the other cries our time would waste—
They cry old wine and new, and bid you taste.

the code of civil laws of the whole of civilised Europe during the twelfth and thirteenth centuries, and which take us back to the most ancient forms of our own civil institutions, make mention in the following manner of the public crier: "Whosoever desires to sell anything by auction, must have it proclaimed by the crier, who is appointed by the lord viscount; and nobody else has a right to make any publication by crying. If anybody causes any such auction to be proclaimed by any other than the public crier, then the lord has a right by assize and custom to claim the property so cried as his own, and the crier shall be at the mercy of the lord. And whoever causes anything to be cried by the appointed public crier in any other way than it ought to be cried, and in any other way than is done by the lord or his representative, the lord may claim the property as his own, and the crier who thus cries it shall be amenable for falsehood, and is at the mercy of the lord, who may take from him all he possesses. But if he [the lord] does not do that, then he shall not suffer any other punishment; and if he be charged, he must be believed on his oath."

From these very stringent and protective regulations it appears, then, that at this early period the public criers, or *præcones*, appointed by the lord, had the exclusive right of proclaiming all sales by auction, not only voluntary, but also judicial, of movables, as well as of fixtures; of "personal," as well as of "real" property.

In England criers appear to have been also a national institution at an early period. They were sworn to sell truly and well to the best of their power and ability. They proclaimed the cause of the condemnation of all criminals, and made proclamations of every kind, except as concerned matters ecclesiastical, which were exclusively the province of the archbishop. They also cried all kinds of goods. In London we find Edmund le Criour mentioned in the documents relating to the Guildhall as early as 1299.

That criers used horns, as in France, appears from the will of a citizen of Bristol, dated 1388, who, disposing of some house property, desires "that the tenements so bequeathed shall be sold separately by the sound of the trumpet at the high cross of Bristol, without any fraud or collusion." In Ipswich it was still customary in the last century to proclaim the meetings of the town council, the previous night at twelve o'clock, by the sound of a large horn, which is still preserved in the town hall of that borough. These horns were provided by the mayors of the different towns.

The public crier, then, was the chief organ by which the mediæval shopkeeper, in the absence of what we now know as "advertising mediums," obtained publicity: it was also customary for most traders to have touters at their doors, who did duty as living advertisements. In low neighbourhoods this system still obtains, especially in connection with cheap photographic establishments, whose "doorsmen" select as a rule the most improbable people for their attentions, but compensate for this by their pertinacity and glibness. Possibly the triumph is the greater when the customer has been persuaded quite out of his or her original intentions. Most trades, in early times, were almost exclusively confined to certain streets, and as all the shops were alike unpretending, and open to the gaze—in fact, were stalls or booths—it behoved the shopkeeper to do something in order to attract customers. This he effected sometimes by means of a glaring sign, sometimes by means of a man or youth standing at the door, and vociferating with the full power of his lungs, "What d'ye lack, sir? what d'ye lack?" Our country is rather deficient in that kind of mediæval literature known in France as *dicts* and *fabliaux*, which teem with allusions to this custom of touting, which is noticeable, though, in Lydgate's ballad of "London Lyckpenny" (Lack-penny), written in the first half of the fifteenth century. There we see the shopmen standing at the door, trying to outbawl each other to gain the custom of the passers-by. The spicer or grocer bids the Kentish countryman to come and buy some spice, pepper, or saffron. In Cheapside, the mercers bewilder him with their velvet, silk, and lawn, and lay violent hands on him, in order to show him their "Paris thread, the finest in the land." Throughout all Canwick (now Cannon Street), he is persecuted by drapers, who offer him cloth; and in other parts, particularly in East Cheap, the keepers of the eating-houses sorely tempt him with their cries of "Hot sheep's feet, fresh maqurel, pies, and ribs of beef." At last he falls a prey to the tempting invitation of a taverner, who makes up to him from his door with a cringing bow, and taking him by the sleeve, pronounces the words, "Sir, will you try our wine?" with such an insinuating and irresistible accent, that the Kentish man enters and spends his only penny in that tempting and hospitable house. Worthy old Stow supposes this interesting incident to have happened at the Pope's Head, in Cornhill, and bids us enjoy the knowledge of the fact, that for his one penny the countryman had a pint of wine, and "for bread nothing did he pay, for that was allowed free" in those good old days. Free luncheons, though rare now, were commonly bestowed in the seventeenth and eighteenth centuries on regular drinkers; and the practice of giving food to those who pay for drink is still current in many parts of the United States. The "Lyckpenny" story is one of the few instances in English literature of this early period, in which the custom of touting at shop doors is distinctly mentioned, but, as before remarked, the French *fabliaux* abound with such allusions. In the story of "Courtois d'Arras"—a travestie of the Prodigal Son in a thirteenth-century garb—Courtois finds the host standing at his door shouting, "Bon vin de Soissons, à six deniers le lot." And in a mediæval mystery entitled "Li Jus de S. Nicolas," the innkeeper, standing on the threshold, roars out, that in his house excellent dinners are to be had, with warm bread and warm herrings, and barrelfuls of Auxerre wine: "Céans il fait bon diner, céans il y a pain chaud et harengs chauds, et vin d'Auxerre à plein tonneau." In the "Trois Aveugles de Compiègne," the thirsty wanderers hear mine host proclaiming in the street that he has "good, cool, and new wine, from Auxerre and from Soissons; bread and meat, and wine and fish: within is a good place to spend your money; within is accommodation for all kind of people; here is good lodging:"—

Ci a bon vin fres et nouvel
Ça d'Auxerre, ça de Soissons,
Pain, et char, et vin, et poissons,
Céens fet bon despendre argent,
Ostel i a à toute gent
Céens fet moult bon heberger.

And in the "Débats et facétieuses rencontres de Gringald et de Guillot Gorgen, son maistre," the servant, who would not pay his reckoning, excuses himself, saying, "The taverner is more to blame than I, for as I passed before his door, and he being seated at it as usual, called to me, saying, 'Will you be pleased to breakfast here? I have good bread, good wine, and good meat.'" "Le tavernier a plus de tort que moy; car, passant devant sa porte, et luy étant assiz (ainsy qu'ils sont ordinairement) il me cria, me disant: Vous plaist-il de dejeuner céans? Il y a de bon pain, de bon vin, et de bonne viande."

Other modes of advertising, of a less obtrusive nature, were, however, in use at the same time, as in Rome, written handbills were affixed in public places; and almost as soon as the art of printing was discovered, it was applied to the purpose of multiplying advertisements of this kind. We may fairly assume that one of the very first posters ever printed in England was that by which Caxton announced, circa 1480, the sale of the "Pyes of Salisbury use,"* at the

* No savoury meat-pies, as some gastronomic reader might think, since they came from the county of sausage celebrity, but a collection of rules, as practised in the diocese of Salisbury, to show the priests

Red Pole, in the Almonry, Westminster. Of this first of broadsides two copies are still extant, one in the Bodleian Library, at Oxford, the other in Earl Spencer's library. Their dimensions are five inches by seven, and their contents as follows:—

If it please ony man spirituel or temporel to bye our pyes of two or thre comemoracio's of Salisburi use, emprynted after the form of this prese't-letre, whiche ben wel and truly correct, late hym come to Westmonester, into the almonestrye at the reed pole and he shal haue them good and chepe:

Supplico stet cedula.

Foreigners appear to have appreciated the boon of this kind of advertising equally rapidly, although, from the fugitive nature of such productions, copies of their posters are rarely to be found. Still an interesting list of books, printed by Coburger at Nuremberg in the fifteenth century, is preserved in the British Museum, to which is attached the following heading: "Cupientes emere libros infra notatos venient ad hospitium subnotatum," &c.—*i.e.*, "Those who wish to buy the books hereunder mentioned, must come to the house now named," &c. The Parisian printers soon went a step further. Long before the invention of the typographic art, the University had compelled the booksellers to advertise in their shop windows any new manuscripts they might obtain. But after the invention of printing they soon commenced to proclaim the wonderful cheapness of the works they produced. It did not strike them, however, that this might have been done effectually on a large scale, and they were content to extol the low price of the work in the book itself. Such notices as the following are common in early books. Ulric Gering, in

how to deal, under every possible variation in Easter, with the concurrence of more than one office on the same day. These rules varied in the different dioceses.

his "Corpus Juris Canonici," 1500, allays the fear of the public with a distich:—"Don't run away on account of the price," he says. "Come rich and poor; this excellent work is sold for a very small sum:"—

> Ne fugite ob pretium: dives pauperque venite
> Hoc opus excellens venditur ære brevi.

Berthold Remboldt subjoins to his edition of "S. Bruno on the Psalms," 1509, the information that he does not lock away his wares (books) like a miser, but that anybody can carry them away for very little money.

> Istas Bertholdus merces non claudit avarus
> Exigius nummis has studiose geres.

And in his "Corpus Juris Canonici," he boasts that this splendid volume is to be had for a trifling sum, after having, with considerable labour, been weeded of its misprints.

> Hoc tibi præclarum modico patet ære volumen
> Abstersum mendis non sine Marte suis.

Thielman Kerver, Jean Petit, and various other printers, give similar intelligence to the purchasers of their works. Sometimes they even resort to the process of having a book puffed on account of its cheapness by editors or scholars of known eminence, who address the public on behalf of the printer. Thus in a work termed by the French savant Chevillier, "Les Opuscules du Docteur Almain," printed by Chevalon and Gourmont, 1518, a certain dignified member of the University condescends to inform the public that they have to be grateful to the publishers for the beautiful and cheap book they have produced:—"Gratias agant Claudio Chevallon et Ægydio Gourmont, qui pulchris typis et characteritus impressum opus hoc vili dant pretio." This, be it observed, is the earliest instance of the puff direct which has so far been discovered.

Meanwhile, though the art of printing had become established, and was daily taking more and more work out of the hands of scribes, writing continued to be almost the only advertising media for wellnigh two centuries longer. Like the ancient advertisement already noticed, that of Venus about her runaway son, they commenced almost invariably with the words "If anybody," or, if in Latin, *Si quis;* and from these last two words they obtained their name. They were posted in the most frequented parts of the towns, preferably near churches; and hence has survived the practice of attaching to church doors lists of voters and various other notifications, particularly in villages. In the metropolis one of the places used for this purpose may probably have been London Stone. In "Pasquil and Marforius," 1589, we read, "Set up this bill at London Stone; let it be done solemnly with drum and trumpet;" and further on in the same pamphlet, "If it please them, these dark winter nights, to stick up these papers upon London Stone." These two allusions are, however, not particularly conclusive.

In the sixteenth and seventeenth centuries the principal place for affixing a *siquis* was in the middle aisle of St Paul's. From the era of the Reformation to the Restoration, all sorts of disorderly conduct was practised in the old cathedral. A lengthy catalogue of improper customs and disgusting practices might be collected from the works of the period, and bills were stuck up in various parts to restrain the grossest abuses. "At every door of this church," says Weever, "was anciently this vers depicted; and in my time [he died in 1632] it might be perfectly read at the great south door, *Hic Locus sacer est, hic nulli mingere fas est.*"

There were also within the sacred edifice tobacco, book, and sempstress' shops; there was a pillar at which serving-men stood for hire, and another place where lawyers had their regular stands, like merchants on 'Change. At the period when Decker wrote his curious "Gull's Horn-Book" (1609), and for many years after, the cathedral was the lounging place for all idlers and hunters after news, as well as of men of almost every profession, cheats, usurers, and knights of the post. The cathedral was likewise a seat of traffic and negotiation, even pimps and procuresses had their stations there; and the font itself, if credit may be given to a black-letter tract on the "Detestable Use of Dice-play," printed early in Elizabeth's reign, was made a place for the advance and payment of loans, and the sealing of indentures and obligations for the security of the moneys borrowed. Such a busy haunt was, of course, the very best place for bills and advertisements to be posted.

No bonâ fide *siquis* has come down to us, but it appears that among them the applications for ecclesiastics were very common, as Bishop Earle in his "Microcosmographia," published in 1629, describes "Paul's Walke" as the "market of young lecturers, whom you may cheapen here at all rates and sizes;" and this allusion is confirmed by a passage in Bishop Hall's "Satires" (B. ii. s. 5), in which also the custom of affixing advertisements to a particular door is distinctly noticed :—

> Saw'st thou ere *siquis* patch'd on Paul's church door
> To seek some vacant vicarage before?
> Who wants a churchman that can service say,
> Read fast and fair his monthly homily,
> And wed, and bury, and make cristen souls,
> Come to the *left side alley* of St Poule's.

But the *siquis* door was not confined to notices of ecclesiastical matters; it was appropriated generally to the variety of applications that is now to be found in the columns of a newspaper or the books of a registry office. Though no authentic specimens of the *siquis* remain, we are possessed of several imitations, as the old dramatists delighted in reproducing the inflated language of these documents. Thus, in Holiday's "Technogamia" (1618), Act i. scene 7, Geographus sets up the following notice :—

If there be any gentleman that, for the accomplishing of his natural endowment, intertaynes a desire of learning the languages; especially the nimble French, maiestik Spanish, courtly Italian, masculine Dutch, happily compounding Greek, mysticall Hebrew, and physicall Arabicke; or that is otherwise transported with the admirable knowledge of forraine policies, complimentall behaviour, naturall dispositions, or whatsoever else belongs to any people or country under heaven; he shall, to his abundant satisfaction, be made happy in his expectation and successe if he please to repair to the signe of the Globe.

Again, Ben Jonson's "Every Man out of his Humour" introduces Shift, "a threadbare shark," whose "profession is skeldring and odling, his bank Paul's." Speaking of Shift in the opening scene of the third act, which the dramatist has laid in "the middle aisle of Paules," Cordatus says that Shift is at that moment in Paules "for the advancement of a *siquis* or two, wherein he hath so varied himselfe, that if any one of them take, he may hull up and doune in the humorous world a little longer." Shift's productions deserved to succeed, as they were masterpieces of their kind, and might even now, though the world is so much older, and professes to be so much wiser, be studied with advantage by gentlemen who cultivate the literature of advertisements in the interest of certain firms. Here are some of his compositions, which would certainly shine among the examples of the present day:—

If there be any lady or gentlewoman of good carriage that is desirous to entertain to her private uses a young, straight, and upright gentleman, of the age of five or six and twenty at the most; who can serve in the nature of a gentleman usher, and hath little legs of purpose,* and a black satin suit of his own to go before her in; which suit, for the more sweetening, now lies in lavender;† and can hide his face with her fan if need require, or sit in the cold at the stair foot for her, as well as another gentleman; let her subscribe her name and place, and diligent respect shall be given.

---

* Small calveless legs are mentioned as characteristic of a gentleman in many of our old plays, and will be observed in most full-length portraits of the sixteenth and seventeenth century.

† To "lie in lavender" was a cant term for being in pawn.

The following is even an improvement :—

If this city, or the suburbs of the same, do afford any young gentleman of the first, second, or third head, more or less, whose friends are but lately deceased, and whose lands are but new come into his hands, that, to be as exactly qualified as the best of our ordinary gallants are, is affected to entertain the most gentlemanlike use of tobacco ; as first to give it the most exquisite perfume ; then to know all the delicate, sweet forms for the assumption of it ; as also the rare corollary and practice of the Cuban ebolition, euripus and whiff,* which we shall receive or take in here at London, and evaporate at Uxbridge, or farther, if it please him. If there be any such generous spirit, that is truly enamour'd of these good faculties ; may it please him but by a note of his hand to specify the place or ordinary where he uses to eat and lie ; and most sweet attendance with tobacco and pipes of the best sort, shall be ministered. *Stet quæso, candide lector.*

It is noticeable that most of these advertisements commence with the English equivalent for the Latin *si quis*, and furthermore that Ben Jonson concludes with the same formula as Caxton, *stet quæso*, imploring the "candid reader" not to tear off the bill. The word *siquis* is of frequent occurrence in the old writers. Green, for instance, in his "Tu Quoque," says of certain women that "they stand like the devil's *siquis* at a tavern or alehouse door." At present the term has more particular reference to ecclesiastical matters. A candidate for holy orders who has not been educated at the University, or has been absent some time from thence, is still obliged to have his intention proclaimed, by having a notice to that effect hung up in the church of the place where he has recently resided. If, after a certain time, no objection is made, a certificate of his *siquis*, signed by the churchwardens, is given to him to be presented to the bishop when he seeks ordination.

At the time when the *siquis* was the most common form

---

* Tricks performed with tobacco smoke were fashionable amongst the gallants of the period, and are recommended in Decker's "Gull's Horn-Book," and commended in many old plays. Making rings of smoke was a favourite amusement in those days.

of advertisement, other methods were used in order to give publicity to certain events. There were the proclamations of the will of the King, and of the Lord Mayor, whose edicts were proclaimed by the common trumpeter. There were also two richly carved and gilt posts at the door of the Sheriff's office,* on which (some annotators of old plays say) it was customary to stick enactments of the Town Council. The common crier further made known matters of minor and commercial importance, and every shopkeeper still kept an apprentice at his door to attract the attention of the passers-by with a continuous "What do you lack, master?" or "mistress," followed by a voluble enumeration of the wares vended by his master. The bookseller, as in ancient Rome, still advertised his new works by placards posted against his shop, or fixed in cleft sticks. This we gather from an epigram of Ben Jonson to his bookseller, in which he enjoins him rather to sell his works to Bucklersbury, to be used for wrappers and bags, than to force their sale by the usual means :—

> Nor have my little leaf on post or walls,
> Or in cleft sticks advancèd to make calls
> For termers or some clerk-like serving-man.

Announcements of shows were given in the manner still followed by the equestrian circus troops in provincial towns, viz., by means of bills and processions. Thus notice of bear-baitings was given by the bears being led about the town, preceded by a flag and some noisy instruments. In the Duke of Newcastle's play of "The Humorous Lovers" (1677), the sham bearward says, "I'll set up my bills, that the gamesters of London, Horseleydown, Southwark, and Newmarket, may come in and bait him before the ladies. But first, boy, go, fetch me a bagpipe; we will walk the streets in triumph, and give the people notice of our sport." Such a procession was, of course, a noisy one, and for that reason

* See prints in "Archæologia," xix. p. 383.

it was one of the plagues the mischievous page sent to torment Morose, "the gentleman that loves no noise," in Ben Jonson's "Silent Woman." "I entreated a bearward one day," says the page, "to come down with the dogs of some four parishes that way, and I thank him he did, and cried his game under Master Morose's window." And in Howard's "English Monsieur" (1674), William, a country youth, says, "I saw two rough-haired things led by the nose with two strings, and a bull like ours in the country, with a brave garland about his head, and an horse, and the least gentleman upon him that ever I saw in my life, and brave bagpipes playing before 'um;" which is explained by Comely as occasioned by its being "bearbaiting day, and he has met with the bull, and the bears, and the jack-an-apes on horseback." Trials of skill in the noble art of self-defence were announced in a similar manner, by the combatants promenading the streets divested of their upper garments, with their sleeves tucked up, sword or cudgel in hand, and preceded by a drum. Finally, for the use of the community at large, there was the bellman or town crier, a character which occupies a prominent place in all the old sets of "Cries of London." In one of the earliest collections of that kind,* engraved early in the seventeenth century, we see him represented with a bunch of keys in his hand, which he no doubt proclaims as "found." Underneath is the following "notice:"—

O yes. Any man or woman that
Can tell any tidings of a little
Mayden-childe of the age of 24
Yeares. Bring word to the cryar
And you shall be pleased for
your labour
And God's blessing.

---

* *Vide* Decker's "Belman of London: Bringing to Light the most notorious Villanies that are now practised in the Kingdome." London, 1608.

O PER SE O, OR A NEW CRYER.

"THE BELMAN OF LONDON."

From Thomas Decker's Lanthorne and Candle Light: or, The Bell-Man's Second Night's Walke. 1608–9.

This was an old joke, which, more or less varied, occurs always under the print of the town crier. The prototype of this venerable witticism may be found in the tragedy of "Soliman and Perseda" (1599), where one of the characters says that he

> —— had but sixpence
> For crying a little wench of thirty yeeres old and upwardes,
> That had lost herself betwixt a taverne and a b——y house.

Notwithstanding the immense development of advertising since the spread of newspapers, the services of the bellman are still used in most of the country towns of the United Kingdom, and even in London there are still bellmen and parish criers, though their offices would appear to be sinecures. The provincial crier's duties are of the most various description, and relate to objects lost or found, sales by public auction or private contract, weddings, christenings, and funerals. Not much more than a century ago the burgh of Lanark was so poor that there was in it only one butcher, and even he dared never venture on killing a sheep till every part of the animal was ordered beforehand. When he felt disposed to engage in such an enterprise, he usually prevailed upon the minister, the provost, and the members of the town council to take a joint each; but when shares were not subscribed for readily, the sheep received a respite. On such occasion the services of the bellman, or "skelligman," as he was there named, were called into request, and that official used to perambulate the streets of Lanark acquainting the lieges with the butcher's intentions in the following rhyme:—

> Bell—ell—ell!
> There's a fat sheep to kill!
> A leg for the provost,
> Another for the priest,
> The bailies and the deacons
> They'll tak' the neist;
> And if the fourth leg we canna sell,
> The sheep it maun leeve, and gae back to the hill!

Sir Walter Scott, in one of his notes, gives a quaint specimen of vocal advertising. In the old days of Scotland, when persons of property (unless they happened to be nonjurors) were as regular as their inferiors in attendance on parochial worship, there was a kind of etiquette in waiting till the patron, or acknowledged great man of the parish, should make his appearance. This ceremonial was so sacred in the eyes of a parish beadle in the Isle of Bute, that the kirk bell being out of order, he is said to have mounted the steeple every Sunday to imitate with his voice the successive summonses which its mouth of metal used to send forth. The first part of this imitative harmony was simply the repetition of the words, "Bell, bell, bell, bell!" two or three times, in a manner as much resembling the sound as throat of flesh could imitate throat of iron. "Bellùm, Bellùm!" was sounded forth in a more urgent manner; but he never sent forth the third and conclusive peal, the varied tone of which is called in Scotland the "ringing-in," until the two principal heritors of the parish approached, when the chime ran thus—

Bellùm Bellèllum,
Bernera and Knockdow's coming!
Bellùm Bellèllum,
Bernera and Knockdow's coming!

A story is also told of an old Welsh beadle, who, having no bell to his church, or the bell being out of order, used to mount the tower before the service on Sundays, and advertise the fact that they were just about to begin, in imitation of the chimes, and in compliment to the most conspicuous patronymics in the congregation list, thus—

Shon Morgan, Shon Shones,
Shon Morgan, Shon Shones,
Shon Shenkin, Shon Morgan, Shon Shenkin,
Shon Shones!

Continued *à discrétion*. And with this most singular form of vocal advertising we will conclude the chapter.

CHAPTER V.

NEWSPAPER ADVERTISING FORESHADOWED—ITS EARLIEST USE—HOUGHTON'S LESSONS.

BY this time, and in various ways, the first transitory glimpses of a system at present all-powerful and universal began to show themselves—vague and uncertain, and often unsatisfactory, it must be admitted, but still the first evidences of the growth of an unparalleled institution; in fact, the base upon which the institution eventually reared itself. With improvements in printing, and the invention of movable type, the supply of pamphlets on current topics—the first rude forerunners of the newspaper as we understand it—began to be enlarged, and this opportunity was not lost on the bold spirits who even in those days could understand the advantages bound to accrue from a system of intercommunication at once advantageous to buyer and seller, and calling for special attention from both. There is a wonderful amount of attraction about these discoloured and moth-eaten papers, with their rude types and quaint spelling, which breathe, as much as do the words themselves, the spirit of a bygone age, and those who are so fond of praising past times might receive a valuable lesson from the perusal of these occasional publications, which are full of the spirit of an age when comfort, as we understand the word, was unknown to even the wealthy; when travelling was a luxury—a woeful luxury, it must be admitted—known only to those possessed of ample means, or others called forth on special or desperate missions; when men lived long, and, as they thought, eventful lives, within a circle of half-a-dozen miles; and when the natural consequences of this isolation, ignorance and intolerance, held almost absolute sway over the length and breadth of the land. And in these old papers, as we get nearer and nearer to modern times, can be traced the gradual benefit which accrued from man's intercourse with man, not only by the construction and improvement of roads, and the introduction of and competition among stage coaches, but by means of the subject of this work,—and very much by their means too,—advertisements.

As early as 1524, pamphlets or small books of news were printed in Vienna and other parts of Germany, but their publication was very irregular, and little or nothing is known of them beyond the fact of their being. It is not easy to determine which nation first found its way towards newspaper advertisements, but there is good reason to believe that France is entitled to the honour, so far as regular and consecutive business is concerned. The *Journal Général d'Affiches*, better known as the *Petites Affiches*, was first published on the 14th of October 1612. It obtained from Louis XIII. by letters-patent sundry privileges which were subsequently confirmed (1628 and 1635). Judging by the title of this publication, it would appear to have been an advertising medium, but this must be left to surmise, there being no opportunity, so far as we are aware, of inspecting the earliest numbers. Two centuries and a half have passed away since the first appearance of this periodical, and the *Petites Affiches* has neither changed its title, nor, it may be fairly presumed, the nature of its publicity. It is now the journal of the domestic wants of France; and servants seeking situations, or persons wanting servants, advertise in it in preference to all others. It is especially the medium for announcing any public or private sales of property, real or personal; and the publication of partnership deeds, articles of association of public companies, and other legal notices, are required to be inserted in the *Journal des Petites Affiches*, which is published in a small octavo form.

The oldest newspaper paragraph approaching to an advertisement yet met with, is in one of those early German newsbooks preserved in the British Museum. It is printed in 1591, without name of place, and contains all the memorable occurrences of the years 1588 and 1589, such as the defeat of the Armada, the murder of King Henry III. of France, and other stale matter of the same kind; a curious instance of the tardiness with which news, whether good or ill, travelled in those times. Among the many signs and tokens which were then supposed to give warning of divine wrath at the general wickedness of mankind, was an unknown plant which had made its appearance in one of the suburbs of the town of Soltwedel. It grew in a garden amongst other plants, but nobody had ever seen its like. A certain Dr Laster thereupon wrote a book describing the plant, and giving a print of it in the frontispiece. "This book," says the pamphlet, "which as yet is not much known, shows and explains all what this plant contains. Magister Cunan has published it, and Matthew Welack has printed it, in Wittemberg. Let whoever does not yet know the meaning of this [portend] buy the book at once, and read it with all possible zeal:"—

Ein wunderlichs Gewechs man hat,
Von Soltwedel der Alten stad,
Der Berber die Vorstadt genand,
Gefunden welchs gar niemand kend.
In einem Garten gewachsen ist,
Bey andern Kreutern ist gewis,
Sein Conterfey und recht gestalt,
Wird auffm Tittel gezeiget bald,
Ein Buch Hoffarts Laster genand,
Welches jetzt noch sehr unbekand
Darin gewiesen und vermied,
Was das gewechse in sich hilt,

Mag: Cunaw hats geben an den Tag
Zu Wittemberg druckts Matths Welack,
Wer des bedeutung noch nicht weis
Kauff das Buch lisz mit allem fleis.

Though this is an advertisement to all intents and purposes, still it is of the kind now best known amongst those most interested as "puff pars," and is similar to those that the early booksellers frequently inserted in their works. It is therefore not unlikely that the book in question and the newsletter were printed at the same shop. Another, in fact, *the* earliest instance of newspaper advertising, is that of Nathaniel Butler; still this also only relates to books. The first genuine miscellaneous advertisements yet discovered occur in a Dutch black-letter newspaper, which was published in the reign of our James I., without name or title. The advertisement in question is inserted at the end of the folio half-sheet which contains the news, November 21, 1626, and, in a type different from the rest of the paper, gives notice that there will be held a sale by auction of articles taken out of prizes, viz., sugar, ivory, pepper, tobacco, and logwood. At that time there appeared two newspapers in Amsterdam, and it is not a little curious that Broer Jansz * occasionally advertised the books he published in the paper of his rival, which was entitled "Courant from Italy and Germany." Gradually the advertisements become more frequent, the following being some of them literally translated. The first is from the *Courante uyt Italien en de Duytschland* of July 23, 1633:—

With the last ships from the East Indies have been brought an elephant, a tiger, and an Indian stag, which are to be seen at the Old Glass house, for the benefit of the poor, where many thousands of people visit them.

---

* Broer Jansz styles himself "Couranteer in the Army of his Princely Excellence," *i.e.*, Prince Frederic Henry, the Stadtholder. Subsequently, in 1630, Jansz commenced a new series, which he entitled "Tidings from Various Quarters."

The *Hollandsche Mercurius*, which was issued more than two hundred years ago, showed great interest in English affairs, especially with regard to the Civil War. It was much inclined to the Royal cause; and when in 1653 Cromwell assumed supreme power, the above was issued as a title, and purported to show the various events which had recently passed in Great Britain.

The heirs of the late Mr Bernardus Paludanus, Doctor, of the City of Enkhuyzen, will sell his world-famed museum in lots, by public auction, or by private contract, on the 1st of August, 1634.

The two following are taken from the *Tydinghen*, the first appearing on May 27, 1634:—

The Burgomasters and Council of the town of Utrecht have been pleased to found in this old and famous town, an illustrious school [university], at which will be taught and explained the sacred Theology and Jurisprudence, besides Philosophy, History, and similar sciences. And it will commence and open at Whitsuntide of this present year.

A few days after, on June 7th, the inauguration of this school is advertised as about to take place on the ensuing Tuesday. There is one instance of an advertisement from a foreign country being inserted in this paper; it runs as follows, and is dated June 2, 1635:—

Licentiate Grim, British preacher and professor at the University of Wesel, has published an extensive treatise against all popish scribblers, entitled "Papal Sanctimony," that is, catholic and authentic proof that Pope John VIII., commonly called Pope Jutte [Joan], was a woman.

In England the first bonâ fide attempt at newspaper work was attempted in 1622, when the outbreak of the great Civil War caused an unusual demand to be made for news, and as the appetite grew by what it fed on, this unwonted request for information may be regarded as the fount-spring of that vast machine which "liners" delight to call "the fourth estate." It was this demand which suggested to one Nathaniel Butler, a bookseller and a pamphleteer of twelve years' standing, the idea of printing a weekly newspaper from the Venetian gazettes, which used to circulate in manuscript. After one or two preliminary attempts, he acquired sufficient confidence in his publication to issue the following advertisement:—

If any gentleman or other accustomed to buy the weekly relations of newes be desirous to continue the same, let them know that the writer, or transcriber rather, of this newes, hath published two former newes, the one dated the 2nd and the other the 13th of August, all of which do carry a like title with the arms of the King of Bohemia on the other side of the title-page, and have dependence one upon another: which manner of writing and printing he doth purpose to continue weekly by God's assistance from the best and most certain intelligence: farewell, this twenty-three of August, 1622.

Like most innovations, this attempt met with an indifferent reception, and was greeted in the literary world with a shower of invective. Even Ben Jonson joined in the outcry, and ridiculed the newspaper office in his "Staple of News," in which, among other notions, he publishes the paradox, as it now appears to us, that the information contained in the gazette "had ceased to be news by being printed." Butler's venture seems to have been anything but a success, and but for the fact that it gave rise to speculation on the subject of newspapers, and laid the foundation of our periodical literature, might, so far at all events as its promoter was concerned, never have had an existence. But the idea lost no ground, and newspapers began to make their way, though they did not assume anything like regularity, or definite shape and character, for nearly half a century. None of these precursors of newspaper history exceeded in size a single small leaf, and the quantity of news contained in fifty of them would be exceeded by a single issue of the present day.

What is generally supposed to be, but is not, the first authenticated advertisement is the following, the political and literary significance of which is apparent at a glance. It appears in the *Mercurius Politicus* for January 1652:—

IRENODIA GRATULATORIA, an Heroick Poem; being a congratulatory panegyrick for my Lord General's late return, summing up his successes in an exquisite manner.

To be sold by John Holden, in the New Exchange, London. Printed by Tho. Newcourt, 1652.

In this chapter we have no intention of giving any specimens beyond those which are striking and characteristic. In subsequent chapters we shall carry the history in an unbroken line to modern times, but our intention is now

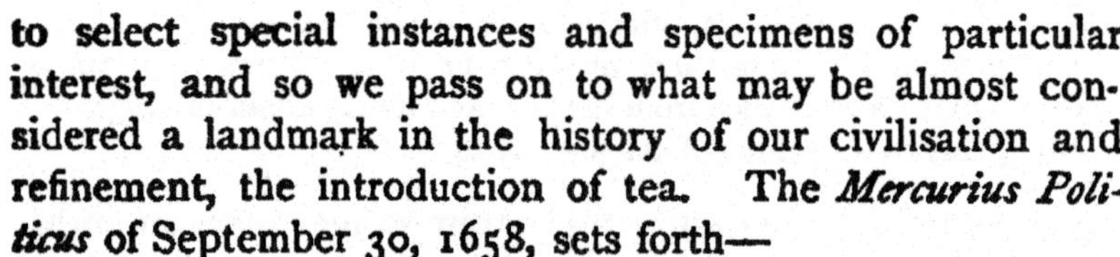

to select special instances and specimens of particular interest, and so we pass on to what may be almost considered a landmark in the history of our civilisation and refinement, the introduction of tea. The *Mercurius Politicus* of September 30, 1658, sets forth—

THAT Excellent, and by all Physicians, approved, *China* drink, called by the Chineans *Tcha*, by other nations *Tay* alias *Tee*, is sold at the Sultaness Head Cophee-House, in Sweeting's Rents, by the Royal Exchange, London.

This announcement then marks an era; it shows that "l'impertinente nouveauté du siècle," as the French physician, Guy Patin, called it in his furious diatribes, has not only made its advent, but is fighting its way forward. Patin is not without followers even in the present day, many people who would be surprised if accused of wanting in sense believing all "slops" to be causes of degeneracy. It must be observed that this is not the first acquaintance of our countrymen with the Chinese leaf—the advertisement simply shows the progress it is making—as tea is said to have been occasionally sold in England as early as 1635, at the exorbitant price of from £6 to £10 per pound. Thomas Garway, a tobacconist and coffee-house keeper in Exchange Alley, the founder of Garraway's Coffee-house, was the first who sold and retailed tea, recommending it, as always has been, and always will be the case with new articles of diet, as a panacea for all disorders flesh is heir to. The following shop-bill, being more curious than any historical account we have of the early use of "the cup that cheers but not inebriates," will be found well worth reading :—

Tea in England hath been sold in the leaf for £6, and sometimes for £10 the pound weight, and in respect of its former scarceness and dearness it hath been only used as a regalia in high treatments and entertainments, and presents made thereof to princes and grandees till the year 1657. The said Garway did purchase a quantity thereof, and first sold the said tea in leaf or drink, made according to the directions of the most knowing merchants into those Eastern countries. On the knowledge of the said Garway's continued care and industry in obtaining the best tea, and making drink thereof very many noblemen, physicians, merchants, &c., have ever since sent to him for the said leaf, and daily resort to his house to drink the drink thereof. He sells tea from 16s. to 50s. a pound.

The opposition beverage, coffee—mention is made of the "cophee-house" in the "Tcha" advertisement—had been known in this country some years before, a Turkey merchant of London, of the name of Edwards, having brought the first bag of coffee to London, and his Greek servant, Pasqua Rosee, was the first to open a coffee-house in London. This was in 1652, the time of the Protectorate, and one Jacobs, a Jew, had opened a similar establishment in Oxford a year or two earlier. Pasqua Rosee's coffee-house was in St Michael's Alley, Cornhill. One of his original handbills is preserved in the British Museum, and is a curious record of a remarkable social innovation. It is here reprinted :—

THE VERTUE OF THE COFFEE DRINK,

First made and publicly sold in England by

PASQUA ROSEE.

The grain or berry called coffee, groweth upon little trees only in the deserts of Arabia. It is brought from thence and drunk generally throughout all the Grand Seignour's dominions. It is a simple, innocent thing, composed into a drink, by being dried in an oven, and ground to powder, and boiled up with spring water, and about half a pint of it to be drunk fasting an hour before, and not eating an hour after, and to be taken as hot as can possibly be endured; the which will never fetch the skin of the mouth, or raise any blisters by reason of that heat.

The Turk's drink at meals and other times is usually water, and their diet consists much of fruit; the acidities whereof are very much corrected by this drink.

The quality of this drink is cold and dry; and though it be a drier; yet it neither heats nor inflames more than hot posset. It so incloseth the orifice of the stomach, and fortifies the heat within, that it is very good to help digestion; and therefore of great use to be taken about three or four o'clock afternoon, as well as in the morning. It much quickens the spirits, and makes the heart lightsome; it is good against sore eyes, and the better if you hold your head over it and take in the steam that way. It suppresseth fumes exceedingly, and therefore is good against the head-ache, and will very much stop any defluxion of rheums that distil from the head upon the stomach, and so prevent and help consumptions and the cough of the lungs.

It is excellent to prevent and cure the dropsy, gout, and scurvy. It is known by experience to be better than any other drying drink for people in years, or children that have any running humours upon them, as the king's evil, &c. It is a most excellent remedy against the spleen, hypochondriac winds, and the like. It will prevent drowsiness, and make one fit for business, if one have occasion to watch, and therefore you are not to drink of it after supper, unless you intend to be watchful, for it will hinder sleep for three or four hours.

It is observed that in Turkey, where this is generally drunk, that they are not troubled with the stone, gout, dropsy, or scurvy, and that their skins are exceeding clear and white. It is neither laxative nor restringent.

Made and Sold in St Michael's Alley, in Cornhill, by Pasqua Rosee, at the sign of his own head.

In addition to tea and coffee, the introduction and acceptance of which had certainly a most marked influence on the progress of civilisation, may be mentioned a third, which, though extensively used, never became quite so great a favourite as the others. Chocolate, the remaining member of the triad, was introduced into England much about the same period. It had been known in Germany as early as 1624, when Johan Frantz Rauch wrote a treatise against that beverage. In England, however, it seems to have been introduced much later, for in 1657 it was still advertised as a new drink. In the *Publick Advertiser* of Tuesday, June 16–22, 1657, we find the following:—

IN Bishopsgate Street, in Queen's Head Alley, at a Frenchman's house, is an excellent West India drink, called chocolate, to be sold, where you may have it ready at any time, and also unmade, at reasonable rates.

Chocolate never, except among exquisites and women of fashion, made anything of a race with its more sturdy opponents, in this country at all events, for while tea and coffee have become naturalised beverages, chocolate has always retained its foreign prejudices.

In the *Kingdom's Intelligencer*, a weekly paper published in 1662, are inserted several curious advertisements giving the prices of tea, coffee, chocolate, &c., one of which is as follows:—

AT the Coffeehouse in Exchange Alley, is sold by retail the right *coffee powder*, from 4s. to 6s. 8d. per pound, as in goodness; that pounded in a mortar at 2s. 6d. per pound, and that termed the East India berry at 18d. per pound. Also that termed the right Turkey berry, well garbled at 3s. per pound, the ungarbled for lesse, with directions gratis how to make and use the same. Likewise there you may have *chocolatta*, the ordinary pound boxes at 2s. 6d. per pound; the perfumed from 4s. to 10s. per pound. Also *sherbets*, made in Turkie, of lemons, roses, and violets perfumed, and *Tea* according to its goodness. For all which, if any gentleman shall write or send, they shall be sure of the best, as they shall order, and, to avoid deceit, warranted under the house-seal—viz., Morat the Great. Further, all gentlemen that are customers and acquaintance, are (the next New Year's day), invited at the sign of the Great Turk, at the new coffee house, in Exchange Alley, where coffee will be on free cost.

Leaving the enticing subject of these new beverages, we find that in May 1657 there appeared a weekly paper which assumed the title of the *Public Advertiser*, the first number being dated 19th to 26th May. It was printed for Newcombe, in Thames Street, and consisted almost wholly of advertisements, including the arrivals and departures of ships, and books to be printed. Soon other papers also commenced to insert more and more advertisements, sometimes stuck in the middle of political items, and announcements of marine disasters, murders, marriages, births, and deaths. Most of the notices at this period related to runaway apprentices and black boys, fairs and cockfights, burglaries and highway robberies, stolen horses, lost dogs, swords, and scent-bottles, and the departure of coaches on long journeys into the provinces, and sometimes even as far as Edinburgh. These announcements are not devoid of interest and curiosity for us who live in the days of railways and fast steamers; and so we quote the following from the *Mercurius Politicus* of April 1, 1658:—

FROM the 26th day of April 1658; there will continue to go Stage Coaches from the *George* Inn, without Aldersgate, *London*, unto the several Cities and Towns, for the Rates and at the times hereafter mentioned and declared.

Every Monday, Wednesday, and Friday.

To Salisbury in two days for xxs. To *Blandford* and *Dorchester* in two days and half for xxxs. To *Burport* in three days for xxxs. To *Exmaster*, *Hunnington*, and *Exeter* in four days for xls.

To *Stamford* in two days for xxs. To *Newark* in two days and a half for xxvs. To *Bawtry* in three days for xxxs. To *Doncaster* and *Ferribridge* for xxxvs. To *York* in four days for xls.

Mondays and *Wednesdays* to *Ockinton* and *Plimouth* for ls.

Every *Monday* to *Helperby* and *Northallerton* for xlvs. To *Darneton* and *Ferryhil* for ls. To *Durham* for lvs. To *Newcastle* for iii£.

Once every fortnight to *Edinburgh* for iv£ a peece—*Mondays.*

Every *Friday*, to *Wakefield* in four days, xls.

All persons who desire to travel unto the Cities, Towns, and Roads herein hereafter mentioned and expressed, namely—to *Coventry*, *Litchfield*, *Stone*, *Namptwich*, *Chester*, *Warrington*, *Wiggan*, *Chorley*, *Preston*, *Gastang*, *Lancaster* and *Kendal;* and also to *Stamford*, *Grantham*, *Newark*, *Tuxford*, *Bawtrey*, *Doncaster*, *Ferriebridge*, *York*, *Helperby*, *Northallerton*, *Darneton*, *Ferryhill*, *Durham*, and *Newcastle*, *Wakefield*, *Leeds*, and *Halifax;* and also to *Salisbury*, *Blandford*, *Dorchester*, *Burput*, *Exmaster*, *Hunnington*, and *Exeter*, *Ockinton*, *Plimouth*, and *Cornwal;* let them repair to the *George* Inn, at *Holborn Bridge*, *London*, and thence they shall be in good Coaches with good Horses, upon every *Monday*, *Wednesday*, and *Fridays*, at and for reasonable Rates.

Among the advertisements which prevailed most extensively in those early times, may, as has been remarked, be ranked those of runaway servants, apprentices, and black boys. England at that time swarmed with negro or mulatto boys, which the wealthy used as pages, in imitation of the Italian nobility. They were either imported from the West Indies, or brought from the Peninsula. The first advertisement of a runaway black page we meet with is dated August 11, 1659, but in this instance the article is advertised as "lost," like a dog, which is after all but natural, the boy being a chattel:—

A Negro-boy, about nine years of age, in a gray Searge suit, his hair cut close to his head, was lost on Tuesday last, *August* 9, at night, in St Nicholas Lane, London. If any one can give notice of him to Mr Tho. Barker, at the Sugar Loaf, in that Lane, they shall be well rewarded for their pains.

It is amusing to see, from this advertisement, that the wool of the negro found no grace in the eye of his Puritan master, who cropped the boy's head as close as his own. Black boys continued in fashion for more than a century after, and were frequently offered for sale, by means of advertisements, in the same manner as slaves used to be, within recent years, in the Southern States of America. Even as late as 1769 sales of human flesh went on in this country. The *Gazetteer*, April 18, of that year, classes together "for sale at the Bull and Gate, Holborn: a chestnut gelding, a trim-whiskey, and a well-made, good-tempered black boy;" whilst a Liverpool paper of ten years later, October 15, 1779, announces as to be sold by auction, "at George Dunbar's offices, on Thursday next, 21st inst., at one o'clock, a black boy about fourteen years old, and a large mountain tiger-cat." This will be news to many blind worshippers of the ideal creature known as "a man and a brother."

Another curiosity of the advertisement literature of the seventeenth century is the number of servants and apprentices absconding with their masters' property. Nearly all those dishonest servants must have had appearances such as in these days might lead to conviction first and trial afterwards. First of all, there is scarcely one of them but is "pock-marked," "pock-pitted," "pock-fretted," "pock-holed," "pit-marked," or "full of pock-holes," a fact which furnishes a significant index of the ravages this terrible sickness must have made amongst our ancestors, and offers a conclusive argument—though argument is unfortunately inadmissible among them—to those blatant and illogical people, the opponents of vaccination. Besides the myriads who annually died of small-pox, it would, perhaps, not be an exaggeration to assume that one-fourth of mankind at that time was pock-marked, and not pock-marked as we understand the term. Whole features were destroyed, and a great percentage of blindness was attributable to this cause. Indeed, so accustomed were the people of those times to pock-marked faces, that these familiar inequalities of the facial surface do not appear to have been considered an absolute drawback even upon the charms of a beauty or a beau. Louis XIV. in his younger days was considered one of the handsomest men of France, notwithstanding that he was pock-marked, and La Vallière and some other famous beauties of that period are known to have laboured under the same disadvantage. This is a hard fact which should destroy many of the ideas raised by fiction. The following is a fair specimen of the descriptions of the dangerous classes given in the early part of the latter half of the seventeenth century, and is taken from the *Mercurius Politicus* of May 1658 :—

A Black-haired Maid, of a middle stature, thick set, with big breasts, having her face full marked with the small-pox, calling herself by the name of *Nan* or *Agnes Hobson*, did, upon Monday, the 28 of May, about six o'Clock in the morning, steal away from her Ladies house in the Pal-Mall, a mingle-coloured wrought Tabby gown of Deer colour and white; a black striped Sattin Gown with four broad bone-black silk Laces, and a plain black watered French Tabby Gown; Also one Scarlet-coloured and one other Pink-coloured Sarcenet Peticoat, and a white watered Tabby Wastcoat, plain; Several Sarcenet, Mode, and thin black Hoods and Scarfs, several fine Holland Shirts, a laced pair of Cuffs and Dressing, one pair of Pink-coloured Worsted Stockings, a Silver Spoon, a Leather bag, &c. She went away in greyish Cloth Wastcoat turned, and a Pink-coloured Paragon upper Peticoat, with a green Tammy under one. If any shall give notice of this person or things at one *Hopkins*, a Shoomaker's, next door to the Vine Tavern, near the Pal-mall end, near Charing Cross, or at Mr *Ostler's*, at the Bull Head in Cornhill, near the Old Exchange, they shall be rewarded for their pains.

In the same style was almost every other description; and

though embarrassed by the quantity as well as quality we have to choose from, we cannot pass over this bit of word-painting, which is rich in description. It is from the *Mercurius Politicus* of July 1658:—

ONE Eleanor Parker (by birth *Haddock*), of a Tawny reddish complexion, a pretty long nose, tall of stature, servant to *Mr Ferderic Howpert*, Kentish Town, upon Saturday last, the *26th of June*, ran away and stole two Silver Spoons; a sweet Tent-work Bag, with gold and silver Lace about it, and lined with Satin; a Bugle work-Cushion, very curiously wrought in all manners of slips and flowers; a Shell cup, with a Lyon's face, and a Ring of silver in its mouth; besides many other things of considerable value, which she took out of her Mistresses Cabinet, which she broke open; as also some Cloaths and Linen of all sorts, to the value of Ten pounds and upwards. If any one do meet with her and please to secure her, and give notice to the said *Ferderic Howpert*, or else to Mr *Malpass*, Leather seller, at the Green Dragon, at the upper end of Lawrence Lane, he shall be thankfully rewarded for his pains.

But besides the ravages of small-pox, the hue and cry raised after felons exhibits an endless catalogue of deformities. Hardly a rogue is described but he is "ugly as sin." In turning over these musty piles of small quarto newspapers which were read by the men of the seventeenth century, a most ill-favoured crowd of evil-doers springs up around us. The rogues cannot avoid detection, if they venture out among good citizens, for they are branded with marks by which all men may know them. Take the following specimens of "men of the time." The first is from the *London Gazette* of January 24–28, 1677:—

ONE John Jones, a Welchman, servant to Mr Gray, of Whitehall, went away the 27th with £50 of his master's in silver. He is aged about 25 years, of a middle stature, something thick, a down black look, purblind, between long and round favoured, something pale of complexion, lank, dark, red hair; a hair-coloured large suit on, something light; a bowe nose a little sharp and reddish, almost beetle brow'd and something deaf, given to slabber in his speech. Whoever secures the said servant and brings him to his master, shall have £5 reward.

This portrait was evidently drawn by an admirer; and

it is with evident pleasure that the artist, after describing the "lank, dark, red hair," and the suit like it, returns to the charge, and gives the finishing touches to the comely features. Here is another pair of beauties, whose descriptions appear in the *Currant Intelligence*, March 6–9, 1682:—

SAMUEL SMITH, Scrivener in Grace Church Street, London, about 26 years old, crook-backed, of short stature, red hair, hath a black periwig and sometimes a light one, pale complexion, Pock-holed full face, a mountier cap with a scarlet Ribbon, and one of the same colour on his cravat and sword, a light coloured campaign coat faced with blue shag, in company with his brother John Smith, who has a slit in his nose, a tall lusty man, red hair, a sad grey campaign coat, a lead colour suit lined with red: they were mounted, one on a flea-bitten grey, the other on a light bay horse.

For powers of description this next is worthy of study. It is contemporary with the other:—

WILLIAM WALTON, a tall young man about sixteen years of age, down-look'd, much disfigured with the Small-pox, strait brown hair, black rotten teeth, having an impediment in his speech, in a sad coloured cloth sute, the coat faced with shag, a white hat with a black ribbon on it, went away from his master, &c. &c.

And so on, as per example; the runaways and missing folk—for all that are advertised are not offenders against the law—seem to have exhausted the whole catalogue of human and inhuman ugliness. By turns the attention of the public is directed to a brown fellow with a long nose, or with full staring grey eyes, countenance very ill-favoured, having lost his right eye, voice loud and shrill, teeth black and rotten, with a wide mouth and a hang-dog look, smutty complexion, a dimple in the top of his nose, or a flat wry nose with a star in it, voice low and disturbed, long visage, down look, and almost every other objectionable peculiarity imaginable. What a milk-and-water being our modern rough is, after all!

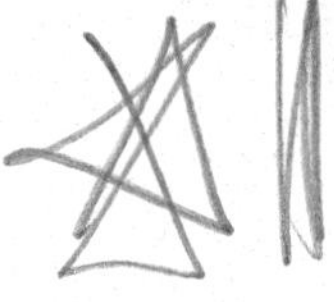

Dr Johnson, in a bantering paper on the art of advertising, published in the *Idler*, No. 40, observes: "The man who first took advantage of the general curiosity that was ex-

cited by a siege or battle to betray the readers of news into the knowledge of the shop where the best puffs and powder were to be sold, was undoubtedly a man of great sagacity, and profound skill in the nature of man. But when he had once shown the way, it was easy to follow him." Yet it took a considerable time before the mass of traders could be brought to understand the real use of advertising, even as the great Doctor understood it. Even he could hardly have comprehended advertising as it is now. The first man who endeavoured to systematically convince the world of the vast uses which might be made of this medium was Sir Roger L'Estrange. That intelligent speculator, in 1663, obtained an appointment to the new office of "Surveyor of the Imprimery and Printing Presses," by which was granted to him the sole privilege of writing, printing, and publishing all narratives, advertisements, mercuries, &c. &c., besides all briefs for collections, playbills, quack-salvers' bills, tickets, &c. &c. On the 1st of August 1663 appeared a paper published by him, under the name of the *Intelligencer*, and on the 24th of the same month the public were warned against the "petty cozenage" of some of the booksellers, who had persuaded their customers that they could not sell the paper under twopence a sheet, though it was sold to them at about a fourth part of that price. The first number of the *Newes* (which was also promoted by Sir Roger L'Estrange) appeared September 3, 1663, and, as we are told by Nicholls in his "Literary Anecdotes," "contained more advertisements of importance than any previous paper." Still, the benefit of the publicity which might be derived from advertising was so little understood by the trading community of the period, that after the Plague and the Great Fire this really valuable means of acquainting the public with new places of abode, the resumption of business, and the thousand and one changes incidental on such calamities, were almost entirely neglected. Though nearly the entire city had been burnt out, and the citizens must necessarily have entered new premises or erected extempore shops, yet hardly any announcements appear in the papers to acquaint the public of the new addresses. The *London Gazette*, October 11–15, 1666, offered its services, but hardly to any effect; little regard being paid to the following invitation:—

Such as have settled in new habitations since the late fire, and desire for the convenience of their correspondence to publish the place of their present abode, or to give notice of goods lost or found, may repair to the corner house in Bloomsbury, or on the east side of the great square [Bloomsbury Square] before the house of the Right Honourable the Lord Treasurer, where there is care taken for the receipt and publication of such advertisements.

Among the very few advertisements relating to those great calamities is the following, produced by the Plague, which is inserted in the *Intelligencer*, June 22–30, 1665:—

THIS is to certify that the master of the Cock and Bottle, commonly called the Cock alehouse, at Temple bar, hath dismissed his servants, and shut up his house for this long vacation, intending (God willing) to return at Michaelmas next, so that all persons who have any accounts or farthings belonging to the said house, are desired to repair thither before the 8th of this instant, July, and they shall receive satisfaction.

Relating to the Fire, the following from the *London Gazette*, March 12, 1672–73, was the notification:—

THESE are to give notice that Edward Barlet, Oxford carrier, hath removed his Inn in London from the Swan at Holborn Bridge to the Oxford Arms in Warwick Lane, where he did inne before the Fire. His coaches and waggons going forth on their usual days, Mondays, Wednesdays, and Fridays. He hath also a hearse, with all things convenient to carry a corpse to any part of England.

There is not, however, a single advertisement relating to any of those temporary conveniences of every kind which invariably arise, as by magic, on any great and unusual emergency. Indeed, about this period, and for a long time after, the *London Gazette*, which was the official organ of the day, appeared frequently without a single advertisement; and till the end of the reign of Charles II., it was only very rarely that that paper contained more than four advertisements of a general kind, very frequently the number being less. The subjects of these were almost exclusively thefts, losses, and runaways. Booksellers' and quacks' advertisements were, however, even then frequent in this paper; their announcements always preceded the others, and were printed in a different type.

In 1668 Mr (afterwards Sir) Roger L'Estrange commenced the *Mercury, or Advertisements concerning Trade,* which does not seem to have answered, for it soon became extinct. Some years after, the now well-known scheme of issuing sheets of advertisements gratuitously, trusting for profit to the number of advertisers, was for the first time attempted. The paper started on this principle was called the *City Mercury*, and appears to have had a hard struggle for existence, since the publishers thought it necessary to insert in No. 52 (March 30, 1673) a notice of this tenor:—

Notwithstanding this paper has been published so long, there are many persons ignorant of the design and advantage of it. And it every week comes to the hand of some, both in City and Country, that never see it before: For which reason the Publisher thinks himself obliged (that all may have benefit by it), to inform them that:—

1. He gives away every *Monday* above a thousand of them to all the *Booksellers, shops* and *inns*, and most of the principal *coffee-houses* in *London* and *Westminster*. Besides they are now sent to most of the cities and principal towns in England.

2. Any person that has anything to insert in it, as the *titles* of *books, houses* or *land* to be *lett* or *sold, persons removing from one place to another*, things *lost* or *stole, physitians' advertisements*, or *inquiries* for *houses* or *lands* to be *lett* or *sold*, for *places* or for *servants*, &c., may bring or send them to the Publisher, *Tho. Howkins*, in *George Yard*, in Lombard Street, London, who will carefully insert them at reasonable rates.

3. That this way of publishing is much more advantageous than giving away *Bills* in the street, is certain, for where there is one of them read, there's twenty is not; and a thousand of these cannot be supposed to be read by less than twenty times the number of persons; and done for at least the twentieth part of the charge, and with much less trouble and greater success; as has been experienced by many persons that have things inserted in it.

This paper lived but a short time; though the fact that

the proprietor undertook to furnish above a thousand copies per week to booksellers, shops, inns, and coffee-houses in London, and that it was sent to "most of the cities and principal towns in England," clearly indicates that the trade began to be aware of the advantages to be derived from publicity. Soon afterwards a paper of the same denomination, but published by another speculator, was commenced. Its appearance and purposes were told to the public in the autumn of 1675 by circulars or handbills, one of which has fortunately been stored up in the British Museum. As this curious document gives a comprehensive outline of the system of newspaper advertising, as it appeared to the most advanced thinkers in the reign of Charles II., we reprint it here *in extenso*:—

ADVERTISEMENT.

WHEREAS divers people are at great expense in printing, publishing, and dispersing of Bills of Advertisements: Observing how practical and Advantagious to Trade and Business, &c. this Method is in parts beyond the Seas.

These are to give notice, That all Persons in such cases concerned henceforth may have published in Print in the Mercury *or* Bills of Advertisements, *which shall come out every week on* Thursday *morning, and be delivered and dispersed in every house where the Bills of Mortallity are received, and elsewhere, the Publications and Advertisements of all the matters following, or any other matter or thing not herein mentioned, that shall relate to the Advancement of Trade, or any lawful business not granted in propriety to any other.*

Notice of all Goods, Merchandizes, and Ships to be sold, the place where to be seen, and day and hour.

Any ships to be let to Freight, and the time of their departure, the place of the Master's habitation, and where to be spoken with before and after Exchange time.

All Ships, their Names, and Burthens, and capacities, and where their Inventaries are to be seen.

All other Parcels and Materials or Furniture for shipping in like manner.

Any Houses to be Let or Sold, or Mortgaged, with Notes of their Contents.

Any Lands or Houses in City or Country, to be Sold or Mortgaged.

The Erection, Alteration, or Removal of any Stage-coach, or any common Carrier.

Advertisements of any considerable Bargains that are offered.

Any curious Invention or Experiment that is to be exposed to the Public view or Sale, may be hereby notified when and where.

Hereby Commissioners upon Commissions against Bankrupts may give large notice.

In like manner any man may give notice as he pleaseth to his Creditors.

Hereby the Settlement or Removal of any Publick Office may be notified.

Hereby all School-masters, and School-mistresses, and Boarding-schools, and Riding-schools or Academies, may publish the place where their Schools are kept.

And in like manner, where any Bathes or Hot-houses are kept.

And the Place or Key at the Waterside, whereto any Hoy or Vessel doth constantly come to bring or carry Goods; as those of *Lee, Favershom*, and *Maidstone*, &c.

AT the Office, which is to be kept for the Advertisements, any Person shall be informed (without any Fee) where any Stage-coach stands, where any common Carrier lies, that comes to any Inn within the Bills of Mortallity, and their daies of coming in and going out.

In like manner all the accustomed Hoys or Vessels that come to the several Keys from the several Ports of England.

All Masters and Owners of the several Stage-coaches, and the Master-Carriers, and the Masters of all the Hoys and Vessels above mentioned, are desired to repair between this and Christmas *day next, to the Office kept for the receipt of the Advertisements, to see if no mistakes be in their several daies and rates, that the said Books may be declared perfect, which shall be no charge to the Persons concerned.*

The Office or Place where any Person may have his desires answered in anything hereby advertised, is kept in St Michael's Alley in Cornhil, London, right against Williams Coffee-house, where constant attendance every day in the Week shall be given, from Nine in the Morning, to Five in the Evening, to receive the desires of all Persons in matters of this nature, carefully to answer them in the same.

With Allowance.

LONDON:

Printed by *Andrew Clark*, in *Aldersgate Street*, 1675.

In accordance with this prospectus, the first number of the *City Mercury* appeared November 4, 1675.

We, who are familiar with the thousand and one tricks resorted to by traders in order to attract attention to their advertisements, may be apt to ridicule the artless manner in which these notices were brought before the public of the seventeenth century. Different types, dividing lines, woodcuts, and other contrivances to catch the wandering eye, were still unknown; and frequently all the advertisements were set forth in one string, without a single break, or even full stop, as in the subjoined specimen from the *Loyal Impartial Mercury*, November 14-17, 1681:—

☞ THE House in the Strand wherein the Morocco Embassador lately resided is to be let, furnished or unfurnished, intirely or in several parts; a house in Marklane fit for a marchant; also very good lodgings not far from the Royal Exchange, fit for any marchant or gentleman to be let, inquire at the North West corner of the Royal Exchange, and there you may know further; inquiry is made at the said office for places to be Stewards of courts, liberties or franchises, or any office at law, or places to be auditor, or receiver, or steward of the household, or gentleman of horse to any nobleman or gentleman; or places to be clarks to brew-houses, or wharfs, or suchlike; also any person that is willing to buy or sell any estates, annuities, or mortgages, or let, or take any house, or borrow money upon the bottom of ships, may be accomodated at the said office.

Conciseness was of course necessary when it is recollected that the paper was only a folio half-sheet, though the news was so scanty that the few advertisements were a boon to the reader, and were sure to be read. This was an advantage peculiar to the early advertisers. So long as the papers were small, and the advertisements few in number, the trade announcements were almost more interesting than the news. But when the papers increased in bulk, and advertisements became common, it behoved those who wished to attract special attention to resort to contrivances which would distinguish them from the surrounding crowd of competitors.

The editor of the *London Mercury*, in 1681, evidently with an eye to making his paper a property on the best of all principles, requests all those who have houses for sale to advertise in his columns, "where," says he, "farther care will be taken for their disposal than the bare publishing them, by persons who make it their business." Consequently we frequently meet in this paper with notices of "A delicate House to lett," agreeably varied with advertisements concerning spruce beer, scurvy grass, Daffy's elixir, and other specifics. Notwithstanding that the utility of advertising as a means of obtaining publicity was as yet hardly understood, the form of an advertisement, according to modern plans, was, it is curious to observe, frequently adopted at this period to expose sentiments in a veiled manner, or to call attention to public grievances. Thus, for instance, the first numbers of the *Heraclitus Ridens*, published in 1681, during the effervescence of the Popish plots, contained almost daily one or more of these political satires, of which the following may serve as examples. The first appears February 4.

IF any person out of natural curiosity desire to be furnished with ships or castles in the air, or any sorts of prodigies, apparitions, or strange sights, the better to fright people out of their senses, and by persuading them there are strange judgments, changes, and revolutions hanging over their heads, thereby to persuade them to pull them down by discontents, fears, jealousies, and seditions; let them repair to Ben Harris, at his shop near the Royal Exchange, where they may be furnished with all sorts and sizes of them, at very cheap and easy rates.

There is also to be seen the strange egg with the comet in it which was laid at Rome, but sent from his Holiness to the said Ben, to make reparations for his damages sustained, and as a mark of esteem for his zeal and sufferings in promoting discord among the English hereticks, and sowing the seeds of sedition among the citizens of London.

The edition of February 15 contains the following:—

IF any protestant dissenter desire this spring time to be furnished with sedition seeds, or the true protestant rue, which they call "herb of grace," or any other hopeful plants of rebellion, let them repair to the famous French gardeners Monsieur F. Smith, Msr. L. Curtis, and Msr. B. Harris; where they may have not only of all the kinds which grew in the garden of the late keepers of the liberty of England; but much new variety raised by the art and industry of the said gardeners, with directions in print when to sow them, and how to cultivate them when they are raised.

You may also have there either green or pickled sallads of rumours and reports, far more grateful to the palate, or over a glass of wine, than your French Champignons or mushrooms, Popish Olives, or Eastland Gherkins.

And on March 1 there was given to the world:—

A MOST ingenious monkey, who can both write, read, and speak as good sense as his master, nursed in the kitchen of the late Commonwealth, and when they broke up housekeeping entertained by Nol Protector, may be seen do all his old tricks over again, for pence apiece, every Wednesday, at his new master's, Ben. Harris, in Cornhill.

This was a species of wit similar to that associated with the imaginary signs adopted in books with secret imprints, in order to express certain political notions, the sentiments of which were embodied in the work; for instance, a pamphlet just before the outbreak of the Civil War is called, "Vox Borealis, or a Northerne Discoverie, etc. Printed by Margery Marprelate, amidst the Babylonians, in Thwack Coat Lane, at the sign of the Crab Tree Cudgell, without any privilege of the Catercaps."

One John Houghton, F.R.S., who combined the business of apothecary with that of dealer in tea, coffee, and chocolate, in Bartholomew Lane, commenced a paper in 1682, entitled *A Collection for the Improvement of Husbandry and Trade*,* which continued to be issued weekly for some time; and though it failed, it was revived again on March 30, 1692. It was modelled on the same plan as the *City Mercury* of 1675, and was rather ambitious in its views. It consisted of one folio half-sheet, and was intended to "lay out for a large

* John Nicholl, in his "Literary Anecdotes," vol. iv. p. 71, calls the editor of this paper Benjamin Harris, a well-known publisher of pamphlets in the reign of Charles II., and says that J. Knighton was the editor in 1692. This last name may be a clerical error for Houghton.

correspondence, and for the advantage of tenant, landlord, corn merchant, mealman, baker, brewer, feeder of cattle, farmer, maltster, buyer and seller of coals, hop merchant, soap merchant, tallow chandler, wood merchant, their customers," &c. But no advertisements proper were mentioned at first; it was a mere bulletin or price-current of the above-named trades and of auctions, besides shipping news and the bills of mortality. The first advertisement appeared in the third number, it was a "book-ad," and figured there all by itself; and it was not till the 8th of June that the second advertisement appeared, which assumed the following shape:—

☞ FOR the further and better Improvement of Husbandry and Trade and for the Encouragement thereof, especially in Middlesex and the bordering counties, a Person, now at my house in Bartholomew Lane, does undertake to make or procure made, as good malt of the barley of these counties, and of that Malt as good Ale as is made at Derby, Nottingham, or any other place now famous for that liquor, and that upon such reasonable terms as shall be to general satisfaction, the extraordinary charge not amounting to above one penny per bushel more than that is now; only thus much I must advise, if provision be not made speedily, the opportunity will be lost for the next malting time.

Under the fostering influence of Houghton, who appears to have been keenly aware of the advantage to be derived from this manner of obtaining publicity, advertisements of every kind began gradually to appear, and ere long the booksellers, who for some time had monopolised this paper, were pushed aside by the other trades; and so the attention of the public is by turns directed to blacking balls, tapestry hangings, spectacles, writing ink, coffins, copper and brass work, &c. &c.; and these notices increased so rapidly that, added to No. 52, which appeared on July 28, 1693, there is a half-sheet of advertisements, which is introduced to the public with the following curious notice:—

My Collection I shall carry on as usual. This part is to give away, and those who like it not, may omit the reading. I believe it will help on Trade, particularly encourage the advertisers to increase the vent of my papers. I shall receive all sorts of advertisements, but shall answer for the reasonableness of none, unless I give thereof a particular character on which (as I shall give it) may be *dependance*, but no argument that others deserve not as well. I am informed that seven or eight thousand gazettes are each time printed, which makes them the most universal Intelligencers; but I 'll suppose mine their first handmaid, because it goes (though not so thick yet) to *most* parts: It 's also lasting to be put into Volumes with indexes, and particularly there shall be an index of all the advertisements, whereby, for ages to come, they may be useful.

This first sheet consists solely of advertisements about newly published books, but it concludes:—

☞ Whither 'tis worth while to give an account of ships sent in for lading or ships arrived, with the like for coaches and carriers; or to give notice of approaching fairs, and what commodities are chiefly sold there, I must submit to the judgment of those concerned.

The advertisements in Houghton's *Collection* may appear strange to the reader accustomed to rounded sentences and glowing periods, but in the reign of William III. the general absence of education rendered the social element more unsophisticated in character. In those old days the advertiser and editor of the paper frequently speak in the first person singular; also the advertiser often speaks through the editor. A few specimens taken at random will give the reader a tolerably good idea of the style then prevalent:—

—— A very eminent brewer, and one I know to be a very honest gentleman, wants an apprentice; I can give an account of him.

—— I want a house keeper rarely well accomplished for that purpose. 'Tis for a suitable gentleman.

—— I know of valuable estates to be sold.

—— I want several apprentices for a valuable tradesman.

—— I can help to ready money for any library great or small or parcels of pictures or household goods.

—— I want a negro man that is a good house carpenter and a good shoemaker.

⁂ I want a young man about 14 or 15 years old that can trim and look after a peruke. 'Tis to wait on a merchant.

—— I want a pritty boy to wait on a gentleman who will take care of him and put him out an apprentice.

—— If any gentleman wants a housekeeper, I believe I can help to the best in England.

—— Many masters want apprentices and many youths want masters. If they apply themselves to me, I'll strive to help them. Also for variety of valuable services.

By reason of my great corresponding, I may help masters to apprentices and Apprentices to Masters. And now is wanting Three Boys, one with £70, one with £30, and a Scholar with £60.

—— I know of several curious women that would wait on ladies to be housekeepers.

—— Now I want a good usher's place in a Grammar school.

—— I want a young man that can write and read, mow and roll a garden, use a gun at a deer, and understand country sports, and to wait at table, and such like.

—— If any young man that plays well on the violin and writes a good hand desires a clerkship, I can help him to £20 a year.

—— I want a complete young man, that will wear livery, to wait on a very valuable gentleman, but he must know how to play on a violin or a flute.

—— I want a genteel footman that can play on the violin to wait on a person of honour.

—— If I can meet with a sober man that has a counter tenor voice, I can help him to a place worth £30 the year or more.

This continual demand for musical servants arose from the fashion of making them take part in musical performances, of which custom we find frequent traces in Pepys. Altogether the most varied accomplishments appear to have been expected from servants; as, for instance,—

—— If any Justice of the Peace wants a clerk, I can help to one that has been so seven years; understands accounts, to be butler, also to receive money. He also can shave and buckle wigs.

The editor frequently gives special testimony as to the respectability of the advertiser:—

—— If any one wants a wet nurse, I can help them, as I am informed, to a very good one.

—— I know a gentlewoman whose family is only her husband herself and maid, and would to keep her company take care of a child, two or three, of three years old or upwards. She is my good friend, and such a one that whoever put their children to her, I am sure will give me thanks, and think themselves happy, let them be what rank they will.

—— I have been to Mr Firmin's work house in Little Britain, and seen a great many pieces of what seems to me excellent linen, made by the poor in and about London. He will sell it at reasonable rates, and I believe whatever house keepers go there to buy will not repent, and on Wednesdays and Saturdays in the forenoon he is always there himself.

—— I have met with a curious gardener that will furnish any body that sends to me for fruit trees, and floreal shrubs, and garden seeds. I have made him promise with all solemnity that whatever he sends shall be purely good, and I verily believe he may be depended on.

—— One that has waited on a lady divers years, and understands all affairs in housekeeping and the needle, desires some such place. She seems a discreet, staid body.

At other times Houghton recommends "a tidy footman," a "quick, well-looking fellow," or "an extraordinary cook-maid;" and observes of a certain ladysmaid, who offered her services through his *Collection*, "and truly she looks and discourses passing well." Occasionally he also guarantees the situation; thus, applying for "a suitable man that can read and write, and will wear a livery," he adds for the information of flunkeys in general: "I believe that 'twill be a very good place, for 'tis to serve a fine gentleman whom I well know, and he will give £5 the year besides a livery." Imagine Jeames of Belgravia being told he should have £5 for his important annual services! Another time "'tis to wait on a very valuable old batchelor gentleman in the City." Again, he recommends a Protestant French gentleman, who is willing to wait on some person of quality, and Houghton adds, "from a valuable divine, my good friend, I have a very good character of him." Of a certain surgeon, whom he advertises, he says, "I have known him, I believe, this twenty years." All these recommendations bear an unmistakable character of truth and honesty on their face, and are very different from the commendatory paragraphs which nowadays appear in the body of a paper because of long advertisements which are to be found in the outer sheet. Nor is the worthy man ever willing to engage his word further than where he can speak by experience; in other cases, an "I believe," or some such cautious expression, invariably appears. Recommending a hairdresser, he says—

—— I know a peruke maker that *pretends* to make perukes extraordinary fashionable, and will sell good pennyworths; I can direct to him.

And once, when a number of quack advertisements had found their way into the paper, old Houghton, with a sly nod and a merry twinkle in his eye, almost apparent as one reads, drily puts his "index" above them, with the following caution:—

☞ Pray, mind the preface to this half sheet. Like lawyers, I take all causes. I may fairly; who likes not may stop here.

A tolerably broad hint of his disbelief in the said nostrums and elixirs. Even booksellers had to undergo the test of his ordeal, and having discovered some of their shortcomings, he warned them—

⁂ I desire all booksellers to send me no new titles to old books, for they will be rejected.

When a book of the right reverend father in God John Wilkins, late Bishop of Chester, was published, Houghton recommended it in patronising terms—

—— I have read this book, and do think it a piece of great ingenuity, becoming the Bishop of Chester, and is useful for a great many purposes, both profit and pleasure.

Of another work he says—

—— With delight have I read over this book, and think it a very good one.

Thus, notwithstanding the primitive form of the advertisements, the benefit to be derived from this mode of publicity began to be more and more understood. It was not without great trouble, however; and it was necessary that Houghton should constantly direct the attention of the trading community to the resources and advantages of advertising, which he did in the most candid manner. He simply and abruptly puts the question and leaves those interested to solve it. Thus :—

—— Whether advertisements of schools, or houses and lodgings about London may be useful, I submit to those concerned.

And the answer came; for a few days after the public were informed that

—— At one Mr Packer's, in Crooked Lane, next the Dolphin, are very good Lodgings to be let, where there is freedom from noise, and a pretty garden.

Freedom from noise and a pretty garden in a street leading from Eastcheap to Fish Street Hill! Shortly after Houghton calmly observes :—

—— I now find advertisements of schools, houses and lodgings in and about London are thought useful.

He then starts other subjects :—

—— I believe some advertisements about bark and timber might be of use both to buyer and seller.

⁂ I find several barbers think it their interest to take in these papers, and I believe the rest will when they understand them.

The barber's shop was then the headquarters of gossip, as it took a long time to shave the whole of a man's beard and curl a sufficient quantum of hair or wig, as worn in those old days, and so the man of suds was expected to entertain his customers or find them entertainment. Next turning his attention to the clergy, Houghton offers that body a helping hand also :—

⁂ I would gladly serve the clergy in all their wants.

How he understood this friendly help soon appeared :—

—— If any divine or their relicts have complete sets of manuscript sermons upon the Epistles and the Gospels, the Catechism or Festivals, I can help them to a customer.

The use of second-hand sermons was not unknown in those days, and detection was of course much less imminent than now. Then—

—— I have sold all the manuscript sermons I had and many more, and if any has any more to dispose of that are good and legibly writ, I believe I can help them to customers.

Possibly the "many more" was a heavy attempt at humour; but anyhow the sermon article was in great demand, and his kindly services did not rest there :—

—— If any incumbent within 20 miles of London will dispose of his living, I can help him to a chapman.

—— A rectory of £100 per annum in as good an air as any in England, 60 miles off, and an easy cure is to be commuted.

—— A vicaridge and another cure which requires service but once a month, value £86. 'Tis in Kent about 60 miles from London.

And so on, proving that the clergy had not refused the friendly offer, and were fully as ready as the tradesman to avail themselves of this means of giving vent to their wants and requirements.

Houghton would occasionally do a little business to oblige a friend, though it is fair to assume that he participated in the profits :—

*** For a friend, I can sell very good flower of brimstone, etc., as cheap or cheaper than any in town does ; and I 'll sell any good commodity for any man of repute if desired.

—— I find publishing for others does them kindness, therefore note : I sell lozenges for 8d. the ounce which good drinkers commend against heartburn, and are excellent for women with child, to prevent miscarriages ; also the true *lapis nephriticus* which is esteemed excellent for the stone by wearing it on the wrist.

—— I would gladly buy for a friend the historical part of Cornelius a Lapide upon the Bible.

Besides the above particular advertisements, the paper frequently contained another kind, which to us may appeai singularly vague and unbusinesslike, but which no doubt perfectly answered their purpose among a comparatively minute metropolitan population, the subjects of William III. We allude to general advertisements such as these:—

Last week was imported
Bacon by *Mr Edwards.*
Cheese by *Mr Francia.*
Corral Beads by *Mr Paggen.*
Crabs Eyes by *Mr Harvey.*
Horse Hair by *Mr Becens.*
Joynted Babies by *Mr Harrison.*
Mapps by *Mr Thompson.*
Orange Flower Water by *Mr Bellamy.*
Prospective Glasses by *Mr Mason.*
Saffron by *Mr Western.*
Sturgeon by *Mr Kett.*
If any desire it other things may be inserted.

In similar style a most extraordinary variety of other things imported are advertised in subsequent numbers, including crystal stones, hops, oxguts, incle, juniper, old pictures, onions, pantiles, quick eels, rushes, spruce beer, sturgeon, trees, brandy, chimney backs, caviar, tobacco-pipes, whale-fins, bugle, canes, sheep's-guts, washballs and snuff, a globe, aqua fortis, shruffe, quills, waxworks, ostrich feathers, scamony, clagiary paste, Scotch coals, sweet soap, onion seed, gherkins, mum, painted sticks, soap-berries, mask-leather, and so on, for a long time, only giving the names of the importers, without ever mentioning their addresses, until at last a bright idea struck this gentleman, who seems to have been one of those vulgarly said to be before their time, but who are in fact the pioneers who pave the way for all improvements; and so the *Collection* was enriched with the following notice:—

—— If desired I'll set down the places of abode, and I am sure 'twill be of good use: for I am often asked it.

Houghton was indeed so well aware of the utility of giving the addresses, that in order to render his paper more permanently useful, he published, apparently on his own account, not only the addresses of some of the principal shops, but also a list of the residences of the leading doctors. From this we gather that in June 1694 there were 93 doctors in and about London, also that Dr (afterwards Sir) Hans Sloane lived at Montague House (now the British Museum), Dr Radcliffe in Bow Street, and Dr Garth, by Duke Street. At the conclusion of this list the publisher says :—

——I shall also go the round, I. of Counsellors and Attorneys; II. of Surgeons and Gardiners; III. of Lawyers and Attorneys; IV. Schools and Woodmongers; V. Brokers, coaches and carriers, and such like, and then round again, beginning with Physitians.

Thus by untiring perseverance, and no small amount of thought and study, Houghton trained his contemporaries in the art of advertising, and made them acquainted with the valuable assistance to be derived from a medium which, as Alexis de Tocqueville remarks, drops the same thought into a thousand minds at almost the same period. Apart from the interest which his papers have on the subject we have been considering, they are full of graphic details which throw a clear and effective light on these old and bygone times. What can give a more vivid picture of the state of the roads in this country in winter-time, nearly two centuries ago, than the following notice extracted from the *Collection for Husbandry and Trade*, March 10, 1693 :—

—— Roads are filled with snow, we are forced to ride with the paquet over hedges and ditches. This day seven-night my boy with the paquet and two gentlemen were seven hours riding from Dunstable to Hockley, but three miles, hardly escaping with their lives, being often in holes and forced to be drawn out with ropes. A man and a woman were found dead within a mile hence. I fear I have lost my letter-carrier, who has not been heard of since Thursday last. Six horses lie dead on the road between Hockley and Brickhill, smothered.

I was told last night that lately was found dead near Beaumarais three men and three horses.

At this picture of those good old times for which people who know nothing about them now weep, we will stop. The rest of the story, so far as the development of advertisements is concerned, will be told in strict chronological order.

CHAPTER VI.

DEVELOPMENT OF ADVERTISING.

WE have now arrived at a period when the value of advertising was beginning to make itself felt among even the most conservative, and when it at last began to dawn upon the minds so unaccustomed to change or improvement, that a new era in the history of trade was about to commence, even if it had not commenced already. So the newspapers of the latter half of the seventeenth century begin to offer fresh inducements to the reader, no matter whether to the antiquarian or simply curious. And he must be a flippant reader indeed who is not impressed by these files of musty and bygone journals, pervaded by the spirit of a former age, and redolent of the busy doings of men who generations ago were not only dead but forgotten. Few things could be more suggestive of the steady progress of Time, and the quite as steady progress of his congeners, Death and Forgetfulness, than these papers. Novelists and essayists have described in most eloquent words the feelings which are aroused by the perusal of suddenly-discovered and long-forgotten letters ; and similar feelings, though of a much more extended description, are evoked by a glance through any volume of these moth-eaten journals. A writer of a few years back, speaking of the advertisements, says, "As we read in the old musty files of newspapers those *naïve* announcements, the very hum of bygone generations seems to rise to the ear. The chapman exhibits his quaint wares, the mountebank capers again upon his stage, we have the living portrait of the highwayman flying from justice, we see the old-china auctions thronged with ladies of quality with their attendant negro-boys, or those by 'inch of candle-light,' forming many a Schalken-like picture of light and shade; or later still we have Hogarthian sketches of the young bloods who swelled of old along the Pall-Mall. We trace the moving panorama of men and manners up to our own less demonstrative, but more earnest times; and all these cabinet pictures are the very daguerreotypes cast by the age which they exhibit, not done for effect, but faithful reflections of those insignificant items of life and things, too small, it would seem, for the generalising eye of the historian, however necessary to clothe and fill in the dry bones of his history." Indeed, turning over these musty volumes of newspapers is for the imaginative mind a pleasure equal to reading the *Tatler* or *Spectator*, or the plays of the period. By their means Cowper's idea of seeing life "through the loopholes of retreat" is realised, and characteristic facts and landmarks of progress in the history of civilisation are brought under our notice, as the busy life of bygone generations bursts full upon us. We see the merchant at his door, and inside the dimly-lit shops observe the fine ladies of the time deep in the mysteries of brocades and other articles of the feminine toilet, whose very names are now lost to even the mercers themselves. And not alone intent on flowered mantuas and paduasoys are they, for we can in fancy see them, keen ever to a fancied bargain, pricing Chinese teapots or Japanese cabinets, and again watch them as, with fluttering hearts, they assist at lotteries for valuables of the quality familiar to "knockouts" of our own time. We hear the lament of the beau who has lost his clouded amber-headed cane or his heart at the playhouse, and listen to the noisy quacks vending their nostrums, each praising his own wares or depreciating those of his rivals. We see the dishonest serving-man rush past us on the road carrying the heterogeneous treasures which have tempted his cupidity. Soon the "Hue and Cry" brings the same ill-favoured malefactor before us in an improved character as horse-stealer and highwayman; and ere long we hear of the conclusion of his short drama at Tyburn. Thus the various advertisements portray, with more or less vividness, lineaments of the times and the characters of the people.

That the newspapers were early used for the purpose of giving contradictions by means of advertisement, or effecting sly puffs, is shown by the following, which was doubtless intended to call attention to the work, and which was published in the form of an ordinary paragraph in the *Modern Intelligence*, April 15–22, 1647:—

There came forth a book this day relating how a divil did appear in the house or yard of Mr Young, mercer in Lombard St., with a great many particulars there related; It is desired by the gentleman of that house, and those of his family, that all that are credulous of those things (which few wise are), may be assured that its all fabulous, and that there was never any such thing. It is true there is a dog, and that dog hath a chain, and the gentleman's son played upon an instrument of music for his recreation,—but these are to be seen, which a spirit sure never was.

There is a logical deduction about the conclusion of this which it is to be hoped forced itself upon the minds of those who were ready to believe not only in the existence but in the visibility of spirits; and if the paragraph was but a lift for the book after all, it surely deserved success, if only for the quaint way in which it admits to the dog and the boy and the musical instrument, a combination equal upon an emergency to the simulation of a very powerful devil. In the very next edition of the same paper we come upon a paragraph which is even more direct in its advertising properties, which, in fact, might have been dictated by editorial "friendship" in these days, instead of in the first half of the seventeenth century. It runs thus:—

You should have had a notable oration made by the Bishop of Angoulesme and Grand Almoner to his Majesty of England, at a Convention in Paris in favour of the Catholicks in England and Ireland, but being

Numb. 2.

The Weekly Account:

Containing,

Certain Special and Remarkable Passages from both Houses of PARLIAMENT; And Collections of severall Letters from the Armies.

This *Account* is Licensed, and Entred into the Register-Book of the Company of *Stationers*; And Printed by BERNARD ALSOP, *According to Order of* PARLIAMENT.

From *Wednesday* the 6. of Jan. to *Wednesday* the 13. of January. 1646.

WEDNESDAY, January 13.

He Commissioners appointed by the Parliament to go to the North, and receive the Kings Person, and then conduct him to Holmeby house, are these

The Earle of Pembroke.
The E. of Denbigh.
The L. Mountague.
Sir Iohn Holland.
Sir Walter Earl.
Sir Iohn Cook.
Sir Iames Harrington.
Major Gen. Brown.
Mr. John Crew.

Two Ministers, *viz.* *Mr. Marshal*, and *Mr. Carol*, go with the Commissioners.

The Commissioners to the Scots Army, are the Earl of Stamford.

 Mr.

overlarge it will be made public the beginning of next week by itself it is worth reading especially by those who are for a generall toleration when they may clearly see it is the broad way to the destruction of these kingdommes.

What is considered by many to be the first *bonâ fide* and open advertisement ever published appears in a paper entitled *Several Proceedings in Parliament*, and is found under the date November 28–December 5, 1650. It runs thus :—

BY the late tumult made the 27 of November, whereof you have the narration before; in the night time in Bexfield, in the county of Norfolk, about 12 Horses were stolen out of the town, whereof a bay-bald Gelding with three white feet, on the near buttock marked with R. F., 9 or 10 years old. A bay-bald Mare with a wall-eye and a red star in her face, the near hind foot white, 7 years old. A black brown Mare, trots all, 6 years old. Whomsoever brings certain intelligence where they are to Mr Badcraft of Bexfield, in Norfolk, they shall have 20s. for each Horse.

The following number of the same paper, that for December 5–12, 1650, contains this :—

A bright Mare, 12 hands high, one white foot behind, a white patch below the saddle, near the side, a black main, a taile cut, a natural ambler, about 10*li.* price, stolne, Decemb. 3. neare Guilford. John Rylands, a butcher, tall and ruddy, flaxen haire, about 30 years of age, is suspected. Mr. Brounloe, a stocking dier, near the Three Craynes, in Thames's Streete, will satisfy those who can make discovery.

In 1655, Lilly the astrologer availed himself of what was then considered the new plan for ventilating a grievance, and accordingly, in the *Perfect Diurnal* of April 9–16, he published the following full-fledged advertisement, one of the earliest extant :—

An Advertisement from Mr William Lilly.

WHEREAS there are several flying reports, and many false and scandalous speeches in the mouth of many people in this City, tending unto this effect, viz. : That I, William Lilly, should predict or say there would be a great Fire in or near the Old Exchange, and another in St John's Street, and another in the Strand near Temple Bar, and in several other parts of the City. These are to certifie the whole City that

I protest before Almighty God, that I never wrote any such thing, I never spoke any such word, or ever thought of any such thing, or any or all of those particular Places or Streets, or any other parts. These untruths are forged by ungodly men and women to disturb the quiet people of this City, to amaze the Nation, and to cast aspersions and scandals on me: God defend this City and all her inhabitants, not only from Fire, but from the Plague, Pestilence, or Famine, or any other accident or mortality that may be prejudicial unto her greatnesse.

This, if noticed and recollected, must have destroyed, or at least damaged, Lilly's fame, when the great fire really did take place; but then eleven years is a long time, long enough indeed to have included many and various prophecies. Certainly modern astrologers would have turned to account the mere fact of having been accused of prophesying such a fire or any portion of it. In a previous chapter we have given a specimen of the earliest advertisements with regard to the coaching arrangements of this time, and now append the following, which would seem to show, singular as it may appear, that the simpler form, in fact the first principle, of travelling by means of saddle-horses, was not arranged until after coaches had been regularly appointed. It appears in the *Mercurius Politicus* toward the end of the year 1658:—

The Postmasters on Chester *Road, petitioning, have received Order, and do accordingly publish the following advertisement:—*

ALL Gentlemen, Merchants, and others, who have occasion to travel between *London* and *Westchester*, *Manchester*, and *Warrington*, or any other town upon that Road, for the accommodation of Trade, dispatch of Business, and ease of Purse, upon every Monday, Wednesday, and Friday Morning, betwixt Six and ten of the Clock, at the house of Mr *Christopher Charteris*, at the sign of the Hart's-Horn, in West-Smithfield, and Post-Master there, and at the Post-Master of *Chester*, at the Post-Master of *Manchester*, and at the Post-master of *Warrington*, may have a good and able single Horse, or more, furnished at Threepence the Mile, without the charge of a Guide; and so likewise at the house of Mr *Thomas Challenor*, Post-Master, at *Stone* in Staffordshire, upon every Tuesday, Thursday, and Saturday's Morning, to go for *London*. And so likewise at all the several Post-Masters upon the Road, who will have all such set days so many Horses with Furniture in readiness to furnish the Riders without any stay to carry them to or from any the places aforesaid, in Four days, as well to *London* as from thence, and to places nearer in less time, according as their occasions shall require, they ingaging at the first Stage where they take Horse, for the safe delivery of the same to the next immediate Stage, and not to ride that Horse without consent of the Post-Master by whom he rides, and so from Stage to Stage to the Journeys end. *All those who intend to ride this way are desired to give a little notice beforehand, if conveniently they can, to the several Post-masters where they first take horse, whereby they may be furnished with so many Horses as the Riders shall require with expedition.* This undertaking began the 28 of *June* 1658 at all the Places abovesaid, and so continues by the several Post-Masters.

It is hard to understand how, even if he received notice beforehand, the first postmaster was enabled to guarantee the readiness of the remaining officials, unless indeed messengers were constantly passing backwards and forwards on each route. The intimation that the three-pence per mile does not include a guide does something to clear up the mystery, and at the same time gives an idea as to the state of the roads at that time. One would imagine from the existence of such a being that the track was across a morass, or by the side of a precipice, and not along a highroad of "merrie England," in those good old times for which so many sigh now. Who, although the necessity for the highway is far less than it was two hundred years ago, can imagine a guide being required nowadays for no other purpose than that of preventing the wayfarer from straying off the beaten track, and losing his horse, and probably himself, in some gigantic slough or quagmire! It is with difficulty one can now realise to himself the fact, that as late as the middle of the seventeenth century, the interior of the country was little better than a wilderness; but that it was so may be easily gathered by a reference to Pepys, who, in the diary of his journey to Bristol and back, makes frequent mention of guides, and finds them far from unnecessary or inexpensive.

The servants of the olden time do not improve upon

acquaintance, as the following specimen advertisement from the *Mercurius Politicus* of July 1658 will show :—

IF any one can give notice of one *Edward Perry*, being about the age of eighteen or nineteen years, of low stature, black hair, full of pock-holes in his face; he weareth a new gray suit trimmed with green and other ribbons, a light Cinnamon-colored cloak, and black hat, who run away lately from his Master; they are desired to bring or send word to *Tho. Firby*, Stationer, at Gray's Inne gate, who will thankfully reward them.

This gay and dashing youth, whose pock-holes were possibly in those days regarded as but beauty-spots, with the additional recommendation of showing that their wearer had passed through the then dreaded and terrible ordeal, was doubtless an idle apprentice travelling in the direction since made famous by one who served his full indentures. Ugly as the young gentleman just described may seem to the hypercritical tastes of the nineteenth century, he, as we will presently show, is a perfect beauty compared with any individual specimen picked out at random from the long lists of criminals published in old newspapers. From these lists some conception may be formed of the ravages of the small-pox, and its effect upon the appearance of the great bulk of the population. Every man and woman seems to have been more or less marked—some slightly, some frightfully pitted or fretted, as the term then was; yet even now we have every day instances of violent and ignorant opposition to vaccination, an opposition which is loud-mouthed and possessed of considerable influence over the lower orders, who are led to believe that vaccination is the primary cause of all epidemic disease, including that which it most professes to prevent.

About this time highwaymen, who during the wars were almost unknown, began to exhibit a strong interest in the portable property of travellers; and as they took horses whenever they could find them, notices of lost, stolen, or strayed animals became frequent. It is much to be feared that the dashing knight of the road, who robbed the rich to give to

the poor, is a complete myth, and that the thieves who infested the highway were neither brave nor handsome, and not above picking up, and keeping, the most trifling things that came in their way. The quality of these riders may be guessed by means of the following, from the *Mercurius Politicus* of February 1659, the subject of which, singularly different from the "prancing prads" of which enthusiasts have written, seems to have been borrowed by one of them:—

A Small black NAG, some ten or eleven years old, no white at all, bob-Tailed, wel forehanded, somewhat thin behind, thick Heels, and goeth crickling and lamish behind at his first going out; the hair is beat off upon his far Hip as broad as a twelvepence; he hath a black leather Saddle trimmed with blew, and covered with a black Calves-skin, its a little torn upon the Pummel; two new Girths of white and green thread, and black Bridle, the Rein whereof is sowed on the off side, and a knot to draw it on the near side, Stoln out of a field at *Chelmsford*, 21 *February* instant, from Mr *Henry Bullen*. Whosoever can bring tidings to the said Mr *Bullen*, at *Bromfield*, or to Mr *Newman* at the Grocer's Arms in *Cornhil*, shall have 20s. for his pains.

It is supposed by some that the great amount of horse-stealing which prevailed during the Commonwealth, and for the next fifty years, was caused by an inordinate scarcity of animals consequent upon casualties in the battle-field. This can hardly be correct, unless, indeed, the object of the foe was always to kill horses and capture men, a state of things hardly possible enough for the most determined theorist. One fact is noticeable, and seems to have been quite in the interest of the thieves—namely, that when at grass most horses were kept ready saddled. This practice may have arisen during the Civil Wars from frequent emergency, a ready-saddled horse being of even greater comparative value than the traditional bird in the hand; and we all know how hard it is to depart from custom which has been once established. That the good man was merciful to his beast in those days hardly appears probable, if we are to take the small black nag as evidence. His furniture, too, seems much more adapted for service than show, despite its variety of colours; and perhaps the animal may have been seized, as was not uncommon, by some messenger of State making the best of his way from one part of the kingdom to another. Before the year 1636 there was no such thing as a postal service for the use of the people. The Court had, it is true, an establishment for the forwarding of despatches, and in Cromwell's time much attention was paid to it; but it was, after all, often in not much better form than when Bryan Tuke wrote as follows during the sixteenth century: "The Kinges Grace hath no mor ordinary postes, ne of many days hathe had, but betweene London and Calais. . . . For, sir, ye knowe well that, except the hackney-horses betweene Gravesende and Dovour, there is no suche usual conveyance in post for men in this realme, as in the accustomed places of France and other partes; ne men can keepe horses in redynes withoute som way to bere the charges; but when placardes be sent for suche cause [to order the immediate forwarding of some State packet], *the constables many tymes be fayne to take horses out of ploues and cartes, wherein can be no extreme diligence.*" In Elizabeth's reign a horse-post was established on each of the great roads for the transmission of the letters for the Court; but the Civil Wars considerably interfered with this, and though in the time of Cromwell public posts and conveyances were arranged, matters were in a generally loose state after his death, and during the reign of his sovereign majesty Charles II. Truly travelling was then a venturesome matter.

In 1659, also, we come upon an advertisement having reference to a work of the great blind bard John Milton. It appears in the *Mercurius Politicus* of September, and is as follows:—

CONSIDERATIONS touching the likeliest means to remove Hirelings out of the Church; wherein is also discours'd of Tithes, Church Fees, Church Revenues, and whether any maintenance of

Ministers can be settled by Law. The author, J. M. Sold by *Livewel Chapman*, at the Crown in Pope's Head Alley.

Here we are, then, brought as it were face to face with one of the brightest names in the brightest list of England's poets. This work is almost swamped amid a host of quaintly and sometimes fiercely titled controversial works, with which the press at that time teemed. The poet seems to have known what was impending, and to have conscientiously put forth his protest. We can guess what weight it had with the hungering crowds anxiously awaiting the coming change, and ready to be or do anything so long as place was provided for them. In something like contrast with the foregoing is this we now select from a number of the same paper in December of the same year:—

George Weale, a Cornish youth, about 18 or 19 years of age, serving as an Apprentice at *Kingston*, with one Mr *Weale*, an Apothecary, and his Uncle, about the time of the rising of the Counties *Kent* and *Surrey*, went secretly from his said Uncle, and is conceived to have engaged in the same, and to be either dead or slain in some of those fights, having never since been heard of, either by his said Uncle or any of his Friends. If any person can give notice of the certainty of the death of the said *George Weale*, let him repair to the said *Mr Graunt* his House in Drum-alley in Drury Lane, *London;* he shall have twenty shillings for his pains.

This speaks volumes for the peculiarities of the times. Nowadays, in the event of war, anxious relatives are soon put out of their suspense by means of careful bulletins and regular returns of killed and wounded; but who can tell the amount of heart-sickness and hope deferred engendered by the "troubles" of the seventeenth century, or of anxious thought turned towards corpses mouldering far away, among whom was most likely George Weale, perhaps the only one of the obscure men slain in "some of those fights," whose name has been rescued from oblivion.

In 1660 we find Milton again in the hands of his publisher, just at the time when the Restoration was considered complete, alone amid the pack that were ready to fall down before the young King, who was to do so much to prove the value of monarchy as compared with the Commonwealth. "The advertisements," says a writer, referring to this period, "which appeared during the time that Monk was temporising and sounding his way to the Restoration, form a capital barometer of the state of feeling among political men at that critical juncture. We see no more of the old Fifth-Monarchy spirit abroad. Ministers of the steeple-houses evidently see the storm coming, and cease their long-winded warnings to a backsliding generation. Every one is either panting to take advantage of the first sunshine of royal favour, or to deprecate its wrath, the coming shadow of which is clearly seen. Meetings are advertised of those persons who have purchased sequestered estates, in order that they may address the King to secure them in possession; Parliamentary aldermen repudiate by the same means charges in the papers that their names are to be found in the list of those persons who 'sat upon the tryal of the late King;' the works of 'late' bishops begin again to air themselves in the Episcopal wind that is clearly setting in; and 'The Tears, Sighs, Complaints, and Prayers of the Church of England' appear in the advertising columns, in place of the sonorous titles of sturdy old Baxter's works. It is clear there is a great commotion at hand; the leaves are rustling, and the dust is moving." In the midst of this, however, there was one still faithful to the "old cause," as Commonwealth matters had got to be called by the Puritans; and on the 8th of March, just when the shadow of the sceptre was once again thrown upon Great Britain, we find the following in the *Mercurius Politicus*:—

THE ready and easie way to establish a free Commonwealth, and the excellence thereof compared with the inconveniences and dangers of readmitting Kingship in this Nation. The Author, J. M. Wherein, by reason of the Printer's haste, the Errata not coming in time, it is desired that the following faults may be amended. Page 9, line 32, for *the Areopagus* read *of Areopagus*. P. 10, l. 3, for *full*

Senate, *true* Senate; l. 4, for fits, is the whole Aristocracy; l. 7, for Provincial States, States of every City. P. 17, l. 29, for *cite*, *citie;* l. 30, for *left*, *felt*. Sold by *Livewel Chapman*, at the Crown, in Pope's-head Alley.

Who would think, while reading these calm corrections, that the poet knew he was in imminent danger, and that in a couple of months he was to be a proscribed fugitive, hiding in the purlieus of Westminster from Royalty's myrmidons? Yet it was so, and the degradation to which literature may be submitted is proved by the fact that within the same space of time his works were, in accordance with an order of the House of Commons, burned by the hangman.

The excessive loyalty exhibited about this time by the lawyers, who were then, as now, quite able to look after their own interests, shows in rather a ludicrous light, viewed through the zealous officiousness of Mr Nicholas Bacon, who must have been the fountspring of the following effusion, which appears in a June, 1660, number of the *Mercurius Politicus*:—

WHEREAS one Capt. *Gouge*, a witness examined against the late King's Majesty, in those Records stiled himself of the Honorable Society of *Gray's* Inne. These are to give notice that the said *Gouge*, being long sought for, was providentially discovered in a disguise, seized in that Society, and now in custody, being apprehended by the help of some spectators that knew him, viewing of a banner with His Majesties arms, set up just at the same time of His Majesties landing, on an high tower in the same Society, by *Nicholas Bacon*, Esq., a member thereof, as a memorial of so great a deliverance, and testimony of his constant loyalty to His Majesty, and that the said *Gouge* upon examination confessed, That he was never admitted not so much as a Clerk of that Society.

The King does not seem to have enjoyed his own very long before he was subjected to loss by the dog-stealers, who, less ready to revere royalty than the lawyers, led to the publication of the following in the *Mercurius Publicus* of June 28, 1660:—

☞ A Smooth Black DOG, less than a Grey-hound, with white under his breast, belonging to the Kings Majesty, was taken from White-hall, the eighteenth day of this instant *June*, or thereabouts. If any one can give notice to *John Ellis*, one of his Majesties servants, or to his Majesties Back-Stairs, shall be well rewarded for their labour.

And one who could very probably afford to be despoiled still less—one of the poor Cavaliers who expected so much from the representative of Divine right, and who were to be so terribly disappointed—is also victimised, his whole stock of bag and baggage being annexed by some of those vagabonds who only see in any public excitement a means to their own enrichment at the expense of others. Fancy the state of mind of the elderly gentleman who is so anxious to present himself at Court, while waiting the return of the articles thus advertised in the *Mercurius Publicus* of July 5, 1660:—

A LEATHERN Portmantle lost at Sittingburn or Rochester, when his Majesty came thither, wherein was a suit of Camolet Holland, with two little laces in a seam, eight pair of white Gloves, and a pair of Does leather; about twenty yards of skie-colourd Ribbon twelvepenny broad, and a whole piece of black Ribbon tenpenny broad, a cloath lead-coloured cloak, with store of linnen; a pair of shooes, slippers, a Montero, and other things; all which belong to a gentleman (a near servant to His Majesty) who hath been too long imprisoned and sequestered to be now robbed, when all men hope to enjoy their own. If any can give notice, they may leave word with Mr *Samuel Merne*, His Majesties Book-binder, at his house in Little Britain, and they shall be thankfully rewarded.

This *Mercurius Publicus* from which we have just quoted is said to be the *Politicus* we have mentioned in reference to earlier advertisements, which turned courtier in imitation of the general example, and changed its name also in emulation of popular practice. All England seemed then to have gone mad with excessive loyalty, and it is no wonder that Charles was surprised that he could have been persuaded to stop away so long. The columns of the *Mercurius Publicus* were placed entirely under the direction of the King, and instead of the slashing articles against malignants, which were wont to appear before its change of title, it contains, under Restoration dates, virulent attacks upon the Puritans, and inquiries after his Majesty's favourite dogs, which had a curious knack of becoming stolen or lost. In addition to the canine advertisement already given, we take the following, which appears during July, and which would seem to have been dictated, if not actually written, by Charles:—

☞ We must call upon you again for a Black Dog, between a Greyhound and a Spaniel, no white about him, onely a streak on his Brest, and Tayl a little bobbed. It is His Majesties own Dog, and doubtless was stoln, for the Dog was not born nor bred in *England*, and would never forsake his Master. Whosoever findes him may acquaint any at Whitehal, for the Dog was better known at Court than those who stole him. Will they never leave robbing His Majesty? must he not keep a Dog? This Dogs place (though better than some imagine) is the only place which nobody offers to beg.

This is evidently the dog advertised before, and seems to have been an especial favourite with the merry monarch, who, one might think, would have had so many dogs that he could not possibly have missed an individual from their number. Pepys about this time describes the King, with a train of spaniels and other dogs at his heels, lounging along and feeding the water-fowl in the Park; and on later occasions he was often seen talking to his favourite Nell Gwyn as she leaned from her garden wall in Pall Mall, whilst his four-footed favourites were grouped about. It was possibly on these occasions that the gentlemen who have such an extraordinary faculty for "finding" dogs, even unto this day, saw their opportunities, and marched off with the choicest specimens. Certainly the dogs were being constantly lost, and just as constantly advertised. In turn we find him inquiring after "a little brindled greyhound bitch, having her two hinder feet white;" for a "white-haired spaniel, smooth-coated, with large red or yellowish spots;" and for a "black mastiff dog, with cropped ears and cut tail." So it would seem that, fond as his Majesty was of dogs, he was not above their being cropped and trimmed in the manner which has of late years caused all the forces of a well-known society to be arrayed against the "fancy" and the "finders." And not alone did the King advertise his lost favourites. As the fashion was set, so it was followed, and the dogmen's lives must then have been cast in pleasant places indeed, for Prince Rupert, "my lord Albemarle," the Duke of Buckingham, and many other potent seigniors, are constantly inquiring after strayed or stolen animals. The change in the general habits of the time is very clearly shown by these advertisements. The Puritans did not like sporting animals of any kind, and it has been said that no dog would have followed a Fifth-Monarchy man. Perhaps this dislike accounts for the total absence of all advertisements having reference to field-sports, or to animals connected therewith, until the return of the Court to England. With its return came in once more an aristocratic amusement which had faded out during the stern days of the Commonwealth, hawking, and we are reminded of this by the following advertisement for a lost lanner, which appears in the *Mercurius Publicus* of September 6, 1660:—

Richard Finney, Esquire, of Alaxton, in Leicestershire, about a fortnight since, lost a LANNER from that place; she hath neither Bells nor Varvels; she is a white Hawk, and her long feathers and sarcels are both in the blood. If any one can give tidings thereof to Mr Lambert at the Golden Key in Fleet-street, they shall have forty shillings for their pains.

If it be true that the *Mercurius* changed its name from *Politicus* to *Publicus* out of compliment to the new King and his Court, second thoughts seem to have been taken, and the original name resumed, for there is a *Mercurius Politicus* in November 1660, from which is the following:—

Gentlemen, you are desired to take notice, That Mr *Theophilus Buckworth* doth at his house on *Mile-end Green* make and expose to sale, for the publick good, those so famous *Lozenges* or

Pectorals, approved for the cure of Consumption, Coughs, Catarrhs, Asthmas, Hoarseness, Strongness of Breath, Colds in general, Diseases incident to the Lungs, and a sovoraign Antidote against the Plague, and all other contagious Diseases, and obstructions of the Stomach: And for more convenience of the people, constantly leaveth them sealed up with his coat of arms on the papers, with Mr *Rich. Lowndes* (as formerly), at the sign of the White Lion, near the little north door of *Pauls Church*; Mr *Henry Seile*, over against *S. Dunstan's* Church in Fleet Street; Mr *William Milward*, at *Westminster* Hall Gate; Mr *John Place*, at *Furnivals Inn Gate* in Holborn; and Mr *Robert Horn*, at the Turk's Head near the entrance of the Royal Exchange, Booksellers, and no others.'

This is published to prevent the designs of divers Pretenders, who counterfeit the said Lozenges, to the disparagement of the said Gentleman, and great abuse of the people.

It will be seen from this that quack medicines are by no means modern inventions—in fact, the wonder is, if our ancestors took a tithe of the articles advertised, that there is any present generation at all; so numerous and, even according to their own showing, powerful were the specifics advertised on every possible opportunity and in connection with every possible disease. As, however, we shall devote special space to charlatans further on, we will here simply pass to the following, which promises rather too much for the price. This is also in the *Mercurius Politicus*, and appears in December 1660:—

MOST Excellent and Approved *Dentifrices* to scour and cleanse the Teeth, making them white as Ivory, preserves from the Toothach; so that, being constantly used, the parties using it are never troubled with the Toothach; it fastens the Teeth, sweetens the Breath, and preserves the mouth and gums from Cankers and Imposthumes. Made by *Robert Turner*, Gentleman; and the right are onely to be had at *Thomas Rookes*, Stationer, at the Holy Lamb at the East end of St Pauls Church, near the School, in sealed papers, at 12d. the paper.

The Reader is desired to beware of counterfeits.

We can now mark the advent of those monstrous flowing wigs which were in fashion for nearly a century, and may be fairly assumed to have made their appearance about the date of this advertisement, which was published in the *Newes* of February 4, 1663 :—

WHEREAS *George Grey*, a Barber and Perrywigge-maker, over against the *Greyhound Tavern*, in *Black Fryers*, *London*, stands obliged to serve some particular Persons of eminent Condition and Quality in his way of Employment: It is therefore Notifyed at his desire, that any one having long flaxen hayr to sell may repayr to him the said *George Grey*, and they shall have 10s. the ounce, and for any other long fine hayr after the Rate of 5s. or 7s. the ounce.

Pepys, in his quaint and humorous manner, describes how Chapman, a periwig-dresser, cut off his hair to make up one of these immense coverings for him, much to the trouble of his servants, Jane and Bessy. He also states that "two perriwiggs, one whereof cost me £3 and the other 40s.," have something to do with the depletion of his ready money on the 30th of October 1663. On November 2nd, he says, "I heard the Duke [Buckingham] say that he was going to wear a perriwigg; and they say the King also will. I never till this day observed that the King is mighty gray." And then on Lord's day, November 8th, he says, with infinite quaintness, "To church, where I found that my coming in a perriwigg did not prove so strange as I was afraid it would, for I thought that all the church would presently have cast their eyes all upon me." Pepys was, it seems, possessed of that rather unpleasant consciousness which prompts a man who wears anything new or strange for the first time to believe that all the world, even that portion of it which has never seen him before, knows he feels anxious and uncomfortable because he has got new clothes on. The price, ten shillings the ounce, shows that there must have been an exceptionally heavy demand for flaxen colour by the wearers of the new-fashioned wigs. Judging by the advertisements just quoted, as well as by those which follow, there can be no controverting the statement that the reign of Charles II. "was characterised by frivolous amusements and by a love of dress and vicious excitement, in the midst of which pestilence stalked like a mocking fiend, and the great conflagration lit up the masquerade with its lurid and angry glare. Together with the emasculate tone of manners, a disposition to personal violence stained the latter part of this and the succeeding reign. The audacious seizure of the crown jewels by Blood; the attack upon the Duke of Ormond by the same desperado, that nobleman having actually been dragged from his coach in St James's Street in the evening, and carried, bound upon the saddle-bow of Blood's horse, as far as Hyde Park Corner, before he could be rescued; the slitting of Sir John Coventry's nose in the Haymarket by the King's guard; and the murder of Sir Edmondbury Godfrey on Primrose Hill, are familiar instances of the prevalence of this lawless spirit." There is still one other memorable and dastardly assault to note, that on "Glorious John," and we shall do so in due course.

The *London Gazette* now appears upon the scene, and this is noticeable, because of all the papers started before, or for a very considerable time after, this is the only one which has still an existence. It has been stated by some writers to have first appeared at Oxford during the time the Court took up its abode there, while the Great Plague was raging, but that this was not so is shown by the following, which is extracted from the *London Gazette* of January 22, 1664, nearly twelve months before the outbreak of the Plague. The fact is that during the residence of the King and Court at Oxford, the official organ changed its title, and was called the *Oxford Gazette*, to resume its original name as soon as it resumed its original publishing office.*

---

* The *London Gazette* was first published 22d August 1642. The first number of the existing "published-by-authority" series was imprinted first at Oxford, where the Court was stationed for fear of the Plague, on November 7, 1665, and afterwards at London on February 5, 1666.

A TRUE representation of the Rhonoserous and Elephant, lately brought from the East Indies to London, drawn after the life, and curiously engraven in Mezzotinto, printed upon a large sheet of paper. Sold by PIERCE TEMPEST, at the Eagle and Child in the Strand, over against Somerset House, Water Gate.

The ignorance of natural history at this time seems to have been somewhat marvellous, and anything in the way of a collection of curiosities was sure to attract a credulous multitude, as is shown by another notice, published in the *News* of a date close to that of the foregoing. The articles are rather scanty, to be sure, but probably the "huge thigh-bone of a giant," whatever it was in reality, was in itself sufficient to attract, to say nothing of the mummy and torpedo.

AT the Mitre, near the west end of St Paul's, is to be seen a rare Collection of Curiosityes, much resorted to and admired by persons of great learning and quality; among which a choyce Egyptian Mummy, with hieroglyphicks; the Ant-Beare of Brasil; a Remora; a Torpedo; the Huge Thighbone of a Giant; a Moon Fish; a Tropic Bird, &c.

Evidently something must have been known of mummies, or how could the exhibitor tell that his was a choïce one? Our next item introduces us to one of those old beliefs which are still to be found in remote parts of the country. The King, like any mountebank or charlatan, advertises the time when he will receive, for the purpose of giving the royal touch, supposed to be sufficient to cure the horrible distemper. Surely he of all people must have known how futile was the experiment; and it is passing strange that a people who had tried, condemned, and executed one king like any common man, should have put faith in such an announcement as that published in the *Public Intelligencer* of May 1664, which runs as follows:—

WHITEHALL, May 14, 1664. His Sacred Majesty, having declared it to be his Royal will and purpose to continue the healing of his people for the Evil during the Month of May, and then to give over till Michaelmas next, I am commanded to give notice thereof, that the people may not come up to Town in the Interim and lose their labour.

Surely such men as Sedley Rochester, Buckingham, and even Charles himself, must have laughed at the infatuation of the multitude; for if ever there was a king whose touch was less likely than another's to cure the evil, that king was, in our humble opinion, "his Sacred Majesty" Charles II. But then people were prepared to go any lengths to make up for their shortcomings in the previous reign. There was possibly a political significance about these manifestations of royal ability and clemency, and some enthusiasts, who believe devoutly in the triumph of mind over matter, think there is reason to believe in the efficacy of the touch in scrofulous affections, and even believe that people did really recover after undergoing the process. Dr Tyler Smith, who has written on the subject, boldly states his belief that the emotion felt by these poor stricken people who came within the influence of the King's "Sacred Majesty" acted upon them as a powerful tonic; though, as the King always bestowed a gold piece upon the patient, we think that if good was derived, it was derived from the comfort procured by that—for those who suffered and believed were generally in the lowest and poorest rank of life—and perhaps travelling and change of air had something to do with it as well. If the arguments of those who believe in the emotional effect are to be admitted, it must be allowed by parity of reasoning that where the touch failed, its failure would be likely to cause the sufferers to become rabid republicans, the Divine right having refused to exhibit itself. Maybe these latter symptoms, like the symptoms of other diseases, did not develop in the individual, but came out in course of generations, which may perhaps account for the large amount of democracy which has exhibited itself during the present century. There is certainly something rather ludicrous in the fact that the practice of touching

H

for the evil ceased with the death of Anne; not because the people had become more enlightened, but because the sovereigns who followed her were supposed to have lost the medicinal virtue through being kings merely by Act of Parliament, and not by Divine right.

The reaction which set in from the strait-laced rule of the Puritans at the time of the Restoration, must have reached its height about 1664, if we may judge by the advertisements then constantly inserted, which reflect the love of pleasure and folly exhibited by all classes, as if they were anxious to make up for previous restrictions. In fact, the chief inquiries are after lacework, or valuables lost at masquerade or water party, announcements of lotteries at Whitehall, of jewels and tapestry, and other things to be sold. The following is a fair specimen of the advertisements of the time, and appears in the *News* of August 4, 1664:—

LOST on the 27th July, about Boswell Yard or Drury Lane, a Ladyes picture set in gold, and three Keys, with divers other little things in a perfumed pocket. Whosoever shall give notice of or bring the said picture to Mr Charles Coakine, Goldsmith, near Staples Inne, Holborn, shall have 4 times the value of the gold for his payns.

There are also about this time all sorts of quack and nostrum advertisements, an "antimonial cup," by means of which every kind of disease was to be cured, being apparently very popular. Sir Kenelm Digby, a learned knight, who is said to have feasted his wife with capons fattened upon serpents for the purpose of making her fair, advertises a book in which is shown a method of curing the severest wounds by a sympathetic powder. But even the knight's efforts pall before the following, which will go far to show the superstitious leaven which still hung about the populace:—

SMALL BAGGS to hang about Children's necks, which are excellent both for the *prevention and cure* of the *Rickets*, and to ease Children in breeding of Teeth, are prepared by Mr Edmund Backworth, and constantly to be had at Mr Philip Clark's, Keeper of the Library in the Fleet, and nowhere else, at 5 shillings a bagge.

We see in the papers of 1665 an increased number of advertisements for lost and stolen animals, mostly those used in connection with sport; but this does not go to prove that more dogs, hawks, &c., were missing, so much as that the advantages of advertising were being discovered throughout the country; and as London was the only place in which at that time a newspaper was published, the cry after stray favourites always came up to town. Strange, indeed, are many of the advertisements about sports long since passed from amongst us, and the very phrases of which have died out of the language. It seems hard to imagine that hawks in all the glory of scarlet hoods were carried upon fair ladies' wrists, or poised themselves when uncovered to view their prey, so late as the time of Charles II., but that it was so, an advertisement already quoted, as well as the following, shows. It is taken from the *Intelligencer* of November 6, 1665:—

LOST on the 30 October, 1665, an intermix'd Barbary Tercel Gentle, engraven in Varvels, Richard Windwood, of Ditton Park, in the county of Bucks, Esq. For more particular marks—if the Varvels be taken off—the 4th feather in one of the wings Imped, and the third pounce of the right foot broke. If any one inform Sir William Roberts, Knight and Baronet (near Harrow-on-the-Hill, in the county of Middlesex), or Mr William Philips, at the King's Head in Paternoster Row, of the Hawk, he shall be sufficiently rewarded.

Inquiries for hawks and goshawks are by no means scarce, and so we may imagine that these implements of hunting were hardly so much to be depended upon as those from the workshop of art and not of nature, which are in use in the present day. Indeed, the falcon seemed to care much less, when once set free, for his keeper, than writers of books are prone to imagine. The King was apparently no more fortunate than the rest of those who indulged in falconry, for in a copy of the *London Gazette*, late in 1667, the following is seen :—

A Sore ger Falcon of His Majesty, lost the 13 of August, who had one Varvel of his Keeper, Roger Higs, of Westminster, Gent. Whosoever hath taken her up and give notice Sir Allan Apsley, Master of His Majesties Hawks at St James's, shall be rewarded for his paines. Back-Stairs in Whitehall.

Sir Allan Apsley was the brother-in-law of the celebrated Colonel Hutchinson, and brother of the devoted wife whose story everybody has read. The next advertisement we shall select is published in the *London Gazette* of May 10, 1666, and has reference to the precautions taken to prevent the spread of the Plague. Long before this all public notices of an idle and frivolous nature have ceased, amusements seem to have lost their charm, and it is evident from a study of the advertisements alone, that some great disturbing cause is at work among the good citizens. No longer does the authorised gambling under the roof of Whitehall go on ; no more are books of Anacreontics published ; stopped are all the assignations but a short time back so frequent ; and no longer are inquiries made after lockets and perfumed bags, dropped during amorous dalliance, or in other pursuit of pleasure. Death, it is evident, is busy at work. The quacks, and the writers of semi-blasphemous pamphlets, have it all to themselves, and doubtless batten well in this time of trouble. The Plague is busy doing its deadly work, and already the city has been deserted by all who can fly thence, and only those who are detained by duty, sickness, poverty, or the want of a clean bill of health, remain. These bills or licences to depart were only granted by the Lord Mayor, and the greatest influence often failed to obtain them, as after the Plague once showed strength it was deemed necessary to prevent by all and every means the spread of the contagion throughout the country. The advertisement chosen gives a singular instance of the manner in which those who had neglected to depart early were penned within the walls:—

Nicholas Hurst, an Upholsterer, over against the Rose Tavern, in Russell-street, Covent-Garden, whose Maid Servant dyed lately of the Sickness, fled on Monday last out of his house, taking with him several Goods and Household Stuff, and was afterwards followed by one Doctor Cary and Richard Bayle with his wife and family, who lodged in the same house; but Bayle having his usual dwelling-house in Waybridge, in Surrey. Whereof we are commanded to give this Public Notice, that diligent search may be made for them, and the houses in which any of their persons or goods shall be found may be shut up by the next Justice of the Peace, or other his Majesty's Officers of Justice, and notice immediately given to some of his Majesty's Privy Councill, or to one of his Majesty's principal Secretaries of State.

A great demand seems at this time to have been made for an electuary much advertised as a certain preventive of the Plague, which was to be drunk at the Green Dragon, Cheapside, at sixpence a pint. This is, however, only one among hundreds of specifics which continued to be thrust upon the public in the columns of the papers, until the real deliverer of the plague-stricken people appeared—a dreadful deliverer, it is true, but the only one. The Great Fire, which commenced on the 2nd of September 1666, and destroyed thirteen thousand houses, rendering myriads of people homeless, penniless, and forlorn, had its good side, inasmuch as by it the Plague was utterly driven out of its stronghold, but not until nearly a hundred thousand persons had perished. Imagine two such calamities coming almost together; but the purgation by fire was the only one which could fairly be expected to prove effectual, as it destroyed the loathsome charnel-houses which would long have held the taint, and removed a great part of the cause which led to the power of the fell epidemic. We have in the preceding chapter referred to the paucity of advertisements which appeared in reference to the new addresses of those who had been burnt out, and a writer a few years back makes the following remark upon the same subject: "Singularly enough, but faint traces of this overwhelming calamity, as it was considered at the time, can be gathered from the current advertisements. Although the entire population of the city was rendered houseless, and had to encamp in the surrounding fields, where they extemporised shops and streets, not one hint of such a circumstance can be found in the public announcements of the period. No circumstance could afford a greater proof of the little use made by the trading community of this means of publicity in the time of Charles II. If a fire only a hundredth part so destructive were to occur in these days, the columns of the press would immediately be full of the new addresses of the burnt-out shopkeepers; and those who were not even damaged by it would take care to 'improve the occasion' to their own advantage. We look in vain through the pages of the *London Gazette* of this and the following year for one such announcement: not even the tavern-keeper tells us the number of his booth in Goodman's-fields, although quack medicine flourished away in its columns as usual." We have already shown that one advertisement at least was published in reference to removal caused by the fire, but as it did not appear till six or seven years afterwards, it is a solitary exception to the rule, indeed. In 1667, notifications occurred now and then of some change in the site of a Government office, caused by the disturbances incident on the fire, or of the intention to rebuild by contract some public structure. Of these the following, which appears in the *London Gazette*, is a good specimen:—

ALL Artificers of the several Trades that must be used in Rebuilding the Royal Exchange may take notice, that the Committee appointed for management of that Work do sit at the end of the long gallery in Gresham Colledge every Monday in the forenoon, there and then to treat with such as are fit to undertake the same.

As nothing occurs in the way of advertisements worthy of remark or collection for the next few years, we will take this convenient opportunity of obtaining a brief breathing space.

CHAPTER VII.

CONCLUSION OF SEVENTEENTH CENTURY.

LET us commence here with the year 1674, a period when the rages and fashions, the plague and fire, and the many things treated of by means of advertisements in the preceding chapter, had plunged England into a most unhappy condition. The reaction from Puritanism was great, but the reaction from royalty and extravagance threatened to be still greater. Speaking of the state of affairs about this time, a famous historian, who has paid particular attention to the latter part of the seventeenth century, says: "A few months after the termination of hostilities on the Continent, came a great crisis in English politics. Towards such a crisis things had been tending during eighteen years. The whole stock of popularity, great as it was, with which the King had commenced his administration, had long been expended. To loyal enthusiasm had succeeded profound disaffection. The public mind had now measured back again the space over which it had passed between 1640 and 1660, and was once more in the state in which it had been when the Long Parliament met. The prevailing discontent was compounded of many feelings. One of these was wounded national pride. That generation had seen England, during a few years, allied on equal terms with France, victorious over Holland and Spain, the mistress of the sea, the terror of Rome, the head of the Protestant interest. Her resources had not diminished; and it might have been expected that she would have been, at least, as highly considered in Europe under a legitimate king, strong in the affection and willing obedience of his subjects, as she had been under an usurper whose utmost vigilance and energy were required to keep down a mutinous people. Yet she had, in consequence of the imbecility and meanness of her rulers, sunk so low, that any German or Italian principality which brought five thousand men into the field, was a more important member of the commonwealth of nations. With the sense of national humiliation was mingled anxiety for civil liberty. Rumours, indistinct indeed, but perhaps the more alarming by reason of their indistinctness, imputed to the Court a deliberate design against all the constitutional rights of Englishmen. It had even been whispered that this design was to be carried into effect by the intervention of foreign arms. The thought of such intervention made the blood, even of the Cavaliers, boil in their veins. Some who had always professed the doctrine of non-resistance in its full extent, were now heard to mutter that there was one limitation to that doctrine. If a foreign force were brought over to coerce the nation, they would not answer for their own patience. But neither national pride nor anxiety for public liberty had so great an influence on the popular mind as hatred of the Roman Catholic religion. That hatred had become one of the ruling passions of the community, and was as strong in the ignorant and profane as in those who were Protestants from conviction. The cruelties of Mary's reign—cruelties which even in the most accurate and sober narrative excite just detestation, and which were neither accurately nor soberly related in the popular martyrologies—the conspiracies against Elizabeth, and above all, the Gunpowder Plot, had left in the minds of the vulgar a deep and bitter feeling, which was kept up by annual commemorations, prayers, bonfires, and processions. It should be added that those classes which were peculiarly distinguished by attachment to the throne, the clergy and the landed gentry, had peculiar reasons for regarding the Church of Rome with aversion. The clergy trembled for their benefices, the landed gentry for their abbeys and great tithes. While the memory of the reign of the Saints was still recent, hatred of Popery had in some degree given place to hatred of Puritanism; but during the eighteen years which had elapsed since the Restoration, the hatred of Puritanism had abated, and the hatred of Popery had increased. . . . The King was suspected by many of a leaning towards Rome. His brother and heir-presumptive was known to be a bigoted Roman Catholic. The first Duchess of York had died a Roman Catholic. James had then, in defiance of the remonstrances of the House of Commons, taken to wife the Princess Mary of Modena, another Roman Catholic. If there should be sons by this marriage, there was reason to fear that they might be bred Roman Catholics, and that a long succession of princes hostile to the established faith might sit on the English throne. The constitution had recently been violated for the purpose of protecting the Roman Catholics from the penal laws. The ally by whom the policy of England had during many years been chiefly governed, was not only a Roman Catholic, but a persecutor of the Reformed Churches. Under such circumstances, it is not strange that the common people should have been inclined to apprehend a return of the times of her whom they called Bloody Mary." Such was the unhappy state of affairs at this period, and though its effect is soon shown in the advertisement columns of the papers, one would think times were piping and peaceful indeed to read the following, extracted from the *London Gazette* of October 15–19, 1674:—

WHITEHALL, *October* 17.—A square Diamond with his Majesty's Arms upon it having been this day lost out of a seal in or about Whitehall, or St James's Park or House; Any person that shall have found the same is required to bring it to *William Chiffinch*, Esq., Keeper of his Majesty's Closet, and he shall have ten pounds for a Reward.

Doubtless this Chiffinch, the degraded being who lived

but to pander to the debauched tastes of his royal and profligate employer, thought nothing of politics or of the signs of the times, and contented himself with the affairs of the Backstairs, caring little for Titus Oates, and less for his victims. Some short time after the foregoing was published (March 20–23, 1675), Chiffinch published another loss in the *Gazette.* This is it:—

FLOWN out of St James's Park, on Thursday night last, a Goose and a Gander, brought from the river Gambo in the East Indies, on the Head, Back and Wings they are of a shining black, under the Throat about the Eyes and the Belly white. They have Spurs on the pinions of the Wings, about an inch in length, the Beaks and Legs of a muddy red; they are shaped like a Muscovy Mallard, but larger and longer legg'd. Whoever gives notice to Mr Chiffinch at Whitehall, shall be well rewarded.

Whether the prince of pimps ever had to give the reward, we are not in a position to state; we should, however, think that his advertisement attracted little attention, for we are now in the midst of the excitement which led to the pretended plots and troubles that made every man suspect his neighbour, and when the cry of Recusant or Papist was almost fatal to him against whom it was directed. That this feeling once roused was not to be subdued even in death, is shown by a notice in the *Domestick Intelligence* of July 22, 1679:—

WHEREAS it was mentioned in the last "Intelligence" that Mr Langhorn was buried in the Temple Church, there was a mistake in it, for it was a Loyal Gentleman, one Colonel Acton, who was at that time buried by his near relations there: And Mr Langhorn was buried that day in the Churchyard of St Giles-in-the-Fields, very near the five Jesuits who were executed last.

John Playford, Clerke to the Temple Church.

Here is intolerance with a vengeance, but in the year 1679 reverence for persons or things was conspicuously absent, and this is best shown by the advertisement which was issued for the purpose of discovering the ruffians, or their patron, who committed the brutal assault upon John Dryden. It appears in the *London Gazette* of December 22, 1679:—

WHEREAS *John Dryden*, Esq., was on Monday, the 18th instant, at night, barbarously assaulted and wounded, in Rose Street in Covent Garden, by divers men unknown; if any person shall make discovery of the said offenders to the said Mr Dryden, or to any Justice of the Peace, he shall not only receive Fifty Pounds, which is deposited in the hands of Mr Blanchard, Goldsmith, next door to Temple Bar, for the said purpose, but if he be a principal or an accessory in the said fact, his Majesty is graciously pleased to promise him his pardon for the same.

Notwithstanding the offer of this money, it was never discovered who were the perpetrators, or who was the instigator of this cudgelling. Some fancy its promoter was Rochester, who was offended at some allusions to him in an "Essay on Satire," written jointly by Dryden and Lord Mulgrove; while others declare that the vanity of the Duchess of Portsmouth, one of the King's many mistresses, having been offended by a *jeu d'esprit* of the poet's, she procured him a rough specimen of her favours. Others, again, have suspected Buckingham, who was never on the best of terms with Dryden, and who sat for the portrait drawn in Zimri ("Absalom and Achitophel"); but profligate and heartless libertine as Villiers was, he was above such a ruffianly reprisal. In the *Domestick Intelligence* of December 23, 1679, the assault is thus described: "Upon the 17th instant in the evening Mr Dryden the great poet, was set upon in Rose Street in Covent Garden, by three persons, who, calling him rogue, and son of a whore, knockt him down and dangerously wounded him, but upon his crying out murther, they made their escape; it is conceived that they had their pay beforehand, and designed not to rob him but to execute on him some *Feminine*, if not *Popish*, vengeance." In a subsequent number of the same paper there is the following advertisement:—

[illegible] Popery (mentioned in our last) the Lord Chancellor has order to prepare Commissions (in which the said Lists are to be Inserted) which do Impower and require the Justices of Peace of the several Countries in *England* and *Wales*, to tender the Oaths of Allegiance and Supremacy to all Persons mentioned therein, and in case of their Denial to take the same, to proceed against them according to Law, in order to their speedy Conviction; with the said Commissions are also to be sent special Instructions for the better direction of the said Justices therein, and also Letters from the Council Board, to require and Encourage them diligently to Execute the said Commissions, and to send up an Account of their proceedings, as likewise the Names of all other Papists and suspected Papists as are not in the said Commissions, And that no Papist shall be allowed a License or Dispensation to stay in Town; Further that a List be taken of all House-keepers, and especially such as entertain Lodgers within the Bills of Mortality, and of all Midwives, Apothecaries and Physicians that are Papists or suspected to be such, and to return the List to the Council: And that no Papist may Harbour in any of His Majesties Palaces, a Commission is ordered for the Green-cloth to offer the Oaths of Allegiance, Supremacy and the Test to all Papists and suspected Papists as shall be found in *Whitehall*, and the Precinct thereof, who upon refusal are to be proceeded against according to Law, And the Messengers and Knight-

[illegible] Chancellor, by His Majesties Command, not to suffer such persons as should sign tumultuous Petitions to go unpunished, but that they should proceed against them, or cause them to be brought before the Council Board to be punished as they deserve, according to a Judgment of all the Judges of *England 2 Jacobi*, we suppose it may gratifie our Readers curiosity, (and prevent his danger too) to see what the Law Books say therein. Judge *Crook in his Reports, folio 37*, saith, That by command from the King, all the Justices of *England*, and divers of the Nobility, with the Archbishop of *Canterbury*, and Bishop of *London*, were Assembled in the *Star-chamber*, when the Lord Chancellor demanded of the Judges, whether it were *an Offence* punishable, and what punishment they deserve, who framed *Petitions*, and Collected a multitude of hands thereto, to present to the King in a publick cause, as the *Puritans* had done, (*which was as it seems for Alteration of the Law* (with an intimation to the King, that if he denied their Suit, many *Thousands* of his Subjects would be *discontented*;) whereto all the Justices answered, "That it was an Offence fineable at "*Discretion*, and very near Treason and *Felony*, in the "punishment, for they tended to the Raising of Sediti-"on, Rebellion, and Discontent among the People, To which Resolution all the Lords agreed, and then many of the Lords declared that some of the *Puritans* had raised a false Rumor of the King, how he intended to to grant a Toleration to *Papists*, which offence the Justices ftices conceived to be highly fineable by the Rules of the Common Law, either in the Kings Bench, or by the *King and his Council*, or now since the Statute of the 3. *Henry* 7. in the *Star-chamber*. The Lords severally declared how the King was discontented with the said false Rumor, and had made but the day before a Protestation unto them, *That he never Intended it, and that he would spend the last Drop of Blood in his body before he would do it, and prayed that before any of his Issue should maintain any other Religion then what he truly professed and maintained, that God would take them out of the world.*

There were Eleven Persons Condemned to dye the last Sessions in the *Old Baily*, six Men and five Women, but one man and three women received a Gracious Reprieve from His Majesty, the other seven suffered at *Tyburn* upon *Friday* last the Nineteenth Instant, whose Names and Crimes follow, *John Parker* by Trade a Watchmaker, for Clipping and Coining, having been formerly Convicted of the like at *Salisbury*; *Benjamin Perry*, a lusty stout man, convicted of being a Notorious Highway-man, and Companion with *French* Executed last Sessions; *John Dell*, who with *Richard Dean*, his Servant were heretofore Tryed, for the Murder of *Dells* wives Brother, and now of his wife, which seemed rather to want Proof then Truth, they were both Condemned for stealing a Mare, and Executed for the same. This [illegible]

pish Plot against His Majesties [illegible] ligion, and for enslaving the Kingdom.

There is a Report that three Suns were lately seen about *Richmond* in *Surrey*, by divers credible persons, of which different observations are made according to the fancy of the People.

This day, *Decemb.* 22. Captain *William Bedlow* one of the Kings Evidence, who has been so instrumental in discovering the *Hellish Popish* Plot, and thereby (under God) for preserving his Majesties Person and the whole Nation, was married to a Lady of a very considerable Fortune.

There being Intimation given, that *Mrs.* Cosier the *Popish* Midwife now a Prisoner in *Newgate*, would make some Discovery both of the Plot, and the Counter Plot; She was brought before the Councill last week, but would confess nothing; whereupon Justice *Warcup* produced some Informations against her taken before him; Upon which she acknowledged the greatest part of what was charged against her, and thereby gave very strong Confirmation to the Truth of Mr. *Thomas Dangerfields* Depositions, concerning that cursed Conspiracy managed by the Lady *Powis*, her self, and several others, for the destruction of many Hundreds of his Majesties Loyal *Protestant* Subjects.

It is reported, that a Quaker fell in love with a Lady of very great Quality, and hath extraordinarily petitioned to obtain her for his Wife.

Upon the [illegible] have 20 *s.* Reward.

London, Printed for *Benjamin Harris* at the *Stationers Armes* in the *Piazza* under the *Royal Exchange* in *Cornhill*, 1679.

WHEREAS *there has been printed of late an Advertisement about the Discovery of those who assaulted* Mr Dryden, *with a promise of pardon and reward to the Discoverer; For his further encouragement, this is to give notice, that if the said Discoverer shall make known the Person who incited them to that unlawful action, not only the Discoverer himself, but any of those who committed the fact, shall be freed from all manner of prosecution.*

As a seasonable illustration we present an exact facsimile of a newspaper containing reference to the attack. It is complete as it appears, being simply a single leaf printed back and front, and so the stories of men repeating a whole newspaper from memory are not so wonderful after all. This year (1679) is memorable among journalists as being the first which saw a rising press emancipated, a fact which is sufficiently interesting to be chronicled here, although our subject is not newspapers, but only the advertisements contained in them.*

During all this time it must not be supposed that the vendors of quack medicines were at all idle. No political or religious disturbance was ever allowed to interfere with them, and their notices appeared as regularly as, or if possible more regularly than, ever. In a paper we have not before met, the *Mercurius Anglicus*, date March 6–10, 1679–80, we are introduced for the first time to the cordial which was destined to become so popular among nurses with whom neither the natural milk nor that of human kindness was plentiful, viz., Daffy's Elixir :—

WHEREAS divers Persons have lately exposed to sale a counterfeit drink called ELIXIR SALUTIS, the true drink so called being first published by Mr Anthony Daffy, who is the only person that rightly and truly prepares it, he having experienced its virtues for above 20 years past, by God's blessing curing multitudes of people

* A nominal censorship was continued till 1695, but the freedom of the press is considered by many to date from the year named above, and an inspection of the papers themselves would seem to justify the opinion.

afflicted with various distempers therewith, the receit whereof he never communicated to any person living; and that these persons the better to colour their deceit, have reported Mr Anthony Daffy to be dead, these are to certify That the said Mr Anthony Daffy is still living and in good health, at his house in Prujean court in the old Bailey, and that only there and at such places as he has appointed in his printed sheets of his Elixir's virtues (which printed sheets are sealed with his seal) the true ELIXIR SALUTIS or choice CORDIAL DRINK OF HEALTH is to be sold.

It is noticeable that about this time people were never sure what year they were in until March, and often during that month; and this is not only so in the dates on newspapers, but is found in Pepys and other writers of the period. Some journals do not give the double date as above, for we have before us as we write two copies of the *Domestick Intelligence; or, News both from City and Country,* "Published to prevent false Reports," No. 49 being dated "Tuesday, Decemb. 23, 1679;" and No. 52, "Friday, January 2, 1679." This has not, as many people have imagined, anything to do with the difference between the New Calendar and the Old, as our alteration of style did not take place till the middle of the next century. It must have been a relic of the old Ecclesiastical year which still affects the financial budget.

That the "agony column" of the present day is the result of slow and laborious growth is shown by an advertisement, cut from a *Domestic Intelligence* of March 1681, which contains an urgent appeal to one who has in umbrage departed from home :—

☞ WHEREAS a Person in London on some discontent did early on Monday morning last retire from his dwelling-house and not yet return'd, it is the earnest request of several of his particular friends, that the said person would speedily repair to some or one of them, that he thinks most fit; it being of absolute necessity, for reasons he does not yet know off.

An advertisement of this kind, without name or initials, might now, like the celebrated appeal to John Smith, apply itself to the minds of so many who had left their families "on some discontent," that there would be quite a stampede for home among the married men making a temporary sojourn away from the domestic hearth and its attendant difficulties. Many of them would perhaps find themselves as unwelcome as unexpected.

Our next selection will be interesting to those who are curious on the subject of insurance, which must have been decidedly in its infancy on July 6, 1685, the day on which the following appeared in the *London Gazette* :—

THERE having happened a Fire on the 24th of the last month by which several houses of the friendly society were burned to the value of 965 pounds, these are to give notice to all persons of the said society that they are desired to pay at the office Faulcon Court in Fleet Street their several proportions of their said loss, which comes to five shillings and one penny for every hundred pounds insured, before the 12th of August next.

Advertisements are so far anything but plentiful, there being rarely more than two or three at most beyond the booksellers' and quack notices; and although nowadays the columns of a newspaper are supposed to be unequalled for affording opportunities for letting houses and apartments, the hereunder notice was, at the time of its publication in the *London Gazette*, August 17, 1685, perfectly unique :—

THE EARL of BERKELEY'S HOUSE, with Garden and Stables, in St John's Lane, not far from Smith Field, is to be Let or Sold for Building. Enquire of Mr Prestworth, a corn chandler, near the said house, and you may know farther.

Any one who passes through St John's Lane now, with its squalid tenements, dirty shops, and half-starved population, will have to be possessed of a powerful imagination indeed to picture an earl's residence as ever standing in the dingy thoroughfare, notwithstanding the neighbourhood has the advantage of a beautiful bran-new meat-market, in place of the old cattle-pens which formerly stood on the open space in front of Bartholomew's Hospital. Yet as proof of the aristocratic meetings which used to be held in St John's Lane, the Hospitallers' Gate still crosses it—the gate which even after the days of chivalry had departed had still a history to make, not of bloodshed and warfare certainly, but of a connection with the highest and finest description of literature.

We now come to the year 1688, when advertising was more common than before, and when Charles having passed away, James held temporary possession of the throne. One, published in the *Gazette* of March 8, is suggestive of the religious tumult which would shortly end in his downfall:—

CATHOLIC LOYALTY, ☞ upon the Subject of Government and Obedience, delivered in a SERMON before the King and Queen, in His Majesties Chapel at Whitehall, on the 13 of June 1687, by the Revnd. Father Edward Scaraisbroke, priest of the Society of Jesus. Published by His Majesty's Command. Sold by Raydal Tevlor near Stationers Hall, London.

Just about this period dreadful outrages were of common occurrence; men were knocked down in the street in open daylight, robbed, and murdered, and not a few deaths were the outcome of private and party hatred. Municipal law was set at defiance, and any small body of desperadoes could do as they liked unchecked, unless they happened to be providentially opposed by equal or superior force, when they generally turned tail, for their practice was not to fight so much as to beat and plunder the defenceless. Here is a notice which speaks volumes for the state of affairs. It is published in the *London Gazette*, and bears date March 29, 1688:—

WHEREAS a Gentleman was, on the eighteenth at night, mortally wounded near Lincoln's Inn, in Chancery Lane, in view as is supposed of the coachman that set him down: these are to give notice that the said coachman shall come in and declare his knowledge of the matter; if any other person shall discover the said coachman to John Hawles, at his chamber in Lincoln's Inn, he shall have 5 guineas reward.

About this time some show is made on behalf of those credulous folk who believe that all highwaymen in the good old times were brave, dashing, highly educated, and extremely handsome; for we find several inquiries after robbers who, before troubles came upon them, held superior positions in society. Here is one of the year 1688:—

WHEREAS *Mr Herbert Jones*, Attorney-at-Law in the Town of Monmouth, well known by being several years together Under-Sheriff of the same County, hath of late divers times robbed the Mail coming from that town to London, and taken out divers letters and writs, and is now fled from justice, and supposed to have sheltered himself in some of the new-raised troops. These are to give notice that whosoever shall secure the said Herbert Jones, so as to be committed in order to answer these said crimes, may give notice thereof to Sir Thomas Fowles, goldsmith, Temple-bar, London, or to Mr Michael Bohune, mercer, in Monmouth, and shall have a guinea's reward.

Mr Jones, culpable as he undoubtedly was, seems to have possessed a sense of honour, and probably he served his friends as well as himself by taking the writs from the mail. The reward offered for his apprehension is so paltry in proportion to the outcry raised, that a disinterested reader, *i.e.*, one who has never felt the smart of highway robbery, cannot help hoping that he got clear off, or that at all events he cheated the gallows by earning a soldier's death "in some of the new-raised troops." Although Mr Jones was a gentleman thief, and had gentlemanly associates, he and his friends are the exceptions to the rule; for robbers generally are described as a very sad as well as a very ugly lot of reprobates. Also in the same eventful year of delivery we find the following, which appears in the *London Gazette*, the subject of it having evidently thought to avail himself of the disturbances of the time, but whether successfully or the reverse, does not appear:—

RUN away from his master, Captain St Lo, the 21st instant, Obdelah Ealias Abraham, a Moor, swarthy complexion, short frizzled hair, a gold ring in his ear, in a black coat and blew breeches.

He took with him a blew Turkish watch-gown, a Turkish suit of clothing that he used to wear about town, and several other things. Whoever brings him to Mr Lozel's house in Green Street shall have one guinea for his charges.

This advertisement is suggestive of the taste in blackamoors, which began to manifest itself about this time, and which had a long run—the coloured creature who was in later times a negro, but in these a Moor, being often regarded as a mere soulless toy, a companion of the pug-dog, or an ornament to be classified with the vases and other china monstrosities which were just then the vogue. The next advertisement we have is of a very different character, and has a distinct bearing upon the political question of the times; it also seems to show that the value of advertising was beginning to be still more understood, and that with the advent of a new sovereign the attention of the commercial classes was once more directed so much to business that even party feeling was to be made a source of profit. The extract is from the *New Observator* of July 17, 1689:—

ORANGE CARDS, representing the late King's reign and expedition of the Prince of Orange; viz. The Earl of Essex Murther, Dr Otes Whipping, Defacing the Monument, My Lord Jeferies in the West hanging of Protestants, Magdalen College, Trial of the Bishops, Castle Maine at Rome, The Popish Midwife, A Jesuit Preaching against our Bible, Consecrated Smock, My Lord Chancellor at the Bed's feet, Birth of the Prince of Wales, The Ordinare Mass-house pulling down and burning by Captain Tom and his Mobile, Mortar pieces in the Tower, The Prince of Orange Landing, The Jesuits Scampering, Father Peter's Transactions, The fight at Reading, The Army going over to the Prince of Orange, Tyrconnel in Ireland, My Lord Chancellor in the Tower. With many other remarkable passages of the Times. To which is added the efigies of our Gracious K. William & Q. Mary, curiously illustrated and engraven in lively figures, done by the performers of the first Popish Plot Cards. Sold by Donnan Newman, the publisher and printer of the New Observator.

This was a popular and rather practical method of celebrating the triumph of the Whigs, and as Bishop Burnet was the editor of the *New Observator*, and these cards were sold by his publisher, he is very likely to have had a hand in their promotion. About now the traffic in African slaves commenced, and these full-blooded blacks gradually displaced the Moors and Arabs, who had formerly been the prevalent coloured "fancy." It is supposed that the taste for these dark-skinned servants was derived from the Venetians, whose intercourse with the traders of India and Africa naturally led to their introduction. Moors are constantly being associated with the sea-girt Republic, both in literature and art, Shakespeare's "Moor of Venice" being somewhat of an instance in point; while Titian and other painters of his school were extremely fond of portraying coloured men of all descriptions. By 1693, however, the negro had not altogether pushed out the Moor, if we may judge by an advertisement dated January 9–12, 1692–93, and appearing in the *London Gazette*:—

THOMAS GOOSEBERRY, a blackamoor, aged about 24 years, a thin slender man, middle stature, wears a periwig: Whoever brings him to Mr John Martin at Guildhall Coffeehouse, shall have two guineas Reward.

Another advertisement, which appears in the same paper a couple of years later, shows that the owners of these chattels considered their rights of property complete, as they put collars round their necks with names and addresses, just the same as they would have placed on a dog, or similar to that worn by "Gurth the thrall of Cedric." This individual seems to have been different from any of the others we have met, as he is evidently a dusky Asiatic who has been purchased from his parents by some adventurous trader, and whose thraldom sits heavily upon him. This is his description:—

A BLACK boy, an Indian, about thirteen years old, run away the 8th instant from Putney, with a collar about his neck with this inscription: 'The Lady Bromfield's black in Lincoln's Inn Fields.'

Whoever brings him to Sir Edward Bromfield's at Putney shall have a guinea reward.

It seems hardly possible that a poor little wretch like this would have run away—for whither could he run with any hope of securing his freedom?—unless he had been unkindly treated. There is little doubt—though we are, through the medium of the pictures of this and a later time, in the habit of regarding the dark-faced, white-turbaned, and white-toothed slaves as personifications of that happiness which is denied to higher intellects and fairer fortunes—that often they were the victims of intense cruelty, and now and then of that worst of all despotisms, the tyranny of an ill-natured and peevish woman.

We now come upon an advertisement, which shows something of the desire that was always felt by residents in the country for the least scintillations of news; and the concoctor of the notice seems fully aware of this desire, as well as possessed of a plan by means of which he may make it a source of profit to himself. It occurs in a copy of the *Flying Post* of the year 1694:—

IF any Gentleman has a mind to oblige his country friend or correspondent, with an account of Public affairs he may have it for twopence of J. Salusbury at the Rising Sun in Cornhill, on a sheet of fine paper, half of which being blank, he may thereon write his own private business or the material news of the day.

By this means the newspaper and the private letter were combined, and it is easy to understand the delight with which a gossiping and scandalising effusion, possessed of the additional advantage of being written on this kind of paper, was received at a lonely country house, by people pining after the gaieties of metropolitan life. The news-letter proper was a very ancient article of intercommunication, and it seems strange that it should have flourished long after the introduction of newspapers, which it certainly did. This may be accounted for by the fact, that during the time of the Rebellion it was much safer to write than to print any news which was intended to be read at a distance, or which had any political significance. It has been remarked that many of these newsletters "were written by strong partisans, and contained information which it was neither desirable nor safe that their opponents should see. They were passed on from hand to hand in secret, and often indorsed by each successive reader. We are told that the Cavaliers, when taken prisoners, have been known to eat their newsletters; and some of Prince Rupert's, which had been intercepted, are still in existence, and bear dark red stains which testify to the desperate manner in which they were defended. It is pretty certain, however, that as a profession newsletter writing began to decline after the Revolution, though we find the editor of the *Evening Post*, as late as the year 1709, reminding its readers that 'there must be three or four pounds a year paid for written news.' At the same time, the public journals, it is clear, had not performed that part of their office which was really more acceptable to the country reader than any other—the retailing the political and social chit-chat of the day. We have only to look into the public papers to convince ourselves how woefully they fell short in a department which must have been the staple of the newswriter." It would seem, therefore, that this effort of Mr Salusbury was to combine the old letter with the modern paper, and thus at once oblige his customers and save a time-honoured institution from passing away. It would seem as if he succeeded, for there are in the British Museum many specimens of papers, half print half manuscript; and as most of the written portions are of an extremely treasonable nature, possibly the opportunity to send the kind of news which suited them best, and thus combine friendship and duty, was eagerly seized by the Jacobites. But how singular after all it seems for an editor to invite his subscribers to write their own news upon their own newspapers!

We are now getting very near the end of the seventeenth century, and among the curious and quaint advertisements which attract attention, as we pore over the old chronicles which mark the close of the eventful cycle which has seen so much of revolution and disaster, and of the worst forms of religious and political fanaticisms carried to their most dreadful extremes, is the following. It appears in Salusbury's *Flying Post* of October 27, 1696, and gives a good idea of manners and customs, which do not so far appear to have altered for the better :—

WHEREAS six gentlemen (all of the same honourable profession), having been more than ordinary put to it for a little pocket-money, did, on the 14th instant, in the evening near Kentish town, borrow of two persons (in a coach) a certain sum of money, without staying to give bond for the repayment: And whereas fancy was taken to the hat, peruke, cravate, sword and cane, of one of the creditors, which were all lent as freely as the money: these are, therefore, to desire the said six worthies, how fond soever they may be of the other loans, to unfancy the cane again, and send it to Will's Coffee-house, in Scotland yard; it being too short for any such proper gentlemen as they are, to walk with, and too small for any of their important uses and withal, only valuable as having been the gift of a friend.

And just about this time we come upon some more applications from our old friend Houghton, who seems to be doing a thriving business, and is as full of wants as even he could almost desire. In a number of his *Collection for the Improvement of Husbandry and Trade* he expresses a wish as follows :—

—— I want an Englishman that can tolerably well speak French (if Dutch too so much the better), and that will be content to sit at home keeping accounts almost his whole time, and give good security for his fidelity, and he shall have a pretty good salary.

And again, his wishes being evidently for the perfection of servants, even to—which is rather an anomaly in domestic servitude—getting security. Many servants must in those days have wished to get security for the honesty of their masters :—

—— I want to wait on a gentleman in the City a young man that writes a pretty good hand, and knows how to go to market, must wait on company that comes to the house and wear a livery, has had the small-pox, and can give some small security for his honesty.

Houghton was noticeable for expressing a decided opinion with regard to the quality of whatever he recommends, and, as we have shown, was not at all modest in his own desires. Even he, however, could rarely have designed such a bargain as this :—

—— One that is fit to keep a warehouse, be a steward or do anything that can be supposed an intelligent man that has been a shopkeeper is fit for, and can give any security that can be desired as far as ten thousand pounds goes, and has some estate of his own, desires an employment of one hundred pounds a year or upwards. I can give an account of him.

This is the last we shall see of old Houghton, who did much good in his time, not only for other people but for himself as well, and who may be fairly regarded as, if not the father, certainly one of the chief promoters of early advertising.

The next public notice we find upon our list is one which directs itself to all who may wish to be cured of madness, though why people who are really and comfortably mad should wish to have the trouble of being sane, we do not profess to understand. However, it is not likely that this gentleman helped them, for he overdoes it, and offers rather too much. The notice appears in the *Post Boy* of January 6–9, 1699 :—

IN Clerkenwell Close, where the figure of Mad People are over the gate, Liveth one who by the Blessing of God, cureth all Lunitck distracted or Mad People, he seldom exceeds 3 months in the cure of the maddest Person that comes in his house, several have been cured in a fortnight and some in less time; he has cured several from

Bedlam and other mad-houses in and about this City and has conveniency for people of what quality soever. No cure no money. He likewise cureth the dropsy infallibly and has taken away from 10, 12, 15, 20 gallons of water with a gentle preparation. He cureth them that are 100 miles off as well as them that are in town, and if any are desirous they may have a note at his house of several that he hath cured.

Notwithstanding the writer's proficiency in the cure of lunatics, he seems to have been sorely exercised with regard to the spelling of the word, and he is ingenious enough in other respects. The remark about no cure no pay, it is noticeable, refers only to the cases of lunacy, and not to those of dropsy, for the evident reason that it is quite possible to make a madman believe he is sane, while it would be rather hard to lead a dropsical person into the impression that he is healthy. Quacks swarm about this period, but as we shall devote special attention to them anon, we will now step into the year 1700, beginning with the *Flying Post* for January 6–9, which contains this, a notice of a regular physician of the time:—

AT the Angel and Crown in Basing-lane near Bow-lane liveth J. Pechey, a Graduate in the University of Oxford, and of many years standing in the College of Physicians in London: where all sick people that come to him, may have for Six pence a faithful account of their diseases, and plain directions for diet and other things they can prepare themselves. And such as have occasion for Medicines may have them of him at any reasonable rates, without paying anything for advice. And he will visit any sick person in London or the Liberties thereof in the day time for two shillings and Six pence, and anywhere else within the Bills of Mortality for Five shillings. And if he be called in by any person as he passes by in any of these places, he will require but one shilling for his advice.

This is cheap enough, in all conscience, and yet there is little doubt that the afflicted infinitely preferred the nostrums so speciously advertised by empirics to treatment according to the pharmacopœia. We have good authority for the statement that faith will move mountains, and it seems, if we are to judge by the testimonials published from time immemorial by vendors of ointment and pills, to have moved mountainous tumours, wens, and carbuncles, for without it soft soap, bread, and bacon fat would be of little use indeed. Glorious John Dryden died early in this year, and a hoaxing advertisement appeared in the *Post Boy* of May 4–7, which called for elegies, &c. :—

THE Death of the famous John Dryden Esq. Poet Laureat to their two late Majesties, King Charles and King James the Second; being a Subject capable of employing the best pens, and several persons of quality and others, having put a stop to his interment, which is to be in Chaucer's grave, in Westminster Abbey : This is to desire the gentlemen of the two famous universities, and others who have a respect for the memory of the deceas'd, and are inclinable to such performances, to send what copies they please as Epigrams, etc. to Henry Playford at his shop at the Temple-Change in Fleet street, and they shall be inserted in a Collection which is design'd after the same nature and in the same method (in what language they shall please) as is usual in the composures which are printed on solemn occasions at the two Universities aforesaid.

Other advertisements followed this, and from them it appears that the shop of Henry Playford was inundated with manuscripts of all lengths and kinds, and in many languages. What became of them does not make itself known, which is a pity, as many must have been equal to any specimen which occurs in the "Rejected Addresses," with the advantage and recommendation of being genuine.

It is strange that so far we have met with no theatrical or musical advertisement or public notice of any forthcoming amusement, for it appeared most probable that as soon as ever advertising became at all popular it would have been devoted to the interest of all pursuits of pleasure. In 1700, however, we come upon what must be considered the really first advertisement issued from a playhouse, and, as a curiosity, reproduce it from the columns of the *Flying Post* of July 4 :—

☞ AT the request and for the Entertainment of several persons of quality at the *New Theatre in Lincolns-Inn-Fields*, to morrow, being Friday the 5th of this instant, *July*, will be acted "The Comical History of *Don Quixote*," both parts made into one by the author. With a new entry by the little boy, being his last time of dancing before he goes to *France*: Also Mrs. *Elford's* new entry, never performed but once and Miss *Evans's* jigg and *Irish* dance: with several new comical dances, composed and performed by Monsier *L'Sac* and others. Together with a new Pastoral Dialogue, by Mr *Gorge* and Mrs *Haynes*, and variety of other singing. It being for the benefit of a gentleman in great distress, and for the relief of his wife and 3 children.

This lead was soon followed by more important houses, and in a very few years we have lists regularly published of the amusements at all theatres. Theatrical managers have in all times been blessed with a strong faculty of imitation, and though it seems immensely developed just now, the lessees of a hundred and seventy years ago were just as keen to follow the scent of anything which had proved fortunate on the venture of any one possessed of pluck or originality.

We have reserved for the end of this chapter two advertisements of an individual who, according to his own showing, would have been invaluable to some of the members of the various school boards of the present, and have enabled them to keep pace with the pupils under their supervision, a consummation devoutly to be wished. However, if we cannot have Mr Switterda, some other *deus ex machinâ* may yet arise. The first is from the *Postman* of July 6–9, and runs thus:—

ALL Gentlemen and Ladies who are desirous in a very short time to learn to speak *Latin*, *French* or *High Dutch* fluently, and that truly and properly without pedantry, according to Grammar rules, and can but spare two hours a week, may faithfully be taught by Mr. *Switterda* or his assistant at his lodgings in *Panton Street*, at the Bunch of Grapes, near *Leicester Fields*, where you may have Latin and French historical cards. Children may come every day, or as often as parents please at his house in *Arundel Street*, next to the *Temple Passage*, chiefly those of discretion, who may be his or her assistant, entring at the same time. And if any Gent. will take two children or half a dozen of equal age, whose capacity are not disproportionable, and let any Gent. take his choice, and leave to the abovenamed S. the other, and he is content to lose his reward, if he or his assistant makes not a greater and more visible improvement of the Latin tongue in the first three months time, than any Gent. whatsoever. Et quamquam nobili Germàno est dedecori linguas profiteri, tamen non abscondi talenta mea quæ Deus mihi largitus est, sed ea per multos annos publicavi, et omnes tam divites quam paupores ad domum meam invitavi, sed surdas semper aures pulsavi, multos mihi invidos conciliavi, quos confidentia et sedulitate jam superavi. Omnes artes mechanicæ quotidie excoluntur, artes vero liberales sunt veluti statua idolatrica quæ addorantur non promoventur. He intends to dispose of two copper plates containing the ground of the Latin tongue, and the highest bidder shall have them. Every one is to pay according to his quality from one guinea to 4 guineas *per* month, but he will readier agree by the great.

It is evident that Mr Switterda was of an accommodating disposition, and doubtless did well not only out of those who agreed by the great—a species of scholastic slang we are unable to understand positively, however much we may surmise—but out of those who were content, or were perforce compelled to put up, with the small. Here is another "high-falutin'" notice which appears in the same paper about a month later, and which shows that the advertiser is also possessed of a power of puffing his own goods which must have aroused the envy and admiration of other quacks, in an age when they were not only numerous but singularly fertile in expedient:—

WHEREAS in this degenerate age, Youth are kept so many years in following only the *Latin* tongue and many of them are quite discouraged Mr. *Switterda* offers a very easy, short, and delightful method, which is full, plain, most expeditious and effectual, without pedantry, resolving all into a laudable and most beneficial practice by which Gent. and Ladies, who can but spare to be but twice in a week with him, may in two years time learn *Latin*, *French* and *High Dutch*, not only to speak them truly and properly, but also to understand a classical author. Antisthenes, an eminent Teacher being ask'd why he had so few scholars? answer'd *Quoniam non compello, sed depello illos virga argentea.* Mr. Switterda who loves *qualitatem non quantitatem* may say the same of a great many, except those who are scholars themselves, and love to give their children extraordinary learning, who have paid not only what he desired, but one, two, or three guineas above their quarteridge, and some more than he asked. He is not willing to be troubled with stubborn boys, or those of 8 or 9 years of age, unless they come along with one of more maturity, that shall be able to instruct them at home, and such as may be serviceable to the public in Divinity, Law and Physick, or teaching school. There is £20 offered for the two copper plates, and he that bids most shall have them. He teacheth Mondays, Wednesdays, and Fridays at his house in Arundel Street, next door above the Temple Passage, and the other three days in Panton Street, at the Bunch of Grapes near Leicester Fields, where you may have Latin and French Historical Cards, and a pack to learn *Copia Verborum*, which is a great want in many gentlemen. Every one is to pay according to his quality, from one Guinea to 4 Guineas *per* month. But poor Gent. and Ladies he will consider, chiefly when they agree by the great, or come to board with him.

How different from the puffing and pretentious announcements just given is the one of the same time which follows, as we read which we can hear the hum of the little country schoolroom, and see the master with his wig all awry, deep in snuff and study, the mistress keenly alive to the disposition of her girls, and the pupils of both sexes, as pupils are often even nowadays, intent upon anything but their lessons or work. London is forty miles away, and the coach is an object of wonder and admiration to the villagers, who look upon the pupils who have come from the great city with awe and reverence, while the master is supposed to diffuse learning from every pore in his body, and to scatter knowledge with every wave of his hand. The mistress is also an object of veneration, but her accomplishments are more within the ken of rustic folk, and she, good simple dame, who imagines her husband to be the most learned man in all the King, God bless him's, dominions, delights to talk about the clergymen they have educated, and has been the principal cause of his inditing and publishing this notice :—

ABOUT forty miles from London is a schoolmaster has had such success with boys as there are almost forty ministers and schoolmasters that were his scholars. His wife also teaches girls lacemaking, plain work, raising paste, sauces, and cookery to a degree of exactness. His price is £10 or £11 the year, with a pair of sheets and one spoon, to be returned if desired; coaches and other conveniencies pass every day within half a mile of the house, and 'tis but an easy journey to or from London.

And with these proofs that the schoolmaster was very much abroad at the time, we will take leave of the seventeenth century.

CHAPTER VIII.

EARLY PART OF EIGHTEENTH CENTURY.

IT is now apparent that advertising has become recognised as a means of communication not only for the conveniencies of trade, but for political, lovemaking, fortune-hunting, swindling, and the thousand and one other purposes which are always ready to assert themselves in a large community. It is also evident that as years have progressed, advertising has become more and more necessary to certain trades, the principals in which a comparatively short time before would have scorned the idea of ventilating their wares through the columns of the public press. So it is therefore as well to notice the rates which were charged by some of the papers. This was before the duty was placed upon advertisements, when the arrangement was simply between one who wished a notice inserted in a paper, and another who possessed the power of making such insertion. It is of course impossible to tell what the rates were on all papers, but as some had notices of price per advertisement stated at foot, a fair estimate may be made. The first advertisements were so few that no notice was called for, and it was not until every newspaper looked forward to the possession of more or less that the plan of stating charges became common. About the period of which we are now writing, long advertisements were unknown; they generally averaged about eight lines of narrow measure, and were paid for at about a shilling each, with fluctuations similar in degree to those of the leading papers of the present day Various rules obtained upon various papers. One journal, the "*Jockey's Intelligencer*, or Weekly Advertisements for Horses and Second-Hand Coaches to be Bought and Sold," which appeared towards the end of the seventeenth century, charged "a shilling for a horse or coach for notification, and sixpence for renewing." Still later, the *County Gentleman's Courant* seems to have been the first paper to charge by the line, and in one of its numbers appears the following rather non-sequitous statement: "Seeing promotion of trade is a matter which ought to be encouraged, the price of advertisements is advanced to twopence per line." Very likely many agreed with the writer, who seems to have had a follower several years afterwards—a corn dealer, who during a great dearth stuck up the following notification: "On account of the great distress in this town, the price of flour will be raised one shilling per peck." But neither of these men meant what he said, though doubtless he thought he did.

The first advertisement with which we open the century is of a semi-religious character, and betrays a very inquiring disposition on the part of the writer. Facts of the kind required are, however, too stubborn to meet with publication at the request of everybody, and if Mr Keith and other controversialists had been trammelled by them, there is every probability that the inquiry we now republish would never have seen the light:—

☞ WHEREAS the World has been told in public papers and otherwise of numerous conversions of quakers to the Church of England, by means of Mr Keith and others, and whereas the quakers give out in their late books and otherwise, that since Mr Keith came out of America, there are not ten persons owned by them that have left their Society, Mr Keith and others will very much oblige the world in publishing a true list of their proselytes.

The foregoing is from the *Postman* of March 1701, and in July the same paper contains a very different notice, which will give an idea of the amusements then in vogue, and rescue from oblivion men whose names, great as they are in the advertisement, seem to have been passed over unduly by writers on ancient sports and pastimes, who seem to regard Figg and Broughton as the fathers of the back-sword and the boxing match:—

A *Tryal of Skill* to be performed at His Majesty's Bear Garden in Hockley-in-the-Hole, on Thursday next, being the 9th instant, betwixt these following masters;—Edmund Button, master of the noble science of defence, *who hath lately cut down* Mr Hasgit and the Champion of the West, *and* 4 *besides*, and James Harris, an Herefordshire man, master of the noble science of defence, who has fought 98 prizes and never was worsted, to exercise the usual weapons, at 2 o'clock in the afternoon precisely.

Exhibitions of swordsmanship and cudgel-play were very frequent in the early part of the eighteenth century, but ultimately pugilism, which at first was merely an auxiliary of the other sports, took the lead, most probably through the invention of mufflers or gloves, first brought into notice by Broughton, who was the most skilful boxer of his time. This was, however, many years subsequent to the date of the foregoing.

The year 1702 is noticeable from the fact that in it was produced the first daily paper with which we have any acquaintance, and, unless the doctrine that nothing is new under the sun holds good in this case, the first daily paper ever published. From it we take the following, which appears on December 1, and which seems—as no name or address is given, and as the advertiser does not even know the name of the gentleman, or anything about him beyond what is told in the advertisement—to have emanated from one of the stews which were even then pretty numerous in London:—

MISSED, on Sunday night, a large hanging coat of Irish frieze, supposed to be taken away (thro' mistake) by a gentleman in a fair campaign wig and light-coloured clothes; if he will please to remember where he took it, and bring it back again, it will be kindly received.

We should imagine that, unless both coats and gentlemen were more plentiful, in proportion to the population, in those days than they are now, the rightful owner, who had probably also been a visitor at the establishment, went without a garment which, judging by the date, must have been peculiarly liable to excite cupidity. Nothing noticeable occurs for a long time, except the growth of raffle advertisements, and notices of lotteries. These arrangements were called sales, though the only things sold were most likely the confiding speculators. Everything possible was during this age put up to be raffled, though, with the exception of the variety of the items, which included eatables, wearing apparel, houses, carriages and horses, &c. &c., there is nothing calling for comment about the style of the notices. In the *Postman* of July 19–22, 1707, we at last come upon this, which is certainly peculiar from more than one point of view :—

MR Benjamin Ferrers, Face-painter, the gentleman that can't neither speak nor hear, is removed from the Crown and Dagger at Charing Cross into Chandois Street, next door to the sign of the Three Tuns in Covent Garden.

This must have been one of the few cases in which physical disability becomes a recommendation. Yet the process of whitening sepulchres must after a time have become monotonous to even a deaf and dumb man. We suppose the highest compliment that could have been paid to his work was, that the ladies who were subjected to it looked "perfect pictures." Just about this time the use of advertisements for the purposes of deliberate puffery began to be discovered by the general trader, and in the *Daily Courant* of March 24, 1707, occurs a notice couched in the style of pure hyperbole, and emanating from the establishment of G. Willdey and T. Brandreth, at the sign of the Archimedes and Globe, on Ludgate Hill, who advertised a microscope which magnified objects more than two million times, and a concave metal that united the sunbeams so vigorously that in a minute's time it melted steel and vitrified the hardest substance. "Also," the notice went on to say, "we do protest we pretend to no impossibilities, and that we scorn to impose on any gentleman or others, but what we make and sell shall be really good, and answer the end we propose in our advertisements." Spectacles by which objects might be discovered at twenty or thirty miles' distance, "modestly speaking," are also mentioned; "and," the ingenious opticians finish off with, "we are now writing a small treatise with the aid of the learned that gives the reasons why they do so, which will be given gratis to our customers." This is an effort which would not have disgraced the more mature puffers of following ages. But it aroused the anger and indignation of the former employers of Willdey and Brandreth, who having duly considered the matter, on April 16 put forth, also in the *Daily Courant*, an opposition statement, which ultimately led to a regular newspaper warfare:—

BY John Yarwell and Ralph Sterrop, Right Spectacles, reading and other optic glasses, etc., were first brought to perfection by our own proper art, and needed not the boasted industry of our two apprentices to recommend them to the world; who by fraudently appropriating to themselves what they never did, and obstinately pretending to what they never can perform, can have no other end in view than to astonish the ignorant, impose on the credulous, and amuse the public. For which reason and at the request of several gentlemen already imposed on, as also to prevent such further abuses as may arise from the repeated advertisements of these two wonderful performers, we John Yarwell and Ralph Sterrop do give public notice, that to any person who shall think it worth his while to make the experiment, we will demonstrate in a minute's time the insufficiency of the instrument and the vanity of the workmen by comparing their miraculous Two-Foot, with our Three and Four Foot Telescopes. And therefore, till such a telescope be made, as shall come up to the character of these unparalleled performers, we must declare it to be a very impossible thing.

Then the old-established and indignant masters proceed

to recommend their own spectacles, perspectives, &c., in more moderate terms than were employed by their late apprentices, but still in an extremely confident manner. This appeared for several days, and at last, on April 25, elicited the following reply:—

WHEREAS Mr Yarwell, Mr Sterrop, and Mr Marshall, the 2 first were our Masters with whom we served our Apprenticeships, and since for several years we have made the best of work for them and Mr Marshall. And now they being envious at our prosperity have published several false, deceitful and malicious advertisements, wherein they assert that we cheat all that buy any of our goods, and that we pretend to many impossibilities, and impose on the public, they having wrested the words and sense of our advertisements, pretend that we affirm that a 2 Foot Telescope of our making will do as much as the best 4 Foot of another man's make, and they fraudulently show in their shops one of their best 4 Foots against our small one, and then cry out against the insufficiency of our instrument. Now we G. Willdey and Th. Brandreth being notoriously abused, declare that we never did assert any such thing, or ever did pretend to impossibilities, but will make good in every particular all those [note, these are their own words] (impossible, incredable, miraculous, wonderful, and astonishing) things mentioned in our advertisements; which things perhaps may be impossible, incredible, miraculous, wonderful, and astonishing to them, but we assure them they are not so to us: For we have small miraculous telescopes, as they are pleased to call them, that do such wonders that they say it is impossible to make such, by the assistance of which we will lay any person £10, that instead of 2 miles mentioned, we will tell them the hour of the day 3 if not 4 miles by such a dial as St James's or Bow.

After this the recalcitrant apprentices repeat all their former boasts, and conclude: "All these things are as they say impossible to them, but are and will be made by G. Willdey and T. Brandreth. . . . Let ingenuity thrive." Willdey and Brandreth now, no doubt, thought that they had turned the tables upon their former masters, and had all the best of the battle; but the duel was not yet over, as the second time this advertisement appeared (*Daily Courant*, April 26), the following was immediately under it:—

A CONFIDENT Mountebank by the help of his bragging speech passes upon the ignorant as a profound doctor, the commonest medicines and the easiest operations in such an one's hand, shall be cried up as miracles. But there are mountebanks in other arts as well as in physick: Glasgrinding it seems is not free from 'em, as it is seen in the vain boastings of Willdey and Brandrith. 'Tis well known to all gentlemen that have had occasion to use optic glasses that J. Yarwell was the true improver of that art, and has deservedly a name for it, in all parts abroad as well as at home. He and R. Sterrop, who lives in the old shop in Ludgate Street, have always and do now make as true and good works of all kinds in that art as any man can do. And we are so far from discouraging any improvement, that we gladly receive from any hand, and will be at any expence to put in practice an invention really advantageous in the art. But Willdey's performances are so far from improvements that we are ready to oppose any of our work to his and stake any wager upon the judgment of a skilful man. And because he talks so particularly of his two foot telescope, to let the world see that there is nothing in that vaunt, we will stake 10 Guineas upon a two-foot telescope of ours against the same of his. And further to take away all pretensions of our preparing one on purpose, if any gentleman that has a two-foot telescope bought of us within a year past, and not injured in the use, will produce it, we will lay 5 Guineas upon its performance against one of theirs of the same date. This is bringing the matter upon the square, and will, we hope, satisfy the world that we are not worse workmen than those we taught.

Again the young men ventured into print (May 1, 1707), to reply, and to defend what they were pleased to call the naked truth, "against the apparent malicious lies and abuse" of their former employers, in whose last advertisement they pointed out some inconsistencies, claimed the invention of the perfected spectacles as theirs, and ended in offering to bet "20 guineas to their 10, that neither they nor Mr Marshall can make a better telescope than we can." This, though rather a descent from the high horse previously occupied by them, was sufficient to rouse the anger of an interested yet hitherto passive spectator, and Mr Marshall presently (May 8) indignantly growled forth:—

THE best method now used for Grinding Spectacles and other glasses, was by me at great charge and pains found out, which I shewed to the Royal Society in the year 1693, and by them approved; being gentlemen the best skilled in optics, for which they gave me their certificate to let the world know what I had done. Since which I have made spectacles, telescopes, and microscopes, for all the Kings and Prince's Courts in Europe. And as for the 2 new spectacle makers, that would insinuate to the world that they were my best workmen for several years: the one I never employed, the other I found as I doubt not but many gentlemen have and will find them both, to be only boasters and not performers of what they advertise, &c. &c.

After pursuing this strain till he had run down, Mr Marshall concludes by saying, "What I have inserted is nothing but truth." At the same time Yarwell and Sterrop overwhelmed the raisers of this hornets' nest with a new attention, in which among other things was the following:—

Mr Willdey and Brandreth have the folly to believe that abundance of words is sufficient to gain applause, and therefore throw 'em out without regard to truth and reason, but as that is an affront to the understanding of gentlemen that use the goods they sell, they being persons of discerning judgment, there needs no other answer to what they have published than to compare one part with another. They set forth with a lying vaunt that their two-foot telescope would perform the same that a common four-foot one would do, and when 'twas replied that was false, and a four-foot one offered to try, they poorly shift off with crying "That's one of your best four-foot ones." Now we profess to make none but best, the glasses of every one being true ground and rightly adjusted, and the difference in price arrises only from the goodness, ornaments, and convenience of the case, neither can he produce a four-foot one of anybody's make, that does not far exceed his two-foot, nor does his two-foot one at all exceed ours, which they don't now pretend. And therefore the lie is all on his side, and the impossibility in his pretensions is as strong as ever, and what we have said is just truth, and his foul language no better than Billingsgate railing. But it seems because we do not treat him in his own way and decry his goods as much as he does other men's, he has the folly to construct it as an acknowledgement that his excel. But we are so far from allowing that, that we do aver they have nothing to brag of but what they learnt of us, and Brandreth was so indifferent a workman that Marshall, who had taken him for a journeyman, was fain to turn him off. The secrets they brag of is all a falsehood, and the microscope the same that any one may have from Culpeper who is the maker. We have already told the world that we will venture any wager upon the performance of our two-foot telescope against theirs, and we would be glad to have it taken up that we might have the opportunity of showing that ours exceeds, and letting the world see that his brags are only such as mountebanks make in medicine.

Finally, in the *Daily Courant* for May 12, 1707, Willdey and Brandreth once again insert their vaunt, and then proceed to demolish their late employers thus :—

We do affirm it [the telescope made by W. & B.] to be the pleasantest and usefullest instrument of this kind, and what our adversaries have said against it is false and proceeds from an ill design; we have already offered to lay them 20 guineas to their 10 that they could not make a better, but they knowing they were not capable to engage us in that particular, said in their answer that there needs no more than to compare one instrument with another that they may have the opportunity of shewing that theirs exceeds; to which proposal we do agree, and to that purpose have bought 3 of their best telescopes that we might be sure of one that was good, though they say in their advertisements that they make none but the best, and we are ready to give our oaths that no damage has been done them since they were bought. And now to bring these matters to an end, we will lay them 20 guineas to their 10, that 3 of our best of the same sizes are better than them; and any gentleman that will may see the experiment tried in an instant at our shop, where they may also see that our best pocket telescope comes not far short of their best large 4 Foot one. And several other curiosities all made to the greatest perfection. And whereas Mr Yarwell, Mr Sterrop, and Mr Marshall have maliciously, falsly, and unjustly insinuated that we are but indifferent workmen, several persons being justly moved by that scandalous aspersion, have offered to give their oaths that they have often heard them say that we were the best of workmen, and that we understood our business as well as themselves. And as such we do each of us challenge them all 3 severally to work with them, who does most and best for £20. As for the Microscope it is our own invention, and 2 of them were made by us before any person saw them, as we can prove by witnesses; as we also can their railing and scandalous aspersions to be false. All persons may be assured that all our instruments do and will answer the character given them in the advertisements of T. Brandreth and G. Willdey, &c. &c.

Whether the game was too expensive, or whether the old

firm was shut up by this, we know not, but anyhow they retired from the contest, and it is to be hoped found that rivalry fosters rather than injures business. We have given particular attention to this conflict of statements, as it shows how soon advertisements, after they had become general, were used for aggressional and objectionable trade purposes. Passing on for a little space, until 1709, the *Tatler* appears on the scene, and commences with a full share of advertisements, and very soon one is found worthy of quotation. This appears on March 21, and is a form of application which soon found favour with the gallants and ladies of pleasure of the day:—

A GENTLEMAN who, the twentieth instant, had the honour to conduct a lady out of a boat at Whitehall Stairs, desires to know when he may wait on her to disclose a matter of concern. A letter directed to Mr Samuel Reeves, to be left with Mr May, at the Golden Head, the upper end of New Southampton Street, Covent Garden.

There are about this time many instances appearing in the notice columns of what has been called love at first sight, though from the fact that advertisements had to bring their influence to bear on the passion, it looks as though the impression took some time to fix itself. Otherwise the declaration might have been made at once, unless, indeed, timidity prevented it. Perhaps, too, the occasional presence of a gentleman companion might have deterred these inflammable youths from prosecuting their suits and persecuting the objects of their temporary adoration. Just after the foregoing we come upon a slave advertisement couched in the following terms:—

A BLACK boy, twelve years of age, fit to wait on a gentleman, to be disposed of at Denis's Coffee house in Finch Lane, near the Royal Exchange.

There is no mincing the matter about this, and as, at the same time, a very extensive traffic was carried on in "white flesh" for the plantations, the advertiser would doubtless have regarded sympathy with his property as not only idiotic but offensive. And then we light on what must be regarded as an advertisement, though it emanates from the editorial sanctum, and is redolent of that humour which, first identified with the *Tatler*, has never yet been surpassed, and, as many still say, never equalled :—

ANY ladies who have any particular stories of their acquaintance which they are willing privately to make public, may send 'em by the penny post to Isaac Bickerstaff, Esq., enclosed to Mr John Morpheu, near Stationers' Hall.

What a chance for the lovers of scandal, and doubtless they readily availed themselves of it. Many a hearty laugh must Steele have had over the communications received, and many of them must have afforded him the groundwork for satires, which at the time must have struck home indeed. In the following year "Isaac Bickerstaff, Esquire," seems to have taken it into his head that John Partridge, the astrologer, ought to be dead, if he really was not, and so inserted a series of advertisements to the effect that that worthy had really departed this life, which, however amusing to the *Tatler* folk and the public, seem to have nearly driven the stargazer wild.* One of the best of this series, which appears on August 10, 1710, runs thus :—

---

* This is Partridge the almanac-maker, who was fortunate enough to be mentioned in the "Rape of the Lock." After the rape has taken place the poem goes on to say—

"This the *beau monde* shall from the Mall survey,
And hail with music its propitious ray;
This the blest lover shall for Venus take,
And send up prayers from Rosamunda's lake;
This Partridge soon shall view in cloudless skies,
When next he looks through Galileo's eyes;
And hence the egregious wizard shall foredoom
The fate of Louis and the fall of Rome."

It would seem, therefore, that the guiding spirits of the *Tatler*, fancying that he had received undue publicity in a favourable manner, were disposed to show Partridge that all advertisements are not necessarily adjuncts to business.

WHEREAS an ignorant Upstart in Astrology has publicly endeavoured to persuade the world that he is the late John Partridge, who died the 28 of March 1718, these are to certify all whom it may concern, that the true John Partridge was not only dead at that time but continues so to the present day. Beware of counterfeits, for such are abroad.

The quiet yet pungent drollery of this is almost irresistible, but it has the effect of making us rather chary of accepting any of the remaining advertisements which look at all like emanations from the quaint fancy of the editor. Take the following, for instance, which is found among a number of others of an ordinary character, undistinguished from them by any peculiarity of type or position. It seems, however, to betray its origin :—

The Charitable Advice Office, where all persons may have the opinion of dignified Clergymen, learned Council, Graduate Physicians, and experienced Surgeons, to any question in Divinity, Morality, Law, Physic, or Surgery, with proper Prescriptions within twelve hours after they have delivered in a state of their case. Those who can't write may have their cases stated at the office. * * The fees are only 1*s.* at delivery or sending your case, and 1*s.* more on re-delivering that and the opinion upon it, being what is thought sufficient to defray the necessary expense of servants and office-rent.

The theory of advertising must about this time have been found considerably interesting to men who were unlikely to participate in its benefits unless it were through the increased prosperity of the newspapers to which they contributed, for essays and letters on the subject, some humorous and others serious, appear quite frequently. Most noticeable among the former is an article from the pen of Addison, which appears in No. 224 of the *Tatler*, date September 14, 1710. It will speak better for itself than we can speak for it:—

"*Materiem superabat opus.*—OVID. MET. ii. 5.
"The matter equall'd not the artist's skill.—R. WYNNE.

"It is my custom, in a dearth of news, to entertain myself with those collections of advertisements that appear at the end of our public prints. These I consider as accounts of news from the little world, in the same manner that the foregoing parts of the paper are from the great. If in one we hear that a sovereign prince is fled from his capital city, in the other we hear of a tradesman who has shut up his shop and run away. If in one we find the victory of a general, in the other we see the desertion of a private soldier. I must confess I have a certain weakness in my temper that is often very much affected by these little domestic occurrences, and have frequently been caught with tears in my eyes over a melancholy advertisement.

"But to consider this subject in its most ridiculous lights, advertisements are of great use to the vulgar. First of all as they are instruments of ambition. A man that is by no means big enough for the Gazette, may easily creep into the advertisements; by which means we often see an apothecary in the same paper of news with a plenipotentiary, or a running footman with an ambassador. An advertisement from Piccadilly goes down to posterity with an article from Madrid, and John Bartlett* of Goodman's Fields is celebrated in the same paper with the Emperor of Germany. Thus the fable tells us, that the wren mounted as high as the eagle, by getting upon his back.

"A second use which this sort of writings have been turned to of late years has been the management of controversy, insomuch that above half the advertisements one meets with nowadays are purely polemical. The inventors of 'Strops for Razors' have written against one another this way for several years, and that with great bitterness;† as

* An advertising trussmaker of that day.

† A specimen advertisement of one of these inventors appears in the *Postman* of January 6–9, 1705 :—

SINCE so many upstarts do daily publish one thing or other to counterfeit the original strops, for setting razors, penknives, lancets, etc., upon, And pretend them to be most excellent; the first author of the

the whole argument *pro* and *con* in the case of the 'Morning Gown' is still carried on after the same manner. I need not mention the several proprietors of Dr Anderson's pills; nor take notice of the many satirical works of this nature so frequently published by Dr Clark, who has had the confidence to advertise upon that learned knight, my very worthy friend, Sir William Read:* but I shall not interpose in their quarrel: Sir William can give him his own in advertisements, that, in the judgment of the impartial, are as well penned as the Doctor's.

"The third and last use of these writings is to inform the world where they may be furnished with almost every thing that is necessary for life. If a man has pains in his head, colics in his bowels, or spots in his clothes, he may here meet with proper cures and remedies. If a man would recover a wife or a horse that is stolen or strayed; if he wants new sermons, electuaries, asses' milk, or anything else,

---

said strops, does hereby testify that all such sort of things are only made in imitation of the true ones, which are permitted to be sold by no one but Mr Shipton, at John's Coffee House, in Exchange Alley, as hath been often mentioned in the Gazettes, to prevent people being further imposed upon.

An opposition notice appears shortly afterwards in the *Daily Courant* of January 11:—

THE *Right Venetian Strops*, being the only fam'd ones made, as appears by the many thousands that have been sold, notwithstanding the many false shams and ridiculous pretences, as "original," etc., that are almost every day published to promote the sale of counterfeits, and to lessen the great and truly wonderful fame of the *Venetian Strops*, which are most certainly the best in the world, for they will give razors, penknives, lancets, etc., such an exquisite fine, smooth, sharp, exact and durable edge, that the like was never known, which has been experienced by thousands of gentlemen in England, Scotland and Ireland. Are sold only at Mr Allcraft's, a toy shop at the Blue Coat Boy, against the Royal Exchange, &c. &c.

* Both oculists of some renown, who advertised largely.

either for his body or mind, this is the place to look for them in.

"The great art in writing advertisements, is the finding out a proper method to catch the reader's eye, without which a good thing may pass unobserved, or be lost among commissions of bankrupt. Asterisks and hands were formerly of great use for this purpose. Of late years the N.B. has been much in fashion, as also little cuts and figures, the invention of which we must ascribe to the author of spring-trusses. I must not here omit the blind Italian character, which being scarce legible, always fixes and detains the eye, and gives the curious reader something like the satisfaction of prying into a secret.

"But the great skill in an advertiser is chiefly seen in the style which he makes use of. He is to mention the 'universal esteem,' or 'general reputation' of things that were never heard of. If he is a physician or astrologer, he must change his lodgings frequently; and though he never saw anybody in them besides his own family, give public notice of it, 'for the information of the nobility and gentry.' Since I am thus usefully employed in writing criticisms on the works of these diminutive authors, I must not pass over in silence an advertisement, which has lately made its appearance and is written altogether in a Ciceronian manner. It was sent to me with five shillings, to be inserted among my advertisements; but as it is a pattern of good writing in this way, I shall give it a place in the body of my paper.

"The highest compounded Spirit of Lavender, the most glorious, if the expression may be used, enlivening scent and flavour that can possibly be, which so raptures the spirits, delights the gusts, and gives such airs to the countenance, as are not to be imagined but by those that have tried it. The meanest sort of the thing is admired by most gentlemen and ladies; but this far more, as by far it exceeds it, to the gaining among all a more than common esteem. It is sold in neat flint bottles, fit for the pocket, only at the Golden Key in Wharton's Court, near Holborn Bars, for three shillings and sixpence, with directions.

"At the same time that I recommend the several flowers

in which this spirit of lavender is wrapped up, if the expression may be used, I cannot excuse my fellow-labourers for admitting into their papers several uncleanly advertisements, not at all proper to appear in the works of polite writers. Among them I must reckon the 'Carminative Wind-Expelling Pills.' If the Doctor had called them 'Carminative Pills,' he had been as cleanly as any one could have wished; but the second word entirely destroys the decency of the first. There are other absurdities of this nature so very gross, that I dare not mention them; and shall therefore dismiss this subject with an admonition to Michael Parrot, that he do not presume any more to mention a certain worm he knows of, which, by the way, has grown seven foot in my memory; for, if I am not much mistaken, it is the same that was but nine feet long about six months ago.

"By the remarks I have here made, it plainly appears, that a collection of advertisements is a kind of miscellany; the writers of which, contrary to all authors, except men of quality, give money to the booksellers who publish their copies. The genius of the bookseller is chiefly shown in his method of ranging and digesting these little tracts. The last paper I took up in my hands places them in the following order:—

"The true Spanish blacking for shoes, etc.

"The beautifying cream for the face, etc.

"Pease and Plasters, etc.

"Nectar and Ambrosia, etc.

"Four freehold tenements of fifteen pounds per annum, etc.

"The present state of England, etc.

"Annotations upon the *Tatler*, etc.

"A commission of Bankrupt being awarded against R. L., bookseller, etc."

This essay probably aroused a good deal of attention, and among the letters of correspondents is one from a

"Self-interested Solicitor," which appears in No. 228, and runs thus:—

"*Mr Bickerstaff.*

"I am going to set up for a scrivener, and have thought of a project which may turn both to your account and mine. It came into my head upon reading that learned and useful paper of yours concerning advertisements. You must understand I have made myself Master in the whole art of advertising, both as to the style and the letter. Now if you and I could so manage it, that nobody should write advertisements besides myself, or print them anywhere but in your paper, we might both of us get estates in a little time. For this end I would likewise propose that you should enlarge the design of advertisements, and have sent you two or three samples of my work in this kind, which I have made for particular friends, and intend to open shop with. The first is for a gentleman who would willingly marry, if he could find a wife to his liking; the second is for a poor Whig, who is lately turned out of his post; and the third for a person of a contrary party, who is willing to get into one.

"Whereas A. B. next door to the Pestle and Mortar, being about thirty years old, of a spare make, with dark-coloured hair, bright eye, and a long nose, has occasion for a good-humoured, tall, fair, young woman, of about £3000 fortune; these are to give notice That if any such young woman has a mind to dispose of herself in marriage to such a person as the above mentioned, she may be provided with a husband, a coach and horses and a proportionable settlement.

"C. D. designing to quit his place, has great quantities of paper, parchment, ink, wax, and wafers to dispose of, which will be sold at very reasonable rates.

"E. F. a person of good behaviour, six foot high, of a black complexion and sound principles, wants an employ. He is an excellent penman and accomptant, and speaks French."

And so on, advertisements being then considered proper sport for wits of all sizes and every peculiarity. In 1711 we come upon the first edition of the *Spectator*, which certainly did not disdain to become a medium for most barefaced quacks, if we may judge by this :—

AN admirable confect which assuredly cures Stuttering and Stammering in children or grown persons, though never so bad, causing them to speak distinct and free without any trouble or difficulty; it remedies all manner of impediments in the speech or disorders of the voice of any kind, proceeding from what cause soever, rendering those persons capable of speaking easily and free, and with a clear voice who before were not able to utter a sentence without hesitation. Its stupendous effects in so quickly and infallibly curing Stammering and all disorders of the voice and difficulty in delivery of the speech are really wonderful. Price 2s. 6d. a pot, with directions. Sold only at Mr Osborn's Toyshop, at the Rose and Crown, under St Dunstan's church Fleet street.

This is a truly marvellous plan for greasing the tongue. The only wonder is that the advertiser did not recommend it as invaluable to public speakers for increasing the fluency to such an extent that the orator had but to open his mouth and let his tongue do as it willed. And certainly the most rebellious and self-willed tongue could hardly give utterance to more remarkable statements, if left entirely to itself, than appears in the following, which is also from the original edition of the *Spectator* :—

LOSS of Memory, or Forgetfulness, certainly cured by a grateful electuary peculiarly adapted for that end; it strikes at the primary source, which few apprehend, of forgetfulness, makes the head clear and easy, the spirits free, active, and undisturbed, corroborates and revives all the noble faculties of the soul, such as thought, judgment, apprehension, reason and memory, which last in particular it so strengthens as to render that faculty exceeding quick and good beyond imagination; thereby enabling those whose memory was before almost totally lost, to remember the minutest circumstances of their affairs, etc. to a wonder. Price 2s. 6d. a pot. Sold only at Mr Payne's, at the Angel and Crown, in St Paul's Churchyard, with directions.

It is sometimes possible to remember too much; and if the specific sold by Mr Payne had but a homœopathic tendency, and caused those who recollected things which never happened to become cured of their propensities, it is a pity its recipe has to be numbered among the lost things of this world. In the beginning of 1712, one Ephraim How seems to have been possessed of a fear that evil folks had been trying to injure him or his business, or else he felt it incumbent on himself to take the hint thrown out in the *Tatler* essay. Accordingly he published in the *Daily Courant* the following:—

WHEREAS several persons who sell knives, for the better vending their bad wares spread reports that Ephraim How, Cutler of London is deceased. This is to certify That he is living, and keeps his business as formerly, with his son in partnership, at the Heart and Crown on Saffron Hill; there being divers imitations, you are desired to observe the mark, which is the Heart Crown and Dagger, with How under it.

About this period shopkeepers were or pretended to be particularly loyal, for a very large percentage of their signs contained the emblem of royalty, coupled with various other figures. Though the Methuen treaty, which favoured the importation of Portuguese wines, and discouraged the use of claret, was signed in 1703, it does not appear to have made much difference in this country for some years, as the first mention we find of the new wine is in a *Postboy* of January 1712, and is caused by the rivalry which sprang up among those who first began to sell it:—

NOTICE is hereby given, That Messieurs Trubey, at the Queen's Arms Tavern, the West End of St Paul's Church, have bought of Sir John Houblon, 76 pipes of *New* natural Oporto Wines, red and white, perfect neat, and shall remain genuine, chosen out of 96 pipes, and did not buy the cast-outs. Also they have bought of other merchants large quantities of *new* natural Oporto wines, with great choice (by the last fleet). And altho' the aforesaid did buy of Messieurs Brook and Hellier, *new* natural Oporto wines of the earliest importation, which they have yet by them; and 'tis not only their own opinion, that the said Sir John Houblon's and other merchant's Oporto wines, which they have bought are superior, and do give us more general satisfaction: for the same is daily confirm'd by gentlemen and others of undoubted judgment and credit. Further this assertion deserves regard, viz. That the said Messieurs Brook and Helliers have bought of several merchants entire parcels of Oporto and Viana wines, red and white, good and bad, thereby continuing retailing, under the specious and fallacious pretences of natural red and neat of their own importing.

N.B.—The intentions of the above-named Vintners are not any way to reproach or diminish the reputation of their brethren, nor insinuate to their detriment, sympathizing with them. Note the aforesaid *new* natural Oporto wines, are to be sold by the aforesaid vintners at £16 per hogshead, at 18d. per quart, without doors, and at 20d. per quart, within their own houses.

Brook & Hellier, whose wine is spoken of so slightingly, kept the Bumper Tavern in Covent Garden, which had formerly belonged to Dick Estcourt. They seem quite able to bear what has been said of them, for they have the *Spectator*, who has evidently tasted, and quite as evidently liked their wines, at their back, one of the numbers of this disinterested periodical being devoted almost entirely to their praise. The *Spectator* was by no means averse to a bit of good genuine puffery, and Peter Motteux, formerly an author who had dedicated a poem or two to Steele, and who at that time kept one of the Indian warehouses so much in fashion, received kindnesses in its columns more than once. So did Renatus Harris the organ-builder, who competed with Smith for the Temple organ, and many others. So it is not extraordinary that their advertisement is found in the *Spectator* very shortly after that just quoted. They seem, however, to have been disinclined to quarrel, as their notice makes no mention of their rivals:—

BROOK and Hellier, &c. having discovered that several gentlemen's servants who have been sent to their taverns and cellars for neat Oporto wines (which is 18d. per quart) have instead thereof bought the small Viana, which is but 15d. a quart; and that some who have been sent directly to the above taverns and cellars have never come there, but carried home (like traitors) something else from other places for Brook and Helliers. Gentlemen are therefore desired, when they suspect themselves imposed on, to send the wine immediately to the place they ordered it from, or a note of what it was they sent for, in order to know the truth, and Brook and Helliers will bear the extraordinary charge of porters on this occasion.

From this and kindred advertisements it looks as though gentlemen were not at the time in the habit of keeping large quantities of wine in the house, but rather of having it in fresh and fresh as required from the tavern, or of going round themselves, and taking it home under their belts. Also the servants of the time do not appear to be possessed of much more honesty than falls to the lot of the domestics of even these degenerate days. The effect of the rage for port as soon as it was once tried, is shown by the following, which also appeared in the January of 1712, in the *Daily Courant*:—

THE first loss is the best especially in the Wine Trade, and upon that consideration Mr John Crooke will now sell his French Claret for 4s. a gallon, to make an end of a troublesome and losing trade. Dated the 7th of January from his vault in Broad street, 5 doors below the Angel and Crown Tavern, behind the Royal Exchange.

JOHN CROOKE.

But this appeal to the lovers of bargains, as well as of claret, was evidently a failure; for three or four days afterwards, and also in the same paper, another, and quite different attempt, is made to draw the unwilling drinkers to the Angel and Crown:—

IT having been represented to Mr John Crooke that notwithstanding the general approbation his French claret has received, yet many of his customers out of a covetous disposition do resort to other places to buy much inferior wine, and afterwards sell the same for Mr Crooke's claret, which practices (if not timely prevented) do manifestly tend to the ruin of his undertaking, and he being firmly resolved to establish and preserve the reputation of his vault, and also willing to give his customers all fitting encouragement; for these causes and others hereunto him moving, he gives notice that from henceforth he will sell his very good French claret for no more than 4s. a gallon at his vault.

The fight between port and claret was very fierce this year, but the new drink had almost from the first the best of the battle, if we may judge from the strenuous appeals put forth by those who have much claret to sell, and who evidently find it very like a drug upon their hands. One individual seems at last to arrive at the conclusion that he may as well ask a high price as a low one for his claret, seeing that people are unwilling to buy in either case. The advertisement occurs in the *Daily Courant* for December 29, 1712. The wily concocter of the plan also thinks that by making three bottles the smallest limit of his sale, the unwary may fancy a favour is being conferred upon them, and buy accordingly :—

THE noblest new French claret that ever was imported, bright, deep, strong and of most delicious flavour, being of the very best growth in France, and never in any cooper or vintner's hands, but purely neat from the grape, bottled off from the lee. All the quality and gentry that taste it, allow it to be the finest flower that ever was drunk. Price 42s. the dozen, bottles and all, which is but 3s. 6d. a bottle, for excellence not to be matched for double that price. None less than 3 bottles. To be had only at the Golden Key, in Haydon Yard, in the Minories, where none but the very best and perfectly neat wine shall ever be sold.

There is good reason to believe that the claret which had been so popular up till this period, was a very different wine from that which is now known by the same name. It was, most probably, a strong well-sweetened drink ; for, as it has ever been necessary to make port thick and sweet for the public taste, it is most likely this was at first done for the purpose of rivalling the claret, and folk would hardly have turned suddenly from one wine to another of a decidedly opposite character. The amount of advertising, probably fostered by the wine rivalry, grew so much this year, that the Ministry were struck with the happy idea of putting a tax upon every notice, and accordingly there is a sudden fall off in the number of advertisements in and after August, the month in which the change took place. In fact, the *Daily Courant* appears several times with only one advertisement, that of Drury Lane Theatre, the average number being hitherto about nine or ten. However, the imposers of the tax were quite right in their estimate of the value of advertisements; as, though checked for a time, they ultimately grew again, though their progress was comparatively slow compared with previous days. We find a characteristic announcement just at the close of the year, one not to be checked by the duty-charge, and so we append it:—

THIS is to give notice That there is a young woman born within 30 miles of London will run for £50 or £100, a mile and an half, with any other woman that has liv'd a year within the same distance; upon any good ground, as the parties concern'd shall agree to.

Unnatural and unfeminine exhibitions, in accordance with this advertisement, of pugilism, foot-racing, cudgel-playing, &c., were at this time not unfrequent, and the spectacle of two women stripped to the waist, and doing their best to injure or wear down each other, was often enjoyed by the bloods of the early eighteenth century. At the same time that the tax was placed on advertisements, the stamp-duty on newspapers became an accomplished fact, and Swift in his journal to Stella of July 9, 1712, says, "Grub Street has but ten days to live, then an Act of Parliament takes place that ruins it by taxing every half-sheet a halfpenny." And just about a month after, he chronicles the effect of this cruelty: "Do you know that Grub Street is dead and gone last week? No more ghosts or murders now for love or money. I plied it close the last fortnight and published at least seven papers of my own, besides some of other people's; but now every single half-sheet pays a halfpenny to the Queen. The *Observator* is fallen; the *Medleys* have jumbled together with the *Flying Post;* the *Examiner* is deadly sick; the *Spectator* keeps up and doubles its price. I know not how long it will hold. Have you seen the red stamp the papers are marked with? Methinks the stamping is worth a halfpenny." Thieves about this time seem to have had delicate susceptibilities, for it was the custom to advertise goods which were undoubtedly stolen as lost. Thus we see constantly in the reign of Queen Anne such notices as this: "Lost out of a room in Russell Street a number of valuable objects. . . . . . Whoever brings them *back* shall have ten guineas reward, or in proportion for any part, and no questions asked." This style of advertising grew so that just about the middle of the century it was found necessary to put a stop to it by Act of Parliament, which took effect on the 21st of June 1752, the penalty being £50 for any one who advertised "no questions asked," and £50 for the publisher who inserted any such notice in his paper. Haydn gives this date as 1754, but a reference to the *General Advertiser* of February 21, 1752, in which the notice of the date on which the law is to come into effect appears, shows that it was two years earlier. Also a reference to any Parliamentary record of forty years before that will show that not in 1713, as Haydn has it, but on the 22nd April 1712, Mr Conyers reported from Committee of the whole House, who were considering further ways and means for raising the supply granted to her Majesty; when among other measures it was resolved that a duty of 12d. be charged for every advertisement in any printed paper, besides the stamp-duty which was at the same time imposed on the newspapers. This and other extra taxes were levied, because France having refused to acknowledge the title of Queen Anne till the peace should be signed, it was resolved to continue the war "till a safe and honourable peace could be obtained." For this purpose money was of course required; and if they never did good any other way, or at any other time, quacks and impostors, libertines and drunkards, did it now, as they mainly contributed all that was gathered for some years by means of the advertisement tax. There seems to have been a good deal of drunkenness going on in the time of Queen Anne, and the tavern keepers contributed in many ways to swell the revenue. But even their advertisements drop off after the imposition of the tax, as do those of promoters of nostrums and lotteries, and the managers of theatres. These public benefactors are, however, not so blind to their own interests, but that they soon return.

Notwithstanding the many important events of the next few years, nothing worthy of chronicling in the way of advertisements is to be found till 1720, when we come upon the following, which is peculiar as being one of the earliest specimens of the ventilation of private quarrels by means of advertisements. It occurs in the *Daily Post* of January 16th :—

WHEREAS an advertisement was lately put in Heathcote's Halfpenny Post, by way of challenge for me to meet a person (whose name to me is unknown) at Old Man's Coffeehouse near Charing Cross, the 28 instant in order to hear that said person make out his assertions in that Dialogue we had in Palace Yard, the 11th of November 1718, This will let that person know that as he would not then tell me his name, nor put it to his advertisement, I conclude he is ashamed to have it in print. When he sends me his name in writing, that I may know who to ask for, I shall be willing to meet him at any convenient time and place, either by ourselves or with two friends on each side, till then I shall have neither list nor leisure to obey his nameless summons. ROBERT CURTIS.

Southwark, Jan. 13th, 1719-20.

Certainly time enough seems to have elapsed between the dialogue and the publication of this advertisement to allow of all angry passions to have subsided; but Robert Curtis, whose name is thus preserved till now, would seem to have been a careful youth, picking his way clear of pitfalls, and with shrewdness sufficient to discover that anonymity but too often disguises foul intent. In that particular matters have not considerably improved even up to the present time

The year 1720 is memorable in the history of England, as seeing the abnormal-growth and consequent explosion of the greatest swindle of comparatively modern times, and one of the most colossal frauds of any time, the South Sea Scheme, which has been best known since as the South Sea Bubble. Its story has been told so often, and in so many ways, that it is hardly necessary to dwell upon it here; but as, though nearly every one has heard of the scheme, there are but few who know anything about it, we may as well give once again a short *résumé* of its business operations. It was started by Harley in 1711, with the view of paying off the floating national debt, which at that time amounted to about £10,000,000. A contemporary writer says: "This debt was taken up by a number of eminent merchants, to whom the Government agreed to guarantee for a certain period the annual payment of £600,000 (being six per cent. interest), a sum which was to be obtained by rendering permanent a number of import duties. The monopoly of the trade to the South Seas was also secured to these merchants, who were accordingly incorporated as the 'South Sea Company,' and at once rose to a high position in the mercantile world. The wondrously extravagant ideas then current respecting the riches of the South American continent were carefully fostered and encouraged by the Company, who also took care to spread the belief that Spain was prepared, on certain liberal conditions, to admit them to a considerable share of its South American trade; and as a necessary consequence, a general avidity to partake in the profits of this most lucrative speculation sprang up in the public mind. It may be well to remark in this place, that the Company's trading projects had no other result than a single voyage of one ship in 1717, and that its prominence in British history is due entirely to its existence as a purely monetary corporation. Notwithstanding the absence of any symptoms of its carrying out its great trading scheme, the Company had obtained a firm hold on popular favour, and its shares rose day by day; and even when the outbreak of war with Spain in 1718 deprived the most sanguine of the slightest hope of sharing in the treasures of the South Seas, the Company continued to flourish. Far from being alarmed at the expected and impending failure of a similar project—the Mississippi Scheme—the South Sea Company believed sincerely in the feasibility of Law's Scheme, and resolved to avoid what they considered as his errors. Trusting to the possibility of pushing credit to its utmost extent without danger, they proposed, in the spring of 1720, to take upon themselves the whole national debt (at that time £30,981,712) on being guaranteed 5 per cent. per annum for seven and a half years, at the end of which time the debt might be redeemed if the Government chose, and the interest reduced to 4 per cent. The directors of the Bank of England, jealous of the prospective benefit and influence which would thus accrue to the South Sea Company, submitted to Government a counter-proposal; but the more dazzling nature of their rival's offer secured its acceptance by Parliament—in the Commons by 172 to 55, and (April 7) in the Lords by 83 to 17; Sir Robert Walpole in the former, and Lords North and Grey, the Duke of Wharton and Earl Cowper in the latter, in vain protesting against it as involving inevitable ruin. During the passing of their bill, the Company's stock rose steadily to 330 on April 7,* falling to 290 on the following day.

* On January 1, 1720, the *Daily Courant*, and other papers, quote South Sea Stock at 127¾, 128⅜, to 128. Bank 150¼. India 200, 200½, to 200. The quotation for Thursday, April 7 (in *Daily Post*, Friday, April 8), is, "Yesterday South Sea Stock was 314, 310, 311, 309, 309½, to 310. Bank 145. India 223." On the 27th May it was 555, and Bank was 205 (*Post Boy*, May 28). It then fell a little, but in the *Daily Courant* of June 2 it is quoted at 610 to 760, Bank 210 to 220, India 290 to 300. The *Daily Post* of Wednesday, June 8, contains the following puff for the scheme: "'Tis said that the South Sea Company being willing to have all the Annuities subscribed to their

Up till this date the scheme had been honestly promoted; but now, seeing before them the prospect of speedily amassing abundant wealth, the directors threw aside all scruples, and made use of every effective means at their command, honest or dishonest, to keep up the factitious value of the stock. Their zealous endeavours were crowned with success; the shares were quoted at 550 on May 28, and 890 on June 1. A general impression having by this time gained ground that the stock had reached its maximum, so many holders rushed to realise that the price fell to 630 on June 3. As this decline did not suit the personal interests of the directors, they sent agents to buy up eagerly; and on the evening of June 3, 750 was the quoted price. This and similar artifices were employed as required, and had the effect of ultimately raising the shares to 1000 in the beginning of August, when the chairman of the Company and some of the principal directors sold out. On this becoming known, a widespread uneasiness seized the holders of stock; every one was eager to part with his shares, and on September 12 they fell to 400, in spite of all the attempts of the directors to bolster up the Company's credit. The consternation of those who had been either unable or unwilling to part with their scrip was now extreme; many capitalists absconded, either to avoid

Stock, now offer forty-five years' purchase for those which have not yet been bought in." And again: "The Annuities which have been subscribed into the South Sea Stock are risen to a very great height, so that what would formerly sell but for £1500, is now worth £8000." In the *Post Boy* of June 23–25, we find this: "Yesterday South Sea Stock was for the opening of the Book 1100. 1st Subscr. 565, 2d Subscr. 610, 3rd Subscr. 200. Bank 265. East India 440." On Friday, June 24, the *Daily Post* says, "We hear that South Sea Stock was sold yesterday at 1000 per cent., and great wagers are laid that it will be currently sold before the opening of the Books at 1200 per cent. exclusive of the Dividend." It is several times after this quoted at 1100, but never over. These compilations show that a higher rate was attained by the stock than is given in the article quoted above, or is generally believed.

ruinous bankruptcy, or to secure their ill-gotten gains, and the Government became seriously alarmed at the excited state of public feeling. Attempts were made to prevail on the Bank to come to the rescue by circulating some millions of Company's bonds; but as the shares still declined, and the Company's chief cashiers, the Sword Blade Company, now stopped payment, the Bank refused to entertain the proposal. The country was now wound up to a most alarming pitch of excitement; the punishment of the fraudulent directors was clamorously demanded, and Parliament was hastily summoned (December 8) to deliberate on the best means of mitigating this great calamity. Both Houses proved, however, to be in as impetuous a mood as the public; and in spite of the moderate counsels of Walpole, it was resolved (December 9) to punish the authors of the national distresses, though hitherto no fraudulent acts had been proved against them. An examination of the proceedings of the Company was at once commenced; and on Walpole's proposal nine millions of South Sea bonds were taken up by the Bank, and a similar amount by the East India Company. The officials of the Company were forbidden to leave the kingdom for twelve months, or to dispose of any of their property or effects. Ultimately various schemes, involving the deepest fraud and villany, were discovered to have been secretly concocted and carried out by the directors; and it was proved that the Earl of Sunderland, the Duchess of Kendal, the Countess Platen and her two nieces, Mr Craggs, M.P., the Company's secretary, Mr Charles Stanhope, a secretary of the Treasury, and the Sword Blade Company, had been bribed to promote the Company's bill in Parliament by a present of £170,000 of South Sea stock. The total amount of fictitious stock created for this and similar purposes was £1,260,000, nearly one-half of which had been disposed of. Equally flagrant iniquity in the allocation of shares was discovered, in which, among others, Mr Aislabie, the Chancellor of the

Exchequer, was implicated. Of these offenders, Mr Stanhope and the Earl of Sunderland were acquitted through the unworthy partiality of the Parliament; but Mr Aislabie, and the other directors who were members of the House of Commons, were expelled; most of the directors were discovered, and all of them suffered confiscation of their possessions. The chairman was allowed to retain only £5000 out of £183,000, and others in proportion to their share in the fraudulent transactions of the Company. At the end of 1720, it being found that £13,300,000 of real stock belonged to the Company, £8,000,000 of this was taken and divided among the losers, giving them a dividend of 33⅓ per cent.; and by other schemes of adjustment the pressure was so fairly and wisely distributed, that the excitement gradually subsided." It will thus be seen that the South Sea Bubble was, after all, not more disastrous in its effects than many modern and comparatively unknown speculations.

It is singular that the South Sea Bubble led to little—almost nothing—in the way of advertisements. When we think of the columns which now herald the advent of any new company, or for the matter of that, any new idea of an old company, or any fresh specific or article of clothing, it seems strange that at a time when the art of advertising was fast becoming fashionable, no invitations to subscribe were published in any of the daily or weekly papers that then existed. Just before the consent of Parliament was obtained we find one or two stray advertisements certainly, but they have no official status, as may be judged by this, which is from the *Post Boy*, April 2–5, 1720:—

+*+ Some Calculations relating to the Proposals made by the South Sea Company and the Bank of England, to the House of Commons; Showing the loss to the New Subscribers, at the several Rates in the said Computations mention'd; and the Gain which will thereby accrue to the Proprietors of the Old South Sea Stock. By a Member of the House of Commons. Sold by J. Morphew near Stationers Hall.

Pr. 1s. Where may be obtained Mr. Hutchison's Answer to Mr. Crookshank's Seasonable Remarks.

In the *Daily Courant* of April 4 is also the following, which shows the immense amount of the stock possessed by private individuals. The reward offered for the recovery of the warrant seems ridiculously small, let its value be what it might to the finder:—

Lost or mislaid, a South Sea Dividend Warrant No. 1343 dated the 25th of February last, made out to John Powell Esq. for 630*l* being for his Half Years Dividend on 21,000*l* stock due the 25th of December last. If offered in Payment or otherwise please to stop it and give Notice to Mr Robert Harris at the South Sea House, and you shall receive 10s Reward, it not being endorsed by the said John Powell Esq. is of no use but to the Owner, Payment being Stopt.

The only official notification in reference to the Bubble is found in the *London Gazette*, "published by authority," of April 5–9, 1720. It is the commencement of a list of Acts passed by the King, and runs thus:—

Westminster, April 7.

HIS Majesty came this Day to the House of Peers, and being in his Royal Robes seated on the Throne with the usual Solemnity, Sir William Saunderson, Gentleman-Usher of the Black Rod, was sent with a Message from His Majesty to the House of Commons, commanding their Attendance in the House of Peers; the Commons being come thither accordingly, His Majesty was pleased to give the Royal Assent to

An Act for enabling the South Sea Company to increase their present Capital Stock and Fund, by redeeming such publick Debts and Incumbrances as are therein mentioned, and for raising Money for lessening several of the publick Debts and Incumbrances, and for calling in the present Exchequer Bills remaining uncancelled, and for making forth new Bills in lieu thereof to be circulated and exchanged upon Demand at or near the Exchequer.

The advertisement then goes on to state what other Acts received the royal assent, but with none of them have we anything to do. In the *Post Boy* of June 25–28 there is a notice of a contract being lost, which runs thus:—

WHereas a Contract for the Delivery of South Sea Stock made between William Byard Grey, Esq. and Mr. William Ferrour is mislaid or dropt: If the Person who is possess'd of it will bring it to the Wheat-Sheaf in Warwick-Lane, he shall have Ten Guineas Reward, and no Questions ask'd.

And in the issue of the same paper for June 30–July 1 we find this, which refers to the Company on which all the South Sea directors' orders were made payable:—

FOund at the South Sea House Saturday the 17th of June a Sword-Blade Company's Note. If the Person that lost it will apply to Mr. Colston's, a Toy Shop at the Flower-de-Luce against the Exchange in Cornhill, and describe the said Note shall have it return'd, paying the Charge of the Advertisement.

These are, however, only incidental advertisements, which might have occurred had the Company been anything but that which it was; and so we have only to remark on the peculiar quietness with which all rigging operations were managed in those days. One of the paragraphs quoted in a note a short distance back will, however, account for the fact that advertisements were not found in the usual places.

The growth of the disgusting system which permitted of public combats between women is exhibited in several advertisements of 1722, the most noticeable among them being one in which a challenge and reply are published as inducements to the public to disburse their cash and witness a spectacle which must have made many a strong man sick:—

CHALLENGE.—I, Elizabeth Wilkinson, of Clerkenwell, having had some words with Hannah Hyfield, and requiring satisfaction, do invite her to meet me upon the stage, and box me for three guineas; each woman holding half a crown in each hand, and the first woman that drops the money to lose the battle.

ANSWER.—I, Hannah Hyfield, of Newgate Market, hearing of the resoluteness of Elizabeth Wilkinson, will not fail, *God willing*, to give her more blows than words, desiring home blows, and from her no favour; she may expect a good thumping!

The precaution taken with the half-crowns to keep the hands clenched and so prevent scratching, shows that even these degraded creatures had not quite forgotten the peculiarities of the sex. And that there is piety in pugilism—even of this kind—is proved by the admittance that the Deity had to give his consent to "the ladies' battle." But Mesdames Wilkinson and Hyfield sink into insignificance when compared with the heroines of the following, which is cut from the *Daily Post* of July 17, 1728:—

AT *Mr. Stokes' Amphitheatre* in Islington Road, this present Monday, being the 7 of October, will be a complete Boxing Match by the two following Championesses:—Whereas I, Ann Field, of Stoke Newington, ass-driver, well known for my abilities in boxing in my own defence wherever it happened in my way, having been affronted by Mrs. Stokes, styled the European Championess, do fairly invite her to a trial of the best skill in boxing for 10 pounds, fair rise and fall; and question not but to give her such proofs of my judgment that shall oblige her to acknowledge me Championess of the Stage, to the entire satisfaction of all my friends.

I, Elizabeth Stokes, of the City of London, have not fought in this way since I fought the famous boxing woman of Billingsgate 29 minutes and gained a complete victory (which is six years ago); but as the famous Stoke Newington ass-woman dares me to fight her for the 10 pounds, I do assure her I will not fail meeting her for the said sum, and doubt not that the blows which I shall present her with will be more difficult for her to digest, than any she ever gave her asses. *Note.*—A man known by the name of Rugged and Tuff, challenges the best man of Stoke Newington to fight him for one guinea to what sum they please to venture. *N.B.*—Attendance will be given at one, and the encounter to begin at four precisely. There will be the diversion of cudgel-playing as usual.

Pugilism was evidently a much valued accomplishment among the lower-class ladies in 1728, and there is no doubt that Mrs Stokes and Mrs Field were considered very estimable persons as well as great athletes in their respective circles. There is, moreover, a suspicion of humour about the reference to the asses in the reply of Mrs Stokes. In the happily-named Rugged and Tuff we see the forerunner of that line of champions of the ring which, commencing with Figg and Broughton, ran unbroken up to comparatively modern days. Other advertisements about this period relate to cock-matches and mains, sometimes specified to "last the week," to bull-baiting in its ordinary and sometimes in its more cruel form of dressing up the beasts with fireworks, so as to excite both them and the savage dogs to their utmost. Perhaps brutality was never so rampant, or affected so many phases of society as it did in the first half of the eighteenth century. Slavery was considered a heaven-born institution, not alone as regards coloured races, for expeditions to the Plantations went on merrily and afforded excellent opportunities for the disposal of any one who happened to make himself objectionable by word or deed, or even by his very existence. The wicked uncle with an eye on the family property had a very good time then, and the rightful heir was often doomed to a slavery almost worse than death. Apropos of slavery, we may as well quote a very short advertisement which shows how the home trade flourished in 1728. It is from the *Daily Journal* of September 28 :—

> TO be sold, a Negro boy, aged eleven years. Enquire of the Virginia Coffee-house in Threadneedle street, behind the Royal Exchange.

Negroes had in 1728 become quite common here, and had pushed out their predecessors, the Moors and Asiatics, who formerly held submissive servitude. This was probably owing to the nefarious traffic commenced in 1680 by Hawkins, which in little more than a hundred years caused the departure from their African homes and the transplanting in Jamaica alone of 910,000 negroes, to say nothing of those who died on the voyage, or who found their way to England and other countries.

CHAPTER IX.

MIDDLE OF EIGHTEENTH CENTURY.

THE further we advance into the years which mark the Hanoverian succession, the more profligate, reckless, and cruel do the people seem to become. Public exhibitions of the most disgusting character are every day advertised; ruffians and swashbucklers abound, and are ready to do anything for a consideration; animals are tortured at set periods for the delectation of the multitude; and we see verified, by means of the notices in the papers, the peculiarities which Hogarth seized and made immortal, and which so many squeamish people consider to be overdrawn nowadays. Assignations of the most immoral character are openly advertised, and men of the time may well have attempted to ignore the existence of female virtue. A recent writer, commenting on this state of affairs, says, in reference to the latter class of shameless advertisements: "We are far from saying that such matters are not managed now through the medium of advertisements, for they are, but in how much more carefully concealed a manner? The perfect contempt of public opinion, or rather the public acquiescence in such infringements of the moral law which it exhibits, proves the general state of morality more than the infringements themselves, which obtain more or less at all times. Two of the causes which led to this low tone of manners with respect to women were doubtless the detestable profligacy of the courts of the two first Georges, and the very defective condition of the existing marriage law.

William and Mary, and Anne, had, by their decorous, not to say frigid lives, redeemed the crown, and in some measure the aristocracy, from the vices of the Restoration. Crown, court, and quality, however, fell into a still worse slough on the accession of the Hanoverian king, who soiled afresh the rising tone of public life by his scandalous connection with the Duchess of Kendal and the Countess of Darlington; whilst his son and successor was absolutely abetted in his vicious courses by his own queen, who promoted his commerce with his two mistresses, the Countesses of Suffolk and Yarmouth. The degrading influence of the royal manners was well seconded by the condition of the law. Keith's Chapel in Mayfair, and that at the Fleet, were the Gretna Greens of the age, where children could get married at any time of the day or night for a couple of crowns. It was said at the time that at the former chapel six thousand persons were annually married in this offhand way; the youngest of the beautiful Miss Gunnings was wedded to the Duke of Hamilton at twelve o'clock at night, with a ring off the bed-curtain, at this very 'marriage-shop.' The fruits of such unions may be imagined. The easy way in which the marriage bond was worn and broken through, is clearly indicated by the advertisements which absolutely crowd the public journals, from the accession of the house of Brunswick up to the time of the third George, of husbands warning the public not to trust their runaway wives." It must not be imagined, though, that wives were the only sinners, or that vice was confined to any particular and exclusive class. It was the luxury of all, and according to their opportunities all enjoyed it.

About this time Fleet marriages, and the scandals consequent upon them, were in full swing. In a number of the *Weekly Journal* this statement is made: "From an inspection into the several registers for marriages kept at the several alehouses, brandy-shops, &c., within the Rules of the Fleet Prison, we find no less than thirty-two couples joined together from Monday to Thursday last without licences, contrary to an express Act of Parliament against clandestine marriages, that lays a severe fine of £200 on the minister so offending, and £100 each on the persons so married in contradiction to the said statute. Several of the above-named brandy-men and victuallers keep clergymen in their houses at 20s. per week, hit or miss; but it is reported that one there will stoop to no such low conditions, but makes at least £500 per annum of Divinity jobs after that manner." A fair specimen of the kind of advertisement published by these gentlemen is this:—

G. R.—At the True Chapel, at the old Red Hand and Mitre, three doors up Fleet Lane, and next door to the White Swan, Marriages are performed by authority by the Rev. Mr. Symson, educated at the University of Cambridge, and late chaplain to the Earl of Rothes.

N.B.—Without imposition.

A curious phase of the dangers of the streets is found in a narrative published in the *Grub Street Journal* of 1735, which is well worth reproducing: "Since midsummer last a young lady of birth and fortune was deluded and forced from her friends, and by the assistance of a wrynecked swearing parson, married to an atheistical wretch, whose life is a continued practice of all manner of vice and debauchery. And since the ruin of my relative, another lady of my acquaintance had like to have been trepanned in the following manner: This lady had appointed to meet a gentlewoman at the Old Playhouse in Drury Lane, but extraordinary business prevented her coming. Being alone when the play was done, she bade a boy call a coach for the city. One dressed like a gentleman helps her into it, and jumps in after her. 'Madam,' says he, 'this coach was called for me, and since the weather is so bad, and there is no other, I beg leave to bear you company; I am going into the City, and will set you down wherever you please.

The lady begged to be excused, but he bade the coachman drive on. Being come to Ludgate Hill, he told her his sister, who waited his coming but five doors up the court, would go with her in two minutes. He went, and returned with his pretended sister, who asked her to step in one minute, and she would wait upon her in the coach. The poor lady foolishly followed her into the house, when instantly the sister vanished, and a tawny fellow in a black coat and a black wig appeared. 'Madam, you are come in good time, the doctor was just agoing!' 'The doctor!' says she, terribly frighted, fearing it was a madhouse; 'what has the doctor to do with me?' 'To marry you to that gentleman. The doctor has waited for you these three hours, and will be paid by you or that gentleman before you go!' 'That gentleman,' says she, recovering herself, 'is worthy a better fortune than mine;' and begged hard to be gone. But Doctor Wryneck swore she should be married; or if she would not he would still have his fee, and register the marriage for that night. The lady finding she could not escape without money or a pledge, told them she liked the gentleman so well she would certainly meet him to-morrow night, and gave them a ring as a pledge, 'which,' says she, 'was my mother's gift on her deathbed, enjoining that, if ever I married, it should be my wedding ring;' by which cunning contrivance she was delivered from the black doctor and his tawny crew." Pennant, in his "Some Account of London," says: "In walking along the street in my youth, on the side next the prison, I have often been tempted by the question, 'Sir, will you be pleased to walk in and be married?' Along this most lawless space was hung up the frequent sign of a male and female hand enjoined, with 'Marriages performed within' written beneath. A dirty fellow invited you in. The parson was seen walking before his shop; a squalid, profligate figure, clad in a tattered plaid nightgown, with a fiery face, and ready to couple you for a dram of gin or a roll of tobacco." Some of the notes found in the registers purchased by Government in 1821, and deposited with the Registrar of the Consistory Court of London, are very amusing. Here are one or two extracts: "June 10, 1729. John Nelson, of ye parish of St George, Hanover, batchelor and gardener, and Mary Barnes, of ye same, sp. married. Cer. dated 5 November 1727, to please their parents." "1742, May 24.—A soldier brought a barber to the Cock, who I think said his name was James, barber by trade, was in part married to Elizabeth: they said they were married enough." "A coachman came, and was half married, and would give but 3s. 6d., and went off." "Edward —— and Elizabeth —— were married, and would not let me know their names." A popular error was current at this time, that if a newly-married woman ran across the street with nothing on but her shift, she would free her husband from all liability as to her debts. More than once the following, or words akin to it, is found: "The woman ran across Ludgate Hill in her shift." Riotous persons often terrified these parsons, such memoranda as the following occurring now and again: "Had a noise for four hours about the money." "Married at a barber's shop one Kerrils, for half a guinea, after which it was extorted out of my pocket, and for fear of my life delivered." "Harrowson swore most bitterly, and was pleased to say that he was fully determined to kill the minister that married him. He came from Gravesend, and was sober." And so on through infinite variety. But to return to our advertisements.

Though advertisements were by no means scarce about this time, the imposition of the duty still told heavily with regard to the regular business community, for in regular trade few things were advertised with the exception of books and quack medicines, all other commercial matters being disposed of by means of agents who advertised in a general manner, of which the following, from the *London Journal* of February 7, 1730, is a fair specimen:—

THE *Public General* CORRESPONDENCE *of affairs, for Improving Money, Trade and Estates, etc.*

Some Persons want to BUY ESTATES HELD BY LEASE from any Bishop, Dean and Chapter, or College, either for Lives or Term of Years.

A Person desires to dispose of considerable SUMS OF MONEY, in such manner as will bring him in the best interest, tho' liable to some uncertainty.

A Rev. Clergyman is willing to EXCHANGE A RECTORY of about £250 a year, in a pleasant cheap country, for a Rectory in or near London, tho' of less value.

Persons who want to raise a considerable sum of money on ESTATES, FREEHOLD or FOR LIFE, may be served therein, and in such a manner as not to be obliged to repayment, if they do not see fit.

ESTATES *which some Persons want to* BUY.

Some Freehold Lands not far from Hertford.—An Estate from £200 to about £500 a year, within 60 miles of London.—A large Estate in Middlesex or Hertfordshire.—A good Farm in Sussex or Surrey.—And several persons want to buy and some to hire other estates.

ESTATES *which some Persons want to* SELL.

Several good Houses in and about London, both Freehold and Leasehold.—A very good house for a Gentleman, pleasantly situated near Bury, with good gardens, etc. and some estate in land.—Several houses fit for gentlemen in the country, within 20 miles of London, some with and some without land.—And several persons want to sell, and some to let other estates.

The Particulars will be given by Mr Thomas Rogers, Agent *for persons who want any such business to be done. He answers letters* Post-paid, *and advertises if desired, not otherwise,* All at his own charge *if not successful.*

He gives Attendance as undermentioned:

Daily except Saturdays from 4 to 6 o'clock at home in Essex Street, then at Rainbow Coffee-house, by the TEMPLE.

At 12 o'clock { Tuesday at Tom's Coffee-house, by the EXCHANGE.
Thursday at Will's Coffee-house, near WHITEHALL.

And on sending for he will go to persons near.

The next advertisement which offers itself for special notice is of a somewhat ludicrous character, and shows into what straits a man may get by means of a highly-developed imagination and an indiscreet tongue. It runs thus :—.

Bristol, January 19, 173⅜.

WHEREAS on or about the 10th day of November last I did say in the Presence of Several People, That Anthony Coller, living at the Sign of the Ship and Dove in the Pithay in Bristol, was sent to Newgate for putting Live Toads in his Beer, in order to fine it; I do solemnly declare, That I never knew any such Thing to have been done by the said Coller nor do I believe he was ever guilty of the aforesaid or any like Practice; I am therefore heartily sorry for what I have said and hereby ask Pardon for the same of the above said Person, who, I fear, has been greatly injur'd by the unguarded Tongue of JOSEPH ROBINS.

To this curious confession, which was evidently extorted from the imaginative but timid Joseph, four witnesses appended their names. The next gentleman to whom our attention is directed was still more unfortunate than Mr Robins, for he received punishment without having committed any particular offence. He, however, seems to have been made of very different mettle from the Bristol man, for he is anxious to try his chances on better terms with those who assaulted him. The advertisement is from the *Daily Post* of January 22, 1739-40:—

WHEREAS on Saturday the 12th instant between six and seven at night, a gentleman coming along the north side of Lincolns Inn fields was set upon by three persons unknown and receiv'd several blows before he could defend himself, upon a presumption, as they said that he was the author of a Satire call'd "the Satirist." This is to inform them that they are greatly mistaken, and that the insulted person is neither the author of that Satire nor of any Satire or Poem whatever, nor knows what the said Satire contains: and therefore has reason to expect, if they are Gentlemen, that they will not refuse him a meeting, by a line to A. Z., to be left at the Bar of Dick's Coffee House, Temple Bar, in order to make him such atonement as shall be judged reasonable by the friends on each side; otherwise he is ready to give any one of them, singly, the satisfaction of a Gentleman, when and wherever shall be appointed, so as he may not have to deal with Numbers.

A. Z. must have been possessed of a considerable amount of faith if he believed that the rufflers who set upon him unawares would consent either to expose themselves, or to give what he and others called, in a thoughtless manner, "the satisfaction of a gentleman." It must have been rare satisfaction at any time to be run through the body or shot through the head, after having been insulted or injured. In the *London Daily Post and General Advertiser*, shortly after this (February 5, 1739–40), is an advertisement which looks suspiciously like a hoax, unless, indeed, it was believed at the time that one swallow would make a summer. As the advertiser was probably devoted to the agricultural interest, this is a not unlikely solution of the problem, more especially as a caged bird would naturally not be expected to possess the desired power:—

IF any person will deliver a Swallow, Swift (commonly called a Jack Squeeler) or Martin, alive to Mr Thomas Meysey, at Bewdley in Worcestershire, before the 22d day of this instant February, he shall have Ten Guineas Reward paid him, and all reasonable charges allowed him for his journey by the said Thomas Meysey: Or if any person will deliver either of the said birds to Mr John Perrins, Distiller, in Butcher Row, London, soon enough to send it to the said Thomas Meysey at Bewdley before the 22d Instant February, and the bird shall be alive when delivered, or come to live after it is delivered to the said Thomas Meysey, he shall have Ten Guineas Reward paid him, and all reasonable charges allowed him by the said John Perrins.

These birds are oftentimes found in the clifts in great rocks, old chimneys, and old houses, seemingly dead; but when they are put before a fire, they will come to life.

N.B.—It must not be a Swallow, Swift or Martin that has been kept in a cage.

There must have been much capturing of small birds, and many may have been roasted alive in attempts to preserve them for the benefit of Thomas Meysey. It certainly does appear as if about this time humour was so rife that it had to find vent in all sorts of strange advertisements, and the quacks were not slow to follow the lead thus set, as is shown by the exercising swindle which follows, and which certainly must have exercised the minds of many who read it at the time. It appears in the same paper as the foregoing, on March 7, 1739–40. (It is almost time by March to know what year one is in.)

FULLER *on* EXERCISE.

(*A Book worth reading*)

NOTHING ought to be thought ridiculous that can afford the least ease or procure health. A very worthy gentleman not long ago had such an odd sort of a cholick, that he found nothing would relieve him so much as lying with his head downwards; which posture prov'd always so advantageous that he had a frame made to which he himself was fastened with Bolts, and then was turned head downwards, after which manner he hung till the pain went off. I hope none will say that this was unbecoming a grave and wise man, to make use of such odd means to get rid of an unsupportable pain. If people would but abstract the benefit got by exercise from the means by which it is got, they would set a great value upon it, if some of the advantages accruing from exercise were to be procured by any other medicine, nothing in the world would be in more esteem than that Medicine.

This is to answer some objections to the book of the Chamber Horse (for exercise) invented by HENRY MARSH, in Clement's Inn Passage, Clare Market; who, it is well known, has had the honour to serve some persons of the greatest distinction in the Kingdom; and he humbly begs the favour of Ladies and Gentlemen to try both the Chamber Horses, which is the only sure way of having the best. This machine may be of great service to children.

Mr Marsh may have been clever at making horses for chamber use, but he doesn't seem to have understood argument much; for whatever pleasure there may be in bolting oneself on to a board, and then standing on one's head, it isn't much in the way of exercise, even though Fuller may have been at the bottom of it. We beg his pardon *on* it. Still, the idea is ingenious, and in a population, the majority of which, we are informed, consists mainly of fools, would succeed now. From this same *London Daily Post and General Advertiser*, which is full of strange and startling announcements, we take another advertisement, that is likely to arouse the attention and excite the envy of all who nowadays suffer from those dwellers in tents and other forms of bedsteads, the "mahogany flats" or Norfolk Howards, who are particularly rapacious in lodgings which are let after a long term of vacancy. This knowledge is the result of actual experience. The date is March 15, 1740:—

MARY SOUTHALL

Successor to John Southall, *the first and only person that ever found out the nature of* BUGGS, *Author of the Treatise of those nauseous venomous Insects, published with the Approbation (and for which he had the honour to receive the unanimous Thanks) of the Royal Society,*

GIVES NOTICE,

THAT since his decease she hath followed the same business, and lives at the house of Mrs Mary Roundhall, in Bearlane, Christ Church Parish, Southwark. Such quality and gentry as are troubled with buggs, and are desirous to be kept free from those vermin, may know, on sending their commands to her lodgings aforesaid, when she will agree with them on easy terms, and at the first sight will justly tell them which of their beds are infested, &c., and which are free, and what is the expense of clearing the infested ones, never putting any one to more expense than necessary.

Persons who cannot afford to pay her price, and is willing to destroy them themselves, may by sending notice to her place of abode aforesaid, be furnish'd with the NON PAREIL LIQUOR, &c. &c.

Bugs are said to have been very little if at all known in the days of our ancestors. It is indeed affirmed in that valuable addition to zoology, Southall's "Treatise of Bugs" (London, 1730, 8vo), referred to in the advertisement just quoted, that this inseet was scarcely known in England before the year 1670, when it was imported among the timber used in rebuilding the city of London after the fire of 1666. That it was, however, known much earlier is not to be doubted, though probably it was far less common than at present, since Dr Thomas Muffet, in the "Theatrum Insectorum," informs us that Dr Penny, one of the early compilers of that history of insects, relates his having been sent for in great haste to Mortlake in Surrey, to visit two noble ladies who imagined themselves seized with symptoms of the plague; but on Penny's demonstrating to them the true cause of their complaint—viz., having been bitten by those insects, and even detecting them in their presence—the whole affair was turned into a jest. This was in the year 1583. It is a somewhat remarkable fact, well known to those whose misfortunes subject them to contiguity with these highly-scented bloodsuckers, that within the past few years bugs have altered considerably. The old, nearly round-bellied, and possibly jovial fellow, has given way to a long dangerous creature who is known to experts as the "omnibus bug," not so much on account of his impartiality as because of his shape. It is believed by some that this change is the result of bugs being discontented with their position, and their natural (and laudable) attempt to become something else in accordance with scientific theory; but we fancy that the true reason of this change is that foreign bugs have been imported in large numbers among cargoes, and not infrequently about passengers, and that the original settlers are being gradually exterminated in a manner similar to that which led to the extirpation of the black rat in this country. There is yet another theory with regard to the change which it would be unfair to pass over. It is that the bugs have altered—it is admitted on all sides that the alteration first exhibited itself at the East End of London—in consequence of feeding on mixed and barbarous races about Ratcliffe Highway and other dock purlieus. Any one who pays his money for this book is at liberty to take his choice of hypotheses, but we can assure him that the change is undoubtedly matter of fact.

The next specimen taken is of a literary turn, and appears in the *Champion, or the Evening Advertiser*, of January 2, 1741. From it we may judge of the number of burlesques and travesties which, some large, some small, were called into existence by the publication of what many consider to be Richardson's masterpiece. Whatever rank "Pamela" may hold as compared with "Clarissa Harlowe," "Sir Charles Grandison," and other works by the same author, it is very little regarded now, while one of the books to which it gave rise is now a representative work of English literature. Here is the literary advertisement of the day:—

This Day is publish'd

(Price One Shilling and Sixpence),

AN APOLOGY for the LIFE of Mrs. SHAMELA ANDREWS, in which the many notorious *Falsehoods* and *Misrepresentations* of a book called *Pamela* are all expos'd and refuted; and the matchless *Arts* of that young Politician set in a true and just light. Together with a full Account of all that passed between her and Parson Arthur Williams, whose character is represented in a Manner somewhat different from what he bears in *Pamela*, the whole being exact Copies of authentick Papers deliver'd to the Editor. Necessary to be had in all Families. With a modern Dedication after the Manner of the Antients, especially CICERO. By Mr. *Conny Keyber*.

Printed for *A. Dodd*, at the Peacock without Temple Bar,

Where may be had, Price 1*s*.,

1. The COURT SECRET, a Melancholy Truth. Translated from the Original *Arabic*. By an Adept in the Oriental Tongues.

Remember that a Prince's Secrets are Balm conceal'd;
But Poison if discover'd. —MASSINGER.

Also, Price 1*s*.,

2. A Faithful Narrative of the Unfortunate Adventures of *Charles Cartwright*, M.D., who in his voyage to *Jamaica* was taken by a Spanish Privateer, and carried into *St Sebastians*. His hard usage there, and wonderful Escape from thence, &c. &c.

The "Court Secret" is possibly a satire on the evil doings which were notorious in connection with high places at that time, but which happily died out with their primary causes; and the other book is doubtless one of those quaint stories of slavery and adventure which form interesting reading even to this day. Next we come upon an advertisement which offers special temptation to the female mind, as it combines the gratification of more than one ruling passion of the time. It is from the *General Advertiser* of April 27, 1745:—

The Interpretation of
WOMEN'S
DREAMS,
With the *Prints* of these DREAMS finely Engraved.

If a *Single* WOMAN *Dreams* the 18th DREAM, it tells when she'll be married. If the 19th, she may make her fortune.—The 35th tells what children she'll have. But if she dreams the 34th DREAM

She may as well wed FARINELLI, *All one*
With a curious print of FARINELLI finely engraved,
Plainly shewing to open and clear view, etc.
The 42d DREAM describes the man she 's to have, and
The 33d tells a WIFE also to LOOK ABOUT HER.
The rest of the DREAMS tell, etc. etc. etc.
To which is added A LOTTERY
For HUSBANDS for young MAIDS,
With the *Prints* of these HUSBANDS, Finely Engraved.
Not one Blank, but ALL Prizes, the *Lowest* of which
Is a very *Handsome* and RICH *Young Gentleman* that keeps his COACH.
—And if she draws of the 6th class of *Tickets*, she is then sure to be
MY LADY.
To be drawn as soon as full—And
Any Maiden that will put off TWO *Tickets*, shall have ONE for *Her Self* to put her in Fortune's way.

'Tis GIVEN GRATIS at Mr BURCHELL'S ANODYNE NECKLACE SHOP in Long Acre, Cutler and Toyshop. The sign of the case of knives next shop to *Drury Lane*,

Where *on the counter it does* Ready *Lie*
For ALL *who'll* step in *for't in Passing by.*

This Mr Burchell of the Anodyne Necklace was a notorious quack of the time, to whom reference is made further on. It is patent to the most casual observer that he is able to dispose his wares in the most tempting manner, and the book, as well as the tickets, must have had a very good sale indeed. Also portraying the tastes and peculiarities of this portion of the eighteenth century is an invitation taken from the *General Advertiser* in October 1745, which displays inordinate vanity on the part of the writer, or, to put it in the mildest form, peculiarity of behaviour on that of the lady to whom he addresses himself:—

WHEREAS a lady last Saturday evening at the playhouse in Drury Lane in one of the left-hand boxes, was observed to take particular notice of a gentleman who sat about the middle of the pit, and as her company would be esteemed the greatest favour, she is humbly desired to send him directions, where and in what manner she would be waited upon, and direct the said letter to be left for P. M. Z. at the Portugal Coffee house near the Exchange.

Notices of this kind—many of the most barefaced, and not a few of a decidedly indelicate description—must have been a fruitful source of income to the proprietors of newspapers; and that professions of adoration for unknown women—most of whom were presumably married, else why all the concealment and strategy?—did not fall off as years progressed is shown by the following, taken from a wealth of the same kind in the commencement of 1748. It is also from the *General Advertiser*:—

WHEREAS a young lady was at Covent Garden playhouse last Tuesday night, and received a blow with a square piece of wood on her breast; if the lady be single and meet me on Sunday at two o'clock, on the Mall in St James's Park, or send a line directed for A. B., to Mr Jones's, at the Sun Tavern at St Paul's Churchyard, where and when I shall wait on her, to inform her of something very much to her advantage on honourable terms, her compliance will be a lasting pleasure to her most obedient servant.

This man, though somewhat rude in his style, and, judging from the description of his adventure at the playhouse, rather coarse in his manners, is noticeable for stipulating that his charmer shall be single. Let us hope that, if his intentions were honourable, he prospered in his suit. If he didn't, then perhaps he felt consoled by the knowledge that virtue is its own reward.

TO THE JOYOUS.—The Bloods are desired to meet together at the house known by the name of the Sir Hugh Middleton, near Saddler's Wells, Islington, which Mr Skeggs has procured for that day for the better entertainment of those Gentlemen who agreed to meet at his own house. Dinner will be on the Table punctually at two o'clock.

The advertisement just given, which appears in the *General Advertiser* for January 13, 1748, is one of the rare instances of anything relating to politics in advertisements. The only time when political significance is given to an advertisement is when party dinners, of which the foregoing seems to be one, are advertised. The Sir Hugh Middleton is still in existence, and a few years back, when Sadler's

Wells was the only home for legitimacy in London, was much frequented by theatrical stars and the lesser lights of the drama. Comparatively recently a music-hall has been added to the establishment, which, however profitable in a pecuniary sense, hardly adds to the reputation of this well-known and once suburban tavern. In another preliminary notice, which appears early in April, attention is directed to another part of the town, and probably to another phase of political and party existence. It is, like the others, from the *General Advertiser*, which at the time was a great medium. The two which follow it are also from the same paper :—

HALF-MOON TAVERN, CHEAPSIDE.—Saturday next, the 16 April, being the anniversary of the Glorious Battle of Culloden, the Stars will assemble in the Moon at six in the evening. Therefore the choice spirits are desired to make their appearance and fill up the joy.

It is not hard to determine the sentiments of those who then called Culloden a glorious battle, though we should think there are few nowadays who, whatever their tastes and sympathies, would affix the adjective to a victory which, however decisive, was marred by one of the most disgraceful and cowardly massacres of any time. But the shame still rests on the memory of that man who was truly a butcher—a butcher of the defenceless, but an impotent officer and arrant coward in the presence of armed equality; and so, as his name leaves a nasty taste in the mouth, we will pass on to a contemporary card put forth by an enterprising tradesman :—

JOHN WARD, STAY-MAKER,

AT the Golden Dove, in Hanover Street, Long Acre, Makes Tabby all over for £1, 13s. od., for large sizes £1, 16s. od.; ticken backs £1, 7s. od., for large sizes two or three shillings advance, with the very best of goods and the very best of work; neither would I accept a ship-load of the second-best bone, and be obliged to use it, to deceive people, nor tabby nor trimming. I am willing to produce receipts in a court of justice for tabby, bone, &c., and be entirely disannulled business, or counted an impostor and a deceiver, if I act contrary to what I propose; which if I did I should be guilty of nothing but deceit, nor nothing less than fraud, and so don't ought to be allowed; but I can give the direct contrary proots; for I can prove I have had eighteen measures at a time by me since Christmas, for people as I have made for several times before, and all the winter never less than five or six in a week, often more, all old customers; and in consideration its all for ready money, it shows a prodigious satisfaction. I buy for ready money, and that commands the best of goods, and the allowance made in consideration thereof.

Mr Ward speaks like a conscientious man, but so do most of the manufacturers of female apparel—or at least they endeavour to—who advertise. The *General Advertiser* was started in 1745, and its title indicates the purpose for which it was intended. It was "the first successful attempt to depend for support upon the advertisements it contained, thereby creating a new era in the newspaper press. From the very outset its columns were filled with them, between fifty and sixty, regularly classified and separated by rules, appearing in each publication; in fact the advertising page put on for the first time a modern look. The departure of ships is constantly notified, and the engravings of these old high-pooped vessels sail in even line down the column. Trading matters have at last got the upper hand. You see 'a pair of leather bags,' 'a scarlet laced coat,' 'a sword,' still inquired after; and theatres make a show, for this was the dawning of the age of Foote, Macklin, Garrick, and most of the other great players of the last century; but, comparatively speaking, the gaieties and follies of the town ceased gradually from this time to proclaim themselves through the medium of advertisements." The great earthquake at Lisbon so frightened people about this time that a law was passed prohibiting masquerades; and the other means of amusement, the china auctions, the rope-dancing, the puppet shows, and the public breakfasts, became scarcer and scarcer as a new generation sprang into being, and the padded, powdered, and patched ladies of high descent and doubtful reputation faded from the world of fashion. This, however, was a work of time, and the crop of noticeable advertisements, though smaller, is still sufficiently large for the purpose of making extracts.

Continuing, then, on our way, we do not travel far from the staymaker's announcement, and are still in the same month, when we drop upon a notice which requires no explanation, so well does it apply itself to the minds of those whom it may concern. It runs thus :—

WHEREAS Ministers of State and other persons in power are often importuned for places and preferments which are not in their disposal, and whereas many Gentlemen waste their lives and fortunes in a long but vain dependance on the Great; This is to give notice, that in order to preserve the suitors, on the one hand, from such disappointments, and the vexation, expense, and loss of time with which they are attended; and men in power, on the other, from being solicited on matters not in their department of business:

At No. 15, one pair of stairs, in the King's-bench Walk, in the Temple, gentlemen at an easy charge may be informed what is in their patrons' power to bestow, and what with consistency and propriety they may ask for; (either civil, ecclesiastical, or military, by land or sea, together with the business of each employment, salaries, fees, &c.) as also by what methods to apply, and obtain a speedy and definite answer.

At the same place the most early and certain intelligence may be had of the vacancies which occur in all public offices. Those who have any business to transact with the Government, may be put into the easiest and readiest way to accomplish it, and those who have places to dispose of may depend on secrecy and always hear of purchasers.

N.B.—At the same place, accompts depending in Chancery, or of any other kind, are adjusted; as likewise the business of a money scrivener transacted, in buying and selling estates, lending money upon proper securities, and proper securities to be had for money.

This agency, if properly conducted, must have been as convenient for patrons as for place applicants, and doubtless the "ministers of State and other persons in power" must often have been astonished to discover what power they really possessed, which discovery would never have been made had it not been for the services of the gentleman up one pair of stairs.

In January 1752, the widow Gatesfield discovered the

advantage likely to accrue from the quotation in an advertisement of any independent testimony, no matter how remote, and so being anxious to acquaint the public with the superiority of the silver spurs, for fighting cocks, manufactured at her establishment, she concluded her announcement in the *Daily Advertiser* as follows:—

☞ Mr. Gatesfield was friend and successor to the late Mr Smith mentioned in Mr Hallam's ingenious poem called the *Cocker*, p. 58.

As curious artists different skill disclose,
The various weapon different temper shows;
Now curving points to soft a temper bear,
And now to hard their brittleness declare.
Now on the plain the treach'rous weapons lye,
Now wing'd in air the shiver'd fragments fly:
Surpris'd, chagrin'd, the others gaze,
And SMITH alone ingenious artist praise.

The following, which appears about the same time, is of a rather doubtful order. It is inserted in the *General Advertiser* of January 6, 1752, and seems to be an attempt to renew a friendship broken off by some frolicsome fair ones at the sacrifice of as little dignity as possible. The advertiser certainly seems to know a good deal about the missing ladies:—

WHEREAS two young ladies of graceful figure, delicate turned limbs and noble aspect, lately absenting themselves from their admirers, are suspected maliciously to have sent an expensive Packet, containing four indecent Words in various Languages, to a gentleman near Hanover Square: This is to give notice whosoever shall induce these ladies to surrender themselves to that gentleman, shall receive a suitable reward. The ladies may depend on the gentleman's discretion.

The tender honour of the fine gentlemen of sixscore years ago is admirably shown by the next two public announcements, the first of which appears in the *General Advertiser* for January 13, 1752:—

DURING the performance on Saturday night at Drury Lane playhouse, a dispute was carried to a great length, between two gentlemen, but all the reparation demanded by the injured party being publicly granted, the affair had no bad consequences.

Three days after, the advertisement was repeated in the same paper with the addition of some particulars :—

DURING the performance on Saturday night at Drury Lane playhouse, a dispute was carried to a great length between Mr V——n and a gentleman unknown; but on the stranger being made sensible of his error, and making public submission and gentleman-like reparation, it was amicably terminated.

Mr V——n was evidently very anxious that his friends should know he had borne himself bravely, and like a gentleman, even at the risk of bloodshed. Nowadays he would have endeavoured to get his advertisement into another portion of the paper, and "Jenkins's" services and leaded type would doubtless have been brought into requisition.

The *General Advertiser* seems to have been a medium for affairs of gallantry, for just at this period we find the annexed :—

A TALL, well-fashion'd, handsome young woman, about eighteen, with a fine bloom in her countenance, a cast in one of her eyes, scarcely discernable ; a well-turned nose, and dark-brown uncurled hair flowing about her neck, which seemed to be newly cut ; walked last new year's day about three o'clock in the afternoon, pretty fast through Long acre, and near the turn into Drury Lane met a young gentleman, wrapp'd up in a blue roccelo cloak, whom she look'd at very steadfastly : He believes he had formerly the pleasure of her acquaintance : If she will send a line directed to H. S. Esq. to be left at the bar of the Prince of Orange Coffeehouse, the corner of Pall Mall, intimating where she can be spoke with, she will be inform'd of something greatly to her advantage. She walked in a dark coloured undressed gown, black hat and capuchin; a low middle-aged woman plainly dressed, and a footman following close behind, seemed to attend her.

It is to be presumed that the hair, and not the neck, is referred to as being newly cut, though at this distance of date it certainly does not matter much which, except for the purpose of discovering probable fresh peculiarities among our very peculiar ancestors. That more than one cunning tradesman began about now to understand the full value of judicious puffery, is well shown by the following ingenious advertisement, in the form of a letter to the editor of the *General Advertiser*, of January 19, 1752, which is a good specimen of that disinterested friendship which people always have for themselves :—

SIR,

Your inserting this in your paper will be of great service to the public, and very much oblige,

Your humble servant, E. G.

That Mr Parsons, staymaker at the Golden Acorn, James Street, Covent Garden, makes stays for those that are crooked, in a perfect easy pleasant manner : so that the wearer is as easy in them, though ever so crooked, as the straitest woman living, and appears so strait and easy a shape that it is not to be perceived by the most intimate acquaintances. As to misses that are crooked or inclined to be so, either by fall, sickness, etc., he always prevents their growing worse, and has often with his care and judgment, in particular methods he has in making their coats and stays, brought them intirely strait, which I can attest, if required, by several which were infants at my boarding School and are now good-shap'd women. I have often persuaded Mr Parsons to let this be published in the Papers, for the good of my sex, for what would not any gentlewoman give, who has this misfortune, either in themselves or their children, to know of a man that can make them appear strait and easy, and their children made strait or preserved from growing worse. But his answer was that he did not like it to be in the Papers ; and not only that, but the Public might think he work'd only for those who have the misfortune of being crook'd. But certainly in mine, and every thinking person's opinion, as he is so ingenious to make such vast additions to a bad shape, he must and can add some beauties to a good one by making a genteel stay. He has been in business for himself to my knowledge 26 years ; consequently has, and does work, for genteel shapes as well as bad. I have several fine-shaped misses in my School that he works for, whose parents always give me thanks for recommending him, and are pleased to say that he makes the genteelest stays, robes, or coats they ever saw ; and I doubt not, but every one that employs him will say the same.

Sir, as the publishing this in the Papers (which I acknowledge was first without your consent), has been of such universal service, therefore I desire you'll permit the continuance of it, for I sincerely do it for the good of my sex, knowing whoever applies to you will receive great benefit thereby.

ELIZABETH GARDINER.

Mrs Gardiner seems to have known just as much about Mr Parsons as Mr Parsons knew about himself, or at all events as much as he cared to let other people know. Very different is the next selection, which goes to show that however unfashionable a thing love at first sight may be now, it had some claims to consideration in 1752, from the *Daily Advertiser* of March 30, in which year, this is taken :—

IF the young gentleman who came into the Oratorio last Wednesday and by irresistible address gained a place for the lady he attended is yet at liberty, Sylvia may still be happy. But, alas! her mind is racked when she reflects on all the tender anxiety he discovered (or she fears she saw) in all his care of her that evening. How much, how deep was all his attention engaged by that too lovely, too happy fair! At all events an interview is earnestly sought, even if it be to talk to me of eternally lasting sorrow. Notice how to direct to him shall not want gratitude. He may remember a circumstance of a lady's mentioning as he passed the sentimental look and sweetness of his eye.

There is just a suspicion of humbug about this, unless, indeed, it emanated from an amorous dame of the Lady Bellaston school, for no young lady of even those days would have penned such an effusion. Of quite a different kind is the following, and yet there is a covert satire upon the doings of the day in it, which suggests a relationship. It is not impossible that both this, which is from the *Daily Advertiser* of October 27, 1752, and that which precedes it, emanate from the same source :—

An Address to the GENTLEMEN.

GENTLEMEN,—It is well known that many of you spare neither pains nor cost when in pursuit of a Woman you have a mind to ruin, or when attâched to one already undone. But I don't remember to have heard of any considerable benevolence conferred by any of you upon a virtuous Woman: I therefore take this method to let you know, that if there should be any among you who have a desire to assist (with a *considerable* present) an agreeable Woman, for no other reason than because she wants it, such Person or Persons (if such there be), may by giving their Address in this Paper, be informed of an occasion to exercise their disinterested Generosity.

There seems to have been no hurry on the part of the gentlemen to respond to this appeal, which might have stirred the heart of a knight-errant, but which had no effect on the bloods and fribbles of the middle of last century. In this year 1752, as previously noticed, the Act was passed forbidding a notification of "no questions asked" in advertising lost or stolen property.* The *Edinburgh Courant* of October 28, 1758, supplies us with our next example, and also shows that the course of true love was as uneven then as now :—

GLASGOW, *Octob.* 23, 1758.

WE Robert M'Nair and Jean Holmes having taken into consideration the way and manner our daughter Jean acted in her Marriage, that she took none of our advice, nor advised us before she married, for which reason we discharged her from our Family, for more than Twelve Months; and being afraid that some or other of our Family may also presume to marry without duly advising us thereof, We, taking the affair into our serious consideration, hereby discharge all and every one of our Children from offering to marry without our special advice and consent first had and obtained ; and if any of our Children should propose or presume to offer Marriage to any, without as aforesaid our advice and consent, they in that case shall be banished from our Family Twelve Months, and if they should go so far as to marry without our advice and consent, in that case they are to be banished from the Family Seven Years ; but whoever advises us of their intention to marry and obtains our consent, shall not only remain Children of the Family, but also shall have a due proportion of our Goods, Gear, and Estate, as we shall think convenient, and as the bargain requires ; and further if any

* This Act seems to have been forgotten, or capable of evasion, for a statute of the 7 & 8 Geo. IV., c. 29, s. 59, imposes a penalty on any person who shall advertise, or print, or publish an advertisement of a reward for the return of property stolen or lost, with words purporting that no questions shall be asked, or promising to pawnbrokers or others the return of money which may have been lent upon objects feloniously acquired.

one of our Children shall marry clandestinely, they, by so doing, shall lose all claim or title to our Effects, Goods, Gear or Estate; and we intimate this to all concerned, that none may pretend ignorance.

There is something original about discharging a member of one's family for twelve months or seven years, and then taking her back again; and so there is in the idea that all members of this same house are not only over-anxious to marry, but that they are unduly sought after. The family must have been, indeed, a large one to necessitate notification through the public press; and though our ignorance may be lamentable, we must confess to not knowing why Mrs M'Nair declined to call herself by her husband's name. We presume—nay, we hope—that Robert and Jean did not upon principle object to wedlock, though the advertisement, coupled with the fact of the dissimilarity of names, might lead any one to suppose so. Marriage was much thought of in 1758, so far as advertisers are concerned, as the following, culled from many of the same kind, which now began to appear in the *Daily Advertiser*, will show:—

A PERSON of character, candour and honour, who has an entire knowledge of the World, and has great Intimacy with both Sexes among the Nobility, Gentry and Persons of Credit and Reputation; and as it often happens, that many deserving Persons of both Sexes are deprived of the opportunity of entering into the state of Matrimony, by being unacquainted with the merit of each other, therefore upon directing a letter to A. Z. of any one's intention of entering into the above State, to the advantage of each, to be left at Mr Perry's, Miller's Court, Aldermanbury, Secrecy and Honour will be observed in bringing to a Conclusion such their Intention. Any Person who shall send a Letter, is desired to order the bearer to put it into the Letter-box for fear it may be mislaid: and it is desired that none but those who are sincere would make any application on the above subject.

That people were, however, quite capable of conducting their own little amours whenever a chance offered, the following, which is another of the love-at-first-sight effusions, and a gem in its way, will show. It is from the *London Chronicle* of August 5, 1758:—

A YOUNG LADY who was at Vauxhall on Thursday night last, in company with two Gentlemen, could not but observe a young Gentleman in blue and a gold-laced hat, who, being near her by the Orchestra during the performance, especially the last song, gazed upon her with the utmost attention. He earnestly hopes (if unmarried) she will favour him with a line directed to A. D. at the bar of the Temple Exchange Coffee-house, Temple-bar, to inform him whether Fortune, Family, and Character, may not entitle him, upon a further knowledge, to hope an interest in her Heart. He begs she will pardon the method he has taken to let her know the situation of his Mind, as, being a Stranger, he despaired of doing it any other way, or even of seeing her more. As his views are founded upon the most honourable Principles, he presumes to hope the occasion will justify it, if she generously breaks through this trifling formality of the Sex, rather than, by a cruel Silence, render unhappy one, who must ever expect to continue so, if debarred from a nearer acquaintance with her, in whose power alone it is to complete his Felicity.

This goes to prove what we have before remarked, that the concocters of these advertisements were in the habit of falling in love with the women whom they saw with other men; and so it is only natural to suppose, that however honourable they may have protested themselves in print, they were in reality mean, cowardly, and contemptible. The well-known Kitty Fisher finds the utility of advertising as a means of clearing her character, and in the *Public Advertiser* of March 30, 1759, puts forth the following petition, which had little effect upon her persecutors, as the little scribblers continued, as little scribblers will even nowadays, and "scurvy malevolence" also held sway over her destinies for a considerable period:—

TO err is a blemish entailed upon Mortality, and Indiscretions seldom or ever escape from Censure; the more heavy as the Character is more remarkable; and doubled, nay trebled, by the World, if the progress of that Character is marked by Success; then Malice shoots

against it all her stings, the snakes of Envy are let loose; to the human and generous Heart then must the injured appeal, and certain relief will be found in impartial Honour. Miss Fisher is forced to sue to that jurisdiction to protect her from the baseness of little Scribblers and scurvy Malevolence; she has been abused in public Papers, exposed in Printshops, and to wind up the whole, some Wretches, mean, ignorant and venal, would impose upon the Public by daring to pretend to publish her Memoirs. She hopes to prevent the success of their endeavours by thus publicly declaring that nothing of that sort has the slightest foundation in Truth. C. FISHER.

We have already referred to an article written by Dr Johnson, in an *Idler* of 1759, on the subject of advertisements. It is very amusing, and in it he says that "whatever is common is despised. Advertisements are now so numerous that they are very negligently perused, and it is therefore become necessary to gain attention by magnificence of promises, and by eloquence sometimes sublime and sometimes pathetic." He then passes in review some of the most inflated puffs of that period, and continues: "Promise, large promise, is the soul of an advertisement. I remember a washball that had a quality truly wonderful—it gave an exquisite edge to the razor. And there are now to be sold, for ready money only, some duvets for bed-coverings, of down, beyond comparison superior to what is called ottar down, and indeed such, that its many excellences cannot be here set forth. With one excellence we are made acquainted—it is warmer than four or five blankets, and lighter than one. There are some, however, that know the prejudice of mankind in favour of modest sincerity. The vendor of the beautifying fluid sells a lotion that repels pimples, washes away freckles, smooths the skin, and plumps the flesh; and yet, with a generous abhorrence of ostentation, confesses that it will not restore the bloom of fifteen to a lady of fifty. The true pathos of advertisements must have sunk deep into the heart of every man that remembers the zeal shown by the seller of the anodyne necklace, for the ease and safety of poor toothing infants, and the affection with which he warned every mother, that she would never forgive herself if her infant should perish without a necklace. I cannot but remark to the celebrated author, who gave, in his notifications of the camel and dromedary, so many specimens of the genuine sublime, that there is now arrived another subject yet more worthy of his pen—A famous Mohawk Indian warrior, who took Dieskaw, the French general, prisoner, dressed in the same manner with the native Indians when they go to war, with his face and body painted, with his scalping knife, tom-axe, and all other implements of war! A sight worthy the curiosity of every true Briton! This is a very powerful description: but a critic of great refinement would say that it conveys rather horror than terror. An Indian, dressed as he goes to war, may bring company together; but if he carries the scalping knife and tom-axe, there are many true Britons that will never be persuaded to see him but through a grate. It has been remarked by the severer judges, that the salutary sorrow of tragic scenes is too soon effaced by the merriment of the epilogue: the same inconvenience arises from the improper disposition of advertisements. The noblest objects may be so associated as to be made ridiculous. The camel and dromedary themselves might have lost much of their dignity between the true flower of mustard and the original Daffy's Elixir; and I could not but feel some indignation when I found this illustrious Indian warrior immediately succeeded by a fresh parcel of Dublin butter. The trade of advertising is now so near to perfection, that it is not easy to propose any improvement. But as every art ought to be exercised in due subordination to the public good, I cannot but propose it as a moral question to these masters of the public ear, Whether they do not sometimes play too wantonly with our passions? as when the registrar of lottery tickets invites us to his shop by an account of the prizes which he sold last year; and whether the advertising controversists do not indulge asperity of language without any adequate provocation? as in the dispute about strops for razors, now happily subsided, and in the altercation which at present subsists concerning Eau de Luce. In an advertisement it is allowed to every man to speak well of himself, but I know not why he should assume the privilege of censuring his neighbour. He may proclaim his own virtue or skill, but ought not to exclude others from the same pretensions. Every man that advertises his own excellence should write with some consciousness of a character which dares to call the attention of the public. He should remember that his name is to stand in the same paper with those of the King of Prussia and the Emperor of Germany, and endeavour to make himself worthy of such association. Some regard is likewise to be paid to posterity. There are men of diligence and curiosity who treasure up the papers of the day merely because others neglect them, and in time they will be scarce. When these collections shall be read in another century, how will numberless contradictions be reconciled; and how shall fame be possibly distributed among the tailors and bodice-makers of the present age?" Judging by the advertisements which continued, the worthy advertisers of 1759 had a very poor opinion of men yet to come, and might have asked, had they thought of it, with the Irish member, "What's posterity ever done for us?"—a query which would have puzzled even Dr Johnson.

The short-sleeved dresses of 1760 must have called for all kinds of apparatus for whitening and beautifying the arms, and among many a kindred and attractive advertisement of the time we take the following from the *Chronicle* of April 19–21:—

Gloves for Ladies.

THE true prepared French Chicken and Dog-skin Gloves, for clearing and whitening the hands and arms, perfumed and plain. As some ladies have had but small confidence in these Gloves, till they have been prevailed upon to wear one Glove for eight or ten Nights, when they have evidently seen to their agreeable satisfaction that hand and arm brought to such a superior degree of whiteness over the other, as though they did not belong to the same Person.

The above Gloves are prepared and sold only by Warren & Co., Perfumers, at the Golden Fleece, in Marybone Street, Golden Square, at 5s. a pair, who import, make and sell, all sorts of perfumery Goods, in the utmost perfection. The Violet-Cream Pomatum, and celebrated quintessence of Lavender, by no other person.

☞ Ladies sending their servants are humbly desired to send a Glove of the size.

N.B.—Just landed, a fine parcel of the famous *India* Pearl.

⁂ The Queen's Royal Marble, at 20s., and Chinese Imperial Wash ball, at 5s., that are so well known to the Nobility, &c. Ladies' Masks and Tippets.

All this effort at decoration and beautifying is very wrong, but we are stopped in our desire to "improve the occasion" by the recollection that no age has been more deep in the mysteries of cosmetic, enamel, pearl powder, and paint than our own, in which quacks abound, and old ladies have been known to submit themselves to the operation of being made beautiful, not for all time, but for ever. A little further on, in the *Evening Post*, we come upon an ambitious author who has attempted to regenerate the drama, and who advertises his work. Shakespeare seems always to have been considered capable of improvement by somebody, but as the mania for touching the immortal bard up, and making him respectable and fit for the understandings of small tradesmen, still goes on, and fortunes are made at it, we will give the following without comment, lest some original author of the present day might think we were obliquely alluding to him :—

In the press and shortly will be published

THE Students, a Comedy, altered from Shakespeare's Love's Labour Lost, and adapted to the stage, with an original Prologue and Epilogue.

Printed for Thomas Hope, opposite the north gate of the Royal Exchange, Threadneedle St.

Deserters are plentiful about this period, our soldiers,

however brave they may have been when put to it, having an evident objection to the pomp and circumstance of war. That was, perhaps, because their share of the latter was unduly large as compared with their participation in the former. The following is from *Lloyd's Evening Post* of April 26–28, and is a fair specimen of the remainder:—

Deserted

FROM the 16th Regiment of Dragoons, Captain Walmesly's troop,
WILLIAM BEVEN,
Aged 16 years, about five feet five inches high, stoops a good deal as he walks, and but very indifferently made; absented himself from his Quarters last Saturday night, the 17th instant; he says he was born in the parish of the *Hays*, in the County of Brecknockshire, and by trade a labourer; he went away with a light horse man's cap, a coarse red frock faced with black, a striped flannel waistcoat, and a pair of leather breeches.

Whoever apprehends and secures the above Deserter, so as he may be committed to any of His Majesty's gaols, shall, by applying to George Ross, Esq., Agent to the regiment, in Conduit Street, London, receive twenty Shillings, over and above the reward given by Act of Parliament.

Those who are in the habit of expressing themselves as to the decadence of the British soldier, and of the British human being generally, will do well to ponder over this advertisement, and judge from it the difference between the defenders of hearths and homes of then and now. Yet, with all his want of size and possession of awkwardness, this same youth, who would not nowadays be admitted into the worst regiment of militia fallbacks in existence, is deemed worthy of an extra reward. So much for "our army" in the middle of the eighteenth century.

CHAPTER X.

THE EDUCATION COMPLETED.

SO far, as has been shown, advertisements have had to struggle against foreign war, internecine disorder, the poverty of the State, and many other drawbacks; but by the commencement of the seventh decade of the eighteenth century, these difficulties have all in turn been surmounted, and the most modern means of obtaining publicity, despite prejudice, and, still worse, taxation, is fixed firmly in the land, and doing much towards the management of its affairs. The country is at peace with the world, so far as Europe is concerned; and even the Canadian campaign is as good as over. Clive has made himself felt and the name of England feared throughout the length and breadth of India, and merchants are beginning to reap the advantages of conquest. George III. has ascended the throne, has been married and crowned, and looks forward to a long and prosperous reign. In fact, everything seems bright and smiling, for never, through many a long year, was the country so free from troubles and anxieties, or with so little to direct her attention from those two great essentials to English existence—profit and pleasure. And so, as marked in the preceding chapter, advertisements of all kinds progressed as the century became older; and when the ordinary style failed, dodges of all kinds were adopted to give a factitious importance to announcements, no matter whether of quacks, of publishers, or of the infinite variety of other trades and professions which just now began to be bitten by the fast-growing mania. Some of the sly puffs were of a most specious order, and attention is called to one of them by the indignation it evoked in the *Monthly Review* (vol. xxvii. 1762). The object of the puff paragraph had been an insipid panegyric on Lord Halifax, called "The Minister of State," which sacrificed on the altar of Halifax the characters of all preceding premiers, from Burleigh to Bute, and the attempt to force its sale evoked the wrath of the *Review*, which commences as follows:—"As the practice of puffing is now arrived at the utmost height of assurance, it will not be improper for the Reviewers occasionally to mark some of the grosser instances that may occur of this kind." Thereupon it notices the "lying paragraph," to which we have already referred, the words within brackets being the comments of the Reviewer:

A noble Peer has absolutely given directions to his Solicitor to commence a Prosecution against the Author of the Poem called, *The Minister of State, a Satire*, as a most licentious and libellous composition.—The writer, no doubt, merits a severer censure of the Law than any of his brethren, because instead of employing those *great talents for poetry and satire for which he is so deservedly celebrated* [what does he not deserve for his effrontery?] in the service of Virtue and his Country, he has *basely* [basely enough!] prostituted them to the unworthy purpose of defaming, lampooning and abusing some of the greatest characters in this Kingdom. [All a puff to excite curiosity.] We think this LITERARY LUMINARY of the age [this illiterate farthing candle!] should pay a greater deference to the words of his predecessor Mr Pope:

"Curs'd be the verse, how smooth soe'er it flow," etc.

[We doubt, however, if any of this *honest* gentleman's readers will think his verses worth a curse, whatever they may think he deserves for his impudence.]

This energetic effort on the part of the *Review* to prevent undue reputations being made by disguised advertisements, had little effect in checking an evil which flourishes unto this day—which will, in fact, flourish as long as a majority exist ready to believe anything they are told, and to be more than usually prompt with their credulity when what they are told is more than usually wrong. The next notification we select is from the *British Chronicle* of January 4-6, 1762, and is of a literary character also, though, judging by the motto adopted, the work is more likely to produce melancholy than amusement:—

This day are published, Price 1s.,

THE Songs of Selma, attempted in English verse, from the original of Ossian, the son of Fingal. . . . . *Quis talia fando Temperet a lacrymis?* . . . . Printed for R. Griffiths, opposite Somerset House in the Strand; C. Henderson, at the Royal Exchange; and G. Woodfall, Charing Cross.

How many books of this kind have been published, thrown aside, and forgotten, or consigned to the pastry-cook and trunkmaker, since the "Songs of Selma" saw the light, is a question easier to ask than to solve. One thing is, though, certain—the number of people who will write, whether they have anything to say or not, increases every year, and in due course we may expect an ingenious Chancellor of the Exchequer to impose a tax on authors; which, after all, will hardly, so far as brilliancy is concerned, be so destructive as the window-tax, or so uncalled for as Mr Robert Lowe's famous "ex luce lucellum" imposition. A couple of weeks later, in the same paper (January 18–20), is the following of a very different character from that which has been already selected:—

READING MACHINE

IS removed from the Three Kings, Piccadilly, to the George Inn, Snow Hill, London; sets out from the *Broad Face, Reading*, every Monday, Wednesday, and Friday, at seven o'clock in the morning, and from the *George Inn, Snow Hill*, every Tuesday, Thursday, and Saturday, at seven o'clock in the morning; carries passengers to and from Reading at 6s. each, children in lap, and outside passengers at 3s.

Performed by { THOMAS MOORE and RICHARD MAPLETON.

N.B.—Takes no charge of Writings, Money, Watches, or Jewels, unless entered and paid for as such.

This machine was evidently a nondescript, partly slow coach, partly waggon, and was extremely reasonable in its rates if it journeyed at any pace, seeing that outside passengers paid no more than present Parliamentary rates, while the insides had no occasion to complain of excessive expenditure. But fancy the journey at seven o'clock on a January morning, with the knowledge that no brisk motion would keep the blood in circulation, that the roads were heavy, the weather indifferent, the society worse, the conversation, if any, very heavy, and the purse proportionally light! Such a company as Roderick Random and Strap fell in with in the waggon, must often have been seen on the outside of the Reading Machine. In the same paper of January 20–22, we find the advertisement of a pamphlet issued for the gratification of a morbid taste which has its representative nowadays — though, by the way, there is more excuse for a little excitement over murder and execution now than there was in the days when every week saw its batch of criminals led forth to take their final dance upon nothing:—

This day was published, price 1s.,

SOME authentic particulars of the life of John Macnaghton, Esq., of Ben ——, who was executed in Ireland, on tuesday the 25th day of December, for the Murder of Miss Mary Anne Knox, the only daughter of Andrew Knox, Esq., of Prehen, representative in the late and present Parliament for the county of Donegal. With a full account of his pretended Connexion with the young Lady; of the measures he took to seize her person previous to the Murder; the circumstances of that fact; the manner of his being apprehended; and his conduct and behaviour from that time till his Death. Compiled from papers communicated by a gentleman in Ireland, to a person of distinction of that Kingdom now residing here.

Printed for H. Payne & W. Croply, at Dryden's Head in Paternoster Row.

John Macnaghton, Esq., was a real gentleman criminal, and though food for the halter was plenty in 1762 and thereabouts, gentlemen were "tucked up" still more rarely than within ordinary recollections; for stern as was the law a hundred years ago, it had very merciful consideration for persons of quality, and the hanging of a landed proprietor for a mere paltry murder was a very noticeable event. In the *London Gazette* of February 23–27, we find a record of the coronation of their illustrious and sacred Majesties, George and Charlotte, which runs thus:—

ALBEMARLE ST., *Feby.* 26, 1762.

THE Gold Medals intended for the Peers and Peeresses who in their robes attended at the Coronation of their Majesties (according to a list obtained from the proper officers) will be delivered at the Earl of Powis's house in Albemarle Street, on Wednesday and Thursday next, from ten to twelve o'clock each day.

It is therefore desired that the Peers and Peeresses, as above mentioned, will send for their Medals; and that the persons who shall be sent for them shall bring Cards, signed by such Peers or Peeresses, as the Medals shall be required for, and sealed with their Arms.

In the same paper we come upon the advertisement of a book which is even now read with interest, though the price at which a modern issue of it is offered is ludicrously small compared with that of the original edition:—

THIS day is published, in small quarto, Price Thirty Shillings, Printed at Strawberry Hill, Anecdotes of Painting in England, with incidental Notes on other Arts. Collected by the late Mr George Vertue, and now first digested and published from his original Manuscripts. By Mr Horace Walpole. Vol. I. and II. With above forty Copper plates, four of which are taken from antient Paintings; the rest, heads of Artists, engraved by Grignion, Muller, Chambers, and Bannerman.

To be had of W. Bathoe, Bookseller, in the Strand, near Exeter Exchange.

As we have no wish whatever to paint the lily, we will, although the subject is a kindred one, leave Horace Walpole's book without a fresh criticism to add to the thousand and odd already passed upon it, and will pass on to the land "where the men are all brave and the women all beautiful," and where, in *Faulkner's Dublin Journal*, also of February 1762, we come upon the cry of a young man for his mother. In the advertisement is the nucleus of a story quite equal to "Tom Jones," provided, of course, that its author possessed the fancy of a Fielding. We are not aware of any literary gentleman who would succeed, though we are acquainted with plenty who would most confidently make the attempt;

their only doubt, if doubt possessed them at all, being not in their own powers, but in the discernment of the reading public. To them, therefore, we present the groundwork of a story which would naturally enlist the sympathies of England and Ireland. A little might also be thrown in for the benefit of Scotland, which would hardly like to be left out of so fascinating a romance:—

WHEREAS a lady who called herself a native of Ireland was in England in the year 1740, and resided some time at a certain village near Bath, where she was delivered of a son, whom she left with a sum of money under the care of a person in the same parish, and promised to fetch him at a certain age, but has not since been heard of; now this is to desire the lady, if living, and this should be so fortunate as to be seen by her, to send a letter, directed to T. E. to be left at the Chapter Coffee house, St Paul's Churchyard, London, wherein she is desired to give an account of herself, and her reasons for concealing this affair: or if the lady should be dead, and any person is privy to the affair, they are likewise desired to direct as above.—*N.B.* This advertisement is published by the person himself, not from motives of necessity, or to court any assistance (he being, by a series of happy circumstances, possessed of an easy and independent fortune) but with a real desire to know his origin.—*P.S.* The strictest secrecy may be depended on.

Foundlings seem to have been better off a hundred years ago than now, for in all stories they come out very well, and in this present instance T. E. seems to have been able to help himself. It is not unlikely, however, that some sharp adventurer, knowing how weak is human nature, had hit upon the expedient of attracting maternal sympathies—Bath was a great place at that time for interesting invalids—with a view to a system of extortion. This may, or may not be, and at this distance of time it is useless to speculate. Accordingly we turn once more to the *London Gazette*, and in a number for April 1762 find this:—

THE following persons being fugitives for debt, and beyond the seas, on or before the twenty-fifth day of October, one thousand seven hundred and sixty, and having surrendered themselves to the Gaolers or

Keepers of the respective Prisons or Gaols hereafter mentioned, do hereby give notice, that they intend to take the benefit of an Act of Parliament passed in the first year of the reign of His present Majesty King George the Third, intituled *An Act for relief of Insolvent Debtors*, at the next General or Quarter Sessions of the Peace, to be held in and for the County, Riding, Division, City, Town, Liberty or Place, or any adjournment thereof, which shall happen next after thirty days from the first Publication of the undermentioned names, viz.,

James Colburn, late of. Smith Street, in the parish of St James, in the county of Middlesex, Baker.

Fugitive surrendered to the Keeper of Whitechapel Prison, in the County of Middlesex.

Second Notice.

Charles Watkins, late of the Bankside, in the parish of St Saviour, Southwark, in the county of Surrey, Waterman.

Fugitive surrendered to the Keeper of the Poultry Compter, in the City of London.

Third Notice.

James Buckley, formerly of Cock Alley, late of Star Alley, in the Parish of Aldgate, Lower Precinct, London, Cordwainer.

This is one of the first notices given of an intention to take the benefit of an Act that was much wanted. The slowness of people to take advantage of any boon, no matter how priceless, is here once again shown, for there are but three claimants for redemption, two of whom had been published before. By the middle of 1762 the Cock Lane ghost had had its two years' run and was discovered, and it must have been just about the time of the trial of Parsons and his family—viz., in June—that the following appeared in the *British Chronicle*:—

This day is published, price 6d.

A TRUE account of the several conversations between the supposed Apparition in Cock Lane, and the Gentlemen who attended. Together with the Death and Funeral of Mrs K——, and many other circumstances not made known to the World.

Published for the conviction of the incredulous.

"I would take the ghost's word for a thousand pounds."

HAMLET.

Printed for E. Cabe, at his Circulating library in Ave Marie lane; and to be had of all Pamphlet shops and News carriers.

It is hard to tell whether the writer is in favour of the ghost's existence or not from the advertisement, for while he in one breath speaks of the supposed apparition, he immediately afterwards refers to the incredulous, and quotes no less an authority than Shakespeare in support of the imposition. Doubtless this was a trick to secure the purchase-money, if not the support, of the partisans of both sides. Next, in the same paper, we come upon a notice of the post-office in reference to the foreign mails of that day, which runs thus:—

GENERAL POST OFFICE, *Aug.* 8, 1762.

PUBLIC Notice is hereby given to all persons corresponding with His Majesty's island of Belleisle, that Letters for the future will be regularly forwarded from Plymouth to and from that Island, by two Vessels, lately hired and appointed for that purpose.

By Order of the Postmaster-General,

HENRY POTTS, *Secretary.*

The mail service across the Atlantic was somewhat different in 1762 from what it is now, when a continuous stream of letters is every day poured forth, either by way of Liverpool or by means of the later delivery at Queenstown. Soldiers seem to have been shorter, too, not only in height but in quantity, about this time, if the evidence of an advertisement of January 1, 1763, is to be taken. We are still quoting from the *British Chronicle*, and shall continue to do so until another journal is named:—

THE Royal Regiment of Horse Guards, commanded by the Right Honourable the Marquis of Granby, is willing to entertain any young Man under 23 years of age, having a good Character, strait and well made, in height from five feet ten, to six feet one inch. Apply to Quarter Master *Campbell*, at the Market Coffee House, Mayfair.

From the same copy we take another notice, which shows that the executors of Mr Ward not only considered it their duty to get rid of his stock at the best possible advantage, but also to continue a defence of the business which had been instituted by the late proprietor against the attacks of an impostor. The reason they give for the republication is curious, unless they fancied its omission would trouble the spirit of the late compounder of drugs :—

THE late Joshua Ward of Whitehall, Esq., having left very considerable quantities of his principal Medicines ready prepared, such and such only as may be applied for by name, will be delivered at his late dwelling-house in Whitehall.

As not the least pretence is made by us, of having any judgment in the application of Medicine, we presume to say no more than that the specified orders shall be delivered with the utmost care and fidelity.—Ralph Ward, Thomas Ward, Executors.

As the following was published by the late Mr Ward it is necessary to adjoin the same.—"Having seen in the public papers that a woman servant discharged from my service advertises herself as (late) my housekeeper and assistant in preparing my medicines. It is a justice I owe the public and myself, to declare, that this woman was hired and lived with me as, and at the wages of a common working servant, keeping no other. And as to what knowledge she may have in preparing my medicines, every living servant in my family, with the same propriety, may pretend to it, being all assistants to me by their manual labour. Signed—Joshua Ward."

Soon after this, February 10–12, comes an announcement which must have filled the lady readers of the *Chronicle*—for ladies ever loved bargains—with anxiety and their husbands with terror. The last paragraph shows that the warehouseman knew well how to bait his trap for the unwary :—

A REAL SALE OF SILKS

AT the Coventry Cross, Chandos Street, Covent Garden. Consisting of a very great assortment of Rich brocades, Tissues, flowered and plain Sattins, Tabbies, Ducapes, black Armozeens, Rasdumores, Mantuas, &c. Being purchased of the executors of an eminent weaver and factor, deceased, and of another left off trade.

Merchants, &c., may be supplied with rich Silks fit for exportation, fresh and fine patterns, greatly under prime cost, for ready money only, the price marked on each piece.

It is hoped Ladies will not be offended that they cannot possibly be waited on at their own Houses.

Within a very short period, little more than a week, we come across an advertisement which we admit fairly puzzles us. We are certainly far more able to believe that the precious balsam does all that is promised for it, than we are to understand the reason for its having but one title. It runs thus :—

WARHAM'S Apopletic Balsam, so well known as an excellent remedy against Fits, Convulsions, &c., cures Deafness, bad Humours in the Eyes, inward Bruises, dissolves hard Lumps in the Breast, and has often cured Cancers, as can be proved by Facts; is a sovereign salve for green Wounds, Burns, &c. Is prepared and sold only by W. Strode, at the Golden Ball, Tottenham Court Road, London.

Who also prepares and sells Warham's Cephalick Snuff, of a most grateful smell, and an effectual remedy for giddiness, nervous pains in the Head, &c.

Also Warham's excellent Mouth water, which certainly cures the toothache, strengthens and preserves the Teeth, takes off all smells proceeding from bad Teeth, &c.

In a number for February 26 to March 1, 1764, there is an announcement of one of those dinners without which no English charity ever has succeeded, or, so long as English nature remains as it is, ever will succeed without. It is noticeable for various reasons, and especially for the notices of "Mr" Handel and the airing of the hall :—

MAGDALEN HOUSE CHARITY.

Prescot Street, Goodman's Fields, Feb. 10, 1764.

THE Anniversary Feast of the Governors of this Charity will be held on Thursday the 18th of March next, at Drapers-Hall, in Throgmorton Street, after a sermon to be preached at the Parish Church of St George, Hanover Square, before the Right Honourable the Earl of Hertford, President; the Vice-Presidents; Treasurer and Governor of this Charity; by the Rev. William Dodd, A.M., Chaplain to the Bishop of St David's.

Prayers will begin at eleven o'clock precisely, and Dinner will be on table at Three o'clock.

Stewards.

The Right Hon. Lord Viscount Spencer.

The Right Hon. Lord Scarsdale.

Joseph Martin, Esq.	John Smith, Esq.
John Weyland, Esq.	Jacob Wilkinson, Esq.
John Barker, Esq.	John Lefevre, Esq.
John Eddows, Esq.	Jacob Bosanquet, Esq.

N.B.—A Te Deum, composed by Mr Handel for the late Duke of Chandos's Chapel, with Jubilate and other Anthems, will be performed by Mr Beard, and a proper Band of the best performers, both vocal and instrumental.

The Hall will be properly aired.

Tickets for the Feast may be had at the following places, at five shillings each, viz., Mr Winterbottom's, the Secretary, in Old Broad Street, and at the following Coffee-Houses; Arthur's, in St James's Street; Mount's, Grosvernor Square; Tom's, in Devereux Court; Richard's, in Fleet Street; Tom's, John's, and Batoon's, in Cornhill; and Waghorn's, at the Court of Requests.

Two ladies Tickets for the Church will be given with each Feast Ticket.

Mr Gibson, whose advertisement appears in the edition for April 5-7, 1764, would have been invaluable to Julia Pastrana and the Bearded Lady, while his aid would have been equally in demand among those anxious to cover themselves with the glory of hirsute appendages. Unfortunately for him, moustaches and beards were not then in demand, nor was baldness so noticeable as now; but the request for his beautifying paste doubtless compensated him for other neglects:—

A CARD TO THE LADIES.

MR GIBSON'S Innocent Composition, so greatly admired for its wonderful effects, in removing by the Roots in half a minute, the most strong Hair growing in any part of the Head or Face, without the least hurt to the finest Skin of Ladies or Children; he sells this useful composition at 5s. an ounce, with such full directions that any Person may use it themselves.

Also his curious Preparation for coaxing Hair to grow on bald Parts when worn off by illness, it being allowed by many who have tried many approved remedies, to fully answer the desired Purpose.

Likewise his Beautifying Paste for the Face, Neck, and Hands, so well known to the Ladies for giving a true Enamel to the Skin; in pots at 10s. 6d. In lesser pots at 5s. each. The above things to be had of him and nowhere else in England, next door to the Golden Star in Lower Cross Street, Hatton Garden, Holborn.—No less a quantity of the composition can be had than one Ounce, nor of the preparation or paste than one Pot.

N.B.—Gibson in gold Letters over the Door.

That the practice of inserting "dummy" advertisements for the purpose of drawing others had been adopted before this, is shown by a caution inserted in the *Public Advertiser* of January 1, 1765, though why theatrical managers should have objected to gratuitous publicity we cannot understand. Misrepresentation of the title of a play to be performed would rarely act detrimentally, while it would often be beneficial. Managers of the present day never object to anything but adverse criticism in a newspaper, and this affects them in various ways. Critics may be as favourable as they like, but let them condemn a piece and they raise a storm not easily allayed. The managerial feeling is then shown at once. Sometimes the advertisement of the theatre is summarily stopped, at others the usual first-night privilege is suspended, and not rarely of late years letters have been written and published showing how utterly biassed the criticism has been. But not one of the whole theatrical fraternity ever objects to a gratuitous advertisement. Even a man who comes on with a message likes it, though he in common with all the outsiders of "the profession" affects to despise criticism, and will, on the slightest provocation, speak about well-known writers for the press in a most contemptuous manner. But here is the advertisement:—

THE Managers of Drury Lane think it proper to give notice that Advertisements of their Plays by their authority are published only in this Paper and the *Daily Courant*, and that the Publishers of all other Papers who presume to insert Advertisements of the same Plays, can do it only by some surreptitious intelligence or hearsay which frequently leads them to commit gross Errors, as mentioning one Play for another, falsely representing the Parts, etc. to the misinformation of the Town and the great detriment of the said Theatre.

As different in style as it is distant in date and place of publication is the next item which attracts our attention. It looks suspiciously like a hoax, for though other Newcastle papers of the time have been rigorously searched, no news is discovered of Mrs Bell having shared the fate which is said to overtake all who pry unduly into the secrets of the Craft for the purpose of making capital out of their information. The advertisement appears in the *Newcastle Courant* of January 4, 1770, and runs as follows:—

THIS is to acquaint the Public, That on Monday the first instant, being the Lodge (or Monthly Meeting) night of the Free and Accepted Masons of the 22d Regiment, held at the Crown, near Newgate (Newcastle) Mrs Bell, the Landlady of the House, broke open a Door (with a Poker) that had not been opened for some Years past, by which means she got into an adjacent Room, made two Holes through the Wall, and by that stratagem discovered the secrets of Masonry; and she, knowing herself to be the first Woman in the World that ever found out the Secret, is willing to make it known to all her Sex. So any Lady who is desirous of learning the Secrets of Free Masonry, by applying to that well-learned Woman (Mrs Bell that lived 15 years in and about Newgate) may be instructed in all the Secrets of Masonry.

Coming back to London again, we find the following announcement published in more papers than one. It is well worthy of perusal, as giving a picture of the loneliness of Chelsea and its approaches a hundred years ago, when it was a little outlying village, and when the whole duty of a watchman was to evade by any and every means in his power, contact with footpads, "high tobymen," or burglars:—

Chelsea, Middlesex, Feb. 20, 1770.

THE Inhabitants of the Parish of Chelsea, being desirous to prevent, as far as in them lies, any Robberies or Felonies being committed in the said Parish, do hereby give Notice, that they have entered into a Subscription, for a Reward for the Discovery of Robberies or Felonies, and have therefore paid into the Hands of Mr Edward Anderson, of Chelsea aforesaid, as Treasurer, a Sum of Money to answer the several Purposes hereafter mentioned, to such Person or Persons who shall, during the Space of one whole Year from the Date hereof, apprehend or take any Offender or Offenders, as are herein after described, the several and respective Rewards hereafter mentioned, in fourteen Days after Conviction, over and above what such Person or Persons may be entitled unto by such Apprehending and Conviction by any Law now in Being.

For every Robbery that shall be committed by any Highwayman or Highwaymen, Footpad or Footpads, within the said Parish (except that Part of the Parish and Road leading from London to Harrow on the Hill, which belongs to the said Parish, the Sum of Ten Pounds.

For any Person or Persons who shall break into the Dwelling House of any Subscriber, or send any Incendiary Letter to any Subscriber, the Sum of Ten Pounds.

For any Person or Persons who shall steal any Horse, Mare, Colt, or other Cattle, belonging to a Subscriber, or commit any Thefts or Robberies in any of their Outhouses, the Sum of Five Pounds.

For every Theft or Robbery that shall be committed in any Garden, Garden-Grounds, or Fields, Orchard, Court Yard, Backside or Fish-ponds, or any Barge or Craft lying ashore, belonging to any of the Subscribers, or shall steal any of their Fruit, Poultry, Fish, Linen, Lead, Iron-Gates, or Gate-Hinges, Pales, or Fences, the Sum of Forty Shillings.

And the Subscribers do hereby promise to pay and discharge the whole, or such Part of the Expence of such Prosecution or Prosecutions of the several Offences above-mentioned, as upon Application to any five or more of the Subscribers, at a Meeting called for that Purpose, shall judge reasonable.

And for the farther Encouragement of all and every the Person and Persons who shall apprehend and convict any Offender or Offenders in any of the Offences aforesaid, the said Subscribers do hereby promise to use their Endeavours for procuring the speedy Payment of such Reward as such Person or Persons may be entitled to by any Law now in Being.

And the said Subscribers do farther promise and agree, That if any Offenders shall, before his or her own Apprehension for any of the Offences aforesaid, voluntarily discover, or apprehend any of his or her Accomplices, so as he, she, or they, be convicted thereof, such Person so apprehending as aforesaid, shall be entitled to, and have such Reward or Sums of Money as before provided for apprehending and taking the said several Offenders as aforesaid, upon Conviction.

The popularity of the *Daily Courant* and *Public Advertiser* with the managers of Drury Lane Theatre seems to have come to a sudden end in 1771, probably for the reasons we have noticed as affecting modern managerial bosoms, for in the *Daily Post* this appears :—

TO prevent any Mistake in future in advertising the Plays and entertainments of Drury Lane Theatre, the Managers think it proper to declare that the Playbills are inserted by their direction in this Paper only.

The *St James's Chronicle* (a weekly paper which is still alive, and as strong in its Toryism as ever), in July 1772, contains an advertisement which for coolness and audacity is very noticeable, even at a time when requests were put forth in the columns of the public press with most unblushing effrontery :—

WANTED immediately, Fifteen Hundred or Two Thousand Pounds by a person not worth a Groat, who having neither Houses, Lands, Annuities or public Funds, can offer no other Security than that of simple Bond, bearing simple interest and engaging the Repayment of the Sum borrowed in five, six or seven Years, as may be agreed upon by the Parties. Whoever this may suit (for it is hoped it will suit somebody) by directing a line to A. Z. in Rochester, shall be immediately replied to or waited on, as may appear necessary.

Benevolence must have been very strongly developed in any one who acceded to the requests of A. Z. But that there was a deal of that commodity afloat at the time of which we are writing, our next specimen, one of disinterestedness and charity, shows. It is from the *Gazetteer* of November 29, 1773 :—

A LADY of strict Honour and Benevolence, who lives in a genteel sphere of Life, influenced by a variety of critical Circumstances, offers her Service as an Advocate to Persons under the most intricate Circumstances, especially to those of her own Sex, whose Troubles she can with a secret Sympathy share, and who will point out certain Means of alleviating their Distress. The Advertiser has a Genteel House to accommodate such Persons, while their Affairs are settled. The greatest

Delicacy, Discretion, and most Inviolable Secrecy may be depended on. Therefore to prevent being made the sport of Curiosity, the Advertiser is determined to answer such Letters only that appear explicit and satisfactory, with the Principal's Name and Place of Abode. Please to address a line (post paid) for Mrs Gladen, at No. 5 Church Row, Aldgate Church, Whitechapel.

Especially those of her own sex. It would be hard to discover what any one of an opposite gender could want as resident with this nice old lady, unless indeed he wished to put in practice the advice given to Nicodemus. But, as for money this benevolent beldame would have done anything, there is little doubt she had plenty of visitors of both sexes. It does not do, however, to be too hard on Mrs Gladen, when it is considered that she has many highly successful and extremely respectable representatives of the present day. We therefore pass on to the latter part of 1774, when it is evident, from a perusal of the advertisements alone, that a general election is impending. In September we find this in the *Morning Post*:—

A GENTLEMAN of Character and considerable Fortune is extremely desirous of a HIGH HONOUR at an approaching Period. Any one who can assist him, or point out an eligible means of succeeding, shall be amply recompensed both at present and in future.—In short, name your Terms; secrecy is all required on his part. A Line to Mr Dormer, at No. 24 Ludgate Hill, will be attended to.

The *Morning Post* seems to have been a particular medium for the process by which legislators were made in the "good old days"—good enough for the rich and unscrupulous, of course—for very shortly afterwards many of the same kind appear. The following stipulates the amount, and with true unselfishness recommends the candidate:—

A GENTLEMAN of Honour, Character, and Fortune, who has £1,500 at his Bankers', has some desire to obtain a Seat. A connection with him will do no discredit to any Man of Rank, or Body of Men. As he is serious, he expects no Application but from such as are so, to Q. at New Lloyd's Coffee-house, Cornhill.

One who follows is much more generous, so far as money is concerned, though he lacks the disinterested recommendation of Q. Still as money and not mind is the desideratum among election agents, there is little fear that the chances were in favour of W. W., though doubtless there was room enough found at St Stephen's for both. Room for two! room for two hundred who had money with which to pave their way:—

A GENTLEMAN of independent fortune is ready to give three Thousand Guineas to be accommodated with a certain purpose to answer the advertiser's end at this Crisis. Any one inclined to treat about the above, may be further informed by Line, or otherwise, directed for W. W., at George's Coffee-house, upper end of the Haymarket.

It must not be supposed that the advertisements in reference to the elections emanated only from persons desirous of writing themselves down M.P.'s. There were plenty anxious as well as willing to assist them for a consideration. From many of that time we select one, still taking the *Morning Post* as our guide:—

ANY Man of Fortune or Family wishing to enjoy an Honourable Station for seven Years, and to accomplish it without the anxiety which generally accompanies the attaining it by Contention, may probably be accommodated to the utmost of his Wishes, by addressing himself to C. C. to be left at the bar of the Chapter Coffee-house, Paternoster Row, and disclosing his Name, the which he may do without the risk of being divulged, as the advertiser pledges himself that the most inviolable Delicacy and Secrecy will be observed.

We commend the foregoing to the notice of the gentlemen who talk of Conservatism as the bulwark of the nation, and rejoice over any so-called political reaction. However, as Conservatism now means "dishing the Whigs" by the most advanced measures, we can put up with it, and so pass on to another specimen from the *Morning Post*, which is published at the same time as the foregoing, and is found snugly ensconced among those of quite a different tendency:—

A YOUNG Gentleman of the most liberal education and a genteel Address, would be happy in having an opportunity of devoting his services to a Lady of real fashion and fortune, who may wish to have some particular deficiencies thoroughly supplied, without subjecting herself to any disagreeable restraint. Any lady to whom such an offer may be suitable, will receive the fullest Explanation, in answer to a letter addressed to A. X. Turk's head Coffee House, Strand.

We will leave this without further comment than the expression of a sad idea that this young gentleman knew what was marketable, as well as a belief that he and others like him may have done much to prevent the titles and fortunes of noblemen and gentlemen who married late in life from passing to remote branches. We have no wish to intrude our opinions, which are strong as our faith in human nature is weak, but the advertisement is only a specimen of many others, and, like its congeners, appears in one of the highest class daily papers of the time. Folk are not so outspoken now as was the fashion a hundred years ago, yet is there any one who will venture to state that we are more virtuous? It will be the natural impulse of many who read the next advertisement, which is also from the now fashionable and severely virtuous *Post* (date January 21, 1775), to cry out against the unnatural guardian who offers to sell his ward. Perhaps though, if they take time to reflect, they may remember instances of marriage for money, which, if not so public, were quite as iniquitous. Listen to a gentleman of honour of the last century:—

A GENTLEMAN of Honour and Property, having in his disposal at present a young Lady of good Family, with a fortune of Sixty Thousand Pounds, on her Marriage with his approbation, would be very happy to treat with a Man of Fashion and Family, who may think it worth his while to give the Advertiser a Gratuity of Five thousand pounds on the day of Marriage. As this is no common advertisement, it is expected no Gentleman will apply whose Family and Connections will not bear the strictest enquiry. The Advertiser having always lived retired from the World, immersed in business, is unacquainted with those of that Rank of Life that the Lady's fortune entitles her to be connected with, for which reason he has made this public application. Letters addressed to L. M., at Tom's Coffee House, Devereux Court, near the Temple, mentioning real Name, and places of Abode, will punctually be attended to.

This is not so bad for a poor innocent who has lived retired from the world. And doubtless, though he was unacquainted with those of that rank of life to which a lady with sixty thousand pounds might well aspire, he was not to be deceived by even the most specious of fortune-hunters, Irishmen included. But here is another notice quite as interesting, though of a very different kind. It is also from the *Morning Post*, and appears a few days after that we have chosen to precede it :—

To the LADIES on MONEY AFFAIRS.

WHEREAS there are sundry Ladies who have Two, Three, or Four thousand pounds, or even more Money at their command, and who, from not knowing how to dispose of the same to the greatest advantage, but by living on the Small Interests which the stocks produce, afford them but a scanty Maintenance, especially to those who have been accustomed to Affluence, and would wish to live so still; the Advertiser (who is a Gentleman of independent Fortune, strict Honour and Character, and above any other reward than the pleasure of serving the Sex) acquaints such Ladies, that if they will favour him with their Name and Address, so as he may wait on them as opportunity best suits, he will put them into a Method by which they may, without any Trouble, and with an absolute Certainty, place out their Money, so as for it to produce them a clear and lawful interest of Ten or Twelve per cent, and that too on equally as good and safe Securities as if in the Funds, or on Mortgage at the common low interest, etc.

Please to direct to R. J. Esq. at the Turks Head Coffee house, opposite Catharine Street, in the Strand, and the same will be duly attended to.

There was no Associate Institute then to look after the interests of unprotected females; and perhaps if there had been, so plausible a rogue would not have attracted the attention of its highly paid officials. But the "weaker vessels" seem able to take their own parts at advertising, for the following is by no means a unique specimen of their effusions. Once again we draw from the *Morning Post*, the date being December 15, 1775:—

A LADY wishes to borrow One Hundred Pounds. The Security, though personal, may probably be very agreeable to a single Gentleman of spirit. Every particular will be communicated with Candour and Sincerity, where confidence is so far reposed as to give the real Name and Address of the party willing to oblige the Advertiser. Gentlemen of real Fortune and liberal Sentiments, and those only, are requested to address a line to Y. N. at Mr Dyke's, Cross Street, Long-Acre.

This lady was modest as well as candid and sincere; it is to be hoped she was pretty also, or else she had small chance. But now comes not virtue but honours in distress, and sufficiently hungry to be satisfied with very dirty pudding. In our own times baronets have seen unpleasantnesses; we remember one who used to do casual reporting, fires, accidents, coroners' inquests, &c., and another who took to the stage, unsuccessfully. But he who advertised in the *Daily Advertiser* of January 23, 1776, was worse off than any titled successor. Judge for yourselves:—

MATRIMONY.

For Fifty Pounds only, may gain One Hundred and Forty Thousand.

A BARONET of Great Britain, that has an eligible chance and right in thirteen distinct Claims to speedily recover the above Sum, or to expect part by a Compromise, inforced by a very little Assistance, will marry any Woman, though with Child, or having Children by a former Husband, that will put such a Fifty-pound ticket in such Lottery; the remainder of her Money, if any, will be settled upon her; his person may not be objected to, and her Attorney may liberally inspect Writings, &c. which in form set forth his expectancies perspicuously; and any young Counsel or others may gain an Advantage, even a Fortune, by offering a small benevolent Assistance. Direct for the Baronet, at No. 2, near Blenheim Steps, in Oxford St., opposite Oxford Market, who has also a profession that may be made very advantageous for any new Adventurer in the physical way, that has a little money to join with him as a Partner. A patient hearing will obviate all Objection, and the strictest Secrecy and Honour may be depended on.

It is noticeable that "the Baronet," like those of his rank already referred to, was not above turning his hand to earn an honest penny. A little way back we invited the attention of Conservatives to an edifying extract; may we now dedicate the baronet's appeal to those who would abolish the laws of primogeniture? Let them be advised in time, unless they should wish to see a duke reduced to despondency, or an earl holding horses for his living. No matter what happens to younger sons. Let them and their younger sons be swallowed up in the middle and lower classes, as they are now, though nobody seems to notice it; but let us preserve, no matter who else suffers, our titled aristocracy in its present exalted position. But what is to become of the scions of nobility who have no claim upon landed estate, when nepotism ceases to exist, sinecures are abolished, and all Government clerkships are matter of open competition! Frankly we do not know, but doubtless Providence will always be tenderly disposed towards persons of good family. Turning once more to the *Morning Post* (February 15, 1776), we come upon an announcement the merits of which are hard to determine. It promises rather too much:—

FEMALE COMPANION.

A LADY of independent Fortune and liberal Sentiments would be glad if, in procuring to herself an agreeable Companion she could at the same time relieve from Distress, and perhaps prevent from utter Ruin, some still deserving although unfortunate fair one; for she can make allowance for the frailty of her own Sex, and knows the base ar's of the other; in a word, a *single faux pas* will be no objection, provided there remain a virtuous Disposition, and that the person wanted be good-natured, affable, and sincere in the account she may give of herself, which for that purpose may at first be anonymous. She must also possess the usual accomplishments required by a good Education; know something of Music, have an agreeable Voice, and a genteel Person, not under twenty nor above the age of twenty-five years. Such as come within this description may apply by letter to B. D. at the York Coffee House, St James's Street, and the apparently most deserving will be enquired after. No kept Mistress or lady of Pleasure need apply.

P

There seems more of the procuress than the patron about this; still there is no knowing what the taste of an elderly single lady who fancied herself injured by the opposite sex would not lead her to do. So leaving the question open, and trusting the reader will be able to satisfy himself as to the purity or the reverse of the advertiser's motives, we will pass on to *Lloyd's Evening Post*, in which, about the same time, we find the following, which is worthy of notice:—

MONEY wanted—when it can be procured—£100. No security can be given for the *Principal*, and possibly the *Interest* may not be punctually paid. Under the above circumstances should any one be found willing to lend the desired Sum, he will much *surprise*, and particularly *oblige* the author of this advertisement.—Direct for A. B. C. George's Coffeehouse, Haymarket.

Even the "author" of this, confident and assured as he must be generally, seems to doubt the readiness of people to part with their money without some inducement, no matter how slight. If A. B. C. had offered something impossible of fulfilment in return for the desired loan, he would very likely have had many applications, whereas it would be hard to believe that in the present instance he had even one. Now, if he had adopted a plan similar to that which is advertised in the *Morning Chronicle* of April 9, 1776, he would have had a much better chance of raising the wind. This must have arrested the attention and diverted the current of pocket-money of many young lovers:—

AFFECTION.

ANY Lady or Gentleman who has made an honourable Connection, may be acquainted if the other party has a reciprocal Affection; and so nice is the method, that it gives in a great measure the degree of esteem. No fortune-telling, nor anything trifling in it, but is a serious and sincere Procedure. To divest any apprehension of discovery of parties, the initials of their names is sufficient. That the meaning of the advertiser may be ascertained, it is only asked for A. B. to know if C. D. has a genuine affection; and of C. D. if A. B. has the like. It is requested that honest Initials be sent, else the deposit of two shillings and sixpence is useless. But to convince those that send for the intelligence of the use of this, they need only to send with the real, other Initials indifferent to them, and they will be satisfied. Absence or distance does not abate the certainty of the then present Esteem and Affection.

Letters (free) directed to S. J., No. 11, Duke-street, Grosvenor Square, will have honest answers left there, or sent conformable to the address, in a day or two after their Receipt.

The next advertisement we find in our collection savours less of affection, for the desire of the inserter seems to be to prevent some one to whom he has an objection inheriting entailed estates. It has its value, in addition to what consideration may be given to it as a specimen of the manners of the last century, as showing the kind of people who then made the laws. Decency must have made a decided advance, look at it from what point we will, since April 16, 1776, when this appeared in the *Public Advertiser* :—

A GENTLEMAN who hath filled two succeeding seats in Parliament, is near sixty years of age, lives in great splendour and hospitality, and from whom a considerable Estate must pass if he dies without issue, hath no objection to marry any Widow or single Lady, provided the party be of genteel birth, polite manners, and five, six, seven, or eight Months gone in her Pregnancy.

Letters directed to —— Brecknock, Esq., at Will's Coffee House, facing the Admiralty, will be honoured with due attention, secrecy, and every possible mark of respect.

In the *Daily Advertiser* of July, in the same year, we find the following, which, though of a much more legitimate character than that just quoted, and directed to the interests of fair and honest trading, will repay perusal :—

TWO Men beg leave to acquaint the Public in general that they keep the cleanest Barber's Shop in all London, where the people can have their Hair cut for 2d., dressed for 3d., and be shaved for 1d. One of these Men can bleed and draw teeth very well ; he bleeds both in the English and German manner, as well at home as abroad, and is exceeding careful. Bleeding 3d., drawing teeth 4d. There is a parlour made in the shop on purpose for bleeding and drawing teeth. The people may depend on being served immediately and well in every respect. No satisfaction, no pay. The above-mentioned Shop is at No. 7 King Street, Seven Dials.

Bleeding nowadays is still done by barbers, though not in the same way, nor so scientifically, as practised by the two clean shopkeepers of King Street. Shaving as a high art is neglected nowadays, a state of affairs traceable to the beard and moustache movement of the last twenty years, which has rendered shaving below the attention of true artists, who now give their attention to "cutting and curling," &c. Any one who doubts this had better trust himself to the untender mercies of half-a-dozen different barbers, in ordinary thoroughfares, and where the prices are fixed at ordinary rates. Before he has tried the sixth establishment he will not only have conformed to our views, but will be a considerably altered, if not an improved, man. In the *Morning Post* of October 13, 1778, we come across an appeal to the short-sighted, which is worthy of the tribes of welchers who in our own times have made large fortunes through advertising in the columns of the sporting papers. This must have been something like the "discretionary investment" dodge, which brought in large sums to swindling firms who professed to govern the turf a few years back, and whose advertisements occupied whole columns in the newspapers :—

A Serious though Surprising Offer.

FOR the compliment of One Hundred Guineas, any enterprizing Gentleman or Lady may have revealed to them an eligible method of converting hundreds into Thousands, in a few weeks, and of continuing so to do yearly. The requiring so inadequate a consideration, is because the proposer is under misfortunes. Only letters with real names and residencies will be regarded. Direct for W. W., at the King's Bench Coffee-House.

In the early part of 1778 (May 7) the *Morning Post* contained the following appeal for an article which has been scarce ever since the world began, which is not valued much when possessed, and which is about the last thing one could hope to obtain through the medium of an advertisement, no matter how cunningly contrived, nor how great the circulation of the paper in which it appeared :—

WANTED immediately, the most difficult thing to be met with in the world, A SINCERE FRIEND, by a person, who, though in the meridian of life, has outlived all he had. He wishes to meet with a Person in whom he may repose the most implicit Confidence; a Person who has a good heart, and abilities to second that goodness of heart; who will give his advice cordially, and assistance readily. The advertiser is a person in a genteel situation of life; has a decent income, but is at present so circumstanced as to want a sincere friend.—Any Person willing (from principles of Friendship, not Curiosity) to reply to the above, by directing a line to T. S., at Mr Sharp's, stationer, facing Somerset House, Strand, will be immediately waited on or properly replied to.

Money, the sincerest of all friends, is probably the object of T. S.'s ambition. If he was not suited in the year '78, an opportunity occurred soon after; for specially directed to the cupidity of persons who desire to get money, and are not at all particular what the means so long as the end is attained, is the following, which appears in the *Morning Post* of March 1779 :—

A GENTLEMAN of Fortune, whom Family reasons oblige to drop a connection which has for some time subsisted between him and an agreeable young Lady, will give a considerable sum of Money with her to any Gentleman, or person in genteel Business, who has good sense and resolution to despise the censures of the World, and will enter with her into the Holy state of Matrimony. Letters addressed to Mr G. H., at the Cecil Street Coffee-House, will be paid due attention to.

As this kind of arrangement has not yet fallen into desuetude, although the aid of advertisements is no longer invoked for it, we had better not give an opinion about its morality, though it is but fair to admit that if the system of selling soiled goods, of which the foregoing is an example, had but been out of date, we should have been loud in our objections. For no vice is so bad as one that has exploded, and the weaknesses which we can regard with complacency while they are current, cause strong emotions of disgust when, their day being over, we look back upon them, and wonder how people could have been so extremely wicked. About the same time, and in the same paper, is another application of a peculiar nature, though in this instance the advertiser wishes not to part with, but to obtain a similar commodity to that advertised by G. H. This is it:—

A SINGLE Gentleman of Fortune, who lives in a genteel private style, is desirous of meeting with an agreeable genteel young Lady, of from 20 to 30 years of age, not older, to superintend and take upon her the management of his House and Servants, for which she will be complimented with board, &c. As the situation will be quite genteel, it will not suit any but such who has had a liberal Education, and who has some independance of her own, so as to enable her always to appear very genteel, and as a relation or particular friend, in which character she will always be esteemed, and have every respect paid her, so as to render the situation and every thing else as agreeable as possible.

Any lady inclining to the above, will please to direct with name and address, to M. H. Esq., to be left at No. 7, the Bookseller's, in Great Newport Street, near St Martin's Lane; she will be waited on, or wrote to, but with the greatest delicacy, and every degree of strict honour and secrecy.

Strict honour and secrecy seems to be an essential to the successful completion of the designs of many advertisers of this time, but they are to be all on one side, in company with an amount of blind credulity which would be wonderful if it were not repeatedly exhibited in modern days. Here is an honourable and secret venture which appears in the *Morning Post* of December 17, 1779, and which was doubtless very successful:—

A GENTLEMAN who knows a Method which reduces it almost to a certainty to obtain a very considerable sum, by insuring of Numbers in the Lottery, is advised by his Friends to offer to communicate it to those who wish to speculate in that Way. The advantage that is procured by proceeding according to his Principles and Directions, will be plainly demonstrated and made perfectly evident to any who chuses to be informed of it. The terms are Ten Guineas each person, and they must engage not to discover the plan for the space of eighteen months. If those who are willing to agree to the above terms will be pleased to address a line to J. R. C. at the Union Coffee-House, Cornhill, or the York Coffee House, St James's Street, they will be immediately informed where to apply. Those who have lost money already (by laying it out improperly) insuring of Numbers, may soon be convinced how much it will be to their advantage to apply as above.

N.B.—This advertisement will be inserted in this morning's Paper only.

A suspicious person would have fancied that the friends of J. R. C., unless they were dissimilar from other friends, would have used the information for their own benefit—but generous and self-abnegating people do turn up in history in the most unexpected and unaccountable ways. Another specimen of the secret and honourable kind, though in it the secrecy and honour have to be on the side of the advertiser, follows. It is in the *Morning Post*, April 18, 1780, and runs thus:—

ANY Lady whose Situation may require a Temporary Retirement, may be accommodated agreeable to her wishes in the house of a Gentleman of eminence in the Profession, where honour and secrecy may be depended on, and where every vestige of Pregnancy is obliterated; or any Lady who wishes to become Pregnant may have the causes of sterility removed in the safest manner. Letters (Post-paid) addressed to A. B. No. 23, Fleet Street, will be attended to.

A. B. offers a double convenience, the second item in which is well worthy of note. The house must have been somewhat similar, except that the accommodation was for human beings, to those establishments advertisements in connection with which frequently appear in the sporting and agricultural papers. Much about the same date as the specimen just quoted appears another of quite a different kind, inserted in several journals. It is rather unique as a way of reminding customers that life is short and debt is long, and is suspiciously sartorial:—

To whom it may Concern.

RICHARD Guy returns thanks to all his good old Friends for their kind Recommendation, which he will always acknowledge with gratitude, by being ready to oblige them on all occasions, but earnestly desires to settle Accounts, to pay and to be paid; which he hopes will be of satisfaction to both parties; for as it is fully observed, short Reckonings keep long Friends; so to preserve good friendship and prevent disputes in Accompts, he always pays ready Money, that is doing as he would be done unto.

N.B.—He courts neither Honour nor Riches, his whole and sole motive being to serve his good old Friends; the sin of Ingratitude he utterly abhors.

The shameless manner in which sinecures in Government offices were bought and sold even so late as 1781 is shown by the following specimen advertisement, which is taken from the *Morning Herald* of September 22:—

A GENTLEMAN of Character who wishes for some Employ under Government merely for the sake of Amusement, would be willing to advance any Nobleman or Gentleman the sum of Three Thousand Pounds, upon Mortgage, upon legal Interest, provided the Mortgager will, thro' his Interest, procure a place in any genteel Department, where the emoluments are not less than two or three hundred Pounds *per annum*. The Advertiser flatters himself this will not be deemed an ineligible Offer, if compared with the present mode of raising Money upon Annuities; as a gentleman must be obliged to grant five hundred *per annum* out of his income to raise the like Sum. If any Gentleman who may be inclined to answer this Advertisement does not know of any Vacancy, the Advertiser will point out several, which may be easily procured by interest. A line addressed to S. X. to be left at the bar of the Chapter Coffee-house, St Paul's, will be attended to. Secrecy may be depended on. No Broker will be treated with.

Those were happy times, indeed, when no such vulgar thing as merit was allowed to interfere with a man's upward progress in life, provided he possessed capital, which could always secure him good interest in more ways than one.

Money was at full value then, and the following, from the *Morning Post* of October 18, 1781, is one among many endeavours to obtain it in larger or smaller quantities :—

WANTED immediately, or as soon as can be met with, that invaluable acquisition (when once gained) A SINCERE Friend, by a person who in the early part of his life had many; but who, from the all-powerful hand of Death and other fortuitous incidents, has been deprived of all those whom he could once call by that sacred Name, and to whom he could apply either for Counsel or Assistance. The author of this Advertisement is a Middle-aged man, in a genteel situation of Life, a Housekeeper, has a decent Income, but yet, is so circumstanced as to have a particular occasion for FIFTY OR SIXTY Pounds, for a Year and a half or thereabouts. He wishes therefore to meet with a Person of liberal and generous Sentiments, who would assist him with the above trifling Sum. He flatters himself he can make the mode of payment quite agreeable to any Gentleman, Lady, or Tradesman of credit, who may be induced to answer this advertisement from a motive arising from the secret satisfaction there is in rendering a Service.—A line directed for S. E., and left at the Morning Post Office, will be immediately attended to.

In 1785 was established the *Daily Universal Register*, a paper which was, under a new title, adopted in 1788, to develop into the greatest and most powerful organ in the world. On the 1st of January, in the last-named year, the *Register* appeared with the following heading: *The Times, or Daily Universal Register, printed Logographically*. The price was threepence, and for many years the *Times* gave no promise of future greatness; but it was always fearless, and very early was fined, while its editor narrowly escaped imprisonment. In 1790 Mr Walter was actually incarcerated in Newgate, where he remained sixteen months, besides being fined £200, for a libel on the Dukes of York and Clarence. He was released eventually at the intercession of the Prince of Wales. The history of the *Times* has been told so often that particulars are hardly needed here; but as showing how its present eminence is due to nothing but perseverance and integrity, as well as the ever-present desire to be first wherever possible, we quote the following from a short notice of the life of one of its proprietors: "It was under John Walter II., born in 1784, that the *Times* rose to the place of the first newspaper in the world. Whilst yet a youth, in 1803 he became joint proprietor and sole manager of the *Times*, and very soon his hand became manifest in the vigour and independence of its politics, and the freshness of its news. Free speech, however, had its penalties. The *Times* denounced the malpractices of Lord Melville, and the Government revenged itself by withdrawing from the Walters the office of printers to the Customs, which had been held by the family for eighteen years. During the war between Napoleon and Austria in 1805, the desire for news was intense. To thwart the *Times* the packets for Walter were stopped at the outports, while those for the ministerial journals were hurried to London. Complaint was made, and the reply was given that the editor might receive his foreign papers as a *favour*; meaning thereby that if the Government was gracious to the *Times*, the *Times* should be gracious to the Government; but Walter would accept no favour on such terms. Thrown on his own resources, he contrived, by means of superior activity and stratagem, to surpass the ministry in early intelligence of events. The capitulation of Flushing in August 1809, was announced by the *Times* two days before the news had arrived through any other channel. In the editorship of the paper he spared neither pains nor expense. The best writers were employed, and wherever a correspondent or a reporter displayed marked ability, he was carefully looked after and his faculty utilised. Correspondents were posted in every great city in the world, and well-qualified reporters were despatched to every scene of public interest. The debates in Parliament, law proceedings, public meetings, and commercial affairs, were all reported with a fulness and accuracy which filled readers with wonder. What a visionary could scarcely dare to ask,

THE TIMES

TUESDAY, JANUARY 1, 1788

(Price Three-pence.)

Theatre Royal, Drury Lane.

By his MAJESTY'S COMPANY.

THIS EVENING,

Will be performed the Tragedy of

JULIA;

OR, THE ITALIAN LOVER.

To which will be added

THE DESERTER.

BY COMMAND OF HIS MAJESTY.

THE Oratorios of SOLOMON, ALEXANDER'S FEAST, ... ACIS and GALATEA, ... MESSIAH, will be performed on the Six FRIDAYS in LENT, at the CONCERT ROOM in TOTTENHAM STREET.

ROYALTY THEATRE,

WELL STREET, NEAR GOODMAN'S FIELDS.

THIS EVENING,

THOMAS and SUSAN; Or, THE GENEROUS TAR.

The ... of NAPLES;

HARLEQUIN MUNGO;

TO BE LETT, OR SOLD.

A CAUTION to prevent IMPOSITION. SHARP'S CONCAVE RAZORS.

KING'S THEATRE, Haymarket.

By PARTICULAR DESIRE, on Thursday next, January 3rd, 1788,

WILL BE PERFORMED THE COMIC OPERA called

IL RE THEODORO in VENEZIA.

The Music composed, in his best style, by the celebrated Sig. PAISIELLO.

Under the Direction of Sig. MAZZINGHI;

And Leader of the Orchestra, Mr. CRAMER.

Painter and Machinist, Sig. GAETANO MARINARI.

Inventor & Maker of the Dresses, Sig. LUPINO.

End of Act I. A NEW DIVERTISEMENT, composed by Mons. CHEVALIER, and performed by Mons. VESTRIS, Mad. COULON, And Mons. CHEVALIER.

And Mad. COULON.

End of the Opera, a new BALLET, composed by Mons. NOVERRE, called

LES OFFRANDES A L'AMOUR.

And Performed by Mons. VESTRIS, Mad. COULON, And Mons. DIDELOT,

Mad. VEDIE.

And MIZZI KES.

NEW MUSIC.

This day is Published,

By LONGMAN and BRODERIP,

Musical Instrument Makers to his Royal Highness the PRINCE of WALES,

No. 26, Cheapside, and No. 13, Haymarket.

THREE SYMPHONIES for a grand Orchestra, dedicated to his Royal Highness the Prince of Wales. Op. 1

NEW MUSIC.

THE SONGS in Robin Hood, ...

OIL AND LAMP WAREHOUSE,

GEORGE DOWNING, Oil Merchant,

CALEDONIAN MACABAU SNUFF

JOHN YOUNG, ...

STATIONARY

ADAM THOMPSON, ...

NEW MUSIC.

This Day is Published,

By LONGMAN and BRODERIP, No. 26, Cheapside; No. 13, Haymarket,

MUSICAL INSTRUMENT MAKERS AND SELLERS TO HIS ROYAL HIGHNESS THE PRINCE OF WALES.

The New Comic Opera, now performing at Covent Garden Theatre, ...

THE OPERA FANS.

To the Subscribers and Frequenters of the KING'S THEATRE.

THE Delivery, however, was put off till the Re-opening of the Opera House next week, ...

HANDEL'S SUBSCRIPTION

Dedicated by Permission to His MAJESTY.

THE ELEVENTH NUMBER OF HANDEL'S WORKS.

AN ABRIDGMENT of the MEMORIAL Addressed to the KING OF FRANCE,

CRAZY KATE A ...

Theatre Royal, Covent Garden.

THIS EVENING

Will be performed the revived Tragedy of

The ROMAN FATHER

The DUMB CAKE;

Or, the REGIONS OF FANCY.

PROPAGATION OF A LIE

W. DICKINSON, Bond Street, has this day published a Print, ...

FESTIVAL OF ANACREON

THE FESTIVAL OF ANACREON, ...

MEDICAL COMMENTARIES for the Year 1787, ...

FAMILIAR and FRIENDLY CORRESPONDENCE of FREDERICK THE SECOND, KING OF PRUSSIA, ...

DR. DERHAM'S PHYSICO and ASTRO THEOLOGY.

The MINIATURE PICTURES.

LETTERS ...

Univerfal Regifter.

A HOLIDAY AT ALL THE PUBLIC OFFICES

To CORRESPONDENTS

TO THE PUBLIC.

LONDON

THE TIMES.

Why change the head?

TIMES.

The Literary,
Political,
Commercial,
Philosophical,
Critical,
Theatrical,
Fashionable,
Humorous,
Witty, &c. &c.

THEATRE.

Drury Lane.

Covent Garden.

THE CUCKOO

This day is published, [illegible]

TIPLER'S CLERICAL and UNIVERSAL ALMANACK, for the year [illegible] [illegible]

London: Printed at the Logographic Press, and sold by all the Booksellers.

GAME OF WHIST.

This day is published, [illegible]

HOYLE'S SHORT RULES of the GAME of WHIST, [illegible]

Printed for John Walter, No. 169, Ludgate Street, [illegible]

EVERY MAN A GOOD CARD PLAYER, [illegible]

By a MEMBER of the JOCKEY CLUB.

VALUABLE NEW YEAR'S GIFTS.

This day was published, [illegible]

A NEW and Beautiful Edition of TOMKINS'S SELECTION OF POEMS, [illegible]

Printed for John Walter, No. 169, Ludgate Street, [illegible]

[illegible]

This day is published, [illegible]

THE INTERESTING MEMOIRS of HENRY MASERS DE LATUDE, [illegible] of FRANCE, [illegible]

[illegible] REMARKS of the TRANSLATOR on the [illegible] of the LETTRES DE CACHET, [illegible]

[illegible]

This day is published, The THIRD EDITION of HISTORIES OF CURES performed by Mr. [illegible]

[illegible]

London: Printed for J. [illegible]

THIS DAY is published, [illegible] Mr. PITT, [illegible]

[illegible]

ANDERSON'S Historical and Chronological Deduction of the ORIGIN of COMMERCE, [illegible]

[illegible]

For the BENEFIT of the PUBLIC.

THE Public are respectfully informed [illegible]

[illegible]

To PARENTS and GUARDIANS.

WANTED, A YOUNG GENTLEMAN of respectable parents, as an APPRENTICE to a LINEN DRAPER in a House of very extensive Business, the West end of the Town. A Genteel premium will be expected, as he will be treated as one of the family.

For particulars, enquire of Mr. Hall, Printing House Square, Blackfriars.

LODGINGS IN SURREY,

Within three or four miles of London Bridge, in a dry, well-sheltered Situation.

TWO Bed-Chambers and a Dining-Room, large, handsome, airy, and well furnished, will be wanted on Monday, the [illegible] of January, for a month's [illegible]

Letters [illegible] to E., at Lloyd's Coffeehouse, [illegible]

TO BE LETT,

And entered upon immediately,

TWO good Dwelling Houses, situated in [illegible] Lane, Lombard Street, late in the possession of [illegible]

Enquire of Mr. John Walter, Printing House Square, Blackfriars.

REFINED LIQUORIC,

For COUGHS, COLDS, ASTHMAS, and DEFLUXIONS of the LUNGS, sold by C. WALSH, [illegible], No. [illegible], STRAND, near LITTLE CHANGE.

THE very great effects in which this Preparation [illegible]

[illegible]

Sold in Boxes, One Shilling each, small ditto, 6d.

ENGLISH STATE LOTTERY.

Begins Drawing FEBRUARY 11, 1788.

RICHARDSON and GOODLUCK respectfully inform the public that the TICKETS are SOLD and divided into Half, Quarter, Eighth, and Sixteenth SHARES, at their Licensed State Lottery Offices, in the Bank Buildings, Cornhill, and opposite the King's Mews, Charing Cross, [illegible]

[illegible]

[illegible]

LOMBARD STREET.

January [illegible], 1788.

MESSRS. SHERGOLD and CO. [illegible]

[illegible]

A PROPOSAL TO THE PUBLIC.

[illegible] LOTTERY TICKETS.

HORNSBY and CO. Licensed pursuant to Act of Parliament, [illegible]

[illegible]

VICTUALLING OFFICE,

19th December, 1787.

THE Commissioners for Victualling his Majesty's Navy do hereby give Notice, That there is money in the hands of the Treasurer of His Majesty's Navy to pay the Principal and Interest of the Bills registered in the course of the Victualling for three months ending the 31st of January, 1787, in order that the Persons possessed of such Bills may bring them to this Office to be assigned for payment.

And all persons who hold the said Bills are desired to subscribe their names and places of abode at the bottom of each Bill.

VICTUALLING OFFICE,

19th December, 1787.

THE Commissioners for Victualling his Majesty's Navy do hereby give Notice, That, on Tuesday, the [illegible] of January next, they will be ready to receive Tenders in writing (sealed up), and treat with such persons as will undertake to supply Fresh Beef and [illegible] Provisions to his Majesty's Ships and Vessels at Liverpool, which will be paid for by Bills in Course.

The Conditions of the Contract may be seen at the Secretary's Office, at this Office, or by applying to the Collector of His Majesty's Customs, at Liverpool.

And all persons who may think proper to make Tenders upon the said occasion are desired to take Notice, That, no Regard will be had to any Tender that shall not be delivered before 1 o'clock on the said [illegible] January next, nor unless the Person who makes the Tender, or some Person on his behalf, attends to answer for him when called for. And that note that contain extravagant prices upon some articles, and prices much inferior to the real value on others, will be considered as proper to be attended to.

CHELSEA HOSPITAL,

Dec. 28th, 1787.

THESE are by Order of the Right Hon. the Lords and others, Commissioners for the Affairs of the Royal Hospital at Chelsea, to give Notice [illegible]

[illegible]

SAMUEL [illegible], Secretary and Register.

NAVY OFFICE,

Dec. 20, 1787.

THE Principal Officers and Commissioners of his Majesty's Navy do hereby give notice that, on Thursday, the 3rd of Jan. next, at one o'clock, they will be ready to treat with such persons as may be willing to contract for supplying the Ship Office here with Deal Cases for packing Ships.

The Particulars may be seen at this Office here. No letter will be received as a tender unless the writer, or an agent for him, attends; nor will any be received after twelve o'clock.

NAVY OFFICE,

December 29, 1787.

THE Principal Officers and Commissioners of his Majesty's Navy do hereby give notice that all Bills registered in the Course of the Navy for the Months of November and December, 1786, and January, 1787, are ordered to be paid in course; that all persons who are possessed of the same may bring them to this office to be assigned to the Treasurer of the Navy for payment.

All persons who hold the said Bills are to subscribe their names and places of abode at the bottom of each Bill.

VICTUALLING OFFICE,

27th December, 1787.

THE Commissioners for Victualling his Majesty's Navy do hereby give Notice, That, on Tuesday, the 29th of January next, they will be ready to receive Tenders in writing (sealed up), and treat with such persons as will undertake to furnish their Agent at Gibraltar with whatever sums of money the service of His Majesty's Victualling that Place may thereafter require.

The Conditions of the Contract may be seen at the Secretary's Office. And all persons who may think proper to make tenders upon the said Occasion are desired to take notice that no regard will be had to any Tender that shall not be delivered to the Board before one o'clock on the said 29th January next; nor unless the person who makes the Tender, or some person on his behalf, attends to answer for him when called for.

FOREIGN INTELLIGENCE.

Yesterday arrived with the Mails from Holland and Flanders.

Warsaw, Dec. 5.

THE Waywodes of Volhinia and Podolia have sent three deputies here to make representations to the King and the permanent Council, with respect to the delivery of the corn that has been demanded by the Russian Army encamped in Poland. These Deputies have had an audience at the last meeting of the Supreme Council, at which they solicited, "That the King and Supreme Council would be pleased to devise means, which by preventing famine, terminating the grievances of the inhabitants, and quieting disorders, might strengthen and give efficacy to the resolutions of the nobility, the more so as their resolutions are conformable to the principles of justice and equity."

These Waywodes had a meeting in pursuance of these resolutions; "For choosing an appointed place to establish a general magazine, to which every person might bring whatever he possesses superfluous, and deliver it to the Directors of the Stores. The Troops of the Republic shall be provided for out of this general depôt of the country, after which what remains will be sold to the Russians at the market price, agreeable to the declaration of Count Romanzow, upon the entry into Poland."

Count Romanzow has taken possession of Tulczyn, nine miles from the frontiers of Turkey, and the army encamped in Poland under his command will winter in the neighbourhood of that place. The Waywode of Russian Lithuania, Count Potocki, has established his general quarters at Mohilow. This patriotic vigilant General takes all the advance posts to protect.

By accounts from our frontiers we learn that eleven commanders who served in the last unfortunate attack upon Kinburn, and to whose imprudence the failure of that enterprise was attributed, have been executed; their heads were cut off and exhibited at the gate of the seraglio, upon spears.

Frankfort, Dec. 14.—On the 11th of this month the reformers established in this city have got permission to follow the forms of their religion in private houses, until their churches shall be finished.

The Elector of Mentz has ordained for the future that Lutherans shall be capable of civil employments, and he has nominated as Counsellor of the present Regency Coburg, a Lutheran Doctor. This is the first example of this kind since 1709.

Constantinople, Nov. 10.—On the 30th of October there was a grand meeting of the principal members for examining the Dispatches that were brought by two couriers, the one from Vienna and the other from Paris; the result of which is that the Porte answers, "That the restoration of a durable peace must be impossible so long as Russia keeps possession of the Crimea, and the chief article of the preliminaries must be that Russia do consent to the re-establishment of the new Chan to all the rights of sovereignty which that prince may claim upon Little Tartary by virtue of his Highness's proclamation."

Paris, Dec. 15.—The Commissioners appointed for the Edict of the Protestants have not as yet concluded their business, although they are very assiduous.

Mr. de Calonne during his administration created forty places of Stockbrokers for transacting financial business, at the rate of 100,000 livres each, who had individually a salary of [illegible]. It is in agitation to augment these offices to 100 by adding 60 more.

Rotterdam, Dec. 15.—Friday morning the Commissioners of his Highness the Stadtholder arrived here for changing the regency; they landed with discharge of cannon and a great concourse of people; they were complimented by the burgomasters.

[illegible]

LOVE, Perfumer to Her Royal Highness the Dutchess of Cumberland, and the principal Nobility, respectfully informs his customers and the Public that he is removed from No. 10, in the Haymarket, to next door, which is numbered 11, [illegible]

MARRIED

[illegible]

DIED

[illegible]

SHIP NEWS

The Hope, Walsh, from Waterford to London, was driven on shore in a heavy gale, the 23d instant, in Youghall harbour. It is feared the ship will go to pieces, but the cargo will be saved.

[illegible]

Mails

Arrived

Two Holland, one French, one Flanders, one Irish.

Due

One Irish.

SHIPS ARRIVED

At Liverpool [illegible]

PRICES OF STOCKS

[illegible]

SMOAKED SALMON and DUTCH HERRINGS, FINE NEW FRENCH OLIVES, and NEW REIN DEER TONGUES.

[illegible]

NEXT PRESENTATIONS TO LIVINGS.

TO be sold, the next Presentation to a Rectory [illegible]

MIDWIFERY

DR. KROHN will commence a New COURSE of LECTURES [illegible]

ANATOMICAL LECTURES.

MR. JOHN ABERNETHY, Assistant-Surgeon to St. Bartholomew's Hospital, will begin a COURSE of ANATOMICAL LECTURES, [illegible]

FREEHOLD IN ESSEX

TO be Sold by Private Contract, [illegible]

To FAMILIES FURNISHING KITCHENS

STONE and Co., No. 134, Oxford Street, [illegible]

[illegible]

DIAMONDS AND WATCHES.

TO be SOLD cheap, [illegible]

TO COWKEEPERS AND FARMERS.

[illegible]

TWENTY young Milch Cows, [illegible]

Sale by Auction.

[illegible]

Sale by Candle.

[illegible] THE following GOODS [illegible]

At the CUSTOM HOUSE, COLCHESTER

[illegible]

Shipping Advertisements.

[illegible]

FOR PRIVATE SALE.

The Ship HOPE.

[illegible]

LONDON: Printed for J. WALTER, at the Logographic Press, Printing House Square, [illegible] the *Times* gave. To other journals imitation alone was left. They might be more consistent politicians, but in the staple of a newspaper, to be nearly as good as the *Times* was their highest praise."

So much for the early struggles of the "Thunderer"—a title given to it from the powerful articles contributed to it by Edward Stirling—and as its later efforts in the cause of justice are shown in the *Times* scholarships at Oxford, as its very appearance betokens its vast importance, and as its history has been given by many much abler pens than ours, we will return to our subject.

In 1798, a house in Stanhope Street having been broken open and robbed, the following singular announcement was issued by the proprietor, and appeared in the *Daily Advertiser*:—

MR. R—— of Stanhope Street, presents his most respectful Compliments to the Gentlemen who did him the honour of eating a couple of roasted Chickens, drinking sundry tankards of ale, and three bottles of old Madeira at his house, on Monday night.

In their haste they took away the Tankard, to which they are heartily welcome; to the Tablespoons and the light Guineas which were in an old red morocco pocket-book, they are also heartily welcome; but in the said Pocket-book there were several loose Papers, which consisted of private Memorandums, Receipts, etc. can be of no use to his kind and friendly Visitors, but are important to him: he therefore hopes and trusts they will be so polite as to take some opportunity of returning them.

For an old family Watch, which was in the same Drawer, he cannot ask on the same terms; but if any could be pointed out by which he could replace it with twice as many heavy Guineas as they can get for it, he would gladly be the Purchaser. W. R.

A few nights after, a packet, with the following letter enclosed, was dropped into the area of the house: "Sir,—You are quite a gemman. Not being used to your Madeira, it got into our upper works, or we should never have cribbed your papers; they be all marched back again with the red book. Your ale was mortal good; the tankard and spoons were made into a white soup, in Duke's Place, two hours afore daylite. The old family watch cases were at the same time made into a brown gravy, and the guts, new christened, are on their voyage to Holland. If they had not been transported, you should have them again, for you are quite the gemman ; but you know, as they have been christened, and got a new name, they would no longer be of your *old* family. And soe, sir, we have nothing more to say, but that we are much obligated to you, and shall be glad to sarve and visit you, by nite or by day, and are your humble sarvants to command." Honour had then, it would appear, not quite departed from among thieves.

At the end of last century a provincial attorney advertised an estate for sale, or to be exchanged for another, stating that he was appointed *Plenipotentiary* to *treat* in the business; that he had ample *credentials*, and was prepared to *ratify his powers;* that he would enter into *preliminaries* either upon the principle of the *statu quo* or *uti possidetis;* that he was ready to receive the *project* of any person desirous to make the purchase or exchange, and to deliver his *contre projet* and *sine quâ non*, and, indeed, at once give his *ultimatum*, assuring the public that as soon as a *definitive treaty* should be *concluded*, it would be *ratified* by his constituent and duly *guaranteed*. He was evidently astonished at his own unexpected importance.

Some curious and amusing statistics of advertising in the second year of this century are given by Mr Daniel Stuart, at one time co-proprietor of the *Morning Post* with Coleridge, when it was in the meridian of its fame. He says: "The *Morning Herald* and the *Times*, then leading papers, were neglected, and the *Morning Post*, by vigilance and activity, rose rapidly. Advertisements flowed in beyond bounds. I encouraged the small miscellaneous advertisements in the front page, preferring them to any others, upon the rule that the more numerous the customers, the more independent and permanent the custom. Besides numerous and various advertisements, I interest numerous and various readers looking out for employment, servants, sales, and purchasers, etc. etc. Advertisements act and react. They attract readers, promote circulation, and circulation attracts advertisements. The *Daily Advertiser*, which sold to the public for twopence halfpenny, after paying a stamp-duty of three-halfpence, never had more than half a column of news; it never noticed Parliament, but it had the best foreign intelligence before the French Revolution. The *Daily Advertiser* lost by its publication, but it gained largely by its advertisements, with which it was crammed full. Shares in it sold by auction at twenty years' purchase. I recollect my brother Peter saying, that on proposing to a tradesman to take shares in a new paper, he was answered with a sneer and a shake of the head—'Ah! none of you can touch the *Daily!*' It was the paper of business, filled with miscellaneous advertisements, conducted at little expense, very profitable, and taken in by all public-houses, coffee-houses, etc., but by scarcely any private families. It fell in a day by the scheme of Grant, a printer, which made all publicans proprietors of a rival, the *Morning Advertiser*, the profits going to a publicans' benefit society; and they, of course, took in their own paper;—an example of the danger of depending on any class. Soon after I joined the *Morning Post*, in the autumn of 1795, Christie, the auctioneer, left it, on account of its low sale, and left a blank, a ruinous proclamation of decline. But in 1802 he came to me again, praying for readmission. At that time particular newspapers were known to possess particular classes of advertisements: the *Morning Post*, horses and carriages; the *Public Ledger*, shipping and sales of wholesale foreign merchandise; the *Morning Herald* and *Times*, auctioneers; the *Morning Chronicle*, books. All papers had all sorts of advertisements, it is true, but some were more remarkable than others for a particular class, and Mr Perry, who aimed at making the *Morning Chronicle* a very literary paper, took pains to produce a striking display of book advertisements. This display had something more solid for its object than vanity. Sixty or seventy short advertisements, filling three columns, by Longman, one day, by Cadell, etc., another—'Bless me, what an extensive business they must have!' The auctioneers to this day stipulate to have all their advertisements inserted at once, that they may impress the public with great ideas of their extensive business. They will not have them dribbled out, a few at a time, as the days of sale approach. The journals have of late years adopted the same rule with the same design. They keep back advertisements, fill up with pamphlets, and other stuff unnecessary to a newspaper, and then come out with a swarm of advertisements in a double sheet to astonish their readers, and strike them with high ideas of the extent of their circulation, which attracts so many advertisers. The meagre days are forgotten, the days of swarm are remembered."

In the same gossiping manner Stuart speaks again of this rage for swarming advertisements: "The booksellers and others crowded to the *Morning Post*, when its circulation and character raised it above all competitors. Each was desirous of having his cloud of advertisements inserted at once in the front page. I would not drive away the short, miscellaneous advertisements by allowing space to be monopolised by any class. When a very long advertisement of a column or two came, I charged enormously high, that it might be taken away without the parties being able to say it was refused admission. I accommodated the booksellers as well as I could with a few new and pressing advertisements at a time. That would not do: they would have the cloud; then, said I, there is no place for the cloud but the last page, where the auctioneers already enjoy that privilege. The booksellers were affronted, indignant. The last page! To obtain the accommodation refused by the *Morning Post*, they set up a morning paper, the *British Press;* and to oppose the *Courier*, an evening one—the *Globe*. Possessed of general influence among literary men, could there be a doubt of success?" The *Globe* has stood the test of time, and though it has seen vicissitudes, and has changed its politics within recent years, it now seems as firmly established as any of its contemporaries that is independent of connection with a morning paper.

We have now reached the end of our journey so far as the education of advertisers and the development of advertisements are concerned. By the commencement of the present century matters were very nearly as we find them now; and so in the following chapters only those examples which have peculiar claims to attention will be submitted.

CHAPTER XI.

CURIOUS AND ECCENTRIC ADVERTISEMENTS.

ADVERTISEMENTS of the kind which form the subject of this chapter have been so often made matter of comment and speculation, have so often received the attention of essayists and the ridicule of comic writers, that it is hard to keep out of the beaten track, and to find anything fresh to say upon a topic which seems utterly exhausted. Yet the store of fun is so great, and the excellence of many old and new stories so undoubted, that courage is easily found for this the most difficult part of the present work. Difficult, because there is an embarrassment of riches, an enormous mine of wealth, at command, and the trouble is not what to put in, but what to leave out, from a chapter on quaint and curious advertisements. Difficult again, because some of the best stories have been told in so many and such various guises, that until arriving at the ends it is hard to tell they have a common origin, and then the claims of each version are as near as possible equal. There is, however, a way out of all difficulties, and the way in this is to verify the advertisements themselves, and pay no attention to the apocrypha to which they give rise; and though it is a tedious proceeding, and one which shows little in return for the pains taken, it may be something to our readers to know, that curious as many of the specimens given are, they are real and original, and that in the course of our researches we have unearthed many impostures in the way of quotations from advertisements

which have never yet appeared, unless private views of still more private copies of papers have been allowed their promulgators. There is, after all, little reason for a display of inventive power, for the real material is so good, and withal so natural, as to completely put the finest fancy to a disadvantage. It has already been remarked that in the whole range of periodical literature there is no greater curiosity than the columns daily devoted to advertisements in the *Times*. From them, says a writer a few years back, "the future historian will be able to glean ample and correct information relative to the social habits, wants, and peculiarities of this empire. How we travel, by land or sea—how we live, and move, and have our being—is fully set forth in the different announcements which appear in a single copy of that journal. The means of gratifying the most boundless desires, or the most fastidious taste, are placed within the knowledge of any one who chooses to consult its crowded columns. Should a man wish to make an excursion to any part of the globe between Cape Horn and the North Pole, to any port in India, to Australia, to Africa, or to China, he can, by the aid of one number of the *Times*, make his arrangements over his breakfast. In the first column he will find which 'A 1 fine, fast-sailing, copper-bottomed' vessel is ready to take him to any of those distant ports. Or, should his travelling aspirations be of a less extended nature, he can inform himself of the names, size, horse-power, times of starting, and fares, of numberless steamers which ply within the limits of British seas. Whether, in short, he wishes to be conveyed five miles—from London to Greenwich—or three thousand—from Liverpool to New York—information equally conclusive is afforded him. The head of the second, or sometimes the third column, is interesting to a more extensive range of readers—namely, to the curious; for it is generally devoted to what may be called the romance of advertising. The advertisements which appear in that place are mysterious as melodramas, and puzzling as rebuses." These incentives to curiosity will receive attention a little further on; meanwhile we will turn to those which are purely curious or eccentric.

The record of these notices to the public is so extensive, and its ramifications so multifarious, that so far as those advertisements which simply contain blunders are concerned, we must be satisfied with a simple summary, and in many cases leave our readers to make their own comments. Here is a batch of those whose comicality is mainly dependent upon sins against the rules of English composition. We will commence with the reward offered for "a keyless lady's gold watch," which is, though, but a faint echo of the "green lady's parasol" and the "brown silk gentleman's umbrella" anecdotes; but the former we give as actually having appeared, while so far the two latter require verification. A lady advertises her desire to obtain a husband with "a Roman nose having strong religious tendencies." A nose with heavenly tendencies we can imagine, but even then it would not be Róman. "A spinster particularly fond of children," informs the public that she "wishes for two or three having none of her own." Then a dissenter from grammar as well as from the Church Established wants "a young man to look after a horse of the Methodist persuasion;" a draper desires to meet with an assistant who would "take an active and energetic interest in a small first-class trade, and in a quiet family;" and a chemist requests that "the gentleman who left his stomach for analysis, will please call and get it, together with the result." Theatrical papers actually teem with advertisements which, either from technology or an ignorance of literary law, are extremely funny, and sometimes alarming, and even the editorial minds seem at times to catch the infection. One of these journals, in a puff preliminary of a benefit, after announcing the names of the performers and a list of the performances, went on: "Of course every one will be there, and for the edification of those who are absent, a full report will be found in our next paper." This is worthy of a place in any collection: "One pound reward—Lost, a cameo brooch, representing Venus and Adonis on the Drumcondra-road, about ten o'clock, on Tuesday evening." And so is this: "The advertiser, having made an advantageous purchase, offers for sale, on very low terms, about six dozen of prime port wine, late the property of a gentleman forty years of age, full in the body and with a high bouquet." The lady spoken of in the following would meet with some attention from the renowned Barnum: "To be sold cheap, a splendid grey horse, calculated for a charger, or would carry a lady with a switch tail." But she would find a formidable rival in the gentleman whose advertisement we place as near as possible, so as to make a pair: "To be sold cheap, a mail phaeton, the property of a gentleman with a moveable head, as good as new." Students of vivisection, and lovers of natural history generally, would have been glad to meet with this specimen of life after decapitation: "Ten shillings reward—Lost by a gentleman, a white terrier dog, except the head, which is black." And as congenial company we append this: "To be sold, an Erard grand piano, the property of a lady, about to travel in a walnut wood case with carved legs."

Differing somewhat, though still of the same kind, is the advertisement of a governess, who, among other things, notifies that "she is a perfect mistress of her own tongue." If she means what she says, she deserves a good situation and a high rate of wages. An anecdote is told of a wealthy widow who advertised for an agent, and, owing to a printer's error, which made it "a gent," she was inundated with applications by letter, and pestered by personal attentions. This story requires, however, a little assistance, and may be taken for what it is worth. Not long ago, a morning paper contained an announcement that a lady going abroad would give "a medical man" £100 a year to look after "a favourite spaniel dog" during her absence. This may not be funny, but it is certainly curious, and in these days, when starvation and misery are rampant, when men are to be found who out of sheer love kill their children rather than trust them to the tender mercies of the parish officials, and when these same officials are proved guilty of constructive homicide, it is indeed noticeable. A kindred advertisement, also real and unexaggerated, asks for "an accomplished poodle nurse. Wages £1 per week." This has double claims upon our attention here, for in addition to the amount offered for such work, there is a doubt as to the actual thing required. Is it a nurse for accomplished poodles, or an accomplished nurse? And, if the latter, what in the name of goodness and common sense is accomplishment at such work? Do poodles require peculiar nursery rhymes and lullabies, or are they nursed, as a vulgar error has it about West-country babies, head downwards? This is not the exact expression used with regard to the infants; but it will do. We will conclude this short list of peculiarities with two which deserve notice. The first is the notice of a marriage, which ends, "No cards, no cake, no wine." This is evidently intended for friends other than those "at a distance," whose polite attention is so constantly invoked. The remaining specimen appeared in the *Irish Times*, and runs thus: "To Insurance Offices.—Whatever office the late William H. O'Connell, M.D. life was insured will please to communicate or call on his widow, 23 South Frederick Street, without delay." One hardly knows which to admire most, the style or the *insouciance* of the demand.

Of curious advertisements which are such independent of errors, selfishness, or moral obliquity, we have in the purely historical part of this work given plenty specimens from olden times; but there are still a few samples of the peculiarities of our ancestors which will bear repetition in this chapter, more especially as most of them have not before been unearthed from their original columns. Before quoting any of those which are purely advertisements in the ordinary sense of the word, we will present to our readers a curious piece of puffery which appeared in an Irish paper for May 30, 1784, and which from its near connection with open and palpable advertising, and from its whimsical character, will not be at all out of place, and will doubtless prove interesting, especially to those of a theatrical turn of mind, as it refers to the gifted Sarah Siddons's first appearance in Dublin. The article runs thus: "On Saturday, Mrs Siddons, about whom all the world has been talking, exposed her beautiful, adamantine, soft, and lovely person, for the first time, at Smock-Alley Theatre, in the bewitching, melting, and all-tearful character of *Isabella*. From the repeated panegyrics in the impartial London newspapers, we were taught to expect the sight of a heavenly angel; but how were we supernaturally surprised into the most awful joy, at beholding a mortal goddess. The house was crowded with hundreds more than it could hold,—with thousands of admiring spectators, that went away without a sight. This extraordinary phenomenon of tragic excellence! this star of Melpomene! this comet of the stage! this sun of the firmament of the Muses! this moon of blank verse! this queen and princess of tears! this Donnellan of the poisoned bowl! this empress of the pistol and dagger! this chaos of Shakspeare! this world of weeping clouds! this Juno of commanding aspects! this Terpsichore of the curtains and scenes! this Proserpine of fire and earthquake! this Katterfelto of wonders! exceeded expectation, went beyond belief, and soared above all the natural powers of description! She was nature itself! She was the most exquisite work of art! She was the very daisy, primrose, tuberose, sweetbrier, furze-blossom, gilliflower, wall-flower, cauliflower, auricula, and rosemary! In short, she was the bouquet of Parnassus! Where expectation was raised so high, it was thought she would be injured by her appearance; but it was the audience who were injured:—several fainted before the curtain drew up! When she came to the scene of parting with her wedding-ring, ah! what a sight was there! the very fiddlers in the orchestra, 'albeit, unused to the melting mood,' blubbered like hungry children crying for their bread and butter; and when the bell rang for music between the acts, the tears ran from the bassoon players' eyes in such plentiful showers, that they choked the finger stops; and making a spout of the instrument, poured in such torrents on the first fiddler's book, that, not seeing the overture was in two sharps, the leader of the band actually played in one flat. But the sobs and sighs of the groaning audience, and the noise of corks drawn from the smelling-bottles, prevented the mistake between flats and sharps being discovered. One hundred and nine ladies fainted! forty-six went into fits! and ninety-five had strong hysterics! The world will scarcely credit the truth, when they are told, that fourteen children, five old women, one hundred tailors, and six common-councilmen, were actually drowned in the inundation of tears that flowed from the galleries, the slips, and the boxes, to increase the briny pond in the pit; the water was three feet deep; and the people that were obliged to stand upon the benches, were in that position up to their ankles in tears! An Act of Parliament against her playing any more will certainly pass." As this effusion appeared almost immediately after the famous actress's first appearance, we are hardly wrong in considering it as half an advertisement. It must certainly have helped to draw good houses during the rest of her stay.

Lovers of the gentle craft may be interested to know that what was perhaps the earliest advertisement of Izaak Walton's famous little book "The Compleat Angler" was published in one of Wharton's Almanacs. It is on the back of the dedication-leaf to "Hemeroscopeion: Anni Æra

Christianæ, 1654." Hemeroscopeion was William Lilly, and the almanac appeared in 1653, the year in which Walton's book was printed. The advertisement says:—

There is published a Booke of Eighteen-pence price, called *The Compleat Angler*, Or, *The Contemplative man's Recreation*: being a Discourse of Fish and Fishing. Not unworthy the perusall. Sold by *Richard Marriot* in S. *Dunstan's* Church-yard, *Fleetstreet*.

The publication of births, marriages, and deaths seems to have begun almost as soon as newspapers were in full swing. At first only the names of the noble and eminent were given, but soon the notices got into much the same form as we now find them. One advantage of the old style was that the amount a man died worth was generally given, though how the exact sum was known directly he died passes our comprehension, unless it was then the fashion to give off the secret with the latest breath. Even under such circumstances we should hesitate to believe some people of our acquaintance, who have tried now and again, but have never yet succeeded in telling the truth about their own affairs or those of their relatives. And doubtless many an heir felt sadly disappointed, on taking his property, to find it amount to less than half of the published sum. Notices of marriages and deaths were frequent before the announcement of births became fashionable; and in advertisements the real order of things has been completely changed, as obituaries began, marriages followed, and births came last of all. In the first number of the *Gentleman's Magazine*, January 1731, we find deaths and marriages published under separate heads, and many papers of the time did likewise. The *Grub Street Journal* gave them among the summary of Domestic News, each particular item having the initials of the paper from which it was taken appended, as was done with all other information under the same head; for which purpose there was at the top of the article the information that C. meant *Daily Courant*, P. *Daily Post-Boy*, D. P. *Daily Post*, D. J. *Daily Journal*, D. A. *Daily Adver-*

tiser, S. J. *St James's Evening Post*, W. E. *Whitehall Evening Post*, and L. E. *London Evening Post*. In the number for February 7, 1734, we find this :—

Died last night at his habitation in Pall-mall, in a very advanced age, count Kilmanseck, who came over from Hanover with King George I. *S. J.*——At his lodgings. *L. E. D. A. Feb.* 1.——Aged about 70. *P. Feb.* 1.——Of the small-pox, after 8 days illness, in his 23d year count Kilmansegg, son of the countess of Kilmansegg, who came over from Hanover the beginning of the last reign. *D. P. Feb.* 1.——He came over with his highness the prince of Orange, as one of his gentlemen. *D. J. Feb.* 1.——*Tho'* Mr Conundrum *cannot* account *for these different* accounts *of these two* German counts, *yet he* counts *it certain, that the younger* count *was the* son of the countess, who came over *from the* county *of* Hanover.

About the same time we find in the same paper another paragraph worthy of notice :—

Died, last week at Acton, George Villers, Esq; formerly page of the preference to queen Anne, said to have died worth 30,000l.——Mr Ryley, a pay-master serjeant, as he was drinking a pint of beer at the Savoy. *D. J.*——On friday Mr Feverel, master of the bear and rummer tavern in Gerard-street, who was head cook to king William and queen Anne, reputed worth 40,000l. *P.*——Mr Favil. *D. P.*——Mr Favel. *D. J.*——Mr Fewell, 21,000l. *D. A.*

On March 14, also of 1734, there is this :—

Died on tuesday in Tavistock-street, Mr Mooring, an eminent mercer, that kept Long's warehouse, said to have died worth 60,000l. *D. J.*——*This was* 5 *days before he did die, and* 40,000l. *more than he* died worth *according to* D. P. *Mar.* 12.

And on the 28th this :—

Died yesterday morning admiral Mighelles. *C.*——Mighells. *P.*——Mighills. *D. P.*——A gentleman belonging to the earl of Grantham was found dead in his bed. *P.*

And so on, there being announcements in every number, many of which showed differences in the daily-paper notices. There are also plenty of marriage announcements, which, as a rule, give the amounts obtained with the ladies, and sometimes the gentlemen's fortunes. The following is from the *G. S. J.* of February 21, 1734:—

Married, yesterday at S. James's church by the right rev. Dr Hen. Egerton, lord bishop of Hereford, the hon. Francis Godolphin, of Scotland-yard, Esq; to the 3d daughter of the countess of Portland, a beautiful lady of 50,000l. fortune. *P.*——Will. Godolphin, Esq; to the lady Barbara Bentinck, &c. *D.P.*——At the chapel-royal, at S. James's: youngest daughter, &c. *D. J. D. A.*

A few weeks later on there is this:—

Married this day the countess of Deloraine, governess to the princesses Mary and Louisa, to Will. Wyndham, Esq; son to the late col. Wyndham. *L. E.*——*They were not* married *'till* 10 at night.

And on April 25 this:—

Married a few days since —— Price, a Buckinghamshire gentleman of near 2000l. per ann. to miss Robinson of the Theatre Royal in Drury-lane. *L. E.*——On tuesday, the lord Visc. Faulkland to the lady Villew, relict of the late lord Faukland, a lady of great merit and fortune. *D. P.*——Mr Price's marriage is entirely false and groundless. *D. A. Ap.* 24.

There are in the *Journal*, as well as in contemporary and earlier papers, occasional references to births as well, but none calling for any comment at our hands. In the *Gentleman's Magazine* of February 1736 there are two notices of deaths, one commencing the list, which is curious, and the other immediately following, which cannot fail to be interesting:—

SIR *Brownlowe Sherard*, Bt in *Burlington* Gardens. He was of a human Disposition, kind to his Servants dislik'd all extravagant Expence, but very liberal of his Fortune, as well to his Relations and Friends, as to Numbers of distressed Objects; and in particular, to St. *George's* Hospital, near *Hyde-Park Corner*.

Bernard Lintott, Esq., formerly an eminent Bookseller in *Fleet-street*. High Sheriff for Sussex, aged 61.

Also the Earl of Derby, and several men who are noted to have died worth sums varying from £13,000 to £100,000, find obituary notices. These give particulars of the lives of the deceased, and the ways in which the various properties are disposed of, very different from the short announcements of modern days. Thus we find that by the death of the Hon. Walter Chetwynd, the barony of Rathdown in the county of Dublin, and viscounty of Chetwynd of Beerhaven in the county of Cork, both in the peerage of Ireland, became extinct, but that his brother, John Chetwynd, was consoled by an estate of £3000 per annum; that Mrs Eliza Barber succumbed to "an illness she had contracted in Newgate on a prosecution of her master, a baronet of Leicestershire, of which being honourably acquitted, and a copy of her indictment granted, she had brought an action of £1000 damages;" that Mr Fellows was an eminent sugar-baker; and that Gilbert Campbell had during his life got himself into trouble for misinterpreting his duties as an attorney. The marriage lists have also the admirable fashion of giving the sums of money obtained with the brides or bridegrooms as the case may be, and in some instances the amounts of revenue.

In the *London Journal* of February 7, 1730, there is the following, which shows that the presentation of advertisement-books gratis is by no means a novelty:—

At the New Masquerade Warehouse *in* Henrietta Street, Covent Garden, *are given gratis.*

PRINTED Speeches, Jokes, Jests, Conundrums and smart Repartees, suited to each Habit, by which Gentlemen and Ladies may be qualified to speak what is proper to their respective Characters. Also some Dialogues for two or more Persons, particularly between a Cardinal and a Milkmaid; a Judge and a Chimney-sweeper; a Venetian Courtezan and a Quaker; with one very remarkable between a Devil, a Lawyer and an Orange Wench. At the same place is to be spoke with Signor ROSARIO, lately arrived from Venice, who teaches Gentlemen and Ladies the behaviour proper for a Devil, a Courtezan, or any other Character. And whereas it is a frequent practice for Gentlemen to appear in the Habits of Ladies, and Ladies in the habits of Gentlemen, Signor ROSARIO teaches the Italian manner of acting in both capacities. The Quality of both Sexes may be waited on and instructed at their Houses.

Also in 1730 two Roman histories, translated from the French by two Jesuit priests, appeared at the same time—one by Mr Ozell, the other by Mr Bundy—which caused the following advertisement to be inserted by the publishers of Ozell's work:—

This Day is Publish'd

What will satisfy such as have bought Mr Ozell's Translation of the ROMAN HISTORY, *and also undeceive such of Mr Bundy's Friends as are more Friends to Truth:*

Number I. of the

HERCULEAN LABOUR: or the AUGÆAN STABLE cleansed of its heaps of historical, philological, and Geographical Trumpery. Being Serious and facetious Remarks by Mr Ozell, on some thousands of capital and comical Mistakes, Oversights, Negligences, Ignorances, Omissions, Misconstructions, Mis-nomers and other Defects, in the folio Translation of the ROMAN HISTORY by the Rev. Mr BUNDY.

A witty Foreigner upon reading an untrue Translation of Cæsar's Commentaries, said: "It was a wicked Translation, for the Translator had not rendered unto Cæsar the things which were Cæsar's."

With equal truth tho' less wit, may it be said the Translator of the ROMAN HISTORY has not paid the Rev. authors the TYTHE of their DUES; which in one of the same cloth is the more unpardonable.

The Money is to be returned by Mr Ozell, to any Gentleman, who, after reading it shall come (or send a letter to him in Arundel Street, in the Strand) and declare upon Honour, he does not think the Book worth the Money.

In the *Bristol Gazette* for Thursday, August 28, 1788, among advertisements of the ordinary kind, some of which are noticeable as emanating from Robert and Thomas Southey, we find the following:—

Swansea and *Bristol* DILIGENCE,
To carry THREE INSIDES.

WILL set out from the Mackworth-Arms, *Swansea*, on Wednesday the 18th of June, and continue every Sunday, Wednesday, and Friday morning at four o'clock; and will arrive early the same evening at the New Passage, where a good boat will be waiting to take the Passengers over, and a Coach ready at eight o'clock the next morning to carry them to *Bristol*.

Also a LIGHT COACH will set out every Tuesday, Thursday, and

Saturday afternoon at five o'clock, from the WHITE LION, to meet the above Diligence.

Fare from Bristol to Swansea 1l. 10s., passage included.

Short passengers the same as the Mail Coach.

N.B.—Parcels carried on moderate terms, and expeditiously delivered; but no parcels will be accounted for above 5l. value, unless entered as such and paid for accordingly.

Performed by

J. LAKE, Mackworth-Arms, Swansea.
C. NOTT, Ship and Castle, Neath.
C. BRADLEY, Bear, Cowbridge.
J. BRADLEY, Angel, Cardiff.
M. HOGGARD, New Passage.
R. CHURCH, New Passage.
W. CARR, White Lion, Bristol.

N.B. A COACH every Monday, Thursday, and Saturday morning, at seven o'clock, from the White Lion to the New Passage.

It is to be presumed that the line about short passengers refers to those who travel short journeys only, though a friend of ours, himself a Welshman, makes several jocular allusions to the conditions that used in the days of travelling by road in and about the Principality to be imposed on people of less than the average height. As these will be some day published in a volume, the title of which is already decided upon—"Cheese and Chuckles; or, Leeks and Laughter"—and which is intended for distribution among the bards at the annual Eisteddfod, we will not discount the sensation then to be derived from their publication, more especially as we have tried in vain and failed to understand them.

For those who take such interest in the poet Southey that anything connected with his family is regarded with favour, we present the following, from the same number of the *Bristol Gazette*, which was kindly forwarded by a gentleman on hearing that this work was in progress:—

DISSOLUTION OF PARTNERSHIP.

THE PARTNERSHIP between ROBERT and THOMAS SOUTHEY, *Linen-drapers*, &c., of this city, was by mutual consent dissolved on the 21st of July last; all persons to whom the said partnership stood indebted, are to send their accounts to ROBERT SOUTHEY, Wine-street, and the persons indebted to them, are respectfully requested to pay the same to the said ROBERT SOUTHEY, who continues the trade as usual.

ROBERT SOUTHEY.
THOMAS SOUTHEY.

BRISTOL, August 8th, 1788.

R. SOUTHEY, thanks his friends in particular and the public in general, for the kind support he has hitherto experienced, and begs leave to inform them, that he is just returned from London with a large assortment of goods; particularly fine printed CALLICOES, MUSLINS, and LACE, which he is determined to sell on as low terms as any person in the trade, and solicits the early inspection of his friends.

N.B.—Part of the old Stock to be sold very cheap.

There is also an advertisement in the paper from Thomas Southey, who has taken up quarters in Close Street, soliciting custom and describing his wares. Our correspondent, who is a gentleman of position at Neath, and whose veracity is undoubted, says: "My father was a correspondent of Southey's, and in one of his letters Southey says he was very nearly settling in our Vale of Neath, in a country house, the owner of which was a strong Tory, but as Southey at that early period of his life was a great Radical, he was not allowed to rent the property! If this had not been so, he says, 'my children would have been *Cam*brian instead of *Cum*brian.'"

Among other old customs now fast falling into desuetude, there is in Cumberland and some other parts of the north of England a practice known as the Bridewain, which consists of the public celebration of weddings. A short time after courtship is commenced—as soon as the date of the marriage is fixed—the lovers give notice of their intentions, and on the day named all their friends for miles around assemble at the intending bridegroom's house, and join in various pastimes. A plate or bowl is generally fixed in a convenient place, where each of the company contributes in proportion to his inclination and ability, and according to the degree of respect the couple are held in. By this custom a worthy pair have frequently been benefited with a sum of from fifty to a hundred pounds. The following advertisement for such a meeting is copied from the *Cumberland Pacquet*, 1786 :—

INVITATION.

Suspend for one day your cares and your labours,
And come to this wedding, kind friends and good neighbours.

NOTICE is hereby given that the marriage of ISAAC PEARSON with FRANCES ATKINSON will be solemnized in due form in the parish church of Lamplugh, in Cumberland, on Tuesday next, the 30th of May inst.; immediately after which the bride and bridegroom with their attendants will proceed to Lonefoot, in the said parish, where the nuptials will be celebrated by a variety of rural entertainments.

Then come one and all
At Hymen's soft call
From Whitehaven, Workington, Harrington, Dean,
Hail, Ponsonby, Blaing and all places between,
From Egremont, Cockermouth, Barton, St Bee's,
Cint, Kinnyside, Calder and parts such as these;
And the country at large may flock in if they please.
Such sports there will be as have seldom been seen,
Such wrestling, and fencing and dancing between,
And races for prizes, for frolick and fun,
By horses, and asses, and dogs will be run
That you'll all go home happy—as sure as a gun.
In a word, such a wedding can ne'er fail please;
For the sports of Olympus were trifles to these.

Nota Bene.—You'll please to observe that the day
Of this grand bridal pomp is the thirtieth of May,
When 'tis hop'd that the sun, to enliven the sight,
Like the flambeau of Hymen, will deign to burn bright.

These invitations were at this period far from rare, and another, calling folk to a similar festival, appeared in the same paper in 1789 :—

BRIDEWAIN.

There let Hymen oft appear
In saffron robe and taper clear,

And pomp and feast and revelry,
With mask and antic pageantry;
Such sights as youthful poets dream,
On summer eves by haunted stream.

GEORGE HAYTON, who married ANNE, the daughter of Joseph and Dinah Colin, of Crosby Mill, purposes having a BRIDE-WAIN at his house, at Crosby near Maryport, on Thursday the 7th day of May next, where he will be happy to see his friends and well-wishers, for whose amusement there will be a variety of races, wrestling matches, etc. etc. The prizes will be—a saddle, two bridles, a pair of *gands d'amour* gloves, which whoever wins is sure to be married within the twelvemonth; a girdle (*ceinture de Venus*) possessing qualities not to be described; and many other articles, sports and pastimes too numerous to mention, but which can never prove tedious in the exhibition.

From fashion's laws and customs free,
We follow sweet variety;
By turns we laugh and dance and sing;
Time's for ever on the wing;
And nymphs and swains of Cumbria's plain
Present the golden age again.

A similar advertisement appears in the *Pacquet* in 1803, and contains some verses of a kind superior to that generally met in these appeals. It is called

A PUBLIC BRIDAL.

JONATHAN and GRACE MUSGRAVE purpose having a PUBLIC BRIDAL at Low Lorton Bridge End, near Cockermouth, on THURSDAY, the 16th of June, 1803; when they will be glad to see their Friends, and all who may please to favour them with their Company;—for whose Amusement there will be various RACES, for Prizes of different kinds; and amongst others, a Saddle, and Bridle; and a Silver-tipt Hunting Horn, for Hounds to run for.—There will also be Leaping, Wrestling, &c. &c.

☛ Commodious ROOMS are likewise engaged for DANCING PARTIES, in the Evening.

Come, haste to the BRIDAL!—to Joys we invite You,
Which, help'd by the Season, to please You can't fail:
But should LOVE, MIRTH, and SPRING strive in vain to delight You,
You've still the *mild* Comforts of LORTON's sweet VALE.

And where does the GODDESS more charmingly revel?
Where ZEPHYR dispense a more health-chearing Gale,

Than where the pure *Cocker*, meandring the Level,
Adorns the calm Prospects of Lorton's sweet VALE?

To the BRIDAL then come;—taste the Sweets of our Valley;
Your Visit, *good Cheer* and *kind Welcome* shall hail.
Round the *Standard* of Old ENGLISH CUSTOM, we'll rally,—
And be blest in *Love, Friendship*, and LORTON'S sweet VALE.

A correspondent, writing in Hone's Table-Book, date August 1827, says it was in the early part of the century "a prevalent custom to have 'bidden weddings' when a couple of respectability and of slender means were on the eve of marriage; in this case they gave publicity to their intentions through the medium of the *Cumberland Pacquet*, a paper published at Whitehaven, and which about twenty-nine years ago was the only newspaper printed in the county. The editor, Mr John Ware, used to set off the invitation in a novel and amusing manner, which never failed to insure a large meeting, and frequently the contributions made on the occasion, by the visitors, were of so much importance to the new-married couple that by care and industry they were enabled to make so good 'a fend as niver to look ahint them.'" That this or a similar custom was practised commonly a generation ago in Wales, where it is even now occasional, a notice issued from Carmarthen shows. It is peculiar, and runs thus:—

CARMARTHEN, April 12, 1836.

AS we intend to enter the MATRIMONIAL STATE on THURSDAY, the 5th of MAY next, we are encouraged by our Friends to make a BIDDING on the occasion the same Day, at the Sign of the ANGEL, situate in LAMMAS-STREET; when and where the favour of your good and agreeable Company is most humbly solicited, and whatever donation you may be pleased to confer on us then, will be thankfully received, warmly acknowledged, and cheerfully repaid whenever called for on a similar occasion,

By your most obedient humble Servants,

DAVID DANIEL
(Shoemaker,)
RUTH EVANS.

THE Young Man, and his Mother, (Mary Daniel,) and his Brother and Sister (Joshua and Anne,) desire that all gifts of the above nature due to them, be returned on the said Day, and will be thankful for all favours granted.

Also, the Young Woman, and her Mother (Sarah Evans,) and her Grand-father and Grand-mother (John and Frances Evans,) desire that all Gifts of the above nature due to them, be returned on the above Day, and will be thankful with her Uncle and Aunt (Benjamin and Margaret Evans, Penrhywcoion,) for all additional favours granted.

The applications made by means of the notes which follow the advertisement show that the promise made by David and Ruth to repay all amounts when called upon is something more than a mere flourish. We should not like, though, to guarantee that these promises were always kept, and have no doubt that the concocters of the foregoing found, as so many others did before them, and not a few have done since, that kindness is generally obtained from the least expected, and often the least valued, quarter. This is a glorious dispensation of providence, and few people who have experienced misfortune, or have been in want of assistance, but have felt how compensating is the hidden power which guides our destinies. Yet writers who constantly rail about the insincerity of friendship make little or no mention of those truest friends, the friends who appear uninvoked, and do whatever has been asked in vain of others who may have promised freely, or who are in fact indebted to those they ignore in the moment of adversity.

Burly old Grose, the friend of Burns, in his "Olio" gives a curious specimen of composition, which he says was the effort of a mayor in one of our University towns, though which is not stated. It tells us that—

WHEREAS, a Multiplicity of Dangers are often incurred by Damage of outrageous Accidents by Fire, we whose Names are undersigned, have thought proper that the Benefit of an Engine, bought by us, for the better Extinguishing of which, by the Accidents of Almighty God, may unto us happen, to make a Rate to gather Benevolence for the better propagating such useful Instruments.

Some clever student of style may be able to tell, by a

clue invisible to the uninitiated, whether this is Oxford or Cambridge. We are not learned in such matters, and so prefer to admire, without troubling ourselves to identify.

Poetical advertisements were not at all uncommon a hundred years ago and less. The demand for space, and the steam-engine rate at which we live now, have, however, destroyed not only the opportunity for them, but their use. Towards the close of the last century there lived in the Canongate, Edinburgh, one Gavin Wilson, a hard-working bootmaker, or, as his sign described him, "Arm, Leg and Boot maker, *but not* to his Royal Highness the Prince of Wales." He was a singular fellow, and was the inventor of an art for hardening and polishing leather, so as to be workable into powder-flasks, snuff-boxes, drinking-mugs, ink-cases, and other articles of a similar kind. His genius did not stop at this rough work, but enabled him to form a German flute and a violin, both of leather, which, for neatness of workmanship and melodiousness of tone, were, friendly critics said, not a bit inferior to any fiddle or flute formed of wood. His greatest triumphs, however, were artificial arms and legs, also made of leather, which not only completely remedied loss of limb, but also closely resembled their human prototypes, being covered with skin, nails, &c. The unexampled success of his endeavours in this way was curiously illustrated by a person who, having lost both his hands by a cannon-shot, was provided with a new and useful pair by Gavin Wilson. This man expressed his gratitude in a letter of thanks, written with the artificial hands, which appeared in the *Caledonian Mercury* for 1779, along with an advertisement of the ingenious mechanic. Wilson had also pretensions to wit, and was occasionally a votary of what Foote once described as the Tuneful Ten. "Nine and one are ten," said Foote one day to an accountant, who was anxious the wit should hear his poetry, and who commenced, "Hear me, O Phœbus and ye Tuneful Nine!" Having got so far, he accused Foote of inattention;

but the latter said, "Nine and one are ten—go on," which was too near the shop to be pleasant. The following advertisement may serve as a specimen of Wilson's poetical attempts :—

G. Wilson humbly as before
Resumes his thankfulness once more
For favours formerly enjoy'd
In, by the public, being employ'd.
And hopes this public intimation
Will meet with candid acceptation.
The world knows well he makes *boots* neatly
And, as times go, he sells them cheaply.
'Tis also known to many a hundred
Who at his late invention wonder'd,
That polish'd *leather boxes, cases*,
So well known now in many places,
With *powder-flasks* and *porter-mugs*,
And jointed *leather arms* and *legs*.
Design'd for use as well as show,
Exempli gratia read below,*
Were his invention ; and no claim
Is just by any other name.
With numbers of production more,
In leather ne'er performed before.
In these dead times being almost idle,
He tried and made a *leather fiddle*.
Of workmanship extremely neat,
Of tone quite true, both soft and sweet.
And finding leather not a mute
He made a *leather German flute*,
Which play'd as well and was as good
As any ever made of wood.
He for an idle hour's amusement
Wrote this exotic advertisement,
Informing you he does reside
In head of Canongate, south side,
Up the first wooden-railed stair,
You're sure to find his Whimship there.
In Britain none can fit you better
Than can your servant the *Bootmaker*.

GAVIN WILSON.

---

* The letter written by the sailor with the artificial hands to the printer of the *Caledonian Mercury*.

Notwithstanding that their day is past, occasional poetical advertisements are to be found in the papers now. They are, as a rule, infinitely bad, and the following is so very different from the general run of them, that we cannot help quoting it. Perhaps it was written after taking a dose of "Lamplough," which is said on authority to have so many beneficial effects, that power over writers of verse in general, and the writer of the following in particular, may easily be included among them. So all minor poets had better study this, which we extract from a "weekly" a year or so ago:—

A DRINKING SONG.

If ever your spirits are damp, low,
  And bilious; you should, I opine,
Just quaff a deep bumper of Lamplough—
  Of Lamplough's Pyretic Saline.

The title is quaint and eccentric—
  Is probably so by design—
But they say for disturbances ventric
  There's nought like Pyretic Saline.

Don't bid me become exegetic,
  Or tell me I'm only a scamp low,
If I can tell you more of Pyretic
  Saline manufactured by Lamplough.

A second good specimen was published in a theatrical paper at the time when Mr J. S. Clarke, an American comedian, whose strength is in his advertisements, and who is well known this side the Atlantic, was playing in "The Rivals." It is entitled

SAVED.

It was a chill November eve and on the busy town
A heavy cloud of yellow fog was sinking slowly down;
Upon the bridge of Waterloo, a prey to mad despair,
There stood a man with heavy brow and deep-lined face of care.

One ling'ring look around he gave, then on the river cast
That sullen stare of rash resolve he meant should be his last.
Far down the old cathedral rose, a shadow grey and dim,
The light of day would dawn on that but ne'er again on him.

One plunge within the murky stream would end the bitter strife.
"What rest's there now," he sobbed aloud, "to bid me cling to life?"
Just then the sound of stamping feet smote on his list'ning ear,
A sandwich-man upon his beat paused 'neath the lamplight clear.

One hurried glance—he read the board that hung upon his back,
He leapt down from the parapet, and smote his thigh a smack.
"I must see that," he cried—the words that put his woe to flight
Were "John S. Clarke as Acres at the Charing Cross to-night."

Another of these effusions, well worthy of insertion here, appeared quite recently in a humorous paper, and is devoted to the interests of Messrs Cook & Son, the tourist agents. Whether or not it was paid for as an advertisement, they must have found it valuable. Despite the sneers of several small wits whom fortune has enabled to travel in the old expensive mode, there are very many who are neither cads nor snobs, whatever the distinction may be, and whose greatest sin is a paucity of income, that have felt the benefit of the popular excursionists' endeavours. The verses are called

COOK'S PERQUISITES.

In longitude six thousand ninety-two,
  Latitude nothing, the good ship, *Salt Beef*,
Caught in a gale, the worst that ever blew,
  Was stranded on a coral island's reef.

Her back was broken, so she went in halves,
  The crew and captain perished, every hand;
Only a pig, some chickens, and two calves,
  And the one passenger, escaped to land.

King Bungaroo, with all the royal suite,
  Was waiting to receive him on the beach;
And seeing he was plump and nice to eat,
  Received him graciously with courteous speech.

The suite, who thus their coming banquet eyed,
  Their gastric regions rubbed with grateful paw,
And wondered if the king would have him fried,
  Or boiled, or roasted,—or just eat him raw!

The hungry passenger their meaning caught
  As hinting dinner in some manner dim,
And smiling at the notion, little thought
  That they meant feasting *on*—and not *with*—him!

But, as you draw a fowl before 'tis drest,
  The suite proceeded first, of everything
The pockets of their victim to divest,
  And laid their plunder down before the king.

The monarch started at some object there—
  Then seized the prisoner's hand and cried aloud,
"Bo, bingo wobli! Chungum raggadare.
  Howinki croblob? Boo! Owchingadowd!"

Which means—"Unhand this kindly gentleman.
  Observe those coupons! Note that small green book!
Put out the fire—hang up the frying-pan!
  We mustn't eat him. He belongs to Cook!"

But turning back to the early times on which we started in quest of amusing advertisements, we come upon a fictitious letter addressed to Sylvanus Urban in the *Gentleman's Magazine* for September 1803, which is signed Maria Elderly, and falls sadly foul of the indecorous announcements then so plentiful. It runs thus: "Good Mr Urban,—You must know, Sir, I am a married woman and a mother (I bless Heaven!) of several not unpromising daughters. We read most of the best English and French authors together as we sit at our work: that is to say one reads aloud whilst the rest draw, sew, or embroider. The hours thus pass more pleasantly; and our amusement I will hope is productive of solid mental profit. It is a proverbial good-natured joke with young gentlemen that curiosity is of the feminine gender. I will not stop to dispute the matter with such acute grammarians; but will rather honestly admit that (although I think otherwise) perhaps 'much may be said on both sides.' Nay, I will own, Sir, that what with the natural timidity of my sex, and the fear of Bonaparte's invasion, I do feel a little hankering or so, to learn how the world of politics is conducted. I therefore have lately taken in a certain fashionable morning newspaper, and was much amused at first with its contents. But, my dear Mr Urban, I fancy I must give up this paper; and as I find you are a married gentleman, I will at once tell you why: I have often been vexed, Sir, at the sight of certain indecorous advertisements. Proof is better than accusation at all times. I will therefore just allude to a few, which, however, I assure you, are not the worst. I know you cannot expect *me* to transcribe them. The first instance I shall notice, is in the paper of April 21, 1803, where 'a lady near 30, wishes to be companion to a single gentleman;' and as a proof of the impropriety of this advertisement, Mr O. of Dover Street (to whom the *lady* referred) thought it necessary pointedly to deny all knowledge of her in another advertisement of April 28. In the paper of May 5, I read that 'a widow-lady *pleasing in her person*, &c., solicits the loan of £40 from a gentleman.' The lady refers to a house in Dean Street, Soho. In that of May 26 'a young female intreats the loan of £130 from a nobleman or gentleman of fortune.' She refers to Curriers' Row, Blackfriars. In that of June 1, a young lady (who refers to the post-office, Blandford Street, Portman Square) inserts a most unqualified proposal indeed. In that of June 16, the proposal is repeated in still more impertinent terms. The lady now refers to Eyre Street, Hatton Garden. In that of June 18, appear two advertisements from females, *of a very curious nature*, addressed to two young men. Both are assignations; and they are expressed too in very intelligible terms, I do assure you. I believe you will agree with me that such advertisements can do no good and may do much harm. I could enlarge my list very greatly, by pointing your eyes to paragraphs of a later date; but the subject is a very unpleasant one, and I at present forbear. 'My poverty, but not my will consents' may do in a play; but it is a sad excuse for the editor of a daily publication: and it is *criminal*, Sir, when we consider how many young minds may thus be empoisoned." We trust this letter will be taken as evidence that we have in the preceding chapter by no means selected the worst specimens of the style which pervaded advertisements at the close of the last century and beginning of the present.

The believers in vested interests may see by an advertisement of the year 1804, that proprietorial rights were respected in those days even among beggars :—

TO be disposed of for the benefit of the poor widow a Blind Man's WALK in a charitable neighbourhood, the comings-in between twenty-five and twenty-six shillings a week, with a dog well drilled, and a staff in good repair. A handsome premium will be expected. For further particulars, inquire at No. 40, Chiswell Street.

The halcyon days of cadgers and crossing-sweepers are over, and we no longer hear of members of either profession leaving fortunes. It has often been source of wonder to us how a right was maintained in any particular crossing or walk. It is presumable, of course, that no action would lie in the event of one man taking another's favourite corner; yet, if story-tellers are to be depended upon, the "good-wills" of these places in days gone by were worth not hundreds alone, but thousands of pounds. The new police and the mendicity societies have considerably disturbed such sinecures, and even those affectionate parents that of late years lived on the earnings of their young, who pretended to sell cigar-lights and newspapers, but who in reality begged freely, have been driven to earn their own meals by the officers of the various school-boards. So passes away the glory of free trade from this over-legislated and effete old country, where no one is allowed to do as he likes if it at all interferes with the comfort of his neighbours—except, of course, when he is rich and the neighbour is poor. Passing on to 1811, we come upon a quaint request for a servant in the *Morning Post* of December 4 :—

A COOK-HOUSEMAID, or HOUSEMAID-COOK is wanted, for the service of a single gentleman, where only one other, a man-servant is kept. The age of the woman wanted must not be less than 25, nor more than 40 years; and it is requisite that she should be equally excellent in the two capacities of Cook and Housemaid. Her character must be unexceptionable for sobriety, honesty and cleanliness. The sobriety, however, which consists in drinking deep without staggering will not do; nor will the honesty suffice which would make up for the possible absence of pilfering by waste. Neither will the cleanliness answer which is content with bustling only before the employer's eyes—a sure symptom of a slattern. The servant advertised for, must be thoroughly and truly cleanly, honest and sober. As it is probable that not a drab out of place who reads this advertisement but will be for imposing herself, though, perhaps, incapable of cooking a sprat, and about as nice as a Hottentot, all such are warned not to give themselves useless trouble. On the other hand, a steady, clean woman, really answering the above description, will, by applying as below, hear of a place not easy equalled in comfort; where the wages are good and constantly increasing, and where servants are treated as fellow-creatures, and with a kindness, which, to the discredit of their class, is seldom merited. Personal application to be made, from one to three o'clock, to Mr Danvers, perfumer, No. 16, Craven Street, Strand.

Here we have the crotchety old bachelor of the novels to the life. This advertiser was evidently a judge of character, and doubtless one of the kindest-hearted of men, but irascible and touchy, subject to twinges of gout, and possessed of a horror of east winds. A man who would scorn to be affected by the most pitiful story, yet whose hand was always in his pocket, and whose sympathy always meant relief as well. Where are all these good old creatures gone? Are they all dead, and is the race extinct? Frankly we must admit that we never met with any one of them, though we should very much like to, as we could in our own person find plenty of opportunity for the disposition of extra benevolence. It is said that the brothers Cheeryble had an actual existence, and perhaps they had, but if so, they managed to conceal their identity extremely successfully. We remember once meeting two brothers in business, who in appearance and manner were exactly like Nickleby's benefactors; but two more astute individuals were not to be found in the three kingdoms. And on the strength of this likeness they possessed a great reputation for a benevolence which never had even a symptom of real being. Apropos of those imaginary philanthropists the Cheerybles, we present one of the advertisements which were called forth by their appearance in the story. It is from the *Times*, and was published February 7, 1844:—

TO THE BROTHERS CHEERYBLE, or any who have hearts like theirs. A clergyman, who will gladly communicate his name and address, desires to introduce the case of a gentleman, equal at least to Nickleby in birth, worthy, like him, for refinement of character, even of the best descent; like him, of spotless integrity, and powerfully beloved by friends who cannot help him, but no longer, like Nickleby, sustained by the warm buoyancy of youthful blood. The widowed father of young children, he has spent his all in the struggles of an unsuccessful but honourable business, and has now for eighteen months been vainly seeking some stipendiary employment.—To all who have ever known him he can refer for commendation. Being well versed in accounts, though possessed of education, talents, and experience, which would render him invaluable as a private secretary, he would accept with gratitude even a clerk's stool and daily bread. Any communication addressed to the Rev. B. C., Post-office, Cambridge, will procure full particulars, ample references, and the introduction of the party, who is now in town, and ignorant of this attempt to serve him.

Dickens, knowing his power at that time, must have laughed in his sleeve at the trick he was playing the professional swindler when he portrayed the brothers; though, if we are to believe what we are told in the preface to a subsequent edition of his book, the noble army of begging-letter writers and suchlike impostors had ample revenge, for he was pestered nearly to death with importunities to reveal the real name and address of purely mythical characters. Inventors of appeals to the benevolent, either by way of letter or advertisement, are a hard-working race, and must find the task of enlisting sympathy much more difficult than it was when Mr Puff tided over a time of misfortune by aid of the charitable and credulous. It is possible even now, despite the efforts of societies and detectives who give themselves entirely to the work of unmasking counterfeits, to find one or two of those heart-stirring appeals to the benevolent which have maintained many an impostor in idleness for years together. Like Puff did in his time, though evidently less and less successfully, these advertisers support themselves upon their inventions by means of the proceeds of addresses "to the charitable and humane," or "to those whom providence has blessed with affluence." The account which Puff gives of his fictitious misfortunes so little exaggerates the advertisements which appear occasionally in the *Times*, that it is well to the point, and worthy of quoting. "I suppose," he says, "never man went through such a series of calamities in the same space of time. I was five times made a bankrupt, and reduced from a state of affluence by a train of unavoidable misfortunes. Then, though a very industrious tradesman, I was twice burnt out, and lost my little all both times. I lived upon those fires a month. I soon after was confined by a most excruciating disorder, and lost the use of my limbs. That told very well; for I had the case strongly attested, and went about to collect the subscriptions myself! Afterwards, I was a close prisoner in the Marshalsea for a debt benevolently contracted to serve a friend. I was then reduced to—oh no!—then I became a widow with six helpless children. Well, at last, what with bankruptcies, fires, gouts, dropsies, imprisonments, and other valuable calamities, having got together a pretty handsome sum, I determined to quit a business which had always gone rather against my conscience."

But leaving "The Critic," and the ideas which the specimens just given have promoted, we will fall back upon an advertisement of a truly humorous nature, which is given to the world as long back as 1816. What householder who has improved his dwelling for the benefit of a grasping proprietor will not sympathise with the writer of this?—

WANTED IMMEDIATELY, to enable me to leave the house which I have for these last five years inhabited, in the same plight and condition in which I found it, 500 LIVE RATS, for which I will gladly pay the sum of £5 sterling; and as I cannot leave the farm attached thereto in the same order in which I got it, without at

least Five Millions of Docks, Dockens (weeds), I do hereby promise a further sum of £5 for said number of Dockens. Apply ——.

Dated, 31 October, 1816.

N.B. The Rats must be full grown, and no cripples.

In close companionship with the above we find another, which for peculiarity is quite as noticeable. The advertiser has evidently studied humanity without receiving much benefit from his researches, unless the knowledge that he is vastly superior to every one else is a benefit. If the advertisement were not a swindle, of which it seems very suggestive, it is not unreasonable to suppose that failure attended upon it, for no man who believed to such an extent in himself could ever be brought to have faith in another :—

IT is the general desire of princes and opulent men to live friendless —they gain obsequiousness, adulation, and dependents, but not friends : the sycophants that surround them disappear when the lure that attracted them is lost: beguiled by blandishments, deceived by hypocrisy, and lulled by professions they do not discover imposture till adversity detects it. The evil is unbounded—they never obtain a sincere opinion, whether regarding pecuniary embarrassment or domestic dissension—in any perplexed or unhappy event they receive no counsel but that which benefits the sinister views of him who gives it. Of what advantage is fortune if it transforms friends into parasites, and we are to live in constant delusion; or isolated and secluded, we must exist like hermits to shun intercourse with our fellow-beings, and escape perfidy? One whose affluence precludes speculation, who has proved himself undaunted in danger and unshaken in fidelity, proffers his friendship to him who deserves it, and will know how to appreciate it; —his reading has not afforded mere abstract knowledge, but has been rendered auxiliary for a vast intercourse with the world; years have furnished experience, reflection has improved it. His advice and aid he hopes is not insignificant, be the station of him who requires them ever so elevated. As there can be no independence where there is not equality of circumstances, no one of inferior condition can be noticed.

Still about the same period we come upon the advertisement of an Irish schoolmaster, which for inflation, pomposity, and ignorance is perhaps unrivalled. It is only fair, while quoting this, to say that Mr Hendrick is not by any means a good specimen of the Irish teacher, who is, as a rule, modest, conscientious, and chokeful of learning. This extract forcibly reminds us of one of Samuel Lover's characters :—

MR HENDRICK'S DEVOIR TO THE GENTRY OF LIMERICK.

WOULD be elated to assign his attention for the instruction of eight or ten Pupils, to attend on their houses each second day, to teach the French language, Geography on the Principles of Astronomy, traversing the Globe by sea and land on the rudiments of a right angle, with a variety of pleasing Problems, attached to Manners, Customs, &c. of different Countries, Trade and Commerce; Phenomenons on Volcanos, Thunder, Sound, Lightning, &c. Such as please to continue, may advance through a Course of Natural Philosophy, and those proficient in French can be taught the above in that Language.

N.B. At intervals would instruct in the Italian Language.

Please to inquire at Mr Barry, Newtown-Perry.

J. HENDRICK, *Philomathos.*

In a Jersey newspaper for December 1821 there is a very funny advertisement for a lost dog—so funny indeed is it that it seems more than likely to have been a hoax, or a hit at the peculiarly broken English identified with the Channel Islands. Still it appears as an advertisement, and so we append it :—

LOSE.—Dere ave bin von doge, dat vil replay to de appel of "Outre ;" he is betwin de couleur of de vite and de bruin, dere is belif he was delay by some personne on propos, as he was vont by de oner on Monday next for to come to de chasse, as he kno vere was de hairs. Applie of de oner at de Printure.

As a companion, here is the following from the *Handelsblad* of Amsterdam. It is much more natural than the Jersey effusion, and is evidently an attempt to write the language known on the Continent and abroad generally as American. It will be recollected that one of the last requests of the Emperor Nicholas during the Crimean war was that, in gratitude for the efforts at assistance made by the good people of the United States, the cadets in the military schools should be taught the American language. This must be near to his idea of it :—

MEDAILLE of SILVER at New-York.
MEDAILLE of GOLD at Paris, London and Berlin.

The very celebrated AMERICAN-BALSAM, notwithstanding the great competition, preserve the preference; wherefore, did is your question because every body is content with his expectation and recommend this balsam indeed.

The under signed have by experience of himself following the working of this balsam and may be rejoicing to offer an his honorables fellow-citizens and compatriots a very excellent remedy to prevent the sally of hair, to dissiporte the erysipelas; and than the greatest desire of man consist to recover the hair upon their bald-spates, it is reading every day in the newspapers, but none annonce, as the under signed has the right to do it with contract *NO HAIR NO MONNEY.*

The prevent imitation none than THEOPHILE is sole agent for the Netherlands, St. Nicholasstreet at Amsterdam. Ladys! Perriwigs! curls, tress shall be dying very beautiful is every colours, of light haired to black.

Bony inspection of a long wigt tress, with teen differents coleurs.

On December 23, 1823, the following droll advertisement appeared in the *Morning Herald.* It was probably a satire on the manners and customs of quasi-fashionables of the day, though why any one should be so anxious to mark his disapprobation of the state of affairs as to pay for the publication of his satires we really are not prepared to say:—

WANTED, for the ensuing London Campaign, a CHAPERON, who will undertake the charge of two young ladies, now making their entrée into fashionable life; she must possess a constitution impervious to fatigue and heat, and be perfectly independent of sleep; *au fait* at the mysteries of Whist and Cassino, and always ready to undertake a round game, with a supper appetite of the most moderate description: any personal charms, which might interfere by her acting as a foil to her charges, will be deemed inadmissible; and she must be totally divested of matrimonial pretensions on her own account, having sufficient experience in the *beau monde* to decide with promptitude on the eligibility of invitations with an instinctive discrimination of Almack men, and eldest sons. Address to Louisa, Twopenny Post Office, Great Mary-le-bone-street.

N.B. No Widow from Bath or Cheltenham will be treated with.

In the *Times*, at the close of the year 1826, an advertisement appeared, which ran as follows:—

TO SCHOOL ASSISTANTS.—Wanted, a respectable GENTLEMAN of good character, capable of TEACHING the CLASSICS as far as Homer and Virgil. Apply ——

There is nothing noticeable in this, the reader will think, nor is there; but the sequel, which is told in a number of the now leading journal a few days afterwards, will perhaps repay perusal. A day or two after the advertisement had appeared, the gentleman to whom application was to be made received a letter as follows: "Sir—With reference to an advertisement which were inserted in the *Times* newspaper a few days since, respecting a school assistant, I beg to state that I should be happy to fill that situation; but as most of my frends reside in London, and not knowing how far Homer and Virgil is from town, I beg to state that I should not like to engage to teach the classics farther than Hammersmith or Turnham Green, or at the very utmost distance farther than Brentford.—Wating your reply, I am, Sir, &c. &c., John Sparks." The errors in orthography and syntax have been copied as in the letter, but we fancy the matter looks suspiciously like a hoax. The editor, however, thinks otherwise, and after appending a few remarks, says, "This puts us in mind of a person who once advertised for a '*strong coal heaver*,' and a poor man calling upon him the day after, saying, 'he had not got such a thing as a *strong coal heaver*, but he had brought a *strong coal scuttle*, made of the best iron; and if that would answer the purpose, he should have it a bargain.'" About this time the following request for a minister was published in the *Monthly Mirror*, and doubtless applications were numerous for the engagement:—

WANTED, for a newly erected Chapel, near Grosvenor Square, a gentleman of elegant manners, and insinuating address, to conduct the theological department to a refined audience. It is not necessary that he believe in the Thirty-nine Articles; but it is expected that he should possess a white hand and a diamond ring; he will be expected to leave out vulgar ideas, and denunciations against polite vices which he may meet with in the Bible; and, upon no account, be guilty of wounding the ears of his auditory with the words h—ll, or d——n. One who lisps, is near-sighted, and who has a due regard for amiable weaknesses, will be preferred.

N.B.—If he is of pleasing and *accommodating* manners, he will have a chance of being introduced to the first company, and three card parties every Sunday evening. One who knows a few college jokes, or who has been Chaplain to the Whip Club, will be preferred. He will have no occasion to administer Baptism, &c. &c. there being an old gentleman employed, who, on account of extreme distress, has agreed, for ten pounds per annum, to preach in the afternoon, and do all the under work.

Letters must be addressed to James Speculate, Esq. Surveyor's Office, New Square, Mary-le-Bone.

Apropos of the foregoing, "The Goodfellow's Calendar," a handbook of humorous anecdote and criticism for nearly every day in the year—some stray leaves of which have found their way into our possession—gives some account of a parson who, it says, would have been eminently fitted for the situation. "The Rev. R. C. Maturin, Curate of St. Peter's, Dublin, and author of one of the most immoral and trumpery tragedies, 'Bertram,' that ever disgraced the stage, or gratified the low taste of an acting manager, died October 30th 1824. This exemplary pillar of the Established Church was exceedingly vain, both of his person and accomplishments, and as his income would not allow him to attract attention by the splendour of his dress and manners, he seldom failed to do so by their singularity. Mr Maturin was tall, slender, but well proportioned, and on the whole a good figure, which he took care to display in a well-made black coat tightly buttoned, and some odd light-coloured stocking-web pantaloons, surmounted, in winter, by a coat of prodigious dimensions, gracefully thrown on, so as not to obscure the symmetry it affected to protect. The Curate of St. Peter's sang and danced, and prided himself on performing the movements and evolutions of the quadrille, certainly equal to any other divine of the Established Church, if not to any private lay gentleman of the three kingdoms. It often happened, too, that Mr

Maturin, either laboured under an attack of gout or met with some accident, which compelled the use of a slipper or bandage on one foot or one leg; and by an unaccountable congruity of mischances he was uniformly compelled on these occasions to appear in the public thoroughfares of Dublin, where the melancholy spectacle of a beautiful limb in pain never failed to excite the sighs and sympathies of all the interesting persons who passed, as well as to prompt their curiosity to make audible remarks or inquiries respecting the possessor." We are much afraid that the vanity of Mr Maturin was not wonderfully peculiar, and with due allowance for those differences in our styles of dress and living which have been made in fifty years, it would not be difficult to find ministers of the gospel who would prove strong rivals to the curate of St Peter's.

In 1825 the *New Times* presented the public with the original of that singular advertisement which has been so often quoted as an Irish bull, but which would appear to be home-bred: "Wanted by a Surgeon residing at Guildford, two apprentices, who will be treated as one of the family." The Hibernian companion to this would most fitly be the Dublin editor's statement, in reference to a newly-invented laundry machine, that by its use every man would probably become his own washerwoman. From washerwomen to general servants is but a step, and so from the *Times* of five-and-twenty years back we extract a model specimen, supposed to emanate from that rarest of *raræ aves*, a pattern domestic:—

DO YOU WANT A SERVANT? Necessity prompts the question. The advertiser OFFERS his SERVICES to any lady or gentleman, company, or others, in want of a truly faithful, confidential servant in any capacity not menial, where a practical knowledge of human nature in various parts of the world would be available. Could undertake any affair of small or great importance, where talent, inviolable secrecy, or good address would be necessary. Has moved in the best and worst societies without being contaminated by either; has never been a servant, begs to recommend himself as one who knows his place; is moral, temperate, middle-aged; no objection to any part of the world. Could advise any capitalist wishing to increase his income and have the control of his own money. Could act as secretary or valet to any lady or gentleman. Can give advice or hold his tongue, sing, dance, play, fence, box, preach a sermon, tell a story, be grave or gay, ridiculous or sublime, or do anything from the curling of a peruke to the storming of a citadel—but never to excel his master. Address ——.

Differing considerably, and yet much in the same line, is the following, which is amusing from the amount of confidence the writer possesses in his own powers, and the small value he sets upon the attainments of those who possess that most valuable qualification of all—property. The offer never to be better than his patron is a condescension indeed from such a paragon:—

TO INDEPENDENT GENTLEMEN.—Wanted by a respectable, modest young man, who can produce a cubic yard of testimonials, a living without a master—that is, he wishes to become a companion to some gentleman, and be his factotum. He can ride, shoot, sing, fish (but never better than his patron without he is wanted), keep accounts, see that servants do their duty, do twenty other things, equally necessary in this life, and make it his whole duty to please and be pleased. Any one seriously wishing such a person, may address, post paid to Z., to be left at ——.

Advertisements from the other side—from employers—are also noticeable now and again, as this will show:—

BOARD AND RESIDENCE FOR WORK.—An old literary gentleman invites two widow ladies, about forty, to assist him in doing without servants, except a charwoman once a week. One lady must undertake entrées, soups, and jellies. Both must be strong and healthy, so that the work may be rather pleasant than irksome; two-thirds of it being for their own comfort, as no company is ever kept. A private sitting-room. Laundry free. All dining together at seven o'clock. References of mercantile exactness required.—Address A. B., —— stating age and full particulars of antecedent position, &c.

This old literary gentleman was wise in his generation, as his offer, though very plausible, meant nothing less than obtaining two servants without wages, and society as well.

Possibly, however, the fact of the ladies being widows was supposed, upon the principle of Tony Weller, to compensate for shortcomings in the way of salary. Other applications for a superior class of servants deserve attention, the following modest offer for a governess being a case in point:—

WANTED, in a gentleman's family, a young lady, as NURSERY GOVERNESS, to instruct two young ladies in French, music, and singing, with the usual branches of education, and to take the entire charge of their wardrobe. She must be of a social disposition and fond of children, and have the manners of a gentlewoman, as she will be treated as one of the family. Salary twelve guineas per annum. Address ——.

All for the small price of twelve guineas per annum, about half what a decent housemaid expects, and with less than half the liberty of a scullion. Yet this advertisement appeared in the *Times*, and is but the representative of others of the same kind, not one of which is supposed to betray meanness or poverty of spirit on the part of its originator. For twelve guineas a year, the poverty-stricken orphan or daughter of some once rich speculator is to teach French, music, singing, writing, arithmetic, geography, history, and other of the "usual branches of education," to two young ladies, who it is only fair to expect would be much more like the brassfounder's daughter who objected to Ruth Pinch than similar to the charge of Becky Sharp when she occupied a governess's position. In addition to the drudgery of teaching, there is the charge of the young ladies' wardrobe, which means an occupation of itself; and then comes—oh, worst of all!—the social disposition, by which is undoubtedly meant a capacity for doing whatever any other member of the family may object to do—for being the drudge of the drawing-room when the little tyrants of the nursery are abed and asleep. By the manners of a gentlewoman is understood a capacity for receiving studied insult without resentment, and by treatment as one of the family such care and comfort as would cause the cook to take her instant departure. And all this for twelve guineas per annum! This may be called an overdrawn picture, but that is what is said of most self-evident facts. And what father worthy of the name would die easily if he thought that his tenderly-nurtured daughters were likely to be grateful for the protection and the salary offered in the foregoing specimen advertisement? Yet many a young girl has suddenly found herself divested of every luxury, and subject to the tender mercies of those who regard a nursery governess as "one of the family." There is an old story in reference to the selection of governesses which is worth repeating here. A lady wrote to her son requesting him to find a teacher for his sisters, and enumerating a long list of qualifications, somewhat similar to those generally expected in a pretentious family. The son seems to have been wiser than his mother, for he replied stating that he had studied the requirements, and that when he found a young lady possessed of them all, he should endeavour to engage her, not as a governess for his sisters, but as a wife for himself. Marriage alters women, however, as the subjoined notice from an Irish paper proves to the most sceptical:—

RUN AWAY FROM PATRICK M'DALLAGH.—Whereas my wife Mrs Bridget M'Dallagh, is again walked away with herself, and left me with her four small children, and her poor old blind mother, and nobody else to look after house and home, and, I hear, has taken up with Tim Guigan, the lame fiddler—the same that was put in the stocks last Easter for stealing Barday Doody's gamecock.—This is to give notice, that I will not pay for bite or sup on her or his account to man or mortal, and that she had better never show the mark of her ten toes near my home again.

PATRICK M'DALLAGH.

N.B. Tim had better keep out of my sight.

Mrs Bridget seems to have been in the habit of straying from the path of virtue and her husband's home, which, if we are to believe Irish poets and orators, must have been very exceptional behaviour in the land of "virtue and Erin." As if to provide against similar emergency, a

Parisian puts forth an advertisement, the translation of which runs thus :—

A gentleman in his twenty-sixth year, tired of the dissipation of the great world, is forming a comfortable establishment in one of the least frequented quarters of the city. His domestics are a coachman, cook, three footmen and a chambermaid. He is in search of a young girl of good family to improve this honourable situation : she must be well educated, accomplished, and of an agreeable figure, and will be entertained in the quality of *demoiselle de compagnie.* She shall receive the utmost attention from the household, and be as well served in every respect as, or even better than, if she were its mistress.

As just now there is constant change of opinion as to what forms the best pavement for the streets with the greatest traffic, as the stones which seemed to be agreed on for ever are every day becoming more and more disliked, and as the main difference now is which is likely to prove the more profitable change, asphalt or wood, the following, from the *Times* of 1851, may not be uninteresting :—

WOOD PAVEMENT.—All poor and distressed cabriolet proprietors and others, wheresoever dispersed, are particularly requested to FORWARD to us immediately PROVED ACCOUNTS in writing of all ACCIDENTS to and DEATHS of HORSES, and Personal and other Casualties, in order that the several parishes may respectfully, in the first place be extra-judicially called on to repay all damages (at our offices), within one calendar month of our respective applications, or otherwise have proceedings taken against them respectively in the County Courts, or under superior jurisdictions, and be so judicially and speedily made to pay on account of entering into ex-parte contracts rendering life and limb and travelling generally unsafe and dangerous in the extreme, and so continuing the bad state of the wood pavement; for no contracts can be lawful and right unless impliedly perused and approved of on behalf of the public generally.

Cole and Scott, Solicitors, 12 Furnival's Inn and Notting Hill.

If the "London stones" become things of the past, they and their advocates will be revenged by the undoubted fact that whatever follows them will, after the novelty has worn off, be just as much abused as its predecessor, and most likely changed much more speedily. Deserving of attention, too, though on a totally different matter, is the following. It seems hard to believe that a London tradesman could believe he was likely to get his note back by informing a man what he must have already known; but such is the case. This must be what is known as "throwing good money after bad:"—

CORAL NECKLACE.—The gentleman who purchased a coral necklace in Bishopsgate-street, on Monday last received in change for a £20 note a FIVE-POUND NOTE too much. He is requested to RETURN it.

Vulgar people would say that the buyer of the coral necklace changed his name to Walker after this. But changes of name are not legal unless duly advertised. Speaking of advertising changes of name, a title by which those lodging-house pests, bugs, are now often known, that of Norfolk Howards, is derived from an advertisement in which one Ephraim Bug avowed his intention of being for the future known as Norfolk Howard. We have never seen this announcement, but have noticed many others, the appended being a specimen, though of a much less sensational kind than that we have just referred to:—

NOTICE.—I, the undersigned THOMAS HUGHES FORDE DAVIES, of Abercery, in the county of Cardigan, Esq., do hereby Give Notice, that I shall, on and after the 1st day of October, 1873, ASSUME the names THOMAS HUGHES FORDE HUGHES, instead of the names of Thomas Hughes Forde Davies, by which last-mentioned names I have hitherto been known and described. And I do hereby request and direct all persons whomsoever to address and describe me as Thomas Hughes Forde Hughes, and not otherwise. And I further Give Notice, that I have executed the necessary Deed Poll in that behalf, and cause the same to be enrolled in her Majesty's High Court of Chancery.—Dated this 29th day of September, 1873.
THOMAS HUGHES FORDE DAVIES.

There is a good deal in a name in the present day, and there are some names which for obvious reasons do not smell as sweet as roses, and therefore require changing. This observation does not, of course, refer to the change from Davies to Hughes, of which we know absolutely nothing, except that it appeared in the *Standard* of October 1873. As there seems little to choose between the two names, it is fair to assume that family reasons or property qualifications led to the alteration. In the interest of those good people who sincerely believe in appearances, we select our next example from the columns of the *Times*. Those, also, who are in the habit of asking what good there is in a University education will do well to ponder over these lines :—

ARTICLED ASSISTANT.—If the GENTLEMAN who called at Messrs —— and —— 29, Poultry, on Thursday the 20th February in answer to an advertisement in that day's *Times* for "An Articled Assistant" will CALL again at the office to which he was referred, and where he stated that he was a Cambridge man &c., no doubt satisfactory arrangements can be made, as appearance is the chief object.

Appearance is indeed the chief object of attention at the present day, and its influence goes much farther than people imagine, even at the very time they are subscribing to it. Not alone does it affect the positions of the drapers' young man, the shop-walker, and the modern *jeune premier*, the latter of whom may be an idiot so long as he is young, tall, slim, and good-looking, but it materially influences a higher class of society. Day after day we see men credited, by means of lying heads and faces, with the qualifications and abilities they do not possess ; and, on the other hand, we as frequently find the mildest and most benevolent of gentlemen regarded as desperate characters or hard-fisted old curmudgeons. No one will nowadays believe that a man who does not look very clever or very foolish can do anything in literature or the arts above the common run ; and the most frequent exclamation to be heard after a real celebrity has been seen is one of disappointment, so little will he bear comparison with the ideal. Appearances were never more deceptive, and never more believed in, than they are now.

Stories of advertising tombstones, some true, some apocryphal, are plentiful, and the best of those in which reliance can be placed is that about the Parisian grocer. It is well known that at the Père la Chaise Cemetery, near Paris, there stands, or stood, in a conspicuous position, a splendid monument to Pierre Cabochard, grocer, with a pathetic inscription, which closes thus :—

His inconsolable widow
dedicates this monument to his memory
and continues the same business at the
old stand, 187, Rue Mouffetard.

A gentleman who had noticed the inscription was led by curiosity to call at the address indicated. Having expressed his desire to see the widow Cabochard, he was immediately ushered into the presence of a fashionably-dressed and full-bearded man, who asked him what was the object of his visit. "I come to see the widow Cabochard." "Well, sir, here she is." "I beg your pardon, but I wish to see the lady in person." "Sir, I am the widow Cabochard." "I don't exactly understand you. I allude to the relict of the late Pierre Cabochard, whose monument I saw yesterday at the Père la Chaise." "I see, I see," was the smiling rejoinder. "Allow me to inform you that Pierre Cabochard is a myth, and therefore never had a wife. The tomb you admired cost me a good deal of money, and, although no one is buried there, it proves a first-rate advertisement, and I have had no cause to regret the expense. Now, sir, what can I sell you in the way of groceries?" The art of mingling mourning and money-making was still better illustrated in the following notice of a death in a Spanish paper :—

This morning our Saviour summoned away the jeweller, Siebald Illmaga, from his shop to another and a better world. The undersigned, his widow, will weep upon his tomb, as will also his two daughters, Hilda and Emma; the former of whom is married, and the latter is open to an offer. The funeral will take place to-morrow. —His disconsolate widow, Veronique Illmaga. P.S. This bereavement will not interrupt our employment which will be carried on as usual, only our place of business will be removed from No. 3, Tessi de Teinturiers to No. 4, Rue de Missionaire, as our grasping landlord has raised our rent.

Advertisements which now and again appear in the *Times* from people who seek employment or money are both curious and eccentric, and in none of them do the writers suffer at all from bashfulness or modest ideas of their own qualifications. In this, which is an appeal for a situation, the constructor describes himself as

A CHARACTER.—The noblemen and gentlemen of England are respectfully informed that the advertiser is a self-taught man—a "genius." He has travelled (chiefly on foot) through the United Kingdom of Great Britain and Ireland, in Holland, Germany, Switzerland, Belgium, France, and Italy. He has conducted a popular periodical, written a work of fiction in three vols., published a system of theology, composed a drama, studied Hamlet, been a political lecturer, a preacher, a village schoolmaster, a pawnbroker, a general shopkeeper; has been acquainted with more than one founder of a sect, and is now (he thanks Providence) in good health, spirits, and character, out of debt, and living in charity with all mankind. During the remainder of his life he thinks he would feel quite at home as secretary, amanuensis, or companion to any nobleman or gentleman who will engage a once erratic but now sedate being, whose chief delight consists in seeing and making those around him cheerful and happy. Address A. Z., at Mr. ——'s, —— Street, Regent's Park.

As a rule, when people break out in this style they are much more in want of the money than the work, although they cloak their actual desires under the guise of applications for situations or employment. There are not a few, however, who come boldly to the point, as the following, also from the *Times*, shows:—

A MAN OF RANK, holding a distinguished public office, moving in the highest society, and with brilliant prospects—has been suddenly called upon to pay some thousands of pounds, owing to the default of a friend for whom he had become guarantee. As his present means are unable to meet this demand, and he can offer no adequate security for a loan, the consequence must be ruin to himself and his family, unless some individual of wealth and munificence will step forward to avert this calamity, by applying £4000 to his rescue. For this he frankly avows that he can, in present circumstances, offer no other return than his gratitude. A personal interview, however painful, will be readily granted, in the confidence that the generosity of his benefactor will be the best guarantee for his delicate observance of secrecy. He hopes his distressing condition will protect him from the prying of heartless curiosity, and to prevent the approaches of money-holders, he begs to repeat that he can give no security. Address to "Anxious," General Post Office, London.

For the benefit of those who are curious about men of rank, and in the interests of those who may like to speculate as to who this holder of a distinguished public office may have been, we will state that the advertisement appeared just thirty years ago. There were then, and have been since, many men in office who wanted four thousand pounds; in fact it would be a hard matter to find a man anywhere to whom that amount—or, for the matter of that, a good bit less—would not be agreeable. That these advertisements were not altogether fruitless, this, from the *Times* of February 1851, would seem to show:—

TRURO.—The generous friend who transmitted from this place under cover to the Secretary, G.P.O. an ENVELOPE containing a SUM of MONEY is gratefully informed that the individual for whom it was intended was relieved by it to an extent of which he can form no conception, and is earnestly entreated COMMUNICATE, if not his name, at least an address to which a letter may be sent. W. H.

Men reduced in circumstances seem to have less and less chance as the world gets older. There would not be much good got out of an advertisement for money nowadays, whatever the original position of advertiser, unless he could promise something in return. His promise might be quite impossible of performance, but still it would be something; and if we are to judge by most of the swindling advertisements which have succeeded in taking in thousands of people, the more improbable the undertaking the more probable the success. Here is another man of high rank, of later date, who only asks for employment. A good pinch of salt must, we think, be taken with the concluding sentence of the application :—

IT WOULD BE A NOBLE ACT OF HUMANITY if any generous and kind-hearted individual would procure or grant EMPLOYMENT to a suffering individual, in whose behalf this appeal is made. He is of high rank, education, and manners, and in every point of view fit to fill any situation. He is without influential friends, and from complicated frauds and misfortunes, is unable to continue the education of eight lovely children. He seeks nothing for himself, except to be so placed, giving to the hands of his kind benefactor all he receives for his children's present and future support. This will save him from a broken heart. Any situation that will enable him to effect this object will be received with heartfelt gratitude, and filled with honour, assiduity, and fidelity. Most respectable reference, &c. N.B. No pecuniary assistance can be received. Address ——.

A man of "high rank, education, and manners," without influential friends, is certainly an anomaly in this country; and the "eight lovely children" forcibly remind us of the large families which begging-letter impostors and cadgers generally have constantly at home, hungering not so much for education as for bread and meat. The mention of high birth reminds us of the many advertisements which have in the course of years appeared from people who, not satisfied with being rich, seek to be fashionable, and who offer free quarters and other advantages to any one possessed of the *entrée* to Society, and yet not over-gifted with the more solid blessings of this world. Of course these generally appear in the most fashionable papers, and the specimen which follows is taken from the *Morning Post* of half-a-dozen years ago. With the exception that it mentions foreign towns, it is almost identical with others which have appeared in reference to our own most exclusive circles :—

SEASONS at SPA and BRUSSELS.—A Lady and Gentleman, well connected, offer to RECEIVE as their GUEST, free of all expense, a lady or a gentleman of family, who, in sole return for the freedom of home, could give the entrée into Belgian society. Spa in the summer, Brussels in the winter. A small establishment. A good cook. The highest references.—Address P. R., Poste Restante, Brussels.

Such notices as this go far to prove the truth of the saying that there are blessings beyond price, that is, of course, always supposing the advertisements were unsuccessful. We shall never in future meet any loud vulgar person in Society—provided we are ever admitted within the sacred portal—without suspecting him of having crawled in by means of bribery. Yet our suspicions may alight upon the very leaders of *ton;* for, so far, the most vulgar men we ever met—among gentlemen—were a horse-racing earl and a coach-driving viscount, and they could have been backed against any four men in that army, the peculiarities of which, while in the Low Countries, will be found recorded in "Tristram Shandy." Among other advertisements in the columns of the leading journal, worthy of notice in this chapter, are those singular effusions which appear at intervals, especially during any period of political effervescence, and which consist of mad schemes, the offspring of enthusiastic patriots and headlong regenerators of the nation, The following is a fair specimen of these :—

TO THE MINISTERS OF STATE, NOBILITY, AND COMMUNITY AT LARGE.—A Remedy for the distresses of England. Every considerate person admits the present condition of society to be perfectly anomalous. A remedy has at length been discovered —a remedy which would effectually arrest the progress of pauperism, confer incalculable benefits upon the industrial community, and diffuse joy and gladness throughout the length and breadth of the land, making England (without exaggeration) the envy of surrounding nations, and the admiration of the world. The plan possesses the peculiar merit of being practicable, and easy of application, without in the slightest degree infringing the rights of property as by law established, or in any way disturbing the present relations of society. The advertiser will communicate his discovery either to the ministers of state, nobility, or those who may take an interest in the wellbeing of society, on condition of his receiving (if his plans are approved, and made available for the purposes contemplated) £100,000. "If the nation be saved, it is not to be saved by the ordinary operations of statesmanship."—Lord Ashley. Address ——.

In this chapter, the mysterious "personal" advertisements which years ago were so frequent and so extraordinary—but which now are rarely noticeable except when devoted to the purposes of puffing tradesmen, or when they are more than ordinarily stupid—must naturally receive attention. Now and again a strange announcement attracts a little curiosity in the present day; but for good specimens of the dark and mysterious advertisement we must go back twenty years, and by so doing we shall be enabled at the same time to give a very good reason why people who correspond through the public papers in cipher or otherwise are careful not to attract particular attention. This reason will exhibit itself by means of two cryptographic specimens selected, which appeared in the *Times*, and were the means of showing that writers of secret signs and passwords must be clever indeed if they would evade the lynx eyes of those who are ever ready for a little mild excitement, and whose hobby it is to solve riddles and discover puzzles. Certainly there must be more pleasure in finding out the meaning of a secret "personal" than in answering the double acrostic charades with which the weekly papers swarm, and which must occupy the attention of thousands, if the quantities of correct and erroneous replies that are received at the various offices may be accepted as evidence. In the early part of 1853 a mad-looking advertisement appeared in the *Times*, which ran thus:—

CENERENTOLA.—N bnxm yt ywd nk dtz hfs wjfi ymnx fsi fr rtxy fscntzx yt mjfw ymf esi bmjs dtz wjyzws, f imtb qtsldtz wjrfns, mjwj It bwnyf f kjb qnsjx jfwqnsl uqjfxj : N mfaj gjjs ajwd kfw kwtr mfund xnshy dtz bjsy fbfd.

Which being interpreted, reads : "Cenerentola, I wish to try if you can read this, and am most anxious to hear the end, when you return, and how long you remain here. Do write a few lines, darling, please. I have been very far from happy since you went away." This appeared in February 2, and some difficulty appears to be in the way, for it is not till the 11th that we find another, which is evidently not in reply, and equally evidently not satisfactory. It says :—

CENERENTOLA.—Zsynq rd mjfwy nx xnhp mfaj ywnji yt kwfrj fs jcugfifynts kwt dtz gzy hfasty. Xnqjshj nx xfs jxy nk ymf ywzj hfzxj nx sty xzx jhyji ; nk ny nx fgg xytwnjx bngg gj xnkyji yt ymj gtyytr. It dtz wjrjrgjw tzw htzxns'x knwxy uwtutxnynts : ymnsp tk ny.

As this system simply consisted in commencing the alphabet with the letter *f* and continuing in regular sequence, the explanation of the last specimen is almost obvious; but so that there should be no difficulty or doubt about it, and so that the intriguers should know they were discovered, some literary lockpicker inserted on the 15th, in the usual personal column of the *Times*, a full translation, correcting all errors of the printer, and concluding with a notice in the secret language, which must have frightened its originators. The explanatory advertisement runs thus :—

CENERENTOLA, until my heart is sick have I tried to frame an explanation for you, but cannot. Silence is safest, if the true cause is not suspected : if it is all stories will be sifted to the bottom, Do you remember our cousin's first proposition? Think of it.—N pstb Dtz.

The cryptogram at the end is a warning, for, subjected to the test, we find it is neither more nor less than "I know you." This seems to have effectually silenced the originals; but the marplots were probably still at work, for on the 19th of February another notification appears, this time in plain English, and running thus :—

CENERENTOLA, what nonsense! Your cousin's proposition is absurd. I have given an explanation—the true one—which has perfectly satisfied both parties—a thing which silence never could have effected. So no more such absurdity.

How miserably small the inventor of this cipher must have felt, and how ridiculous those most interested must have appeared to each other, we leave to the imaginations of those readers who have suddenly been stopped in any grand flight to find themselves as idiotic as they had before considered themselves ingenious. Doubtless the Cenerentolans will not want for sympathisers even amongst those who affect most to ridicule them. Much about the same time as the instance we have given, and while the rage for secret advertising was in its meridian, one of the most remarkable samples of the kind appeared—remarkable as much for its want of reason as for anything else. On February 20, 1852, we are told by the *Quarterly*, there appeared in the *Times* the following mysterious lines :—

TIG tjohw it tig jfhiirvola og tig psgvw.
F. D. N.

This was a little above the ordinary hand, and many attempts at deciphering it failed. At last the following explanation was published in the *Quarterly*. If we take the first word of the sentence, Tig, and place under its second letter, i, the one which alphabetically precedes it, and treat the next letters in a similar manner, we shall have the following combination :—

```
T i g
  h f
    e
```

Reading the first letters obliquely, we have the article "The ;" if we treat the second word in the same manner, the following will be the result :—

```
T j o h w
  i n g v
    m f u
      e t
        s
```

which read in the same slanting way produces the word *Times.* So far our authority is correct, and here we leave him. The following participle and article are of course evident, and then comes the principal word of the sentence, which the transcriber makes to be Jefferies, which it is doubtless intended to be; but in his hurry the inventor or solver has made a mistake, as is shown upon an attempt at the same conclusion :—

```
J f h i i r v o l a
  e g h h q u n k z
    f g g p t m j y
      f f o s l i x
        e n r k h w
          m q j g v
            p i f u
              h e t
                d s
                  r
```

This gives the word as Jeffemphdr, an expression which, if it can be expressed at all, is very dissimilar from that we expected, after being told that the sentence read—

The Times is the Jefferies of the press.

We have taken this trouble and used this space in the endeavour to see if the letters would make "Jefferies," because we have always had a suspicion that the first explainer was also the originator. The advertisement, without being rendered into English, could not have gratified the malice or satisfied the spite of its writer; and as, if any one else had discovered the key and made the attempt, he would have remarked the error, it is but fair to assume that "F. D. N.," whoever else he may have been, was the individual whom a writer in the *Quarterly Review*, a couple of years or so afterwards, described as the friend who "was curious and intelligent enough to extract the plain English out of it," and whose design we commenced with. Was he an author who had been slated in the *Times?* However, as the advertiser evidently meant Jeffreys, however he may have fancied to spell it, the explanation may be taken as all right.* This and the preceding advertisement must have set people thinking that it was hardly safe to trust to secrets in the papers, no matter how carefully disguised; but the crowning blow to cryptographic communication was given by means of the "Flo" intrigue, which created some little sensation, and was the cause of a good deal of amusement at the close of the year 1853 and the beginning of 1854. On November 29 of the first-named year the following was first seen in the *Times*:—

FLO.—1821 82374 09 30 84541. 844532 18140650. 8 54584 2401 322650 526 08555 94400 021 12 30 84541 22 05114650. 726 85400 021.

It may be as well to premise that the idea of the "Flo" system was to make an alphabet with the nine numerals and the cipher, and the correspondents evidently prided themselves, poor innocents, on having arranged the letters arbitrarily and not in regular order, and fixed the tell-tale capital I when standing alone at 8:—

0	1	2	3	4	5	6	7	8	9
y	u	o	i	e	a	d	k	h	f
s	t	n	m	r	l	q	g	w	p
x							c	b	
								v	

So the communication read: "Flo, thou voice of my

---

* Our information of this advertisement, and the clue to its explanation, was, as already stated, obtained from an article in the *Quarterly Review*. On reference to the *Times* to discover whether the Jefferies portion was right or not, we could not for a long time find the particular notice we were in search of. At last, after the above was written, under date February 10, it was found; and then we saw that the word was "Jfhiiwola," which subjected to the process as above, will give the required name. We have preferred to explain this in full, as the *Quarterly* is undoubtedly entitled to the merit of deciphering the puzzle, if not to anything else; and any alteration or correction of ours would have detracted from such merit, which is original, and without which the quaint libel might still have remained in obscurity. Besides, it shows how a small printer's error may spoil the calculations of a week, in matters like this.

heart! Berlin, Thursday. I leave next Monday, and shall press you to my heart on Saturday. God bless you." How they communicated for the next month does not appear, but judging by the quotation just given, it is to be supposed personally, and that another separation occurred soon after, for on December 21 there is this:—

FLO.—1821 82374 29 30 84541 8 53 02 522450. 8 3300 021 3244 1852 4844. 8 5227 51 0214 9371144 48440 23781. 8 0426 021 52 326352 08585 12 8459 42116 021 88354 505449 59144 632244. 31 8355 7449 021 8543 526 021 3101 95270 1851 31 5430 544 42126 021. 726 85400 021.

Which, errors included, reads: "Flo, thou voice of my heart, I am so lonely. I miss you more than ever. I look at your picture every night. I send you an Indian shawl to wrap roud you while asleep after dinner. It will keep you warm, and you must fancy that m/ arms are round you. God bless you." Two days afterwards the next appears, though the translation hardly gives a substantial reason for the repetition:—

FLO.—184 5501 850 84227 8 449451 31. 1821 82374 29 30 84541 8 53 02 522450. 8 3300 021 3244 1852 4844. 8 5227 51 0214 9371144 48140 23781. 8 0426 021 52 326352 08585 12 8459 42126 021 88354 505449 59144 63224 31 8355 7449 021 8543 526 021 3101 95270 1851 30 5430 544 42126 021. 726 85400 021. 828 8 62 5284 021.

This makes: "Flo, the last was wrong, I repeat it. Thou voice of my heart, I am so lonely. I miss you more than ever. I look at your picture evwry night. I send you an Indian shawl to wrap round you while asleep after dinnr. It will keep you warm, and you must fancy my arms are round you. God bless you. How I do love you!" It will be hard to discover, if the last was wrong, how this can be right, as for each error he corrects he makes another. Then we go on to the new year, and on January 2 recommence with the following:—

FLO.—30 282 5284 853 85990 57532 31 30 5374 5857327 9423 5 856 64453. 021 544 30 5334 12 7228 1851 18444 305 785274 29 044327 021 12 8454 9423 021 12 62 183270 12 422178. 8 08555 140 526 044 021 0222 84314 12 34 50 29142 50 021 752 726 85400 021 1821 82174 29 30 84541.

Difficulties seem to have been removed by this time, for when the magic of the key has been tried upon it the advertisement just quoted says this: "Flo, my own love, I am happy again; it is like awakening from a bad dream. You are, my li*m*e [? life], to know that there is a chance of seeing you, to hear from you, to do things to enough [there is an evident bungle here]. I shall try and see you soon. Write to me as often as you can. God bless you, thou vo*u*ce of my heart!" The wise men who had been content to understand this so far, now thought it time that these turtle-doves should know they were not so wise as they supposed, and that their cipher was being read regularly. So on January 6 the *Times* contained the following:—

FLO.—1821 82374 29 39 84541. 828 8 62 5284 021. 828 544 021 08555 021 84 5536 19 1830 094 327. 8 752 044 021 8557327 8318 0214 6545327 8851 8 82156 7384 12 84 8318 021. 185270 924 0314 5501 541144 8 9454 2218327 811 0495 451322 9423 021 021 544 30 82456 30 5394 30 8294. 1821 3244 1852 5394 95448455 726 85400 021.

And this when read must have caused some feeling of consternation, as it was an evident burlesque of the real correspondent's style: "Flo, thou voice of my heart! How I do love you! How are you? Shall you be laid up this spring? I can see you walking with your darling. What would I give to be with, you! Thanks for your last letter. I fear nothing but separation from you. You are my world, my life, my hope. Thou more than life, farewell! God bless you!" The natural effect of this was to cause an alarm to be given, and so on the following day the following was inserted in the famous private column:—

FLO.—8 9454 6454401 214 739 844 30 6307284446. 84314 51 2274 12 0214 943426 "326352 08585." 9. 2. 8177327853. 81770.

Which drops the curtain upon "Flo" and her lover, who is more than likely not to have been her husband—and this without affecting the question as to her being married. It is translated in these words: "Flo.—I fear, dearest, our cipher is discovered. Write at once to your friend, "Indian Shawl," P. O., Buckingham, Bucks." So much for secret correspondences, which are not often to be seen nowadays, though when any one is found foolish enough to confide in the press under these circumstances, the comic papers almost invariably make capital out of the communications, and give to their less acute readers full information. Here is one we fell across the other day in the *Telegraph*. We must admit to a decided ignorance as to what it means, but perhaps the reader, profiting by the foregoing, will be able to decipher it:—

KANGAROO revived by bones, though nearly choked by a piece of one after swallowing five hard biscuits. Troubled. Four cat two six camel five two one eight pig one boar in every way. Four nine leopard one four elephant three four seven boar. Faithful until death.

This looks like an attempt to set the cryptographists on a wrong scent, and probably means nothing. If it really is a genuine communication, its scope must be extremely limited. Many of the mysterious advertisements which appear in the usual style are very noticeable, though of late the art has fallen a prey to the vendors of quack medicines and cheap books, and the managers of some theatres and music-halls. What has been characterised, and with every probability of truth, as the most ghastly advertisement that ever appeared in a public journal is the following, which is taken from the *Times* of the year 1845. It certainly is a most frightful paragraph:—

TO THE PARTY WHO POSTS HIS LETTERS IN PRINCE'S STREET, LEICESTER SQUARE. — Your family is now in a state of excitement unbearable. Your attention is called to an advertisement in Wednesday's Morning Advertiser, headed "A body found drowned at Deptford." After your avowal to your friend as to what you might do, he has been to see the decomposed remains, accompanied by others. The features are gone; but there are marks on the arm; so that unless they hear from you to-day, it will satisfy them that the remains are those of their misguided relative, and steps will be directly taken to place them in the family vault, as they cannot bear the idea of a pauper's funeral.

The most horrible subject has, however, a ludicrous side, and the idea of the decomposed remains objecting to parochial interference is as dreadfully funny as the matter generally is dreadfully shocking. In another notice, five years later, there is, as it were, a plaintive moan, the cry of a weak and distressed woman, who has no "strong mind" to enable her to bear up against infidelity and loss. Listen to it:—

THE one-winged Dove must die unless the Crane returns to be a shield against her enemies.

Far different is the next, which is a couple of years later, and which displays as much strength of purpose and self-dependence as its forerunner betrays weakness:—

IT is enough; one man alone upon earth have I found noble. Away from me for ever! Cold heart and mean spirit, you have lost what millions—empires—could not have bought, but which a single word truthfully and nobly spoken might have made your own to all eternity. Yet are you forgiven: depart in peace: I rest in my Redeemer.

The reader can imagine the flashing eyes and indignant face of a proud and wronged woman, as this is read; and it might well be taken as the text for a whole volume of a modern novel. The next which we select is still from the *Times*, and appeared several days in succession in February 1853. It forms a good companion to that which precedes it:

TO M. L. L.—M. L. L., you have chosen your own lot: may it be a happy one! and if it be so I would not have you think of the desolate heart you leave behind; but oh! my child, if sorrow should ever overtake you, if you should find, when too late, that you have been leaning on a broken reed; then, my Maria, come back to her whose heart has ever cherished you; she will always be ready to receive you.

Maybe M. L. L. has proved herself devoid of gratitude, and left a kind home to follow the fortunes of some adventurer. But the good heart of the advertiser does not turn sour, nor does she give vent to repining; and so even in advertisements do we see the finest as well as the worst sides of human nature. In the same paper that contained the address just given we stumbled across one of the most laconic notices ever seen. It says—

IF H. R. will Return, I will forgive him.
E. R.

This is evidently from a relenting parent, whose sternness has been subdued by the continued absence of his prodigal. Most likely the latter returned, and went away again as soon as "the guv'nor" showed signs of resuming sway. And so on through one of those wretched dramas with which all people must be acquainted, in which the principal characters are a broken-hearted mother, a worn-out and prematurely old father, and an utterly demoralised, drunken, and perhaps dishonest son, who is most likely a brutal husband as well. Of quite another kind is this, which is also from the *Times*:—

TO EQUATOR.—Fortuna audaces juvat. Vincit omnia veritas.—
E. W.

As we have before remarked, the newspapers of to-day give us no such specimens of secret and mysterious advertising as those we have unearthed, although the opportunities are far more numerous than—and we presume the occasions quite as frequent as—they were twenty years ago, for every daily paper, and a good many of the weeklies, now keep special columns for the display of private announcements. Quite unique, however, in its way is one which appeared in *Lloyd's* half-a-dozen years ago. It says that

HARRIET AND HARRY COMPTON

ARE well.—124, Stamford-street, Lambeth.

The ignorance may be crass, but we are bound to confess that even now we are not aware of the claims upon publicity of Mr and Mrs Compton. The information is given in style worthy of a royal bulletin, and doubtless it much interested all whom it may have concerned. A very faint attempt at cryptography is made in an advertisement which appeared comparatively recently in one of the penny papers, the writer of which must have had great faith in the dulness of the British public if he thought that backward writing would not be at once detected. This is it:—

LUCKY 6d. and 4d.!!—Came back by train a few minutes after meeting you that forenoon, the only real reason for my coming. Always the same feeling for you as expressed. Od etirw ecno ot pihs ot yas uoy evah nees siht. Quite efas Rolias. Will sometimes advertise.

The next is a specimen of the present day, and is from the *Times*. Want of logical consequence is its chief characteristic:—

CANNOT mistake the decision of continued exceeding courtesy. Awaited, but could not identify. Forgive, dear, if I have been too superstitious. 'Tis the first fault, though twice repeated, and you still hold the lash.

Readers may possibly remember two rather singular advertisements which appeared in the *Telegraph* quite recently, and were full of gratitude to the firm which had unwittingly led to a pleasant if questionable acquaintance between two persons. After this luncheon-baskets will probably be carried by all gentlemen anxious for adventure—that is, when they travel on lines the authorities of which graciously permit their caterers to supply them. Here is the first:—

THE lady who travelled from Bedford to London by Midland train on the night of the 4th inst., can now MEET the GENTLEMAN who shared with her the contents of his railway luncheon basket. She enjoys the recollection of that pleasant meal, and would like to know if he is going on another journey. Will keep any appointment made at the Criterion in Piccadilly.—Answer to A.

The application seems to have had the desired effect, for a day or two afterwards this was published:—

A. will meet you at the Criterion, on Wednesday, at three. Am going on another journey shortly, and will provide luncheon-basket.—F. M.

Any one who has travelled a distance by Midland or any other of the lines supplied with refreshments by Spiers & Pond, must have noted what a great boon to the traveller is the well-stocked basket, which can be taken in full at one station and delivered out wholly or partially empty, according as appetite serves, at another. Yet the luncheon-basket is a very small item in the revolutionisers' total. Those who have suffered under the old system of railway refreshments, will admit that Spiers & Pond fully deserve whatever credit has been given them for their efforts in the public interest. Ten years ago no man in his senses would have dreamt of applying for food or drink at a railway buffet while he could go elsewhere; now Spiers & Pond daily serve thousands who desert the old familiar taverns and crowd the bars at the various City stations. Among the many great feats in the way of providing for the hungry and the thirsty performed by this firm is one which has claims for particular notice, as it is told in an official report of a Wimbledon meeting. For the camping-time the following is the record: Of bread there were eaten 25,000 lbs.; of butter 3 tons; of cheese 1 ton; of bacon 11 cwt.; of hams 3 tons; of eggs 23,350; of rolls 52,677; of flour 36 sacks; of tea 1967 lbs.; and of coffee 2240 lbs.; 15 tons weight of meat were eaten, and 1446 fowls, with 626 ducklings, and 304 goslings. In the way of fish, the consumption of salmon reached 6200 lbs., with 1667 soles, 400 turbot, 80 brill, and 2330 lobsters. Vegetables were devoured to the amount of 12 tons, to which must be added 40,000 lettuces and 500 quarts of shelled peas. In fancy pastry 5000 pieces were made, with 1120 lbs. of biscuits, and 2460 quarts of cream and water ice. Add to these 720 baskets of strawberries, 75 lbs. of grapes, 400 pine-apples, 287 tongues, 10,800 bottles of aerated waters,

896 plus 522 gallons of wine, 130 dozen and 312 gallons of spirits, 348 hogsheads of beer, 275 lbs. of tobacco, 300 boxes of cigars, 67 gallons of salad oil, 1½ hogshead of vinegar, 150 lbs. of mustard, 6000 gallons of claret cup, 13 cases of lemons, 84 tons of ice brought direct from the ship's side from Norway, 33 gallons of various sauces, 120 gallons of pickles, 25,000 sandwiches, 24 tons of sugar, 30 cwt. of currants, and 25,000 lbs. of "Volunteer" plumcake. In addition to these, large quantities of wines, spirits, &c., were supplied to sutlers, messmen, and volunteers. On subsequent occasions, when, for reasons best known to themselves, the Rifle Association has provided its own commissariat, it has been discovered that the efforts of Spiers & Pond were by no means overpraised at the time, and that the laudatory notices received by the men who came from Australia to teach the mother country a profitable lesson were well deserved. Spiers & Pond have, it is true, met ample recognition from the press; yet now and again those gentlemen who consider it the whole duty of a journalist to sneer at everybody and everything have had their usual fling, and have written about pretentious eating-house keepers, forgetful of the fact that a dozen years or so ago they were crying their eyes out because the weary traveller in Great Britain could nowhere find the accommodation he was so anxious to pay for. We have been careful not to stray into the opposite extreme, though a long course of railway journeying under the old *régime* of mouldy pork-pies and stale Banbury cakes has made us feel very well disposed to a firm whose name has already passed into a proverb.

Some little interest was exhibited in the annexed, which appeared in the *Times* a few weeks back, and, according to the side espoused, looks like just indignation or brutal intolerance :—

SHOULD this meet the eye of the lady who got into the 12.30 train at New Cross Station on Friday, May 15, with two boys, one of whom was evidently just recovering from an illness, she may be pleased to learn that three of the four young ladies who were in the carriage are very ill with the measles, and the health of the fourth is far from what her relations could desire.

It has been quite the fashion to say how wrong it was of the lady with the sick boys to get into a train and spread infection; and nobody seems to have thought that the poor lads wanted change of air—had perhaps been ordered it. As no special provision is made for the travelling sick—or for the matter of that, for the travelling healthy—the fault, if fault there be, lies not with the mother, who was anxious for the recovery of her children, but with the railway authorities. Judging from the tone of the advertisement, we should think that the advertiser would have resented any interference had his or her young ladies been travelling as invalids, instead of being in that state of health which is most subject to the attacks of disease. The case is hard, argued from either side, but it seems very unfair to cast the blame all one way.

The last example we shall give of this kind of advertising shows that extended space is used for "personals," without any extension of interest, the following being but a mild kind of raving on the part of a weak-minded man after an obstinate woman. It appeared early during the present year (1874) in the *Telegraph*:—

MARY ANN C.—Do return home. You labour under an illusion. What you wish to accuse me with does not exist. This I solemnly declare. I have at last a good position, but am so wretched that I cannot attend to my duties properly. Many happier returns of the 1st. God's blessing be with thee, and that He may tend thy heart to believe me in truth. Put six years of love and happiness against your accusation, and you must feel that you are wrong. Oh, you are very, very wrong. Do write and give me an appointment, so that happiness may be re-established. You must be very unhappy, but for God's sake do not be so strong-minded. My love and devotion are unaltered. For your own peace, my sweet, pretty, good wife, come back. When death parts it is sad enough, but to part while living, and without true cause, creates and leaves wretchedness to both. Come back to your unhappy but true-loving husband.

These last extracts are quite sufficient to show the style which now obtains in this class of advertisements, and to prove that what a score of years ago promised to be a never-ending source of amusement has become sadly deficient of its original properties.

Familiar to many people, among curious announcements, will be the following, which is one of many similar that have from time to time appeared in the leading journal :—

THE CHANCELLOR of the EXCHEQUER acknowledges the receipt of the first halves of two £10 notes, conscience-money, for unpaid Income-Tax.

The man who sends conscience-money for income-tax must have been virtuous indeed, if the evasion of that impost has been through life his worst sin. There are many otherwise estimable persons whose greatest pride it is that they have never paid income-tax unless compelled. Yet these men have in ordinary matters the greatest abhorrence of anything mean or paltry, and their general conduct might be safely contrasted with that of the bestowers of conscience-money. So, after all, there is something more than a joke in the humourist's idea of a grand new patriotic song called "Never pay your taxes till you're summoned, my boys!"

Those who wear artificial teeth must have been now and again indescribably shocked by advertisements like the following, which, scarce a short time back, are getting more and more frequent, so that what at first appeared a revolting riddle to the many, may have now developed into a lucrative pursuit for the few. Is it right to suppose that new sets of teeth are made up from second-hand materials? If so, how horrible!

WANTED to PURCHASE some OLD ARTIFICIAL TEETH. Persons having the above to sell can apply, with the teeth, or, if forwarded by post their value will be sent per return.—Mr ——.

Theatrical advertisements are, as has been remarked, often very funny, and whether from ignorance on the part of the writers, or the prevalence of technology, the columns of the *Era* absolutely teem with startling notices, which when coupled with the really remarkable as well as "original" correspondence, and the provincial critiques, make the chief theatrical organ one of the most genuine among comic papers, and this is none the less so because the *Era's* comicality is unintentional. A fair specimen of the general style is given in an advertisement appearing in March 1874, and if our reproducing it will be of any use to Messrs Gonza & Volta, they are quite welcome. In fact it would be sad to think that such an effort should go unrewarded :—

Nil Admirari.

GONZA and VOLTA!!!
GONZA and VOLTA!!!
GONZA and VOLTA!!!

The Modern Hercules and Achilles. The Goliathan Gymnasts. The Champions of Olympia Resuscitated. The greatest Athletes since the Christian Era.

M. DE GONZA, the famous Mexican Athlete of the Golden Wing and Olympic Club; also of Crystal Palace, Cirques Napoleon and de l'Imperatrice celebrity, and late Proprietor of Gonza's Transatlantic Combination Company, has much pleasure in announcing that the Colossal Sensation he is about submitting to the World's criticism is in course of progression, and that he has secured the services of EDOUIN VOLTA, the grandest Aerial Bar Performer of the period, who will have the honour of making his First Appearance in England in conjunction with M. DE GONZA'S New Aerial Athletic Performance. M. DE GONZA, without desiring to eulogise, prognosticates that his coming achievement will introduce an astonishing epoch in gymnastics. In ancient days mythological conceptions were framed by senile philosophers for the wonder and delectation of the inhabitants of the world B.C., more particularly during the existence of Rome under the Empire, when the stupendous Colosseum lived in its glory, and where myriads witnessed the famous gladiatorial combats. In those mighty days of heroism, when the great pan-Hellenic festivals were held, every fourth year in Olympia, instituted by Iphitus, King of Elis, the ninth century B.C., when Athletic revels and Icarian games were as prevalent as cigar smoking in this generation, people were more prone to countenance the possible existence and marvellous exploits of the gods and goddesses.

Evanescent ages have flown by, and in the sentiments of millions there **now subsists** a certain amount of familiarity with the intrepid and **valiant deeds** of those illustrious mythological gods Hercules and **Achilles.** They have been quoted and spoken of so often that their fictitiousness is forgotten. They have ingratiated their fabulous selves **into the good** graces of mankind, and become entwined around their **minds like the** ivy around the gnarled and knotted oak; and, although **centuries have** passed away, this nurtured concatenation of deep-rooted **imaginations** have not proven altogether futile, for these legendary **and dauntless** heroes actually do exist in the persons of

GONZA and VOLTA,

The Cyclopean Athletes of the Age.

Anchorites, ascetics, persons of secluded and fastidious natures, **stoics, and** misanthropists, all will be metamorphosed into congenial **spirits, and** be reconciled to the world and its pleasures after witnessing **these** gigantillos and wonders of creation in the most surprising **and** surpassingly elegant gymnastic exhibition hitherto placed before **an** appreciative nation, the production of which due notice will be **given.** Meanwhile all communications are to be addressed to M. DE GONZA, ——.

Turning from such extremely professional exponents of art and literature, we are reminded of one who stands in quite an opposite position to that of the Cyclopean athletes, Dr Vellère, the champion and foremost representative of the "unacted and unread," of the theorists who would regenerate the drama with their own works, and, if they could only once be performed, would mark an epoch in the history of the stage. Doubtless they would. About five years ago the enthusiastic Doctor—who, being a foreigner, has a perfect right to regenerate the British drama, as well as the British Constitution—burst forth in the *Times*, and at once placed himself at the head of that glorious minority which, owing to the iniquitous "ring" formed by a clique of authors, managers, and critics, cannot get its plays, marvellously good as they are, produced; and thus not only they, but the great British public are sufferers under a system which Vellère & Co. will yet expose or perish in the attempt. The first advertisement of the regenerator appeared on October 2, 1869. It ran thus:—

TO the PATRONS of the LEGITIMATE DRAMA and to the PLAY-GOING PUBLIC in GENERAL.

Ladies and Gentlemen,—As a general outcry arose some considerable time ago that there was a great dearth of good, original English dramas, and as the recent so-called original productions of English dramatists have failed to stifle it—because they have either traduced English society or have been simply adaptations from the French respecting a state of society which cannot exist here, and in both cases have proved unpalatable to the English, and, therefore, unsuccessful—I, who am a writer in more than one language, resolved to produce a drama on purely English topics, and I was guided by the dictum of your immortal poet, Byron, that "Truth is stranger than fiction," because all fictitious situations prove less "sensational" (pardon me the vernacular), as produced by those dramatists, with all the powerful accessories and machinery of the stage, than the simplest police report from the daily papers. It took me more than a year of my half-holidays to write the drama "Stern Realities," and in about five months I wrote the play "Trust." Now, I have been trying for the last eighteen months to have one of these pieces accepted, but all my endeavours have been in vain. The excuse was, that I am not known (a circumstance which, by-the-by, happened once to Shakespeare also), and that it is far preferable to produce the works of authors already known to the public, even if their more recent efforts have proved a failure in more than one respect. It is now for the public of this great country to decide whether this arrangement between Managers of Theatres and a certain small clique of authors is a monopoly that is to go on for ever; or whether it is only a false and preconceived notion on the part of the former regarding the want of good taste for superior productions on the part of the public. Though I am a foreigner I consider myself as one of the public who has endeavoured to amuse his fellow-citizens, but to whom no opportunity has hitherto been afforded. However, as the author of a collection of songs, of which some are written in English, French, and German, or English and German, or simply in English poetry, and which volume is entitled "Honi soit qui mal y pense," and was collectively dedicated to the Queen, and accepted by her Majesty, containing dedications also, by special commission, to ladies of the highest titles, and to others equally exalted in attainments, I beg you to believe me, when I assure you, on the word of a gentleman, author, and schoolmaster, that the two pieces I have written will meet with your approbation. I appeal now to you, ladies and gentlemen, to assist me in bringing out one of the two pieces; and, in my humble opinion, the most effectual way, perhaps, in which this could be done, would be in addressing me a note, kindly informing me which of the two pieces, "Stern Realities" or "Trust," should in your opinion be performed first, and that you promise you will come to see either or both. Receiving thus from you a great quantity of letters, I shall, armed with such a phalanx of patronage, present myself as the bearer of the popular will to the Manager of one of the London Theatres, and—we shall see! A letter simply addressed thus, "Dr. Vellère, Harrow," will safely reach me. Trusting to hear from you at your earliest convenience, I remain, ladies and gentlemen, very faithfully yours,

E. R. W. VELLERE.

The English and Continental College,
Harrow, October 1st, 1869.

Before the attention directed to this novelty in literature had died away, another similar effusion appeared, and for about a twelvemonth the *Times* contained every three or four weeks a message of direful import from Dr Vellère on dramatic monopoly and its probable ultimate effect on dramatic literature and the stage generally, varied by requests similar to those given here. Iniquity was still triumphant, however, and the patrons of the legitimate must have been unwilling to interfere, for at the end of the year Dr Vellère was yet unacted. He is still busy writing plays, for he believes that success must come in the end; and if his literary ability be in any way proportioned to his pertinacity, the chief of the Elizabethan roll of dramatists has at last met a worthy rival. Happily there is a way out of the difficulty with which Dr Vellère and his friends are encompassed. Let them take a theatre, engage actors, and play each other's dramas in turn. If they can only agree as to the order of production, and the relative merits of the pieces, they are sure to succeed; for if our experience goes for anything, the unacted and unread are sufficiently numerous to support any house of moderate pretensions. But they mustn't all want to be put on the free list. That great distinction must be left for Dr Vellère and a chosen few—composed, say, of friendly critics, and managers distraught with the knowledge that priceless gems have been discarded, and that the new era has at last arrived.

CHAPTER XII.

SWINDLES AND HOAXES.

IT is of course only natural that as soon as advertising became general, that portion of the community which regards the other portion as its oyster, was not slow to discover the advantages which were soon to accrue in the way of increased facilities for publishing new dodges, or of giving extended scope to those which were old, but had so far attained only limited circulation. This has been so conclusively shown by specimens already given, and references made, that there is no necessity to discuss the question anew, and therefore we will at once plunge into the thick of those advertisements which have special qualifications for treatment different from that given to the milder classes of rogues and scoundrels. The first transaction which calls for attention is in connection with Queen Anne's farthings. No popular delusion has perhaps made more dupes than that relating to these coins. Innumerable people believe that there never were but three farthings of this description, two of which have found their way in due course to the British Museum, the third only being still abroad; and it is also believed that the Museum authorities would give a very large sum for the possession of the missing token. Now there are no less than six distinct varieties of Anne's farthings known to exist, and specimens of them are not at all rare. Some of them may be procured at the coin-dealers, for ten or twelve shillings; but there is one variety, struck in 1713, which is extremely rare, and would bring from £5 to £10.

There is also a small brass medal or counter of Queen Anne, about the size of a farthing, of which there are hundreds. A publican once procured one of these, and placed it in his window, ticketed as "*the* real farthing of Queen Anne." Credulous persons came from far and near to view this wonderful curiosity, and the owner turned his deception to good account.

Sometime about the first quarter of this century, a man in Ireland received twelve months' imprisonment for secreting a Queen Anne's farthing. He was shopman to a confectioner in Dublin, and having taken the farthing over the counter, he substituted a common one for it. Unfortunately for him, he told his master how he had obtained it, and offered it to him for sale. The master demanded the treasure as his property, the shopman refused to give it up, was brought into the Recorder's Court, and there received the above sentence. When rogues fall out, honest men know what they have lost. It is wrong to assume that because thieves quarrel, their natural enemies "get their own." At all events, experience has never taught us so, and the proverb, as generally read, is wrong.

Numerous are the instances of people having travelled from distant counties to London, in order to dispose in the best market of the supposed valuable farthing. The custodian of the medals in the British Museum used to be besieged by applicants from all parts of the country, offering Queen Anne's farthings and imitations of them for sale, and of course the dealers in coin even now receive a liberal share of the same annoyance. Whence the treacherous fable originally sprung has never been satisfactorily explained. It is certain that Anne's farthings never were very common, though of one variety, coined in 1714, not less than from 300 to 500 must have been put in circulation. But the others were mere patterns, and were never struck for currency: all of them were coins of great beauty, and for this reason, as well as on account of their being the only copper coins struck in the reign of Queen Anne, it is probable that they were soon hoarded and preserved as curiosities, thereby acquiring an imaginary value, which grew rapidly as soon as some sharp fellow saw how useful the figment might be made. But the immediate cause of the popular fallacy concerning the scarcity and great value may be found in the fact, that at the end of the last century a lady of Yorkshire having lost one of these coins, offered a large reward for it. Probably it was valuable to her as a souvenir of some departed friend; but the advertisement, and the comparative scarcity of these farthings, gradually led to the report that there was only one such token in circulation, and that the unique coin was of course of almost priceless value. Long before this, however, advertisements in reference to Anne's farthings had found their way into the papers. So far as we can discover, the first of these appeared in the *General Advertiser* of April 19, 1745, and ran as follows:—

WHEREAS about seven years ago an Advertisement was published in some of the Daily Papers offering a Reward for a Queen Anne's Farthing struct in the year 1714.

This is to inform the CURIOUS

That a Farthing of Queen Anne of that year of a very beautiful dye may be seen at the Bar of the Pensylvania Coffeehouse in Birchin Lane. The impression is no ways defaced but as entire as from the Mint.

This, probably, just at the time when a furor was in existence with regard to the farthings, must have given a fillip to the business at the Pennsylvania Coffee-house; and must have done a great deal to spread the belief that a Queen Anne's coin was much more desirable than the wonderful lamp of Eastern story, or the more modern but quite as powerful four-leaved shamrock. That in 1802 the fiction was still lively is shown by an advertisement which appeared in the February of that year. This was disguised so as to appear like an ordinary paragraph:—

The Queen Anne's farthing, advertised to be disposed of in Pall

Mall, proves to be an original. There were only *two* coined in that Queen's reign, and not *three* as has been erroneously stated. That which was sold by the sergeant from Chatham for £400, was purchased by a noble viscount, curious in his selection of coins, &c. Seven Hundred guineas was the price asked for the one advertised last week. Five hundred was offered for it and refused. The owner lives at Lynn, in Norfolk. The offer was made by the son of a baronet, who wants to complete his collection.

Attention and credulity were so excited by the above paragraph, and many others of the same tendency, that no one thought of doubting that a Queen Anne's farthing was worth more than a Jew's eye; nor was it till some time after that the whole was discovered to be a fabrication, intended either to impose upon the credulity of the public, or, what is more likely, to enhance the value of such a coin to the holder, who was quietly waiting to realise. Whether he did so or not does not appear, but it is more than likely that he did not allow his opportunity to slip, but hooked one of those unconsciously greedy people who are always falling victims to their own selfishness as much as to the sharpers, and who, as soon as they are deluded, look for sympathy and redress to those very laws they were prepared to outrage when anything was apparently to be got by so doing. The belief that Queen Anne's farthings are very valuable still obtains among the vulgar, notwithstanding the many times its absurdity has been exposed; and there is no particular reason for imagining that it will become at all exploded until some fresher but quite as illogical a fiction is ready to supply its place.

One of the most notorious swindlers of the early part of the present century was Joseph Ady, who used to profess that he knew "something to your advantage." As he did not deal in advertisements, perhaps he has no right here; but as about 1830 he was constantly being referred to in newspaper paragraphs, and was a feature of the time among sharpers, he is entitled to passing notice, if only as a newspaper celebrity. At the period we mention, "Ady was a decent-looking elderly man, a Quaker, with the external respectability attached to the condition of a housekeeper, and to all appearance considered himself as pursuing a perfectly legitimate course of life. His *métier* consisted in this. He was accustomed to examine, so far as the means were afforded him, lists of unclaimed dividends, estates or bequests waiting for the proper owners, and unclaimed property generally. Noting the names, he sent letters to individuals bearing the same appellatives, stating that, on their remitting to him his fee of a guinea, they would be informed of 'something to their advantage.' When any one complied, he duly sent a second letter, acquainting him that in such a list was a sum or an estate due to a person of his name, and on which he might have claims worthy of being investigated. It was undeniable that the information *might* prove to the advantage of Ady's correspondent. Between this *might be* and the unconditional promise of something to the advantage of the correspondent, lay the debatable ground on which it might be argued that Ady was practising a dishonest business. It was rather too narrow a margin for legal purposes; and so Joseph went on from year to year reaping the guineas of the unwary—seldom three months out of a police court and its reports—till his name became a byword; and still, out of the multitudes whom he addressed, finding a sufficient number of persons ignorant of his craft, and ready to be imposed upon—and these, still more strange to say, often belonging to the well-educated part of society."* In all the police cases we have come across, in which Ady was concerned, he seems to have considerably "sat upon" the magistrates, the "great unpaid" of the City being quite unable to hold their own with him, notwithstanding the disadvantage at which Joseph was placed.

The claims for precedence of the two most important

* Book of Days.

advertising swindles of the present day are so equally divided, that it is hard to say which has caused the greater amount of ruin among credulous persons who have invested their last few coins in the hope of the certain success, or which has returned most profit to the exchequers of its wily promoters. The two claimants are the Turf-Circular and the Home-Employment swindles, both of which have been allowed full play. We will give the "home-employment" arrangement preference of treatment, as it appeals to wider sympathies, the victims being mostly credulous only, and not selfishly and idiotically greedy for other folk's goods; and being, as well, mostly poor hard-working women, and not a few children. One of the most notorious of these advertisers flourished half-a-dozen years ago. He used to insert a small notice in the daily papers, informing those who had leisure that he could find ample remunerative employment for them, and directing applications to be made by letter at a given address, enclosing a stamped addressed envelope. Then the swindle commenced, the reply being as follows:—

GROVE HOUSE, TOTTENHAM ROAD.

ISLINGTON, LONDON, N.

In reply to your application as per my Notice (Leisure Time, *&c.*, *&c.*,) *I very respectfully inform you that it has now become impossible to describe my Advertisement on employing leisure time fully in the Newspaper in which the little abridged notice appeared, owing to the enormous charge demanded for inserting it, namely £2 16s. for each time it appears. So that in consequence I am compelled, reluctantly, to trouble my correspondents to forward their envelope for the purpose of an extended explanation, which I think cannot be clearer done than my forwarding in print, as under, a copy of the intended announcement, which after reading, and you deciding on sending for the packet, please deduct from the number (eighteen) the three Penny Postage Stamps you will necessarily have used, and only enclose (fifteen) which trifling outlay I think you, like others, will have no cause to regret. Yours faithfully,*

EVERETT MAY.

THE UNDER WILL BEST EXPLAIN:—

LEISURE TIME.—FOUR GUINEAS PER WEEK.—HOW TO REALISE THIS AT YOUR OWN HOMES.

MR EVERETT MAY, of Kingsland, begs to apprise the Public that he is sending off as rapidly as possible by every post his far-famed Packet, the contents of which will show the many plans of getting money most honourably by either sex employing leisure hours at their own homes. £2 to £6 weekly may be most certainly realised by all industrious persons, without five shillings outlay or any risk, by following the easy, respectable and clear instructions. Sent by Mr Everett May, of Grove House, Tottenham-grove, Kingsland, London, N. This is no visionary theory. The Present Season highly suitable. Enclose eighteen penny stamps, and you will receive post free punctually per return THIS PROVED BOON TO THE INDUSTRIOUS OF BOTH SEXES.

But to remove any doubt that sceptical persons may entertain as to the truth of the above, I here insert the under six letters received, with hundreds of others. The parties are very respectable and each well-known in the towns they reside.

Calverton, near Nottingham.

Dear Sir,—I beg to inform you that your packet came quite safe, and I was surprised and highly pleased with its contents. Like others who doubted the truth, I was ready to conclude it was only to catch those foolish enough to try it. But I have now proved otherwise, and can testify that you are no other than a true and faithful man. The contents of your indeed famed packet are well worth twenty times as much, and whoever the party may be receiving it will have no cause to repent. Yours very truly, SETH BINCH.

Another—Spettisbury, Blanford, Dorset.

Dear Sir,—I beg to inform you that the Packet ordered arrived safely, and allow me to tender you my sincere thanks for it. Your plans for getting money so honourably are indeed excellent. Anyone having a doubt may most certainly remove such doubt. Hoping you may long continue in your good work is the earnest wish of your obedient servant, W. OAKLEY.

Then follow the remaining four letters, which have an astonishing family likeness to the two chosen, and as these six were only inserted to show what the careful May would have done had he been able to launch into lavish expenditure in the interests of his clients, he gives a statement after the last epistle :—

Such is the exact copy of the advertisement I intended to have placed before the public by inserting in the Newspapers had the charge not been so high, but as I now do so by this circular I can add a few more of my correspondents' approval letters, in furtherance of a still more convincing proof of the value of this esteemed Money Making Packet.

After this he gives a string of letters, which must have demanded great ingenuity on the part of their writer, if only on account of the number of signatures he must have invented. Occasionally he breaks down, however, and has to fall back on initials. We should like to reproduce a lot of these expressions of gratitude as forms to be used at any time when thanks are required for any great benefit, but space will not allow of it, and we must be content with two, which are redolent of truly Christian thankfulness:—

Short Heath Road, Erdington, near Birmingham, December 13th, 1867.

Mr. May, Dear Sir,—I have received your Packet, and am at a loss how, adequately, to express to you what I think about it—suffice it to say that I consider your Packet to be an inestimable boon to the unemployed of every class. Thousands will, doubtless, make money by it. It professes only to be a guide to the employment of leisure hours, but in reality it is a guide to the employment of a whole life, and an easy path to opulence. "Whoever receives it will have no cause to regret." "It is worth twenty times as much." "Anyone having a doubt may most certainly remove such doubt." I heartily re-echo these testimonials, and recommend your Packet to every unemployed person, this is no more than I am in equity bound to do. I am, Dear Sir, faithfully yours, THOMAS JONSON, JUN.

1, Vincent Terrace, Frome, October 5th, 1867.

Dear Sir,—I have carefully examined the contents of your excellent Packet, and am astonished and delighted with them. He or she would indeed be difficult to please who could not select from so extensive a stock some profitable employment congenial to their taste. The instructions are explicit, and the minute details in each case fully and clearly explained. A person of moderate industry and perseverance, furnished with your Packet may attain, if not a fortune, at least a very comfortable living. It ought to be widely known, and I for my part shall not fail to recommend it. I admit I answered your advertisement merely from a curious desire to know what was the latest dodge (pardon the word) for hoaxing the public, and I am now heartily glad I did answer it, though ashamed of the motive that induced me to do so. I am, Dear Sir, faithfully yours, JOSEPH JOHNSON, Schoolmaster.

The poor gulls, after reading these effusions, which all play on the same strings of wonder, satisfaction, and gratitude, are of course anxious to participate in the benefits of lucrative employment, and off go the stamps. If the mischief ended there, the matter would not be so bad; but these advertising scoundrels have various courses open to them. If they judge that nothing more is to be obtained from the sender, they calmly pocket the stamps and take no further notice. In the event of continued "annoyance," or threats of exposure, they will send forth a circular which states that a packet was posted, and must have been lost or stolen in transit. This circular speaks of the post-office, and other institutions, in the most disparaging manner, and of the transactions of its writers as not only just, but infallible. One of them winds up thus:—

Another matter I wish to inform you upon, namely, an error prevails regarding the punctual and prompt conveyance of Packets by the Post Office. This is at times impossible. If the letter mails are heavy, Packets are sometimes left until the following day. So that I cannot guarantee it will be delivered at your residence by return, but you may fully expect it by the second if not by the first mail, postage free, well packed, and secure from observation. These remarks may appear trifling, but they are really necessary, and while on the subject I will name another, also of importance, it is this—several of my correspondents when applying for these particulars send only their name and address on a stamped envelope, and when ordering the Packet enclose their name and omit the address, and this not being retained by me renders it impossible to forward it. So that a distinct name and address is, in the second instance, absolutely necessary. It is required for no other object than to enable me to promptly forward the order, which I can do to any address in the United Kingdom.

The correspondent who dates from a good address, or whose letter looks promising, is likely to be despoiled still more. The stamps are acknowledged, and at the same time information is tendered that a special order for the peculiar fancy goods upon which the income is to be made has just come in; and that if the intending employée will send a fee, say five shillings, for registration, and a deposit, say five pounds, for security, she will receive a packet containing the work—which is very easy—and ample instructions. A little delay enables these wandering tribes to change both names and addresses, and to appear in greater force than ever in the advertisement columns. No wonder the writers we have quoted show such gratitude for the receipt of promised parcels! But we did know two real people who got what they bargained for. One, who only paid the eighteenpence, obtained, after a good long time, and the expenditure of many threats, some scraps of brown paper, which were said to be patterns for pen-wipers, "the manufacture of which would be found to yield a lucrative profit, if a market could be found for them." There is much virtue in an *if* in this case. The paper went on to say that there were many shopkeepers who would be glad to sell them on commission, "the article being extremely rare." It is noticeable that the circular received on this occasion was printed, with blanks left for description of the patterns and the name of the work for which they were to be used. A man of imaginative mind might in the course of the day have run through a considerable list of trades; and as the reference to the demand for the article and the sales by commission would be the same in all the notices, the demand upon truth was evidently not particularly excessive. The other successful applicant was a lady who began by writing out of mere curiosity, and who gradually got on until she had parted with not much less than ten pounds. A sharp letter from a solicitor brought no answer to him, but succeeded in sending the long-expected parcel to his client. It was heavy, and accompanied by a short letter, which said:—

BIRMINGHAM, October 7, 1869.

MADAM,

We beg to inform you that some little delay has been caused by the failure of a company to whom we entrusted the manufacture of a large quantity of articles. We have now however great pleasure in forwarding you a sample of an enamelled leather child's button boot, with lasts and leather for you to follow model. As soon as we receive from you specimen equal to pattern we shall be glad to afford you constant employment.

Yours obediently,
VENTNOR AND MORRIS.

The parcel contained some old odd lasts, a really well-made little boot, and some queer bits of leather, which the cleverest man in the world could have done nothing with; a shoemaker's knife, an awl, and a lump of cobbler's wax! This expedient enabled the swindlers to tide over the time till a new name and a fresh address were decided on. It is worthy of note—and we shall refer to it a little further on—that the statement of one of these scoundrels would lead to the impression that extra prices are charged for these swindling advertisements. If larger prices are charged to men because their advertisements are fraudulent, no amount of false logic or forensic oratory can dispose of the fact that the proprietors of the papers are accessories in any robbery or swindle that is committed; and the insertion of such advertisements, knowing them to be traps for the unwary, at a price which denotes the guilty knowledge of the proprietors, is as gross a breach of the trust reposed in them by the public as was ever committed by smug, well-fed, Sabbath-observing sinners. There is, unfortunately, but too much reason to believe that extra prices are charged for these fool-traps, and that in the most pious and pretentious papers. At the time of the baby-farming disclosures which led to the execution of Margaret Waters, one paper openly accused another—a daily of large circulation—with charging three or four hundred per cent. over the ordinary tariff price for the short applications for nurse children which were then usual. Perhaps the accusation was not worth disproval—at all events it remains uncontradicted till this day. These murderous advertisements presented no particularly destructive features, they simply said in each case that a nurse child was wanted at a certain address; and sometimes an offer would be made to take a baby altogether for a lump sum. This is one of a lot taken from a leading daily paper :—

ADOPTION.—Child Wanted to NURSE, or can be LEFT ALTOGETHER. Terms moderate. Can be taken from birth. Address ——.

Sometimes the terms were mentioned, and, as a rule, the sum named showed that even the tender mercies experienced by Oliver Twist and his friend Dick at the farming establishment inhabited by them could hardly have been expected by the most confiding of parents. Thus :—

A RESPECTABLE Woman wishes to adopt a CHILD. Premium £6. Will be taken altogether and no further trouble necessary. Apply ——.

As some of these establishments may be still in existence, we refrain from republishing the addresses. These specimens, as advertisements, simply call for no comment at our hands, and so we will get on with the more pronounced, though less guilty, swindlers. Here is a specimen which doubtless gave the postman some extra work :—

GENTLEMEN having a respectable circle of acquaintance may hear of means of INCREASING their INCOME without the slightest pecuniary risk, or of having (by any chance) their feelings wounded. Apply for particulars by letter, stating their position &c. to W. R. 37, W—— Street C—— Square.

To such an advertisement as this—one of exactly the same kidney—which appeared in *Lloyd's*, under the head of "How to make Two pounds per Week by the outlay of Ten Shillings," and asking for thirty stamps in return for the information, the following belongs. It is sent in reply to the letter enclosing the fee, and is too good a specimen of the humour possessed by these rogues to be passed over :—

"First purchase 1 cwt. of large-sized potatoes which may be obtained for the sum of 4s., then purchase a large basket, which will cost say another 4s., then buy 2s. worth of flannel blanketting and this will comprise your stock in trade, of which the total cost is 10s. A large-sized potato weighs about half-a-pound, consequently there are 224 potatoes in a cwt. Take half the above quantity of potatoes each evening to a baker's and have them baked; when properly cooked put them in your basket, well wrapped up in the flannel to keep them hot, and sally forth and offer them for sale at one penny each. Numbers will be glad to purchase them at that price, and you will for certain be able to sell half a cwt. every evening. From the calculation made below you will see by that means you will be able to earn £2 per week. The best plan is to frequent the most crowded thoroughfares, and make good use of your lungs, thus letting people know what you have for sale. You could also call in at each public-house on your way and solicit the patronage of the customers, many of whom would be certain to buy of you. Should you have too much pride to transact the business yourself (though no one need be ashamed of pursuing an honest calling), you could hire a boy for a few shillings a week who could do the work for you, and you could still make a handsome profit weekly. The following calculation proves that £2 per week can be made by selling baked potatoes:—

	£	s.	d.
"1 cwt. containing 224 potatoes sold in two evenings at 1d. each, ...	£0	18	8
Deduct cost, .	0	4	0
	£0	14	8
			3
Six evenings' sale,	2	4	0
Pay baker at the rate of 8d. per evening for baking potatoes, . .	0	4	0
Nett profit per week.	£2	0	0."

Many and most curious are the answers received from time to time by persons with sufficient faith to make application to these advertisers, the foregoing being by no means unique. One reply received in return for half-a-crown's worth of stamps, which were to have purchased much wisdom in the way of money-saving, was this: "Never pay a boy to look after your shadow while you climb a tree to see into the middle of next week." A man who would send his money to such evident scamps, could hardly see into the middle of anything, no matter where he chose his vantage-ground. Fortunately for the interests of the community at large, these tricksters now and again are made to feel that there is justice in the land. Twenty years ago, a City magistrate did good service by exposing a man who lived abroad in splendour at the expense of the poor governesses he managed to victimise through the advertising columns of the *Times*. This rascal used, by means of the most specious promises, to drag young girls to a foreign land, and there leave them to become a prey to other villains, or to make their way back accordingly as circumstances permitted. But as at the present time there are streams of foreign girls decoyed to London under all sorts of pretexts for the vilest purposes, the least said as to the criminality of one single individual among the shoals of scoundrels who live by means of advertisements the better. Since Mr Fynn was unmasked many other hawks have been captured, and only recently two have found their way into the obscurity of penal servitude under circumstances worthy of mention. *Place aux dames:* we will give precedence to Mistress Margaret Annie Dellair, though her retirement was subsequent to that of the other claimant on our attention. The difference of date is, however, extremely small. Mrs Dellair lived at Croydon, and for a long time lived in peace and plenty on the post-office orders, or rather the cash received in exchange for them, obtained by means of the following advertisement:—

HOME EMPLOYMENT.—Ladies in town or country wishing for Remunerative EMPLOYMENT in Laces, Church Needlework, &c., should apply at once to M. D., Fern House, West Croydon, enclosing a directed envelope. Reference to ladies employed by permission.

This must have been a fruitful source of income to M. D., who seems to have considered that people were calmly content to part with their money, as she made no attempt to put off the day of reckoning which was bound to arrive. So in due course Mrs Dellair found herself charged with fraud before the Croydon bench, and ultimately she appeared at the bar of the Central Criminal Court in April of the present year. Her mode of procedure, described during the trial, was this. Applicants in due time, after sending in their stamped and addressed envelopes, received circulars, stating that the work which the sender was able to furnish comprised braiding, point lace, tatting, church needlework, and Berlin-wool. The needlework was to be done at the ladies' homes, and they were never to earn less than eightpence or a shilling per hour. To secure employment the applicants were informed that the payment of one guinea "for registration fee, materials, and instruction," was required, half of which sum was to be returned when the employment was resigned. Post-office orders were to be made payable at the office, Windmill Street, Croydon, to Margaret Dellair. "There is," says a writer at the time commenting on this case, "something quite admirable in this calm repudiation of the anonymous, in this wearing of the heart upon the sleeve, on the part of Mistress Dellair. The bait she threw out was swallowed with avidity by many young ladies — some with more money than wit, others painfully anxious to secure bread-winning employment; others less solicitous about procuring work for themselves than inquisitive to discover, for the benefit of society in general and their friends in particular, whether the transaction was *bonâ fide*. Then the curtain rose on the second act of the drama. Some ladies sent post-office orders to Windmill Road; others took the train to Croydon, and had personal interviews with the benevolent recluse of Fern House—a little cottage near a wood—who did not fail to represent that she was extensively employed by some eminent firms of church furnishers in the metropolis." One young lady having sent her guinea, received, after a lapse of some weeks, and after repeated communications on her part, ten toilet-mats, with the materials for braiding them. There was not enough braiding, and so she wrote for more, but received no reply. Then she finished the mats with materials purchased by herself, and despatched the articles to Croydon; but neither reply nor payment was forthcoming. After many more weeks Mrs Dellair wrote to say that she was in ill-health. Seeing, however, that the advertisement was continued in the papers, the defrauded young lady wrote to Fern Cottage, demanding the return of ten shillings, being one-half of the sum she had disbursed for "registration fee, materials, and instruction." No answer was returned, of course; and the victim not only lost her money, but her time and her labour, to say nothing of postage, worry of mind, and other incidental expenses. One of the principal witnesses against Dellair was the Croydon postmaster, who stated that he had known her a year and a half. She had been in the habit of bringing post-office orders to his office to cash. She had brought between three and four hundred orders since July 1872, principally for guineas, but there were some for half-crowns and some for half-guineas. They were brought principally by her daughter, but sometimes by a servant. On the 30th of October 1873 a post-office order (produced) was brought to him, and the payee's signature was that of the prisoner. He paid the money to the person who brought it. The house at which the prisoner lived was a small private house, called Fern Cottage, and there was no show of business kept up there. On cross-examination by prisoner's counsel, the postmaster stated that the fact of so many orders being cashed by Mrs Dellair excited his suspicion. He, however, knew that she was getting her living by sending parcels of needlework by post, and since he had ascertained that fact, he did not think it so extraordinary. Mrs Dellair was in the habit of purchasing postage stamps in large quantities of him. She sometimes purchased ten shillings' worth, and once or twice had bought them to a larger extent. At the trial the entire seat in front of the jury-box was filled by young women who attended to prosecute, some of whom had been prudent enough to ask for references, but imprudent enough to part with their guineas, although the testimonials received were not quite satisfactory. Some applicants had interviews with Dellair at Croydon, and then she gave the names of one or two eminent firms as her employers, but at the trial representatives of these firms swore that she was totally unknown to them. One of the most peculiar points in this trial was the line taken by the counsel for the defence, who argued that although the victims of his client might be deserving of sympathy, they had parted with their guineas in a foolish and careless manner, and the real question was whether the accused was guilty of a fraudulent pretence or not. The advocate raised the curious point in favour of his client, that although she had avowedly four hundred transactions with different persons, it was extraordinary that she had not been discovered and prosecuted before; but he forgot how much more extraordinary it was that for her defence the prisoner was unable to bring forward out of her four hundred clients a single witness who could swear to receiving remunerative employment from her. The defence was original, and originality in defence has a good deal to do with success when a case is being tried by a common jury; but it did not succeed, and Mrs Margaret Annie Dellair was found guilty. The woman was an impudent and abandoned swindler, who had been systematically preying for years upon a class that can, of all classes, the least afford to be cheated—decently-educated young women of small means, who fill respectable positions, and whose consequent need of employment which will enable them to earn a little something above their ordinary salaries is always pressing and frequently imperative. Before sentence was passed an inspector from Scotland Yard stated that the prisoner and her husband had formerly lived at Finchley under another name; that they had afterwards kept a shop in Bloomsbury under the title of "Fuller & Co.," where they advertised to give "remunerative employment" both to young ladies and young gentlemen; that in May 1872 the husband was sentenced at the Middlesex Sessions to five years' imprisonment for fraud; that on his conviction the woman removed to Fern Cottage; and that after her arrest, and its consequent publication in the papers, upwards of eighty letters had been received by the police complaining of her dealings. All that Margaret Annie Dellair could do when she was called up for sentence was to plead that she had been left in an all but penniless condition with seven young children; that she had tried in vain to obtain an honest livelihood by keeping a stall in a bazaar; and that her crime was caused by a desire to avert starvation from her innocent offspring. A good deal of sympathy was of course expressed by the public—especially by those who have nothing to lose—not for the victims, but for the victimiser. The interest taken in criminals nowadays, when they have the slightest claims to be out of the common order, would be regarded as quite overdrawn if described in a novel.

The other delinquent was not so interesting, and being only a man, did not find any hearts to bleed for him even among those who had not been deceived. His practices were provincial, his advertisement, of which the following is a copy, being inserted in the Warwickshire and London papers:—

HOME EMPLOYMENT.—Ladies (several) wanted to COPY manuscript SERMONS for supply to the clergy. Reasonable terms. Apply by letter only to R. H., 39, New-buildings, Coventry.

R. H. was Robert Hemmings, who was eventually tried at the Warwick Assizes of last March, and whose *modus operandi* was then described. Several young ladies seeing the advertisements, and wishing for employment, wrote to the address given, in answer to which they received the "Prospectus of the Private Office for the Supply of Sermons and Lectures to Clergymen and Public Speakers." In this highly-titled and pretentious document, clergymen "who find the composition of sermons too heavy a tax on their ingenuity, are invited to subscribe for manuscript sermons, arranged according to the three schools of thought in the English Church. The High Church section is subdivided into Ritualistic and moderate Anglican. The subscription for three sermons weekly is four guineas per annum, payable in advance. The same sermon will not be sent to any two clergymen within twenty miles of each other." It also states, that the business of the office rendering necessary the employment of copyists, it has been decided to employ ladies only, the reason being that home occupation to gentlewomen of limited income is such a great desideratum of our times. Then it goes on to say that "the ordinary avenues for respectable women desiring to replenish their scanty purses are so overstocked that the limited number we are able to employ will gladly welcome the opportunity of turning a fair handwriting to a profitable account. The remuneration paid will be 2d. per 100 words. To avoid the possibility of unscrupulous persons obtaining valuable sermons on pretence of copying, a guarantee of 10s. will be required from each copyist before MSS. are sent, to be returned when she may discontinue working. Applicants for employment should enclose 2s. 6d. on account of their deposit, which will either be returned or a notification of engagement sent. In the latter case the balance must then be remitted, in order that the first parcel may be supplied. All communications to be sent to Mr Robert Hemmings, 39, New-buildings, Coventry." One young lady resident in London, who gave evidence, sent the half-crown, and then received a letter stating that she would be employed on forwarding a post-office order to Birmingham for 7s. 6d. She did not do so, but many other ladies were not so wise. The prisoner having obtained the money, ceased to communicate with the applicants. The jury found the prisoner guilty, and the judge sentenced him to twelve months' imprisonment with hard labour.

A more fortunate rogue was one who came into notice at the Sussex Assizes four or five years back. Justice may or may not have overtaken him since, for these fellows have so many and such various aliases that unless you happen to see one tried and hear him sentenced, there is no way of telling who he is or what he may have been. The object of our care at the present moment was known at Bognor in Sussex as Henry Watkis, though as he admitted to one more name, the suggestive one of Walker, even there, it would be difficult to say what might be his name in London or any other large town. He used to advertise to procure situations in London daily and weekly papers, and some complaints having been made to the police, he was taken into custody on a warrant, and appeared at the Chichester Quarter Sessions. From a newspaper report of the time we take some of the following particulars of what must be considered a decided miscarriage of justice.

Watkis lived at 6 Jessamine Cottages, Bognor, and when the superintendent of police from Chichester searched his cottage, he found under the stairs 530 letters, consisting of testimonials, replies to, and drafts of advertisements; and in another part of the house he found about 150 envelopes, apparently sent for replies, from which stamps had been cut. When Watkis was apprehended, he acknowledged that he was the person who had been advertising in the name of

"B. C., Post-office, Chichester," by which it seems that he had still another alias, though not in Bognor. On that day he sent a lad to the Chichester post-office, and a large bundle of letters, addressed as above, was brought back from the office. In the course of a few days after Watkis's apprehension, between seven and eight hundred letters were received at the post-office all directed in the same way. Evidence was given that advertisements were inserted in the *Daily Telegraph* and *Lloyd's* in consequence of orders received in letters signed "Hy. Watkis," and "Hy. Walker." About 500 letters were received at Chichester, addressed "X. Y. Z," in accordance with one of the advertisements, and a very large number were also received at Emsworth under still a fresh set of initials. Altogether nearly 20,000 letters are supposed to have been sent to the two offices for the accused. It was proved that 34s. worth of stamps, all singles, had been sold by Watkis. At the conclusion of the address for the prosecution, the deputy recorder ruled that there was no case to go to the jury as far as the law was concerned. There was no proof that Watkis had, either on his own part or on that of others, no such situations to offer as had been advertised. The jury were not satisfied without hearing the evidence that the prisoner was not guilty. The deputy recorder said they had placed him in a very difficult position, and he must tell them again that the indictment could not be maintained in point of law. Therefore they would be doing a very irregular thing to go into the case. It was for them to find a verdict in accordance with the ruling of the court on the point of law. After some discussion the jury returned into court, and the foreman, in answer to the usual question, said, "If we are obliged to say not guilty, we must; but the jury wish to express a strong opinion." By advice of the deputy recorder, however, this opinion was not recorded, and the prisoner was accordingly discharged.

We will wind up this portion of our list of swindles with

an advertisement of the same order, which succeeded in realising a good income for its promoter :—

LADIES and EDUCATED WOMEN are respectfully invited to consult Mrs. EGGLESTON'S SERIES of 60 HOME and other NEW EMPLOYMENTS, which are beginning to attract a large share of public interest for their marked superiority over very unremunerative pursuits usually engaged in.—Enclose an addressed stamped envelope to Mrs Eggleston, ——, Ramsgate, for prospectus.

Sixty different businesses to choose from for home employment! Dollseye and leather-apron weaving was doubtless among them; and in sorting out those occupations most suited to her various correspondents, Mrs Eggleston doubtless passed a pleasant time at the seaside, even if she did not lay up riches against the time she returned to London.

Turf-swindlers are next upon our list, and no one will doubt that these gentry are well deserving of attention, the more so as, partly by themselves, and partly by means of the shortsightedness peculiar to the public, which causes it to form judgments on subjects it does not understand, welchers and thieves who advertise the most impossible "certainties" have been in numerous instances taken to represent the respectable and honourable turfite. We know it is the custom now to assume that a man is bound to be dishonourable if he be professionally connected with racing in any capacity; and any effort made to contradict wholesale and thoughtless accusations is supposed to be the outcome of self-interest, or the blind devotion of quixotry. Men who are cool and calculating enough when discussing ordinary subjects, become almost rabid when the turf is mentioned; and in most articles which have been written on the subject of sporting advertisements, it is assumed that the scheming concocters of baits for fools are fair representatives of the bookmaking class, and all are alike denounced. Surely it would be as just to assume that the baby-farmers and promoters of home employment whose effusions we have quoted were fair representatives of ordinary commerce, as that the "discretionary-investment" promoter is in any way connected with the legitimate bookmaker. We have no wish here to argue for or against betting; but we cannot help noticing that even in Parliament—which is never supposed to legislate upon what it does not understand!—notorious thieves have been taken to represent the principal advertising bookmakers, and long arguments as to the equity of the Betting-House Act framed on the assumption. During the present year there has been considerable discussion in the House of Commons with reference to the Act which was passed in 1853, Scotland being at the time exempt from its operation. The effect of leaving the "land of cakes" in the position of one who is known to be too virtuous to need protection was not visible for some years; for though the Act of Sir Alexander Cockburn had the effect of clearing away the numerous betting-offices, which were undoubtedly at the time public nuisances and open lures to men whose speculative disposition was in inverse proportion to its means of gratification, the better-class agents, whose business was carried on through the post only, continued to flourish or decay, according to circumstances, until 1869. The attention of the police being then drawn to numerous advertisements which appeared in the London and provincial papers on the subject of betting, a raid was made on a large establishment near Covent Garden: books and papers, clerks and managers, were seized and conveyed to Bow Street; and though the employés were ultimately discharged, the proprietor was ultimately fined heavily, the decision of the magistrate being eventually endorsed by the judges to whom the case was referred on appeal. A flight of betting men resulted, the resting-place of some being Glasgow, and of others Edinburgh; from both of which places they put forth their advertisements as before, safe in the knowledge that so far, at all events, the law was on their side. The extension of the Act of 1853 was of course only matter of time; but the first two or three efforts failed signally, principally on account of the blind animosity of the promoters of the measure, which caused them to frame bills which, for intolerance and hopeless stupidity, have perhaps never been equalled. Another cause was a feeling that, while one form of betting was allowed at Tattersall's and the chief sporting clubs—a form which had shown itself equal to ruining several peers and hundreds of young men of less degree—it was impolitic to over-legislate with regard to the half-crowns and half-sovereigns of working men and small tradesmen, and to say to them, while yet the terrible "plunging" years were fresh in memory, "Dukes and marquises only shall ruin themselves at will, you, the common people, must be saving as well as industrious."

At last Mr Anderson, one of the members for Glasgow, introduced his Extension Bill (1874), and though his arguments were eminently ridiculous, as he assumed that every advertiser was a swindler, his legislative attempt was a much greater success than any former effort had been in the same direction, and his bill, with a few modifications, eventually became law. As an instance of the feeling to which this measure gave rise, we quote part of a criticism upon it from the most able of the sporting papers which make the turf their principal study, the *Sportsman*, the first journal that refused the advertisements of swindlers whose intentions were evident, a method of self-abnegation which might be studied to advantage by many virtuous newspapers, which, while they weep over the iniquity of sporting advertisements, are strangely oblivious as to the character or effect of those which appear in their own columns. It must be remembered that the "ring" and Tattersall's betting—of which mention is made in the following—is not interfered with by law, because nothing is staked before the decision of the race but "honour." This, being often deeply mortgaged, is found insufficient for the demand when settling-day arrives.

Says the writer in the *Sportsman*, after demolishing several of the charges made against ready-money betting: "Take the case of those who bet in the ring, or at Tattersall's, or in the clubs. What guarantee is there between the contracting parties that there shall be no element of fraud, and consequently no immorality in the transaction? And what guarantee is there that one or other of the contracting parties who is induced to bet is not a person who cannot afford to lose? There is an inducement to bet on either side: on the side of the layer and on the side of the backer, and will any one acquainted with the subject be prepared to say that in scores of cases there is not on both parts a total inability to pay in the event of loss? What man is there who, having seen much of the ring, cannot recall many instances of layers betting to such an extent that they could never pay if the fates were against them, and of backers 'having' the ring all round without a sovereign in their pockets? Nay, cannot even the general public who are not initiated into such mysteries remember numbers of men who have ruined themselves and others under the system in which Mr Anderson 'does not feel there is any immorality,' because in it 'the element of fraud is not introduced,' and because under it 'people who cannot afford to lose' are not induced to bet? The result of his bill will be that he will drive men from one style of betting, in which they lose or win, knowing the extent of their gains or their losses, to another, under which they may be drawn into hopeless speculation, and perhaps concomitant fraud, simply because they are not called on for ready money. We do not propose to follow Mr Anderson through his ingenious and amusing descriptions of the advertisements of tipsters and 'discretionary-investment' people. He was good enough to introduce ourselves as a striking example of the facility with which such persons could foist their schemes on the public, and of the large profits which were derived by certain newspaper proprietors from them. He had the honesty to acknowledge that we had refused to take any further announcements with respect to 'discretionary investments,' and that we had persistently cautioned our readers to have nothing to do with them. . . . . As for tipsters, who merely offer to give information for a shilling's worth of stamps, what immorality can there be in that which is not to be found in the 'selections' of the daily newspapers? Even the *Times*, in a roundabout 'respectable' way, now and then indicates horses which, in the opinion of its sporting writer, will win certain races, and there is hardly a daily paper in town or country which has not its regular 'prophet,' who from day to day lifts up his voice or his pen and offers inducements to the public to bet. Can any one of such journals say to us, 'I am holier than thou, because I sell my prophecies for a penny, and thou insertest the advertisements of men who want a dozen stamps for theirs'? But the whole policy of objecting to certain classes of advertisements is absurd. If the proprietor of a newspaper were to inquire, even superficially, into the *bona fides* of all the announcements he makes every day, his journal could not be conducted. If he were even to confine his attention to the examination of the prospectuses of joint-stock companies—and this will appeal to Mr Anderson—he would be in the Bankruptcy Court in six months. Suppose the directors of any one of hundreds of bubble concerns which every year carry away the public with 'bogus' announcements were to appear before the manager of the *Times* with their prospectuses, what would they think if he said, 'Gentlemen, before I insert this you must prove to me that it is not a gross swindle;' and how would they proceed to do so?"

We admit to a weakness for reading the sporting papers, and can therefore vouch for the truth of what the *Sportsman* says about its own action. It would have been well, however, if other papers had been as careful, for we happen to know that all the contemporaries of the journal from which we have quoted did not come out with quite such clean hands. Some not only continued to insert the advertisements, despite numerous complaints, but actually *doubled the usual tariff price* to the thieves. This seems to have been a pretty general proceeding when the discretionary movement was at its height, all papers which continued to insert the specious swindles after the exposures had begun being very careful to be well paid for their trouble. As in these days the plain truth is often the most desperate of libels, we must refrain from particularising; but we should think that no one in his sober senses will dispute the evident fact that such newspaper proprietors as took double pay from men because they knew they were assisting them in robbery, were morally far and away more guilty than the robbers themselves. If any apology is needed for our going so far into the betting subject, it will be found in the almost total ignorance, as well as the blind prejudice, which is every day manifested about the difference between the commission agents and their greatest enemies, the advertising welchers.

The raid which drove the bookmakers from London to the principal towns in Scotland seems almost to have been organised by the authorities in the interest of the scamps of the betting world. It certainly was considerably to the latter's advantage. In the hurry and turmoil which eventuated from the hegira, it was hard for people who were not experts to tell the good men from the bad; and as, the more unfounded a man's pretensions, the greater were his promises, letters containing remittances almost swarmed into the offices least worthy of confidence. One good, however, resulted from this. The conversion of sinners we have the best authority for regarding as a blessing, and it must be admitted that owing to the manner in which money poured in upon them, and one or two subsequent bits of luck in the way of unbacked horses' victories, men who went to

Glasgow and Edinburgh as adventurers, if not as actual thieves, remained to become not only solvent, but strictly virtuous. It was not, however, until affairs had somewhat settled down in the North, until Scotland began to be regarded as the permanent abode of the layer of odds, that advertisements which on the face of them were gigantic swindles appeared. Hitherto the attempts of impostors had been confined to a semblance of really fair and legitimate business, the firm being existent as long as there was nothing to pay, and *non est* immediately the blow came. And people who imagine that a bookmaker has nothing to do but take money, would respect him rather more than they do now if after one or two big races they could see his account, and note the scrupulous manner in which every debt is paid, if he bids for respectability in his vocation. A delay of a day in his settlement would lead to unpleasant results, for the very contiguity of the thieves makes the honest men more exact in their transactions. So it is usual, when a man has money to receive by post from a commission agent, for him to get it at once, or most likely not at all. The tipstering and touting fraternities had, while the headquarters of advertising turfites remained in London, been satisfied with short paragraphs intimating their absolute knowledge of the future, and their willingness to communicate such knowledge to the British public for a consideration in the way of stamps, or a percentage on winnings. But when once ready money had been tasted, it seemed to act on these people as blood is said to on tigers, and they determined to have more at all risks. It was useless to try for it a year or so after the migration by applications couched in the ordinary style, for the run of business was by that time divided among certain firms, and the old slow way of giving advice for shillings and sixpences was abhorrent to minds that soared after bank-notes and post-office orders; besides, it had very nearly worn itself out. Fresh moves were therefore necessary, and they were made in various ways, each of which was more or less successful. The most important of them all, and the one with which we have to do now, was the discretionary-investment dodge, which was for a time a complete success, and which would have lasted much longer than it did, had it not been for the faculty of imitation possessed by thieves other than those who inaugurated the venture. Imitation may be the sincerest form of flattery, but even flattery must be painful when it is destructive, and Messrs Balliee & Walter could doubtless have dispensed with the crowds who followed in their wake, and almost made the fortunes of all papers who would take their advertisements. We are not aware whether the system was invented by Balliee & Walter, either or both; but, anyhow, they were its first promoters to any extent, and became thoroughly identified with it. Rumour states that Balliee was a kind of Mrs Harris, and that Walter was the firm. This is nothing to us, though, however much it may be to those who were despoiled of their cash by the discretionary swindle. The advertisements put forth for the benefit of those willing to trust their money blindly into the hands of men of whom they knew nothing must have been very successful, for it is admitted that the letters received in Glasgow for Balliee & Walter were so enormous in quantity that special arrangements had often to be made for their delivery. It is noticeable that swindlers of this description always assume that their firm is not only long established but well known, and the following, taken from the first page of the *Sporting Life* of the Derby-day 1871, will show that the particular people in question had no scruple about inventing facts for the purpose of substantiating their arguments:—

THE KINGSCLERE LONDON AND GLASGOW TURF COMMISSION AGENCY.

Messrs. BALLIEE and WALTER beg to inform their subscribers and the sporting public that, in consequence of increase of business, they have opened a Commission Agency in Glasgow, where in future all commissions will be executed.

Gentlemen may rely on liberal treatment and prompt settlement of all claims. All letters answered same day as received.

MESSRS. BALLIEE AND WALTER
(Members of the principal West-End Clubs),
62, JAMAICA STREET, GLASGOW.

As heretofore, Commissions of every description, and to any amount, will be undertaken, the following being the leading features:—

INVESTMENTS ON FORTHCOMING EVENTS effected at the best Market Prices.

FIRST FAVOURITES backed at the post, and the rate of odds guaranteed as quoted by the sporting paper the investor chooses to adopt.

JOCKEYS' MOUNTS invested upon in accordance with any scale or principle.

POST COMMISSIONS for EPSOM MEETING will meet with prompt attention.

THE EPSOM CARNIVAL.
THE OAKS A CERTAINTY.

"So if to be a millionaire at present is your aim,
Don't hesitate, but join at once our systematic gains."
Shakspeare, revised and improved.

A SAFE INVESTMENT.—WINNING A CERTAINTY.

KINGSCLERE RACING CIRCULAR
DISCRETIONARY INVESTMENTS.
Messrs. BALLIEE and WALTER, Proprietors
(Members of the principal West-End Clubs).

The only recognised method by which backers of horses can win large sums at all the principal meetings.

PROSPECTUSES FREE ON RECEIPT OF ADDRESS.

MESSRS. BALLIEE and WALTER draw the attention of investors to the all-important fact that they alone of all firms who undertake Discretionary Investments are to be seen personally in the Ring, and are represented at the lists outside, at every meeting throughout the racing season. Some firms, although they state they are present, are never to be seen.

SELECTED MORTEMER TO WIN AND A PLACE
FOR CHESTER CUP;

THE DWARF,
GREAT NORTHERN;
LORD HAWTHORN,
FLYING DUTCHMAN;
STANLEY,
DONCASTER SPRING HANDICAP;
With nearly every other winner at York and Newmarket.
We defy contradiction, and court inquiry.

RESULTS OF LATE MEETINGS:—

Each £10 investor at York was remitted by Friday's post (May 12) £108 nett winnings.

Each £5 investor at Doncaster was remitted by Monday's post, £85.

Being exclusive of stake and nett return after commission (5 per cent.) had been deducted.

Newmarket accounts and winnings were forwarded by Tuesday's post, May 16.

Gentlemen of capital and backers of horses can now judge of the intrinsic value of this infallible system of backing our Final Selection at the post.

MESSRS. BALLIEE and WALTER will continue their highly successful system of DISCRETIONARY INVESTMENTS at the

EPSOM MEETING,

where they personally attend, and as such a great influx of business is expected during the Derby Week, they have engaged three extra Commissioners to assist them in carrying out the system, and again are sanguine of realising a gold-achieving victory.

AT EPSOM MEETING LAST SUMMER, SEASON 1870,
Each £25 investor was returned £703 nett Winnings, in addition to stake deposited.

Each investor of £20 in 1868 realised £487.
" £25 " 1869 " £324 15s.
" £50 " 1870 " £1,406.

The above sums were paid to each investor of the specified amounts, and this season we with confidence assert that the investments will be more remunerative to the investor.

The Oaks this season will be won by, comparatively speaking, an outsider. Last season's subscribers will remember our warning them against Hester, and we assure our readers that Hannah will, like all the Baron's favourites, be doomed to defeat. A clever Northern division have a filly the beau ideal of Blink Bonny, as being tried a 7lb better animal than Bothwell, and with health must win the fillies' race in a canter. The owner most unfortunately omitted to enter her for the Two Thousand and Derby, or we should have seen her credited with the first-named event, and first favourite for Blue Riband honours.

SEVERAL RODS ARE IN PICKLE

for the minor events. Particulars were given in our last week's Circular (May 12), and even at this distant period we are enabled to predict the success of six certain winners.

HAVING HORSES OF OUR OWN,

and others identical with our interests, running at this meeting, coupled with the important commissions we have the working of at EPSOM.

Our knowledge of market movements, the intimate terms we are on with the various owners, jockeys, and trainers, our social position with the élite of the racing world, enables us to ascertain the intentions of other owners and the chances their respective candidates possess—information far beyond the reach of other advertisers.

This is by no means all; we merely pause to take breath and recover self-possession, after a steady perusal of Mr Walter's benefactions. It is noticeable that the standard of verse employed by these philanthropists is about on a par with their standard of morality. It seems wonderful that any sane person should believe in the existence of a certain guide to the winning-post, and the idea that, if there had been such a thing, Messrs Balliee & Walter would have assuredly used it for themselves alone, never seems to have entered into the heads of their victims, at all events until too late. After the vaunt about position and information, the intimates of "the *élite* of the racing world" go on :—

MESSRS. BALLIEE and WALTER, alone of all firms that undertake Discretionary Investments, are to be seen personally in the Ring, and they wish to draw the attention of Turf speculators to the fact that NO OTHER ADVERTISERS ARE OWNERS OF HORSES, despite what they may say to the contrary. If their systems equalled ours, would they not accept the challenge given by us for the past twelve months in the various sporting papers? Vide commencement of advertisement.

So sanguine are we of success at Epsom, the innumerable and peculiar advantages presented, and every facility being offered for the successful working of our

DISCRETIONARY METHOD,

that we are enabled to

GUARANTEE AGAINST LOSS,
and assert with confidence that
WINNING IS REDUCED TO AN ABSOLUTE CERTAINTY.

DEPOSIT REQUIRED FOR DISCRETIONARY INVESTMENTS AT THE
EPSOM SUMMER MEETING:—
£500, £100, £50, £25, £10, or £5.

By investing in accordance with this infallible method of backing our final selections at the post, loss is simply an impossibility, and guaranteed against,

WINNING BEING REDUCED TO AN ABSOLUTE CERTAINTY.

This often-repeated assertion (and not once contradicted for the past five years), and the winnings realised weekly for subscribers who patronise this system, is sufficient to prove its intrinsic value.

This is just the sort and class of meeting for gentlemen of capital and systematic investors to invest a £500 or £1,000 bank, being indeed a golden opportunity that all should embrace. The fact of our guaranteeing

A WIN EQUAL TO OUR SUCCESS OF LAST SUMMER,
and, as previously stated,
GUARANTEE TO HOLD THE INVESTOR AGAINST LOSS OF EVEN A FRACTIONAL PART OF CAPITAL EMPLOYED,

should be sufficient to convince gentlemen of the true character and value of this infallible method of backing our final selections at the post.

CAN ANY SYSTEM BE SO LUCRATIVE TO THE INVESTOR?

Our position as owners of horses and proprietors of "THE KINGSCLERE RACING CIRCULAR," the most successful medium of all Turf advices, and has treble the circulation of any other circular published; the flattering encomiums passed on our "Infallible Method" by the Sporting Press of the United Kingdom, and being recommended by them as

"The only recognised method by which backers of horses can win large sums at all the principal meetings;"

coupled with our position as the most influential Commission Agents both in the London and Manchester Markets, ensure gentlemen entrusting us with Discretionary Investments being fairly and honestly dealt with, and the successes that we promise and achieve meeting after meeting in the columns of this and other papers.

FACTS ARE STUBBORN THINGS.

The following average results speak volumes in favour of this method :—

The following successes have been achieved this season by

THE KINGSCLERE RACING CIRCULAR'S
INFALLIBLE METHOD
OF
DISCRETIONARY INVESTMENTS.

Each £25 investor at Enfield received nett winnings value £200.

Each £10 investor at Lichfield was remitted by Thursday's post (April 13) £82 10s., being winnings and stake included, after the 5 per cent. commission had been deducted.

Each investor of a £10 stake at the Lincoln Meeting received nett winnings of £180 10s. by Tuesday's post, March 28.

Each investor at Liverpool in accordance with this system, on two investments, viz.,

THE LAMB..................Win,
SCARRINGTON............A place,

realised £75 with each £10 invested.

A £10 stake realised £200 nett winnings at the Burton (Lincoln) Meeting.

A £25 stake invested on Waterloo Cup realised £300,

MASTER McGRATH

being selected right throughout the piece, and again in finals with Pretender.

A £10 stake realised at the Cambridgeshire Meeting the sum of £240 nett winnings.

A £5 stake at the West Drayton Meeting realised £30 nett winnings.

Bromley and several other meetings were also highly successful.

At Croxton Park each £10 invested realised £102 nett.

Each £25 invested at Thirsk realised £150.

THE ABOVE AMOUNTS HAVE BEEN PAID THIS SEASON TO ALL PATRONS WHO ENTRUSTED US WITH DISCRETIONARY INVESTMENTS OVER THESE MEETINGS, again proving the value of this method over all others advertised.

The past augurs well for the future, as the above successes testify. We personally attend EPSOM, and are always successful at this meeting.

A LOSS HAS NEVER OCCURRED TO FOLLOWERS

OF OUR SYSTEM, and this season we are even more than ever confident of success.

Cash reaching us on Thursday will be in time for two days' investments; and cash arriving by Friday's first post will be invested on Oaks winner and the last day of the meeting.

Five per cent. deducted from all winnings.

THE LARGER THE STAKE, THE GREATER SCOPE IS AVAILABLE FOR LUCRATIVE SPECULATION.

LOSS OF STAKE IS IN ALL CASES GUARANTEED AGAINST.

The opulent winnings realised weekly throughout the season cannot fail to convince systematic speculators that this system is the par excellence of all methods for winning large sums at each and every important race-gathering.

Winnings and account of investments will be forwarded on Monday, May 29.

Investors can have their winnings (less 5 per cent.) remitted by open cheque or bank notes, as preferred, by signifying their wishes on that point when remitting cash for investment.

One trial is sufficient to prove to the most sceptical the value of this method over all others advertised. Gentlemen who have lost their money in the so-called winning modus swindles, or through following their own fancies, advice of puffing tipsters, newspaper selections, backing first favourites, jockeys' mounts, or any other system, should give our infallible method a trial at the Epsom Meeting. Cash should be forwarded to reach us on or before Tuesday, addressed to Mr W. H. WALTER, 62 Jamaica-street, Glasgow. If after that date, address letters, &c., &c., W. H. WALTER (of Kingsclere), Box 20, Post-office, Epsom, where due precaution has been taken for their safe delivery.

Cheques to be crossed, Bank, Newbury. Letters containing gold or notes to be registered. Scotch and Irish notes taken as cash. Stamps, 20s. 6d. to the pound. P.O. Orders in all cases to be made payable to W. H. WALTER, and drawn on the Post-office, Newbury, Berkshire.

*** The successes we achieve weekly, our social status on the Turf, the years we have been before the public, the fact of our being promoters of Discretionary Investments, our selecting Jack Spigot for City and Suburban, Vulcan for Lincoln Handicap, the Lamb for Grand National, Bothwell for Two Thousand, Mortemer (a place), Chester Cup, the Dwarf for Great Northern Handicap; Lord Hawthorn, Flying Dutchman's Handicap; Stanley, Doncaster Handicap, with nearly every other winner at York and Doncaster, &c., prove the value of our information and the integrity and value of our system of backing Discretionary Investments.

THE

KINGSCLERE RACING CIRCULAR of Friday next (May 26), price 1s., will contain a Review of the Derby running, and the WINNER OF THE ASCOT STAKES, with some important notes anent ROYAL HUNT CUP and ST. LEGER, with selections and keys for all races at the Manchester, Scarborough, Winchester, West Drayton, and Wye Meetings. Notes on the Two Year Old Form of the Season, and a Bird's-eye View of the Middle Park Plate, being particulars of Walter's Visit to the Dark Two Year Olds at their Training Grounds. Terms:—Season, 21s.—Address orders and letters, W. H. WALTER (of Kingsclere), Ravenscourt Park, Hammersmith, London, W.

In thanking our Derby subscribers for their past support, we respectfully solicit a continuance of their favours on the above terms.

The Private Telegraphic Key Book will be issued to Season Subscribers only in the course of a few days. Those that intend renewing their subscriptions should do so at once.

It must not be imagined that this advertisement was intended to obtain one large haul before the business was abandoned. With little alteration it ran for a very considerable time in many papers, and the expenses of advertising alone must have been enormous. For it is not to be expected that any blind credulity exhibited itself in the various publishing offices, and hard cash, and plenty of it, had to be expended before a line of Balliee & Walter's was allowed to appear. It will be seen by what we have quoted that winnings and accounts of investments are promised on Monday, and in true business-like style every depositor received his envelope. With what feverish anxiety many must have torn open the enclosure! So many men, so many minds, says the proverb, and the ways of expressing wrath must have been various indeed. We are, however, not in a position to furnish any particulars as to how the news was received, it is enough to know what the information was. And, as may be guessed, it was not satisfactory. The circulars were always neatly constructed, and set forth with a regret that owing to a combination of untoward circumstances the hopes of the chief investor, "the man at the post," had been dashed, and for that week—always the first week of such an occurrence—matters had resulted disastrously. Then would follow a statement of account, in which it was shown that investments had been fortunate at the outset, that then they had changed, and that by placing too much money on an apparent certainty, so as to recover the losings, the whole bulk of the bank had departed, never to return. The sums received by Messrs Balliee & Walter were of course various, and according to the amonnt, so was the table arranged; but there was a great family likeness about them all, the principle being to show that the horses, when they did not win, were very close up, and so seconds, with now and again a third, were nearly always chosen! Thus one £10 stake for the Derby week of 1871—the week in which the advertisement given appears—was accounted for thus:—

Epsom, Tuesday, May 23.	Won.	Lost.
Trial Stakes, Manille,	—	£0 10 0
Horton Stakes, Trident,	—	1 0 0
Maiden Plate, Queen Bee,	—	2 0 0
Rous Stakes, Banderolle,	—	0 10 0
Woodcote Stakes, Cremorne (11 to 8 on),	£0 14 6	—
Wednesday.		
Bentinck Plate, Lady Atholstone,	—	0 10 0
Derby, King of the Forest,	—	1 0 0
Stanley Stakes, Hamilton,	—	2 0 0
Match, Lizzie Cowl (5 to 4 on),	0 8 0	—
Manor Stakes, Holdenby,	—	0 10 0
Town Plate, Banderolle,	—	1 0 0
Thursday.		
Glasgow Plate, Countryman (2 to 1 on),	0 5 0	—
High Level Handicap, Free Trade,	—	0 10 0
Two-year-old Stakes, Clotilde filly,	—	1 0 0
Tadworth Stakes, Manna,	—	2 0 0
	£1 7 6	£12 10 0

With five per cent. commission charged on the winnings, this left a balance ot £1, 3s. 9½d. due to Messrs Balliee

& Walter, which it was hoped would be at once remitted. This was cruel, but crueller still was the statement, that had the stake been larger, affairs would have arranged themselves satisfactorily, as a great change took place at the close of Thursday and on Friday, and those whose banks lasted over the first run of ill-luck left off winners of large sums. With the demand for payment of balance came a request which, from its very coolness, must have staggered those who, being once victimised, could see through the swindle, though in very many instances—as if in corroboration of Mr Carlyle's theory—it was complied with. This was a desire for a fresh trial, and positive security from loss was guaranteed. It is noticeable in the table given that by a judicious selection of races and horses the winnings were bound to be always low, as animals with odds on are selected, and that when stakes are lowest. When on the doubling principle the stake on the chosen winner would be inconveniently large a race was omitted. The returns made were necessarily various, but that given is an accurate representative of the system.

Balliee & Walter continued to flourish for a long time; but whether it was that they became individually greedy, whether newspaper proprietors became exorbitant in their demands on the spoil, or whether rivalry affected them, we know not, all we do know is that they committed a most openly outrageous act on a race-course, and the bubble at once burst. It may seem strange that anything discretionary-investment agents, who had been gradually becoming a byword and a reproach, could do would affect their position; but our duty is to record the fact, and not to allow it to be disputed on any theoretic grounds. If they had calmly continued to merely swindle, they might have advertised till now; but they outraged the sanctity of the British race-course, and were damned for all time, if not to all eternity. They had become possessed by some means or other of a hurdle-racer called Goodfellow, and two or three weeks before one of the suburban gate-money meetings they made a match for him to run a race at it against a very moderate mare. Immediately this was done they circularised all customers, telling them to be sure and back Goodfellow, as he could not possibly lose, and stating that on account of very heavy investments already made, they could afford, as a favour to their clients, to return them double the odds which would be laid against Goodfellow on the day. In the *Kingsclere Racing Circular*, a weekly pamphlet issued by these honourable gentlemen, we find under date March 10, 1871, the following ingenious application. This, it has been since proved, brought heavy sums to the Ravenscourt Park exchequer, whence it was not allowed to depart, Messrs Balliee & Walter, like true and legitimate bookmakers, preferring to lay the 6 to 4's against their own horse themselves, rather than that their patrons should be inconvenienced by having to take shorter prices from others :—

CROYDON SPECIAL INVESTMENT.

The match—Goodfellow v. Harriett—will come off at Croydon on Tuesday next. It is simply a matter of putting the coin down and picking it up again. It is any odds on our horse, and as we wish our Subscribers to participate in this certainty, we will undertake to obtain for them 6 to 4 for all cash sent, which must reach Mr Walter, Ravenscourt Park, if possible by Monday evening, and not later than Tuesday's first post. Gibson is sure to back Harriett for a 1000, and probably bring her favourite. The sole reason of us wishing Subscribers to allow us to invest for them, is to prevent them rushing on and spoiling the market, which will be to their interest as well as our own. We have engaged one of the cleverest cross country riders of the day to ride Goodfellow, and our horse never was so fit and well as at the present time. Daniels will have the mount of Harriett. Such a chance may not occur again throughout the season. Investors should speculate a £50 or £100 Bank. We cannot undertake to invest more than £300 for any one of our patrons.

By this means Balliee & Walter obtained from their purblind dupes a large amount of money with which to back Goodfellow, and of this they of course placed as much as they could upon Harriett, the opposing candidate. In the race, if race so iniquitous a transaction can be called, the discretionary-investment horse was, as might have been expected, "pulled," so that Balliee & Walter had all the money they received to the good, besides what they won from the unsuspecting by backing the animal they had pretended to oppose. This led to their gradually disappearing from the front pages of the newspapers, though they continued their business under an *alias* very successfully. Walter was eventually fined a hundred pounds at one of the metropolitan courts, under the Betting-House Act, 1853, for having carried on a part of his business at Hammersmith. It seems rather ludicrous that a man should have been fined for what he in reality never did. But lawyers and magistrates could not distinguish the difference between betting and only pretending to bet, so they fined Mr Walter just as they would have done if he had been a really honourable man, and had therefore deserved punishment.

From the discretionary-investment class of turf-swindler we will now pass on to another, quite as ingenious and very often as dangerous. A few years back, when opportunity served—that is, when the honest layer of odds was harassed by the police and driven from London, and when good men and bad were almost irremediably mixed up—a sharp rogue hit upon an idea for making the tipstering and private-advice business a means to quite a new phase of imposition. This was known among those who profited by it as "forcing the voucher," and a very pretty little game it was while it lasted, though the profits of pioneers were of course considerably diminished as soon as ever the secret got wind, by the imitative faculty to which reference has been already made. Commencing, as usual, with small advertisements and large profits, forcers in time found themselves, by stress of competition, obliged to spend a good share of their hard earnings in specially-tempting invitations to those who would go any but the right way towards being wealthy; or else to seek other courses. So in 1872 we find three or four firms occupying a large share of the papers, and giving forth promises without stint. Whether the original forcer was in any of these partnerships it is impossible to tell, as the names were, as a rule, fictitious, and often changed; but whether or not, it is certain that those who advertised heaviest drove all small thieves from the field, and so, two years back, the business, as far as we are concerned, was carried on chiefly by Adkins & Wood, Robert Danby & Co., Marshall & Grant, and James Rawlings & Co., who advertised quite separately, but whose notifications might very easily have been the work of one pen. We will therefore take Rawlings & Co. to represent the fraternity, and in their advertisement which appeared at the end of April 1872 will be found the peculiarities of all the others. This is it:—

DIGBY GRAND sent to every season subscriber, and for a place at 6 to 1, to every reader of

THE PREMIER RACING CIRCULAR.

Proprietors,

JAMES RAWLINGS and Co.,

65, YORK PLACE,

EDINBURGH.

Published by the Proprietors every Saturday, at their chief office, 65 York Place, Edinburgh.

THE PREMIER RACING CIRCULAR still maintains its well-merited reputation as the only infallible and unerringly-successful winning guide, by the aid of which private backers can and do, week by week, realise hundreds of pounds with perfect safety over the principal races throughout the kingdom. The uninterrupted series of successes which have attended its vaticinations during past seasons have been gloriously crowned by the success of every special investment advised in its pages this season, as will be seen by the following list of winners already given:—

Race.	Selection.	Result.	Price at which clients were put on.
Croydon	Footman	Won...	15 to 1
Lincoln Handicap	Guy Dayrell	Won...	20 to 1
Grand National	Casse Tête	Won...	25 to 1
Nottingham Handicap	Flurry	Won...	10 to 1
Great Warwick Handicap	Cedric the Saxon	Won...	12 to 1
Warwick Grand Annual	Snowstorm	Won...	7 to 1
Northamptonshire Stakes	Messager	Won...	8 to 1
City and Suburban	Digby Grand	Won...	25 to 1

Thus a £10 stake on each of our selections already made this season has now won the handsome sum of £1,164 after deducting our commission of 5 per cent.

If one statement of the above glorious triumph is untrue, we boldly invite our subscribers and clients to expose us in the fullest manner in the sporting papers. Promptitude, despatch, exactitude, and liberality, as in the past, will ever be our watchwords in the future.

Every reader of "The Sporting Life" is earnestly invited to send at once for this week's number, as the information therein contained will enable everyone to win a little fortune over that splendid and highly lucrative mode of investment—

A DOUBLE EVENT

That cannot be upset.

The positive Winners of

THE TWO THOUSAND

and

ONE THOUSAND GUINEAS.

It is rarely that we advise this method of investing, but when we have sent out to our clients a double event it has never failed to come off. Last year we advised a double event for these races—

Two Thousand	Bothwell	Won
One Thousand	Hannah	Won

And this year both our selections are, if possible, greater and more undeniable certainties.

THE TWO THOUSAND GUINEAS.

Of all the good things that in the course of a long and varied experience on the Turf it has ever been our good fortune to be possessed of, we cannot recall a single occasion on which every attendant circumstance combined so surely to render, as in the present instance, the race such an absolute foregone conclusion for our selection. The trial which took place this week was unprecedented in its severity, and, to the surprise of owner and trainer, the animal performed so far beyond their most sanguine expectations or hopes as to show them that success is reduced to the greatest moral certainty ever known in the history of the English Turf. This is an opportunity similar to those that have made the fortunes of many of our most wealthy speculators, for whom, as in the present instance, victory is a foregone conclusion and defeat a moral impossibility. Everyone should seize the opportunity of reaping the rich harvest of golden fruit that awaits the bold speculator of foregone conclusions like this.

THE ONE THOUSAND GUINEAS.

It is to us an easy task to select the winner of this race, as the immense superiority she enjoys over every other animal engaged (known only to owner, trainer, and ourselves) is so vast that this race will be little more than an exercise canter for this speedy filly. So quietly has this good thing been nursed by the shrewd division to which the mare belongs, that a real good price is now to be had, though when this superb specimen of an English thoroughbred is seen at the post, we are confident that even money will be eagerly snapped up by those who till then neglect to back her.

THE DOUBLE EVENT,

as stated above, is as sure to come off as these lines are in print. Send then at once for this week's number, and do not delay an hour if you wish to land a fortune over these two genuine certainties.

We could wish no better opportunity to display the genuine good things sent out by the "Premier Racing Circular" than these two races present, and we beg that everyone will at once send six stamps and stamped addressed envelope for this week's number, and stand these morals to win them a fortune.

Address—

JAMES RAWLINGS and Co.,
65, YORK PLACE,
EDINBURGH.

If we were not certain that these men got large sums of money from willing victims, it would seem almost impossible that people could be found credulous enough to believe that absolute certainty could be secured on the turf. Certainty of losing is naturally much easier than certainty of winning, and yet even loss cannot be reduced to less than imminent probability so long as a horse goes to the post unphysicked, and the jockey is not allowed to openly pull him. And so, though no one will attempt to defend Messrs Rawlings & Co., their dupes deserve but the smallest amount of pity; for even the most foolish of them must have known that certainty of winning to them must have meant certainty of losing to the other side, and that therefore, even if the contract had been carried out, somebody must have been swindled. If it were not for the greed and avarice which mainly direct the actions of those who are generally known as fools, magsmen, sharpers, discretionary-investment commissioners, and voucher-forcers would have to take to honest employment. This may seem a truism, yet when a skittle-sharper or "street-mugger" is tried in a police court, and convicted for having victimised a "flat," it never seems to strike the magistrate or the general public that the prisoner simply swindled a man who had all the will but not the ability to swindle him. And there can be no reasonable doubt—we should much like to see the matter tried—that the principal supports of rogues are the most grasping, selfish, and hard-hearted of mortals, and not at all the soft, good-natured bumpkins that they are generally depicted. We should not like to trust to either the honour or the honesty of any man who had been concerned even as a victim in one of the transactions which now and again appear in the police reports; and if we had any sympathy, which is not very likely, to bestow on either side, it would certainly be given to the man who gets sent to prison.

Rawlings & Co. seem to have managed the spring campaign of 1872 very successfully, for while other members of the same brotherhood had to drop out of the papers or to appear in new guise after April, we find our heroes still merrily addressing the public from the front page of the sporting papers of June 8, and as able to guarantee freedom from loss as ever. And though it may not seem long from the end ot April to this early part of June, it must be recollected that within that space several very important meetings are held, and that dismal gaps are found in the ranks of both "wrong" and "right" men after a Derby, especially after such a Derby as Cremorne's, which found out the weak spots in a good many big books, and altered the prospects of many a turfite, professional and amateur. So finding Rawlings so well through, we were tempted at the time to communicate with him, and discover the principle upon which he "forced the voucher." Here is his advertisement of June 8, in which he glories in past triumphs and feels confident of future successes:—

CREMORNE, QUEEN'S MESSENGER, AND REINE.

JAMES RAWLINGS and Co., the oldest established Turf advisers in Great Britain; proprietors of

THE PREMIER RACING CIRCULAR,

the most successful winning guide extant.

THE PREMIER RACING CIRCULAR, selected Cremorne and Reine.

THE PREMIER RACING CIRCULAR of this day contains three certainties.

THE PREMIER RACING CIRCULAR'S selections pulled off the double event for the Derby and Oaks, likewise Queen's Messenger for a place at 4 to 1.

THE PREMIER RACING CIRCULAR has this season selected each and every important winner, as may be seen by referring to back numbers of this publication, invaluable alike to large and small speculators. The proprietors beg respectfully to draw the attention of that section of the public who have neglected to take advantage of the opportunities that they have, for the past three months, weekly drawn attention to in the columns of this and other journals, that this week's number of the Premier Racing Circular will contain three of the greatest morals and most undeniable certainties ever known in this or any other era of the Turf's history, namely, the winner of

THE ASCOT STAKES,

a real good thing, at a real good price. Over this race any gentleman may safely invest as heavily as he may think fit, as we know that our selection cannot be beaten; the course is peculiarly adapted to the animal's action, and the stable have satisfied themselves, past question

or doubt, that he possesses both speed and stamina to land this event with the utmost ease.

THE ROYAL HUNT CUP

is equally a certainty for a veritable flyer, whose merits have hitherto been so cleverly concealed by the owner, that the handicapper has no idea of his sterling excellence. He is undergoing a special preparation for this race, the best light-weight in the world will be in the saddle, and a long price is now to be had.

THE NORTHUMBERLAND PLATE.

We have never yet missed selecting the winner of this race, and as the cleverest division on the Turf, as to whose movements we are always au fait, have specially laid themselves out to secure this prize, the public may rely upon it that, as in past years, we shall again select the winner.

This week's number contains full particulars of these undeniable and gold-producing morals, in addition to a mass of other information invaluable to backers. No one should invest a shilling on any one of the above races without first forwarding us six stamps and stamped directed envelope for this week's issue.

Address—

JAMES RAWLINGS and Co.,
65, York Place,
Edinburgh.

Six stamps and a stamped directed envelope were accordingly sent, and in return we received a copy of the *Premier Racing Circular*, dated June 6, which was full of congratulations, and which promised far more than even the advertisements did. One paragraph in it was specially worthy of attention. It ran thus: "*We have several commissions still unsettled over the Derby and Oaks. Gentlemen holding winning vouchers will please send them in at once.*" What could be more fair, honourable, and straightforward than this; and who would think of suspecting Rawlings of unfair dealing? Yet, at the very time the invitation we have quoted appeared, the people who sent in their winning vouchers received in return, not money, but the following circular, which we reprint exactly, and which, with the alteration of the signature and the name of the meeting, will do for any firm and any week's racing the reader may choose. This is one of a lot we have collected at times from many victims:—

65 York Place, Edinburgh.

SIR,

We regret to inform you that, in consequence of some of our important Accounts not having been settled at Epsom this week, we must unavoidably postpone the settlement. This is the first time that such an unpleasantness has occurred, but we can assure you that we have done all in our power in the matter. No one regrets this unfortunate affair more than ourselves, after serving the public so faithfully for such a number of years, and all we can do is to remit you immediately we receive winnings from the temporarily embarrassed Commissioners.

Meanwhile, We remain,

Yours faithfully,

JAMES RAWLINGS & CO.

There is no boast in the statement, that when we received the *Premier Racing Circular*, we were pretty well acquainted with the manner in which Rawlings conducted his business—it would be a poor thing to boast about—and so we turned to the envelope to look for the vouchers we knew would be there. And there they were, enclosed in a piece of paper, on which was the information, that owing to the large sums they had invested when the horses were at long shots, they could afford to return odds considerably over the current market; and winding up with a request that intending backers would at once forward the amounts for which the vouchers were filled in, or any part of it which would suit them. Yes, there they were, three in number, looking like cheques—the first, No. 32,323, being for the Ascot Stakes, and bearing the bet of £200 to £10 against Palmerston for the Ascot Stakes. The second was numbered 36,162, and said £300 to £10 Pitchfork for the Royal Hunt Cup; and the third was 39,346, and was to the tune of £400 to £20 Minerve for the Northumberland Plate. And this is the advice with regard to them, given in the *Circular*, without the alteration of even a letter:—

THE PITCHFORK, PALMERSTON, AND MINERVE COMMISSION.

We have been able to work the Commission (Pitchfork, Palmerston, and Minerve), at an unusual liberal price, and we herewith offer for your acceptance, as per enclosed vouchers, the very advantageous bets about these absolute morals. Should you accept the whole (which we strongly recommend), you will please forward stake money by return and retain vouchers; if only a portion, return same, with stake money, and a corrected voucher to amount of stake will be at once forwarded to you. In the remote contingency of your not accepting any portion of either bet, you will please return vouchers without a moment's delay, that we may have an opportunity of offering the bets to other clients.

Those who wish to back Pitchfork, Palmerston, and Minerve for a place, can be on at one-fourth the odds, but to no greater amount than a £50 stake.

The secret of forcing the voucher, therefore, lay in the fact of offering far longer prices than could be obtained of any one who intended to pay when the races were over; for on June 6th, 1872, the day on which the vouchers were drawn, the market prices, as quoted in the papers Mr Rawlings advertised in, were 10 to 1 against Palmerston for the Ascot Stakes; 15 to 1 against Pitchfork for the Royal Hunt Cup; and 10 to 1 against Minerve for the Northumberland Plate. Now as double the fair price is offered, and as the quoted market represents the odds which are laid at the chief clubs by the chief men, who can say that the victims of Rawlings deserve pity? The ability of Rawlings & Co. as tipsters is strangely shown in this transaction. In their circular, Pitchfork, Palmerston, and Minerve are their selections for the several races, even to people who only accepted their advice and did not intrust them with commissions. They assert that they have positive information that these horses cannot lose. Under the head of "Royal Hunt Cup," and perfectly independent of anything but the private-advice department, they say, in reference to Pitchfork: "This is a 'Woodyeates moral,' and all must be on. Every now and then this influential coterie throws in for a fortune, and when they do, the good thing invariably comes off. We have never missed the winner of this race, and now, with all confidence, we assure every client that no better opportunity could possibly occur of landing a rich and substantial stake. Some of our clients will neglect the opportunities we frequently lay before them; but on this occasion as the price is so liberal, we do heartily hope that one and all will go in for a rattling good stake." Then about Palmerston for the Ascot Stakes, they tell us that "previous to the great Epsom event, Palmerston performed such a wonderful feat with the Brother to Flurry as to show the stable that the Ascot Stakes were completely at their mercy. Mr Payne and the owners who train at Fyfield look upon defeat as impossible, and will stand their horses to win a very large stake. We cannot recollect a more genuine investment, and must urge all to stand this moral freely." For the Northumberland Plate they are, if anything, still more confident, their article on it containing this: "Another triumph awaits the French contingent in the Northumberland Plate, as Minerve, own sister to Miss Hervine, is certain to carry off this event." Rawlings's prophecies might have turned out right if they had had a chance, but he does not seem to have possessed even a hint as to what would be started for the various stables, for not one of the three selected ever saw the course on which victory was to be so easily obtained. What sorry rogues make fortunes nowadays! It is more than likely that Rawlings, or whatever this trickster's name was, like his own selections on this particular occasion, had never seen a race-course. Strange as this may seem, it is not at all improbable; for there are lots of men who live by the turf, and who are as conversant with pedigrees and performances of horses as can be, yet who know nothing beyond what they see on paper, and who, authorities on racing when in Fleet Street, would be quite nonplussed if taken to Newmarket among the horses whose names they know so well.

We trust we have now made plain the two greatest swindles in connection with the turf, and at the same time shown the unworthiness of even the pretence to knowledge made by them. But we have no wish that readers, forgetting the scamps with whom we set out, shall conclude this chapter with the impression that there are no thieves so bad as sporting thieves, and so we will fall back on some swindling advertisements of the general kind, from the general papers, which are not only as roguish, but as ignorant of the subjects selected as the effusions of Rawlings himself. Here is one from the *Weekly Times* of a couple of years or so back :—

WONDERS OF THE HOROSCOPE.—Any person sending an addressed envelope, age, height, colour of hair and eyes, together with 13 stamps, will receive within 24 hours a correct likeness of their future husband or wife, and date of marriage.—Address, A. WEMYSS, 2, Drake-street, Red Lion-square, London.

We don't mind giving Mr Wemyss—what an aristocratic name, by the way!—a gratuitous advertisement, though we hope that the first customer he gets through our instrumentality will be the reverse of profitable. Wemyss can do better still at a better price, as other advertisements show. He is a milder form of rascal than Methralton, who makes offer as follows in several of the weekly papers, and who is not content with his effect on the mind, but actually wishes to interfere with the matter :—

WONDROUS ARTS.—Your future revealed—Seven years, six stamps; lifetime twelve stamps. State age. Love Charm, sixteen stamps. Medicine for removing Gravel and Private diseases in a few days, without injuring the constitution, sixty stamps. Methralton's Bible Key, twenty-six stamps. Book of Spirits, 408 pages, thirty-two stamps. Millennial Prophecies, Gratis. METHRALTON, the Seer, Daventry.

Another kind of scoundrel, whose victims are like those of the home-employment robbers, mostly poor helpless girls, and whose villany is far greater than that of the discreet Walter or the forcible Rawlings, is the fellow who advertises constantly for actors and actresses, who may be perfectly inexperienced, but who are to get salaried engagements through his influence. His form varies, but this is one of his concoctions, and is from the *Daily Telegraph*:—

THE STAGE.—WANTED, TWELVE LADIES and GENTLEMEN (ages 16 to 40) for salaried engagements. Totally inexperienced persons may apply.—Communicate, by letter only, enclosing photograph and thirteen stamps, Histrionicus ——.

This is either a swindle on the girls, or else on the members of the British public who pay their money to see acting. It is rumoured that now and again women moving in a certain hemisphere give large sums for the purpose of appearing on the stage. This may be, but we fancy the managers are quite shrewd enough not to let outsiders like the advertiser, Histrionicus, interfere in such delicate matters. It might be as well to ask why the "promotion in absentiâ" dodges are still allowed to parade themselves in the leading papers, or in fact why people should be permitted to take upon themselves titles they have no right to. Possibly the matter is thought too ridiculous to call for interference, but there are other qualities besides those of ridicule and contempt to be found in connection with the following, which is an advertisement having no particularly distinctive features, and therefore will represent the thousands of the same order that appear during the year, and for payment of which a considerable number of spurious degrees must be manufactured:—

PROMOTION IN ABSENTIÂ.—Qualified surgeons, chemists, dentists, oculists, chiropodists, and professors of music or arts aspiring to a doctor's degree, may communicate by letter to Professor ——.

Qualified, forsooth! why, any one who liked to pay could obtain the most honourable degree for the biggest idiot in Earlswood Asylum. One of the chief difficulties to be encountered over such a bad business as this is that the good and the sham degree holders very often get irretrievably mixed up in certain phases of society. Physicians, surgeons, and gentlemen in similar position are protected, and so little dealing is done in medical, surgical, or chemical degrees; but bachelors and masters of arts and doctors of laws are made by the score, the recipients of honours being in a majority of cases men whose ignorance must be probed before it is appreciated, but whose depth requires no delving whatever. Now, when a man of this kind elects to call himself doctor, or puts B.A. or M.A. after his name, even those who know what little right he has to the degree are hardly quixotic enough to decline giving him the title he covets; so in a year or so, Dr Brown or Dr Jones has as firm a hold upon his title as if he had obtained it by a personal examination under the most rigorous system; and strangers who are unable to discover for themselves the unworthiness of the pretender, give him all the honours which belong to the learned. Sometimes the applicant swindles the professor, and we not long back heard of an aspiring youth who paid for the degrees of M.A. and LL.D. with a cheque and a bill, each being for £20, and both being dishonoured. It is a pity that these two scamps cannot be treated to three months in the House of Correction, just to encourage all other professors and practisers of small and paltry swindles.

There is yet another kind of rogue for whom we have room, who addresses his victims by means of advertisements. This is the sorrowful Christian, who makes the profession of religion his stock-in-trade, and finds it profitable. Under the guise of sanctity there is hardly anything at which he will stick—he is the foulest and nastiest of all the foul and nasty birds who have supplied material for this chapter. He is as great an impostor in his pretences as any of the other swindlers are in theirs, and so it would be just as fair to blame religion for the existence of the sanctimonious scoundrel, or commerce for the home-employment agent, as it is to blame racing for the welcher and the forcer. Here is a sample of the whining and despicable hound, compared with whom, to our taste, the ordinary pickpocket is a gentleman :—

TO THE LORD'S PEOPLE.—A dear Christian tradesman, who about four months ago drew from the Savings' Bank £60, his all therein, to give to a fellow Christian who urgently required that sum, "thus lending and hoping for nothing again" but from a bountiful "God whose name is Love," is now in WANT OF FORTY POUNDS to pay all demands upon him, ere he accepts a call to the ministry of the Everlasting Gospel, which he believes his Heavenly Father is about to make known unto him. A lady, his friend in Christ the Lord as revealed, in the power of God the Holy Ghost, thus ventures in simple faith to try the door of Providence in his behalf; and would leave the issue in the hands of Him who has heart, hand, breath and purse of men at sovereign command. The smallest help will be gratefully acknowledged by the Advertiser. Address to ——.

If this is not blasphemy, what is it? Imagine the greasy smirk of satisfaction with which the coin of the faithful was received and divided between the dear Christian tradesman and his lady friend. There is something suspiciously jocular about the wind-up of the application; but then, as an old proverb informs us, people who are doing well can afford the luxury of laughter. Another plan of the religious rascal is to answer applications for loans, and under the guise of philanthropy and Christianity to offer the required accommodation. By this means, and by the exhibition of certain forms, he obtains a deposit from the unfortunate would-be borrower, and decamps. This is, however, but a means of relaxation, and is simply indulged in at intervals, just to keep the hand in while more important business is in course of projection. The loan-office advertisements may to a certain extent be regarded as swindles, especially when they promise money without security. Depend upon it, no professional money-lender is likely to let out his cash without security any more than without interest. Still loan-office advertisers are not swindlers absolutely, as they do lend money and to some extent perform their contracts. The papers at the present time swarm with their advertisements, and the curious reader may inspect them as they appear, as for obvious reasons we must decline making a selection, which might be the reverse of judicious, more especially as the notices do not come strictly within our limits. Now and again temporary offices are started, generally in poor neighbourhoods, for the purpose of bagging the inquiry fees, and with no intention whatever of lending money. Their general ultimatum is, "Security offered insufficient;" and a good story is told of a gentleman who from motives of curiosity applied for a loan of £5, and gave as guarantors two of the most notoriously wealthy bankers of the City. In due course he received the usual notification, that the security offered was not sufficiently "responsible," and that the accommodation could not therefore be afforded.

This brings us to the end of our list of swindlers and thieves; and if we have succeeded in our endeavour to show that the advertising rogue belongs to no particular class or profession, and that it is idle to assume that any rank or class is answerable for him, we shall be well satisfied. To our mind, and we have studied the subject rather closely, the advertising swindler is a swindler *per se*, and attaches himself to anything which offers a return, without caring what its title so long as it has claims to attention. It would be a great pity, therefore, to assume that these men have anything to do with the respectable forms of the professions—from sporting to religion—they from time to time adopt, and a great blunder to blame any body of respectable men because a lot of rogues choose to assume their business. As long as there are advertising swindlers, some profession or other must have the discredit of them.

There are, however, still advertisement swindles of a totally different description from any that have been here mentioned or referred to. There is the swindle of the newspaper proprietor who guarantees a circulation which has no existence, and who, when he takes the money of those who insert notices in his journal, knows that he is committing a deliberate and barefaced robbery. There are in London, at the present time, papers that have absolutely no circulation, in the proper sense of the word, whatever; and of which only a sufficient number of copies is printed to supply those who advertise in them, according to the custom observed in many offices. The readers, therefore, pay a rather heavy premium for the privilege of perusing each other's announcements. It may seem that this state of affairs cannot possibly continue long; but whatever theorists may make of it, we can speak with confidence of more than six papers which to our knowledge have possessed no buyers whatever for more than six years, yet their proprietors get good livings out of them—better, perhaps, than they would if sale and not swindle was the reason of their being—and calculate on continuing this state of things for their time at all events. After them the deluge may come as soon as it likes. We remember quite well an office in which six of these newspapers were printed —that is, supposed to be printed, for with the exception of an alteration of title and a rearrangement of columns, and with, very rarely, the substitution of a new leading article for an old one, these six newspapers were all one and the same to the printers. Now, of course, had there been any chance of one man buying two copies of this instrument of robbery under any two of its distinct names, the swindle would have run some risk of being exposed; but so far as we could discover, there was no desire ever shown to buy even one, the circulation being exclusively among the advertisers. A very small circulation which finds its way in any particular direction may often be far more useful to one who wishes his notice to travel that way than would the largest circulation in the world; but the intensest of optimists could hardly discern any likelihood of benefit in the system just noticed.

Still another kind of advertisement swindle—still more distinct from the general run of swindles—is that by which certain ambitious persons try to obtain a spurious notoriety. Their desire is in no way connected with trade, though as it has in its effect the passing off of inferior wares upon the public as though they were of first-class quality, the word swindle very properly applies to their little trickery. These men pine for recognition in the public prints, and so long as their names are mentioned, no matter how, they regard the task of achieving a cheap immortality as progressing towards completion. Literature and the various phases of art suffer most from these impostors, who very often not only attain notoriety by means of the specious puffery they exercise, but by it obtain money as well. No one can be blind to the manner in which some very small literary lights manage to keep their names continually paraded before the public; and the puffs are so worded that the unthinking are bound to believe that these rushlight writers are the souls of the literature and journalism of the present day. Said the publisher of a magazine, who is not renowned for either taste or education, when it was proposed that a really eminent man should write him an article, "No; I dessay he's very good, but I want men with names. I can get Montague Smith and Chumley Jones and Montmorency Thomson, all famous, and all glad to write for two pound a sheet—why, I never heard of your man, and yet he wants ten times as much. I never see his name in the papers." This was the publisher who is said to have refused to pay for the refrain of a set of verses except where it first occurred, and demanded that the rest should be measured off and deducted from the price originally agreed upon. So not only in the case of the publisher, but in that of the public do these small potatoes, who have a knack of glossing over their mean surnames with high-sounding prefixes, render themselves representatives of an institution the real leaders in which are often quite unknown out of their own circles.

For every thousand familiar with the name of Shakespeare Green, the writer of "awfuls," there is not one who can tell you who are the editors of the leading daily papers and principal reviews. The anonymity of journalism has its advantages, and very likely the directors of public opinion are content to remain behind its curtain; but it is through this same anonymous arrangement that the smallest of small fry measured on their merits are enabled to parade themselves as they do. There are, we know, many deservedly well and widely known writers for newspapers and serials who are really what they profess to be, and who depend upon nothing so much as merit for success; but even they must admit the truth of what we have said, and must often feel very like the apples did as they went down stream in the fable.

It might be as well here to say a few words about the advertisement swindles that are perpetrated by means of photographs. It has long been a crying evil that at certain theatres shameless women who wear many diamonds and few clothes are allowed to appear upon the stage and play at acting. Much training enables them now and again to deliver half-a-dozen lines without displaying their ignorance and peculiarity of aspiration too glaringly; but they cannot be depended on to do even this much with certainty. Sometimes they sing in the smallest of small voices, and a few of them have mastered the breakdown and the *can-can;* but their chief attraction consists, to the audience, in their lavish display of limbs and "neck," and, to the manager, in their requiring but nominal salaries. One would have thought it sufficient that such creatures should exhibit themselves to the people who choose to go and see them; but it is not so, they get themselves photographed in the most extraordinary attitudes, and their counterfeit presentments leer out from the shop windows upon passers-by in much the same manner as in the flesh—sometimes in very much of it—they leer at their friends in the stalls and boxes. Now and again we see the portrait of one real and justly-celebrated actress surrounded by these demireps, but of late what are known as actresses' portraits consist mainly of those to whom the title is convenient, or of those who combine a little of the actress with a great deal of the courtesan. Those artists whose portraits should grace the photographers' show-cases hardly care to run the risk of being mixed up in the questionable society they see there; and we can vouch for the fact that in a leading thoroughfare, of twenty-five English portraits exhibited in a window as those of actresses, at which we were looking but recently, there were not five that were really what they pretended to be.

Of hoaxes which come within our scope a very noticeable one took place in August 1815. A short time previous to the departure of the French Emperor from our coast on his last journey, to St Helena, a respectably-dressed man caused a quantity of handbills to be distributed through Chester, in which he informed the public that a great number of genteel families had embarked at Plymouth, and would certainly proceed with the British regiment appointed to accompany the ex-Emperor to St Helena: he added further, that the island being dreadfully infested with rats, his Majesty's ministers had determined that it should be forthwith effectually cleared of those noxious animals. To facilitate this important purpose, he had been deputed to purchase as many cats and thriving kittens as could possibly be procured for money, in a short space of time; and therefore he publicly offered in his handbills "sixteen shillings for every *athletic full-grown tom-cat*, ten shillings for every *adult female puss*, and half-a-crown for every thriving *vigorous kitten* that could *swill* milk, pursue a ball of thread, or fasten its young fangs in a dying mouse." On the evening of the third day after this advertisement had been distributed, the people of Chester were astonished by an irruption of a multitude of old women, boys, and girls into their streets, each of whom carried on his or her shoulders either a bag or a basket, which appeared to contain some restless animal. Every road, every lane, was thronged with this comical procession; and before night a congregation of nearly three thousand cats was collected in Chester. The happy bearers of these sweet-voiced creatures proceeded (as directed by the advertisement) towards one street with their delectable burdens. Here they became closely wedged together. A vocal concert soon ensued. The women screamed; the cats squalled; the boys and girls shrieked aloud, and the dogs of the street howled to match, so that it soon became difficult for the nicest ear to ascertain whether the canine, the feline, or the human tones were predominant. Some of the cat-bearing ladies, whose dispositions were not of the most placid nature, finding themselves annoyed by their neighbours, soon cast down their burdens and began to box. A battle royal ensued. The cats sounded the war-whoop with might and main. Meanwhile the boys of the town, who seemed mightily to relish the sport, were actively employed in opening the mouths of the deserted sacks, and liberating the cats from their forlorn situations. The enraged animals bounded immediately on the shoulders and heads of the combatants, and ran spitting, squalling, and clawing along the undulating sea of skulls, towards the walls of the houses of the good people of Chester. The citizens, attracted by the noise, had opened the windows to gaze at the fun. The cats, rushing with the rapidity of lightning up the pillars, and then across the balustrades and galleries, for which the town is so famous, leaped slap-dash through the open windows into the apartments. Never, since the days of the celebrated Hugh Lupus, were the drawing-rooms of Chester filled with such a crowd of unwelcome guests. Now were heard the crashes of broken china; the howling of affrighted dogs; the cries of distressed damsels, and the groans of well-fed citizens. All Chester was soon in arms; and dire were the deeds of vengeance executed on the feline race. Next morning above five hundred dead bodies were seen floating on the river Dee, where they had been ignominiously thrown by the two-legged victors. The rest of the invading host having evacuated the town, dispersed in the utmost confusion to their respective homes.

In 1826 the following handbill was circulated in Norwich and its neighbourhood for some days previous to the date mentioned in it, and caused great excitement:—

St James's Hill, back of the Horse Barracks.

The Public are respectfully informed that Signor CARLO GRAM VILLECROP, the celebrated Swiss Mountain Flyer, from Geneva and Mont Blanc, is just arrived in this City, and will exhibit with a Tyrolese Pole, fifty feet long, his most astonishing Gymnastic Flights, never before witnessed in this country. Signor Villecrop has had the great honour of exhibiting his most extraordinary Feats on the Continent before the King of Prussia, Emperor of Austria, the Grand Duke of Tuscany, and all the resident Nobility in Switzerland. He begs to inform the Ladies and Gentlemen of this City that he has selected St James's Hill and the adjoining hills for his performances, and will first display his remarkable strength in running up the hill with his Tyrolese Pole between his teeth. He will next lay on his back, and balance the same Pole on his nose, chin, and different parts of his body. He will climb upon it with the astonishing swiftness of a cat, and stand on his head at the top; on a sudden he will leap three feet from the Pole without falling, suspending himself by a shenese cord only. He will also walk on his head up and down the hill, balancing the Pole on one foot. Many other feats will be exhibited, in which Signor Villecrop will display to the audience the much-admired art of toppling, peculiar only to the Peasantry of Switzerland. He will conclude his performance by repeated flights in the air, up and down the hill, with a velocity almost imperceptible, assisted only by his Pole, with which he will frequently jump the astonishing distance of Forty and Fifty Yards at a time. Signor Villecrop begs to assure the ladies and gentlemen who honour him with their company that no money will be collected till after the exhibition, feeling convinced that his exertions will be liberally rewarded by their generosity. The Exhibition to commence on Monday, the 28th of August 1826, precisely at half-past five o'clock in the evening.

On the evening of the 28th August there were more than twenty thousand people assembled at the foot of the hill, on foot, on horseback, and in every kind of conveyance. Of course Signor Carlo Gram Villecrop did not put in an appearance, for that best of all the reasons that could be given—his having no existence out of the minds of the perpetrators of the swindle.

We had intended to introduce as a congenial subject the great bottle-trick hoax, but as we have already run to such length, and as this famous piece of humbug will stand well alone, we give it a chapter to itself.

CHAPTER XIII.

THE GREAT BOTTLE-TRICK SWINDLE.

AT the close of the year 1748, or in the beginning of 1749, the Duke of Montague, Lord Portman, and some other noblemen were talking about the gullibility of the people, and the Duke offered to wager that, let a man advertise the most impossible thing in the world, he would find fools enough in London to fill a playhouse, and pay handsomely for the privilege of being there. "Surely," said the Earl of Chesterfield, "if a man should say that he would jump into a quart bottle, nobody would believe that." The Duke was somewhat staggered at this, but for the sake of the jest determined to make the experiment. Accordingly the following advertisement was inserted in the papers of the first week in January 1749:—

AT the New Theatre in the Hay market, on Monday next, the 12th instant, is to be seen a Person who performs the several most surprising things following, viz.—1st. He takes a common walking Cane from any of the Spectators, and thereon plays the music of every Instrument now in use, and likewise sings to surprising perfection.—2dly. He presents you with a common Wine Bottle, which any of the spectators may first examine; this Bottle is placed on a Table in the middle of the Stage, and he (without any equivocation) goes into it, in the sight of all the Spectators, and sings in it; during his stay in the bottle, any Person may handle it, and see plainly that it does not exceed a common Tavern Bottle.—Those on the Stage, or in the Boxes, may come in masked habits (if agreeable to them); and the Performer, if desired, will inform them who they are.—Stage, 7s. 6d. Boxes, 5s. Pit, 3s. Gallery, 2s. Tickets to be had at the Theatre:—To begin at half an hour after six o'clock. The performance continues about two hours and a half.

Note.—If any Gentlemen or Ladies (after the above Performance) either single or in company, in or out of mask, is desirous of seeing a representation of any deceased Person, such as Husband or Wife, Sister or Brother, or any intimate Friend of either sex, upon making a gratuity to the Performer, shall be gratified by seeing and conversing with them for some minutes, as if alive; likewise, if desired, he will tell you your most secret thoughts in your past Life, and give you a full view of persons who have injured you, whether dead or alive. For those Gentlemen and Ladies who are desirous of seeing this last part, there is a private Room provided.

These performances have been seen by most of the crowned Heads of Asia, Africa, and Europe, and never appeared public any where but once; but will wait on any at their Houses, and perform as above, for five Pounds each time. A proper guard is appointed to prevent disorder.

On the appointed day the theatre was crowded to excess, but as there was not even a single fiddle provided to keep the audience in good-humour, signs of impatience soon began to manifest themselves. When the hour was past at which the conjuror had to make his appearance, there arose a horrible uproar, and the loud cat-calls, heightened by cries and beating of sticks, soon brought a person on the stage, who, amidst endless bowing and scraping, declared that if the performer did not appear within a quarter of an hour, the money should be returned. At the same time a wag in the pit exclaimed that if the ladies and gentlemen would give double prices he would creep into a pint bottle. Scarcely was the quarter of an hour's grace elapsed, when a gentleman in one of the boxes seized a lighted candle and threw it on the stage. This was the signal for a general outbreak, the benches were torn up and everything that could be moved was thrown about. The greater part of the audience made the best of their way out of the house, the rush to the doors being so dreadful that wigs, hats, cloaks, and dresses, were left behind and lost. Meantime the mob remained and almost gutted the building: the wood was carried into the street and made into a mighty bonfire, whilst the curtain was hoisted upon a pole by way of a flag. Of the conjuror nothing was ever heard, but the affair gave rise to a number of curious advertisements. The Duke of Cumberland having lost his sword in the general panic, it was advertised in the following manner:—

LOST, last Monday night at the Little Play house in the Hay market, a Sword with a gold Hilt and cutting Blade, with a crimson and gold Swordknot tied round the Hilt. Whoever brings it to Mr Chevenix's Toy shop, over against Great Suffolk Street, near Chearing Cross, shall receive thirty Guineas reward, and no Questions asked.

It was probably a Jacobite who answered this by the following:—

FOUND entangled in the slit of a Lady's demolished smock Petticoat, a gold hilted Sword, of martial length and temper, nothing worse for wear, with the Spey curiously wrought on one side of the blade, and the Scheldt on the other; supposed to have been stolen from the plump side of a great General, in his precipitate retreat from the Battle of Bottle-Noodles, at Station Foote. Enquire at the Quart Bottle and Musical Cane in Potter's Row.

N.B.—Every word of a certain late advertisement is true, except all the advertisement.

Foote having been blamed by many for the occurrence of this disgraceful hoax, excused himself by an advertisement, in which he threw the blame upon Potter, the proprietor of the playhouse, whom Foote had warned that he thought a fraud on the public was intended. To this Potter replied by a counter-advertisement, explaining the precautions he had taken: how he had not allowed the conjuror or any of his men to take the money, but placed his own servants at the door, and how he would have returned it all, but that the house was sacked and the takings stolen. On the 20th of January there appeared an advertisement of Potter's, which ran as follows:—

WHEREAS a letter signed S. M. dated the 18th instant, was sent yesterday by the Penny Post, directed to Mr Potter, in the Hay market; which by the contents seems to come from the person who took Mr Potter's Theatre, for Monday last; wherein he complains of much ill usage, and insists that the Man can perform the things he advertised, and would have performed them, and was actually in a Coach in order to come, but was intimidated by two Gentlemen who came from the Gun Tavern, who told him he would be taken up if he performed: and in his Letter he threatens, that in case Mr Potter will not give him £22, which he says he was out of pocket, that he will apply to some Court of Law or Equity, for justice: He also desires an answer in this Paper—In answer to which, S. M. is desired to appear personally and to give an Account of his Name and place of Abode; and he shall have such Satisfaction as in justice deserves.

JOHN POTTER.

The same paper also contained the following exculpation:—

WHEREAS the Public was on Monday last basely abused by an Impostor, who pretended to perform what was impracticable, at the Theatre in the Hay market; the same imposition some evil-minded villains imagined John Coustos, Lapidary, to be the author of: This is to assure the Public that the said John Coustos had never such Design, nor ever hired or caused to be hired, the House on any occasion whatever; and to caution those his Enemies, who are the Authors of this Report, not to assert a thing which they know to be a gross Falsity: And there are those who are ready to attest on Oath that he was in their company that Evening, and was at the Theatre as a spectator only.

JOHN COUSTOS.

Many attempts were made to fathom the depth and discover the origin of this hoax, and several humorous explanations were given in the papers, among them being the following:—

WHEREAS various stories have been told the Public, about the Man and the Bottle, the following account seems to be the best as yet given of that odd Affair; viz. A Gentleman went to him the same evening he was to perform in the Haymarket, and asking him what he must have to perform to him in private, he said £5, on which they agreed; and the Conjuror getting ready to go into the Bottle, which was set on a Table, the gentleman having provided a Parcel of Corks, fitted one to the Bottle; then the Conjuror, having darkened the Room as much as was necessary, at last with much squeezing got into the Bottle, which, in a moment the Gentleman corked up, and whipt into his Pocket, and in great haste and seeming confusion, went out of the House, telling the Servants who waited at the door, that their Master had bewitched him, and bid them go in and take care of him. Thus the poor Man being bit himself, in being confined in the Bottle and in a Gentleman's Pocket, could not be in another Place; for he never advertised he would go into two Bottles at one and the same time. He is still in the Gentleman's custody, who uncorks him now and then to feed him; but his long Confinement has so damped his Spirits, that instead of singing and dancing, he is perpetually crying and cursing his ill Fate. But though the Town have been disappointed of seeing him go into the Bottle, in a few days they will have the pleasure of seeing him come out of the Bottle; of which timely notice will be given in the daily Papers.

Pamphlets ridiculing the public for its gullibility issued from the press with alarming rapidity, and advertisements of performances equally impossible as the bottle-hoax continued to be inserted in the papers for several weeks after. Among them were the following :—

Lately arrived from Italy,

SIGNOR CAPITELLO JUMPEDO a surprising Dwarf, no taller than a common *Tavern Tobacco Pipe:* who can perform many wonderful Equilibres on the slack or tight Rope: likewise he will transform his Body in above ten thousand different Shapes and Postures, and after he has diverted the Spectators two hours and a half, *he will open his Mouth wide* and jump down his own Throat! He being the most wonderfullest Wonder of Wonders, as ever the World wondered at, would be willing to join in performance with that surprising Musician, on Monday next in the Hay market. He is to be spoke with at the Black Raven in Golden Lane, every day from seven till twelve, and from two to all day long.

This was also an emanation caused by the current excitement, and was published January 27, 1749:—

DON JOHN DE NASAQUITINE, sworn Brother and Companion to the Man that was to have jumped into the Bottle at the Little Theatre in the Hay market, on Monday the 16th past; hereby invites all such as were then disappointed to repair to the Theatre aforesaid on Monday the 30th; and *that* shall be exhibited unto them, which never has heretofore, nor ever will be hereafter seen. All such as shall swear upon the Book of Wisdom that they paid for seeing the Bottle Man will be admitted gratis; the rest at Gotham prices.

And then the public were treated to this, for the purpose of keeping up the interest :—

Lately arrived from Ethiopia,

THE most wonderful and surprising Doctor BENIMBE ZAMMANPOANGO, Oculist and Body Surgeon to Emperor of Monoemungi, who will perform on Sunday next, at the little T—— in the Hay market, the following surprising Operations; viz. 1st, He desires any one of the Spectators only to pull out his own Eyes, which as soon as he has done, the Doctor will shew them to any Lady or Gentleman then present, to convince them there is no Cheat, and then replace them in the Sockets, as perfect and entire as ever. 2dly, He desires any officer or other, to rip up his own Belly, which when he has done, he (without any Equivocation) takes out his Bowels, washes them, and returns them to their place, without the Person's suffering the least hurt. 3dly, He opens the head of a J—— of P——, takes out his Brains, and exchanges them for those of a Calf; the Brains of a Beaü for those of an Ass, and the Heart of a Bully for that of a Sheep: which Operations will render the Persons more sociable and rational Creatures than they ever were in their Lives. And to convince the town that no imposition is intended, he desires no Money until the Performance is over. Boxes, 5 güin. Pit 3. Gallery 2.

N.B.—The famous Oculist will be there, and honest S—— F—— H—— will come if he can. Ladies may come masked, so may Fribbles. The Faculty and Clergy gratis. The Orator would be there, but is engaged.

Money seems to have been at least as plentiful as wit in those days, for, from a lot of other notices bearing on this subject, we take this:—

This is to inform the Public,

THAT notwithstanding the great Abuse that has been put upon the Gentry, there is now in Town a Man, who instead of creeping into a Quart or Pint Bottle, *will change himself into a Rattle;* which he hopes will please both young and old. If this Person meets with encouragement to this Advertisement, he will then acquaint the Gentry where and when he performs.

Strange as it may seem, and notwithstanding all the expenditure of wit and humour upon the credulity of the times that had been made, one showman still thought there was room left for a further attempt at attracting the public with the tenant of a bottle. Very soon after the great hoax he published the following advertisement, which shows the desire some industrious people have to avail themselves of the general disposition of the time. The faculty of imitation is very largely developed nowadays, as witness what follows as soon as any enterprising theatrical manager makes "a hit," and so it is pleasant to find that an honest penny was turned in humble imitation of the great bottle swindle:—

To be seen at MR LEADER'S, *the Old Horseshoe, in Wood Street, Cheapside, from Nine till Twelve, and from Four to Seven o'Clock, Lately brought from France,*

A FULL grown MOUSE alive, confined in a small two ounce Phial, the Neck of which is not a quarter of an inch Diameter. This amusing Creature has lived in the Phial three Years and a half without Drink or any Sustenance but Bread only. It cleans out its little Habitation, and hath many other pretty Actions, as surprising as agreeable; but particularly creates wonderful diversion with a Fly, and is allowed to be an extraordinary Curiosity, never before seen in England; at the Expense of 6d. each Person.

Note.—Gentlemen or Ladies who don't chuse to come, it shall be carried to them, by sending a line to MR LEADER.

Like everything else of its kind, the excitement in connection with the bottle-hoax soon gave way to fresh topics of public interest. The trick has, however, been revived occasionally with more or less effect; and Theodore Hook's cruel, and not particularly clever, hoax, which made a house in Berners Street notorious and its occupants miserable, was but a phase of the swindle just related; and being so, loses whatever merit it possessed in the eyes of those who will sacrifice anything to a joke, so long, of course, as it is original and does not interfere with their own comfort or convenience. Deprived of its originality, Hook's exploit stands forth as a trick hardly excusable in a boy, and utterly at variance with the character of a gentleman. Now in the bottle-hoax there was quite a different element; people were invited to the theatre to see that which they must have known was utterly impossible. In obedience to the laws which govern human nature, they readily accepted the invitation, and also, in accordance with the same laws, they resented the affront they considered had been put upon them. A moral might be deduced from this, were it not for the fact, that if any hoax analogous to the bottle-trick were to be advertised to-morrow in a conspicuous manner, the proportion of dupes would be at least as great as it was in 1749. Perhaps greater.

CHAPTER XIV.

QUACKS AND IMPOSTORS.

QUACKS have been in existence so long, have received so much of the confidence of the people, and have afforded such capital to satirists and humourists, that they have become almost a necessity of our existence, from a literary as well as from a domestic point of view. They also add considerably to the revenue, if only through the impost upon patent medicines; for though many may be astonished and horrified to hear it, all patent medicines—*i.e.*, all medicines which bear the inland-revenue stamp—are of necessity quack, and although many partisans may endeavour to prove that in the particular case each may select, this is not so, the qualification must fairly be applied, if applied to anything, to all medicines which are supposed to specifically remedy various diseases in various systems, no matter what the peculiarities of either. It can hardly matter whether the inventor of the general remedy be learned doctor or impudent charlatan, the medicine, as soon as ever it assumes specific powers, and is to be administered by or to anybody, is quack, not only in the proper acceptation of the term, but in its original signification. Quacks are, with a few notable exceptions, a very different body now from what they were in the last century, when they killed more than they cured, and when drugs were compounded with a recklessness which seems quite impossible in these moderate days. Just and proper legislation has clipped the wings of the vile impostors who used to trade upon the weaknesses of human nature, and with the exception of those pestiferous practitioners whose advertisements are as noxious as their prescriptions, and who find the fittest possible media for publication, quacks are no longer in existence except as purveyors of patent medicines, pills, ointment, and plasters; and so if there is no cure there is also no kill. Formerly the quack prescribed and compounded, and then he was indeed dangerous, and we cannot better prove this than by means of a remark in the *Gentleman's Magazine* of July 1734 about Joshua Ward, an advertisement in reference to whom is to be found in the historical part of this book. The paragraph in the old magazine runs: "There was an extraordinary advertisement in the newspapers this month concerning the great cures in all distempers performed with one medicine, a pill or drop, by Joshua Ward, Esq., lately arrived from Paris, where he had done the like cures. 'Twas said our physicians, particularly Sir Hans Sloane, had found out his secret, but 'twas judged so violent a prescription, that it would be deemed malepractice to apply it as a dose to old and young and in all cases." And again, in the Obituary in the same periodical for 1736, there is an advertisement bearing on this so-called remedy rather unfavourably. It runs thus:—

Vesey Hart, Esq. of *Lincoln's Inn*. About 15 Months ago he took the celebrated Pill, which had at first such violent effects as to throw him into Convulsions and deprive him of his Sight. On recovery he fell into Consumption.

Joshua Ward was rather a celebrity about that time, even among quacks, as the following lines from the *Gentleman's Magazine* of July 1734 will show. The heading is—

UNIV. SPEC. ON WARD'*s Drops.*

EGregious *Ward*, you boast with success sure,
That your *one drop* can *all* distempers cure:
When it in *S——n cures* ambition's *pain*
Or ends the *Megrims* of Sir *James*' brain,

Of *wounded conscience* when it *heals* the *smart*,
And on *reflexion* glads the statesman's heart;
When it to women palls old *M—ar—'s gust*,
And *cools* 'fore death the *fever* of his *lust;*
When *F——d* it can give of *wit* a *taste*,
Make *Harriot* pious or *lorima* chaste;
Make scribbling *B—dg— deviate* into *sense*,
Or give to *Pope* more wit and excellence;
Then will I think that your ONE DROP will save
Ten thousand dying patients from the *grave.*

In the *Daily Advertiser* of June 10, 1736, there is a puff advertisement for Ward, which runs:—

We hear that by the Queen's appointment, Joshua Ward, Esq; and eight or ten persons, who in extraordinary Cases have receiv'd great benefit by taking his remedies, attended at the Court at Kensington on monday night last, and his patients were examin'd before her Majesty by three eminent surgeons, several persons of quality being present, when her Majesty was graciously pleas'd to order money to be distributed amongst the patients, and congratulated Mr Ward on his great success.

In the *Grub Street Journal* of June 24 of the same year is an article on the paragraph, in which it is stated that only seven persons attended at the palace, and that these were proved to be impostors who were in collusion with Ward. The *Journal* is very strong against the quack, and the article concludes with the following lines, which are in fact a summary of what has been said in the criticism upon Ward's fresh attempt to gull the public:—

Seven wonderful Cures.

One felt his sharp rheumatic pains no more:
A Second saw much better than before:
Three cur'd of stone, a dire disease much sadder,
Who still, 'tis thought, have each a stone in bladder:
A Sixth brought gravel bottled up and cork'd,
Which *Drop and Pill*, he say'd, by urine work'd;
But Questions, ask'd the Patient, all unravell'd;
Much more than whom the Doctor then was gravell'd.
The last a little Woman but great glutton,
Who at one meal eat two raw legs of mutton:

Nor wonder, since within her stomach lay
A Wolf, that gap'd for victuals night and day:
But when he smelt the Pill, he strait for shelter
Run slap into her belly helter skelter.

There is no necessity to take trouble for the purpose of discovering the origin of quacks. It is evident that they "came natural" as soon as ever there was a chance for them, and it is but right to suppose that before quackery became a question of money-making, it had an existence, the outcome of a love people have innately for prescribing and administering to each other, relics of which may still be seen in out-of-the-way parts of the country. Some people imagine that quackery and the belief, still current in various parts of Great Britain, that a seventh son, particularly if the son of a seventh son, possesses medical powers, had originally something to do with each other. That quackery in general was caused by this quaint conceit is not to be supposed, yet the belief in the seventh-son doctrine is well worthy of note. The vulgar mind seems from the earliest ages to have been impressed by the number seven, and there are various ways of accounting for this. Chambers, in his "Book of Days," says that it is easy to see in what way the Mosaic narrative gave sanctity to this number in connection with the days of the week, and led to usages which influence the social life of all the countries of Europe. "But a sort of mystical goodness or power has attached itself to the number in many other ways. Seven wise men, seven champions of Christendom, seven sleepers, seven-league boots, seven ages of man, seven hills, seven senses, seven planets, seven metals, seven sisters, seven stars, seven wonders of the world—all have had their day of favour; albeit that the number has been awkwardly interfered with by modern discoveries concerning metals, planets, stars, and wonders of the world. Added to the above list is the group of seven sons, especially in relation to the youngest or seventh of the seven; and more especially still if this person happen to be the seventh son of a seventh son. It is now perhaps impossible to discover in what country, or at what time, the notion originated, but a notion there certainly is, chiefly in provincial districts, that a seventh son has something peculiar about him. For the most part, the imputed peculiarity is a healing power, a faculty of curing diseases by the touch, or by some other means. The instances of this belief are numerous enough. There is a rare pamphlet called 'The Quack Doctor's Speech,' published in the time of Charles II. The reckless Earl of Rochester delivered this speech on one occasion, when dressed in character, and mounted on a stage as a charlatan. The speech, amid much that suited that licentious age, but would be frowned down by modern society, contained an enumeration of the doctor's wonderful qualities, among which was that of being a 'seventh son of a seventh son,' and therefore clever as a curer of bodily ills. The matter is only mentioned as affording a sort of proof of the existence of a sort of popular belief. In Cornwall, the peasants and the miners entertain this notion; they believe that a seventh son can cure the king's evil by the touch. The mode of proceeding usually is to stroke the part affected thrice gently, to blow upon it thrice, to repeat a form of words, and to give a perforated coin, or some other object, to be worn as an amulet. At Bristol, about forty years ago, there was a man who was always called 'doctor' simply because he was the seventh son of a seventh son. The family of the Joneses of Muddfi, in Wales, is said to have presented seven sons to each of many successive generations, of whom the seventh son always became a doctor —apparently from a conviction that he had an inherited qualification to start with. In Ireland, the seventh son of a seventh son is believed to possess prophetical as well as healing power. A few years ago a Dublin shopkeeper finding his errand-boy to be generally very dilatory in his duties, inquired into the cause, and found that the boy, being the seventh son of a seventh son, his services were often in requisition among the poorer neighbours, in a way that brought in a good many pieces of silver. Early in the present century there was a man in Hampshire, the seventh son of a seventh son, who was consulted by the villagers as a doctor, and who carried about with him a collection of crutches and sticks, purporting to have once belonged to persons whom he had cured of lameness. Cases are not wanting, also, in which the seventh daughter is placed upon a similar pinnacle of greatness. In Scotland the spaewife or fortune-teller frequently announces herself as the seventh daughter of a seventh daughter, to enhance her claims to prophetic power. Even so late as 1851, an inscription was seen on a window in Plymouth, denoting that a certain doctress was the third seventh daughter!—which the world was probably intended to interpret as the seventh daughter of the seventh daughter of a seventh daughter. . . . . France, as well as our own country, has a belief in the seventh-son mystery. The *Journal de Loiret*, a French provincial newspaper, in 1854 stated that, in Orleans, if a family has seven sons and no daughter, the seventh is called a *Marcou*, is branded with a fleur-de-lis, and is believed to possess the power of curing the king's evil. The Marcou breathes on the part affected, or else the patient touches the Marcou's fleur-de-lis. In the year above named there was a famous Marcou in Orleans named Foulon; he was a cooper by trade, and was known as 'le beau Marcou.' Simple peasants used to come to visit him from many leagues in all directions, particularly in Passion-week, when his ministrations were believed to be most efficacious. On the night of Good Friday, from midnight to sunrise, the chance of cure was supposed to be especially good, and on this account four or five hundred persons would assemble. Great disturbances hence arose; and as there was evidence, to all except the silly dupes themselves, that Foulon made use of their superstition to enrich himself, the police succeeded, but not without much opposition, in preventing these assemblages. In some of the states of Germany there used formerly to be a custom for the reigning prince to stand sponsor to a seventh son (no daughter intervening) of any of his subjects. Whether still acted upon is doubtful; but there was an incident lately which bore on the old custom in a curious way. A West-Hartlepool newspaper stated that Mr J. V. Curths, a German, residing in that busy colliery town, became, towards the close of 1857, the father of one of those prodigies—a seventh son. Probably he himself was a Saxe-Gothan by birth; at any rate he wrote to the Prince Consort, reminding him of the old German custom, and soliciting the honour of his Royal Highness's sponsorship to the child. The Prince was doubtless a little puzzled by this appeal, as he often must have been by the strange appeals made to him. Nevertheless, a reply was sent in the Prince's name, very complimentary to his countryman, and enclosing a substantial souvenir for the little child; but the newspaper paragraph is not sufficiently clear for us to be certain whether the sponsorship really was assented to, and, if so, how it was performed." It is not at all likely, proud as the late Prince was of his countrymen, and of Germans generally, that he took upon himself the pains and penalties of sponsorship to this miraculous infant, whose father was doubtless well satisfied with the douceur he received, and never expected even that.

Saffold was an early humbug who depended mainly upon doggerel rhyme for attraction. It is to be hoped that his wares were better than his numbers, or else the deaths of many must have lain heavy on his soul. One of his bills, enumerating his address and claims upon the attention of the public, informs us that of him

The Sick may have Advice for Nothing,
And good Medicines cheap, if so they please
For to cure any curable Disease.

It's *Saffold's* Pills, much better than the Rest,
Deservedly have gained the Name of best
In curing by the Cause, quite purging out
Of Scurvy, Dropsie, Agues, Stone and Gout.
The Head, Stomach, Belly and the Reins, they
Will cleanse and cure, while you may work or play.
His Pills have often, to their Maker's Praise,
Cur'd in all Weathers, yea, in the Dog-Days.
In short, no purging Med'cine is made, can
Cure more Diseases in Man or Woman,
Than his cheap Pills, but three Shillings the Box.
Each Box contains Thirty-six Pills I'm sure.
As good as e'er were made Scurvy to cure.
The half Box eighteen Pills, for eighteen Pence,
Tho' 't is too cheap, in any Man's own Sense.

At the foot of the bill, after a lot of puffery, he breaks out into rhyme once more :—

Some envious Men being griev'd may say,
What needs Bills thus still be given away?
Answer: New People come to London every Day.
Believing Solomon's Advice is right,
I will do what I do with all my might.
Also, unless an English Proverb lies
Practice brings Experience and makes wise.
Experimental Knowledge, I protest,
In lawful Arts and Science is the best,
Instead of *Finis* Saffold ends with Rest.

Another of his bills, which were various and plentiful, began thus :—

Dear Friends, let your Disease be what God will,
Pray to Him for a Cure, try Saffold's Skill;
Who may be such a healing Instrument,
As will cure you to your own Heart's Content.
His Medicines are cheap and truly good.
Being full as safe as your daily Food—
Saffold he can do what may be done, by
Either Physick or true Astrology.
His best Pills, rare Elixir and Powder,
Do each Day praise him louder and louder.
Dear Countrymen, I pray be you so wise

When Men backbite him, believe not their Lies,
But go, see him, and believe your own Eyes.
Then he will say you are honest and kind.
Try before you judge and speak as you find.

At another time the muse informs us, among other things in connection with the great Saffold, that

He knows some who are Knaves in Grain,
And have more Gall and Spleen than Brain,
Will ill reward his Skill and Pain.

He hath practised Astrology above 15 Years, and hath License to practise Physick, and he thanks God for it, hath great Experience and wonderful Success in both those Arts, giving to doubtful People and by God's Blessing, cureth the Sick of any Age or Sex or Distemper though given over by Others, and never so bad (if curable); therefore let none despair of a Cure, but try him.

Yet some conceited Fools will ask how he came to be able to do such great Cures, and to foretell such strange Things, and to know how to make such rare and powerful Medicines, as his best *Pills*, *Elixir* and *Diet Drinks* are, and wherefore he doth publish the same in Print? But he will answer such dark Animals thus:

It hath so pleased God, the King of Heaven,
Being He to him hath Knowledge given,
And in him there can be no greater Sin,
Than to hide his Talent in a Napkin.
His Candle is Light and he will not under
A Bushel put it, let the World wonder:
Though he be traduced by such like Tools,
As have Knaves' Hearts, Lackbrains are Fools.

☞ **I request a favourable Construction upon this Publick way of Practice (And** *as I am a Graduate Physician) should wholly omit to appear in Print, as well in this Disease as I have at all Times in all other Diseases, only in Opposition to the Ignorant, that pretend to Cure, and to prevent the ruine of them that suffer and I see daily throw themselves upon ignorant and outlandish Pretenders and others, to the Patient's utter ruine of Body and Purse.* AND *upon this Consideration alone, I was persuaded rather to adventure the censure of* some, than conceal that which may be of great use to many.

One other specimen of this artist's verse and we will let him follow his predecessors. It may be as well to mention that when Saffold left the scene of his labours, "his mantle" was supposed to fall on one John Case, who followed in his footsteps so closely that the lines which had done for one quack were often made to do for the other.

> Saffold resolves, as in his Bills exprest,
> When asked in good Earnest, not in Jest;
> He can cure when God Almighty pleases,
> But cannot protect against Diseases.
> If Men will live intemperate and sin,
> He cannot help 't if they be sick agen.
> This great Truth unto the World he will tell
> None can cure sooner, who cures half so well.

Dr John Case was a contemporary of Dr Radcliffe, and a noted quack who united the professions of an astrologer and a physician. He took the house in which Lilly had resided, and over his door was a vile distich which was said to have brought him more money than Dryden earned by all his works. Upon his pill-boxes he placed the following curious rhyme :—

> Here's 14 Pills for 3 Pence
> Enough is every Man's own Con-sci-ence.

It is almost impossible to find out when quacks were not, and as we have before remarked, as long as there have been advertisements, whether in newspapers or elsewhere, these cunning rogues have been fully awake to their advantages and uses. One effusion, published as a handbill in the time of William and Mary, is noticeable, as, though the advertisers call themselves physicians, there is reason to doubt their right to the title, and to believe that the college was anything but what we now understand by the word. The bill proclaims itself as an

ADVERTISEMENT.

The Physitians of the Colledge, that us'd to consult twice a Week for the benefit of the Sick at the Consultation House, at the Carved Angel and Crown in King-street, near Guildhall, meet now four times a Week ; and therefore give Publick Notice, that on Mondays, Wednesdays, Thursdays and Fridays, from two in the afternoon till six, they may be advised by the known Poor, and meaner Families for nothing; and that their Expectations and Demands from the middle Rank shall be moderate: but as for the Rich and Noble, Liberality is inseparable from their Quality and Breeding.

This is, to say the least, peculiar, the quaint use of the word "advised" seeming very strange, while the wind-up shows that whoever and whatever the physicians may have been, they were not likely to lose sight of the main chance. But their notice is feeble compared with another handbill of the same period, which is of the most dogmatic order, and is called

A friendly and seasonable Advertisement concerning the Dog-days, by Nath. Merry, Philo-Chim.

In regard that there are many that perish in and about this City, &c. through an evil custom, arising from a false opinion That it is not safe to take Physick in the Extreams of Heat and Cold or in the Dog days; and some exclude old People, Women with Child and little Children, from the use of Medicine; which is as much as to say, That God hath ordained no Medicine for such Times and such Ages, which would be absurd to imagine, seeing we know there is no Time, Age nor Disease exempted from proper homogenial and effectual Means (with God's Blessing) only against Death there is no Medicine, the Time of which to us is uncertain. From the aforesaid Mistakes many labour under the tyranny of their Diseases, till the Catastrophe end in Death (before the Time come which they have alotted for their Cure) which might by timely and suitable Remedies be prevented. It's granted *pro confesso* that there is a sort of *Dogmatical Medicines*, that is unfit to be exhibited in those Times, and are not innocent at any Time, being impregnated with venomenous Beams, which by their virulent Hostility invade the vital Œconomy of the Body. But you may have Archeal or Vital medicines, truly adapted for all Times; being divested of their Crudities and heterogene Qualities, by a true Separation of the pure from the impure, and impregnated with Beams of Light, which give their Influences and refreshing Glances upon the vital Faculties, expels Venoms, alters Ferments, co-unites with Nature and re-unites its powers to their due Œconomy, and such Medicines being most natural and most powerful in the most deplorable Diseases being timely taken are most effectual, and are no more to be omitted at any time than foods, and are altogether as safe.

And so on at length, until Nath. Merry divulges the secret that he is the man for the dog-days, and that all others are impostors, which in common with many remarks of the kind, found in most advertisements of the same and other times issued by pretended curers of all known and many unknown disorders, lead us to the belief that however willing quacks have always been to impose upon the credulous themselves, they have been careful enough to expose the presumption of their rivals: a merciful dispensation of providence, which has enabled the statements of one rogue to be balanced, and to a certain extent neutralised, by those of another, and so the remedy is found in the disease when at its worst. Had it not been for the attacks made by empirics upon each other throughout the last century, qualified medical men would have stood a very bad chance, and as it is they seem to have often been obliged to join the ranks of the rascals from sheer inability to get a living without pandering to the popular taste for infallible remedies and things generally unknown to the pharmacopœia. Here is the commencement of an appeal made just prior to the year 1700 by one quack, which consists in a warning against all others of the same profession, and which shows how anxious the writer is for the public benefit, except where his own is immediately concerned:—

A CAUTION TO THE UNWARY.

'Tis generally acknowledged throughout all Europe, that no Nation has been so fortunate in producing such eminent Physicians, as this Kingdom of ours; and 'tis as obvious to every Eye, that no Country was ever pestered with so many ignorant Quacks or Empirics. The Enthusiast in Divinity having no sooner acted his Part, and had his *Exit*, but on the same Stage, from his Shop (or some worse Place) enters the Enthusiast in Physicks: yesterday a Taylor, Heelmaker, Barber, Serving Man, Rope Dancer, etc., to-day *per saltum* a learned Doctor, able to instruct Esculapius himself, for he never obliged Mankind yet with a *Panacæa*, an universal Pill or Powder that could cure all Diseases, which now every Post can direct you to, though it proves only the Hangman's Remedy for all Diseases by Death. *Pudet hæc opprobria dici;* for shame, my dear Countrymen, reassume your Reasons, and expose not your Bodies and Purses to the handling of such illiterate Fellows, who never had the Education of a Grammar-School, much less of an University.

Nor be ye so irrational as to imagine anything extraordinary (unless it be Ignorance) in a Pair of outlandish Whiskers, tho' he's so impudent to tell you he has been Physician to 3 Emperours and 9 Kings when in his own Country he durst not give Physick to a Cobbler.

Nor be gulled with another sort of Impostor, who allures you to him with CURE WITHOUT MONEY, but when he once has got you into his Clutches, he handles you as unmercifully as he does unskilfully.

Nor be ye imposed on by the Pretence of any *Herculean* Medicine, that shall with four Doses at 5s. a Dose, cure the most inveterate Complaint, and Distempers not to be eradicated (in the Opinion of the most learned in all Ages) with less than a Renovation of all the Humours in the whole Body.

These and the like Abuses (too numerous here to be mentioned) have induced me to continue this public Way of Information, that you may be honestly dealt with, and perfectly cured, repairing to him, who with God's Blessing on his Studies and 20 Years successful Practice in this City of London hath attained to the easiest and speediest way of curing.

Then follows the puff which this disinterested person gives to his own wares and powers, and if it is to be believed, he certainly proves to demonstration that he is as good as the others are bad. The next item we have is a bill of the early eighteenth century, headed by a rude woodcut of a unicorn's horn. There is no address on it, and it looks as though used while travelling round the country, in which case the High-German's lodging for the time being would be written or printed on the back, or supplemented in one of the ways usual among itinerant charlatans:—

The High-German, Master of the Waxwork,

Hath an Unicorn's Horn that was found in the Deserts of Arabia, the Powder whereof does several wonderful Cures, whereof I was advised by several Doctors to Publish the same in Print; the Cures that it has done are as follow:

I have in my Travels, by the Virtues of this Powder, saved the Lives of several Gentlewomen in Child-Bed, which could not be Delivered before they took the Powder.

About October the Fifth, 1702, I was in the Town of Hampton, in the County of Gloucester, at Mr Gardners, at the Sign of the White-Hart, where I heard that one Mrs Webb was in Child-Bed and could not be Delivered, so that Doctor Farr of the said Town, the Midwife and all Women left her off for Dead, upon which I sent my Landlady with a little of this Powder, the Quantity whereof would lie upon a Six-pence, which the Gentlewoman took, and was Delivered in less than a Quarter of an Hour; Doctor Farr has given it under his Hand, and some other Gentlemen of the Town can testify, that this Powder was the saving of her Life (under God).

Likewise this Powder is a certain Cure for the Kings-Evil, when it breaks and runs: The Powder must be put on a Linnen Cloath and applied to the Place, and take as much as will lie on a Six-pence for two Mornings in warm Ale.

The College of Physitians in London, hearing of this Powder, they came to my Lodging, on purpose to see this Horn, and desired me to let them have some Experience to try if it would Expel Poyson, upon which they sent for two Dogs and Poysoned them both, and asked me if I could save one of them, whereupon I took a little Powder of this Horn in a Spoonful of Milk, and gave it to one of them, that which I gave it to was saved, and the other died in their Presence, after which the Doctors offered me a great Sum of Money for this Horn, which I was not willing to part with.

If there are any Gentlewomen desirous to Buy any of this Powder, I Sell it at Reasonable Rates, and it may be kept Ten Years and not lose its Virtue.

FINIS.

In Queen Anne's time, and during the first years of the Hanoverian succession, quackery does not seem to have impaired its professors' positions in society, providing they had other claims to consideration, and even the most impudent impostors obtained rank and celebrity under circumstances which hardly seem possible. Listen to the following: "Sir William Read, originally a tailor or a cobbler, became progressively a mountebank and a quack doctor, and gained, in his case, the equivocal honour of knighthood from Queen Anne. He is said to have practised by 'the light of nature;' and though he could not read, he could ride in his own chariot, and treat his company with good punch out of a golden bowl. He had an uncommon share of impudence;

a few scraps of Latin in his bills made the ignorant suppose him to be wonderfully learned. He did not seek his reputation in small places, but practised at that high seat of learning, Oxford; and in one of his addresses he called upon the Vice-Chancellor, University, and the City, to vouch for his cures—as, indeed, he did upon the people of the three kingdoms. Blindness vanished before him, and he even deigned to practise in other distempers; but he defied all competition as an oculist. Queen Anne and George I. honoured Read with the care of their eyes; from which one would have thought the rulers, like the ruled, as dark intellectually as Taylor's (his brother quack) coach-horses were corporeally, of which it was said five were blind in consequence of their master having exercised his skill upon them." Dr Radcliffe mentions this humbug as "Read the mountebank, who has assurance enough to come to our table up-stairs at Garraway's, swears he'll stake his coach and six horses, his two blacks, and as many silver trumpets, against a dinner at Pontack's." Read died at Rochester, May 24, 1715. After Queen Anne had knighted him and Dr Hannes, the following lines were published:—

> The Queen, like Heav'n, shines equally on all,
> Her favours now without distinction fall:
> Great Read and slender Hannes, both knighted, show
> That none their honours shall to merit owe.
> That Popish doctrine is exploded quite,
> Or Ralph had been no duke and Read no knight.
> That none may virtue or their learning plead,
> This has no grace and that can hardly read.

The Ralph referred to here is the first Duke of Montague, a title that has already appeared conspicuously in these pages. In the matter of the bestowal of titles, especially knighthoods and baronetcies, we have no particular reason to congratulate ourselves now, but we have certainly improved since the days when rank was sold or bestowed upon the most audacious adventurers. So far as merit is concerned, we are, however, much in the same position as we were in the days of Read and Ralph; but ability always was an unmarketable commodity, and now it seems to secure its unhappy possessors the decided enmity of those more favoured beings whose dependence is upon patronage, and not upon personal powers, and who, in humble imitation of the fox of fable, affect to despise any such common thing as cleverness. And unfortunately this observation has a far wider bearing than on the mere bestowal of titles. It refers to things generally, and to the means by which many clever men are deprived of their subsistence, and driven to the wall by the nepotism and friendly feeling so often exercised in favour of the most arrant impostors, or on behalf of those who are just clever enough to conceal their ignorance and inability, to rob others of their ideas, or to foist second-hand notions upon a credulous and misjudging public.

In "A Journey through England," published in 1723, we get the following picture of a travelling quack of that time: "I cannot leave Winchester without telling you of a pleasant incident that happened there. As I was sitting at the George Inn, I saw a coach with six bay horses, a calash and four, a chaise and four, enter the inn, in a yellow livery turned up with red; four gentlemen on horseback, in blue trimmed with silver; and as yellow is the colour given by the dukes in England, I went out to see what duke it was; but there was no coronet on the coach, only a plain coat-of-arms on each with this motto '*Argento laborat Faber.*' Upon inquiry I found this great equipage belonged to a mountebank, and his name being Smith, the motto was a pun upon his name. The footmen in yellow were his tumblers and trumpeters, and those in blue his merry-andrew, his apothecary and spokesman. He was dressed in black velvet, and had in his coach a woman that danced on the ropes. He cures all diseases and sells his packets for sixpence apiece. He erected stages in all the market towns twenty miles round; and it is a prodigy how so wise a people as the English are gulled by such pickpockets. But his amusements on the stage are worth the sixpence without the pills. In the morning he is dressed up in a fine brochade nightgown, for his chamber practice, when he gives advice and gets larger fees."

Although the papers of the early eighteenth century actually teem with the advertisements of quacksalvers, few of the applications to the unwary possess any distinctive features, and those which do are of the grossest possible description. In the *Daily Post* of July 14, 1736, there is a curious testimonial to the abilities of a City practitioner who advertised very considerably about that period. His advertisements all take the form of recommendations from those who have received benefit at his hands and from his medicines, and the one we have chosen will give a fair idea of the others, which in many cases refer to the disorders of the gentler sex :—

THESE are to certify, that I Richard Sandford, Waterman, dwelling in Horsely-down-street, near the Dipping Pond, have a Son, who for a considerable Time was troubled with a *Pain in his Stomach, a Sleepiness and Giddiness,* whereupon I calling to Mind that some Years since my Wife's Mother, betwixt 60 and 70 years of Age, *afflicted with a Palsy or Hemeplegia, or loss of the Use of one Side of her Body, had been cured by*

Mr. JOHN MOORE, *Apothecary,*

At the Pestle and Mortar in Laurence-Pountney's Lane, the first Great Gates on the Left-Hand from Cannon-street,

I applied to him for Relief of my Son, who after having taken a few of his Worm-Powders, they brought from him a WORM (or INSECT) like a Hog-Louse, with Legs and hairy, or a Kind of Down all over it, and very probably more, but he going to a common Vault they were lost; upon which he is amended as to his former Illnesses, and I desire this may be printed for the Good of others.

Witness RICHARD SANDFORD.

Oct. 6, 1735.

N.B. The said JOHN MOORE's Worm Medicines and Green-Sickness Powder, are sold at Mrs. Reader's at the Nine Sugar-Loaves, a Chandler's Shop in Hungerford-Market, sealed with his Coat of

Arms, being a Cross, with the Words, *John Moore's Worm-Powders*, &c., inscribed round it: And if any are Sold at any place, except at his own House, without that Seal and Inscription, they are Counterfeits.

He sells Byfield's Sal Volatile Oliosum, at 6d. per Ounce.

To be had at the said J. Moore's,

COLUMBARIUM; or, The Pigeon-House: Being an Introduction to a Natural History of Tame Pigeons, giving an Account of the several Species known in England, with the Method of breeding them, their Distempers and Cures.

The two chief Advantages, which a real Acquaintance with Nature brings to our Minds, are first, by instructing our Understandings and gratifying our Curiosities; and next by exciting and cherishing our Devotion. Boyle's Experimental Philosophy, p. 3.

Mr Sandford's ideas on natural history were rather confused, and his powers of description evidently bothered by the astonishing "insect" which had so annoyed his son. What a pity so curious a specimen was not preserved for the benefit of Moore and "the good of others"! There was now a sore battle being fought between the quacks and the regular practitioners, the latter being bound to come forward and defend what they considered to be their rights by all and every means. That they did not disdain the use of advertisements, the following, which had its origin in a small gossiping paragraph, shows. It appears in the *Daily Journal* of July 22, 1734, but was originally published a few days before, without the two paragraphs after signature:—

WHEREAS in the Papers of Saturday last there was a Paragraph relating to a Dispute that happened at Child's Coffee-house, between a Doctor and a Surgeon; I think it my Duty to tell the Fact that occasioned this Dispute, truly as it is.

On Wednesday the 10th of July I sent to Mr. Nourse; when he came I told him I had a Swelling and great Pain in my Leg; he saw it, said it was much inflamed, and that I must be blooded, take some Physick, and that he would send something that was proper to be applied; I was immediately let Blood; and he writ a Purge for me, to be taken the next Day, which I took, and am thereby, I thank God, much better. Afterwards, in the same Conversation, he ask'd me how long I had been ill? my Answer was, ten Days; he reply'd, have you been ill so long, and had no Advice? I then told him, I had, some Days before, been to the Jew Doctor's House; his Answer was, I suppose you mean Dr. Schamberg, and pray what has he ordered for you? I said, I could not tell; but being desirous that Dr. Nourse should see the Prescription, I sent to the Apothecary's for it by my Son, who brought it directly into the Room, where there was not anybody but Mr. Nourse and myself; Mr. Nourse looked upon the Bill, and told me I must take none of these Things now; nor the Spaw Water, said I? (for that was Part of the Prescription); his Answer was No, and laid the Bill down upon the Table, without saying anything more. This is the whole Truth, and I'm ready to attest it by an Affidavit.

N.B. When I sent to Mr. Nourse I was determined to apply no more to Dr. Schamberg, he being in a manner a Stranger to me, and I have been much worse every Day, from the Time I began to take his Medicines. B. J. KNIGHT.

Leadenhall Market, 15 July.

The Propriety of Æsculapius's Prescription judge of by the Effect.

Q. Whether Steel steep'd in Brandy, and Spa Water, are proper for a Shortness of Breath, or an Inflammation.

After this had been published once or twice, the advertiser, who could hardly have taken so much trouble out of pure gratitude, inserted another notice in the form of an affidavit, containing the foregoing and other particulars, the most important of which is that which discovers her sex. At least we presume that Bridget was a woman's name in 1734. The difficulties between the doctors and apothecaries—the latter, when not quacks themselves, being their special agents—and the demand made for the far-famed Jesuits' Bark, are both shown in the following handbill, which is of about the same date as the foregoing:—

WHEREAS it has been of late the Endeavour of several Members of the Physicians College, to reform the Abuses of the Apothecaries, as well in the Prizes as in the Composition of their Medicines, This is to give Notice for the public Good, that a superfine Sort of *Jesuits Bark* ready powder'd and paper'd into Doses, with or without Directions for the Use of it, is to be had at Dr. Charles Goodal's at the Coach and Horses, in Physician's Colledge in Warwick Lane, at 4s. per Ounce, or for a Quantity together at £3 per Pound; for the Reasonableness of which Prizes, (considering the Loss and Trouble in powdering) we appeal to all the Druggists and Apothecaries themselves in Town, and particularly to Mr. Thair, Druggist in Newgate Street, to whom we paid full 9s. per Pound for a considerable Quantity for the Use of our self and our friends.

And for the Excellency and Efficacy of this particular Bark enquire of Dr. Morton in Grey Friars.

I am to be spoken with at Prayers at S. Sepulchre's every Day, *but the Lord's Day, at Seven in the Morning, and at Home from Eight in the Morning till Ten at Night.*

The Poor may have Advice (*that is,* Nothing) *for* Nothing.

"Nothing for nothing" is a rate of exchange which is current even to this day, and was very likely known long before the time of this physician, whose effort could hardly have been expected to prove disastrous to the empirics, as he, among other peculiarities, regards what should have been his strong point of dissimilarity from them as "nothing." Another bill of the same period is noticeable for the explicitness of the address given in it:—

When you are in *Baldwin's Gardens,* that you may not mistake, ask for *Leopard's Court,* and there at the Sign of the *Moon and Stars,* you will find the *Louvain Doctor* from 8 in the Morning till 7 at Night. As you pass by the end of Leopard's Court you may see the Sign of the *Moon and Stars,* which, pray, observe, least you mistake: for there are several Pretenders, therefore keep this bill. *Baldwin's Gardens* are near *Holborn.*

Baldwin's Gardens would hardly be a good address in these times for even the veriest quack. It is now about the foulest specimen extant of that kind of backslum or alley where, a generation back, according to Hood, pigs and Irish were wont to rally. The pigs, except in the form of hocks, "Jerry Lynch" heads, and other portions of bacon, have been removed by Act of Parliament since the poet sang his simple lay of "The Lost Child," but the Irish have increased and multiplied with an activity unknown to them in other pursuits. The powers of the finest peasantry in the world are undoubted in one particular of philoprogenitiveness under any circumstances, and they seem to exert them to the utmost when least required and most inconvenient—when they are "pigged up" in small rooms and festering courts, and when every fresh birth is an outrage upon the sanatory laws supposed to govern us, and upon their own sense of decency. We are in the habit of hearing most of our domestic and civic misfortunes ascribed to the higher wages and increased leisure of the labouring classes of the present, as compared with those of twenty or thirty years back. Is this the case with regard to the rapid development of inhabitants for Baldwin's Gardens, Leather Lane, Saffron Hill, and neighbouring purlieus? There may be increased leisure there, but if the wages are higher now than they were, in proportion to the higher price of provisions, they must have suffered worse than starvation in years gone by. So unhealthily crowded—in fact, pestilent—is the neighbourhood we have mentioned, that no number of quacks could have done more to shorten life than the inhabitants now do for themselves. But even these poor wretches are made the groundwork for a new system of quackery—the quackery of the mock philanthropist, who builds model lodging-houses, ostensibly and with much flourishing of trumpets, for the very poor, and then lets them to people who never did dwell in rookeries; to those people who can afford to pay good rents, and so keep up the dividends which are the modern reward of so-called charity.

Notwithstanding the many stirring events of the early part of the last century, there is little or nothing to read in any of the papers. This may be accounted for by the difficulty of obtaining news from distant or even from any parts a hundred and thirty years or so back; but whatever the reason, this is certain, the advertisements are by far the best reading in the journals, daily or weekly. Though the newspapers were to our notions wonderfully small, their editors seem to have had the greatest difficulty in filling the little space they had at command with news, and provincial journals were sometimes put to strange shifts, even the now common work of the liner, that of inventing facts, being then unknown. It is by no means unusual to find a chapter of the Bible put in to fill up the columns; and even as late as 1740 the *London and County Journal* gratified its readers with the History of the Old and New Testaments, while other papers filled up their front pages with occasional extracts from the histories of England and other countries, or selections from books of travel. Singular as this may seem, it is true. Its truth is perhaps the most singular thing about it.

Among the many specifics of the last century was snuff, which in various forms is advertised as possessing the power not only of curing all bodily but many mental evils. In the *General Advertiser* for June 21, 1749, there is an advertisement of a snuff which was supposed to cure lunacy. Certainly it has an effect on the ideas with regard to the construction of sentences, as the proprietor himself shows:—

GENTLEMEN,

ONCE more I desire you to remember, I have published my *Imperial Snuff*, for all Disorders in the Head; and I think I might have gone further, and said, for all Disorders of Body and Mind. It hath set a great many to rights that was never expected, but there is but few, or none, that careth to have it published they were a little out of their Senses, although it be really an Ailment that none can help; but there is present Relief, if not a Cure; but I hope both, as by God's Assistance it hath been performed already on many. And I think it my Duty to let the World know it, that they may not bear so many miserable Ailments that is capable of curing. I hear it is reported abroad I am dead, and that the World is imposed on; but, thank God, I am alive and put my Dependance on him, that he will give me leave to do some more Service before I go hence. But suppose I was dead, my Snuff is alive, and I hope it will live after I am dead, as it is capable of keeping the World in sprightly Life and Health, which must be allowed to be the greatest Blessing in the World. But what is Riches without that? And what would some have given for some of these Reliefs before it was advertised. But you are all heartily welcome at this Price of Sixpence, at present, but I should be glad of more from the Rich. I do assure you it is sold at this Price in regard to the Poor only.

I am yours, etc.

SAMUEL MAJOR.

In Swedland Court, against the end of Half-Moon-Alley, Bishopsgate Street.

The next gentleman upon the list is Mr Patence, who combined in himself many valuable qualifications, and was according to his own showing a decided benefactor to humanity. In December 1771 we find the following in the *Gazetteer*:—

MR Patence, Dentist and Dancing Master, No. 8, Bolt Court, Fleet Street, whose Ingenuity in making artificial Teeth, and fixing them without the least Pain, can be attested by several of the Nobility, and hopes to be honoured by the rest of the Great—may depend his Study shall be devoted to the good of every Individual. His whole Sets, with a Fine enamel on, is a Proof of his excelling all Operators. He charges ten Guineas for a whole, five for an upper or under Set, and half-a-Guinea for a single Tooth.—His Rose Powder for preserving the Teeth, is worthy to grace and perfume the chamber of a Prince.—His Medicines for preventing all Infections and sore Throats have been experienced by several.—As for dancing, he leaves that to the multitude of Ladies and Gentlemen whom he has taught, and desires to be rewarded no more than his Merit deserves, nor no less. Public School nights, Monday, Wednesday, and Friday Evenings; Tuesday Evenings set apart for Cotillons only.—*N.B.* His Rose Dentrifice may be had at Mr Nesbit's Toy Shop Bishopsgate Street, and at his House, at 2s. 6d. the box.

The conjunction of practices seems somewhat odd, and, as many may think, rather ominous—for the patients. But Mr Patence evidently flourished, and found plenty money to spend in advertisements. He promises much, but his strong point is secrecy. Advice is as usual offered gratis, which was a fair charge for it, considering that the applicant was sure to be advised to buy some of the nostrums purveyed by Patence. By his skill he repeatedly offers to stand or fall, and about the date we have given he publishes the following as evidence of it. It will be noticed that the address has been shifted, possibly on account of increased business:—

No. 3 *Ludgate Hill.*

THIS Week a Lady applied to Mr. *Patence*, No. 3 Ludgate Hill, who had her Jaw-Bone broke by having a Tooth extracted, by another Lady, with a sound front Tooth in her Hand, and two others just ready to drop from their Sockets, by having four wretched artificial ones set in by another: her Teeth are all loose. By Tincture, a Gentleman with Teeth set in as brown as a Walnut, that never answered any End; and several other Persons in different Cases. Mr. *Patence* therefore begs leave to add, that it is not his Intent to take away or lessen the Merit of any one particular Person; but how shocking it is to see Ladies and Gentlemen imposed on, a good set of Teeth ruined, and left at Leisure to lament the Loss in Pain, by Pretenders; for, of all Things artificial Teeth badly set in, is the most destructive of the good next them: but if performed in that masterly Manner that human Nature requires, they are a Preservation, and will answer the End which a humane Man would wish for, or a skilful Dentist desire. —Advice given daily in Cases ordinary, and extraordinary. No Cure no Pay.

After this Patence goes on merrily telling us now that his "works, cures, and operations confirm his supremacy over every dentist in this kingdom; also physicians, curing man, woman, and child, when not one of them can give relief;" and then that he sells "teeth comprised of six different enamels, warranted never to turn black." Teeth were, however, but small things in his practice, as he guarantees to replace "fallen noses," and challenges all known and unknown diseases, being, as he states, "mechanically accurated and anatomically perfect in the human structure." To say less, he tells us, would be "doing an act unjust to himself, his patients, and his Maker, whose gifts are disposed of to whom he pleases." In the *Morning Post* of 1775 he publishes the following, having in the meantime once again changed his residence:—

To the *Nobility*, *Gentry*, and Others.

PATENCE, Surgeon by Birth, and Dentist, having had ten Years Practice, performs every Operation on the Teeth, Gums, &c., with superior Skill, and whose Cures are not excelled or even equalled by any Dentist whatever. And as a Confirmation of the same, please to observe the following :—

October 5. A Gentleman who had lost all his Teeth, his Gums ulcerated and scorbutic, in five Days made a perfect Cure, fixed him in a whole set of natural Teeth, without Springs or any Fastening.

October 16. A Lady whose Jaw was fractured by a Barber, her Teeth loose, her Gums ulcerated, attended with a running Matter, and an inflammation in her Cheeks, with a callous Swelling, cured without poulticing or cutting.

October 20. A Lady that had lost all her upper Teeth by using Powders and Tinctures that are advertised to cure Everything, her Mouth ulcerated, and her Breath nauseous, is now delicately Clean, and replaced the Teeth with those that never change their Colour.

Sunday, October 29. Perfectly relieved a Person that had lost both Palate and Speech; when he drank or eat it came out at his Nostrils, and had been in that state three Years; he had applied to Surgeons and several Hospitals, who deemed him incurable, and told him, one and all, he could have no Relief; he now speaks articulate, eats and drinks with Pleasure, which if any one should doubt, he can refer them to the Man. These, with upwards of three thousand Operations and Cures, have been accomplished by your humble Servant, M. PATENCE.

At No. 403, in the Strand, near *Southampton Street*, London. Where the Teeth, though ever so foul, are made delicately white in six Minutes, and Medicines given for their preservation, for half a Guinea, any hour after ten in the Morning. Advice gratis, and profound Secrecy if required.

☞ Envy may snarl, but superior Abilities assists the Afflicted.

There must be something very ambitious about a man who, not satisfied with being dentist and dancing-master, assumes the title of "surgeon by birth." It is noticeable that though Patence was born a surgeon, he did not discover it till he had been at dentistry and dancing for some years.* But in 1775 and thereabouts quacks were not very particular as to their statements. In September 1776 the *Morning Post* contains a very lengthy advertisement, put forth by one Lattese, a Piedmontese,

* After all Patence was only an imitator in this particular. In the *Gentleman's Magazine* of 1735, there is a reference to the "Unborn Doctor of Moorfields," who flourished very early in the eighteenth century. This man upon being asked to explain his mysterious title, replied, "Why, I was'nt born a doctor, was I?"

who states that he has "by a long course of experiments discovered the wonderful secret of procreating either sex at the joint option of the parents. Should their desire be to have a girl, the success cannot be warranted with absolute certainty, though the chances will be highly in favour of such an event; but should they concur in their wishes to have a son, they may rely that by strictly conforming to a few easy and natural directions, they will positively have a boy." Mr Lattese is so satisfied with the result of his experience that he is satisfied to await the result, and, no satisfaction, no pay. However much we may have advanced in some directions since the days of Patence and Lattese—though we now have railroads, steamboats, tramways, electric telegraphs, a penny post, vote by ballot, asphalt pavement, and good-templarism—it must be admitted that we have, in grasping at mere bubbles, lost many true arts. Among those unfortunately forgotten must, we are sorry to assume, be ranked those of breeding boys at will and surgeons *à discrétion*.

It is curious how anxious many of the quacks are that they shall not be confounded with their rivals, and their addresses are often given with wonderful exactness. Of this we will add another example, which, though some years later than the one about Baldwin's Gardens, is in no way less distinct. It would seem, from many references in old newspapers, that the term Maypole was used for a certain portion of the Strand long after the shaft itself had been removed :—

IN the Strand, over against the Maypole, on the left Hand coming from Temple-Bar, at the Sign of the Golden Cross, between a Sword Cuttlers and a Milliner's Shop, the Sign of the Sugar Loaf and Barber's Pole, within four Doors of the Mitre Tavern: Where you may see a large Red coloured Lanthorn, with Eleven Candles in it; and a white Sign written upon with red Letters DUTCH DOCTOR, **Licensed by his most Excellent Majesty**: and a long Entry with a Hatch and a Knocker on it. Where you may come in privately, and speak with him, and need not be ashamed, he having not any in his House but himself and his Family.

The sign of the Sugar-loaf and Barber's Pole must have been unique even in the days of signboards, when incongruity was an advantage. Signs remind us of a noted quack of last century, Van Butchell, who painted a wonderful inscription over the front of his house. He was a great advertiser, too, and his effusions are found in most of the papers. When his wife died he had her embalmed, and used to let his patients see the body. He made her very useful as a means of publicity, one of his notices—in the *St. James's Chronicle* for October 1776—running thus :—

VAN BUTCHELL (not willing to be unpleasantly circumstanced, and wishing to convince some good Minds they have been misinformed) acquaints the Curious no Stranger can see his embalmed Wife, unless (by a Friend or personally) introduced to himself, any Day between Nine and One, Sundays excepted.

Van Butchell, though he lost no opportunity of looking after the main chance, had a mad way of conducting his business, which caused people to regard him as quite out of the ordinary level of charlatans, and his eccentricities in time got him a reputation for both cleverness and conscientiousness. He lived in Mount Street, and on his house and part of the next the following strange inscription was painted :—

BY

HIS MAJESTY'S

Thus, said sneaking Jack, I'll be first ; if I get my Money, ROYAL speaking like himself, I don't care who suffers.

LETTERS PATENT,

MARTIN

VAN BUTCHELL'S

NEW INVENTED

With caustic care—and old Phim.

SPRING BANDS

AND FASTENINGS

Sometimes in six days, and always in ten—the Fistula in Ano.

FOR
THE APPAREL
AND FURNITURE
July 6.
OF
Licensed to deal in Perfumery, i. e.
HUMAN BEINGS
Hydrophobia cured in thirty days.
AND
BRUTE CREATURES.
Made of Milk and Honey.

His next-door neighbour, however, thinking proper to rebuild part of his front, obliterated half of the notice, which, as remarked, ran across both houses. At one time Van Butchell had a famous dun horse, and having some dispute with the stable-keeper, it was detained by the latter to pay for his keep, and was at length sold at Tattersall's, where, from the character given him by Van Butchell, he brought a good price. This affair was the occasion of a lawsuit, and caused the Doctor to add in small gold letters as quoted, nearly at the top of his notice, the words, "Thus said sneaking Jack," &c. Of Van Butchell's literary and advertising talents, the reader will be best able to form a conclusion after a perusal of the following specimen, taken from various newspapers at various times :—

Causes of Crim. Con. Also Barreness—And the King's Evil: Advice—new—Guinea; come from Ten till One: for I go to none. The Anatomist and Sympathizer who never poisons — nor sheds human blood: Balm is always good.

Corresponding—Lads—Remember Judas :—And the year 80! *Last Monday morning at Seven o'clock,* Doctor Merryman, *of Queen Street, Mayfair, presented* Elizabeth, the wife of Martin van Butchell *with her Fifth fine Boy, at his* House *in* Mount Street, Grosvenor Square, and—they—all—are—well. Post Masters General for Ten Thousand Pounds (—We mean Gentlemen's—Not a Penny less—) I will soon construct —Such Mail-Coach—Perch Bolts, as shall never break!

Tender—hearted—Man—User of the Knife,—Would'st thou cut thy Wife? (—Unless two* were by?—Fearing she might die?—) Is—not —Blood—the Life? If the Empress of Russia—the Emperor of Germany—the King of Prussia—an Immaculate,—or the Pope of Rome —were sorely smitten—with bad Fistulæ and tormenting Piles—visited Martin to be made quite whole:—*Without Confinement—Fomentation—Risk—Infection—Poultice—Caustic—or Cutting:* — *bringing* two per Cent. of Five Years Profit.—☞ Less *is* not *his* fee. Nor would he suffer a third person to be in the room. Not wanting help,—he won't be hinder'd; by half-willed spies; slavish informers: nor sad alarmists. All his patients live: and—Jehovah—praise.

To the Editor—of a Morning Paper—*Ego—Secundus.*—Of God every man—hath his proper gift: glory be to him—that of mine is healing: —(Not miraculous,—nor by Satan's aid:)—being vigilant—while gay lads gamed at the Tennis Court—I found it in schools anatomical—Fistulæ and Piles—best my genius fit—Very broad is art—narrow human wit: tho' man was complete (—As he ought to be with an hairy chin.)—Lovely women hate fops effeminate.—Time approaches when among certain men—in another age—beards—will—be—the—rage!

To many I refer—for my character: each will have the grace—to write out his case; soon as he is well—an history tell: for the public good;—so save human blood: as—all—true—folk—shou'd. Sharkish people may—keep themselves away—*Those that use men ill—I never can heal; being forbidden—to cast pearls to pigs; lest—they—turn—and —tear. Wisdom makes dainty: patients come to me, with heavy guineas —between ten and one: but—I—go—to—none.*

Mender of mankind; in a manly way.

Fistulæ—Patients—Fee—is—according—to ability! let those—who have much give—without grudging!—(heavy guineas—down: I don't like paper;—unless—from the Bank of good Old England)—Plain folk—do comply—very readily: so shall—the gaudy:—or keep their complaints! Many—are in want of food;—and raiment, for large families. Such—will be made whole—just so speedily as the most wealthy; that's "one right of man," and he shall have it; while God grants me health!—(Philosophers—say—Mankind—are equal:—and pure religion—kindly—promotes—good.)—Lofty ones—read this;—

* This refers to the regular mode of eminent Surgeons, who seldom cut for Fistulæ or Piles, but in the presence of their assistants: because some patients have died under the operation, and others some days after.

then pause a little: down your dust—must lay; promises—won't do; I can't go away—to receive some pay from other people!

British Christian *Lads.* ("Behold—now is the day—of salvation." Get understanding:—as the highest gain.—) Cease looking boyish:—become quite manly!—(*Girls* are fond of *hair*:—it is natural.)—Let your beards grow long: that ye may be strong:—in mind—and in body: as were great grand dads: centuries ago; when John did not owe—a single penny: more—than—he—could—pay.

Phi—lo—so—fie—*sirs.*—"Heaven gives a will:—then directs the way." Honor your maker:—And "*Be swift to hear: slow*—to—*speak:* —or—*wrath.*" Leave off *de*forming:—each—himself—*re*form: wear—the—marks—of—men—*In-con-tes-ti-ble!* Jesus—did not shave:—for He—knew better. Had it been proper—our chins should be bare, would hair—be put there:—by wise Jehovah?—Who—made—all—things—good.

Sympathising—Minds!—"Blessed are they that consider the poor." Princes—Dukes—Lords—Knights—Esquires—Ladies—"Or the Lord knows who," are hapless mortals!—Many do need me—to give them comfort! Am not I—the first—healer—(at this Day)—of bad Fistulæ? —(with—an handsome Beard)—like Hippocrates! The combing—I sell—one guinea—each hair?—(of use—to the Fair, that want fine children:—I can—tell them how;—it—is a secret—) Some—are quite—auburn;—others—silver white:—full—half quarter—long, growing—(day and night)—only—fifteen—months! Ye must hither come,—(As I go to none)—and bring—one per cent. of five years' profit:—that's my settled fee; it—shall be return'd if I do not cure—(in a little time)—the worst Fistulæ: let who will—have failed! Lie telling—is bad:—sotting—makes folk sad! see—(Ananias)—Beginning Acts v. Pot-I-cary—bow—thy—frizz'd—mealy pate! "Despisers, —behold—wonder—and perish!" "God—gives grace to man! Glory—be to God! He—doth all things well!"

Fistulæ—and—Piles, by *the* help *of* God—*we* eradicate, *Having* wit *enough* to *heal* those *complaints,* my *small* fee *must* be—*twelve* heavy *guineas:* large *six* score *thousand:* We *mean* 2 *pr* cent. *on* five *years* profit—*put* it *in* rouleaus *of* an *hundred* each.—*Come* from *ten* till *one:* —for—*I*—go—*to*—none.

No one, after reading these extracts, will be inclined to doubt that Van Butchell was an original. His notoriety was such that many used to visit his house, not so much for the purpose of receiving advice as to see and converse with him. The success which he and contemporary quacks made led to the tax on "patent medicines," which was imposed in 1783, and has now for over ninety years been a fruitful source of revenue. Of Van Butchell's contemporaries, one of the most worthy of note was Katerfelto, of whom Cowper speaks in "The Task"—

> And Katerfelto, with his hair an end
> At his own wonders, wondering for his bread.

Katerfelto was a foreigner who had "seen service," and according to his own showing was both brave and learned. A notice of him which appears in an article on quacks says: "In a pamphlet on quackery, published at Kingston-upon-Hull, in 1805, it is stated that Dr Katerfelto practised on the people of London in the influenza of 1782; that he added to his nostrums the fascinations of hocus-pocus; and that with the services of some extraordinary *black cats* he astonished the vulgar. In 1790, or 1791, he visited the city of Durham, accompanied by his wife and daughter. His travelling equipage consisted of an old rumbling coach, drawn by a pair of sorry hacks; and his two black servants wore green liveries with red collars. They were sent round the town, blowing trumpets and delivering bills of their master's performances. These were—in the daytime, a microscope; in the evening, electrical experiments, in which the black cats—'the doctor's devils'—played their parts in yielding electric sparks; tricks of legerdemain concluded the entertainments. He was a tall, thin man, dressed in a black gown and square cap; he is said to have been originally a soldier in the Prussian service. In one of his advertisements he states that he was a colonel in the 'Death's Head' regiment of hussars, a terrific prognostic of his ultimate profession. He had many mishaps in his conjuring career; once he sent up a fire balloon, which, falling upon a hay-stack, set it on fire, and it was consumed, when Katerfelto was sued for its value, and was sent to prison in default of payment. And not long before his death, he was committed by the Mayor of Shrewsbury to the House of Correction in that city as a vagrant and impostor. Katerfelto mixed up with his quackery some real science, and by the aid of the solar microscope astonished the world with insect wonders. In one of his advertisements in the *Morning Post*, of July 1782, he says that, by its aid, the insects on the hedges will be seen larger than ever, and those insects which caused the late influenza will be seen as large as a bird; and in a drop of water the size of a pin's head there will be seen above 50,000 insects; the same in beer, milk, vinegar, blood, flour, cheese, etc., etc., and there will be seen many surprising indifferent vegetables, and above 200 other dead objects. He obtained good prices for his show:—'The admittance to see these wonderful works of Providence is only—front seats, three shillings; second seats, two shillings; and back seats, one shilling only, from eight o'clock in the morning till six in the afternoon, at No. 22 Piccadilly.' He fully understood the advantages of puffing, and one of his advertisements commences with a story of 'a gentleman of the faculty belonging to Oxford University, who, finding it likely to prove a fine day, set out for London purposely to see those great wonders which are advertised so much by that famous philosopher, Mr Katerfelto;' that the said gentleman declared, 'if he had come three hundred miles on purpose, the knowledge he had then received would amply reward him; and that he should not wonder that some of the nobility should come from the remotest part of Scotland to hear Mr Katerfelto, as the people of that country in particular are always searching after knowledge.' He elsewhere declares himself 'the greatest philosopher in this kingdom since Sir Isaac Newton.' 'And Mr Katerfelto, as a divine and moral philosopher, begs leave to say that all persons on earth live in darkness, if they are able to see, but will not see his wonderful exhibition.'" Katerfelto, who had been in trouble both in his own country and in France, showed an aptitude for distinguishing himself in a similar way here, not only in the ways we have already quoted, but with regard to impositions practised on the confiding. He obtained £2000 from a Captain Paterson, but had to return it. This he afterwards referred to as instance of his generosity and love of honesty, and his admiration for this country is shown by his avowed desire to stay in it, "though unpensioned, notwithstanding the many offers from the Queen of France, the request of his friend and correspondent Dr Franklin, and the positive commands of his liege lord the King of Prussia."

Mention of the Queen of France reminds us of another impostor, perhaps the greatest in his way that ever lived, Joseph Balsamo. As, however, he had little or nothing to do with advertising, and as he has already afforded work for many able and vigorous pens, we will be content to quote a few lines from Carlyle regarding the arch-quack's description and personal appearance: "The quack of quacks, the most perfect scoundrel that in these latter ages has marked the world's history, we have found in the Count Alessandro di Cagliostro, pupil of the sage Althotas, foster child of the Scherif of Mecca, probably son of the last king of Trebizonde; named also Acharat, and unfortunate child of nature; by profession healer of diseases, abolisher of wrinkles, friend of the poor and impotent, grand-master of the Egyptian mason-lodge of high science, spirit-summoner, gold-cook, grand cophta, prophet, priest, and thaumaturgic moralist and swindler; really a liar of the first magnitude, thorough-paced in all provinces of lying, what one may call the king of liars. . . . One of the most authentic documents preserved of Joseph Balsamo is the picture of his visage. An effigy once universally diffused in oil paint, aquatint, marble, stucco, and perhaps gingerbread, decorating millions of apartments. Fittest of visitors, worthy to be worn by the quack of quacks! A most portentous face of scoundrelism: a fat, snub, abominable face; dew-lapped, flat-nosed, greasy, full of greediness, sensuality, ox-like obstinacy; a forehead impudent, refusing to be ashamed; and then two eyes turned up seraphically languishing, as if in divine contemplation and adoration; a touch of quiz, too; on the whole, perhaps the most perfect quack-face produced by the eighteenth century." The subject of this flattering portrait was born in 1743, and died in the fortress of St Leo, Rome, after an imprisonment of six years, aged fifty-two.

The system of showing on oneself the effect of one's own specifics has had many admirers and practisers. A Mrs Harden, in Newman Street, Oxford Street, used to advertise some years ago a hair-dye, the effect of which was to be seen on her own hair at her private residence, or at ladies' own residences if preferred. In a similar manner a quack in the time of King Charles II. commenced his handbill with this statement: "Salvator Winter, an Italian of the city of Naples, aged 98 years, yet by the blessing of God, finds himself in health and as strong as any one of fifty, as to the sensitive part. Which first he attributes to God, and then to his *Elixir Vitæ*, which he always carries in his pocket adayes, and at night under his pillow. And when he finds himself distempered he taketh a spoonful or two, according as need requireth." He then goes on to state that people should call and see its effect on him, and purchase so as to ensure health.

A most original, unique, and successful humbug, quite worthy of mention here, though not a dealer in medicines, was the late Monsieur Mangin of Paris. While passing through the public streets, there was nothing in his personal appearance to distinguish him from any ordinary gentleman. He drove a pair of bay horses, attached to an open carriage with two seats, the back one always occupied by his valet. Sometimes he would take up his stand in the Champs Elysées; at other times near the column in the Place Vendôme; but usually he was seen in the afternoon in the Place de la Bastille, or the Place de la Madeleine. On Sundays his favourite locality was the Place de la Bourse.

Mangin was a well-formed, stately-looking individual, with a most self-satisfied countenance, which seemed to say, "I am master here; and all that my auditors have to do is, to listen and obey." Arriving at his destined stopping-place, his carriage halted. His servant handed him a case from which he took several large portraits of himself, which he hung prominently upon the sides of his carriage, and also placed in front of him a vase filled with medals bearing his likeness on one side, and a description of the blacklead pencils in which he traded on the other. He then leisurely commenced a change of costume. His round hat was replaced by a magnificent burnished helmet, mounted with rich plumes of various brilliant colours. His overcoat was laid aside, and he donned in its stead a costly velvet tunic with gold fringes. He then drew a pair of polished steel gauntlets upon his hands, covered his breast with a brilliant cuirass, and placed a richly-mounted sword at his side. His servant watched him closely, and upon receiving a sign from his master he too put on his official costume, which consisted of a velvet robe and a helmet. The servant then struck up a tune on the richly-toned organ which always formed a part of Mangin's apparatus. The grotesque appearance of these individuals, and the music, soon drew together an admiring crowd. Then the charlatan stood up. His manner was calm, dignified, imposing, indeed, almost solemn, for his face was as serious as that of the chief mourner at a funeral. His sharp, intelligent eye scrutinised the throng which was pressing around his carriage, until it rested apparently upon some particular individual, then he gave a start; then, with a dark, angry expression, as if the sight was repulsive, he abruptly dropped the visor of his helmet and thus covered his face from the gaze of the anxious crowd. Thus far he had not spoken a word. At last the prelude ended, and the comedy commenced. Stepping forward again to the front of the carriage, he exclaimed —"Gentlemen, you look astonished! You seem to wonder and ask yourselves, who is this modern Quixote? What mean this costume of bygone centuries—this golden chariot—these richly-caparisoned steeds? What is the name, what the purpose of this curious knight-errant? Gentlemen, I will condescend to answer your queries. I am Monsieur Mangin, the great charlatan of France! Yes, gentlemen, I am a charlatan—a mountebank; it is my profession, not from choice, but from necessity. You, gentlemen, created that necessity! You would not patronise true, unpretending, honest merit, but you are attracted by my glittering casque, my sweeping crest, my waving plumes. You are captivated by din and glitter, and therein lies my strength. Years ago I hired a modest shop in the Rue Rivoli, but I could not sell pencils enough to pay my rent, whereas, by assuming this disguise—it is nothing else—I have succeeded in attracting general attention, and in selling literally millions of my pencils; and I assure you, there is at this moment scarcely an artist in France or in Great Britain who does not know that I manufacture by far the best blacklead pencils ever seen." And Mangin so far differed from other mountebanks in the fact that his wares were everywhere said to be superior to any others.

Speaking of Mangin reminds us of another French itinerant who forms the central figure of a rather amusing story. In July 1817 a man of imposing figure, wearing a large sabre and immense moustache, arrived at one of the principal inns of a provincial city in France, with a female of agreeable shape and enchanting mien. He alighted at the moment the dinner was being served up at the *table d'hôte*. His martial appearance and bearing caused all the guests to rise with respect; they felt assured he must be a lieutenant-general or a major-general at least. A new governor was expected in the province about this time, and everybody believed that it was he who had arrived incognito. The officer of *gens d'armes* gave him the place of honour, the comptroller of the customs and the receiver of taxes sat each by the side of madame, and exerted their wit and gallantry to the utmost. All the tit-bits, all the most exquisite wines, were placed before the fortunate couple. At length the party broke up, and every one ran to report through the city that M. le Gouverneur had arrived. But, oh, what was their surprise, when the next day his Excellency, clad in a scarlet coat, and his august companion, dressed out in a gown glittering with tinsel, mounted a small open calash, and preceded by some musicians, went about the squares and public ways selling Swiss tea and balm of Mecca! Imagine the fury of the guests! They complained to the *maire*, and demanded that the audacious quack should be compelled to lay aside the characteristic mark of the brave. The prudent magistrate assembled the common council; and those respectable persons, after a long deliberation, considering that nothing in the charter forbad a citizen to let his beard grow on his upper lip, dismissed the complaint altogether. The same evening the supposed governor gave a serenade to the offended diners, and the next day took his leave, and continued his journey amid the acclamations of the populace.

It would be interesting to know what quack—for a quack it certainly must have been—was first responsible for the belief that a child's caul would save a man from drowning. The origin of this fiction is, however, hidden under the dust of ages. It is customary for people who assume what they wish to believe, to state that the superstition went out when education came in; but that such is not the case a perusal of the advertisement sheets of current journals will show. Here is a rather curious specimen of a generation ago :—

A CHILD'S CAUL to be disposed of, particularly recommended to persons going to the Continent on pleasure or business, officers in his Majesty's navy, merchants trading to the East and West Indies, and all other parts of the globe, being exposed to the dangers of the seas, having the caul in their possession their life will most assuredly always be preserved. Address by letter only, prepaid, to Mr W., Temple Chambers, Falcon Court, Fleet Street.

It must be admitted that the demand for these extremely portable life-preservers has quite gone so far as advertisements are concerned, all that we have seen of modern years being in reference to cauls that the owners wished to part with. When these preventives were fully believed in, an ancient mariner must have been as much surprised as afraid when he went down to the bottom. Captain Marryat tells a rather funny story of a pair of canvas inexpressibles that refused to sink because they had a caul in one of the pockets; and in the days of Howe, Collingwood, and Nelson, a rare trade was driven in cauls, real and imitation, which then fetched fancy prices.

The motives will be apparent which prevent our entering on the merits and demerits of quacks and quack medicines of the present day. Some of the latter are doubtless concocted with skill, and, under peculiar circumstances, are productive of much good, while others are quite the reverse in all particulars. Into this subject we cannot go, as we have no wish to advertise any one nostrum at the expense of another, or to subject ourselves to the expense and unpleasantness which too often attends on outspokenness. We shall rest content with the facts that the most impudent empirics confine themselves to "certain diseases" and hole-and-corner advertisements, and that analytical chemists and comparatively recent legislation have provided for us remedies for any excess on the part of the patent-medicine manufacturers, any one of whom a single false step would irretrievably ruin. Besides, the curious need look no further than the current newspapers for any quantity of average specimens.

Graham and his Celestial Bed are worthy of a chapter to themselves, especially as we have already run to such length on the subject of quacks and quackery.

CHAPTER XV.

GRAHAM AND HIS CELESTIAL BED.

IN the year 1775 there commenced practice in London one of the most extraordinary empirics of any time, whose name was Graham. He was the son of a saddler in the Cowgate, Edinburgh, where he was born in 1745. Having graduated as a doctor of medicine at the University of the modern Athens, he practised for some time at Pontefract. After a short residence in that town, Dr Graham went to America, where he figured as a philanthropic physician, travelling for the benefit of mankind, to administer relief in the most desperate diseases to patients whose cases had hitherto puzzled ordinary physicians. And here he picked up a deal of experience, which he put to the test on his return. Having the advantage of a handsome person, a polite address, an agreeable conversation, and great fluency of speech, he obtained admission into the first circles, particularly in New England, where, as he himself stated, he reaped "golden opinions." Returning to England, he made an excursion through the country, and according to his own account, was eminently successful in curing many individuals whose cases had been considered desperate. In 1775 Graham settled in London, opening a house in Pall Mall, "nearly opposite the King's Palace," where he devoted his attention specially to disorders of the ear and eye, and inserted advertisements to that effect in the daily papers. These advertisements, though by no means couched in so bombastic a style as Graham's later productions, still have an undeniable spice of quackery about them. They are, however, rather too lengthy for insertion. One of them which appeared on February 9, 1776, after stating that from motives of delicacy the Doctor made it an invariable rule never on any account to mention the cure, however extraordinary, of any person, poor or rich, gives the following particulars of his practice :—

Dr Graham began to practise in London, Feb. 1, 1775, and the following is the general state of his Practice in disorders of the Eye and Ear : from that time to November 1, being a period of nine Months, cures or relieved 281 ; refused as incurable on their first Application, 317 ; after a short Trial (by desire) found incurable 47 ; dismissed for Neglect, etc. 57 ; country, foreign, and other Patients, events unknown, 381.

After residing in London for some time, he visited Scotland, and was employed by people of the first quality, who were tempted to put themselves under his care by the fascination of his manner and the fame of his wondrous cures. So popular was he that he might have settled in Edinburgh to great advantage, but he preferred returning to England. He fixed his abode in London, where he set on foot one of the most original and extravagant institutions that could well be imagined, the object of which was, according to the *ipsissima verba* of one of the Doctor's advertisements, "the propagation of a much more strong, beautiful, active, healthy, wise, and virtuous race of human beings, than the present puny, insignificant, foolish, peevish, vicious, and nonsensical race of Christians, who quarrel, fight, bite, devour, and cut one another's throat about they know not what." The idea was original and singular in the highest degree; but he founded his hopes on a perfect knowledge of human nature, and the success which attended his experiment proved that he had calculated with judgment. It has been assumed by some that he really believed in his own statements. That must have been the result of repeating them so often, and in this particular he was by no means singular. In May 1779 he opened what he called "The Temple of Health" in the Adelphi, the purposes of which may be best understood from one of his advertisements which appeared in the *Morning Herald* and other newspapers pretty constantly between 1778 and 1781 :—

TEMPLE OF HEALTH, Adelphi.

To their Excellencies the Foreign Ambassadors, to the Nobility, Gentry, and to Persons of Learning and of Taste.

By Particular Desire, the Exhibitions at the TEMPLE of HEALTH will be continued as usual every TUESDAY, THURSDAY, and SATURDAY Evenings, till the TEMPLE of HYMEN be opened, which will be announced in the Public Papers.

THE CELESTIAL BRILLIANCY of the Medico-Electrical Apparatus in all the apartments of the Temple, will be exhibited

By Dr. GRAHAM himself

Who will have the honour of explaining the true Nature and Effects of Electricity, Air, Music, and Magnetism when applied to the Human Body.

In the Introductory Oration, the whole Art of enjoying Health and vigour of Body and of Mind, and of preserving and exalting personal beauty and loveliness; or in other words of living with Health, Honour, and Happiness, in this world for at least an hundred years, is pointed out and warmly inculcated. Previous to the display of the Electrical Fire, the Doctor will delicately touch upon the CELESTIAL BEDS which are soon to be opened in the Temple of Hymen, in Pall Mall, for the propagation of Beings, rational and far stronger and more beautiful in mental as well as in bodily Endowments, than the present puny, feeble and nonsensical race of Christians — probationary immortals, which crawl and fret, and cut one anothers throat for nothing at all, on most parts of this terraqueous globe.

This Apparatus which visibly displays, as it were, the various facilities of the material Soul of universal and eternal Nature, is acknowledged by all who have seen it, to be by far the largest, most useful and most magnificent that now is or that ever was in the world. Admittance 5s.

But in order that Persons of every Rank may have a View of this most magnificent Apparatus, the Temple of Health may be viewed every Day this Week, from two o'Clock in the Afternoon till eight at Night. Admittance 1s.

N.B.—A Pamphlet is now published, (by permission) with the particulars of several hundred Cures in confirmed Diseases, lately performed at the Temple of Health, with the Names and Residence of the Patients, at their own particular Desire, to be had of the Porter at the Temple, price only 3d.

As a further attraction to his establishment, Graham secured the services of a beautiful young woman, whom he styled "Vestina, the Rosy Goddess of Health," who presided over the evening lectures, and, according to the advertisements, assisted "at the display of the Celestial Meteors, and of that sacred Vital Fire over which she watches, and whose application in the cure of diseases, she daily has the honour of directing." The lady who acted this part subsequently became notorious as the wife of Sir William Hamilton, ambassador to the Court of Naples. Her name was Emma Hart, and before she was raised to the dignity of Goddess of Health, she had officiated in the more humble capacity of nursery and lady's maid in gentlemen's families. Eventually, after having sat as model to Romney and other painters, and having lived under the protection of different gentlemen, she was finally married in 1791 at St George's, Hanover Square, to Sir William Hamilton. Her subsequent connection with Lord Nelson, and her power over that great naval hero but weak human being, as well as the humiliating positions in which she placed her dotard of a husband, form part of the history of this country.

In another of his advertisements Graham offers to explain "the whole art of enjoying health and vigour of body and mind, and of preserving and exalting personal beauty and loveliness; or, in other words, of living with health, honour, and happiness in this world, for at least a hundred years." One of the means for ensuring this end was the constant use of mud baths; and that the Doctor might be observed to practise what he preached, he was to be seen, on stated occasions, immersed in mud to the chin, accompanied by Vestina, who had only then recently left off nursing children and attending on ladies. Her beauty attracted general attention, and brought Graham a deal of practice. While she remained in the mud bath, she had her hair elaborately dressed in the prevailing fashion, with powder, flowers, feathers, and ropes of pearls; Graham appearing in an equally elaborate wig.

In the spring of 1781 the Temple of Health was removed to Schomberg House (now the Ordnance Office), Pall Mall, and the "Temple of Hymen" and "Celestial Bed" were exhibited to the gaze of the profane and the curious. Altogether the establishment was of a very extraordinary description. The front was ornamented with an enormous gilt sun, a statue of Hygieia, and other attractive emblems; the suites of rooms were superbly furnished, and the walls decorated with mirrors, so as to confer on the place an effect like that of an enchanted palace. All the exertions of the painter and sculptor, all the enchantments of vocal and instrumental music, all the powers of electricity and magnetism, were called into operation to enliven and heighten the scene. In a word, all that could delight the eye or ravish the ear, all that could please the smell, give poignancy to the taste, or gratify the touch, were combined to give effect to the whole—at least such was his own account. As a further means of attraction, he hired two men of extraordinary stature, two sons of Anak, whom he appareled in showy and startling liveries, and each of whom wore an enormous cocked-hat, whose business it was to distribute bills from house to house through the town. These handbills were curiously suggestive of the wonderful Doctor's general bombastic style. Here is one of them:—

Temple of Health and of Hymen. Pall Mall.

THE LECTURE at the above place having been received by very numerous, polite and brilliant audiences of Ladies and Gentlemen with unbounded applause, it will be repeated This and every Evening this Week; and precisely at 8 o'clock the Gentleman Usher of the Rosy Rod, assisted by the High Priestess, will conduct the rosy, the gigantic, the stupendous Goddess of Health to the Celestial Throne.

The blooming PRIESTESS of the TEMPLE will endeavour to entertain Ladies and Gentlemen of candour and good nature, by reading a Lecture on the simplest and most efficacious means of preserving health, beauty, and personal loveliness, and serene mental brilliancy, even to the extremest old age.

VESTINA, the GIGANTIC! on the Celestial Throne, as the Goddess of Health, will exhibit in her own person, a proof of the all-blessing effects of virtue, temperance, regularity, simplicity, and moderation; and in these luxurious, artificial, and effeminate times, to recommend those great virtues.

The Temple (which exhibits more riches, more elegance, and more brilliancy than any royal Palace in the world) will as usual be sweetly illuminated with wax, in the highest, most dazzling, and most celestial magnificence from 7 till 10 o'clock, This evening and every Evening this week, and the Lecture will begin precisely at eight. Both before and after the Lecture, one of Vestina's Fairy Train will warble forth sweet celestial sounds.—*Admittance only* ONE SHILLING.

The magnificent Electrical Apparatus, and the supremely brilliant and *unique* decorations of this magical Edifice—of this enchanting Elysian Palace! where wit and mirth, love and beauty—all that can delight the soul, and all that can ravish the senses, will hold their court, This and every Evening this week, in chaste and joyous assemblage.

*** Ladies of rank and character are assured, that nothing will be said or seen, which can give even the smallest offence to the chastest and most delicate female eye or ear, and that every thing will be conducted with the most perfect decency and decorum.—Ladies are requested to come early, in order that they may be agreeably accommodated with seats.

*** A very few copies still remaining of Dr. Graham's Private Advisers (*sealed up, price One Guinea*) to those Ladies and Gentlemen who wish to have children, or to become snowy pillars of Health and Beauty, studded as it were with roses, and streaked with celestial blue, may now be had at only Half a Guinea; his other curious and eccentric works, containing full descriptions of his Travels, Discoveries, Improvements, Principles, Cures, Electrical Apparatus, etc.—formerly 3s. 6d., now only 1s. 9d., and VESTINA, the rosy Goddess's warm Lecture, price 2s. 6d.

☞ All Dr. Graham's Medicines to be had as usual, at the Temple of Health.

Note. Ladies and Gentlemen Electrified.

All went well for a time, and the Temple was nightly crowded with silly people who paid their half-guineas, for the shilling of the advertisements only just admitted to the "body of the hall." Sometimes there were magnificent illuminations and Elysian promenades for both ladies and gentlemen, to which persons in masks were also admitted. "The enchanting glory of these seemingly magical scenes," said the advertisements, "will break forth about seven, and die away about ten o'clock; during which time Oriental odours and ætherial essences will perfume the air, while the hymænal sopha blazes forth with the plenitude of the soft lambent celestial fire." Having opened such scenes to the eyes of the wondering world, the Doctor thus addresses his contemporaries in another advertisement:—

TEMPLE OF HEALTH AND HYMEN,
PALL MALL,
Near the King's Palace.

IF there be one human Being, rich or poor, Male or Female, or of the doubtful Gender, in or near this great Metropolis of the World, who has not had the good Fortune and the Happiness of hearing the celebrated Lecture, and of seeing the grand celestial Bed, the magnificent electrical Apparatus, and the supremely brilliant and unique Decorations of this magical Edifice, of this enchanting Elysian Palace! —where Wit and Mirth, Love and Beauty—all that can delight the Soul and all that can ravish the Senses—will hold their Court, this, and every Evening this week, in chaste and joyous Assemblage—let them now come forth, or for ever afterwards let them blame themselves and bewail their irremediable Misfortune.

But the most important feature of Dr Graham's establishment was the Celestial Bed. This wonder-working piece of furniture was made by one Denton,* a tinman, who lived in Coventry Street, and subsequently kept a bookseller's shop in High Holborn, and it was said to have cost £12,000. It was beautifully carved and gilt, covered with silk damask,

* This Denton was a man of great mechanical skill, who made some very curious automaton figures. He was afterwards tried for coining, and acquitted on that charge, but was found guilty on a second count of having implements of coining in his possession. For this crime he was executed at Tyburn, on which occasion Dr Graham was present.

supported by twenty-eight glass pillars, and surmounted by a richly carved and gilt canopy, from which crimson silk curtains with fringe and tassels were suspended. Graham pretended that married couples without children might have heirs by sleeping in this bed, for which privilege he demanded one hundred pounds per night; and such is the folly of wealth, that persons of high rank were named who had acceded to these terms. This modern Æsculapius sold also for half a guinea a "Treatise on Health," which was intended to render marriages happy, and entered into full particulars of the means to ensure this great and important object. After a long list of preliminary and necessary preparations, the principal of which was the utmost attention to cleanliness, the writer insisted on certain regulations. He recommended particularly the practice of early hours for rising and for retiring to rest. He advised that in bed-chambers the light, especially that of the moon, should not be excluded by curtains. He confessed he could give no sufficient reason for this predilection for the lunar rays, but observed that there are a thousand things in nature which exist without our being able to explain the reasons of their existence. He also advised married people to sing sometimes. "Music," said he, "softens the mind of a happy couple, makes them all love, all harmony; their bodies, their souls unite, their existence is melted into a single being, which yields itself up with rapture to divine transports, and loses itself in an Elysium of bliss. In this state, this incessantly progressive enjoyment, the happy couple imagine themselves raised above this world, and become inhabitants of a superior region." Thus he continued, till coming at last to the principal part of his discourse: "When the preliminary regimen which I have just described has been scrupulously observed and followed, and a new vigour has been acquired by drinking of the divine balm, which for the benefit of the human race, I have concocted with my own hand, and which, however, costs only a guinea a bottle, and when all these means have not proved sufficient for arriving at the end proposed, the last must then be absolutely applied to, that most extraordinary expedient which I alone possess, and which cannot fail. This agent is a most marvellous celestial bed, which I call magnetico-electric; it is the first, the only one in the world, or that ever existed. It is placed on the second floor, in a large and elegant hall, on the right hand of my orchestra, and immediately before my charming hermitage. In a neighbouring closet is placed a cylinder by which I communicate the celestial fire to the bed-chamber, that fluid which animates and vivifies all, and those cherishing vapours and Oriental perfumes, which I convey thither by means of tubes of glass. The celestial bed rests on six massy and transparent columns; coverings of purple, and curtains of celestial blue surround it, and the bed-clothes are perfumed with the most costly essences of Arabia: it is exactly similar to those that adorn the palaces in Persia, and to that of the favourite sultana in the seraglio of the Grand Turk. This bed is the fruit of the most laborious industry, and of the most indefatigable zeal. I will not mention the sums it has cost me: they are immense. I shall only add that I have omitted none of those precautions which decency and delicacy have a right to exact. Neither I, nor any of my people, are entitled to ask who are the persons that rest in this chamber, which I have denominated the Holy of Holies. This bed is never shown to those who come only to view the accessory parts. This precaution is as proper as it is delicate; for is there a being frigid enough to resist the influence of that pleasure, of those transports which this enchanting place inspires? It furnishes the grossest imagination with the means of refining its enjoyments, of multiplying its pleasures, and of carrying them to their highest degree. But the consequences are cruel; such dangerous refinements on the pleasures of the senses abridge the period of life, and relax the springs both of body and mind. Persons, however, who would penetrate to this throne of pleasure, are intreated to signify their desire to me in writing, and having appointed the night, and enclosed a bank-bill for fifty pounds, I shall furnish them with an admission ticket." Ultimately, as the demand decreased, the price was reduced to twenty-five pounds, and it is said that even less was at times taken.

It is not to be supposed that Graham's contemporaries, except the weakest and most idiotic, believed in the marvellous effects attributed to this bed, or supposed that the Doctor had any motive in making his statements other than those which generally actuate quacks, and lead them into exaggerations. He and certain rich voluptuaries worked very well together with regard to this couch, as may be gathered from various satirical allusions in newspapers of the time, caricatures, &c. It is certain that spendthrifts and men of pleasure were the most profitable customers of the great empiric. The more the "Holy of Holies" began to be visited, the more did Graham add to the luxury and magnificence of the place; but in the month of March 1784 the farce was played out, the Temple of Health was shut, and all the furniture and apparatus put up for public sale. All the paraphernalia which had cost so much money, and with which he was identified—the superb temple of Apollo, the immense electrical machine, the instruments of music which played incessantly, and even the famous celestial bed itself—all fell in one common ruin under the ruthless hammer of the auctioneer.

In a note which serves as a supplement to the description of the Celestial Bed, the Doctor adds: "Nothing is more surprising than the truly divine energy of this celestial and electric fire, which fills every part of the bed, as well as the magnetic fluid, both of them calculated to give the necessary degree of strength and exertion to the nerves. Besides the melodious tones of the harmonica, the soft sounds of a flute, the charms of an agreeable voice, and the harmonious notes of the organ, being all joined, how can the power and virtue of such a happy conjunction fail in raising sentiments of admiration and pleasure in the soul of the philosopher, and even of the physician?"

According to the advertisements, the descriptive exhibition of the apparatus in the daytime was conducted by an "officiating junior priest." This office was filled by a young medical man named Mitford, afterwards well known as, among other things, father of the celebrated authoress. Graham's expenses were very heavy, and when after a time his advertisements failed to draw he fell into poverty, and it is said died in very straitened circumstances near Glasgow.

CHAPTER XVI.

LOTTERIES AND LOTTERY INSURANCES.

THERE have been few things which in their time have had more intimate connection with advertising than Lotteries. In fact almost all we can now discover about them is by means of the notices which were published before and after a drawing, as the system of picturesque descriptive writing now applied to everything had not come into fashion during the existence of this legalised species of gambling, which was for generations most ruinous and demoralising in its effects, but which was continued mainly because it added to the revenue, and perhaps because it was considered unfair to stop the speculation of the people while gaming under so many forms and in so many varieties was indulged in by the higher classes. In these days the Legislature has got over any such squeamish feelings—even if it ever possessed them—for though gambling is carried on to as great lengths as ever under certain forms, though within the past few years great scandals have leaked out from clubs and private hells, and though on the turf many noble names have been dragged through the mire, the rank and file of the community are rigidly guarded from any chance of giving way to the temptations of gambling, either by means of the racehorse or the milder forms of speculation which up till recently were allowed in public-houses, and are very properly compelled to be virtuous whether they like it or no.

The origin of lotteries is involved in obscurity, but it is generally believed that the first of them was held in Italy early in the sixteenth century, and that in due course the plan found favour over here, and was gradually taken up by the State. From 1569 down to 1826 (except for a short time following upon an Act of the reign of Anne) lotteries continued to be a source of revenue to the English Government. Some interesting particulars are given by Hone and Chambers, the latter of whom says: "It seems strange that so glaringly immoral a project should have been kept up with such sanction so long. The younger people of the present day may be at a loss to believe that, in the days of their fathers, there were large and imposing offices in London, and pretentious agencies in the provinces, for the sale of lottery tickets; while flaming advertisements on walls, in new books, and in public journals, proclaimed the preferableness of such and such 'lucky' offices—this one having sold two-sixteenths of the last twenty-thousand-pounds prize; that one a half of the same; another having sold an entire thirty-thousand-pound ticket the year before; and so on. It was found possible to persuade the public, or a portion of it, that where a blessing had once lighted it was the more likely to light again. The State lottery was framed on the simple principle, that the State held forth a certain sum to be repaid by a larger. The transaction was usually managed thus. 'The Government gave £10 in prizes for every share taken on an average. A great many blanks or of prizes under £10, left, of course, a surplus for the creation of a few magnificent prizes wherewith to attract the unwary public. Certain firms in the City, known as lottery-office keepers, contracted for the lottery, each taking a certain number of shares; the sum paid by them was always more than £10 per share; and the excess constituted the Government profit. It was customary, for many years, for the contractors to give about £16 to the Government, and then to charge the public from £20 to £22. It was made lawful for the contractors to divide the shares into halves, quarters, eighths, and sixteenths; and the contractors always charged relatively more for these aliquot parts. A man with thirty shillings to spare could buy a sixteenth; and the contractors made a large portion of their profit out of such customers. The Government sometimes paid the prizes in terminable annuities instead of cash; and the loan system and the lottery system were occasionally combined in a very odd way. Thus in 1780, every subscriber of £1000 towards a loan of £12,000,000, at four per cent., received a bonus of four lottery tickets, the value of each of which was £10, and any one of which might be the fortunate number for a twenty or thirty thousand pounds prize. Among the lottery offices, the competition for business was intense. One firm, finding an old woman in the country named Goodluck, gave her £50 a year on condition that she would join them as a nominal partner, for the sake of the attractive effect of her name. In their advertisements each was sedulous to tell how many of the grand prizes had in former years fallen to the lot of persons who had bought at his shop. Woodcuts and copies of verses were abundant, suited to attract the uneducated."

The first lottery in this country, so far as is known, took place in 1569. Dr Rawlinson, a distinguished antiquary of the last century, produced before the Antiquarian Society in 1748 the following:—

A Proposal for a very rich Lottery, general without any Blankes, contayning a great N° of good prices, as well of redy money as of Plate and certain sorts of Merchandizes, having been valued and prised by the Commandment of the Queenes most excellent Majesties order, to the extent that such Commodities as may chance to arise thereof, after the charges borne, may be converted towards the reparations of the Havens and Strength of the realme, and towards such other public good workes. The N of lotts shall be foure hundred thousand, and no more; and every lott shall be the summe of tenne shillings sterling only, a d no more. To be filled by the feast of St Bartholomew. The shew of Prises ar to be seen in Cheapside, at the sign of the Queenes armes, the house of Mr. Dericke, Goldsmith, Servant to the Queen.

Some other Orders about it in 1567-8.

Printed by Hen. Bynneman.

According to Stow the drawing of this lottery was commenced at the west door of St Paul's Cathedral on the 11th of January 1569, and continued day and night until the 6th of May. It was originally intended to be drawn at Dericke's house, but most likely, as preparations were made, it was discovered that a private establishment would be hardly the place for so continuous a piece of business. Maitland in his "London" says, "Whether this lottery was on account of the public, or the selfish views of private persons, my author* does not mention; but it is evident, by the time it took up in drawing, it must have been of great concern. This I have remarked as being the first of the kind I read in England." By these remarks it would seem that neither Stow nor Maitland had seen the "Proposal" we have quoted above, which gives the reason for the lottery.

In 1586 there was another drawing, about which we are quaintly told: "A Lotterie, for marvellous rich and beautiful armor, was begunne to be drawn at London, in S. Paules churchyard, at the great west gate, (an house of timber and boord being there erected for that purpose) on St. Peter's Day in the morning, which Lotterie continued in Drawing day and night for the space of two or three daies."† Of this lottery Lord Burleigh says in his diary at the end of Munden's State Papers: "June 1586, the Lottery of Armour under the charge of John Calthorp determined." About the year 1612 James I., "in special favour for the plantation of English colonies in Virginia, granted a lottery to be held at the west end of St Paul's; whereof one Thomas Sharplys, a taylor of London, had the chief prize, which was four thousand crowns in fair plate."‡

A correspondent of the *Gentleman's Magazine* in 1778 gives Mr Urban some particulars regarding a lottery "held in London for the present plantation of English colonies in Virginia" in 1619. The writer says: "It may be found,

---

* Stow. † Stow's Annals. ‡ Baker's Chronicle.

perhaps, upon strict enquiry that this mode of raising money was authorized in many wealthy towns, as well as in the capital; and that it was attended with beneficial effects, not only to the colony of Virginia, but likewise to the town itself where the lottery was held. In proof of this supposition I send you the following authentic extract from the Register of charitable Gifts to the Corporation of Reading:"—

Whereas at a Lottery held within the Borough of Reading in the Year of our Ld. God 1619, Gabriel Barber Gent. Agent in the sd. Lottery for the Councell & Company of Virginia, of his own good Will & Charity towarde poor Tradesmen ffreemen & Inhabitants of the sd. Borough of Reading, & for the better enabling such poor Tradesmen to support & bear their Charges in their several Places & Callings in the sd. Corporation from time to time for ever freely gave & delivered to the Mayor & Burgesses of this Corporation the sum of forty Pounds of lawfull Money of England Upon Special Trust & Confidence, that the sd. Mayor & Burgesses & their Successors shall from time to time for ever dispose & lend these 40l. to & amongst Six poor Tradesmen after the rate 06l. 13s. 4d. to each Man for the Term of five Years gratis And after those five Years ended to dispose & lend the sd. 40l. by Such Soms to Six other poor Tradesmen for other five Years & so from five years to five years Successively upon good Security for ever Neverthelesse provided & upon Condition that none of those to whom the sd. Summs of money shall be lent during that Term of five years shall keep either Inn or Tavern or dwell forth of the sd. Borough, but there during that time and terme, shall as other Inhabitants of the sd. Borough reside & dwell.

Memorand. that the sd. Sum of 40l. came not into the hands & charge of the Mayor & Burgesses until April 1626.

The writer then concludes with the following somewhat puzzling sentence: "If it be asked what is become of it now? *gone*, it is supposed, *where the chickens went before* during the pious Protectorship of Cromwell."

Hone in his "Everyday-Book" says that "in 1630, 6th Charles I., there was a project 'for the conveying of certain springs of water into London and Westminster, from within a mile and a half of Hodsdon, in Hertfordshire, by the undertakers, Sir Edward Stradling and John Lyde.' The author of this project was one Michael Parker. 'For defraying the expenses whereof, King Charles grants them a special licence to erect and publish a lottery or lotteries; *according,*' says this record, '*to the course of other lotteries* heretofore used or practised.' This is the first mention of lotteries either in the *Fœdera* or Statute-book. 'And for the sole privilege of bringing the said waters in aqueducts to London, they were to pay four thousand pounds per annum into the king's exchequer: and, the better to enable them to make the said large annual payment, the king grants them leave to bring their aqueducts through any of his parks, chases, lands, &c., and to dig up the same gratis.'" In 1653 there was a lottery at Grocers' Hall, which has escaped the observation of the earliest inquirers on this subject. In an old weekly paper, called *Perfect Account of the Daily Intelligence,* November 16–23, 1653, there is the following:—

Advertisement.

At the Committee for Claims for Lands in Ireland,

Ordered, that a Lottery be at Grocers-Hall, London, on Thursday 15 Decem. 1653, both for Provinces and Counties, to begin at 8 of the Clock in the forenoon of the same day; and all persons concerned therein are to take notice thereof. *W. Tibbs.*

After the Restoration, Charles, whose ideas of rewarding fidelity were always peculiar, granted plate lotteries "with a view to reward those adherents of the Crown who resided within the bills of mortality, and had served with fidelity during the interregnum." By this is to be understood a gift of plate from the Crown to be disposed of by lot, certain persons—most likely those who had no claim whatever on the score of fidelity—having the privilege of selling tickets. The *Gazette* tells us that in 1669 Charles II., the Duke of York, and many of the nobility were present "at the grand plate lottery, which, by his Majesty's command, was then opened at the sign of the Mermaid, over against the mews." Even if this had been a proper way to reward the faithful, the faithfullest must have felt it had been left rather late. From this plate lottery sprang many successors, the most noticeable of which was the Royal Oak, whose title explains itself. The rapid growth of the institution may be judged by the following, which, according to Anderson in his "History of Commerce," was published shortly after the drawing to which we have referred :—

THIS is to give Notice, that any Persons who are desirous to farm any of the Counties within the Kingdom of England, or Dominion of Wales, in Order to the setting up of a Plate Lottery, or any other Lottery whatsoever, may repair to the Lottery Office, at Mr. Philips's House, in Mermaid Court over against the Mews; where they may contract with the Trustees commissioned by his Majesties Letters Patent for the Management of the said Patent, on the Behalf of the truly Loyal Indigent Officers.

It is stated that "the Crown exceeded its prerogative by issuing these patents, and the law was not put in motion to question them." This was not the only point upon which the royal rights were extended, but the tide of loyalty had set in strongly, and Charles was not likely to miss any of the current's strength. Book lotteries were before this time much in fashion, and with the kinds which came in afterwards, were drawn at the theatres. At Vere Street theatre, which stood in Bear Yard, to which there was an entrance through a passage at the south-west corner of Lincoln's Inn Fields, another from Vere Street, and a third from Clare Market, Killigrew's company performed during the seasons of 1661 and 1662, and part of 1663, when they removed to the newly-built theatre in Drury Lane; the Vere Street theatre was then probably unoccupied until Mr Ogilby, the author of the "Itinerarum Angliæ, or Book of Roads," adopted it, as standing in a populous neighbourhood, for the temporary purpose of drawing a lottery of books, which took place in 1668. Books were often the species of property held out as a lure to adventurers, by way of lottery, for the benefit of the suffering Loyalists. In the *Gazette* of May 18, 1668, is the following advertisement :—

MR. Ogilby's Lottery of Books opens on Monday the 25th instant, at the old Theatre between Lincoln's Inn Fields and Vere street, where all Persons concerned may repair on Monday May 18, and see the Volumes, and put in their Money.

But the business being much better than was anticipated, the drawing had to be postponed, and so in the number of the *Gazette* for May 25 there is this :—

MR Ogilby's Lottery of Books (Adventurers coming in so fast that they cannot in so short Time be methodically registered) opens not till Tuesday the 2d of June ; then not failing to draw ; at the old Theatre between Lincoln's Inn Fields and Vere street.

Ogilby had had a venture before this, about which there seems to have been some little difficulty, as in his "Proposal" for this same lottery he refers to aspersions which have been made. A correspondent of the *Gentleman's Magazine* of nearly a hundred years ago gives as a curiosity even then a copy of this "Proposal," which, though rather long, is very interesting, and so we subjoin it :—

A SECOND PROPOSAL, by the Author, for the better and more speedy Vendition of several Volumes, (his own Works,) by the way of a standing *Lottery*, licensed by his Royal Highness the Duke of York, and Assistants at the Corporation of the royal Fishing.

WHEREAS *John Ogilby*, esq., erected a standing Lottery of Books, and completely furnished the same with very large, fair, and special Volumes, all of his own Designment and Composure, at vast Expense, Labour and Study of twenty Years ; the like Impressions never before exhibited in the English Tongue. Which according to the appointed Time, on the 10th of May, 1665, opened ; and to the general Satisfaction of the Adventurers, with no less Hopes of a clear Despatch and fair Advantage to the Author, was several Days in Drawing : when its Proceedings were stopt by the then growing Sickness and lay discontinued under the Arrest of that common Calamity, till the next Year's more violent and sudden Visitation, the late dreadful and surprising Conflagration, swallowed the Remainder, being two Parts of three, to the Value of three thousand Pounds and upward, in that unimaginable Deluge. Therefore, to repair in some Manner his so much commiserated Losses, by the Advice of so many his Patrons, Friends, and especially by the Incitations of his former Adventurers, he resolves, and hath already prepared, not only to reprint all his own former Editions, but others that are new, of equal Value, and like Estimation by their Embellishments, and never yet Published; with some remains of the first Impressions, Relics preserved in several Hands from the Fire; to set up a second standing Lottery, where such the Discrimination of Fortune shall be, that few or None shall return with a dissatisfying Chance. The whole Draught being of greater Advantage by much (to the Adventurers) than the former. And accordingly, after Publication, the Author opened his Office, where they might put in their first Encouragements (*viz.*) twenty Shillings, and twenty more at the reception of their Fortune, and also see those several magnificent Volumes, which their varied Fortune (none being bad) should present them.

* But the Author now finding more difficulty than he expected, since many of his Promisers (who also received great Store of Tickets to dispose of, towards promotion of his Business) though seeming well resolved and very willing, yet straining Courtesy not to go foremost in paying their monies, linger out, driving it off till near the time appointed for Drawing; which Dilatoriness: (since Despatch is the soul and life to his Proposal, his only Advantage a speedy Vendition:) and also observing how that a Money Dearth, a Silver Famine, slackens and cools the Courage of Adventurers: through which hazy humours magnifying medium Shillings loome like Crowns, and each forty Shillings a ten Pound Heap. Therefore, according to the present Humour now reigning, he intends to adequate his Design; and this seeming too large-roomed, standing Lottery, modelled into many less and more likely to be taken Tenements, which shall not open only a larger Prospect of pleasing Hopes, but more real Advantage to the Adventurer. Which are now to be disposed of thus: the whole Mass of Books or Volumes, being the same without Addition or Diminution, amounting according to their known Value (being the Prices they have been usually disposed at) to thirteen thousand seven hundred Pounds; so that the Adventurers will have the above said Volumes (if all are drawn) for less

---

* Whereas, some give out that they could never receive their Books after they were drawn in the first Lottery, the Author declares, and it will be attested, that of seven hundred Prizes that were drawn there were not six remaining Prizes that suffered with his in the Fire; for the Drawing being on the 10th of May, 1665, the Office did then continue open for the Delivery of the same (though the Contagion much raged) until the latter End of July following; and opened again, to attend the Delivery, in April, 1666, whither Persons repaired daily for their Prizes, and continued open until the Fire.

than two-thirds of what they would yield in Process of Time, Book by Book. He now resolves to attempter, or mingle each Prize with four allaying Blanks; so bringing down, by this Means, the Market from double Pounds to single Crowns.

THE PROPOSITIONS.—First, whosoever will be pleased to put in five Shillings shall draw a Lot, his Fortune to receive the greatest or meanest Prize, or throw away his intended spending Money on a Blank. Secondly, whoever will adventure deeper, putting in twenty-five Shillings, shall receive, if such his bad Fortune be that he draws all Blanks, a Prize presented to him by the Author of more value than his Money (if offered to be sold) though proffered ware, &c. Thirdly, who thinks fit to put in for eight Lots forty Shillings shall receive nine, and the advantage of their free Choice (of all Blanks) of either of the Works complete, *viz.* Homer's Iliads and Odysses, or Æsop the first and second Volumes, the China Book, or Virgil. Of which,

The First and greatest Prize contains

1 Lot, Number 1.

An imperial Bible with Chorographical and an hundred historical Sculps, valued at.........25*l.*
Virgil translated, with Sculps and Annotations, val.........5*l.*
Homer's Iliads, adorned with Sculps, val.........5*l.*
Homer's Odysses, adorned with Sculps, val.........4*l.*
Æsop's Fables paraphrased and Sculped, in Folio, val.........3*l.*
A second Collection of Æsopick Fables, adorned with Sculps, never

[*Rest imperfect.*]

His Majestie's Entertainment passing through the city of London, and Coronation.
These are one of each, of all the Books contained in the Lottery, the whole value 51*l.*

The Second Prize contains

1 Lot, Num. 2.

One imperial Bible with all the Sculps, val. ....25*l.*
Homer complete, in English, val. ....9*l.*
Virgil, val. ....5*l.*
Æsop complete, val. ....6*l.*
The Description of China, val.........4*l.*

In all 49 Pound.

The Third Prize contains

1 Lot, Num. 3.

One royal Bible with all the Sculps ....10*l.*
Homer's Works in English, val.........9*l.*
Virgil translated, with Scu'ps and Annotations, val.........5*l.*
The first and second Vol. of Æsop, val.........6*l.*
The Description of China, val.........4*l.*
Entertainment, val. ....2*l.*

In all 36 Pound.

1 Lot, Num. 4.

One imperial Bible with all the Sculps, val. ....25*l.*
Æsop's Fables the first and second Vol. val. ....6*l.*
In all 31 Pound.

1 Lot, Num. 5.

One imperial Bible with all the Sculps, val. ....25*l.*
Virgil translated, with Sculps, val. ....5*l.*
In all 30 Pound.

1 Lot, Num. 6.

One imperial Bible with all the Sculps, val. ....25*l.*
And a Description of China, val. ....4*l.*
In all 29 Pound.

1 Lot, Num. 7.

One imperial Bible with all the Sculps and a new Æsop, val. ....28*l.*

1 Lot, Num. 8.

One imperial Bible with all the Sculps, val. ....25*l.*

1 Lot, Num. 9.

A royal Bible with all the Sculps, val. ....10*l.*
A Description of China, val. ....4*l.*
And a Homer complete, val... ....9*l.*
In all 23 Pound.

1 Lot, Num. 10.

A royal Bible with all the Sculps, val. ....10*l.*
A Virgil complete, val. ....5*l.*
Æsop's Fables the first and second Vols. val ....6*l.*
In all 21 Pound.

1 Lot, Num. 11.

One royal Bible with all the Sculps, val. ....10*l.*
And a Homer's Works complete, val. ....9*l.*
In all 19 Pound.

1 Lot, Num. 12.

One royal Bible with all the Sculps, val. ....10*l.*
And both the Æsops, val. ....6*l.*
In all 16 Pound.

1 Lot, Num. 13.

One royal Bible with all the Sculps, val. ....10*l.*
A Virgil complete in English, val. ....5*l.*
In all 15 Pound.

1 Lot, Num. 14.

One royal Bible with all the Sculps, val. ....10*l.*
A Description of China, val. ....4*l.*
In all 14 Pound.

[*No.* 15 *imperfect.*]

1 Lot, Num. 16.

One royal Bible with all the Sculps ....10*l.*
The second Volume of Æsop, val. ....3*l.*
In all 13 Pound.

1 Lot, Num. 17.

One royal Bible with all the Sculps, val..........10*l.*
And an Entertainment, val..........2*l.*

In all 12 Pound.

1 Lot, Num. 18.

One royal Bible with all the Sculps, val..........10*l.*

1 Lot, Num. 19.

One royal Bible with Chorographical Sculps, val..........5*l.*
One Virgil complete, val..........5*l.*

In all 10 Pound.

1 Lot, Num. 20.

One royal Bible with Chorographical Sculps, val..........5*l.*
And a Homer's Iliads, val..........5*l.*

In all 10 Pound.

1 Lot, Num. 21.

One royal Bible with Chorographical Sculps, val..........5*l.*
And a Homer's Odysses, val..........4*l.*

In all 9 Pound.

1 Lot, Num. 22.

One royal Bible with Chorographical Sculps, val..........5*l.*
And a Description of China, val..........4*l.*

In all 9 Pound.

1 Lot, Num. 23.

One royal Bible with Chorographical Sculps..........5*l.*
And Æsop complete, val..........6*l.*

In all 11 Pound.

1 Lot, Num. 24.

A royal Bible with Chorographical Sculps, val..........5*l.*
And Æsop the first Volume, val..........3*l.*

In all 8 Pound.

1 Lot, Num. 25.

A royal Bible with Chorographical Sculps, val..........5*l.*
And Æsop the second Volume, val..........3*l.*

In all 8 Pound.

1 Lot, Num. 26.

A royal Bible, ruled, with Chorographical Sculps, val..........6*l.*

1 Lot, Num. 27.

A royal Bible, with Chorographical Sculps, ruled, val..........6*l.*

1 Lot, Num. 28.

One royal Bible with Chorographical Sculps, val..........5*l.*

10 Lot, Num. 29.

Each a Homer complete, val..........9*l.*

10 Lot, Num. 30.

Each a double Æsop complete, val..........6*l.*

520 Lot, Num. 31.

Each a Homer's Iliads, val. .... 5*l.*

520 Lot, Num. 32.

Each a Homer's Odysses, val. .... 4*l.*

570 Lot, Num. 33.

Each a Virgil complete, val. .... 5*l.*

570 Lot, Num. 34.

Each a China Book, val. .... 4*l.*

570 Lot, Num. 35.

Each the first Volume of Æsop, val. .... 3*l.*

570 Lot, Num. 36.

Each the second Volume of Æsop, val. .... 3*l.*

The whole Number of the Lots three thousand, three hundred, and sixty-eight. The Number of the Blanks as above ordered; so that the Total received is but four thousand, one hundred, and ten Pounds.

The Office where their Monies are to be paid in, and they receive their Tickets, and where the several Volumes or Prizes may be daily seen, (by which visual Speculation understanding their real Worth better than by the Ear or printed Paper,) is kept at the Black Boy, over against St. Dunstan's Church, Fleet Street. The Adventurers may also repair for their better Convenience, to pay in their Monies, to Mr. Peter Cleyton, over against the Dutch Church, in Austin Friars, and to Mr. Baker, near Broad Street, entering the South door of the Exchange, and to Mr. Roycroft, in Bartholomew Close.

The certain Day of Drawing, the Author promiseth (though but half full) to be the twenty-third of May next. Therefore all Persons that are willing to Adventure, are desired to bring or send in their Monies with their Names, or what other Inscription or Motto they will, by which to know their own, by the ninth of May next, it being Whitson Eve, that the Author may have Time to put up the Lots and Inscriptions into their respective Boxes.

Notwithstanding the positive promise given as to the date of the drawing, there seems, judging by the advertisements first quoted, to have been two alterations in the time. Mr Ogilby assorted his wares in the most tempting manner, and it is interesting to know what were considered the most marketable books, with their relative values, over two hundred years ago. Even then, and long before either became familiar to the bulk of English readers, the Iliad was worth a pound more than the Odyssey. Æsop was rated, entire, at more than the best of the Homeric books, but divided, he was inferior to either, and Virgil complete was worth exactly the same amount as the Iliad. A contributor to the *Gentleman's Magazine*, about a hundred years back, states that he had seen a then very old but undated "Address to the Learned, or an advantageous lottery for books in quires; wherein each adventurer of a guinea is sure of a prize of two pounds value; and it is but four to one that he has a prize of three, six, eight, twelve, or fifty pounds." The proposals for this lottery were, one thousand four hundred lots, at a guinea each, to be drawn with the lots out of two glasses, superintended by John Lilly and Edward Darrel, Esqs., Mr Deputy Collins, and Mr William Proctor, stationer; two lots of £50, ten of £12, twenty of £8, sixty-eight of £6, two hundred of £5, and one thousand two hundred of £3. Letters-patent on behalf of the promoters of Lotteries were from time to time renewed, and from the *Gazette* of October 11, 1675, it appears by those dated June 19 and December 17, 1674, there were granted for thirteen years to come, "all lotteries whatsoever invented or to be invented, to several truly loyal and indigent officers, in consideration of their many faithful services and sufferings, with prohibition to all others to use or set up the said lotteries." These officers were also granted powers to give licences and name agents.

In the *Examiner*, about the time when Lotteries were suppressed, there is much information concerning them, and the writer among other things finds, from a copy of the *London Gazette* of May 17, 1688, that "Ogilby, the better to carry on his 'Britannia,' had a lottery of books at Garraway's Coffeehouse in 'Change Alley." Lotteries of various kinds seem to have been very general before this date; indeed so much so that Government issued a notice in the *London Gazette*, September 27, 1683, to prevent the drawing of any lotteries (and especially a newly-invented lottery under the name of the riffling, or raffling, lottery) "except those under his Majesty's letters-patent, for thirteen years, granted to persons for their sufferings, and have their seal of office with this inscription, '*Meliora Designavi.*'" In 1683, Prince Rupert dying rather poor, a plan was devised to obtain money by disposing of all his jewels; but as the public were not satisfied with the mode of drawing the lotteries, on account of the many cheats practised on them, they would not listen to any proposals until the King himself guaranteed to see that all was fair, and also that Mr Francis Child, the goldsmith at Temple Bar, would be answerable for their several adventures, as appears by the *London Gazette*, October 1, 1683:—

THESE are to give notice, that the Jewels of his late Royal Highness Prince Rupert have been particularly valued and appraised by Mr. Isaac Legouch, Mr Christopher Rosse, and Mr. Richard Beauvoir, Jewellers, the whole amounting to Twenty Thousand Pounds, and will be sold by way of Lottery, each Lot to be Five Pounds. The biggest Prize will be a great Pearl Necklace, valued at 8,000*l.*, and none less than 100*l.* A printed Particular of the said Appraisement, with their Divisions into Lots, will be delivered gratis by Mr. Francis Child, at Temple Bar, London, into whose Hands, such as are willing to be Adventurers are desired to pay their Money, on or before the 1st Day of November next. As soon as the whole Sum is paid in, a short Day will be appointed which, (it is hoped, will be before Christmas) and notified in the *Gazette*, for the Drawing thereof, which will be done in his Majesty's Presence, who is pleased to declare, that *he himself will see all the Prizes put in among the Blanks*, and that the whole will be managed with Equity and Fairness, Nothing being intended but the sale of the said Jewels at a moderate Value. And it is further notified, for the Satisfaction of all as shall be Adventurers, that the said Mr. *Child* shall and will stand obliged to Each of them for their several Adventures. And that each Adventurer shall receive their Money back if the said Lottery be not drawn and finished before the first Day of February next.

This Mr Child is said to have been the first regular banker. He began business soon after the Restoration, and received the honour of knighthood. He lived in Fleet Street, where the shop still continues in a state of the highest respectability.* A subsequent notice says that

The King will probably, to-morrow, in the Banquetting House, see all the Blanks told over, that they may not exceed their Number; and that the Papers on which the Prizes are to be written shall be rolled up in his Presence; and that a Child, appointed, either by his Majesty or the Adventurers, shall draw the Prizes.

The most popular of all the schemes of the time was that drawn at the Dorset Garden Theatre, near Salisbury Square, Fleet Street, with the capital prize of a thousand pounds for a penny. The drawing began on October 19, 1698; and in the *Protestant Mercury* of the following day its fairness was said to give universal content to all that were concerned. In the next number is found an inconsistent story as to the possessor of the prize. It runs thus: "Sometime since, a boy near Branford going to school one morning, met an old woman, who asked his charity; the boy replied, he had nothing to give her but a piece of bread and butter, which she accepted. Sometime after, she met the boy again, and told him she had good luck after his bread and butter, and therefore would give him a penny which, after some years keeping, would produce many pounds: he accordingly kept it a great while, and at last, with some friends' advice, put it into the Penny Lottery, and we are informed that on Tuesday last, the said lot came up with £1000 prize." This is a very fair specimen of the stories which were always afloat concerning the chief prizes in the principal lotteries, and which had always some superstitious current underlying them, much to the benefit of the vendors of tickets. The scheme of the Penny Lottery was assailed in a tract entitled "The Wheel of Fortune, or Nothing for a Penny; being Remarks on the Drawing of the Penny Lottery at the Theatre Royal, in

---

* *Examiner*, October 22, 1826.

Dorset Garden." (1698, 4to.) Afterwards this theatre was used for exhibitions of sword-and-cudgel players, prize-fighters, &c.; but the building was totally deserted in 1703. In the last years of the century, schemes were started called "The Lucky Adventure; or, Fortunate Chance, being 2000*l.* for a groat, or 3000*l.* for a shilling;" and "Fortunatus, or another Adventure of 1000*l.* for a Penny;" but purchasers were more wary, and the promoters' plans in both cases fell to the ground. The royal patentees also advertised against the "Marble Board, alias Woollich Board lotteries; the Figure Board, alias the Whimsey Board and the Wyre Board lotteries." The patentees were, in addition, always quarrelling among themselves; and the following lines from the *Post-Boy*, January 3, 1698, were very popular at the time, as giving an estimate of the disputes between the legalised rogues:—

A DIALOGUE *betwixt the* NEW LOTTERIES *and the* ROYAL OAK.

New Lott. To you the Mother of our Schools,
Where knaves by license manage Fools,
Finding fit Juncture and Occasion,
To pick the Pockets of the Nation;
We come to know how we must treat 'em,
And to their hearts' content may cheat 'em.

Oak. It cheers my aged Heart to see
So numerous a Progeny;
I find by you, that 'tis Heaven's will
That knavery should flourish still;
You have docility and wit,
And Fools were never wanting yet.
Observe the crafty Auctioneer
His art to sell waste Paper dear;
When he for Salmon baits his Hooks,
That Cormorant of Offal books,
Who bites, as sure as Maggots breed,
Or Carrion Crows on Horseflesh feed;
Fair specious Titles him deceive,
To sweep what Sl—— and T——n leave.
If greedy gulls you would ensnare,
Make 'em Proposals wondrous fair;

Tell him strange Golden Show'rs shall fall,
And promise Mountains to 'em all.

New Lott. That Craft we've already taught,
And by that Trick have millions caught;
Books, Baubles, Toys, all sorts of Stuff,
Have gone off this way well enough.
Nay, Music, too, invades our Art,
And to some Tune wou'd play her Part.
I'll show you now what we are doing,
For we have divers Wheels agoing.
We now have found out richer Lands,
Than Asia's Hills, or Afric's Sands,
And to vast Treasures must give Birth,
Deep hid in Bowels of the Earth;
In fertile Wales, and God knows where,
Rich mines of Gold and Silver are,
From whence we draw prodigious Store
Of Silver coin'd, tho' none in Ore,
Which down our Throats rich Coxcombs pour,
In hopes to make us vomit more.

Oak. This Project surely must be good
Because not eas'ly understood;
Besides, it gives a mighty Scope
To the Fool's Argument—vain Hope.
No Eagle's Eye the Cheat can see,
Thro' Hope thus back'd by Mystery.

New Lott. We have, besides, a thousand more,
For Great or Small, for Rich and Poor,
From him that can his Thousands spare,
Down to the Penny Customer.

Oak. The silly Mob in Crowds will run,
To be at easy Rates undone.
A gimcrack Show draws in the Rout,
Thousands their all by Pence lay out.

New Lott. We, by Experience, find it true,
But we have Methods wholly new,
Strange late-invented Ways to thrive,
To make Men pay for what they give,
To get the Rents into our Hands
Of their hereditary Lands,
And out of what does thence arise,
To make 'em buy Annuities.

We've mathematick Combination,
To cheat Folks by plain Demonstration,
Which shall be fairly manag'd too,
The Undertaker knows not how.
Besides——
Oak. Pray, hold a little, here's enough,
To beggar Europe of this Stuff.
Go on, and prosper, and be great,
I am to you a puny Cheat.

The Royal Oak Lottery came in for a great share of public odium, it being regarded as the parent of all the others. A very curious tract of 1699 sets forth the various charges against it in the form of a trial. The pamphlet is called "The Arraignment, Trial and Condemnation of *Squire Lottery*, alias *Royal-Oak Lottery*." The various charges, defences, and counter-charges are very funny, and we regret that we have only room here for the jury list, which shows that the "British palladium" possessed then many of its present features, judged by the characters and pretensions of the jurymen. The descriptions of these latter would fit pretty well even in these days:—

The Jurors' Names.

Mr. *Positive*, a Draper in *Covent Garden*.
Mr. *Squander*, an Oilman in *Fleet Street*.
Mr. *Pert*, a Tobacconist, *ditto*.
Mr. *Captious*, a Milliner in *Paternoster Row*.
Mr. *Feeble*, a Coffeeman near the *Change*.
Mr. *Altrick*, a Merchant in *Gracechurch Street*.
Mr. *Haughty*, a Vintner by *Grays-Inn*, *Holborn*.
Mr. *Jealous*, a Cutler at *Charing Cross*.
Mr. *Peevish*, a Bookseller in *St. Paul's Churchyard*.
Mr. *Spilbook*, near *Fleet Bridge*.
Mr. *Noysie*, a Silkman upon *Ludgate Hill*.
Mr. *Finical*, a Barber in *Cheapside*.

It is noticeable that during the whole of the trial no individual interferes with either the Court or the witnesses, there being no mention in the report of "a Juror;" and as might have been anticipated, the trial ends with the wholesale condemnation of Squire Lottery, and an order for his immediate execution. Private and fallacious lotteries had by this time become so common, not only in London, but in most other great cities and towns of England, whereby the lower people and the servants and children of good families were defrauded, that an Act of Parliament was therefore passed, 10 and 11 William III. c. 17, for suppressing such lotteries, "even although they might be set up under colour of patents or grants under the Great Seal. Which said grants, or patents," says the preamble, "are against the common good, welfare, and peace of the kingdom, and are void and against law." A penalty, therefore, of five hundred pounds was laid on the proprietors of any such lotteries, and of twenty pounds on every adventurer in them. Notwithstanding this, the like disposition to fraud and gaming prevailed again till fresh laws were enacted for their suppression. The public, or, as they were called, the Parliamentary, lotteries, went on, however, as merrily as before, though they were every now and again threatened—indeed for nearly a hundred and thirty years lotteries were always on the point of being abolished. The promoters of lotteries, even in the early days, thoroughly knew the value of advertising by means of puffs, and many of their paragraphs are found given as ordinary news, for the more effectual trapping of the gulls. Such a one is this from the *Post-Boy* of December 27, 1710:—

We are informed that the Parliamentary Lottery will be fixed in this Manner:—150,000 Tickets will be delivered out at 10*l*. each Ticket, making in all the Sum of 1,500,000*l*. Sterling; the Principal thereof is to be sunk, the Parliament allowing nine per cent. Interest for the whole during the Term of thirty-two Years, which Interest is to be divided as follows: 3750 Tickets will be Prizes from 1000*l*. to 5*l*. per annum, during the said thirty-two Years; all the other Tickets will be Blanks, so that there will be thirty-nine of these to one Prize, but then each Blank Ticket will be entitled to fourteen Shillings a year for the Term of thirty-two Years, which is better than an Annuity for life at ten per cent. over and above chance of getting a prize.

Such was the eagerness of the public to secure shares in this great and liberal undertaking on the part of a beneficent Legislature, that Mercers' Hall was literally crowded, and the clerks were found incompetent to receive the influx of names. Six hundred thousand pounds was subscribed by January 21; and on the 28th of February the required amount of a million and a half had been taken out in shares. This rage for speculation had much to do with the success of the South-Sea Bubble, which was attended by myriad smaller bubbles that in the grand collapse of the most magnificent swindle of modern times have been quite forgotten. But many large fortunes were made by small means. In the height of the speculative fever, hardly a day, certainly not a week, passed without fresh projects, recommended by pompous paragraphs in the newspapers, directing where to subscribe to them. On some six per cent. was paid down, on others one shilling per thousand at the time of subscribing. Some of the obscure keepers of these books of subscription, contenting themselves with what they had netted in the morning, by the registration of one or two millions, disappeared in the afternoon, the rooms they had hired being shut up, and they and their subscription-books being never heard of more. On others of these projects, two shillings, and two-and-sixpence, were paid down; for some few even half a sovereign per cent. was deposited, but this was only in the case of those who could find some person of standing to recommend them in Exchange Alley. Some were divided into shares instead of hundreds and thousands, upon each of which so much was paid down. Any impudent impostor, while the delusion was at its greatest height, needed only to hire a room near the alley for a few hours, and open a subscription-book for a pretended scheme relating to commerce, manufacture, plantation, or some supposed invention, having first advertised it in the newspapers of the preceding day, and he might in a few hours find subscribers for one or two millions of imaginary stock. Yet many of the subscribers were far from believing the project feasible; it was enough for their purpose that there would soon be a premium on the receipts for the subscriptions, when they could easily get rid of them in the crowded alley to others more credulous than themselves. Indeed some of these bubbles were so barefaced and palpably gross as not to have the shadow of anything like feasibility: such, for instance, were an insurance against divorces; a scheme to learn men to cast nativities; another for making butter from beech-trees; a project for a flying machine; a company for fattening hogs; and a proposal for a more inoffensive method of emptying or cleansing necessary-houses.

Addison, of course, availed himself of the opportunity afforded by the great lottery mania, and in the *Spectator* for Tuesday, October 9, 1711, he comments on the peculiarities of investors. "When a man has a mind to venture his money in a lottery," says he, "every figure of it appears equally alluring, and as likely to succeed as any of its fellows. They all of them have the same pretensions to good luck, stand upon the same foot of competition, and no manner of reason can be given why a man should prefer one to the other before the lottery is drawn. In this case, therefore, caprice very often acts in the place of reason, and forms to itself some groundless imaginary motive, where real and substantial ones are wanting. I know a well-meaning man that is very well pleased to risk his good fortune upon the number 1711, because it is the year of our Lord. I am acquainted with a tacker that would give a good deal for the number 134. On the contrary, I have been told of a certain zealous dissenter, who being a great enemy to Popery, and believing that bad men are the most fortunate in this world, will lay two to one on the number 666 against any other number, because, says he, it is the number of the Beast. Several would prefer the number 12,000 before any other, as it is the number of the pounds in the great prize.

In short, some are pleased to find their own age in their number; some that have got a number which makes a pretty appearance in the ciphers; and others because it is the same number that succeeded in the last lottery. Each of these, upon no other grounds, thinks he stands fairest for the great lot, and that he is possessed of what may not be improbably called—'the golden number.'"

The reference to the number 134 is made on account of a bill which was brought into the House of Commons against occasional Conformity; and so that it should pass through the Lords, it was proposed to tack it to a money bill. This proposal caused some warm debates, and at last, on being put to the vote, it was found that 134 were for tacking. A large majority was, however, against it, and the motion fell through. The Beast's number is, of course, a reference to Revelation xiii. 18; and the final allusion in the paragraph we will not insult the reader by attempting to explain. Addison then goes on: "These principles of election are the pastimes and extravagances of human reason, which is of so busy a nature, that it will be exerting itself in the meanest trifles, and working even where it wants materials. The wisest of men are sometimes acted by such unaccountable motives, as the life of the fool and the superstitious is guided by nothing else. I am surprised that none of the fortune-tellers, or, as the French call them, the *Diseurs de bonne Aventure*, who publish their bills in every quarter of the town, have turned our lotteries to their advantage. Did any of them set up for a caster of fortunate figures, what might he not get by his pretended discoveries and predictions? I remember, among the advertisements in the *Post-Boy* of September the 27th, I was surprised to see the following one:—

This is to give Notice that ten Shillings over and above the Market Price, will be given for the Ticket in the 1,500,000*l. Lottery, No.* 132, by Nath. Cliff, *at the* Bible and Three Crowns *in Cheapside.*

"This advertisement has given great matter of speculation

to coffee-house theorists. Mr. Cliff's principles and conversation have been canvassed upon this occasion, and various conjectures made why he should thus set his heart upon No. 132. I have examined all the powers in those numbers, broken them into fractions, extracted the square and cube root, divided and multiplied them all ways, but could not arrive at the secret until about three days ago, when I received the following letter from an unknown hand, by which I find that Mr. Nath. Cliff is only the agent, and not the principal, in this advertisement. 'Mr. Spectator,—I am the person that lately advertised I would give ten shillings more than the current price for the ticket No. 132, in the lottery now drawing, which is a secret I have communicated to some friends, who rally me incessantly upon that account. You must know I have but one ticket, for which reason, and a certain dream I have lately had more than once, I resolved it should be the number I most approved. I am so positive that I have pitched upon the great lot, that I could almost lay all I am worth upon it. My visions are so frequent and strong upon this occasion, that I have not only possessed the lot, but disposed of the money which in all probability it will sell for. This morning in particular I set up an equipage which I look upon to be the gayest in the town; the liveries are very rich, but not gaudy. I should be very glad to see a speculation or two upon lottery subjects, in which you would oblige all people concerned, and in particular, your most humble servant George Gosling. P.S. Dear Spec, if I get the 12,000*l.* I'll make thee a handsome present.' After having wished my correspondent good luck, and thanked him for his intended kindness, I shall for this time dismiss the subject of the lottery, and only observe, that the greatest part of mankind are in some degree guilty of my friend Gosling's extravagance. We are apt to rely upon future prospects, and become really expensive while we are only rich in possibility. We live up to our expectations, not to our possessions, and make a figure proportionable to what we may be, not what we are. We outrun our present income, as not doubting to disburse ourselves out of the profits of some future place, project, or reversion that we have in view. It is through this temper of mind, which is so common among us, that we see tradesmen break, who have met with no misfortunes in their business; and men of estate reduced to poverty, who have never suffered from losses or repairs, tenants, taxes, or lawsuits. In short, it is this foolish sanguine temper, this depending upon contingent futurities, that occasions romantic generosity, chimerical grandeur, senseless ostentation, and generally ends in beggary and ruin. The man who will live above his present circumstances, is in great danger of living in a little time much beneath them; or, as the Italian proverb runs, 'the man who lives by hope will die by hunger.' It should be an indispensable rule in life to contract our desires to our present condition, and, whatever may be our expectations, to live within the compass of what we actually possess. It will be time enough to enjoy an estate when it comes into our hands; but if we anticipate our good fortune, we shall lose the pleasure of it when it arrives, and may possibly never possess what we have so foolishly counted upon." We have quoted nearly at length, and offer no excuse; for those who are familiar with the lesson can do no harm by reading it anew, while those who are not may be tempted to dip deeper, and find in the pages of the *Spectator* many new delights. We can offer no remarks of our own on the superstitions of "adventurers" fit to be placed by those we have extracted, and so will pass on to fresh incidents.

Lotteries abounded to such an extent about this time that we really have too much tempting material to choose from. There were the Greenwich Hospital Adventure, sanctioned by Act of Parliament; the Land Lottery, the promoter of which declared it was "found very difficult and troublesome for the adventurers for to search and find out what prizes they have come up in their number-tickets, from the badness of the print, the many errors in them, and the great quantity of prizes;" as well as the Twelvepenny, or Nonsuch, the Fortunatus, and the Deer Lotteries, all flourishing; to say nothing of the smaller swindles, which, despite Parliament, were connived at by the minor authorities. The Hamburgh Lottery caused in 1723 some trouble in the House of Commons. It was ostensibly a scheme for promoting trade between Great Britain and the Elbe territories, but was as gross an imposition as even a lottery system could produce, and was ultimately suppressed by special Act, John Viscount Barrington being expelled the House for complicity in the snare. He was not the only man of rank who dabbled with dirty water, many members of the Commons being more or less openly convicted of fraud in connection with lotteries. George Robinson, Esq., member for Marlowe, disappeared mysteriously in 1731, and it was found that with him went all the hopes of the Charitable Corporation Society, who discovered upon investigation that the half million capital they thought themselves possessed of had been embezzled. Two other M.P.'s, Sir Archibald Grant and Sir Robert Sutton, were found to be concerned, in common with many other persons of position, in the defalcation, and were expelled from their seats, while their property was attached. A lottery was instituted for the benefit of the sufferers, and in 1734 they received nine shillings and ninepence in the pound. This is an advertisement published in the *Daily Courant*, July 1, 1734, with regard to the distribution of prizes in this same lottery:—

Lottery-Office, 28 June 1734.

THE Managers appointed by an Act of Parliament for exchanging the Tickets in the Charitable Corporation Lottery give Notice, That Certificates for all Tickets in the said Lottery, which have been entered at their Office in the New Palace Yard, near the Receipt of his Majesty's Exchequer, to the 29th Day of June, 1734, *will be delivered out at their said Office, in Exchange for the said Tickets, on Wednesday and Thurs-*

day next, from Ten in the Forenoon 'till Two in the Afternoon of each Day; and that the Business of taking in the Tickets will be suspended 'till Friday the 5th Day of July.

And whereas Tickets have been brought to be entered for Certificates, that have been altered from Blanks to Numbers intituled to Benefits (which Tickets have been detected) The Managers do hereby give Notice, that the same is declared Felony by the Act.

It is worthy of notice that sharpers of a description other than the promoters of lotteries were anxious to get all they could out of the ventures, and so winning numbers were very often fabricated; and in more than one instance the utterers being detected, were with the forgers tried and cast for death. A notable instance of this kind of fraud was made public in 1777, in the January of which year two Jews, Joseph Arones and Samuel Noah, were examined at Guildhall before the Lord Mayor, charged with counterfeiting the lottery ticket No. 25,590, a prize of £2000, with intent to defraud Mr Keyser, an office-keeper, who had examined the ticket carefully, and had taken it into the Stock Exchange to sell, when Mr Shewell happened to come into the same box, and hearing the office-keeper's offer, asked to look at the ticket, as he recollected buying one of the same number a day or two before. This very fortunately led to the discovery of the fraud, and the two Jews were committed to take their trial. The number was so artfully altered from 23,590 that not the least erasure could be discerned. Arones was but just come to England, and Noah was said to be a man of property. In the February the two were tried at the Old Bailey for forgery and fraud. Their defence was that Arones found the ticket, and persons were produced to swear to the fact, which they did positively and circumstantially, that the prisoners were discharged. At the same sessions Daniel Denny was tried for forging, counterfeiting, and altering a lottery ticket with intent to defraud; and being found guilty, was condemned. In later days the small cards given on race-courses—and a few years back in the streets—by turf bookmakers to their customers were very successfully imitated, sometimes the number of a ticket which was known to be held by a winner being counterfeited, while at others the brazen-visaged presenter would simply depend upon his ability to "bounce" the layer of odds into the belief that the entry was wrong as to the amount or name of horse. In these latter cases the ingenuity exhibited was great—was in fact of the kind which judges are in the habit of instancing as worthy of better application. As if judges—and juries too, when they have sense—did not know that the only outlet for ability nine times out of ten in certain conditions of society is in a criminal direction. The kind of skill which brings a man to the Central Criminal Court is not likely to find much of an opening so far as money-getting is concerned, and from the ingenuity of the great bank-forgers of 1873, down to that of Counsellor Kelly and Jim the Penman of watch-robbery recollection, there is a wide field of skill for which virtue has small market, and which therefore turns to vice for its reward. We say this without any wish to be regarded as encouragers of crime in any shape or form, but because we consider the words of the judge humbug, and the leaders in certain papers which always break out upon such occasions as we have referred to as cant of the most flagitious character. There is hardly a man now languishing in prison for being ingenious who will not tell you that ingenuity has been his bane, not alone because he yielded to temptation, but because he found the market overstocked with people quite as clever as himself who had additional advantages. This simply proves that the ability which looks so great when it has been devoted to the purposes of robbery is of a very small order after all, and shows itself in its true light when in its proper channel. What, if estimated at their proper value, were the qualifications of the American forgers or the English burglars? Are there not scores of confidential clerks and dozens of skilled mechanics who could have done as well or better than either if they had chosen so to do? Yes, decidedly. Yet in both cases, as well as in many others, the judge and jury, the public and the press, affected to be horror-struck at such a waste of talent. But, as they say in the novels, this is a digression.

In 1736 an Act was passed to build Westminster Bridge by means of a lottery, and by means of advertisement the following scheme was submitted to the public:—

LOTTERY 1736, *for raising* 100000*l*. *for building a Bridge at* Westminster, *consisting of* 125000 *Tickets at* 5*l*. *each.*

Prizes 1	of	20000*l*.	is	20000*l*.
2	"	10000	"	20000
3	"	5000	"	15000
10	"	3000	"	30000
40	"	1000	"	40000
60	"	500	"	30000
100	"	200	"	20000
200	"	100	"	20000
400	"	50	"	20000
1000	"	20	"	20000
2880	"	10	"	288000
30616	Prizes, amounting to		.	523000
94384	Blanks.			
	First Drawn		.	1000
	Last Drawn		.	1000
125000				525000

The Prizes to be paid at the Bank in 40 Days after Drawing, without Deduction. N.B. *There is little more than Three* Blanks *to a* Prize.

Other lotteries were granted for the same purpose before the bridge was completed. Its structure must have been as rotten as the system on which it was built, as for many years before it was pulled down it was a disgrace to the neighbourhood; and as it was anything but old when it was demolished, it must have gone to decay almost as soon as it was opened. Almost every imaginable article was at this period disposed of by raffle or lottery, and Horace Walpole, writing about one for an organ, says: "I am now in pursuit of getting the finest piece of music that ever was heard; it is a thing that will play eight tunes. Handel and all the great musicians say, that it is beyond anything they can do; and this may be performed by the most ignorant person; and when you are weary of those eight tunes, you may have them changed for any other that you like. This I think much better than going to an Italian opera or an assembly. This performance has been lately put into a lottery, and all the royal family choose to have a great many tickets rather than to buy it, the price being I think £1000, infinitely a less sum than some bishoprics have been sold for. And a gentleman won it, who I am in hopes will sell it, and if he will, I will buy it, for I cannot live to have another made, and I will carry it into the country with me." As Walpole lived for sixty years after this, he must have lived to see much more wonderful instruments built, and possibly offered as prizes in lotteries. In June 1743 the price of lottery tickets rose from £10 to £11, 10s., the prizes being in no way increased, and a hint to the unwary was published, in which it was shown that adventurers "gamed at 50 per cent. loss; paying at that price 2s. 6d. to play for 5s.; the money played for being only three pound, besides discount and deductions." The practice of giving £1000 each to the first and last drawn tickets led to a curious difficulty in 1774. On the 5th of January, at the conclusion of drawing the State Lottery at Guildhall, No. 11,053, as the last-drawn ticket, was declared to be entitled to the thousand pounds, and was so printed in the paper of benefits by order of the commissioners. It was, beside, a prize of a hundred pounds. But after the wheels were carried back to Whitehall, and there opened, the ticket No. 72,248 was found sticking in a crevice of the wheel. And, being the next-drawn ticket after all the prizes were drawn, was advertised by the commissioners' order as entitled to the thousand pounds, as the last-drawn ticket; "which affair," we are told by the *Gentleman's Magazine*, "made a great deal of noise." The State Lottery of 1751 met with much opposition from the press, and an article in the *London Magazine* gives the following computation of its chances :—

IN THE LOTTERY 1751 IT IS

69998 to	2 or 34999 to 1	against a	£10000 Prize
69994 to	6 or 11665 to 1	against a	5000 or upwards
69989 to	11 or 6363 to 1	against a	3000
69981 to	19 or 3683 to 1	against a	2000
69961 to	39 or 1794 to 1	against a	1000
69920 to	80 or 874 to 1	against a	500
69720 to	280 or 249 to 1	against a	100
69300 to	700 or 99 to 1	against a	50
60000 to	10000 or 6 to 1	against a	20 or any Prize.

The writer then goes on to say: "I would beg the favour of all gentlemen, tradesmen, and others, to take the pains to explain to such as any way depend upon their judgment, that one must buy no less than seven tickets to have an even chance for any prize at all; that with only one ticket it is six to one, and with half a ticket twelve to one, against any prize; and ninety-nine or a hundred to one that the prize, if it comes, will not be above £50; and no less than thirty-five thousand to one that the owner of a single ticket will not obtain one of the greatest prizes. No lottery is proper for persons of very small fortunes, to whom the loss of five or six pounds is of great consequence, besides the disturbance of their minds; much less is it advisable or desirable for either poor or rich to contribute to the exorbitant tax of more than two hundred thousand pounds, which the first engrossers of lottery tickets, and the brokers and dealers, strive to raise out of the pockets of the poor chiefly, and the silly rich partly, by artfully enhancing the price of tickets above the original cost." The first price of tickets in this lottery was ten pounds. On their rise a Mr Holland publicly offered in an advertisement to wager four hundred guineas that four hundred tickets when drawn did not amount to nine pounds fifteen shillings on an average, prizes and blanks. As might have been expected, his challenge was never accepted. On the 11th of the next month (November) the drawing began, and notwithstanding the public-spirited efforts of individuals, societies, and papers which did not receive any benefit in the way of advertisements, to check the exorbitancy of the ticket-mongers, the price rose steadily and ultimately to sixteen guineas a ticket. All means were tried by the disinterested to cure this infatuation by writing and advertising; and on the first day of drawing, it was publicly averred that near eight thousand tickets were in the South Sea House, and upwards of thirty thousand pawned at bankers, &c., that nine out of ten of the ticket-holders were not able to go to the wheel, and that not one of them durst stand the drawing above six days. These dealers seem to have had an awkward knack of selling the same ticket to two buyers, or disposing of more than the proper fractional parts of one ticket, in the hope of its turning up a blank, thus "going for the gloves" in a style imitated in modern days by votaries of Tattersall's and other betting institutions with much success. This arrangement, with others of a similar nature, led to the establishment of insurances offices, which, at first an ostensible protection by guaranteeing special numbers, and thereby preventing fraud on the part of sellers, became in time greater swindles than those they were supposed to prevent.

To prevent the monopoly of tickets in the State Lottery, and the consequent upheaval of rates, it had been enacted that persons charged with the delivery of tickets should not sell more than twenty to one person. This provision was evaded by the use of pretended lists, which defeated the object of Parliament, and injured public credit, insomuch that in 1754 more tickets were subscribed for than the holders of the lists had cash to purchase, and there was a deficiency in the first payment. The mischief and notoriety of these practices occasioned the House of Commons to prosecute an inquiry into the circumstances, which, though opposed by a scandalous cabal that endeavoured to screen the delinquents, ended in a report, by the committee, that Peter Leheup, Esq., had privately disposed of a great number of tickets before the office was opened to which the public were directed by advertisement to apply; that he also delivered great numbers to particular persons, upon lists of names which he knew to be fictitious; and that, in particular, Sampson Gideon became proprietor of more than six thousand, which he sold at a premium. Upon report of these and other illegal acts, the House resolved that Leheup was guilty of a violation of the Act and a breach of trust, and presented an address to his Majesty praying that he would direct the Attorney-General to prosecute him in the most effectual manner for his offences. An information was accordingly filed, and, on a trial at bar in the Court of King's Bench, Leheup, as one of the receivers of the last lottery of three hundred thousand pounds, was found guilty (1) of receiving subscriptions before the day and hour advertised; (2) of permitting the subscribers to use different names to cover an excess of twenty tickets; and (3) of disposing of the tickets which had been bespoke, and not claimed, or were double charged, instead of returning them to the managers. In Trinity Term, Leheup was brought up for judgment, and fined a thousand pounds, which was at once paid. This was one of the grossest miscarriages of justice known with regard to the lottery frauds, as in the course of the evidence given it was discovered that the defendant had amassed by his trickery over forty thousand pounds for his own share. Another instance of the horrible effect these instruments of gambling had on the public mind is found in the madness of many successful speculators, as well as in the continuous suicides of the unsuccessful. On November 5, 1757, Mr Keys, a clerk, who had absented himself from business ever since the 7th of October, on which day was drawn the ten-thousand-pound prize, supposed to be his property, was found in the streets raving mad, having been robbed of his pocket-book and ticket.

The very small parts into which shares were divided more than a hundred years ago is shown by the following advertisement, published in several papers of November 1766:—

DAME FORTUNE presents her Respects to the Public, and assures them that she has fixed her Residence for the Present at CORBETT'S State Lottery Office, opposite St. Dunstan's Church, Fleet Street; and, to enable many Families to partake of her Favours, she has ordered not only the Tickets to be sold at the lowest Prices, but also that they be *divided into Shares at the following low Rates*,—viz.:—

	£	*s.*	*d.*
A Sixty-fourth	0	4	0
Thirty-second	0	7	6
Sixteenth	0	15	0
An Eighth	1	10	0
A Fourth	3	0	0
A Half	6	0	0

By which may be gained from upwards of one hundred and fifty to upwards of five thousand Guineas, at her said Office No. 30.

As another instance of the superstition prevalent during the lottery mania we will give the following anecdote, which though old will bear repetition. A gentlewoman whose husband had presented her with a ticket, put up prayers in the church, the day before drawing, in the following manner: "The prayers of the congregation are desired for the success of a person engaged in a new undertaking." Lottery tickets were often presented by gentlemen to ladies, and it is recorded that a lady falling in love with an actor, finding that the many letters of passionate admiration she sent him passed unnoticed, accompanied one of them with a gift of four lottery tickets. Whether they were successful, either as regards moving his obdurate heart or providing him with a prize, we are unfortunately not able to say. Anyhow, it doesn't much matter, as the recipient of the favours died shortly afterwards; and most likely the unknown lady consoled herself with another and more willing lover, or else with a lottery.

Between 1770 and 1775 the tricks of the insurers occupied a great deal of attention, and almost left the ordinary office-keepers unnoticed. The two businesses were, however, pretty well mixed up by this time. An important trial took place at Guildhall for the purpose of deciding the legality of insuring on March 1, 1773, the Lord Mayor being plaintiff, and Messrs Barnes & Golightly defendants, but on account of an error in the declaration the plaintiff was nonsuited. On June 26, 1775, a cause came on in the Court of Common Pleas, Guildhall, between a gentleman, plaintiff, and a lottery office-keeper, defendant. The cause of the action was, that the gentleman, passing by the lottery office, observed a woman and a boy crying, on which he asked the reason of their tears. They informed him that they had insured a number in the lottery on the overnight, and upon inquiry at another office, found it to have been drawn five days before, and therefore wanted their money returned. The gentleman taking their part was assaulted and beaten by the office-keeper, and the jury, after hearing the evidence, gave a verdict in favour of the gentleman with five pounds damages.

In 1775 some of the Bluecoat boys appointed to assist in the drawing of the State Lottery were tampered with for the purpose of inducing them to commit a fraud. These attempts were successful in one instance that became known, and doubtless in many others that did not. This discovery led to certain regulations, which were carried out with great vigour. On the 1st of June a man was brought before the Lord Mayor for attempting to bribe the two boys who drew the Museum Lottery at Guildhall to conceal a ticket, and to bring it to him, promising that he would at once return it. His intention was to insure it in all the offices with a view to defraud the keepers. The boys were so frightened at the proposition that they gave notice to the managers of the lottery, and pointed out the delinquent, who was, however, discharged, as there was no law by which to punish him. On the 5th of December another of the boys engaged to draw the numbers in the State Lottery at Guildhall was examined before Sir Charles Asgill relative to a number that had been drawn out the Friday before, on which an assurance had been made in almost every office in London. The boy confessed that he was prevailed upon to conceal the ticket No. 21,481, by a man who paid him for so doing; that the man copied the number; and that the next day he followed the man's instructions, and put his hand into the wheel as usual, with the ticket in it, and then pretended to draw it from among the rest. The instigator of the offence had actually received £400 of the insurance-office keepers. Had all of them paid him, the whole sum would have amounted to £3000; but some of them suspected a fraud had been committed, and caused the inquiry which led to the boy's confessing both the temptation and his folly. On the next day the man who insured the ticket was examined. He was clerk to a hop-factor in Goodman's Fields; but not being the person who had persuaded the boy to secrete the ticket and pretend to draw it in the usual manner, and no evidence appearing to connect him with the actual seducer, the prisoner was discharged, though it was ascertained that he had insured the number already mentioned ninety-one times in one day. In consequence of the circumstances which led to this examination, the Lords of the Treasury inquired further and deliberated on the means of preventing a recurrence of such transactions. The result of their conference was the following order, which was, however, but privately circulated, and was never published in any periodical, book, or newspaper until after the abolition of Lotteries:—

ORDER *of December* 12, 1775.

A DISCOVERY having been made that WILLIAM TRAMPLETT, one of the Boys employed in drawing the Lottery had, at the Instigation of one CHARLES LOWNDES, (since absconded) at different Times in former Rolls, *taken out of the Number Wheel* THREE *numbered Tickets, which were at* THREE *several Times returned by him into the said Wheel, and drawn without his parting with them*, so as to give them the Appearance of being fairly drawn *to answer the purpose of defrauding by insurance:*

IT IS THEREFORE ORDERED, for preventing the like wicked Practices in future, that every Boy, before he is suffered to put his Hand into either Wheel, be brought by the Proclaimer to the Managers on Duty, for them to see that *the Bosoms and Sleeves of his Coat be closely buttoned, his Pockets sewed up, and his Hands examined;* and that during the Time of his being on Duty, *he shall keep his left Hand in his Girdle behind him, and his right Hand open with his Fingers extended;* and the Proclaimer is not to suffer him at any Time to leave the Wheel, without being first examined by the Manager nearest him.

The Observance of the foregoing Order is recommended by the Managers on this Roll to those on the succeeding Rolls, till the matter shall be more fully discussed at a general Meeting.

It is noticeable that though only one ticket was spoken of in the police case, the secret instructions refer to three. It is likely that if it had been known that more than one had been tampered with, a general unpleasantness would have resulted, and the whole of the drawing been declared null and void. As it was, there was some difficulty in keeping the matter within bounds; and the trifling proportion of the attempted cheat, as compared with the magnitude of the general issue, was the strong point of the lottery managers. The exposure of the attempted, and so far as two tickets were concerned apparently successful, fraud, would have led to a vast amount of trouble and expense, and would have considerably added to the unpopularity of lotteries—a feeling which, as it was, made itself now and again very manifest. Anyhow the secret was kept for over sixty years, as it was never divulged until the general dissolution of the lottery system in 1826, when the following on the same subject was also for the first time made public:—

ORDER *at* GENERAL MEETING.

A PLAN OF RULES AND REGULATIONS to be observed in order *to prevent the Boys committing Frauds, &c.*, in the Drawing of the Lottery, agreeable to *Directions* received by Mr. Johnson on Tuesday the 16th of January 1776, from the LORDS OF THE TREASURY.

THAT ten Managers be always on the Roll at Guildhall, two of whom are to be conveniently placed opposite the two Boys at the Wheels, in order to observe that they strictly conform themselves to the Rules and Orders directed by the Committee at Guildhall, on Tuesday, December 12, 1775.

THAT *it be requested of the* TREASURER OF CHRIST'S HOSPITAL *not to make known who are the twelve Boys nominated for drawing the Lottery till the morning the Drawing begins; which said Boys are all to attend every Day, and the two who are to go on Duty at the Wheels are to be taken promiscuously from amongst the whole Number* by either of the Secretaries, *without observing any regular Course or Order; so that no Boy shall know when it will be his turn to go to either Wheel.*

THIS METHOD, though attended with considerable additional Expense, by the extra Attendance of two Managers and six Boys, will, it is presumed, effectually prevent any Attempt being made to corrupt or bribe any of the Boys to commit the Fraud practised in the last Lottery.

In July 1778 there was tried before Lord Mansfield at Guildhall a case wherein a merchant was plaintiff and a lottery-office keeper defendant. The action was for the purpose of recovering damages against the office-keeper for suffering plaintiff's apprentice, a youth, to insure during the drawing of the last lottery, contrary to the statute; whereby the lad lost a considerable sum, the property of his master. The jury, without leaving their box, gave a verdict for the plaintiff, and the judge ordered the defendant to pay £500 penalty and be imprisoned for three months. During the same year, Parliament having discussed the evil of insuring, and the mischievous subdivision of the shares of tickets, passed an Act for the regulation of lottery offices, by which it was enacted that every office-keeper should pay £50 for a licence, and give tangible security not to infringe any part of the Act; that no smaller portion of any ticket than a sixteenth should be disposed of under a penalty of £50; that any person disposing of goods or merchandise upon any chance relating to the drawing of any ticket should be liable to a fine of £20; and that all shares should be stamped at an office established under the said Act, the original tickets being kept at the office till after the drawing. Many other regulations were made in the same law, and in the following year the question was again subject of legislation; but notwithstanding all the efforts of the Commons, the ruinous practice of insuring was still conducted with dexterity and great profit by the office-keepers. This is one of their plans for evading the law:—

November 7, 1781.

MODE OF INSURANCE,

WHICH continues the whole Time of drawing the Lottery, at CARRICK'S STATE LOTTERY OFFICE, King's Arms, 72, Threadneedle Street. *At one Guinea each* NUMBERS *are taken*, to return three Twenty Pound Prizes, value Sixty Pounds, for every given Number that shall be drawn any Prize whatever above Twenty Pounds during the whole drawing.

*** *Numbers at half a Guinea to receive half the above.*

And here is another of about the same date, which openly violates the spirit if not the letter of the law:—

J. COOK respectfully solicits the Public will favour the following *incomparably advantageous plan* with attention, by which *upwards of thirty-two thousand Chances for obtaining a Prize (out of the forty-eight thousand Tickets) are given in one Policy.*

POLICIES OF FIVE GUINEAS *with three Numbers*, with the first Number will gain

20000	if a Prize of	£20000
10000	"	£10000
5000	"	£5000

with the second Number will gain

6000	guineas if	20000
3000	"	10000
1500	"	5000

with the third Number will gain

3000	guineas if	20000
1500	„	10000
1200	„	5000

Then follow the address and other tempting inducements. In 1781 an Act was passed to prevent the insurance of tickets by any method. The office-keepers continued to insure notwithstanding, and many prosecutions resulted; but as the profits were greater than the fines, business continued to run briskly. One man was in 1784 fined fifteen hundred pounds, and he brought an action in 1785 to recover the money from the sheriff who had levied the amount on his goods. The case was tried in the Court of King's Bench, and ended in an almost immediate nonsuit. In February 1793 the Commissioners of the Lottery, in order to abate insuring, determined that no persons should be suffered to take down numbers except the clerks of licensed offices known to the Commissioners. No slips were to be sent out; but the numbers were to be taken down by one clerk in one book; Steel's list of lottery numbers was to be abolished, and a recompense made for it; and the magistrates resolved to apprehend all suspicious persons who should be seen taking early numbers. Yet in 1796 there was a class of sharpers who took lottery insurances, and this gambling among the higher and middle classes was carried on to an extent exceeding all credibility, producing consequences to many private families of great worth and respectability, of the most distressing nature.

The insurance offices in London numbered over four hundred. To many of them persons were attached called Morocco men, who went from house to house among their customers, or attended in the back parlours of public-houses, for the purpose of making insurances. It was calculated that at these offices (exclusive of what was done at the licensed offices) insurances were made to the extent ot eight hundred thousand pounds, in premiums, during the

Irish Lottery, and above one million during the English, upon which it was calculated that the insurers made from fifteen to twenty-five per cent. profit. This confederacy, during the English Lottery of the year 1796, supported about two thousand agents and clerks, and nearly eight thousand Morocco men, "including a considerable number of ruffians and bludgeon men, paid by a general association of the principal proprietors of the establishments, who regularly met in committee in a well-known public-house in Oxford Market, twice or thrice a week during the drawing of the lottery, for the purpose of concerting measures to defeat the exertions of the magistrates by forcibly resisting or bribing the officers of justice."

Lotteries were declared by the Parliamentary reports of 1807 to be inseparable from illegal insurances. The reports further state that "the Lottery is so radically vicious, that under no system of regulations which can be devised will it be possible for Parliament to adopt it as an efficient source of revenue, and at the same time divest it of all the evils and calamities of which it has hitherto been so baneful a source." Among these evils and calamities the Committees of Parliament enumerate that "idleness, dissipation, and poverty were increased,—the most sacred and confidential trusts were betrayed,— domestic comfort was destroyed, madness was often created, suicide itself was produced, and crimes subjecting the perpetrators of them to death were committed." Sir Nathaniel Conant, who in 1816 was chief magistrate of Bow Street, stated to a committee of the House of Commons that the Lottery was one of the predisposing causes by which the people of the metropolis were vitiated; that it led to theft, to supply losses and disappointments occasioned by speculating on its chances; and that illegal insurances continued to be effected. "There are," he says, "people in the background, who, having got forty or fifty thousand pounds by that, employ people of the lowest order, and give them a con-mission for what they bring; there is, *a wheel within a wheel.*" Another magistrate giving evidence before the same committee, said, "It is a scandal to the Government, thus to excite people to practise the vice of gaming for the purpose of drawing a revenue from their ruin. It is an anomalous proceeding by law to declare gambling infamous; to hunt out petty gamblers in their recesses, and cast them into prison; and by law also to set up the giant gambling of the State Lottery, and encourage persons to resort to it by the most captivating devices which ingenuity uncontrolled by moral rectitude can invent." This evidence may be regarded as the ultimate cause of the suppression of lotteries, which might have dragged on an existence for a few more years had it not been for the atrocities of the insurance-mongers. We will now turn towards the closing scenes in this eventful drama.

Seldom was human ingenuity more exercised than in giving public notoriety to lottery schemes. The originators or proprietors of lotteries used to employ a number of persons, frequently of considerable literary ability and talent, to attract the public attention by verses, ingenious advertisements, and decoy paragraphs in the newspapers, engaging the attention of the readers by smart allusions to political topics or other matters of interest, which entrapped the unwary into lottery puffs. Thirteen thousand pounds was usually paid into the Exchequer for duties on these and other methods of advertising practised by the lottery people, and some of the agents spent as much as £20,000 in puffing and advertisements. Take the following as a specimen of the puffing which marked the later days of the Lottery:—

Before the time of Sir Isaac Newton, various notions were entertained concerning colours. Plato said colour was a flame issuing from bodies, the Indians of America believed the same, and when any person read a letter they believed it spoke, and blessed the paper in proportion as they were moved by it. What emotions would the following billet excite? "The bearer may receive one hundred thousand pounds." This would make a deep impression on the natives of every country, and may now be realised; for by the present Grand Lottery a single ticket may bestow on the Bearer One Hundred Thousand Pounds.

Here is another of the same ingenious description, which kept the trap constantly baited for the unsuspecting :—

DUEL.—On Friday last a meeting took place near Plymouth, between Capt. G—— and Lieut. R——, both of the Royal Navy, when, after exchanging shots, happily without effect, the seconds interfered and amicably adjusted the dispute. The following is said to have been the cause of the duel :—Lieut. R—— had dreamt three successive nights that a certain number would be a prize of £3000, in the ensuing lottery, which he mentioned to Captain G——, but never intimated any intention of having that ticket; he, however, wrote up to his agent in London to procure it, who found the Captain was beforehand with him, as he had got it the day before, and refused to give it up. By the intercession of the seconds, it is settled that they are each to have half the ticket, and as they are both very meritorious officers, we sincerely wish they may have one of the numerous Capital Prizes with which the scheme abounds.

The most stupendous efforts were made to promote the success of the last lottery, which, however, languished sadly. The price of tickets was arbitrarily raised, to induce a belief that they were in great demand, "at the very moment when," says Hone, writing immediately afterwards, "their sale was notoriously at a stand; and the lagging attention of the public of the metropolis was endeavoured to be quickened by all sorts of stratagems to the 18th of July, as the very last chance that would occur in England of gaining 'Six 30,000*l.* besides other Capitals,' which it was positively affirmed were 'all to be drawn' on that fatal day." Besides the dispersion of innumerable bills and aspersions on Government for extinguishing the Lottery, those most interested in its preservation caused London and the suburbs to be paraded by a most magnificent procession, in which was a band of music which played to attract attention, and then a man stepped forward, and ringing a bell, announced the

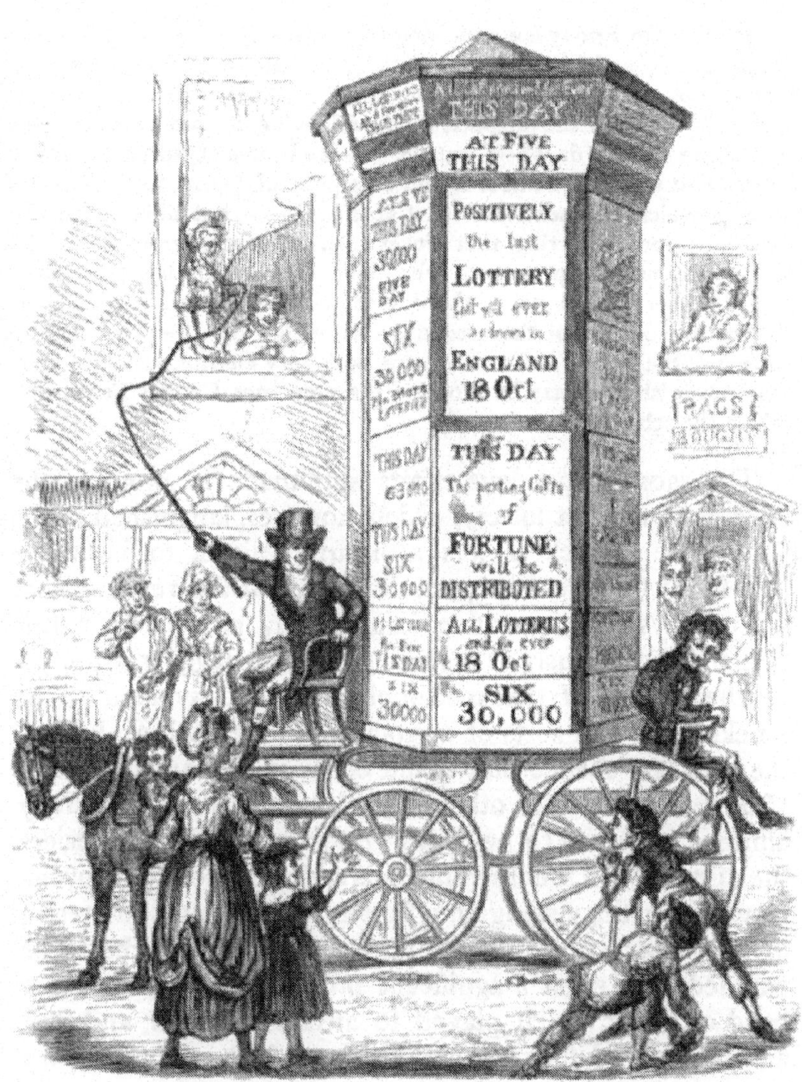

ADVERTISING THE LAST STATE LOTTERY DRAWN IN ENGLAND. 1826.

By the purchase of a Ticket or Share in the New Lottery, to be all drawn in Two Days, 5th and 18th OCTOBER. Two of £20,000, Two of £10,000, &c. All Sterling Money. All the 4500 Tickets drawn the First Day are sure to be Prizes. Two of £10,000 in the First Quarter of an Hour. Only 7000 Tickets.

(See the Scheme.)

If you *are a man struggling to get through the world, or surrounded by crosses;* or if you *wish* to lay *by a Fortune for your Children,* go to *BISH* or his *Agents,* who may make you *independent, and* above the frowns of the world.

Tickets and Shares are selling by

BISH CONTRACTOR FOR ANOTHER LOTTERY

4, CORNHILL, & 9, CHARING-CROSS, LONDON, and by

ALL HIS AGENTS IN THE COUNTRY.

death of the Lottery. Cartloads of bills were showered down areas and thrust under doors, and no effort was spared to make the end crown the work of centuries.

Chief among the office-keepers of the period was a Mr T. Bish—one of whose earlier prospectuses we present in exact facsimile—who showered millions of bills and miles of doggerel verse upon London just before the final draw took place. He had been a considerable adept in the art of puffing by means of the mock news-paragraphs to which reference has just been made, one of his best being that which follows :—

A laughable circumstance occurred at the Opera House a few evenings since. The Honourable Mrs H—— C—— in the confusion that takes place in the lobby on quitting the theatre, dropped her reticule, and was some minutes before she regained it; when on looking at its contents she exclaimed: "I have lost my duplicates!" This created surprise, not that the company had any doubt when the lady pledged her word, but they thought she had pledged her jewels. However, on enquiry, it was found that the lost duplicates were Two Tickets of one number (which she had purchased that evening) in the Lottery to be drawn the next Tuesday; luckily she soon after found them, and anticipates getting £20,000, as she had procured them at Bish's well-known office, Charing Cross.

It would be impossible here to give the many specimens which have been preserved of Bish's handiwork just before the close of the lotteries, but from an *embarras de richesses* we select the following :—

BISH.

The Last Man.

In reminding his best friends, the public, that the State Lottery will be drawn this day, 3d May, Bish acquaints them that it is the *very last but one* that will ever take place in this kingdom; and he is

THE LAST CONTRACTOR

whose name will appear *singly* before the public, as the very last will be a coalition of all the usual contractors. Bish being "the last man" who appears singly, has been particularly anxious to make an excellent scheme, and flatters himself the one he has the honour to submit must meet universal approbation.

At the back of the bill were some verses after the style of the "Cajolery Duet." This is one of them:—

To-day, or Not at All.

Run, Neighbours, Run!

Run, neighbours, run! To-day it is the Lott'ry draws,
You still may be in time if your purse be low;
Rhino, we all know, will stop of poverty the flaws.
Possessed of that, you'll find no one to serve you slow.
The ministers in Parliament of lotteries have toll'd the knell,
And have declared from Cooper's Hall dame Fortune soon they will expel;
The Blue-coat boys no more will shout that they have drawn a capital!
Nor run as though their necks they'd break to *Lucky Bish* the news to tell.
Run, neighbours, run, &c.

Although the last lottery was expected to take place on the 18th of July, it was not until the 18th of October that the closing scene in an eventful history took place. For this Bish, among many other handbills, produced the following:—

THE AMBULATOR'S GUIDE
To the Land of Plenty.

By Purchasing a TICKET
in the present Lottery

You may *reap* a golden *harvest* in *Cornhill*, and pick up the *bullion* in *Silver*-street, have an interest in *Bank-buildings*, possess a *Mansion-house* in *Golden-square*, and an estate like a *Little Britain;* never be in *Hunger*ford-market, but all your life continue a *Mayfair.*

By Purchasing a HALF,

You need never be confined within *London Wall*, but become the proprietor of many a *Long Acre;* represent a *Borough* or an *Aldermanbury*, and have a share in *Threadneedle-street.*

By Purchasing a QUARTER,

Your affairs need never be in *Crooked-lane*, nor your legs in *Fetter-lane;* you may avoid *Paper-buildings*, steer clear of the *King's Bench*, and defy the *Marshalsea;* if your heart is in *Love-lane* you may soon get into *Sweeting's Alley*, obtain your lover's consent for *Matrimony-place*, and always live in a *High-street.*

By Purchasing an EIGHTH,

You may secure plenty of *provision* for *Swallow-street;* finger the *Cole* in *Coleman-street;* and may never be troubled with *Chancery-lane.* You may cast *anchor* in *Cable-street;* set up business in a *Fore-street;* and need never be confined within a *Narrow-wall.*

By Purchasing a SIXTEENTH,

You may live *frugal* in *Cheapside;* get merry in *Liquorpond-street;* soak your *hide* in *Leather-lane;* be a *wet sole* in *Shoe-lane;* turn *maltster* in *Beer-lane*, or *hammer* away in *Smithfield.*

In short, life must indeed be a *Long-lane* if it's without *a turning.* Therefore, if you are wise, without *Mincing* the matter, go *Pall-mall* to *Cornhill* or *Charing-cross,* and enroll your name in the *Temple* of Fortune,

BISH'S.

Advertisements in the newspapers were not, however, plentiful. The office-keepers seemed to prefer the pomp and circumstance of processions and bands and funeral speeches, to the cold respectability which was just then part of the newspaper system. Bish had many eccentric illustrations in his handbills, and some of his verses went beyond even the bounds of eccentricity. As the eventful day approached, the efforts in the handbill line redoubled, and people were provided with waste paper for an indefinite period; but there was little to notice in the columns of any of the chief journals. On October 7, 1826, a public notice appeared on the front page of the *Times*, in company with the advertisements of Swift and Eyton, two office-keepers; but whether it was placed there by order of the "powers that be," or was in the interests of the dealers, we must leave our readers to judge for themselves. The latter seems most probable :—

PUBLIC NOTICE.—The Licenses granted by 4th Geo. IV. cap. 60, to the Lottery-office-keepers, to sell and divide into shares State Lottery Tickets, will cease and determine on Wednesday the 18th of this month, when all the Six Prizes of £30,000, and every other prize, amounting to £389,000, must be decided, and all Lotteries end in this kingdom. Government, having already given extra time for the sale of tickets, will not grant an hour beyond the 18th instant.

Hazard was the rather appropriate name of another promoter whose advertisements are published just at this time; but they are, as are the others, small and unpretentious when in the newspapers, and are only noticeable as records of the finishing days of the great State Lottery. In the *Times* of October 13 there is this notice, which was repeated on the 16th and 17th, on the last-named date having the word "to-morrow" inserted instead of "next Wednesday:"—

DRAWING of the LOTTERY. — Whereas it is maliciously asserted by an Anonymous Correspondent in the Morning Chronicle of this day, that application would be made to the Lords of the Treasury for a further Postponement of the Lottery, the Public are most unequivocally and positively assured by the Contractors that no such application has been made, nor even contemplated; but on the contrary, it is absolutely and inevitably determined by Government, that this last of all lotteries shall and must be decided NEXT WEDNESDAY, 18th instant.

On the day before the drawing, the advertisements in the *Times* showed that great apathy existed, and that the tickets had not gone off well, as the office-keepers had evidently many yet left on hand. Even the advertisements have a dispirited appearance:—

FINISH of LOTTERIES.—SWIFT and Co. respectfully inform the Public that the last and only day of drawing the STATE LOTTERY is Wednesday the 18th of this month, when 6 prizes of 30,000l. and all the other capitals in the scheme will be determined. Every ticket will receive 5l. independent of any sum to which it may be entitled. In the last Lottery containing 30,000l. prizes Swift and Co. sold two out of four of them at their offices 11, Poultry; 1, Strand; and 31 Aldgate High-street.

It is almost evident that the Lottery was "played out" on its own merits, and that the interference of Parliament only hastened the end so far as concerns the important events. Another firm of contractors put forth a final appeal thus:—

THE LAST of ALL, TO-MORROW, 18th October.—J. and J. SIVEWRIGHT, Contractors, most positively assure the Public that—

To-morrow, Six of 30,000l. must be drawn.
To-morrow, 389,000l. will be decided.
To-morrow, all Lotteries end in this kingdom.

To gain a Prize of 30,000l. you must buy THIS DAY.

Tickets and Shares are selling by J. and J. SIVEWRIGHT, Contractors, 37, Cornhill; 11, Holborn; and 38, Haymarket; who shared and sold 12,478, a prize of 30,000l.; 3,613, 21,055l.; and in the last Lottery, 1,783, a prize of 21,000l.; and 3,925, a prize of 21,000l.

On the fatal day itself the only noticeable advertisement in the *Times* is that of Bish, which is the same as had been running for some little time, and which on the 18th of October 1826, with the word "this day," instead of what had appeared before, stood thus, a specimen of the last newspaper appeal in regard to a forthcoming State lottery:—

THE inevitable and absolute FINISH of LOTTERIES, THIS DAY.—BISH, in soliciting for the last time the favours of his best friends, the Public, assures them that,

This Day, a Ticket must gain . .	£30,000
This Day, a Half must gain . .	15,000
This Day a Quarter must gain .	7,500
This Day an Eighth must gain .	3,750
This Day a Sixteenth must gain .	1,875

This Day, all the Six of £30,000 will be drawn, every number decided, and every ticket a Prize.

This Day, 18th instant, all lotteries end for ever.

Tickets and Shares are selling by BISH, Stockbroker, 4, Cornhill, and 9, Charing-cross, who shared and sold, within the last 12 months, 5 prizes of 30,000l. and 9 of 20,000l., and in the very last drawing, 3d of May, No. 1,833 (Class B), 21,000l., and 3,925 (Class A), 21,000l.

The following is the record of the last drawing, as published in the Thursday's papers: "Yesterday afternoon, about half-past six o'clock, that old servant of the State, the lottery, breathed its last, having for a long period of years, ever since the days of Queen Anne, contributed largely towards the public revenue of the country. This event took place at Cooper's Hall, Basinghall Street; and such was the anxiety on the part of the public to witness the last drawing of the lottery, that great numbers of persons were attracted to the spot, independently of those who had an interest in the proceedings. The gallery of Cooper's Hall was crowded to excess long before the period fixed for the drawing (five o'clock), and the utmost anxiety was felt by those who had shares in the lottery for the arrival of the appointed hour. The annihilation of lotteries, it will be recollected, was determined on in the session of Parliament before last; and thus a source of revenue, bringing into the treasury the sums of £250,000 and £300,000 per annum will be dried up. This determination on the part of the Legislature is hailed by far the greatest portion of the public with joy, as it will put an end to a system which many believe to have fostered and encouraged the late speculations, the effects of which have been and are still severely felt. A deficiency in the public revenue to the extent of £250,000 annually will, however, be the consequence of the annihilation of lotteries, and it must remain for those who have strenuously supported the putting a stop to lotteries to provide for the deficiency."—"Although that which ended yesterday was the last, if we are informed correctly the lottery-office keepers have been left with a great number of tickets remaining on their hands—a pretty strong proof that the public in general have now no relish for these schemes."—"The concourse of persons in Basinghall Street was very great; indeed, the street was almost impassable, and everybody seemed desirous of ascertaining the fortunate numbers. In the gallery the greatest interest was excited, as the various prizes were drawn from the wheel; and as soon as a numbered ticket was drawn from the number wheel, every one looked with anxiety to his share, in order to ascertain if Fortune smiled on him. Only one instance occurred where a prize was drawn and a number held by

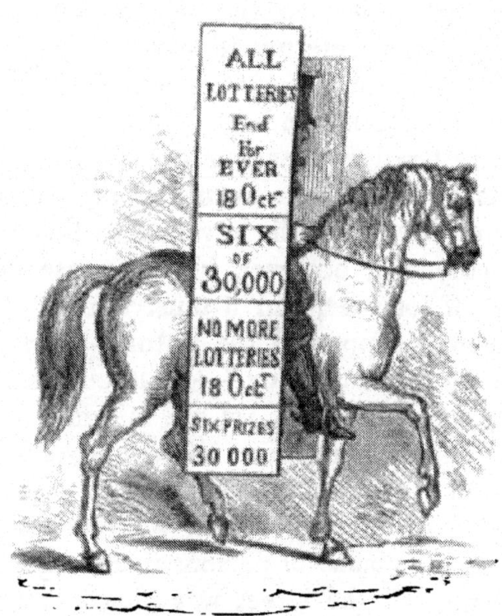

THE LAST OF THE LOTTERIES.

any individual present. The fortunate person was a little man, who no sooner had learned that his number was a grand prize, than he buttoned up his coat, and coolly walked off without uttering a word. As the drawing proceeded disappointment began to succeed the hopes indulged by those who were present. On their entrance to the hall every face wore a cheerful appearance; but on the termination of the drawing a strong contrast was exhibited, and the features of each were strongly marked with dissatisfaction. The drawing commenced shortly after five o'clock, and ended at twenty minutes past six. The doors of the various lottery offices were also surrounded by persons awaiting the issue of the drawing."

The *Times*, in a short leader—short and few were the leaders in the *Times* of that day—published on the Thursday, says: "Yesterday terminated the lotteries in this country —may we say for ever? We know not. Such a result will depend upon the wants of Government, and the morality of its ministers. However, we rejoice at their suspension,—a suspension which we hope we have in some degree assisted in effecting,—yet rejoice with fear. Looking at the Stock Exchange, at the time bargains, and at all the iniquities practised there, we have only to hope that the place of the lotteries may not be supplied by some more mischievous system of knavery. Time was when all the robberies were committed on the king's highway. The lighting, watching, and general improvement of our roads, have nearly put an end to this practice; but housebreaking has unfortunately taken its place! And yet the people of England is not a gambling people like the French, as is evident from the fate of the last lottery. We have heard that hardly half the tickets were sold; from which it is evident, that the spirit of lottery-gambling was extinct before the system; and if that spirit had not been kept alive by incessant stimuli, it would have expired long ago."

It may be as well to mention, though it is generally known, that an Act of the 9th and 10th Vict. was passed for legalising Art Union Lotteries within certain limits and under certain conditions. Though our chapter has run over its length, we can hardly conclude without quoting the wise words of Adam Smith on the subject of lotteries. "The chance of gain," says he, "is by every man more or less overvalued, and the chance of loss is by most men undervalued. . . . The world neither ever saw, or ever will see, a perfectly fair lottery, or one in which the whole gain compensated the whole loss; because the undertaker could make nothing by it. In the State lotteries the tickets are really not worth the price which is paid by the original subscribers, and yet commonly sell in the market for twenty, thirty, and sometimes forty per cent. advance. The vain hope of gaining some of the greatest prizes is the sole cause of this demand. The soberest people scarce look upon it as a folly to pay a small sum for the chance of gaining ten or twenty thousand pounds; though they know that even that small sum is perhaps twenty or thirty per cent. more than the chance is worth. In a lottery in which no prize exceeds twenty pounds, though in other respects it approach much nearer to a perfectly fair one than the common State lotteries, there would not be the same demand for tickets. In order to have a better chance for some of the great prizes, some people purchase several tickets, and others small shares in a still greater number. There is not, however, a more certain proposition in mathematics, than that the more tickets you adventure upon the more likely you are to be a loser. Adventure upon all the tickets in the lottery, and you lose for certain; and the greater the number of your tickets the nearer you approach to this certainty." Though this was written in reference to a state of affairs long past, the lesson is not without value nowadays.

October 18, 1826, saw the last of the State lotteries, but

it was long before the smaller fry were eradicated. Conducted very quietly at first, but after a while their promoters growing bolder, lotteries for clothes, furniture, and, especially at Christmas-time, for food and drink, were openly advertised under the title of "sweeps" up to comparatively recent times. A few police prosecutions about a dozen years back improved these relics of a past day off the face of the earth. There were, however, still left what were called "specs," which violated both the Betting-House Act and the Lottery Act, and the promoters of the chief of them in turn suffered under the majesty of the law about the period of the raid on the commission agents referred to in a previous chapter. Under the guises of picture and circular sales these turf lotteries are still continued, an advertisement in a sporting paper of June 1874 giving an address in Glasgow, informing all those whom it most concerns that the "East End Circular" has for disposal

30,000 circulars, at 1*s.* each; the profits, about £800, will be distributed on

THE DERBY.

2000 PRIZES. FIRST, £300.

This circular needs no recommendation. It is a fortune to all who invest in it. The winners of all the large races have been sent in it. Every purchaser has a fair chance of securing the £200. For circulars, 1*s.* each, apply at once to E. Jones, 128, Renfield Street, Glasgow, or in person to any of his well-known agents.

Then follows a list of names of people living in various parts of the kingdom who are empowered to sell the circulars. Within the past twelvemonth certain small papers which added to their circulation by the presentation of coupons entitling the holders to shares in lotteries for prizes of all descriptions, received solemn warning from the Home Office, and had to discontinue their projects. That this was wise, considering the innocence of the arrangement, we do not think; that it was not impartial, the notice from which we have just quoted proves. For the Lottery Act extends to Scotland, even if the Betting Act does not.*

---

* Since the above was written the Betting-House Extension Act of 1874 has become law, and, curiously enough, has caused the cessation of a procedure which was rendered illegal by an Act passed nearly fifty years before, a fact which our detectives with proverbial dulness were unable to discover. This was perhaps because there was nothing to be got by the discovery.

CHAPTER XVII.

MATRIMONIAL ADVERTISEMENTS AND AGENCIES.

IT will not be at all out of the way to assume that as long as the world has been populated it has possessed people anxious to get married. Marriage is the correct condition of life; indeed we have the best authority for regarding it as one of the principal reasons of our being, and so there is no need for wonder that many of the best-known customs of the ancients bear upon marital rites and festivities. Marriage comes in due course to the majority, male and female; but there are, naturally, those who have no desire for it, and again those who have to make effort to obtain it. There are various ways of exhibiting one's wares and attractions, and chief among them comes the object of our attention—advertising. Of late years there seems, in addition to the ordinary courses open to advertisers, to have been special arrangements made on behalf of the unmatched, who are allowed to express their desires and recommendations free, gratis, for nothing, in the columns of certain cheap periodicals—the described being all beauty or virtue, or both, when not possessed of capital. Would-be lovers are not generally deficient in either particular when the circulating medium is thrown into the balance as well. So that by means of the weekly publications referred to, marriage seems a much better commercial arrangement than that mentioned by a modern author, who, speaking of the Babylonians, says that "Herodotus records one of their customs, which, whether in jest or earnest, he declares to be the wisest he ever heard of. This was their wife-auction, by which they managed to find husbands for all their young women. The greatest beauty was put up first, and knocked down to the highest bidder; then the next in the order of comeliness—and so on to the damsel who was equidistant between beauty and plainness, who was given away gratis. Then the least plain was put up, and knocked down to the gallant who would marry her for the smallest consideration,—and so on till even the plainest was got rid of to some cynical worthy who decidedly preferred lucre to looks. By transferring to the scale of the ill-favoured the prices paid for the fair, beauty was made to endow ugliness, and the rich man's taste was the poor man's gain."

But in the representations of the wistful lovers who confide their secrets to certain editors, ugliness has no existence among the ladies, vice or laziness is unknown to the gentlemen, and money seems plentiful with both, so that it remains quite a mystery how any of the intending suitors have managed to evade Hymen for any length of time, so superior are they to the commonplace people whom we are in the habit of seeing settled down in sober domesticity. A writer in a miscellany a few years back catalogued a lot of the claimants for matrimony, first in the list being Sincere Polly, who describes herself as dark, high-spirited, and handsome; next is Evangelina, eighteen, handsome and accomplished, who will have £300 a year when of age; Fanny declares herself to be a sweet-tempered and pretty girl, just seventeen; Annie Everard endeavours to attract by her modesty in saying that she is eighteen, and not beautiful, only pretty; and Viola offers inducement in describing herself as seventeen, and Irish, merry, lively, and inclined to be stout. These ask for the carte-de-visite of a Captain Compass who advertised previously. Following these young and lovely females comes Blanche, who describes herself as a slight, graceful girl of eighteen, with dreamy violet eyes and golden rippling hair, shading a face of rare and delicate loveliness. She is a great admirer of soldiers, a lover of the chase, and all field sports. This enchanting creature is very anxious for Albert's carte-de-visite. Who is Albert, and what has he done, that he of all men should be singled out to carry off this flower of creation? "But," says the writer to whom we have referred, who seems quite unable to swallow the description, in which he is very different from ourselves, as we would never contradict a lady, "the morbid curiosity of the human mind goes a step farther, and seeks to picture Blanche—not the Blanche of Blanche's vivid imagination, but Blanche herself. Two alternatives present themselves. She may be a stout little milliner in a Camden-town shop; or—*horribile dictu!*—a waggish cook, with a turned-up nose, underdone arms and cheeks to match. The ideal Blanche fades away as we contemplate these possibilities. We pity Albert. We hope he will not waste his hardly-earned money in the vanities of photography, and cordially wish him a comfortable married state with a more earthly maiden, now that this too celestial vision dies back into dream-land. There is but one young person who approaches the ideal Blanche; and she calls herself 'Sparkling with Gems.' She is (on her own authority, be it always understood) a young, pretty, and accomplished Irish girl, with blue eyes, pearly teeth, and a wealth of golden ringlets, who is considered very stylish and graceful-looking, is of a loving disposition, and will have an income in her own right, and she wishes for the carte-de-visite of a young gentleman, who must be tall, dark, and handsome, of good family and position, and either of the military or medical profession. 'Kill or cure' is this young lady's principle in choosing a husband; but we should say that so attractive a bride, with a wealth of golden ringlets, an income in her own right, and what not, ought certainly to fall into the hands (or arms) of a dashing young officer, whose want of an income in his own right is generally the chief drawback from the amenities of his profession." Constance is already possessed of £500 a year, and limits her hopes to a husband with £200 of income. But he must be fair, of the middle height, and nice-looking. Eunice has no money at all; but she has very dark hair and eyes, rosy complexion, and is domestic. Here again our cynic shows his scepticism: "Had the indefinite article been placed before the last word in her catalogue of qualities, the description would probably have been complete." Poor Jane says: "Why should I become a nun against my wish, merely because my father wishes it? I suppose he wishes to get married again, and I am in his way. I can say without flattery that I am near twenty, have a very graceful figure, very handsome, and between the medium height, a first-class pianist, and capable of making any gentleman a good wife. I possess no money. I am a lady, very domestic, and am quite certain that I am worthy of a good husband." Poor Jane! her notions of the descriptive are rather vague, and so are her ideas of what is a lady. But as we once knew a writer of stories for the periodical in which her description appears who considered it beneath the dignity of a gentleman to spell properly, Jane is, perhaps, quite right in her estimate of herself according to the code under which she was instructed.

Some of the gentlemen in this same catalogue deserve attention. As a rule, they seem to consider "proputty" the best qualification, though if other advantages are thrown in they will not be objected to. Let us pick out from the herd Gauntlet, who says that he is a gentleman of good standing in society, a widower, forty, but looks much younger, of middle height, highly respected in his own neighbourhood, and is possessed of upwards of £8000 at command; he wishes to meet with a lady younger than himself, and with means equal to his own. Then there is R. S., who has £100 a year, is of like opinion as to the proportion of money his bride ought to bring, and would like to become acquainted with a young lady of similar income, or one who has a talent for elocution or singing. Our author, after exhausting his list, admits that the young gentlemen who advertise in the penny journals are far less mercenary than the young ladies. "The latter betray quite a rapacity with regard to a good income, are very explicit about it, and put down in plain figures the precise sum which they think their charms are worth. By what means the acquaintanceship begun in these advertising columns is continued and completed we are unable to say. As a preliminary the editor kindly undertakes the charge of photographs; but of the steps by which the contracting parties advance to the goal of their wishes we know nothing. We should think that the proprietors of the journal ought to keep an attorney on the premises, to see that the gentlemen who offer £8000 are acting in good faith." Had further inspection been given to the page in which these requisitions appear, the critic would have learned that, when second steps are taken, communication is made through a newspaper belonging to the same proprietary as the penny journal, and would have seen that "all advertisements must be prepaid." But we are beginning at the wrong end, and must retrace our steps for the purpose of renewing acquaintance with our old friend Houghton, the father of English advertising, who, in his *Collection* of July 19, 1695, says:—

⁂ I have undertaken to advertize all sorts of Things that are honourable, and what follows is not otherwise, and I am well paid for it:

☞ A Gentleman about 30 Years of Age, that says he has a Very Good Estate, would willingly Match Himself to some Young Gentlewoman that has a Fortune of £3000 or thereabout, And he will make Settlement to content.

When it shall appear that I am candid and no otherwise concerned than in bringing two Elderly Persons to a Treaty; and the nine Days Wonder and Laughter (usually attending new Things) are over, and that Nobody shall know Anything of the Matter, but where I shall reasonably believe they are in good earnest; then 'tis probable such Advertisements may prove very useful.

A Young Man about 25 Years of Age, in a very good Trade, and whose Father will make him worth £1000, would willingly embrace a suitable Match. He has been brought up a Dissenter with his Parents, and is a sober Man.

It seems the public either did not believe in the reality of these advertisements, or were suspicious of the advertisers, for a few weeks after the editor thought necessary to declare again :—

*** These Proposals for Matches are real, and I do promise to manage them and such like with so much Secresie and Prudence that none shall discourse with their best Friends, with more Confidence of Fidelity than with me, let them be of what Rank soever.*

Notwithstanding these honest statements, Houghton appears to have been sadly teased on account of this innovation, for shortly after the above he once more attempted an explanation :—

I thought what I said before about Matches, was very intelligible, but I find otherwise : The Case is thus :

A. comes to me and says : his Friend has a Kinsman that he would be glad to have match'd, and he is a sober, well-bred, comely, understanding Man, and in so good an Employment, that with his Fortune he shall deserve a vertuous, well-bred, discreet, comely Wife with a Fortune of £1000, but his Kinsman has not much Acquaintance and is bashful. This I publish and then comes B. and says his Friend has a Kinswoman qualified as above, and he would gladly match her to such if it be real. Upon this I bring the two that speak to me, together, and if they can understand each other they carry on the Match: and if it succeed, I shall expect some small Consideration, and this is what I intend to be concerned in the Matter.

This explanation seems to have been thought satisfactory, and no doubt eligible parties left their names and addresses with him, for a few weeks after the *Collection for Improvement of Husbandry and Trade* contained the following :—

I know of several Men and Women whose Friends would gladly have them match'd, which I'll endeavour to do, as from Time to Time I shall hear of such whose Circumstances are likely to agree ; and I'll assure such as will come to me it shall be done with all the Honour and Secrecy imaginable. Their own Parents shall not manage it more to their Satisfaction, and the more comes to me the better I shall be able to serve them.

We have already, in an early portion of this book, dilated on the claims Houghton has on the gratitude of past and present advertisers, and so we will pass on to the next specimen on our list, which appears in the *Gazetteer* of December 14, 1771:—

To Gentlemen of Fortune.

A MOST advantageous Opportunity now offers to any young Gentleman of Character and independent Fortune; the Advertiser of this will introduce such to a most accomplished young Lady of Fortune, and greater Expectancy. None but a real Gentleman will succeed: therefore it is desired no other would apply. Letters directed to P. L. at the Nottingham Coffee-house, opposite Great Turnstile, Holborn, mentioning their present Condition, and where to inquire of the specified Particulars, signed with their own Name, will have due Regard and Honour, and Secrecy observed as it is required.

From this and kindred notices in the papers of a hundred years ago or so, it would appear that certain young ladies were kept, like the fabled damsels of old, each in an enchanted castle, until some knight should appear to break the spell. With just this difference, that not chivalry but cheque-books was the requisition, and that the dragon, instead of being punished by the avenging sword, was rewarded with the "usual percentage." In 1775 the following handbill must have been pretty familiar to residents in London:—

No. 2, Dover Street, St. James's.

Marriage Treaties

Carried on, and solely calculated for such Persons as can give the best Proof of being (totally) at their own Disposal.

THE open undisguised Manner in which this truly important Business is pursued, will best appear by the following Plan, which is humbly submitted to the Judgment of the Public. Negociation of Money is also transacted at the House, where widow Ladies, Clergy, and other Gentlemen, may possibly be accommodated with Sums on granting Annuities, or otherwise, as may be agreed upon.

The great Utility of this Undertaking, especially that Department of it relative to Marriage, is so very striking, that it seems to bespeak the Approbation of this great Metropolis, where *Business* may almost be said to have rivall'd *Marriage;* for it not only robs the Gentlemen of their Time, but the Ladies of their Lovers. Now this House in Dover Street is established to supply the Time that is wanting; and Courtships may be carried on by Way of Proxy to their final Issue: thus will the Gentleman save his Time, and the Lady gain a Husband; and it will be readily allowed that happy Marriages are the very Cement of Society, the Promoters of Virtue, and may be truly said to strike at the very Root of Dissipation.

Upon these honourable, these eligible Principles, it is that the Managers of this Undertaking ground all their Hopes; nor have they ventured to announce it to the Public without the maturest Deliberation, after having considered it in every Point of View; and dare assure the World, that the most upright Conduct, greatest Delicacy and inviolable Secrecy shall be observed in all their Proceedings; and as this Plan bids fair for the Happiness of Thousands, so will it soon put a Stop to those futile, trifling (not to say dangerous) Advertisements that so frequently invade the public Ear, and which seem but too often calculated to deceive.

As to the Proprietors themselves, some of them are well known in the City, and others are not totally Strangers in the polite Circle; which puts it still more in their Power to promote the Design, and that not more upon the Principles of Love and Honour, than those of Sense and Discretion.

Each Person who appears at Dover Street (aforesaid) will be shown into a separate Apartment. Such as cannot attend in Person, are requested to signify their Intention by their Friend in Writing; and it is hoped and presumed that such Recital will be made with the utmost Exactness; and not only the Situation in Life, but the Age, Constitution, and Religion of the Party set forth with all possible Accuracy and Candour.

It hardly seems needful to add, that so much Time and Thought cannot be supposed to have been laid out without a reasonable Recompense; therefore it will be quite necessary, when the Principals do not appear (which may not unfrequently happen), that their Agents shall have been apprised that the Terms upon which this truly important Matter is commenced, is no more than FIVE GUINEAS, to be paid to the Managers on taking down the Minutes of the Business; and no more is to be paid till after the Matter is completed, either by supplying the Sum of Money according to Agreement, or by the Marriage of the Parties in Question: and although the Managers claim no more than FIVE GUINEAS, yet (it is presumed) so small a Sum will not be deemed an adequate Compensation, when Business of Consequence is to be done, and Persons of Condition and liberal Sentiment concerned.

The Proprietors are to be spoken with from eleven in the Morning till four in the Afternoon, and from seven in the Evening till ten at Night (as many cannot attend before that Time) every Day, Sunday excepted; and as it is manifest that many Gentlemen both in Court and City, are so absorbed in Business, that though they are happy in the Thought of Marriage, and every Way qualified to engage in it, yet may have neither Time nor Temper for the tedious Forms of Courtship; and as it is also manifest that many excellent Women are, in a great Measure, lost to Society, lost (as we may say) to the tender Joys of Hymen; and who, tied down by Custom to be passive, cannot be first Movers in a Point so delicate; to shun, therefore, all unnecessary Forms (for true Sincerity, we know, cannot exist with too much Ceremony), it is hoped that the above Expedient will be adopted, and that each Person, in Town or Country, who employs an Agent, will signify their Intention so clearly, and candidly, that the Managers may have it in their Power to compleat the Business, and that as soon as possible.

And although it is said above that the Ladies cannot be first Movers in some certain Points, yet, sure, they are not debarred the use of Agents; nor does true Modesty demand the Sacrifice of Sense.

Note, Sums of Money, from Five Hundred Pounds to any Amount whatsoever, may be had, and that upon the shortest Notice, and most equitable Terms. Every Proposal that is practicable will be compleated without Trifling or Delay.

It would be superfluous to trouble the Public about the Characters of the Proprietors of this House for Honour and Delicacy, as it could not possibly subsist without such a Foundation; therefore the Nobility, Gentry, and other Persons may depend on being accommodated with any Sum, as above, without Loss of Time.

Persons who have Monies to lend, as well as those who have Occasion to borrow, may both be accommodated at Dover Street aforesaid.

These handbills being largely circulated, and advertisements being inserted in the principal newspapers at the same time, the establishment enjoyed its full share of notice. At a masked ball given by Mrs Cornelys,* on the 16th of

---

* This Mrs Cornelys was a notoriety of the period. She lived at Carlisle House, Soho Square, where she, coming from Germany, of which country she was a native, settled in or about 1756. Her business was to entertain "the votaries of fashion of both sexes" with masked

July 1776, one of the characters was a Jew, with a label in his hat inscribed with the words "Marriage Treaties," who delivered to the company the following card:—

THE MARRIAGE BROKER

Accommodates Ladies and Gentlemen with everything in the matrimonial way which their Hearts can wish for (Virtue and Money only excepted), and that at first sight of the Parties, having fitted up a variety of very commodious Apartments.——He deals either in the ton or City Stile. If a difficult case, apply to our Attorney General, who attends me here in Person. N.B. I only charge five Guineas poundage per couple.

MARRIAGE TREATIES.

Ye Nymphs forlorn, who pine away in Shades!
Ye mournful Widows, wailing for—Brocades!
Coxcombs who sigh for—Mode! and sighing Wits!
Bucks of St. James's! and ye Half-moon'd Cits!

---

and other balls, and suchlike festivities. Mrs Cornelys seems to have thoroughly understood the advantages of judicious puffery, and her advertisements usually appeared as news paragraphs. On February 18, 1763, there appeared a good specimen of the kind of notice she most affected. It says, "On Saturday last Mrs Cornelys gave a ball at Carlisle House, to the upper servants of persons of fashion, as a token of the sense she has of her obligations to the nobility and gentry, for their generous subscription to her assembly. The company consisted of 220 persons, who made up fourscore couple in country dances; and as scarce anybody was idle on this occasion, the rest sat down to cards." Carlisle House was kept open by means of annual subscriptions, and the fast young men of the period, and not a few older sinners, patronised the establishment. Rules and regulations were published, and from them we learn that members' tickets were transferable provided the name of the holder was written on the back. There are in the papers between 1757 and 1772 frequent references to the grand doings at this notorious place of assignation; but notwithstanding all her customers and her various ways of making money, Mrs Cornelys's name appears in a *Gazette* of November in the latter year among the bankrupts. She is described as "Teresa Cornelys, Carlisle House, St Ann, Soho, dealer." This, however, says very little as to her success or the want of it, for bankruptcy meant anything but ruin a hundred years ago, if one had only money enough to break properly.

Ye old and young—the ugly and the fair!
To Hymen's Shrine haste, sacrifice despair.
Let Law divorce, tyrannic Husbands rail,
Hence dare their Ire!—for here's enough for sale.
Let Virtue's mask the Wife awhile pursue,
Here's fresh Supply—here Wives of ev'ry Hue!
Black, white, red, grey—the bright, the dull, the witty!
Here's Dames for Courtiers, misses for the City!

In the August number of the *Town and Country Magazine*, 1776, a correspondent who signs himself "Lothario," wrote a letter to warn the public against the Dover Street Marriage Office. It states that, having paid his five guineas, he had his name entered on the list of candidates for matrimony, and that in due course of time he received a letter, intimating that a lady, conforming minutely to the conditions for which he had stipulated, wanted a husband exactly like himself. The lady, after some formalities, gave him an appointment in Gray's Inn Gardens, describing her dress; and in order that she might not be mistaken in the gentleman (for till then the parties had not seen each other), she desired that he should have a large nosegay in his hand, bound round with a blue ribbon, which he was to present to her as an introduction to their conference. Unfortunately the lady turned out to be an old acquaintance of the gay Lothario, and by no means the sort of person he could have desired for a wife. This exposition of the matrimonial swindle was answered by the company, with the following advertisement in the *Morning Post*, October 17, 1776:—

TO THE CANDID AND IMPARTIAL.

ON perusing the Town and Country Magazine of August last, Page 408, there appears a Letter in which the Author throws out a very illiberal, unjust Assertion, viz., that any new Plan or Scheme that is offered to the Public is founded upon Imposition; and then goes on to recite an elaborate Tale of his having paid five Guineas to the Managers of the Marriage-Plan, and of his obtaining the promise of a Wife with £10,000 on declaring himself worth treble that Sum. Now the Managers of that Undertaking are called upon to assert, that they are equally unacquainted with the Villa or with the Lady he mentions (not but it would be their Pride and Boast for such as resolve to return to the Paths of Virtue and Honour); and they further declare that every Line of this Letter that reflects the least Dishonour on them, and that does not set their Undertaking in the fairest Point of View, is utterly groundless.

Note, The Managers of said Plan, in Dover Street, finding that the Payment of five Guineas has been thought by some too much on the Commencement, have resolved to reduce that Payment to the Sum of two Guineas for the Future to each Gentleman who may apply; and to give the World some Proof that the Managers are no Deceivers, they will return, on Demand, the three Guineas overplus, to such who have paid the five above mentioned.

Ladies of Reputation are invited gratis, and the Managers shall think themselves highly honoured, as well as amply rewarded, by their Appearance, which must add true Dignity to a Plan where their Felicity is consulted, without trespassing on their Delicacy.

⁂ Counsellor Taite, one of the Managers, will carefully answer all Letters, or other Applications relative to Money Negotiations, and has the Disposal of several large Sums for that Purpose.

Like its predecessors and followers in quackery and cheating, the Dover Street establishment died of itself in due course, and its promoters doubtless turned their attention to new swindles. In the *Daily Advertiser* of 1777 the following is discovered, and is noticeable for the horse-couping manner in which the young gentleman speaks of the future bride who is to assist him in setting up house-keeping. He must have had some trouble in finding such a thoroughbred filly as he requires :—

MATRIMONY.

WANTED, by a young Gentleman just beginning House-keeping, a Lady, between eighteen and twenty-five Years of Age, with a good Education, and a Fortune not less than 5,000*l.*; sound Wind and Limb, Five Feet Four Inches without her Shoes; not fat, nor yet too lean; a clear Skin; sweet Breath, with good Set of Teeth; no Pride, nor Affectation; not very talkative, nor one that is deemed no Scold; but of a Spirit to resent an Affront; of a charitable Disposition; not over fond of Dress, though always decent and clean; that will entertain her Husband's Friends with Affability and Cheerfulness, and prefer his Company to public Diversions and gadding about; one who can keep his Secrets, that he may open his Heart to her without reserve on all Occasions; that can extend domestic Expenses with Economy, as

Prosperity advances, without Ostentation; and retrench them with Cheerfulness, if Occasion should require.

Any Lady disposed to Matrimony, answering this Description, is desired to direct for Y. Z. at the Baptist's Head Coffee-House, Aldermanbury.

N.B. None but Principals will be treated with, nor need any apply that are deficient in any one Particular: the Gentleman can make adequate Return, and is, in every Respect, deserving a Lady with the above Qualifications.

Getting on towards the present day, we come across an advertisement in the *Courier* of May 1815 from a lady who, like the gentleman we have just attended to, wants a good deal for the money. Unlike him, however, she is not young, and so should know better than to ask for a combination of impossibilities in a husband, when, according to her own showing, she should be glad to get a very ordinary creature indeed:—

MATRIMONY.—A Lady, tremblingly alive to the impropriety of this address, is nevertheless compelled, from the family discomforts she now endures, to adopt this method of obtaining a friend and protector; and she is quite certain, that a candid explanation of her situation, will excuse, with a liberal mind, this apparently indecorous appeal. The Advertiser has been married, is middle-aged, of pleasing appearance, highly educated, and accomplished; but, she flatters herself, the regulations of her heart and mind exceed all outward recommendation: her income is very small, and only just sufficient to enable her to make the appearance of a gentlewoman. The being she is desirous of looking up to for happiness, must be, by birth, far above the middling class of society; and all professions, except the Church, the Army, or Navy, will be objected to; about forty, but not under that age; very tall, of gentlemanlike appearance, and possessing that polish, and those habits, that are only to be acquired in good company; of an unimpeached, moral, respectable, and honourable character, fond of retirement and domestic life. Fortune not being the object of the Advertiser, she requires his income only to be equal to his own wants; and she will never lessen it. As the most serious and painful causes have occasioned this Address, it is earnestly solicited that no one will reply to it from curiosity or amusement; and persons who seek fortune, connections, or any other worldly advantage, will only be disappointed by noticing it; but should it meet the eye of a being whose mind is sufficiently cultivated to consider a well-born, elegant, and accomplished companion, and sincere friend, the first treasure in life, from such she will be glad to hear; and real names and addresses will be considered a pledge of sincerity that will not be abused. Letters must be post paid, and addressed to O. P. Q., Two-penny Post-office, Blandford-street, Portman-square.

In December 1818 there appeared in *Galignani* an application from the scion of a distinguished though unfortunate family who was anxious to enter into the holy state. It was called

OFFER OF MARRIAGE.

COUNT SARSFIELD, Lord Lucan, descendant of the royal branches of Lorraine and Capet, and other sovereigns of Europe, wishes to contract an alliance with a lady capable from her rank and talents of supporting the dignity and titles, which an alliance so honourable would confer on her. Address, Poste Restante à Paris.

The name of Sarsfield is highly distinguished in the military annals of Ireland: during the eventful period subsequent to the expulsion of James II. from England, Sarsfield was General-in-Chief of the Irish troops, and was one of those who took advantage of the capitulation of Limerick to transfer himself and family to another country. But for all his great name and historical associations, this Sarsfield was but a poor adventurer; for he did not succeed in getting any rich parvenue to nibble at his bait, as is evidenced by this, which seven years afterwards appeared in a London newspaper :—

COUNT SARSFIELD LUCAN, lineal descendant of the royal line of Lorraine and Capet, and other sovereigns of Europe, desires to join in an alliance of marriage with a lady whose qualities and abilities will enable her to support the rank and titles she will obtain by this honourable alliance. Address to Count Sarsfield Lucan, Poste Restante à Paris.

In a handbill circulated about the year 1820, a "new matrimonial plan" is ventilated. The advertiser states that he possesses "an establishment where persons of all classes who are anxious to sweeten life by repairing to the *altar of Hymen*, have an opportunity of meeting with proper partners. . . . Their personal attendance is not absolutely necessary, a statement of facts is all that is required at first." The method propounded was for all anxious to secure husbands or wives to become subscribers to the institution, the amount of subscription to be regulated according to the class in which they place themselves, the classes being described thus in the plan :—

Ladies.

1st Class. I am twenty years of age, heiress to an estate in the county of Essex of the value of 30,000*l.*, well educated, and of domestic habits; of an agreeable, lively disposition, and genteel figure. Religion that of my future husband.

2nd Class. I am thirty years of age, a widow, in the grocery line in London—have children; of middle stature, full made, fair complexion and hair, temper agreeable, worth 3,000*l.*

3rd Class. I am tall and thin, a little lame in the hip, of a lively disposition, conversible, twenty years of age, live with my father, who, if I marry with his consent, will give me 1,000*l.*

4th Class. I am twenty years of age; mild disposition and manners; allowed to be personable.

5th Class. I am sixty years of age; income limited; active, and rather agreeable.

Gentlemen.

1st Class. A young gentleman with dark eyes and hair; stout made; well educated; have an estate of 500*l.* per annum in the county of Kent; besides 10,000*l.* in three per cent. consolidated annuities; am of an affable disposition, and very affectionate.

2nd Class. I am forty years of age, tall and slender, fair complexion and hair, well tempered and of sober habits, have a situation in the Excise, of 300*l.* per annum, and a small estate in Wales of the annual value of 150*l.*

3rd Class. A tradesman in the city of Bristol, in a ready-money business, turning 150*l.* per week at a profit of 10 per cent., pretty well tempered, lively, and fond of home.

4th Class. I am fifty-eight years of age; a widower, without encumbrance; retired from business upon a small income; healthy constitution; and of domestic habits.

5th Class. I am twenty-five years of age; a mechanic of sober habits; industrious, and of respectable connections.

It is presumed that the public will not find any difficulty in describing themselves; if they should, they will have the assistance of the managers, who will be in attendance at the office, No. 5, Great St. Helens, Bishopsgate Street, on Mondays, Wednesdays, and Fridays, between the hours of eleven and three o'clock.—Please to inquire for Mr Jameson, up one pair of stairs. All letters to be post paid.

The subscribers are to be furnished with a list of descriptions, and when one occurs likely to suit, the parties may correspond; and if mutually approved, the interview may be afterwards arranged.

About 1840, some adventurers anxious to emulate the success achieved by matrimonial agencies in Paris and other towns on the Continent, set up an office in the neighbourhood of Cavendish Square, and issued a prospectus, which stated that it was written by a clergyman of the Church of England, who was also a graduate of the University of Oxford—a kind of double guarantee as to purity of morals and excellence of style—and which, after setting forth the advantages of such an establishment properly conducted, and the success which had attended on similar ventures in other countries where people were less prejudiced, went on thus:—

It is conducted by a gentleman and his wife, both persons of the highest character, respectability, and connexions. They have separate houses at some distance from each other, at which the husband gives interviews to gentlemen and his wife to ladies. The negotiations are conducted in conformity with printed rules, from which not the slightest deviation will be allowed, and everything is managed in a manner which cannot offend the most fastidious delicacy, or deter the most easily excited diffidence. It is quite impossible that ladies or gentlemen applying to the establishment can see each other, until a meeting be finally and satisfactorily arranged, and all effects of idle curiosity are effectually checked. The rules are to be published for ten shillings—the price is set upon them for no other reason than as some guard against the thoughtless, the idle or the ill disposed—at Mr Proudfoot's, 63, Mortimer Street, Cavendish Square, and they entitle the purchaser to a speedy interview.

In the same year an advertisement was published in the papers directing the ignorant in such matters where to apply in the event of their wishing to obtain the benefits of the agency and the services of the clergyman of the Church of England and graduate of the University of Oxford :—

MATRIMONIAL ALLIANCE.—The Pamphlets, Rules, and Regulations of this Establishment for promoting Matrimonial Alliances, may be obtained by applying to A. B. care of Mr. Proudfoot, 63, Mortimer Street, Cavendish Square. Price of the pamphlet one shilling. The Portfolio of February is now ready, containing letters from gentlemen in every sphere of life, possessing property from £400 to £3000 per annum, and may be purchased or inspected by ladies, free of charge, at the agent's, 63, Mortimer Street, as above.

Notwithstanding the honours of the clergyman and the contents of the portfolio, the old-fashioned and insulated notions of English folk were too much for the Alliance, which in due course faded from sight and recollection. Possibly the graduate sought those happier climes to which he refers in his exordium, and there made two into one as often as he could wish. Ten years or more after Mr Proudfoot and his reverend friend had departed from the scene, the following, which is suggestive of a still smaller agency, appeared. It is a unique specimen of the use to which artful and designing folks can under any set professions put advertisements :—

TO GIRLS OF FORTUNE.—MATRIMONY.—A bachelor, young, amiable, handsome, of good family, and accustomed to move in the highest sphere of society, is embarrassed in his circumstances. Marriage is his only hope of extrication. This advertisement is inserted by one of his friends. Ingratitude was never one of his faults, and he will study for the remainder of his life to prove his estimation of the confidence placed in him. Address, post paid L. L. H. L., 47 King Street, Soho.—N.B. The witticisms of cockney scribblers deprecated.

This was evidently concocted by a man who knew what would be most likely to attract silly spinsters of a romantic turn of mind and independent means. Did he succeed? We cannot say, but sincerely hope not, as the professions are too good to be sincere, and his pretensions are pitched too high to be genuine. The following has been already compared with the handsome bachelor's effusion :—

MATRIMONIAL ADVERTISEMENT. I hereby give notice to all unmarried women that I, John Hobnail, am at this writing five and forty, a widower, and in want of a wife. As I wish no one to be mistaken, I have a good cottage with a couple of acres of land, for which I pay 2*l*. a-year. I have five children, four of them old enough to be in employment; three sides of bacon and some pigs ready for market. I should like to have a woman fit to take care of her house when I am out. I want no second family. She may be between 40 and 50 if she likes. A good sterling woman would be preferred, who would take care of the pigs.

This was originally given in *Blackwood* over twenty years ago. John Hobnail is plain-spoken, but he is evidently honest, and no greater contrast could be afforded to L. L. H. L. than John's desires for a mate. Here is no high-falutin' nonsense, and romance-reading young ladies were doubtlessly horrified at the use to which John would put a "good sterling woman." But there may, after all, be heroism in pig-feeding; and many a brave lady would quail before a hungry sow and her litter. Some might also object to the contiguity in which Mr Hobnail places his porkers and his children. Differing from John Hobnail very widely, yet in the same agricultural interest, is the author of the next application, which a good many years nearer the present time than the *Blackwood* specimen, appeared in a Yorkshire journal. The effusion is in its way almost as curious as the two are which immediately precede it—at least we think so, whatever our readers may do :—

WANTED a WIFE, by a handsome young FARMER who is desirous of becoming domesticated, and of enjoying the society of a young, good-tempered female, who would tempt him away from his market festivities by her pleasing and gently persuasive manners. She must not exceed 20, unless she be a widow, whose family must not exceed six. Want of beauty would be no kind of objection, provided she possessed from 1,000*l*. to 2,000*l*. His rent, tithes, and taxes are all paid up, and he is wholly free from debt. All that he requires is love, peace, and happiness. Apply —— near Tenbury.

All he requires is love, peace, and happiness. Love of course includes beauty; and so we can manage to understand that his object really is love and beauty, or a thousand pounds, and two if possible. How he can expect peace, to say nothing of happiness, when he gives a widow with six children a chance, passes our comprehension. But some men will do anything for money, and we regret to say that this handsome young farmer appears, after all, to be of a most mercenary description. While we are so far north, we may as well turn to Sheffield, in which town, about five years ago, a very amusing police case, having its origin in a matrimonial advertisement, was heard. The complaint was laid against three young men of the town of blades, named respectively George Herd, Joseph Fidler, and Arthur Harrop, who were charged by John Wilmer Lambert, "for that they did unlawfully, maliciously, and knowingly, with intent to provoke a breach of the peace, cause to be inserted in a certain public newspaper, called the *Sheffield Independent*, a certain false, scandalous, and defamatory statement of libel of and concerning one John Wilmer Lambert, and against the peace of our Lady the Queen." The libel thus described was as follows :—

TO SINGLE YOUNG WOMEN.—A young man wishes to meet with a partner for life. Any young lady feeling disposed, apply by letter, WILMER LAMBERT, auger filer, St Mary's-road, Sheffield.

The following are some of the answers the unhappy Wilmer received from the fair ones of Sheffield: "Aperil 5, 1869. Sir—seeing Advertisement In the *Independent* that you are in Wants a partner for *life* so i hoffer myself as a Candate But Befoare there Is much More caressponденc I should like an intearew with *you*. Notes the adress. . . ." A more dignified lady says: "Wilmer Lambert: The under singed quite feel disposed as *you call it*. I am considered by my friends good looking and they think I shall make a good wife. I am the age 22 and dark. If W. L.

answers this pleas to send cart de visite. Address by letter."

The next correspondent is anxious to make a match, if not to find a husband for herself: "Sir,—I with pleasure saw it advertised in the *Independent* to-day you was in wants of a partner and would be obliged if you will acpt Miss A. M. A——, tall, dark hair, dark eyes, and what the world calls good looking (age 23), or my sister who is (24) good looking. A widdow no children. A fortune at her own disposal willed to her by her late husband Mr. R——, or if you would Prefer a light young lady my friend Miss C. M. C——, who is at present residing in sheffield, but is scotch, light hair, blue eyes, and affectionate will accept you please to answer in Tuesday *Independent* and you shall hear fearther from me.—Please not delay as I shall be ancouse to know which you prefer." This lady's anxiety to rush in and try her hand at match-making will perhaps in some way account for the contemptuous tone of the "but is scotch," though, continuing the description, we find that even the Scotch young lady has forgotten the caution peculiar to her people, and so distasteful to her match-making friend, and has decided to accept the auger-filer.

A fifth is also affectionate, but cautious: "My dear fren Iv Sean in to Day Nuse Paper you Wanting A wife I shall be glad for a good husborn But I should Be very Glad to now you age firs 2 I should like to now Wether you are Good temper. My age is 24 years and a little Incom for Life and if you are Really in Wants of A Wife I should be happy to seay you after you Have Sent you Liknes and then I will meat you at my sisters and then We Will talk the Matter Over. Short aquantress Som times makes Long Repentnc. But, I Would Mak you Comfortable Wile I Liv and A Little After I am Dead Weakly Incom PS Excuse my Riting PS Anserr by Next Post." This is indeed a gem which would have gladdened the heart of Isaac Pitman; and with a wife who will make her husband comfortable after death, we must conclude our examples. There are other letters, one from "a publican's daughter, twenty-three years of age, and as no objection to be a Partner if bouth sides sues tgether;" and several which bear the appearance of having been written for the purpose of hoaxing. After some little time spent in hearing the case, the defendants agreed to apologise and pay the costs, upon which Wilmer Lambert, auger-filer, felt that his honour was appeased, and stated that he would withdraw from the prosecution.

In *Belgravia*, of six or seven years back, there is an article on matrimonial advertisements and the answers to correspondents which are peculiar to certain of the penny periodicals. It enters so thoroughly into the subject, and contains so much information as well as amusement, that a selection from it will be found agreeable. Speaking of the "answers," the writer says, after alluding to one or two of a different sort: "By far the greater number of correspondents are, however, concerned about matrimonial affairs. The *London Journal* is, perhaps, the periodical which does the largest business of this kind. In a single copy there are no fewer than twenty-three paragraphs relating to this subject, many of them referring to four or five separate correspondents, besides two long lists of announcements of cartes-de-visite wanted and received. The study of these paragraphs is curious and edifying. 'P. Y. R.,' who seems to be a favoured personage, has in some previous number asked for a wife. In reply he is told that 'Nellie Vernon, twenty-two, accomplished, rather tall, dark, and considered handsome; an English Gem, nineteen, pretty, lady-like, and the daughter of an independent gentleman; Emilie R., twenty, handsome, and of good family; and Eveline de Courcy, eighteen, fair and pretty, and will have a nice fortune—wish to correspond and receive the carte-de-visite of the favoured one.' Next comes the announcement of a forlorn swain. He tells the sympathetic readers of his favourite 'weekly' that he 'is twenty-three, tall, dark, and good-tempered, and has an income of £500 a year,' and he asks to correspond with 'a pretty and amiable young lady.' One of the softer sex comes next. 'Emma G., a well-informed girl of nineteen, rather dark, genteel, five feet eight inches in height, a domestic servant, is very much in want of some one to love.' The domestic servant is, however, eclipsed by the lady whose announcement of her wishes is to be found in the same column. 'Queen Adeline' flies at higher game—evidently desires, in a word, one of the earls or marquises who figure so magnificently in the serial novels of the journal—and thus expresses her wishes: she is, she says, 'tall, dark, handsome, and has £400 a year,' and she would like to have 'the carte-de-visite of a tall, dark, and handsome man, not too old. She is twenty-two. He must have well-formed and small hands and feet, and plenty of money.' It is difficult to imagine that these announcements and their like are published in good faith. Of course, we can understand why 'Emma G.' or 'Sergeant D.,' a non-commissioned officer of the line, should publish their wants in this very open way; but as for the ladies and gentlemen with £400 and £500 a year, who appeal to the editor for partners for life, *que diable viennent-ils faire dans cette galère?* Is it possible that there are people in the world who, unless they have some irremovable stain upon their characters, find any difficulty in disposing of their incomes and themselves amongst their own friends?

"This is probably a sufficiently business-like way of arranging a 'matrimonial alliance' for the tastes of most people, but there are even more commercial methods in existence. People who want wives or husbands sometimes find it advisable to make their wants public by advertisement—a method of proceeding which is very commonly practised in some of the northern and manufacturing districts. Matrimonial advertisements are excluded from the respectable journals of the metropolis, but the scarcely less influential and respectable journals of the cotton capital insert them readily and receive the answers. They are generally very matter-of-fact—romance would, indeed, be out of place in such a connection. Now and then some of them are, however, comic enough. 'A handsome young gentleman, aged twenty-three, wishes to correspond with a young lady with not less than £300 a year,' was an advertisement which appeared several times in one of the journals of Cottonopolis. Whether the advertiser's expectations were ever realised the present writer is, of course, unable to say; but from his own experience he is inclined to think it rather doubtful. Some few months back, having nothing very particular to do, he inserted an advertisement in a certain Manchester newspaper, stating that 'a young professional man, handsome, amiable, and intelligent, and possessing an income of £500 a year, was anxious to meet with a suitable mate.' The replies came in shoals. Within four days, between sixty and seventy letters were received, all, with one exception, evidently *bonâ fide*. The exception was a high-flown composition written in a disguised hand, and on paper profusely scented with musk. Of the remainder, the majority were rather touching. A great many came from servant girls, who always included two things in their applications: first, they declared that their parents were eminently respectable—generally professional men—and that it was only through family misfortunes that they had been compelled to 'go to service;' and secondly, they treated their correspondent to a great deal of bad spelling and worse grammar. The following is a verbatim copy of one of these communications:—'Dear Sir. Having notised your advertizment we beg to offer ourselves. Are 2 sisters Lottie twenty one and dark hand tall and Tottie fair and pritty which I never hexpected to go to survice having always been brought up quite genteel. I am Sir Yours and c. —— ——. P.S. Please adress your letter *Miss* ——.' Young ladies in shops and warehouses contributed somewhat liberally to the batch of answers. They generally wrote the flashy hand taught at 'young ladies' seminaries,' and sometimes quoted poetry of a tender character. The grammar of their epistles was, however, somewhat dubious, and their spelling worse than that of a charity-school boy. Strangest of all was the following, which was written in a beautifully firm and lady-like hand upon good paper :—'I have seen your challenge to the ladies in the ——, and I fancy it must be genuine, and that you expect it to be taken up in all frankness. . . . I am twenty-five, and am the daughter of a solicitor. I have been well educated, and you may judge of my personal appearance by the enclosed carte-de-visite. I shall be entitled on my marriage to about £5,000 in the funds, and at my mother's death I expect to receive a similar amount. My reason for this bold and perhaps imprudent letter is that I am tired of home, which is too stiff and formal for me. If you would like to know more about me you must give me all particulars about yourself. Write to Miss ——, under cover to ——.' The portrait enclosed was that of a really handsome girl of about the age mentioned in the letter. The name given was one not altogether unknown to the writer, and the person under cover to whom the reply was to be sent was evidently a servant. It need scarcely be said that the matter went no further, and that the carte was returned forthwith. Still, it is rather melancholy to think of what may be the fate of this girl. She evidently suspected no harm, and she confided in an utter stranger with singular frankness and simplicity. In all human probability she would become the prey of the first fortune-hunting scoundrel who came across her path, unless she had, as the writer sincerely hopes, a big brother with a strong arm and a thick stick."

We have before us at the present moment an accumulation of the very extraordinary applications for wives and husbands which are constantly appearing in the cheap publications of the day, but the specimens already given will doubtless be found sufficient for the purpose. Two from our heap, however, we feel in duty bound to give, not because they are very different from the rest we have garnered, but because they are fair samples of a style often adopted by the Benedicks and Beatrices of the *London Journal*. One is from a lady and the other from a gentleman. Let us take the lady first:—

AGENORIA says that she has natural golden-brown hair, fair oval face, laughing mischievous eyes, dark arched eyebrows, roguish expression of countenance, is eighteen, ladylike, sensible, merry, good-natured, highly respectable, and has good expectations. She longs to be married to a tall, studious, benevolent, affectionate, well-principled gentleman, who would think it a pleasure to instruct and assist her endeavours to obtain a thorough knowledge of English, French, and drawing; and in return she would try to be an apt pupil, and a loving and obedient wife.

The pseudonyms adopted by these young ladies are often provokingly funny: sometimes loving hearts take the name of a favourite heroine, whose virtues and temptations, joys and sorrows, are at the time attracting their attention in the *Journal;* but sometimes they take higher flights, and in attempting high-sounding names they have heard, succeed in inventing others, just as the old chemists, in trying to discover the philosopher's stone, found things much more valuable —with the difference, of course, that the new titles are only valuable to future writers of the fiction believed in most by the fair correspondents. Agenoria requires a good deal, but her effort is of the weakest compared with that of our next friend, who, provided he had a big stick, would prove himself a true hero—say on a box of eggs:—

L. S. W., twenty-one, dark, and considered handsome, lithe in figure, of the medium height, and of a good family, would like to receive the carte-de-visite of a young lady, a blond preferred. He is shortly going abroad, probably to Mexico, or some of the republics adjacent, where he intends to make a name and fortune. He is very ambitious, and intends joining an army wnere there is active service. He wants a wife who would encourage his plans and undertakings. One who would share with him the toils of a camp life, or who would rule in Courts. One who would receive homage from the savage tribes of Northern and Central America, or would maintain her husband's position as an officer and gentleman of honour both at home and at Court. He is of a very loving disposition, though rather hasty, and to a lady who would do as he wished he would be an affectionate, loving husband, companion, and protector.

That matrimonial clubs or agencies are still in existence is shown by a case tried quite recently before Sir James Hannen in the Divorce Court—a wife's petition for a judicial separation on the ground of her husband's cruelty. The counsel for the petitioner stated that she was a lady of property, residing in Liverpool, and that the respondent was a clerk in a firm in the same town. He was a member of a Matrimonial Club, whose object was to secure for its members wives with good fortunes; and as an instance of what kind of alliances result from the interference of these establishments, we give some of the evidence. The respondent, whose chief object was to get money, was very violent on finding soon after the marriage that his wife had not nearly so much as he had anticipated. He was guilty of drunkenness and assaults, and treated his wife in a very brutal manner. The petitioner said that her father died on Christmas Day, 1866. On his death she had an income of £400 for her separate use. She made the acquaintance of the respondent some two or three years before, and he was at that time a clerk in a firm of shipbrokers. At the marriage no settlement was made; but a few days after the respondent asked for any papers she might have. She gave him them. She had £675 in a building society, and he wrote out a form that she signed, and the money was transferred to him. He often said that £400 per annum was a very paltry sum, and that if he had a few thousands he could go into business. Petitioner's mother had a considerable sum, and her name being the same, had led the defendant into the error of marrying a woman with only a "paltry £400 a year," instead of a lot of ready money. Soon after the marriage he took to drinking, and was violent in his language. The latter, the petitioner believed, arose from his being disappointed at the smallness of her fortune. She found a letter of a very immoral character addressed to her husband. She was much annoyed, and sent the letter to the office. When the respondent returned he brought a friend with him, and used most violent language. After the friend had gone to bed the respondent pulled her on to the floor, bit her in the neck, ground her beads into powder, and bit a piece out of a glass. This latter act, it must be admitted, is a rather novel way of showing disappointment, even in matters like these. The friend was at once called for, and assisted to hold the disappointed man down. In August 1870 defendant tore a piece of skin from her arm. He had been drinking for some time, and tried to prevent her seeing her mother, who only lived a few hundred yards away. The mother was doubtless a sore point with him. He said that once a month was often enough to see her, but witness went more frequently. The family doctor saw the injuries which she sustained. In the same month the respondent called her very foul names, and threatened to strangle her and throw her out of the window. His threats were so violent that she never expected to see the morning. On one occasion he came home drunk, and partook of three large bottles of champagne. This would be a dangerous experiment for a sober man to make in these degenerate days. Afterwards he fell backwards, and she had to stay with him all night. In March 1871 she went to her mother's to tea, and when she returned he used very bad language, and made all sorts of charges about her conduct, which were false. When sober, he said she ought not to take any notice of this. Her first child was born in 1870, and her medical adviser told her to go away. She was anxious to take the child with her, which her husband would not allow, and during her absence he sent it from home. On hearing of this she at once returned, and he refused to tell her where the child was, until she wrote a letter which he forced her to write. On a Sunday after this he returned home drunk, and when she remonstrated with him, he said that he was not half drunk, but soon would be so. He then took the decanters out of the cupboard, and threw them at her. This was, to say the least, eccentric, as a means to the end of drunkenness. She was so frightened at his conduct that she had to seek protection amongst neighbours. On the 20th of December witness was in the house alone with respondent, who threatened to kill her, stating that he often wished to do so, and now that they were alone there was a good opportunity. He then got hold of the carving-knife, and stood over her with it. He then said that would not do, but a pistol or razor would. Corroborative evidence as to the violence was given by the doctor who attended the petitioner, and noticed bruises on her; and by a servant who formerly lived with the parties to the suit. His lordship granted a decree of judicial separation, with costs, the wife to have the custody of the child. Marriage for money and money alone, without any consideration as to whether the contracting persons are at all suited to each other, is almost bound to end in unpleasantness, more especially when the fortune-hunter finds that he has married the daughter instead of the mother, and has only a "paltry £400 a year" and a little ready money to subsist on.

There is at the present time in London a weekly newspaper specially devoted to the interests of those who wish to marry or to give in marriage, and as the copy we have before us under date May 9, 1874, is numbered 214, and is full of advertisements all referring to the holy state of matrimony, it is to be presumed that the supply is caused by a most undoubted demand for an organ of intercommunication between kindred souls which scorn to be trammelled by ordinary social restrictions, or to which conventionalities can bring no balm. Love is a fierce flame, and people who feel it burning within them, and know no object on whom to bestow the priceless blessing, are apt to try any short cut that offers itself, instead of biding their time and going the ordinary slow-coach road which lumbering old-fashioned etiquette suggests. Therefore we take up our paper with interest, and receive with pleasure the intimation that it is "a weekly journal devoted to the promotion of marriage and conjugal felicity." We say pleasure advisedly, for most editors would have been satisfied to promote marriage, and have let the subsequent felicity look after itself. We must admit that we fail to find any further reference to the future happiness of couples in our copy; perhaps it is to be secured by a regular supply of the newspaper, so that those already done for may see how the remaining lovers are getting on. On the front page there are ten "rules and regulations" to be complied with by advertisers, the most important of which seems to be that "*bona fide* notices from ladies and gentlemen desirous of marrying will be inserted at the rate of twelve stamps per forty words," with a reduction by taking a quantity, and that "all introductions are given on the understanding that the lady and gentleman shall each pay a fee to the editor within a month after marriage." Why these are called rules and regulations we don't pretend to know. The editor also offers, as one of the rules, to give advice on the subject of courtship or marriage, by which it would appear that he has had an extended experience of both. Yet this supposition is hardly borne out by a request—also one of the ten regulations—for contributions "calculated to enlighten the public mind in reference to marriage and other kindred subjects." Maybe, great as is the editor's own knowledge of marriage "and other kindred subjects," he cannot write equal to the demands of such a topic. Certainly he and his advertisers have the most original ideas of both orthography and syntax. Maybe also, the "address to the public," which adds to the front-page glories, has been enough for him in the way of hard literary labour. It is certainly very nice, though short; and we regret that no such cunning hand could be obtained to give a few opening lines for the present chapter. But better late than never, and so we will borrow the "address" now. "Marriage," says the editor, "is such an ancient institution, and has in all ages excited such universal interest among the human family, that in offering to the public a journal specially devoted to the promotion of marital felicity, we feel sure we are only supplying a national want. Civilisation, combined with the cold formalities of society and the rules of etiquette, imposes such restrictions on the sexes, that there are thousands of marriageable men and women, of all ages, capable of making each other happy, who never have a chance of meeting, either in town or country; therefore, the desirability of having some organ through which ladies and gentlemen aspiring to marriage can be honourably brought into communication, is too obvious to need demonstration; and as we are resolved to devote our best energies to advance the interests and happiness of our readers and correspondents, we feel sure the *Matrimonial News* will meet with a generous support." This appeal seems to have met with a good response, as there are no less than 331 advertisements of various lengths, all relating to marriage, in the number before us. It is noticeable, however, that many of them have a striking family likeness, and a peculiarity of constructive style is evidenced by a great number in each column. It is hardly fair to suppose that half-a-dozen ladies of forty anxious for husbands would describe themselves as orphans, yet we find no less than eight ladies in one page, all content with that classification, whose united ages amount to 313 years, one being thirty-five, another thirty-eight, and six admitting to be forty each; but these are insignificant compared with a poor young thing who appears close by, and whose application runs thus :—

227 **AN orphan LADY, aged 52, of good connexions, and an income of £160 a year, wishes to hear from a gentleman not under 60. Address with Editor.**

This orphan business may be partly an intimation that there are no mothers-in-law to fear, besides being an appeal to the charitable to prevent giddy young creatures straying into harm's way. The columns of this unique journal are also strong in the military, several colonels and some other officers being anxious to commit matrimony.

From 331 advertisements, all peculiar, it is hard to make anything like a judicial selection; but there are a few specimens we have determined on giving, even though others must suffer and be left in the cold shade of neglect. We will commence with

245 **A WIDOWER, aged 60, healthy and active, with a business of about £150 a year, wishes to correspond with a well educated lady, from 40 to 50 with a view to early marriage. Address with Editor.**

This will doubtless throw a new light on the question of early marriages, which seems to have been hitherto handled in a selfish and one-sided manner. Sixty and fifty can hardly ever be "too early wed." Next we come upon

124 **CATHLEEN, aged 30, a Widow LADY, without children, income £7,000, residing in a handsome house, surrounded by a park of 200 acres, within 50 miles of London, would correspond with a Nobleman or Gentleman of position, with a view to marriage. Address with Editor.**

Probably there are many noblemen and gentlemen with whom Cathleen mixes in daily intercourse who do not dream that she wishes to be married again, and she is of course too much a lady to let them know the state of her feelings. Which accounts for her confiding in the editor, who must be a perfect Pantechnicon of secrets. The intelligent foreigner is not blind to the advantages of advertising for what he requires, as witness

9982 A Spanish GENTLEMAN, aged 30 years, residing at Seville (Andalusia), tall, good looking, very swell, rather a meriodinal type, an income of £1,000. He knows English thoroughly, and would like to correspond with the following ladies: Nos. 9442, 9697, 9646, and 9710. Address with Editor.

He knows English better than we do in England, if he understands what a "meriodinal type" is; and the editor doesn't offer to explain. But the latter is evidently too interested in the following to trouble himself with small and foreign fry :—

195 A BACHELOR, 32, height 6 feet, strong, fair and considered good looking, closely connected with nobility, and moving in the best county society, one brother inherits entailed estates and two in the army, a member of one of the most particular west-end clubs, residence family mansion beautifully situated on the bank of a large river, disposition amiable and energetic, would not mind getting married, if I could meet a suitable wife. She must be of a loveable disposition, good figure and pleasing face, and have a fortune of not less than £10,000 to enable me to buy out the other partner in a large manufactory which cost £23,000, and yealds over £3,000 per annum, without which I will not become a benedict for years. Would like communicate with 9920, 9852, or 9803. Address L. M. A., Editor M. N., 282, Strand.

These figures refer, of course, to young ladies who have advertised for the connections of the nobility in previous numbers. When the School Board has done with the children of costermongers and other plebeians, it will have to turn its attention to the members of particular West-End clubs, whose education seems to have been somewhat neglected, so far as grammar is concerned. Should the fair creatures referred to by L. M. A. be already suited, or the inducements held out be insufficient for them, our next may be worthy of his attention :—

284 A Young LADY, tall, fair, and beautiful, with a great profusion of golden hair, and an income of £800 a year, wishes to correspond with a gentleman of position with a view to marriage. Editor has address.

Quite a modern Miss Kilmansegg, with the advantage of

having the typical adornment in the shape of golden hair instead of a golden leg. This reference to poetry is of great advantage, as it puts us in a proper frame to consider the following :—

> "Oh, woman, in our hours of ease,
> Uncertain, coy, and hard to please;
> When pain or sickness rend the brow,
> A ministering angel thou."

9828 A Young WIDOW, highly connected, dark hair and eyes, considered pretty, good income, desires to marry, she does not deny that she might at times realize the two first lines of the couplet quoted above, but she can assure any gentleman willing to make the experiment that she is as certain to be true to the conclusion. Address with Editor.

Even Scott has to succumb to the grammatical requirements of the marriage advocate and its readers; but the alteration from the original is as nothing compared with the reference to "the two first lines of the couplet." There is poetry of a different kind in the next specimen, which deserves particular attention :—

45 I am a BACHELOR, 28, tall and gentlemanly. My income being £150 only (though prospects good), I seek an amiable, educated wife, with private means. Should 10,000, 9920, 9851, 9960, Geraldine, Miss Kate, Miss Maxwell, 9852, 9828, 9878, 9885, or other lady under 28, with at least £2,000 in own control, deem my position compatible with her views, I should much like to correspond. I am well educated, of refined and intellectual tastes, fond of literature and home, of sound moral principles, eschewing smoking, drinking, gambling, and all fast life delusions, of undoubted respectability, unquestionable honour and integrity, of equable temper, and kind, generous heart. Believing a true wife to be man's greatest blessing, I fully intend being a good husband or none at all, and shall treat my wife not merely with the courtesy due to a lady, but with the respectful consideration to a woman. As this is bona fide, inviolable honour observed and expected. Particulars of age, income, and disposition respectfully solicited. Address with Editor.

O true poetic soul longing for a mate! O noble heart of undoubted respectability and unquestionable honour!

may you go on and prosper! Even teetotalism can be fervid, and an equable temper may become quickened, when matrimony stirs up the feelings; and so catching is the impulse, that we should like to fold this young man to our breast, and present him with our favourite daughter. But she hasn't got £2000, and so, regretting the circumstance, we pass on to

8672 A PHYSICIAN of noble lineage (of French and English extraction), of statue about 5ft. 8 inches, aged 36 years, of dark complexion, with black hair and eyes, possessing a strong and healthy constitution, desires to form the acquaintance, with a view to matrimony, of a Lady from 19 to 23 or 24 years, who must be of a noble family or the upper class; brunette preferred, if not of a medium complexion with black or dark hair, and eyes having a fine physique, with some embonpoint,. pretty, of an affectione disposition, with a heart true and loving, talented, speaking or understanding French and Italian, or the other foreign languages; in height about 5 feet 6 to 8 inches. Also must possess in her own right considerable fortune, and having no incumbrance preferred. In effect a Girl who can ever love a man with an affectionate disposition. Photograph and address with Editor.

This noble physician evidently wishes for a wife whom he may eventually stuff and exhibit, even if he does not take her "round the country" during life. Few people would object to paying sixpence or so to see, among other things, eyes having a fine physique; and so we trust 8672 may get the wife he wishes for. She would, however, if existent, as a matter of natural selection prefer our next friend, and then they could mutually rejoice over each other's tastes and peculiarities:—

9971 VEGETARIAN, a young man who does not use flesh as food; a Roman Catholic, humble, well-educated, and connected. A lover of temperance, truth, literature, fruit, flowers, and economy, income about £80 a year, wishes for a wife with similar tastes, principles, and income, or as nearly so as possible.—The address with Editor.

The fact of being connected is such an entirely new

qualification, that we feel compelled to pause and wonder; and this will be an opportunity for withdrawing from a perusal which is very fascinating, but which threatens to prolong this chapter unduly. There are many more noticeable advertisements, but those we have given will be sufficient to show the character of the newspaper from which we have selected them, as well as the credulity of its public, who are either gulled into paying for matrimonial applications, or deluded into purchasing it in the hope that by its means husbands or wives may be secured. That Oxford "double firsts," Cambridge wranglers, members of Parliament, military and naval officers of high rank, peers of the realm, and beneficed clergymen, would send twaddling and ungrammatical advertisements to this paper, so as to secure wives, we no more believe than we do that eminent authoresses and ladies of rank and property would avail themselves of its services to secure to themselves husbands. If we are wrong, and these advertisements are all *bonâ fide,* and what they profess to be, then a paternal Government, which legislates against betting and strong drink, which puts a tax on quack medicines, and subscribes to compulsory education, should fulfil its *métier* by preventing the public exposure of idiotcy we have just been contemplating, more especially as no good can possibly be the outcome of it.

CHAPTER XVIII.

HANDBILLS, INSCRIPTIONS, ETC.

UNDER this head it is our intention to give some slight insight into peculiarities of a kind of advertising unconnected with newspapers, and independent of any of the subjects treated in preceding chapters. We set forth with a great variety of handbills, which seemed almost too extensive for use in this volume; but we have already got rid of so many that the task of disposal is considerably lightened—so lightened, indeed, by the absorption of many of the most characteristic into preceding pages, that by comparison with the original collection our present supply seems rather meagre. It will doubtless, however, be found sufficient for the requirements of readers. We have already given an outline of the history of advertising by means of bills and posters, and have referred to the gradual growth of the system of "billing" until it has attained its present proportions. This system, though regarded by the Board of Works as very objectionable, is far pleasanter than that adopted twenty years ago, when every billsticker considered it his bounden duty to overstick the placards of opponents, and when nothing but a long course of education, or a most vivid imagination, would enable the passer-by to read what was upon the dead walls and hoardings. The Board of Works certainly took the initiative at the wrong time—at the time when improvement was vast and apparent to every one; but as it failed in its object, we may consider that public opinion has admitted the improvement, and no longer regards wall-advertising as a nuisance. The Board doubtless started on the idea at a time when placarding was a most decided scandal, but it—like most other committees—took so long to bring the idea to perfection, that the scandal had abolished itself long before the Board was ready to abolish it. Having already entered into full particulars as to the modes formerly adopted, and contrasted them with those in use at the present time, individual efforts at illuminating the public mind will now be found amply sufficient for our purpose. Some of these are, as all the world knows, extremely funny on account of the vagueness of the writers, and in that particular resemble many of those we have instanced from the columns of newspapers. A very few examples of this kind will suffice, and will pave the way for the heavier material. One of the best of those inscriptions, the comicality of which is founded upon ignorance, appeared in 1821, and was posted up by order of Lord Camden in that portion of the county of Kent which called him owner. It said:—

> Notice is hereby given, that the Marquis of Camden (on account of the backwardness of the harvest) will not shoot himself, nor any of his tenants, till the 14th of September.

We don't suppose that the Marquis had anything to do with the actual wording of the notice, but he has always been identified with it, and doubtless was cruelly badgered about it at the time. Another lordly notice of a similar kind appeared a few years back at Osterly Park, near Brentford, the seat of the Earl of Jersey, which gave the public this information: "Ten shillings reward.—Any person found trespassing on these lands or damaging these fences on conviction will receive the above reward. Dogs poisoned." Somebody once said that nobody expects to find education or ability in a lord, but that is because his household are expected to fulfil his duties properly. Lords would seem in imminent danger of having to pick up a little scholarship, and use it in the interest of their dependants. If so, polo and pigeon-shooting will languish, and West-End night-schools may become fashionable. But getting away from the aristocracy, and turning our attention to the other side of the social sphere, we don't find matters anyway improved, if we are to judge by the specimens of literary ability which now and then address themselves to the curious pedestrian. In Lambeth the latter might some short time back have been terrified by an announcement in a baker's shop, which informed all whom it might concern that *vitals* were baked there. Not so terrible, but more comical, is the following, which is copied from an announcement in the window of a shop at Chatham: "The public are requested not to confound this shop with that of another swindler who has established himself on the other side of the way." There is a story told of two rival shoemakers, one of whom astonished his opponent by the inscription, "Mens conscia recti." He was not allowed his triumph unalloyed, for the other, after puzzling over the notice for some days, divined that it was some new name for "understandings," and feeling sure there was nothing in the opposition shop that was not in his own, replied with this, "Men's and women's conscia recti may be obtained here." This story, however, requires confirmation, as does that of the two provincial photographers. One is said to have placed over his studio, "The acme of photography," to which his enemy and neighbour replied, "Photography in the very height of acme." Salt seems necessary to both of these, but we are informed on good authority that the next one is quite true. A correspondent says that the following is a verbatim copy of a sign formerly to be seen over a shoemaker's shop in the village of Heallan, near Denbigh, Wales. The schoolmaster would seem to have been a long way abroad when the sign was composed:—

Pryce Dyas, Coblar, daler in Bacco Shag and Pig tail, Bacon and Ginarbread Eggs laid every morning by me, and very good Paradise, in the Summer, Gentlemen and Lady can have good Tae and Crumquets and Strawburry with a scim milk, because I can't get no cream.—N.B. Shuse and Boots mended very well.

Of a similar kind is the following, which was, years back, copied from a bill in the window of a small house near Lancaster :—

James Williams, parish clerk, saxtone, town crier, and bellman, makes and sells all sorts of haberdasharies, groceries, &c.; likewise, hair and wigs drest and cut on the shortest notice. N.B.—I keeps an evening scool, where I teach, at reasonable rates, reading, riting, and rithmitic, and singing. N.B.—I play the hooboy occasionally if wanted. N.B.—My shop is next door, where I bleed, draw teeth, and shoo horses, with the greatest scil. N.B.—Children taut to dance if agreeable at 6d. per week, by me, J. Williams, who buy and sell old iron, and coats—boots and shoos cleaned and mended. N.B.—A hat and pr of stockens to be cudgelled for, the best in 5, on Shrof Tushday. For particulars encuire within, or at the horse shoo and bell, near the church, on t'other side the way. N.B.—Look over the dore for the sign of the 3 pidgeons. N.B.—I sells good ayle, and sometimes cyder. Lodgings for single men. N.B.—I teach jografy, algebry, and them outlandish kind of things. A ball on Wednesdays and Fridays.

The next quaint window inscription, which treats of the troubles of a small shopkeeper, may also be depended upon, it being an exact copy of a written card suspended in the shop window of a tradesman in Horsemarket Street, Warrington. One can conceive the amount of provocation undergone and the indignation felt by the honest purveyor of mousetraps, whose blood must have been at boiling point when he penned this :—

Notice I dont keep twelve hole mousetrap nor penney ones what i keep I sell to respectable people not to impudent Boys Hand Bad Girls that comes to rob me and annoy me and has bad parents those that come into my shop shall be severely beat and put into the celler and took before the magistrates those that come into a shop and ask for article that is not made they must come to steal.

Examples like this are manifold, and could be extended to great length, but those we have given are quite enough to afford a vivid idea of the danger of venturing upon literature without the precaution of first learning the rudiments of education, and of the ridicule likely to attend upon any more than usually ambitious effort, which succeeds in landing its perpetrator quite out of his depth.

Old playbills offer a fruitful subject to the investigator, but their actual origin is hidden in the obscurity of ages. So far as their history goes, however, they are plentiful, and mention of them is made in works of a period far anterior to the date of any specimens extant. The modern drama had its origin in an attempt to commemorate the mysteries of the Incarnation, from whence the plays were called mysteries; and it is recorded that one Gregory Nazianzen, an early father of the Christian Church, constructed a drama on the Passion, for the purpose of counteracting the profanities of the ancient plays, about the year of our Lord 364. We have to pass over eight hundred years for the next mention of dramatic representations, and then it is met in Fitzstephen, who states that "London had for its theatrical exhibitions holy plays, and the representation of miracles wrote by holy confessors." This would be towards the close of the twelfth century; and next we come to the Chester Mysteries, which were performed about 1270. These have been reprinted during the present century, and the application of the word mystery is explained in the two subjoined verses from the proclamation or prologue to the Whitsun Plays, a title by which the famous Chester Mysteries were also known. The "moonke" mentioned is Done Rondali, of Chester Abbey, who founded the plays:—

> This moonke, moonke-like in Scriptures well seene
> In storyes travelled with the best sorte;
> In pagentes set fourth, apparently to all eyne,
> The Olde and Newe Testament with livelye comforte;
> Intermynglinge therewith, onely to make Sporte,
> Some things not warranted by any writt,
> Which, to glad the hearers, he woulde men to take yt.
>
> Now, you worshippfull Tanners, that of custome olde
> The fall of Lucifer did set out,

> Some writers awarrante your matter; therefore be boulde,
> Lustily to playe the same to all the rowtte;
> And yf any thereof stande in any doubte,
> Your author his author hath, your shewe let bee,
> Good speech, fyne players, with apparill comelye.

With the history of plays we have nothing to do, and need only state that the first regular English tragedy was "Ferrex and Porrex," which was acted before Queen Elizabeth on the 18th of January 1561 by the gentlemen of the Inner Temple. This same play was tried at one of the minor theatres in 1854, but had no claim upon the tastes of the time. From a passage in Strype's Life of Archbishop Grindall, it has been assumed that the custom of issuing bills, giving information concerning the time, place, and nature of plays to be acted, came in with the plays themselves, as it is there shown to exist prior to the year 1563. In alluding to Grindall's objections to dramatic representations, Strype mentions that the Archbishop complained to Queen Elizabeth's secretary that the players "did then daily, but especially on the holidays, set up their *bills*, inviting to plays." This, however, is a somewhat curious error of Strype's, into which Mr Payne Collier has also fallen. The Bishop did not write *bills* but *booths;* his words are as follows: "Common players, now daylie, but speciallye on holy dayes, set up *boothes* whereunto the youthe resorteth excessively." There is, however, other evidence to prove that playbills were in use not long after the above date; for John Northbrooke, in his treatise against theatrical performances, printed about 1579, says: "They use to set up their bills upon posts some certain days before, to admonish people to make resort to their theatres." At that time the Stationers' Company had the right of giving licences for the printing of playbills, and in the year 1587 its Court of Assistants conferred upon John Charlewood the privilege of being the sole printer of bills for players. Before that time they were printed by one James Roberts, who names "the bills for the players" amongst his publications as early as 1573—six years before Northbrooke's mention of them—and, authorised no doubt by Charlewood, he continued to print them until after the year 1600. This right of printing playbills was at a subsequent period assumed by the Crown. A broadside, dated 1620, is preserved in the Library of the Society of Antiquaries, by which this privilege was granted to a printing firm by James I. It is entitled "An Abstract of his Majesty's Letters Patent granted unto Roger Wood and Thomas Symcocke, for the sole printing of paper and parchment on the one side." Among the articles enumerated as coming under this category are, "Bills for Playes, Pastimes, Showes, Challenges, Prizes, or Sportes whatsoever." At the end the public are informed that if they may want any work of that description, they need only repair to Edward Allde (Wood and Symcocke's assignee), "in the Old Change at the Golden Anchor, over against Carter Lane end, where they shall be reasonably dealt with for the same."

According to Malone these early playbills did not contain a list of the characters or of the names of the actors by whom they were represented. But that the name of the author was sometimes, if not always, on the playbill may be inferred from a passage in the anonymous play of "Histriomastix" (1610), act iv., in which Belch, speaking of Post-hast the playwriter, says, "It is as dangerous to read his name at a play dore, as a printed bill on a plague dore," the allusion being to the practice of writing "Lord have mercy upon us" on the doors of houses in which the plague had broken out, which words of course were a caution, and made people pass on hurriedly. In the same play also we find a curious illustration of our subject in a reference to the part of one of the inferior actors. In act iii. the stage direction says, "Enter Belch setting up bills." And it may not be out of place to remark that the word poster is evidently derived from the custom of sticking bills on posts. That bills were stuck on posts for choice, many of them at stated or customary places, there is plenty of evidence. Sometimes they were ordered to be stuck upon doors and gates, as in the following, though this very possibly means door or gate post. From the *Moderate Intelligencer*, March 18–25, 1647, we discover that in the time of civil war, when the bishops' lands and palaces were sold, the following places were appointed by Parliament to be used for affixing bills concerning the sales. Upon the outer gate and upon the hall door of Sir Richard Gourney's house in the Old Jewry (this was the office where the committee charged with those sales held their sitting), upon the north door of St Paul's Church, upon the gate of Guildhall, and upon the gate of Blackwell Hall.

As long as they have had an existence — from the sixteenth century—these bills have gone by the name of playbills. In the prologue to the anonymous tragedy of "A Warning for Fair Women" (1599), Tragedy whips History and Comedy from the stage, exclaiming :—

'Tis you have kept the theatre so long
Painted in Play bills upon every post,
While I am scornèd of the multitude.

They have also, however, in various places and at various times, been called "text bills for plays." The natural and shorter title, though, always overruled its more pretentious rival. From the prologue to Shirley's "Cardinal" (1652) it appears that it was usual to add on the bill whether the piece was a comedy or a tragedy. This "Cardinal" being a tragedy, the author apologises in the following words for only calling it "a play" in the bills :—

Think what you please, we call it but a "play."
Whether the comic muse, or lady's love,
Romance, or direful tragedy it prove,
The bill determines not : and you would be
Persuaded I would have't a comedy
For all the purple in the name.

From which it may be inferred that the names of tragedies, for greater distinction, were usually, or at all events occasionally, printed in red ink. That the custom of posting playbills continued in the reign of Charles II. may be inferred from the following entry in Pepys' Diary: "I went to see if any play was acted and I found none upon the posts, it being Passion Weeke."

During the Civil Wars the drama had a hard struggle not to be swamped in the deluge which destroyed all things appertaining to the pomp and luxury of the Court, or connected with pleasure generally. The face of the Parliament was turned against stage-plays, and when the war broke out, one of the first measures was that which led to the publication of the following bill :—

Ordinance of the Lords and Commons concerning Stage-Plays.

Whereas,

The distressed Estate of Ireland, steeped in her own Blood, and the distracted Estate of England, threatened with a Cloud of Blood by a civil War, call for all possible Means to appease and avert the Wrath of God, appearing in these Judgements; amongst which Fasting and Prayer, having been often tried to be very effectual, have been lately, and are still, enjoined; And whereas public Sports do not well agree with public Calamities, nor public Stage-plays with the Seasons of Humiliation, this being an exercise of sad and pious Solemnity, and the other being Spectacles of Pleasure too commonly expressing lascivious Mirth and Levity; It is therefore thought fit, and ordered by the Lords and Commons in this Parliament assembled, That while these sad Causes and set Times of Humiliation do continue, public Stage-plays shall cease and be forborne. Instead of which are recommended to the People of this Land the profitable and seasonable consideration of Repentance, Reconciliation, and Peace with God, which probably will produce outward Peace and Prosperity, and bring again Times of Joy and Gladness to these Nations.

This intimation was of course received with much outcry, and "The Actors' Remonstrance" was soon published. In it the writer complains naturally of a law which robs the poor player of his livelihood, and allows bear-gardens and suchlike places to remain unmolested to the delectation of "boisterous butchers, cutting cobblers, hard-handed masons, and the like riotous disturbers of the public peace." The playhouses are defended against sundry charges brought against them, and a promise is made that no female whatsoever shall be admitted unless accompanied by her husband or some male relative; besides which the use of tobacco is to be forbidden even in the threepenny galleries, except in the case of "the pure Spanish leaf." It may thus be readily guessed that something worse even than the cheap "sensation smokes" of the present day was often misnamed tobacco. This is hard to believe, however. The promise extends to the expulsion of all ribaldry from the stage; and the actors say, "We will so demean ourselves as none shall esteem us of the ungodly, or have cause to repine at our actions or interludes; we will not entertain any comedian that shall speak his part in a tone as if he did it in derision of some of the pious, but reform all our disorders and amend all our amisses." During the Commonwealth, stage-plays were almost openly connived at; and the licence indulged in during the Restoration days is too well known to require notice here.

An interesting epoch in the history of the drama is the first appearance of David Garrick, and it is noticeable that the playbill which commemorates the event does not contain his name. Neither, for the matter of that, does it contain the name of the author of the play, who, if Shakespeare, must have been improved and amended. The monopoly of the patent theatres was such that these plays had to be advertised and regarded as simply interludes to a musical entertainment. As witness:—

October 19, 1741.

GOODMAN'S FIELDS.

At the late Theatre in Goodman's Fields, this Day will be perform'd a *Concert* of *Vocal* and *Instrumental Music*, divided into two Parts.

Tickets at Three, Two and One Shilling.

Places for the Boxes to be taken at the Fleece Tavern, near the Theatre.

N.B. Between the two Parts will be presented an Historical Play, called the Life and Death of

KING RICHARD THE THIRD,

containing the Distresses of

KING HENRY VI.

The Artful Acquisition of the Crown by

KING RICHARD,

The Murder of the young King Edward V. and his Brother, in the Tower,

The Landing of the Earl of Richmond,

And the Death of King Richard in the memorable Battle of Bosworth Field, being the last that was fought between the Houses of York and Lancaster.

With many other true historical Passages.

The Part of KING RICHARD *by a Gentleman.*

(*Who never appeared on any Stage.*)

King Henry, by Mr. Giffard; Richmond, Mr. Marshall; Prince Edward, by Miss Hippisley; Duke of York, Miss Naylor; Duke of Buckingham, Mr. Peterson; Duke of Norfolk, Mr. Blades; Lord Stanley, Mr. Pagett; Oxford, Mr. Vaughan; Tressel, Mr. W. Giffard; Catesby, Mr. Marr; Rutcliff, Mr. Crofts; Blunt, Mr. Naylor; Tyrrell, Mr. Puttenham; Lord Mayor, Mr. Dunstall; The Queen, Mrs. Steel; Duchess of York, Mrs. Yates;

And the Part of Lady ANNE

By Mrs GIFFARD.

With Entertainments of Dancing

By Mons. Fromet, Madame Duvall, and the two Masters and Miss Granier.

To which will be added a *Ballad Opera* of one Act, called

THE VIRGIN UNMASK'D.

The Part of Lucy by Miss HIPPISLEY.

Both of which will be performed Gratis by Persons for their Diversion.

The Concert will begin exactly at Six o'Clock.

This bill would seem to contradict an inscription in the large room at the St John's Gate Tavern, Clerkenwell, which is to the effect that Garrick made his first appearance on any stage there. The first appearance of David on any stage was at Ipswich, also in 1741, "where, under the assumed name of Lyddul, he appeared as Aboan in the tragedy of 'Oroonoko.'" His acting at the East End of

London was a decided success, and the performances were continued for what was then considered an almost fabulous period. "The other theatres were quickly deserted, and Goodman's Fields became the resort of people of fashion, even from the West End, till that theatre was shut up." The last performance at Goodman's Fields is said to have taken place on a Sunday. Another playbill of the middle of the eighteenth century may be found interesting, though for no such reasons as are found in that of Goodman's Fields. It is redolent of the pride and poverty which seem to be ever associated with the drama in days gone by, and is given by Boaden in his "Life of Mrs Siddons:"—

At the Old Theatre, in East Grinstead, on Saturday, May, 1758, will be represented (by particular desire, and for the benefit of Mrs. P.) the deep and affecting tragedy of

"THEODOSIUS, OR THE FORCE OF LOVE,"

with magnificent scenes, dresses, &c.

Varanes by Mr. P., who will strive, as far as possible, to support the character of the fiery Persian Prince, in which he was so much admired and applauded at Hastings, Arundel, Petworth, Midworth, Lewes, &c.

Theodosius by a young Gentleman from the University of Oxford, who never appeared on any Stage.

Athenais by Mrs. P. Though her present Condition will not permit her to wait on Gentlemen and Ladies out of the town with Tickets, she hopes, as on former Occasions, for their Liberality and Support.

Nothing in Italy can exceed the Altar, in the first scene of the Play; nevertheless should any of the Nobility or Gentry wish to see it ornamented with Flowers, the Bearer will bring away as many as they choose to favour him with.

As the coronation of Athenais, to be introduced in the fifth Act, contains a number of Personages, more than sufficient to fill all the dressing Rooms, &c., it is hoped no Gentlemen and Ladies will be offended being refused admission behind the Scenes.

N.B. The great yard Dog, that made so much noise on Thursday night, during the last Act of King Richard the Third, will be sent to a Neighbour's over the way; and on account of the prodigious demand for places, part of the Stable will be laid into the Boxes on one side, and the Granary be open for the same purpose on the other.

Vivat Rex.

Those who are curious in the matter of playbills in all languages will perhaps accept the annexed as a compromise, and as the nearest thing in a general way we can manage in the space at command. Those also who are good at riddles may like to try their skill on it :—

NOTICE.

SAturday 30 and on Sunday 31 of the corrent, in the Royal Theatre of St. Charles will be represented by the Italian Company the famous Holy Drama intitled

IL TRIONFO DI GIUDITTA

O SIA

LA MORTE D' OLOFERNE.

In the interval of the first to the second act it shall have a new and pompous Ball of the composition of John Baptista Gianini, who has by title :

IL SACRIFICIO D' ABRAMO

in which will enter all the excellent corp of Ball, who dance at present in the said Royal Theatre ; the spetacle will be finished with the second act and Ball analog to the same Drama, all with the nessessary decoration.

This is who is offered to the Respectable Publick of whom is waited all the proctetion and concurrence :

It will begin at 8 o'clok.

Na officina de Simão Thaddeo Ferreira. 1811. Com licenca.

We next append a bill of the far-famed Richardson's Theatre under date 1825 — one of those distributed during the Bartlemy Fair of that year. Hone describes the theatre thus : "The outside of this show was in height upwards of thirty feet, and occupied one hundred feet in width. The platform on the outside was very elevated ; the back of it was lined with green baize, and festooned with deeply-fringed crimson curtains, except at two places, where the money-takers sat, which were wide and roomy projections, fitted up like Gothic shrine-work, with columns and pinnacles. There were fifteen hundred variegated illumination-lamps disposed over various parts of the platform, some of them depending from the top in the shape of chandeliers and lustres, and others in wreaths and festoons. A band of ten performers in scarlet dresses, similar to those worn by beefeaters, continually played on clarionets, violins, trombones, and the long drum; while the performers paraded in their gayest 'properties' before the gazing multitude. Audiences rapidly ascended on each performance being over, and paying their money to the receivers in their Gothic seats, had tickets in return; which being taken at the doors, admitted them to descend into the 'theatre.'" The bill is as follows:—

*** Change of Performance each Day.

RICHARDSON'S
THEATRE.

This Day will be performed, an entire New Melo-Drama, called the
WANDERING
O U T L A W,
Or, the Hour of Retribution.

Gustavus, Elector of Saxony ...	*Mr. Wright.*
Orsina, Baron of Holstein	*Mr. Cooper.*
Ulric and Albert, Vassals to Orsina	*Messrs. Grove and Moore.*
St. Clair, the Wandering Outlaw	*Mr. Smith.*
Rinalda, the Accusing Spirit ...	*Mr. Darling.*

Monks, Vassals, Hunters, &c.

Rosabella, Wife to the Outlaw ... *Mrs. Smith.*

Nuns and Ladies.

The Piece concludes with the DEATH of ORSINA, and the Appearance of the
ACCUSING SPIRIT.

The Entertainments to conclude with a New Comic Harlequinade, with New Scenery, Tricks, Dresses, and Decorations, called
HARLEQUIN
FAUSTUS!
OR, THE
DEVIL WILL HAVE HIS OWN.
Luciferno, Mr. THOMAS.
Dæmon Amozor, afterwards Pantaloon, Mr. WILKINSON.—Dæmon

Ziokos, afterwards Clown, Mr. HAYWARD.—Violoncello Player, Mr. HARTEM.—Baker, Mr. THOMPSON.—Landlord, Mr. WILKINS.—Fisherman, Mr. RAE.—Dr. Faustus, afterwards Harlequin, Mr. SALTER.

Adelada, afterwards Columbine,
Miss WILMOT.
Attendant Dæmons, Sprites, Fairies, Ballad Singers, Flower Girls, &c. &c.

The Pantomime will finish with
A SPLENDID PANORAMA
Painted by the First Artists.

BOXES, *2s.* PIT, *1s.* GALLERY, *6d.*

Of show advertisements of a different kind, we have preserved one or two notable specimens. The first is of the time of William and Mary, and gives itself in two languages, though, unlike the opera bill given a page or so back, it keeps them separate:—

A Raritie in Nature.

Surpassing all Prodigies and strange Births that ever were seen, more admired by the Learned than any sort of Creature that ever was brought to England, *whose Body is of different Colours, part white, part brown and smooth, part Hairy like a Satyr, with admirable unusual growings out, that no reason can be given for. This Maid is about* 16 *years of age, of a comely Countenance, proportionable Body, hath an excellent head of Hair, speaketh good English, is Ingenious and Modest. Any particular Company may see her at any hour of the day in* Bell Savage Yard *on* Ludgate Hill, London.

God save the KING.

Vne Rareile en la Nature, viz.

Une Fille tres Admirable, elle est belle, agée de seize ans, son visage, Col, mameles, Bras & Mains, sont de Coleur Blanche, merques de beaucoup taches naturelles, les jambs, & pieds toutes de mesmes, le rest du Corps est de divers Coleurs, avec des Excrescenes fort estranges on n'a jamais veue une telle. L'on la voit en toutes heures du jour dans *Bell-savage-yard* on *Ludgate Hill, London.*

VIVAT REX.

It is noticeable that the showman uses the common Latin

form of "Vivat Rex" under his French, and adopts an English equivalent in his other column. About twenty years ago a similar creature was shown in London, and those who had her in charge vamped up most marvellous stories to account for the *lusus naturæ*, both decency and probability being outraged in the attempt to excite a "sensation." The next bill is, though of the show series, of a totally different character, and refers to one of the exhibitions of the famous Figg, the swordsman and pugilist. It is now the fashion to decry such adventures as that advertised; but it is hard to believe that both Figg and Sutton were not far more respectable characters than many who practise the licensed and misnamed sport of modern times. For ourselves, we could have looked at such free agents as the rapier and backsword men, or even the more degraded pugilists, doing their best and their worst on each other, rather than sit out an aristocratic pigeon match, assist at a battue, or be party to the coursing of trapped hares and rabbits.

G. R.

At Mr. FIGG's New Amphitheatre.

Joyning to his House, the Sign of the City of *Oxford*, in *Oxford Road, Marybone Fields*, on *Wednesday* next, being the *8th* of *June*, 1726. *Will be Perform'd a Tryal of Skill by the following* Masters.

WHereas I *EDWARD SUTTON*, Pipemaker from *Gravesend*, and *Kentish* Professor of the Noble Science of Defence, having, under a Sleeveless Pretence been deny'd a Combat by and with the Extoll'd Mr. FIGG; which I take to be occasioned through fear of his having that Glory Eclipsed by me, wherewith the Eyes of all Spectators have been so much dazzled: Therefore, to make appear, that the Great Applause which has so much puff'd up this Hero, has proceeded

only from his Foyling such who are not worthy the name of Swordsmen, as also that he may be without any farther Excuse; I do hereby dare the said Mr. FIGG to meet as above, and dispute with me the Superiority of Judgment in the Sword (which will best appear by Cuts, *&c.*) at all the Weapons he is or shall be then Capable of Performing on the Stage.

I *JAMES FIGG, Oxonian* Professor of the said Science, will not fail giving this daring *Kentish* Champion an Opportunity to make good his Allegations; when, it is to be hop'd, if he finds himself Foyl'd he will then change his Tone, and not think himself one of the Number who are not worthy the Name of Swordsmen, as he is pleased to signifie by his Expression: However, as the most significant Way of deciding these Controversies is by Action, I shall defer what I have farther to Act till the Time above specified; when I shall take care not to deviate from my usual Custom, in making all such Bravadoes sensible of their Error, as also in giving all Spectators intire Satisfaction.

N.B. *The Doors will be open'd at Four, and the Masters mount between Six and Seven exactly.* *VIVAT REX.*

Sutton does not seem to have made much but hard knocks by his desire to uphold the honour of pipemakers and Kentish men, for Figg is generally characterised as retiring undefeated, and Captain Godfrey, the great amateur of his day, makes reference to the defeat of Sutton in his "Treatise upon the Useful Science of Defence" (1747). Speaking of the Oxford professor, he says: "Fig was the atlas of the sword, and may he remain the gladiating statue! In him, strength, resolution, and unparalleled judgment conspired to form a matchless master. There was a majesty shone in his countenance, and blazed in all his actions, beyond all I ever saw. His right leg bold and firm, and his left, which could hardly ever be disturbed, gave him the surprising advantage already proved, and struck his adversary with despair and panic. He had that peculiar way of stepping in I spoke of in a parry; he knew his arm and its just time of moving, put a firm faith in that, and never let his adversary escape his parry. He was just as much a greater master than any other I ever saw, as he was a greater judge of time and measure." Of Sutton the enthusiastic captain tells us that "he was a resolute, pushing, awkward swordsman; but by his busy intruding arm, and scrambling legs, there were few judgments but what were disordered and disconcerted. Fig managed him the best of any by his charming distinction of time and measure, in which he far excelled all, and sufficiently proved these two be the sword's true foundation." Figg was also a great bruiser, and was regarded as the champion of the boxers as well as the master of the swordsmen. He was a genial good-tempered fellow, and was the boon companion of many eminent authors and artists of his time.

So much for show and play bills, and the celebrities to whom they have introduced us. We will now turn to handbill and poster advertisements of various descriptions. Tickets and bills containing the information that apartments were to be let were set up over doors at least as early as 1665. In the "Pillulæ Pestilentialis" of the Rev. Richard Hingston, preacher, of St James's, Clerkenwell, there is the following in reference to the Plague and the practice just mentioned:—

No Papers then o'er our Doors were set
With "Chambers ready furnished to be Let,"
But a sad "Lord have Mercy upon us" and
A bloody Cross as fatal Marks did stand.

At the end of a pamphlet, printed in 1673, entitled "An Essay to revive the Ancient Education of Gentlewomen, in Religion, Manners, and Tongues," there is a postscript, containing an advertisement of a boarding school at Tottenham High Cross. This establishment was under the management of Mrs Makin, who had been tutoress to the Princess Elizabeth, daughter of Charles I., and who put forth part of her prospectus in the following manner:—

Here by the blessing of God, Gentlewomen may be instructed in the principles of Religion, and in all manner of sober and virtuous Education: more especially in all Things ordinarily taught in Schools for the other Sex; as in

Works of all sorts,
Dancing,
Music,
Singing,
Writing,
Keeping Accounts.

Half the Time is to be spent in these Things, and the other half to be employed in gaining the Latin and French Tongues, and those that please may learn Greek and Hebrew, the Italian and Spanish; in all which this Gentlewoman hath a competent knowledge.

Gentlewomen of eight or nine Years old, that can read well, may be instructed in a Year or two (according to their Parts) in the Latin and French Tongues, by plain and short Rules accommodated to the English Tongue.

Those that will bestow a longer Time may learn the other Languages before mentioned, if they please.

Repositories also for Visibles shall be prepared, by which from beholding the things, Gentlewomen may learn the Names, Natures, Values, and Uses of Herbs, Shrubs, Trees, mineral Juices, Metals and Stones.

Those that please may learn Limning, Preserving, Pastry, and Cookery, etc.

The rate shall be certain £20 per Annum; but if a competent improvement be made in the Tongues, and the other Things before mentioned, as shall be agreed upon them, something more will be expected. But the Parents shall judge what shall be deserved by the Undertaker.

Sterne, who knew as much about struggles and adversity as most people, used to tell this story about his young days: "I happened to be acquainted with a young man from Yorkshire, who rented a window in one of the paved alleys near Cornhill, for the sale of stationery. I hired one of the panes of glass from my friend, and stuck up the following advertisement with wafers:—

Epigrams, Anagrams, Paragrams, Chronograms, Monograms, Epitaphs, Epithalamiums, Prologues, Epilogues, Madrigals, Interludes, Advertisements, Letters, Petitions, Memorials, on every occasion, Essays on every subject, Pamphlets for and against Ministers, Sermons upon any Text or for any Sect, to be written here, on reasonable terms, by

A. B. Philologer.

"The uncommonness of the titles occasioned numerous applications, and at night I used privately to glide into the office to digest the notes or heads of the day, and receive the earnest which was directed always to be left with the memorandums, the writing to be paid for on delivery, according to the subject." Yorick speedily became disgusted with this employment, however, and as soon as he possibly could retired from it.

Another of the triumphs which have unfortunately not come down to the present generation, and which many will consider to be hardly compensated for by gas, steam, and electricity, the postal service and the police system, is that of Mr Nunn, whose bill, published to the world in the latter portion of the eighteenth century, runs thus :—

Breeches Making improved by Geometry.

Thomas Nunn, Breeches-Maker, No. 29, Wigmore Street, Cavendish Square, has invented a System on a mathematical Principle, by which Difficulties are solved, and Errors corrected; its usefulness for Ease and Neatness in fitting is incomparable, and is the only perfect Rule for that Work ever discovered. Several hundreds (Noblemen, Gentlemen, and Others) who have had Proof of its Utility, allow it to excel all they ever made Trial of.

N.B. An approved Method is adopted for keeping them clean without discommoding by Dust.

In some future day, when personal comfort again becomes one of the fine arts, one of the chief tests for a wranglership may be the making of mathematical breeches. If the age is very material, perhaps the approved method of cleaning them may stand in stead of classics, which are already going much out of fashion. Our next specimen comes from the Emerald Isle, and though short is well marked with both of the most prominent characteristics of the natives. It was given away and posted up in various parts of Dublin at the end of July 1781 :—

This is to certify that I, Daniel O'Flannaghan, am not the Person that was tarred and feathered by the Liberty Mob, on Tuesday last; and I am ready to give 20 Guineas to any one that will lay me 50, that I am the other Man who goes by my Name.

Witness my Hand, this 30th July. DANIEL O'FLANNAGHAN.

A man who can afford to lay seventy guineas to thirty that he is himself, and nobody else, deserves credit for his boldness, if not for his ingenuity. Another bill from Ireland, of a few years later on, next claims our attention. It refers to a house to let in Coleraine, and is a specimen of quite another kind of Hibernian humour:—

To be Let

To an OPPIDAN, a RURICOLIST, or a COSMOPOLITAN, and may be entered upon immediately.

The House in STONE ROW, lately possessed by Capt. Siree. To avoid verbosity the proprietor with compendiosity will give a perfunctory description of the premises, in the compagination of which he has sedulously studied the convenience of the occupant—it is free from opacity, tenebrosity, fumidity, and injucundity, and no building can have greater pellucidity or translucency—in short, its diaphaneity even in the crepuscule makes it like a pharos, and without laud, for its agglutimation and amenity, it is a most delectable commorance; and whoever lives in it will find that the neighbours have none of the truculence, the immanity, the torvity, the spinosity, the putidness, the pügnacity, nor the fugacity observable in other parts of the town; their propinquity and consanguinity occasions jucundity and pudicity—from which, and the redolence of the place (even in the dog days) they are remarkable for longevity. For terms and particulars apply to JAMES HUTCHISON, opposite the MARKET HOUSE.

Coleraine, 30th September, 1790.

We commend this to that rather numerous class of people who like words with plenty of sound, and regard sense as quite a secondary consideration. Dogberry would have been delighted with it, and the writer could have commanded his own price as a contributor to certain newspapers, or as a sporting tipster. We have already given our readers an advertising tombstone, which was a swindle, inasmuch as it was placed up to the memory of a person who never existed. We now give another, which is really what it pretends to be—an improvement of the opportunity to combine business, not with pleasure, but with mourning. It stood, we are told, in a burial-ground belonging to one of our old ivy-clad churches in the North, and was an elegantly-carved memorial stone, the inscription being:—

Sacred to the Memory
of
JOHN ROBERTS,
Stonemason and Tombcutter,
Who died on Saturday, October the 8th, 1800.
N. B.—The business carried on by the Widow at No. 1, Freshfield place.

Perhaps her being in the "tombstone line" may be an excuse for the widow Roberts. We don't suppose she needed one, however, for any one who would do what she did would be quite callous as to the world's opinions. Of the two we much prefer the Frenchman who erected the stone to an entirely supposititious person, to the widow who

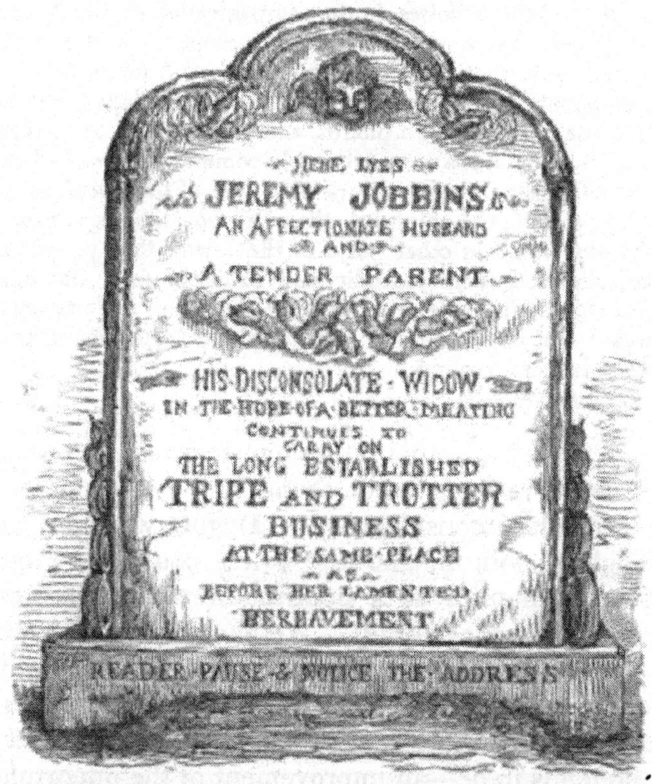
HERE LYES
JEREMY JOBBINS
AN AFFECTIONATE HUSBAND
AND
A TENDER PARENT
HIS DISCONSOLATE WIDOW
IN THE HOPE OF A BETTER MEATING
CONTINUES TO
CARRY ON
THE LONG ESTABLISHED
TRIPE AND TROTTER
BUSINESS
AT THE SAME PLACE
AS
BEFORE HER LAMENTED
BEREAVEMENT
READER PAUSE & NOTICE THE ADDRESS

traded on her husband's grave. This reminds us that we have received, among many communications, one containing the above sketch of an advertising tombstone, which the writer, who dates from a well-known town in the north, Gateshead, states positively stood in a neighbouring churchyard within his recollection. The address, he says, was on the footstone. We give the illustration "without prejudice." Do tripe and trotters after all produce a prosaic condition of the human mind suggested by this tombstone, or would the relict of Jeremy have done as she did had her wares been of a different kind? In the interests of the edibles referred to, for which we must confess a weakness, we trust she would. But who shall say?

At the time of the marriage of George the Third's eldest daughter to the Duke of Wurtemburg, a curious little handbill was given away about London. It was printed on both sides, and looked like a tract. Its contents were to the following effect:—

FRAGMENT *of a* CHAPTER *concerning the curious* MANGLE of BEETHAM *appointed to be read by all the* LADIES *and* LAUNDRESSES *of the land of Albion.*

By His Majesty's special command.

CHAP. I.

1 *Beetham's fame and diligence.* 3 *his marvellous mill.* 6 *he constructs a mangle which surprises the World.* 8 *The Princesses visit his museum and praise the curious Machinery.* 16 *He is mimiced by others.* 18 *The King grants his royal patent to the Artist.* 22 *Beetham is recompensed by the nobles and the people.*

NOW it came to pass, even towards the close of the eighteenth century, that there lived in the great city which is called London a certain man of the name of Beetham who had many curious inventions.

2 The same mechanic while the world waged war against *Albion* cultivated with all diligence the arts of Peace in the ways of wisdom.

3 When therefore he saw that his washing mill pleased the people and was daily employed by all throughout the regions of Britain and her colonies.

4 Behold he also constructed another machine more marvellous than the first which is called a *Mangle* even to this day. 5 Neither adhered

he to the old gothic plan of his predecessors but formed it new and surprising in simplicity so that a little maiden could set it in motion.

6 And it came to pass when a great company of ladies and laundresses beheld the infant turn the wheel with wonderful ease and moreover saw the wheel move backwards as well as the way of the wheel whose revolution was always the same and also saw it move as by self instinct.

7 That they cried aloud with one voice saying, great and marvellous is the *Mangle* of *Beetham*.

8 And in process of time, the princesses and the nobles accompanied a certain great prince who came from a far country to carry away a royal beauty, even the eldest daughter of the King.

9 And behold as they passed on their way to view the wonders of the great temple of *Paul*, one of the damsels lifted up her azure eyes and beheld the Museum of *Beetham* fronting the temple of *Dunstan*.

10 At that instant the child was turning the wonderful *Mill* which laved the fine linen clean and white in the twinkling of an eye;

11 Also another child by its feeble arm was moving the newly invented *Mangle*.

12 And lo, one of the nobles cried, wherefore should we pass on further into the city, let us step aside and see this miracle.

13 Now it came to pass that the company alighted from their gilded chariots and went into the *Museum*, and marvelled much at the curious machines.

14 And when they saw the *Mill* and the *Mangle*, the *Wringer* also, and the machine for the *Churning* of *Milk*, which even *Solomon* with all his wisdom never invented.

15 They all with one accord commanded the master of the Museum to prepare for the *Princess* one of each of these curious machines; to the end she might spread the fame of the inventor all over the land, in which she was soon to be a sojourner.

16 ¶ Now—the *Mimic Machinists* of those days by their enchantments strove to surpass *Beetham*, but failed by falling into the great *chaos* of complication:

17 So that, like the builders of Babel they were confounded; crying aloud, surely all machination against Beetham must fail, neither can we imitate the simplicity of his Mangle.

18 And word was carried to the King in those days, even concerning the new invention of the artist of London.

19 Which prevailed upon him when he also heard of the utility of the *Mangle* in tender kindness to all the laundresses of the land to cause his Royal signet to be set on a certain parchment called a patent.

20 So that until twice seven seasons should pass no man should imitate the machine but by the consent of *Beetham* the Proprietor thereof.

21 And when the King had so done, lo there was prepared many machines of various sizes in order that the high and the low, the rich and the poor, might use the same throughout the land, but Beetham was the vender of them all.

22 And for those which the Princess and the Lords and Ladies of the Land did cause to be sent to them which were made of Oak whose duration shall far exceed the years of the generations of the sons of men and which were for smoothing all the linen of the Households of the mighty nobles, Beetham received certain pieces of money which being counted in the coin of Albion amounted to Ten guineas.

23 And for such as were made of the wood called Beech he received nine pieces of gold and for others eight pieces of the like coin, but for less than eight pieces Beetham sent not the *Mangle* forth among the inhabitants of the land.

24 And behold all the people rejoiced extremely and the fame of the Mangle was spread abroad among all the isles of Britain even to the remotest part thereof; and the ships of the sea were laden with the same machines to the Colonies abroad, and in all those parts of the Earth where Economy is an object, where Convenience is desirable, and where Cleanliness is esteemed next to Godliness.

Mr. BEETHAM's

NEW PATENT PORTABLE WASHING MILL

IS so universally used and Economical, that it deserves the serious attention of the Public in general.

1 It renders the linen whiter and cleaner than it can be made by any other method.

2 It will wash more in one hour than ten women can in the same time.

3 It is so saving, that for Five Shillings it will wash as much as will cost One Guinea in the common mode.

4 The price of the Mill is very soon cleared by what it saves in soap, coals, manual labour and the preservation of the linen.

This invaluable invention may be seen from Eleven until Two every day.

A Mill large enough to wash 8 shirts 4l. 4s. 14, 4l. 14s. 6d. 18, 5l. 5s. 24, 6l. 6s.

One to first and second, 10l. 10s. Wringer, 1l. 1s.

This Beetham was the grandfather, on her mother's side, of Miss Reed, the celebrated old lady of Stamford Street, whose houses were for many years in a notoriously dismantled and dilapidated condition, and who not very long since left a hundred thousand pounds to the Brompton Hospital. Her mother was a pupil of Opie's, and before she married Mr Reed, a solicitor, some of her pictures were exhibited as those of her master. She late in life became eccentric, but not to such an extent as her daughter, whose name was at one time almost a household word. Another tradesman of the City, who was well known for his devotion to the art of advertising, early in the present century put forth this, which is rather magniloquent, considering the subject which forms its basis:—

MAY THE WINGS OF EXTRAVAGANCE *be clipped by the Scissars of Economy*—was the constant toast of a person who knew very well the value of a sixpence. To all good economists would Romanis wish to be recommended, though but a bad practitioner himself, (he is a little like the clergy—"Don't do as I do, but as I tell you to do.") When you want real good Stockings at a low price, come to the Sign of the Regent, 33 in Cheapside—there you have them in perfection, and I am certain sixpence in a pair is worth saving; and any one that is possest of the least spark of parsimony will give their assent. Frugality is certainly a good thing—it enables a people to pay taxes—to pay their armies—to thrash the French—to make peace on good terms—to extend commerce—to make people live long and comfortable:

FOR STOCKINGS

Romanis against the whole World, at his Mart, 33 Cheapside.

From small beginnings great events arise—only see what benefit to the nation as well as to private individuals accrued from the purchase of cheap stockings. Romanis has never been mentioned in conjunction with Wellington, yet he seems to have had a good deal to do towards building up the victory of Waterloo, and ought to have been remembered, say as much as Blucher, who has been immortalised in the way of boots while the stocking-seller has been clean forgotten.

Another curious advertiser was William Hall of Lynn, who flourished early in the present century. According to Hone, Hall was a celebrated antiquarian bookseller, and received the alias of Will Will-be-So. He was also an auctioneer, and on the market-day he would knock down his lots in great style, and with many whimsical remarks. He had a craze for verse, and in such as follows all his advertisements were written :—

LYNN, 19*th* SEPTEMBER, 1810.

First Tuesday in the next October,
Now do not doubt but we'll be sober!
If Providence permits us action,
You may depend upon
AN AUCTION,
At the stall
That's occupied by WILLIAM HALL.

To enumerate a task would be—
The best way is to come and see;
But not to come too vague an errand,
We'll give a sketch which we will warrant.
About *one hundred books*, in due lots,
And pretty near the same in *shoe-lasts;*
Coats, *waistcoats*, *breeches*, shining *buttons*,
Perhaps ten thousand *leather cuttings*,
Sold at per pound—your lot but ask it,
Shall be weighed to you in a basket;
Some lot of *tools* to make a try on,
About one hundred-weight of *iron;*
Scales, *earthenware*, *arm-chairs*, a *tea-urn*,
Tea-chests, a *herring-tub*, and so on;
With various more that's our intention,
Which are too tedious here to mention.
N.B.—To undeceive, 'fore you come nigher,
The duty charged upon the buyer;
And, should we find we're not perplext,
We'll keep it up the Tuesday next.

We have two more specimens of the English peculiar to Continentalists, the first being of about the same period as Hall's verse. It is an exact copy of a card circulated by the landlord of an hotel at Ghent :—

Mr. Dewitt, in the Golden Apple, out of the Bruges Gate at Ghent, has the honour to prevent the Persons who would come at his house, that they shall find there always good and spacious Lodgings, a Table served at their taste, Wine of any quality, etc. Besides he hires Horses and Chaises, which shall be of a great conveniency for the Travellers; the Bark of Bruges depart and arrives every day before his door. He dares flatter himself, that they shall be satisfied, as well with the cheapness of the price, as with the cares such an establishment requires.

This and the next, which was given to the world in 1822, may cause English people who fancy they have the most correct knowledge of French, as well as the true Parisian accent, to be a little cautious in their belief, for there is no doubt that the authors of both notices were very strong on their powers of "spiking the English," as many French announcements have it:—

M. MARLOTEAU et Cie.

Manufacturers from Paris,

37, MONTMORENCY-STREET,

To London 14 *Broad Street, Oxford street.*

Acquaint the Trade in general, that they have just established in LONDON.

A Warhouse for FRENCH FLOWERS, for each Season, feathar from hat ladies of their own Manufacture elegant fans of the NEWEST TASTE.

And of Manufactures of PARIS, complette sets ornaments for balls, snuff boxes scale gold and silver, boxes toilette, ribbons and embroidered, hat et cap, from Ladies of the newest Taste, China, all sorts, etc.

He commit generally the articles from Paris, Manufacturers.

And send in all BRITISH CITY.

Attandance from Nine o'Clock in the Morning till five in the Afternoon.

Before and during the year 1825 a man used to stand at the corner of Fleet Market, and deliver handbills in the interest of a society which had for its object the genteel and comfortable interment of its members. One of these advertisements has been preserved, and a copy of it is appended. Its commencement is curious, and must at times have somewhat disconcerted incautious readers, who in the midst of their business cares or pleasure pursuits suddenly had the notice of death thrust upon them. Sir Thomas Browne, who professed to know all about mortality, says that "man is a noble animal, splendid in ashes, and pompous in the grave." Whoever drew up the handbill was certainly aware of the craving which exists in many minds, especially among the lower orders, for a good funeral, and made abundant provision for it. Really a *tædium vitæ* almost creeps over one upon reading it. Who would not be willing to die, in death to be attended as is promised? Two rows all round of close-drove best black japanned nails feelingly invite and almost irresistibly persuade us to come and be screwed down. What aching head can resist the temptation to repose presented by the handsome crape shroud, the cap, and pillow? What sting is there in death which handles with wrought gripes are not calculated to pluck away? What victory in the grave which the drops and the velvet pall do not render at least extremely disputable? And, above all, a pretty emblematic plate, with the angel above and the flower beneath, is utterly irresistible. But we in our rhapsody had forgotten to copy the bill :—

BURIAL SOCIETY.

A favourable opportunity now offers to any person, of either sex, who would wish to be buried in a genteel manner, by paying one shilling entrance, and twopence per week for the benefit of the stock. Members to be free in six months. The money to be paid at Mr. Middleton's at the sign of "the First and Last," Stonecutter Street, Fleet Market. The deceased to be furnished as follows: a strong elm coffin, covered with superfine black, and finished with two rows, all round, close drove, best black japanned nails, and adorned with ornamental drops, a handsome plate of inscription, angel above, and flower beneath, and four pair of handsome handles, with wrought gripes; the coffin to be well pitched, lined, and ruffled with fine crape; a handsome crape shroud, cap, and pillow. For use, a handsome velvet pall, three gentlemen's cloaks, three crape hatbands, three hoods and scarfs, and six pair of gloves; two porters equipped to attend the funeral, a man to attend the same with band and gloves; also the burial fees paid, if not exceeding one guinea.

The notice further informed the public, that though the society had only been established a very few years, upwards of eleven hundred persons had put down their names. It is worthy of remark that so many people of the industrious classes should have clubbed their twopences to avoid what they considered the disgrace of a parish funeral, and should doubtless have rejoiced when their six months had expired, and they stood face to face with the handsome velvet pall and etceteras. The very poor are to this day very particular about their funerals, and many a savoury morsel is the living body deprived of that the lifeless one may go comfortably to its last home. A labouring man's greatest pride often is that he gave wife, parent, or child a good funeral; and this feeling is perfectly independent of the wake peculiarities and festivities that obtain among a certain section of the lower orders. Readers must be warned against an idea which they may be apt to form about the place whence these proposals issued. From the sign of the "First and Last," they might conclude that Mr Middleton was a publican who, in assembling a club of the above description at his house, had a view to his own interest altogether foreign to the purpose for which the society was instituted. Mr Middleton was no publican, though he hung out a sign, but an honest undertaker, who also dealt in wicker ware, and who, by the exhibition of both cradle and coffin as a device, attracted attention to which the motto "First and Last" contributed in no small measure.

The following humorous handbill was about 1825 given away by a publican in the neighbourhood of the Strand. It is certainly a gem in its way, and shows an originality which was more likely to have been possessed by one of the needy and seedy customers hanging about in the vicinity of the theatres fifty years back, than by the well-fed, well-clad, and probably bumptious "bung," who ought to have made the writer free of his various entertainments during the long "run" they doubtless obtained if the performance was in any way as good as the programme:—

Licensed by Act of Parliament.
And under the immediate Patronage of the Public.
THEATRE OF EPICUREAN VARIETY
at the
KING OF PRUSSIA
Wych Street.

W. Trampton has the honor of informing his friends and the public that his compact comfortable snug and *cosey* little Theatre is now open for the Winter Season; where from the well known excellence of the company engaged he trusts to meet with a share of that encouragement it will be his endeavour to merit and his pride to acknowledge.

A peculiar advantage attending this Theatre will no doubt be justly appreciated by the public, namely that tickets of admission may be had for the separate branches of the entertainment, the price of which together with the hours of performance are specified in the following bill:—

During the Week the following Entertainments will be presented.
A favourite Burletta in One Act, called
SOMETHING LIKE BREAKFAST.
The chief characters by the celebrated foreign performers,
Signiors TEA COFFEE SUGAR etc.
Price of admission 10d. Hours from 8 to 10 A.M.

After which, a Bagatelle, or Interlude in One Act, called
IF YOU LIKE IT, LUNCH IT.
The characters by
Messrs CHESCHIRE GLOUCESTER CRUST
KIDNEY RAREBIT etc.
And other well known Performers who will be found ever ready at the call of the Public.

At the Hour of three P.M. a Grand Melodrama in two Acts called
HOW SHALL I DINE?
The chief Character on Monday by the celebrated old Roscius of the Epicurean Stage,
ROAST BEEF.

The other Characters by the celebrated *Murphys* etc., assisted by the *Little Pickles* etc.

Guards, Messrs *Cayenne* etc. Scenery by Messrs *Diaper and Assistants.* Dresses by *Mrs Cook.*

Music (a *joint* composition of *Handel* and *Stick*) by Messrs *Knife and Fork.*

Price of Admission One Shilling.

The principal Character in the above-mentioned Piece will be sustained by different Actors of celebrity during the week, viz.

Tuesday *Boiled Mutton*, Wednesday *Roast or Boiled Pork*, Thursday *Veal and Bacon*, Friday *Boiled Beef*, Saturday *Roast Mutton.*

At Eight P.M. every evening the well known eccentric Pat Murphy (in company with his friend Pat Butter) will have the honour of making his appearance in his much admired hot-jacket of brown.

Theatre closed every Evening at half past Eleven.

N.B. A stout and venerable white-headed Porter from the office of Messrs Goodwyn & Co. will attend the Theatre for the purpose of keeping good order during the performance.

The whole got up under the immediate care of
Stage Manager *W. Trampton.*

Between forty and fifty years ago there was an amusing contest going on between two tradespeople in the City: both were hairdressers, and lived opposite each other. Seeing that the one throve by selling pomade made of bear's grease, the other, knowing that it was just as good and more profitable to sell any other material in pots with "bear's grease" on the label, started in opposition, using similar pots to those sold by his opponent, filled with an inexpensive unguent. The first dealer, who was known to keep bears in his cellar, and who had himself taken up once a week before the sitting alderman as a nuisance, by way of advertisement, killed a bear upon this, and hung him up whole in full sight in his shop. He also wrote in the window, "A fresh bear killed this day!" The other, who had but one bear in all the world, which he privately led out of his house after dark every night, and brought him back in the morning (to seem like a new supply going on), continued his sale, and announced in his window, "Our fresh bear will be killed to-morrow." The original vendor then, determined to cut off his rival's last shift, kept his actual bears, defunct, with the skins only half off, like calves at a butcher's, hanging up always at his door, proclaimed that "all bear's grease sold in pots was a vile imposture," and desired his customers to walk in "and see theirs with their own eyes, cut and weighed from the animal." This seemed conclusive for two days; but on the third, the cunning opposition was again to the fore, with a placard "founded on the opinion of nine doctors of physic," which stated that bear's grease "obtained from the animal in a tamed or domesticated state, will not make anybody's hair grow at all." In consequence of which, he went on to say, "he has formed an establishment in Russia (where all the best bears come from), for catching them wild, cutting the fat off immediately, and potting it down for London consumption." And the rogue actually ruined the business of his antagonist, without going to the expense of killing a single bear, by writing all over his house, "Licensed by the Imperial Government—Here, and at Archangel."

George Robins, the auctioneer, was a profound believer in the value of advertisements, and exercised all his ingenuity and ability, both of which were considerable, to devise fresh schemes for attracting public notice. His powers of producing a good bill were remarkable, as was also his facility of description. Robins's style has been so often commented upon, and his work so often copied and burlesqued, that it is hardly worth while our touching upon either him or his bills. As, however, such a book as this would be hardly complete without a reference to the puffing genius of modern days, we select a portion—and only a portion, mind—of his description of the Colosseum in Regent's Park, one of the greatest failures of speculative enthusiasts known, which, despite Robins and his panegyric, and despite the strenuous efforts which have been made to cultivate an unwilling populace into believing in it as a place of amusement, is now being demolished to make way for a set of dwelling-houses planned upon the site on which was reared the building described by the poetically-fancied auctioneer as, among many other things, a

CYCLOPÆAN STRUCTURE,

WHERE DESCRIPTION FAILS TO PORTRAY

"Its eloquent proportions,
Its mighty graduations,"

WHICH, EVEN WHEN SEEN,

"Thou seest not all, but piecemeal thou must break,
To separate contemplation, the great whole."

THE EXQUISITE PROPORTIONS OF

THE CLASSIC PORTICO,

One of the finest specimens of

THE GREEK DORIC,

TOGETHER WITH

"The Dome, the vast and wondrous Dome,"

WHICH PROUDLY

"——————————Vies
In air with earth's chief structures,"

Win our admiration, while there is nothing of ancient or modern days that can compete with it either in

Classic Elegance, Grandeur of Effect, or Beauty of Proportion;

And it must remain to future ages a monument of the genius of the architect, as an

"Outshining and o'erwhelming edifice."

The stupendous purpose for which the COLOSSEUM was erected is too well known to need description.

THOUSANDS AND TENS OF THOUSANDS

Having been attracted by

THE PICTURE OF LONDON,

Which covers the interior of the external wall,

THE MODERN BABYLON,

Which occupied the artist upwards of four years in delineating its endless details from the dome of St. Paul's at the quiet hour of morning, when the buildings of this great metropolis were unobscured by smoke, and the early mists dispersed by the sun's vicegerent power,—this picture now

"Stands within the Colosseum's wall."

THE BUILDING CONTAINS

A GRAND SALOON OF ART,

Surrounding the interior of the whole edifice,

"All musical in its immensities,
Rich marbles—richer painting—"

Stored with productions of modern artists, models of ingenious machinery, and a variety of scientific experiments to attract the spectator, and is well calculated for any and every exhibition of an extensive nature.

"Enter—————thy mind,
Expanded by the genius of the spot,
Has grown colossal!"

On the outside of the main building are magnificent Conservatories filled with every kind of exotic, and decorated with

FOUNTAINS AND JETS D'EAU,

Equalling in beauty the most celebrated

Fountains of Versailles & St. Ildefonso.

Two Thousand Eight Hundred Persons

HAVE PAID FOR ADMISSION DURING ONE DAY

To view this extraordinary and incomparable work of art.

THE COLOSSEUM'S GRANDEUR

ENCOMPASSED THEM WITH WONDER—A SUBLIME CREATIVE SPIRIT IN THIS WORLD OF MIRACLES.

It may be well to observe that continued success will be rendered certain by a change of scene, and the purchaser has only to call to his aid

THE MAGIC INFLUENCE OF STANFIELD'S PENCIL

To create a new sensation, and enlist thousands to partake of the refreshing delight created by his versatile and unrivalled talent. Indeed, it will not be requisite to tax ingenuity very greatly to think of an

infinite variety of ways by which a large fortune may be made. It has for years past produced from

Three to Five Thousand Pounds a Year,

And this without any artificial aid, or so much of industry and tact as this wonderful building seems especially to have invited.

Robins's eloquence very often led him to describe things as they were not, and now and again he had to recant and make amends. He is generally credited with having referred to a gallows which stood upon part of an estate, as a unique and elegant hanging wood, and thereby obtaining a considerably larger sum for the property than it was in any way worth. Among Robins's many eccentricities this must not be reckoned, as the hanging-wood episode, though true in itself, belongs to an earlier time, the trick having been played during the last century. When a man gets credit for the possession of any peculiarity, every story that can be raked up of a suitable kind takes him for its originator or leading spirit, and innumerable tales were at one time current with regard to the great auctioneer, of which he was perfectly innocent. So it is in other things. What did Foote, Garrick, Sheridan, Hook, Sydney Smith, Hood, Barham, Rogers, Jerrold, and numerous other of our celebrated wits, know of a quarter the sayings and doings that have been ascribed to them? Little indeed, we fancy. But there are some things which Robins did say and do which have not been recorded. In answer to a lady who remarked to him that in his graphic descriptions he must have used up the entire dictionary, Robins said, "Madam, I'll give five pounds to any charitable society you like to name if you can find me a word I have not used." Mrs Macauley might have taken him at his word, and would doubtless have won the money, but the lady we speak of declined the contest. There is not much in this, except as showing to what an extent his powers of description led him. Having given one of his sayings, we will conclude with an item from his doings, a description of the villa and garden of W.

Harrison, Esq., Q.C. We trust we shall cause no one to be discontented with his or her present abode by giving this description—rather do we hope that one of the new race of picturesque reporters may be tempted by it to study under Robins, and thereby improve his condition :—

In attempting an adequate representation of what has been aptly termed

A LITTLE HEAVEN UPON EARTH,

Much of the difficulty Mr. ROBINS feared to encounter he is happily relieved from by the extraordinary renown which the late worthy possessor has imparted to this incomparable retreat.

"Thus far we sail before the wind,"

Exclaims the individual who is flattered by having been selected for this interesting Sale, but fear and trembling now succeeds in encountering the Herculean task of pourtraying the countless beauties that are congregated

Within the Grounds of this Elysium.

It would puzzle much higher talent than he can bring, adequately to describe this Landscape, but it must be attempted; and Mr. ROBINS prays that the reader will bear with him a little longer, under the assurance that condensity shall be his motto, at the same time avoiding that cloudy region entered by the witty Flaccus, who,

"Aiming at brevity became obscure."

THE GROUNDS

Extend to near Five Acres, and the extraordinary tact that must have presided in arriving at this scene of perfection, must be viewed, it must be seen to feel and appreciate what seems to partake of Fairy Land. Mr. LOUDON has indulged the public with Twenty-two Vignettes and Plans to hand down to posterity a faint idea of

The Velvet Ornamental Lawn,

On which is congregated the most rare and extensive assemblage of Plants and Flowering Shrubs that is to be met with in England. From all

THE FLORICULTURAL EXHIBITIONS

The treasures were quite sure to find a home at Cheshunt, indeed the late Proprietor's judgment in the Cultivation of Rare and Valuable Plants was quite unique, and his Gardener, Mr. PRATT, a prototype of his employer. It would fatigue the reader to give in detail the host of Rare Plants that adorn these Grounds, the value of which is past belief—more than a Thousand Pounds have been consumed alone in rare Exotics; the masses of Growing Plants, the French Garden, and all this (by the way) is relieved and varied by

THE ORNAMENTAL WATERS AND ISLAND,

Varying and necessarily improving this beauteous scene. Perpetual breaks and peeps are contrived, by different views, to look on the Waters, in which Thousands of Gold and Silver Fish enjoy their "sportive gambols." Correct judgment is made very manifest in the disposition of these Grounds, by avoiding the whole being seen, except by slow degrees. Then there are dispersedly dotted about throughout the Lawn—The Rustic Alcoves, the Chinese Temple, Grottos, and covered Seats, Orchidaceus and Fern Houses, and Aviary.

A Mount is devoted to the Show of Aloes during the Summer, rendering the *ensemble* most captivating; a Hermit's Cave, covered with Ivy; a Gravel Walk, belted by American Borders of Rare Plants; a beautiful Grotto, adorned by a fine piece of Statuary; a Rustic Summer House, fitted up in the Indian style; a smaller Grotto, fitted in Stone, of grotesque and rustic masonry; in fact, everything that sagacity or the human mind could well conceive, seems to have been achieved here, to render this spot

A PERFECT PARADISE.

From the Terrace Walk that environs it, a perpetually interesting scene of the Lawn, in varied forms of beauty (the Church Steeple peeping out in the distance, to vary the scene) is disclosed, and is so ingeniously and cleverly managed that the deciduous Trees, during the Summer, afford constant protection from the heat of the sun, and during the Winter (being then naked) admit the genial warmth of the sun to keep dry the Gravel Walks.

From the canny North Country we get two bills, the first of which is likely to shake the belief of those who imagine that swindlers and impostors have little chance in the border counties, where the babies are said to be born with their wisdom teeth ready cut, and to "know their way about" before they are out of leading-strings. J. A. was fully possessed of his share of artfulness, and though his name has not come down to us, it being just the same in the bill as here printed, his initials were well known some years back, and his practice was very successful :—

THE WHOLE ART OF FORTUNE-TELLING,
BY J——n A——k, BARTON.

Deep in the dismal Regions, void of Light,
Three Witches, for Consultation, meet to Night;
So, sacred Sisters, your secret Mysteries state,
The Witches leaders, and their great Powers relate.

WHO begs most respectfully to acquaint his Friends that he has, for the Benefit of the Public, commenced the above Business; and, from the long Time he had studied under the different Masters of the Magical Mysteries in the present Age, also, in all the ancient and modern Books in Astrology, Nicromancy, Divinations, and all the magical Charms, Spells, Rites, Enchantments, and hidden Mysteries in past and future Events, flatters himself that he has become Proficient in his Art.

Hail, Medea, hail! if still he scorn the Spell,
By Fate, I'll force him to the Gates of Hell!
Such potent Sorceries an Assyrian taught,
As to a magic Charm the Drugs he wrought.

J. A. can break any Charm caused by Enchantment; can also immediately name the Planet under which a Person is born; and will also inform any Person whether he or she will be married, and to whom; and can inform all married Men, to their Satisfaction, in all the secret Transactions which they may suppose to have taken place with their Wives; can also conjure back any stolen Goods, and bewitch any Person or Animal who has done any one an Injury, &c. &c.

Hail, Hecate! and give my rising Spell
Ev'n Appollonius's Sorceries to excel:
Bid my strong Witchery match ev'n Circe's Skill,
O'er the dire Rites,—my Mysteries fulfil.

J. A. also begs to add that he has not spared any Expence to make himself Master of all the magical Mysteries, and is confident of his own Abilities in being able to give every Satisfaction to those who may favour him with a Consultation will meet with due Attention, but their Letters must be post-paid, inclosing a Post-office Order for 5s. The Age of the Applicant must be stated. Persons attending will be charged 2s. only. J. A. is also a Dealer in Talismanick Charms, engraved with magical Characters, 10s. 6d. each.

A man who commences a sorcery business for the benefit of the public deserves to succeed, especially when he can break any charm caused by enchantment, conjure back stolen goods, and so play the avenger's part as to bewitch any person or animal who has done any one an injury. It is a pity J. A. did not get some of his mysterious agents to put his lines a little in order. The other is a Tyneside advertisement, and shows also a partiality for verse—indeed consists of nothing else, if we except the name and address; but its theme is far more material than that of its companion. Unlike in the case of the publican of Wych Street, we will not assume that Mr Catcheside employed any one over the following effusion, of which he is welcome to all the credit:—

JOHN CATCHESIDE,

GROCER & TEA-DEALER,

BIGG-MARKET,

NEWCASTLE.

YE gentlemen of town and country,
A shop, next door to Whitfield's entry,
Is just fit up for your inspection,
By Mr Catcheside's direction;
Good ladies, too, I crave your favours,—
To please you shall be my endeavours.
Without the fairer sex are pleas'd,
The mind of man is never eas'd.
But ladies, pray, and gentlemen,
Call, and I'll please you if I can.
I've Teas of all sorts you can mention—
To keep them good is my intention:
All from the India-house direct,
Warranted genuine you may expect;
Which I do sell on lowest terms,
And not as gentlemen let farms;
I've Sugars too, the same to sweeten,
As good as ever yet were eaten;
Loaves, well refin'd as 'ere you saw,
Which boiling water scarce will thaw.
I've Treacle, Juice, and Sugar-Candy,
And Turkey Coffee strong as brandy;
The very best Plantation ditto,
With Fry's and White's best Patent Cocoa,
And Churchman's Patent Chocolate,—
All which I sell at a low rate.
I've fine Tobacco, Patent Shag,
Twist, Saffron Cut, and Common Rag;
And Snuff, whatever kind you choose,
To clear your brain, and warm your nose:
Zant Currants, commonly call'd Spice,
Orange and Lemon Peel, and Rice;
Malaga Raisins, too, I sell,
With Bloom, and Sun, and Muscatell,
With which you well may stuff your wigs;
Or here's French Plumbs, or Turkey Figs;
Or Prunes, if you do think them fitter,
With Almonds, Jordan, Shell, and Bitter;
Nutmegs, Cloves, Cinnamon, and Mace,
Good as you'll get at any place;
Season your syllabubs and custards;
For beef, I've Vinegar and Mustards.
All kinds of Pepper, too, I'll sell ye,
Macaroni and Vermacelli:

Anchovies, Cassia, and Cassia-buds,
And many other sorts of goods,
Prepar'd for puddings, pies, and sauces:—
Come, buy them cheap, ye bonny lasses!
And if your birds for seeds do gape,
I have Canary, Hemp, and Rape;
And further down you need not wander
For Annis, Carraway, and Coriander;
Of Ginger, too, I'm never scant,
For any purpose you may want.
I've Sago fine, and Capers both,
And famous Barley for your broth!
Salt Petre, Bay and Basket Salt,
To make your hams without a fault;
With Picked Isinglass and Staple,
To make your ale fit for the table:—
Then what can man desire more,
Than beef, and broth, and ale in store?
But dinner's done; come, draw the table,
Here's Soap to wash while you are able;
But if you think that will not do,
Here's Poland Starch and Powder Blue;
And if you'd have some coarser washes,
I have good Pearl and Comby Ashes;
Should you incline to wash by night,
I've Candles, too, will shew you light.
To spin dry wool you need not toil,
I've plenty Whale and Florence Oil.
Set by your wheels, your tongs, and poker
And paint your nooks with Yellow Ochre.
Put all your dye-pots to one side,
When with fresh Indigo supplied;
Then paint above your lintel-head
And chimney-pieces with Black-Lead.
If still materials you do lack,
I've Fuller's Earth and Ivory Black,
Logwood, Copperas, and Whiting,
Yea many more things not worth writing.
Once more your favours I solicit,
I'm ready waiting for a visit;
Most due attendance will be given
From seven at morn till eight at even;
Or later, if it seems expedient,
By your most humble and obedient,
JOHN CATCHESIDE.

Getting back to London, we come upon a bill of the kind now and then adopted with regard to posters, the idea in which is to convey a different notion at sight from that which is given by close inspection. In the following the plan has been carried out with great nicety, the author's endeavour being to make the notice look like a Government proclamation, and as one of the best specimens of the kind we have ever seen it is presented to the reader:—

PROCLAMATION!

Whereas,

It being Our Royal Will and Pleasure that our well-beloved, trusty and loyal subject HARRY JOHNSON, should for the Amusement of our well-beloved, trusty and loyal subjects of Hoxton and its Vicinity, give a grand entertainment on ASH WEDNESDAY, the 9th of February, 1842, for the BENEFIT of Himself, when he trusts from the Talent he has selected on this occasion, and the well-known respectability and celebrity of all parties, he cannot fail of securing a TREAT

TO THE

British Public.

H. J. feels proud and happy to announce that many Professional Friends have, in the most handsome manner, proffered their valuable Services: they are enabled to do this with greater facility as no other Place of Amusement in London is open on that Evening. Their Names will transpire in future bills. Miss PHILLIPS will on this night sing, in her usual sweet and inimitable style,

WANTED

A GOVERNESS

The Beneficiare will also sing,

FOR THE

First time, the Young

PRINCE OF WALES.

A Gentleman has kindly consented on this occasion to sing an Entire New Comic Song, to be called "Comfort is all my View; or

SALARY

Is no object!!" Mr. H. PARKER will also sing his much admired ballad of Had I

£1,000 A-YEAR!!!

A Lady will sing

NO FOLLOWERS ALLOWED.

ALL APPLICATIONS TO BE MADE (FOR TICKETS) ON OR BEFORE

ASH WEDNESDAY, FEBRU. 9, 1842,

AT THE OFFICE

ROYAL BRITANNIA SALOON, HOXTON OLD TOWN.

The Ceremony of* IN-STALL-ING *to commence at Half Past* SIX *o'clock Precisely.

GOD SAVE THE QUEEN!!!

The attention of readers will probably be attracted by the advertisement so elaborately concocted and carefully worked out. If its promoters received any extra support because of it, they certainly deserved what they got, as the plan is difficult to connect with any but large bills. The next item we have brings us to the year 1853, and is again from the county of Northumberland. It is far more pretentious than the composition of Mr John Catcheside, but by no means so successful. It is from the pen of a general shopkeeper, who evidently considered he had done something when he had been through his proofs, seen this to press, and forwarded copies to unsuspecting, and, as it turned out, unsympathising, families about G——, a small place not very far from Newcastle :—

To the inhabitants of G—— and its neighbourhood.

The present age is teeming with advantages which no preceding era in the history of mankind has afforded to the human family. New schemes are projecting to enlighten and extend civilisation, Railways have been projected and carried out by an enterprising and spirited nation, while Science in its gigantic power (simple yet sublime) affords to the human mind so many facilities to explore its rich resources, the Seasons roll on in their usual course producing light and heat, the vivifying rays of the sun and the fructifying influences of nature producing food and happiness to the Sons of Toil, while to the people of G—— and its neighbourhood a rich and extensive variety of Fashionable Goods is to be found in my Warehouse, which have just been selected with the greatest care. The earliest visit is requested to convey to the mind an adequate idea of the great extent of his purchases, comprising, as it does, all that is elegant and useful, cheap and substantial to the light-hearted votaries of Matrimony, the Matrons of Reflection, the Man of Industry, and the Disconsolate Victims of Bereavement.

This composition having been printed and distributed, the author waited impatiently for its powerful effect, and when to his great astonishment he discovered that it had produced none, he, with the irritability that nearly always accompanies neglected genius, resolved to get back and destroy every copy of his essay, and thereby deny to posterity what his own generation could not appreciate. Fortunately for ourselves, and for ages yet unborn, a copy was preserved, and printed in *Notes and Queries*.

Most dwellers for any time in London remember Lord Chief Baron Nicholson and his Judge and Jury Society, which used to be held at the Coal Hole in the Strand. Virtuous readers may shudder at the mention of such a place; but time was when the deliberations and decisions of the jury, as well as the directions of the judge and the peculiarities of the witnesses, were productive of mirth independent of *double entendre* among an audience composed of anything but roysterers and howling cads. In such halcyon days, when Nicholson was in the flesh, looking much more like a chief baron than nine-tenths of the possessors of the title ever did, the following handbill was printed:—

The Lord Chief Baron

NICHOLSON

Begs to inform his best friends, the Public, that he and the learned Gentlemen of the JUDGE AND JURY SOCIETY, have left the Garrick's Head in Bow Street, and now hold their Forensic Sittings at the celebrated COAL HOLE TAVERN, Fountain Court, Strand, every Evening.

A JUDGE!—and in a Coal Hole too!
Quoth rustic John, I can't believe thee.
That sounds too funny to be true,
Come NICHOLSON, now don't deceive me.

I wont deceive thee in the path,
So at the ancient Coal Hole meet me,
BLACKSTONE and COKE burn on the hearth,
And LAW flares up, my lad, to greet thee.

DO NOT FORGET TO REMEMBER
THE COAL HOLE
IN THE STRAND.

Law was the proprietor of the establishment, and he "flared up" to some tune, so far as the production of suppers required flaring. And suppers were both numerous and excellent at the Coal Hole; the stewed or scalloped oyster, the devilled kidney, the broiled bone, and the modest "rabbit" receiving considerable attention during the progress of the mock trials. Subsequently the Coal Hole became a resort for journalists and actors, who used to be admitted to a snug old room behind the bar; but all that is changed now, an ambitious landlord having modernised the place and driven forth its old *habitués.* Not by violence or through incivility, but by means of plate-glass, electro tankards, and other goods, the unwonted and unwelcome aspect of which has made wanderers of the old warm-hearted coterie. Why will people "restore" and improve the few comfortable old taverns still left about London, and drive honest folk from the snug and unpretending corners they have occupied for years? This same restoration is shortsighted and impolitic. The houses become nondescript; they are too modern, and perhaps too respectable, for the old customers, not glaring and gassy enough for the new; and so they stand, with just sufficient about them to remind us of the joys that are past, and not enough to tempt us to renew them in the future.

Turning from taverns, coal-holey and otherwise, we have finally to notice that kind of advertising which is the result of an attempt to make profit out of others' misfortunes. At the time, but a very few years back, of the Overend and Gurney failure, an enterprising linen-draper in the North-West district of London put forth the following hand-bill (p. 555), which was of large size, surrounded by a thick black mourning border, and which, in addition to being given away, was sent about by post. For reasons which are obvious, we have changed the names, and have no hesitation in giving an opinion that the proceeding was a very sharp bit of business, worthy of the hero of the wooden nutmegs.

It was followed by a long list of the goods to be sold, with the market prices and those at which they were offered, the practice of making up two sets of figures on goods having been found very efficacious of late years. This brings us well up to the present time, and as that is quite capable of taking care of itself without any assistance from us, we will conclude, in the hope that, though we have perforce passed many interesting specimens by, our selection, considering the space at command, has not been in any way injudicious.

The Overend Gurney & Co. Disaster.

LAMENTABLE CASE OF RUIN AND DEATH.

THE "STANDARD" of the 29th ultimo, truly observes—

"Difficult indeed would it be to exaggerate the extent of the mischief that was done by the fall of the great house which had for generations stood firm as a rock * * * * nor would it be easy to adequately describe the woe and desolation, the loss and ruin, consequent upon the suspension and disastrous liquidation of the Company."

A more distressing case than the one in question it is impossible to conceive.—It is briefly told.—An old-established Linen Draper of the City of London, (Mr. JOB HUCKABACK), had invested the Savings of a life-time in the Overend Gurney Scheme. The result is known. Still his Business remained, and he might have struggled on, but further calls being imminent, his last hope was crushed, so, Bankrupt and broken-hearted, he died,—leaving a wife and five young children to the mercy of fate.—

The Trade Creditors have done what they can by waiving all claims upon the Estate, and have generously resolved that the Stock shall be sold for the benefit of the Widow and Children.

THE STOCK, WHICH IS HIGHLY CHOICE AND VALUABLE, HAS BEEN ENTRUSTED TO

MR. CHARLES MARTEL,

With prompt Orders TO REALISE AT ONCE ON ANY TERMS.

THE FIRST GRAND SALE OF SELECTED GOODS WILL BE HELD IN THE

Large Assembly Room of the —— Hotel, N.W.

(☞ Ladies may avoid passing through the Hotel, by presenting enclosed Card to Messenger at Private Door.)

On Monday, 1st, Tuesday, 2nd, Wednesday, 3rd, and Thursday, 4th March,

From Ten a.m. till Dusk each Day, closing on Thursday, at 5 p.m., prompt, *not a minute later.*

The Sale will be by Private Treaty, thus affording Ladies leisure to freely inspect. Although prices are quoted as a guide, NO OFFER WILL BE REJECTED, AS EVERYTHING MUST BE SOLD IN THE BRIEF TIME SPECIFIED.

CHAPTER XIX.

AMERICAN AND COLONIAL ADVERTISEMENTS.

IN such a go-ahead nation as the United States, it is only natural that advertising should be a very important feature of its business arrangements; and in perusing most of the papers which have travelled across the Atlantic, we find that our cousins have what are called much broader notions concerning the duties of advertisements than we have. The word broader we use in its conventional sense, and without any wish to take responsibility upon ourselves; for the so-called broader view is, after all, only the view which will be found expressed in those of our pages which contain notices published a hundred years ago. So that perhaps, after all, the broader view is our modern view; for it is, or certainly should be, the improved view. In course of time the American press may adopt the plan now in use here so far as regards all the papers which we consider representative, that of having an outward and visible show of decency in the advertisement columns, no matter what darkness or danger lurks beneath. With very few exceptions, the papers which come from the United States—we refer not to the hole-and-corner but to the high-class, which are widely read and disseminated among family circles—contain advertisements which would be rejected by the gutter journals of this country. A hundred years ago, as we have said and instanced, our papers were not at all particular, so long as they could get advertisements, what they took; now a sense of what is right and proper compels them to refuse many notices which would be highly paid for—would be paid any price for—and in time the American press will doubtless follow the self-abnegating example. The broadened view we think, therefore, is ours, yet our style is often referred to as narrow-minded. The narrow mind is that which sacrifices its honour and credit in its greed for immediate profit and hunger after the almighty dollar.

For many reasons there is a great difficulty in dealing with American advertisements. Sometimes they are too long for quotation, at other times they are too broad; and very often one is not quite sure whether or not it is a really *bona fide* advertisement he is reading, or only an expression of gratitude from an editor for the favours he has received or fondly anticipates. American editors have peculiar notions on the subject of advertisements and the duties of advertisers. In a New York journal which boldly announces itself as the American Gentleman's Newspaper, there is, or used to be, an editorial notice which informs all whom it most concerns, that, so as to meet the requirements of the family circle, and so that the paper may be left upon every gentleman's breakfast-table, the use of the name of the Deity is expressly forbidden in the advertising or other columns. We quote from memory, but if these are not the exact words, the line of argument—if argument such a *non sequitur* can be called—is identical with that used by Mr Wilkes, the proprietor and editor of this model and gentlemanly paper. It would be well, however, if the American lady's newspaper erred in no greater particular than the American gentleman's does. For the honour of America it is to be sincerely hoped that its ladies know nothing of the sheets which are flaunted here with the names of women as the editors, and which are said to be written especially for women. It is hard to believe that any sane creature, much more a woman, could write such festering scurrility, such fatuous blasphemy, and such shameless indecency and advocacy of open adultery as appear in the columns of one at least of these women's journals; but it is easy to imagine that a few besotted females, suffering from erotic and other dementia, should exhibit themselves to the scornful gaze of the virtuous or the only moderately vicious for the purpose of obtaining notoriety—far easier than to believe that the women of America are the readers of and subscribers to these papers and their opinions. We are quite sure that no woman worthy of the name would look a second time at the organ of Victoria C. Woodhull and Tennie C. Claflin—quite as sure as that the two persons we have named are, with their followers, quite unfit to be regarded as women. We have referred to this paper and its "editors" because it and they represent a class of journals and journalists which are, unfortunately for Americans, too apt to be taken as standard representatives of the type, and from no desire to accord them the spurious celebrity they so anxiously covet.

Still, without wishing to impute anything like iniquity to American newspapers generally, it must be admitted that the vast majority of them have rather lax notions of propriety, and their motto being "Get money," they are apt to ignore the existence of ill in any advertisement, provided the presenter of it has his "pile" ready, and will "come down handsome." This is evident throughout the whole of the transatlantic news world; and though there are, we feel bound and are glad to admit, very honourable exceptions, they are but the exceptions which prove the rule. As the editors and proprietors generally accuse each other, they cannot feel annoyed if we, standing afar off, make our notes according to what they give us If they prefer to feel angry, however, we shall not stand in their way; but doubtless the majority are too intent on getting money to care much for what is said about them. Indeed there are many who exult in the notion of making capital by all kinds of advertisements, from the puff preliminary to the nauseating display of vile quackery or undisguised immorality, and vary this with agreeable little interludes in the way of black-mail. In several American newspapers open and undisguised announcements have been published that their columns are to be bought, and that for a price they will advocate any cause or take any side of a disputed question.

But throughout all this there is a great spice of humour, and in the general run of American advertisements it is much to be feared, and only natural to assume, that a stricter code of morality would result in a vast increase of dulness, the general concomitant of prim respectability. Yet it is possible to be wise as well as witty, and even now a good percentage of American advertisers prove this. From these we shall endeavour to select our stock, and so give all the humour without intruding the unpleasantness, except where it is absolutely necessary for the purpose of giving a fair idea of the American system. A good instance of ingenuity is that of the grocer in Pennsylvania, who on the fence of a graveyard inscribed in large white letters, "Use Jones's bottled ale if you would keep out of here." Grave subjects are often chosen as opportunities for advertising, one thing frequently offered being "Port wine as pure as the tears which fall upon a sister's grave." A firm engaged in the "statuary line" state that "those who buy tombstones of us look with pride and satisfaction upon the graves of their friends;" and from a large upholstery establishment the following emanates :—

Their parlor furniture is elegant,
Their bedroom furniture is rich,
Their mattresses are downy,
Their coffins are comfortable.

There is, after all, not much opportunity for the display of novelty in advertisements nowadays; but a merchant in Newark, New York State, succeeded very well by leaving his column entirely blank with the exception of this note, in very small type, at the bottom: "This space was sold to

A. E. Brennan and Co., but as their business is sufficiently brisk already they decline to use it." This anecdote in its progress has been related of most large houses in or about New York and Boston, but Brennan was the man who gave rise to it. Quite as business-like, and rather more cynical, was the Ohio tradesman who, in large print, gave the following forth: "Ministers of the Gospel supplied with goods at cost, if they agree to mention the fact to their congregations." And though the next is a purely private communication, the author of it was evidently a born advertiser: "If the party who took a fancy to my overcoat was influenced by the inclemency of the weather, all right; but if by commercial considerations, I am ready to negotiate for its return." In an advertisement headed "Full-dress funeral," which appears in a Philadelphia paper, is the intimation that "all the gentlemen friends of the late Mr Smith desirous of participating in the funeral will appear in full-dress suit and white gloves at Happy Hall, at nine o'clock a.m. on Friday morning, Jan. 29, and proceed from thence in a body to the house of the deceased." This peculiarity of a.m. in the morning reminds us of the announcement on a bridge at Denver, Colorado, which states that "no vehicle drawn by more than one animal is allowed to cross this bridge in opposite directions at the same time;" though our intention, while touching on funerals, was to give the subjoined letter from an enterprising undertaker in Illinois to a sick man: "Dear sir, having positive proof that you are rapidly approaching Death's gate, I have, therefore, thought it not imprudent to call your attention to the inclosed advertisement of my abundant stock of ready-made coffins, and desire to make the suggestion that you signify to your friends a wish for the purchase of your burial outfit at my establishment." And thereon followed an elaborate list of the essentials to a first-class funeral, the reader having nothing to do but to supply the corpse. Apropos of supply, the following from a Chicago confectioner's notice is worthy of remark: "Families supplied by the quart or gallon." This ostensibly refers to olives, but to us it seems very suggestive of olive branches. Occasionally, in running through the papers, one is surprised at the appetite of a lady who wants "to take a gentleman for breakfast and tea;" at the single-mindedness of a boarding-house keeper who advertises that "single gentlemen are furnished with pleasant rooms, also one or two gentlemen with wives;" or the boldness of a merchant who, in a free country, openly gives notice that there is "wanted—a woman to sell on commission."

We have already referred to the "editorials" which have a more or less remote connection with advertisements, and now select two examples with which to illustrate our meaning. They are of very opposite characters, and will serve to give both extremes, between which all sorts of puffs may find classification. The first is very common. Says the editor of a Yankee paper:—

A correspondent wants to know what kind of a broom the young lady in the novel used when she swept back the ringlets from her classic brow. We don't know, and shouldn't answer if we did. We only undertake to answer queries of a practical and useful character. If our correspondent, who we presume is a gentleman, had asked who was the best and most popular hatter in the city, we would have promptly and unhesitatingly answered, James H. Chard of Broadwalk.

This tradesman had evidently supplied, or promised to supply, a new covering for the editorial head, with perhaps a little light refreshment as well. The other specimen is far more deliberate, and at the same time more respectable. It is from a Buffalo paper of half-a-dozen years back, and is not at all unlike the very earliest advertisement recommendations of our own country:—

We are assured that the firm of Eastman & Kendall, 65, Hanover Street, Boston, Mass., advertised in our columns, is trustworthy and reliable. For 10 cents they send a patent pen fountain and a check describing an article to be sold for $1. Their club system of selling goods is becoming quite popular, particularly with the ladies. It is worthy of a trial.

Two specimens of editorial personal advertisements will doubtless suffice. One was published by an Illinois journalist on assuming the duties of chief of the staff, and it gives a very good idea of the plan upon which he intended to "run" his paper. It says:—

Sensational, distressing details of revolting murders and shocking suicides respectfully solicited. Bible class presentations and ministerial donation parties will be "done" with promptness and despatch. Keno banks and their operations made a speciality. Accurate reports of Sunday School anniversaries guaranteed. The local editor will cheerfully walk 17 miles after Sunday school to see and report a prize fight. Funerals and all other melancholy occasions written up in a manner to challenge admiration. Horse races reported in the highest style of the reportorial art. Domestic broils and conjugal felicities sought for with untiring avidity. Police court proceedings and sermons reported in a manner well calculated to astonish the prisoner, magistrate, and preacher.

The other is the opposite of the foregoing, and was penned under very different circumstances. It is from a Keithsburg journal, and first saw the light under the head reserved for notices of deaths:—

About two and a-half years ago we took possession of this paper. It was then in the very act of pegging out, having neither friends, money, nor credit. We tried to breathe into it the breath of life; we put into it all our own money and everybody else's we could get hold of; but it was no go; either the people of Keithsburg don't appreciate our efforts, or we don't know how to run a paper. We went into the business with confidence, determined to run it or burst. We have busted. During our connection with the *Observer* we have made some friends and numerous enemies. The former will have our gratitude while life lasts. The latter are affectionately requested to go to the deuce.

Occasionally these advertising notices take a widely different form, and refer to the benefits which are to be found from a use of the columns in which they appear. Take the following as an instance of the kind of work we mean :—

THE NEW YORK DAILY NEWS has the largest circulation of any daily paper published in the United States, and, with the exception of one in England and one in France, the largest in the world. We will contract for advertisements in the NEWS upon the following terms: Three (3) cents per line for every (10) ten thousand of our circulation. Every bill when presented to be accompanied with the sworn affidavit of the pressman who prints the paper, the clerk who delivers the paper, and the cashier who receives the money. No paper to be counted as circulation except those that are actually sold and paid for. Believing this to be the most fair and equitable plan ever offered to advertisers, we make the proposition.

This is a fair and equitable idea which none but the proprietors of rival journals could object to. And that rivals do have their say about each other's advertisements, the following article, which is called "Ensnaring the Simple," and which at one stroke deals two blows—one in the journalistic and the other in the electioneering interest—will show. It is from a New York daily, and runs thus : "*The Sunday Mercury* is published by Cauldwell & Whitney, Editors and Proprietors. Its senior editor is William Cauldwell, late Senator from the IXth District, comprising Westchester, Putnam, and Rockland Counties, and now the Democratic candidate for re-election. From yesterday's issue of that *Sunday Mercury*, we copy the following advertisements, omitting only the addresses of the respective advertisers :—

TWO YOUNG MEN, residents of New-York, of some means, are desirous of forming the acquaintance of two ladies between the ages of sixteen and twenty-two, with a view to sociability and quiet enjoyment. To those that are worthy, pecuniary assistance will be willingly rendered, if necessary. Those employed in some light occupation preferred. Address, appointing interview, —— and ——, Mercury office.

A GENTLEMAN, aged twenty-five, would be pleased to form the acquaintance of a young lady, or widow, under twenty-five years of age. Must be educated, and of good reputation. One engaged during the day preferred. A desirable party will meet with a permanent friend. Disreputable parties need not answer this. Address in confidence for ten days, —— ——, Mercury office.

A GENTLEMAN of means, alone in this city, desires the acquaintance of a respectable, genteel young lady of refinement, who is, like himself, friendless and alone; the most honorable secrecy observed. Address, with full particulars, ——, Mercury office, 128 Fulton-st., New-York.

A FRENCH GENTLEMAN, newly arrived in this country and lonely, wishes to form the acquaintance of a lady who could prove as true a friend to him as he would be to her. Address, in confidence, as discretion will be absolute, ——, Mercury office.

A YOUNG GENTLEMAN would like to make the acquaintance of an affectionate and sociable young lady who would appreciate a true friend; one residing in Brooklyn preferred. Address ——, box 3, 761 New-York P.O.

A GENTLEMAN OF MEANS wishes to make the acquaintance of a young lady of sixteen to eighteen years (blonde preferred); one who would appreciate a companion and friend may find one by addressing ——, Mercury office.

A YOUNG WIDOW would like to make the acquaintance of an elderly gentleman of means, who would be willing to assist her, in return for true friendship. No triflers need answer. Address ——, Station E.

A GENTLEMAN, thirty years of age, with some leisure time at his disposal, would like the acquaintance of a handsome young lady, resident of Brooklyn. Address, stating age and other particulars, ——, Mercury office.

A KIND, ELDERLY GENTLEMAN, a stranger, wishes to enjoy the society of an agreeable young lady. Address ——, Mercury office.

A GENTLEMAN of position desires the society of a young lady or widow. Would afford moderate pecuniary aid to a respectable and deserving person. Address, with particulars, appointing interview, ——, Mercury office.

A STRANGER in New-York desires a few lady correspondents whom he can call upon, and who would be pleased to accompany him to theatres, &c. Address ——, New-York University.

A YOUNG MAN of refined taste would like to meet with a good-looking lady (not above twenty) who is engaged during the day. Address, appointing interview, ——, No. 4, Mercury office.

A LADY would like to meet with a gentleman who would thoroughly appreciate her exclusive society. For particulars, address ——, Box 2, No. 688 Broadway.

"These are but fair specimens of columns of such advertisements which have for years appeared in the successive issues of *The Mercury*. The publishers put over them the head 'Matrimonial,' but the advertisers do not countenance that fraud. They use *The Mercury* and pay for it as though it were a house of infamous resort; and, if there be any moral difference between permitting this use and keeping a house of ill-fame, we cannot see it. We do not doubt that at least One Thousand foolish girls have been ruined through the instrumentality of these shameful advertisements. Must not that be a monstrous dispensation of justice which, while Rosenzweig is (most righteously) sent to State Prison, should send Cauldwell to the Senate? What do you think of it? Electors of Westchester, Putnam, and Rockland Counties! read the above advertisements carefully, and say whether you can aid the election of Cauldwell to the Senate without sharing his guilt? Do not pretend ignorance of his iniquities: for above is the evidence which no man can gainsay. There are more such in this week's issue, as there have been in every issue of that sheet for years. Fathers, brothers, pure men of every degree! read those infamous advertisements carefully, and then judge if you can vote to send their publisher to the Senate!" This is all very well, and extremely virtuous, but in the high-class daily journal from which it is taken there are plenty of advertisements of a character anything but beyond reproach. We are far from wishing to uphold the character of the *Mercury*, which is no more and no less than a Pandarus among papers, but the axiom, "Physician, heal thyself," will apply to the champion of outraged innocence just quoted.

An astonishingly elaborate way of bringing the "puff pars" of enterprising and liberal tradesmen under immediate notice is shown in a weekly, possessed of considerable notoriety, that is published in California. This paper, the *San Francisco Newsletter*, has several times with pleasing candour informed the world that its opinions and advocacy are within easy purchase. Which means that those who do not think its friendship worth buying had better beware of its animosity. For those who doubt this we reproduce the following, which was probably placed on the front page of the *Newsletter* because the directors of the company referred to refused to patronise that organ of publicity, and which has now been running for some time:—

A PERMANENT PARAGRAPHIC ADVERTISEMENT.

[RESPECTFULLY DEDICATED TO THE SPRING VALLEY WATER WORKS.]

A miner's inch of water is about twenty thousand gallons. The usual price for an inch of water in the mines is ten cents. The Spring Valley Company sells water in large quantities at seventy-five cents per thousand gallons, or at fifteen dollars seventy-five cents per inch—which is one hundred and fifty-seven times the price which miners pay. Furnished in small quantities to housekeepers, the Company charges from thirty to fifty dollars an inch—five hundred times the miners' rates. IGNOTUS.

The *Newsletter* was originally known in England as the vehicle of a vein of humour peculiar even in America, and mainly dependent upon a contempt for all religious formalities and observances, an affectation of atheism, and an evident desire to render all those things ridiculous that believers hold most sacred. Through all this ran a vein of ability which even those who objected most to the degradation of it were bound to admit, and the smart utterances of the chief writer on the staff were not only quoted widely throughout America, but now and again found supporters among advanced journalists in England. How different now is the *Newsletter!* Its flippancy is as rampant as ever, but its attempts to make fun out of the doctrines of faith in general and Christianity in particular are of the dreariest, while in place of the cleverness which once made its columns readable there is a scurrility worthy of the typical *Stabber* or *Rowdy Journal.* And the more its ability becomes deteriorated, the more do its abuse, its blasphemy, and its blackmailing qualities exhibit themselves. It is evident that the old leader has departed, and left in his place one whose servile imitation must have been his best credential for the office of successor.* But it was in reference to the *Newsletter's* advertisements that we commenced; though they are in truth so mixed up with its other matter that the distinction is subtle indeed. The construction of the paper is unique. Each page is complete in itself, and in the "backs" and "gutters"—the inside margins, in fact—there are numerous advertisements. The chief peculiarity, however, of the paper is that of spreading its puffs and notices about among the ordinary matter. The following extract will give some idea of the prevailing plan :—

* It is only fair to Americans in general, to state that the proprietor of this the most American of all American papers is an Englishman. At least, we are informed so by men who remember him in London.

"**Tell me,** O, thou ancient warrior,
How it is you look so strong.
Full well I know, for four-score years
You've wandered round—say, am I wrong?"

"I have lived for four-score years, sir,
Drinking naught but Cutter's best.
If you want to live as long, sir,
I advise you to invest."

Shortening a Telegram.—A gentleman took the following telegram to a telegraph office:—"Mrs Brown, Liverpool street.—I announce with grief the death of uncle James. Come quickly to read will. I believe we are his heirs.—John Black." The clerk, having counted the words, said, "There are two words too many, sir." "All right, cut out 'with grief,'" was the reply.

The other afternoon I strayed,
About the hour of four,
To see if in the town I'd find
A first-class carpet store.

I wandered round for a long time,
Until a friend did tell
Where was the only place in town—
The store of Plum & Bell.

San Francisco ... candour informed the world ... are within easy purchase. W... do not think its friendship worth b... of its animosity. For those who d... the following, which was probably place... of the *Newsletter* because the director... referred to refused to patronise that orga... which has now been running for some time

...train stopped at the station, an old gentle-
...stepped out on the platform, and
...claimed, "Isn't this invigorat-
...ied the conscientious porter.
...seat in the carriage.
...gentleness and purity:
...y & Rulofson made
... to worship at her

A PERMANENT PARAGRAPHIC ADVERT...

[RESPECTFULLY DEDICATED TO THE SPRING ... WATER WORKS.]

...an who struck
...t an election;
... "I am the
...tepping to the
...re," answered
...t well!"

A miner's inch of water is about twenty thousa... usual price for an inch of water in the mines is ten cen... Valley Company sells water in large quantities at se... per thousand gallons, or at fifteen dollars seventy-five ce... which is one hundred and fifty-seven times the p... pay. Furnished in small quantities to housekee... charges from thirty to fifty dollars an inch—five... miners' rates.

Mr. John Owens, who lately died at Jackson, aged 114, was in some respects a remarkable man. He blushingly admitted that he had used whisky since he was ten years old, and had chewed tobacco and smoked, more or less, for one hundred and three years, but he never claimed that he had seen Washington.

Wherever Minerva, the Goddess of Wisdom, presides, or Pomona, or Ceres require book work to be done, there will be found the school and office furniture made by Gilbert & Moore. It is universally acknowledged to be the best that is made in this or any other State. If once used, no other desks, stools, forms, garden seats, etc., will ever meet with any favour. Their patent school desk, with seat attached, is the most perfect thing we ever saw, and is as strong as it is neat.

A Yankee editor has just had his family reinforced, whereupon he indulges in the following poetic outburst :—

"Ring out, wild bells — and tame ones too—
Ring out the lover's moon !
Ring out the little slips and socks,
Ring in the bib and spoon !
Ring out the Muse, ring in the nurse—
Ring in the milk and water !
Away with paper, pens, and ink—
My daughter, oh, my daughter !"

The philosopher's stone has not yet been discovered, but modern science has found out a means by which the energy of youth can be imparted to those who have long passed the meridian of life. Such a boon to mankind is the Elixir Damiana, that the well known Doctor Jose Juniga, from whose prescription it is made, has earned a name not soon to be forgotten. The Elixir can be procured at Chas. Langley's, the agent, and at all drug stores.

Edmund Munger, speaking of the time when he was a boy, says it was the custom of school children as you passed a school-house, to make a bow ; but in these later days, as you pass a school-house, you must keep your eye peeled, or you will get a snowball or a brick-bat at the side of your head.

Help me to sing, ye muses Nine,
In praises of that house on Pine,
Which by its name, the Saddle Rock,
All praise and say the finest stock
Of oysters in the town are there ;
Both raw, and cooked with greatest care.

Mr. Redpath applied to Mr. Warner, author of "My Summer in a Garden," to enter the lecturing field. The genial author replied that there was less prospect now than ever of his consenting to do so. "It seems to me," he wrote, "that the older I grow, the wiser I grow."

The Six-Mile House, on the San Bruno Road, is the favourite calling place on the road. No one ever thinks of passing without stopping to have a word with Harry Blanken.

Twenty-eight different kinds of "bitters" sold in Rhode Island for "strictly medicinal use" are undergoing analysis by the State Chemist from an excise point of view.

This is the best part of the paper at the present time, and the best part of this—that is, the most original—is formed by the advertisements. There must now and again be a great run upon that edition of "Joe Miller" the proprietor keeps in his room, when the "exchanges" refuse to give out new or second-hand humorous paragraphs. We will conclude this section of our cousins' peculiarities with the following, picked out from a Boston sheet, where it was nestled close by the biggest of the advertisements:—

Keep on Advertising.

Don't fear to have a small advertisement by the side of a larger competing one. The big one can't eat it up.

Which, freely translated, means, "Keep on advertising, and don't be afraid. We'll take you, big or little, so long as you have the money, and of course we're quite disinterested."

In the year 1795, an English paper, speaking of the transatlantic journalism of the time, says: "As one proof of the commerce and trade of America, there are four daily papers printed in the city of New York; and it is not uncommon to enumerate 350 advertisements in a single paper. The price of an advertisement is from 1s. to 1s. 6d., and a paper sells for one penny. But what injures the beauty and authenticity of their papers is the want of a little red mark at one corner of the sheet; a blessing that has been withheld from them since the imprudent declaration of independence." The last remark is evidently satirical. It was sixty years after this that we got rid of our glorious red mark. But we have an advertisement of some years before the declaration of independence, which is subjoined:—

Bush Creek, Frederick's County, Maryland, Oct. 11, 1771.

RUN away from the subscriber, a Servant Maid named Sarah Wilson, but has changed her name to Lady Susanna Carolina Matilda, which made the public believe that she was her Majesty's Sister; she has a blemish in her right Eye, black rolled Hair, stoops in her shoulders, makes a common practice of writing and marking her cloaths with a Crown and a B. Whoever secures the said Servant Woman, or takes her home, shall receive five Pistoles, besides all cost and charges. WILLIAM DEVALL.

I entitle Michael Dalton to search the city of Philadelphia and from thence to Charles-Town, for the said Woman. W. D.

Sarah Wilson, who was quite an extraordinary adventuress, had been lady's-maid to the Hon. Miss Vernon, sister to Lady Grosvenor, and whilst in her service found means to obtain admittance into the royal apartments, where she broke open a cabinet and robbed it of some jewellery of value. For this she was apprehended, tried, and sentenced to death, but through the interposition of her former mistress was reprieved, and transported to Maryland, where on her arrival she was exposed for sale, and purchased by the Mr Devall above named. She soon, however, managed to make her escape into Virginia, travelled through that colony, and through North into South Carolina. When at a proper distance from Mr Devall, she assumed the title of Princess Susanna Carolina Matilda, and passed herself off as a sister to the Queen. She was dressed in a manner likely to favour the deception, and as she had with her part of the stolen jewels, and a miniature portrait of the Queen, which by some means she had managed to conceal before her trial and during her subsequent journey, she succeeded in deceiving many of the planters. Thus she travelled from one gentleman's house to another, affecting the manners of royalty, and admitting many of the gentry to the honour of kissing her royal hand. To some she promised governments, to others regiments, with promotions of all kinds in the Army, Navy, and Treasury. In short, she acted her part so plausibly that very few suspected her of being a deceiver. During the period of her imposture she levied heavy contributions upon some people of the highest rank in the southern colonies. At length the above advertisement appeared in the papers, and Mr Michael Dalton made his appearance in Charlestown, raising a loud hue and cry. Seeing that the game was up, her Serene Highness disappeared, and for a short time baffled the exertions of the police; but in the end she was captured and suffered condign punishment.

While on the subject of runaway slaves we will skip a few years, and so give a companion to this Cleopatra in the person of one Anthony, certainly a congenial spirit. The following is from a Raleigh paper of February 1815, in which it is preceded by the figure of a runaway negro. Anthony is evidently a paragon possessed of all a paragon's failings, and Caleb Quotem, so renowned in farce, scarcely equalled the subject of this advertisement in the variety and whimsical nature of his accomplishments:—

TWENTY-FIVE DOLLARS REWARD.

RAN away from Raleigh, a month or two ago, a mulatto man, named ***Anthony***, well known in Raleigh, and many parts of the State, as having been, for several years, the body servant of General Jones, and mine lately as a pressman and news-carrier in the Star office. Anthony is about twenty-five or twenty-six years of age, five feet eight or ten inches high, is a mongrel white, has a tolerably large aquiline nose, bushy hair, a scar on one of his cheeks; when in good humour has a pleasing countenance.

He works and walks fast, is lively and talkative, full of anecdote, which he tells in character with much humour; is an excellent pressman, indifferent at distributing types, a tolerable carpenter and joiner, a plain painter, an excellent manager of horses, drives well and rides elegantly, having been accustomed to race riding; is fond of cock-fighting (and of man-fighting when drunk), and is said to *heel* and *pit* with skill; he can bleed and pull teeth, knows something of medicines, is a rough barber, a bad but conceited cook, a good sawyer, can lay bricks, has worked in the corn fields, and can scratch a little on the fiddle.

He can do many other things; and what he cannot do, he *pretends* to have a knowledge of. His trades and qualities are thus detailed, because his vanity will undoubtedly lead to a display of them. His master-vice, or rather, the parent of all his vices, is a fondness for *strong drink*, though sometimes he will abstain for months. His clothes cannot be described, but he carried away few or none, and 'tis expected will appear shabbily. He is an artful fellow, and if taken up will tell a most plausible story, and possibly show a forged pass.

In 1806 the *Connecticut Courant* contained the following, which gives an unpleasant idea of what many wives might say in reply to the warning advertisements of desperate husbands if they only thought it worth while, or rather if they thought of it at all:—

East Windsor, U.S.

THOMAS Hutchins has advertised, that I have absented myself from *his bed and board*, and forbid all persons trusting me on his account, and cautioned all persons against making me any payment on his account. I now advertise the public, that the same Thomas Hutchins came as a fortune-teller into this town about a year ago, with a recommendation, which, with some artful falsehoods, induced me to marry him. Of the four wives he had before me, the last he quarrelled away; how the other three came by their deaths, he can best inform the public: but I caution all widows or maidens against marrying him, be their desire for matrimony ever so strong. Should he make his advances under a feigned name, they may look out for a little, strutting, talkative, feeble, meagre, hatchet-faced fellow, with spindle shanks, and a little warped in the back. Thankful Hutchins.

There are a good many more notices in the American papers which show that conjugal infelicity is no great rarity over there. The following exquisite effusion appeared in the *Port Gibson Correspondent* in November 1825:—

O matrimony! thou art like
To Jeremiah's figs—
The good are very good indeed,
The bad—too sour for pigs!

WHEREAS, thank God! my wife Rachel has left my bed and board for the hereafter mentioned provocation: this is to give notice that I will pay no debts of her contracting after this date.—We were married young; the match was not of our own choosing, but a made-up one between our parents. "My dear," says her mother, with a nose like a gourdhandle, to her best beloved, "now if we can get our neighbour Charles to consent to a marriage between our Rachel and his son, we shall have no more care upon our hands, and live the rest of our days in undisturbed repose." Here my beloved began to whimper; the truth is, she loved tenderly, loved another—and they knew it; he had no property, however, and that was their only idea of happiness: but she could not conceive how they could feast in joy upon her misery. "Hold your tongue," says her surly father, "don't you think your parents know better how to direct your attachments than you do yourself?" "Yes, my dear," says the mother, "you should always be governed by your parents—they are old and experienced and you are too young to think for yourself." The old dad and mam forgot that they were a runaway love match at the age of nineteen. But poor Rachel said not a word for she was afraid of her daddy's cowhide, that he had used sixteen years on nobody's back but his daughter's. She seemed reckless of her fate, was almost stupid, and did not know that she could alter it for the worse. My father, by persuasion and argument, dazzled my fancy with the eight negroes that would be her portion, "which," said he, "put upon the quarter section which I shall give you, will render you independent, and you are a fool if you do not live happily with such an angel."—"Angel!" said I, but I said no more, for my dad (in peace rest his ashes!) would have flown into a passion with the rapidity that powder catches fire; and its ebullition, like the blaze, would scorch me, I well knew.—We were married. I thought, as her father had ruled her with so tough a whip, I could do it with a hickory switch, and for my leniency gain her everlasting gratitude. We have now lived together six years, and have had no offspring except a hearty quarrel every little while. In truth I found her more spirited than I imagined; she was always ready to tally word for word, and blow for blow; but I never used a switch till the other day, always taking my open hand. The other day, coming home from work, very much fatigued and hungry, I found my wife in rather an unusual fit of passion, scolding some pigs that had overset the buttermilk. "Rachel," says I, "make me some coffee."—"Go to ——!" says she. I could not stand this; I had never heard her swear before. "I will chastise you for that," says I. Villain," said she, "I'm determined to bear no more of your ill usage. Instead of using the mild and conciliating language which a husband ought to use, you always endeavour to beat me into measures—touch me with that whip,

I will leave your house, and take my niggers with me too, so I will." She had said such things so often that I did not regard her, and belaboured her handsomely. The next morning after I had gone out to work, away she bundles sure enough, and when I came home at noon, I found the house emptied of bag and baggage, and all the negroes taken but the three that were at work with me. I have lived *happily* since, however; and she may keep all she took, if she will stay at her crooked-nose mammy's and never trouble my house again.

J. JOHNSTONE.

Laurence County, Miss.
Nov. 1, 1825.

This is a vigorous specimen of condensation, and contains, according to the present standard, quite enough plot for a three-volume novel, with special opportunities for essays on the horrors of slavery. If any rising authoress —we will give way to a lady—should happen to stumble across this book, and see her opportunity, we will waive all rights, as, after trying to sketch out the story, it was abandoned in despair, owing to our inability to keep our wandering attention from the next advertisement, which gives a companion picture, though the complaint is this time laid by the woman:—

$100 REWARD—For the apprehension of Lewis Turtle, a tall man, about 50 years, has considerable money and a high forehead, long face and lantern jawed man, a bad man, with a fist like a giant, and has often beat me, and I want him to end his days in the Penitentiary where he belongs, and he wears a grey coat, with a very large mouth, and one blue eye, and one blind blue eye, and a hideous looking man, and now living with the 7th woman, and me having one child to him, and he has gone off, and I want him brought slap up in the law, with blue pants. He ought to be arrested and has a $100 of my money, and a bald headed rascal, full of flattery and receipt, and she is a bad woman, and her little girl calls him "papa" and is called Eliza Jane Tillis, and a boy blind of one eye, and he is not a man who has got any too much sense, nor her. And he stole $100 from me, and some of my gold and silver, and ought to be caught and I will never live with him again, no never, he is a disgrace. And I would like to have him caught up and compelled to maintain me and his child, as I am his lawful wedded wife, and have the certificate of marriage in my possession.

NANCY TURTLE.

Coherency was evidently not Nancy's forte, and if she entertained her turtle-dove with much conversation as per sample, he was hardly to be blamed for trying a little change. In 1853 a sad and suffering husband sought consolation from the Muse, and published his lines in a Connecticut paper. Though not strictly in accordance with the rules laid down by authorities, they contain a good deal in a small space :—

Julia, my wife, has grown quite rude ;
She has left me in a lonesome mood;
She has left my board,
She has took my bed,
She has gave away my meat and bread,
She has left me in spite of friends and church,
She has carried with her all my shirts.
Now ye who read this paper,
Since she cut this reckless caper,
I will not pay one single fraction
For any debt of her contraction.

LEVI ROCKWELL.

East Windsor, Conn. Aug. 4, 1853.

Another husband also flies to verse for consolation, and records both his experiences and his determination in the following notice :—

Whereas my pet, my pretty toy,
   My wife, my Lizzie J.,
Has left my bed and my employ,
   With other men to stray.
I, therefore, take this to forewarn
   You not to trust her with a straw,
For I will never pay her corn,
   Unless compelled by law.

HENRY KA

BIG SUAMICO, Oct. 13, 1870.

Still another husband, after publishing some supposed grievances in the public prints, is made to see the error of his ways, and eats the leek in the following manner, and in a New York paper. Verse is here the sign not of the disease but of the remedy :—

WHEREAS I, Daniel Clay, through misrepresentation, was induced to post my wife, Rhoda, in the papers; now I beg leave to inform the public, that I have again taken her to wife, after settling all our domestic broils in an amicable manner; so that everything, as usual, goes on like clockwork.

Divorc'd like scissars rent in twain,
Each mourn'd the rivet out:
Now whet and riveted again,
They'll make the old shears cut.

With a notification from a maligned as well as injured wife, this selection will probably be considered complete :—

NOTICE.

WHEREAS my husband Chas. F. Sandford, has thought proper to post me, and accuse me of having left his bed and board without cause, etc., I wish to make it known that the said Charlie never had a bed, the bed and furniture belonging to me, given to me by my father; the room and board he pretended to furnish me were in Providence, where he left me alone, while he staid at the Valley with his "Ma." He offered me $200 to leave him and go home, telling at the same time that I could not stay at the place he had provided for me, and as I have never seen the named sum, I suppose he will let me have it if I can earn the amount. It was useless for Charlie to warn the public against trusting me on his account, as my father has paid my bills since my marriage, as before.

Moral.—Girls, never marry a man not weaned from his "Ma," and don't marry the whole family.

ELEANOR J. SANDFORD.

North Providence, July 1, 1871.

From such advertisements as the foregoing to those which emanate from persons desirous of becoming married is but a step; though, as has been already shown, most of the applications which come under the head of Matrimonial in the New York papers hardly justify the selection. Here is one, of a fair and honourable type enough, but it is fifty years old, being from the *New York Morning Herald* of July 2, 1824. This probably accounts for its really meaning marriage, and nothing else :—

WANTED immediately a young LADY of the following description (as a wife) with about 2000 dollars as a patrimony: Sweet temper, spend little, be a good housewife and born in America; and as I am not more than 25 years of age I hope it will not be difficult to find a good wife.

N.B.—I take my dwelling in South Second Street, No. 273. Any lady that answers the above description will please to leave her card.

This swain in his anxiety has forgotten to give either name or initials, so we cannot take steps to see whether or not he succeeded in getting a "rale Yankee gal." The advertisements of the present day are mainly of the character already quoted from the *Sunday Mercury*, in proof whereof we take one cut at random from a paper published three thousand miles away from that estimable journal, viz., the *San Francisco Chronicle*:—

TWO FUN-LOVING YOUNG LADIES would like to correspond with an unlimited number of young gentlemen; object, fun. Address, Roxey Hastings and Gracie Baker, Virginia, Nevada.

jy17 2t*

This is barefaced enough, in all conscience; but it is by no means out of the way, and will stand as a fair example of the rest.

From the *Waverley Magazine*, Boston—which is not a magazine as we understand the term, but a large broadsheet periodical—of four years back, we extract a batch of communications, which for convenience might be called matrimonial, but which have little to do with marriage:—

CORRESPONDENCE.

Two Dollars Each Address For One Insertion.

A YOUNG MAN of good standing in society, of refinement and education, desires an unlimited number of young-lady correspondents. Respectability and education the only requisites. Object, agreeable amusement during these long winter evenings. All letters answered. Photographs exchanged if desired. Address GEORGE MEADE, box 125, Middleburg, Schoharie County, N.Y.

Two young gentlemen would like to correspond with a number of young ladies, for improvement and amusement. Both are good-looking and in good circumstances. None but members of the National Matrimonial Association need reply. Address CASKER PLATT, box 2442, New-York City.

LADIES and gentlemen who wish correspondents will please send their photograph and ten cents for particulars and photograph of correspondent. Address "CENTRAL PERSONAL AGENCY," Garrettsville, O.

A YOUNG gentleman of good character and habits desires to correspond with some young lady, for amusement, mutual benefit, and perhaps matrimony. Address FRED S. LORING, box 1356, St. Paul, Minn.

A YOUNG gentleman wishes a lady correspondent. Object, cultivation of the heart and mind. Address, ARTHUR C. STANLEY, box 27, Letter Depot No. 54, East Twelfth Street, New-York City.

WILL "Mac," of Cambridge, who has a lady's privilege of changing her mind, please send her full address to J. S. W., now of Poitland, Me.? J. S. W.

ATTENTION.—Ladies, when you have nothing else to do write to me. Address EDWARD BELL, box 27, Sheffield, Mass.

The same paper also contains the following. As it is published early in the year, February 5, 1870, there must have been a rare rush of the amorous to enlist themselves under its banners :—

NATIONAL MATRIMONIAL ASSOCIATION.

HAVE you joined the National Matrimonial Association? Every young lady and gentleman will learn of many privileges and advantages to be gained by joining the association. 13,400 members since Nov. 9. Monthly meeting of members in different sections of the Union alternating for convenience. Members, though strangers, can recognize each other by means of the grip and secret signs of the association. The circular of the association, giving all particulars, will be sent postpaid upon receipt of ten cents. A young lady and gentleman are wanted as agents in towns where none have been appointed. Members wishing any information at any time need not inclose stamp. Address "Box 686," Hartford, Conn. Nos. 6, 8.

Falling back from matrimony and its substitutes into the regular channel, we take a declaration which contains a theory doubtless often promulgated nowadays at Bethlehem Hospital, Colney Hatch, and maybe Earlswood. Perhaps, though, it will be considered worthy the attention of philosophers, seeing that just now any new or startling view is sure to command not only regard but remuneration :—

Light developes light—*ad infinitum.*
St. Louis (Missouri Territory) North America.
April 10, A.D. 1818.

TO ALL THE WORLD.—I declare the earth to be hollow, and habitable within; containing a number of concentric spheres, one within the other, and that their poles are open twelve or sixteen degrees. I pledge my life in support of this truth, and am ready to explore the concave, if the world will support and aid me in the undertaking. JOHN CLEVES SYMMES
of Ohio, late Captain of Infantry.

I ask one hundred brave companions, well equipped, to start for Siberia, in autumn, with reindeer and sledges, on the ice of the frozen sea. I engage we find a warm country and rich land, stocked with thrifty vegetables and animals, if not men, on reaching about sixty-nine miles northward of latitude 82°. We will return in the succeeding spring.—J. C. S.

Captain Symmes seems pretty positive about getting back, though how he intended to get up again after getting down into one of the lower spheres he doesn't say. Perhaps a hundred brave companions, standing on each other's heads, might manage it, and if that was the idea, one of our own learned societies might look into it. Good thick heads would of course be necessary to bear the strain, and that may be, after all, the reason why they are so plentiful. *Quien sabe?* Far more within the ken of ordinary mortals is the following, which comes from Connecticut, and is well worthy of even that land of "notions :"—

THE SUBSCRIBER

BEING determined not to move from this State, requests all persons indebted to pay particular attention to his

New definition of an *Old* Grammar, viz.

Present Tense.

I am. Thou art. He is.

I am *	In want of money.
Thou art †	Indebted to me.
He is ‡	Shortly to be authorized, for the want thereof to take the body.

Unless immediate payment is made, you must expect to take a lecture upon my *new plural.*

The Subscriber offers for sale, at his Store, two rods south of the Fish-market, the following articles, viz.

Solid Arguments.

Hot Oysters, Boiled Lobsters, Ham and Eggs, Butter and Cheese, &c.

Agitations.

Cider, Vinegar, Salt, Pickles, etc.

Grievances.

Pepper-Sauce, Mustard, Cayenne-Pepper.

Punishments.

Rum, Brandy, Gin, Bitters, etc.

Superfluities.

Snuff, Tobacco, Segars, Pomatum, etc.

Extraordinaries.

Sea Serpent's Bones, Wooden Shoes, Waterwitches, etc.

N.B. The above articles will be exchanged for

Necessaries, vis.

Bank-Bills at par, Crowns, Dollars, Half ditto, Quarter ditto, Pistareens, Nine penny pieces, Four-penny half-penny ditto, or Cents.

---

* Andrew Smith. † Any one the coat fits. ‡ Hezekiah Goddard, Sheriff's Deputy.

Terms of Payment :

One half the sum down, and the other half on the delivery of the articles.

Rudiments gratis, viz.

Those indebted for	Arguments
Must not be	Agitated ;
Nor think it a	Grievance
If they should meet	Punishment
For calling such	Superfluities ;
Nor think it	Extraordinary
That I find it	Necessary
To demand immediate . . .	Payment.

ANDREW SMITH.

The smallest favour thankfully received.

New London,
March 1, 1819.

It seems a pity that such genius as that of "the subscriber" should have been wasted upon trifles; but possibly in such a country as the United States, where nothing is beyond a man's reach if his head is only long enough, he reaped the honours and rewards to which his talents entitled him. So many famous people have been called Smith, in America as well as here, that it would be vain to attempt a discovery of his subsequent career. Maybe he went to New York, and composed the following advertisement, which is just of three years' later date, and seems strange to those who know the Empire City in its present condition only :—

ANY person in want of a DEAD PIG may find one, that will probably answer his purpose, in the middle of Broadway, between Broome and Spring Streets. Applicants need not be in any great haste, as it is expected that he will lie there several days; and if the warm weather should last, and the carriages will let him alone, he will grow —*bigger and bigger*.

Getting nearer to modern times—1822 is very old for American notions—we find a New Yorker who speaks his mind freely, and treats his customers with moral illustration as well as business detail :—

GEORGE OTT, 262, North Second Street, respectfully informs his customers and friends in general, that his bakehouse is in full operation, and that he is always prepared to supply them with loaf-bread, crackers, pilot-bread, fresh rusks, &c. &c.

Having disposed of his list of wares, our baker proceeds, and no one can accuse him of mincing the matter:—

On his part nothing shall be left undone to give complete satisfaction to his customers, and in return he expects them to *pay punctually* when their bills are presented. Experience having taught him, that a disorderly soldier in the ranks and a bad paymaster in a baker's list of customers, are the most troublesome customers a man can have anything to do with, he requests those who do not calculate on paying promptly, to oblige him so far as to give their custom to a more accommodating baker.

Being anxious to take a journey for the benefit of his health, which is much impaired, those indebted to him would oblige him very much by making immediate payment; and he requests those who may have claims against him to call and receive their money.

Payment of quite a different kind is treated of in the next advertisement, which few boys, old or young, will read without feeling interested. It is, though in such few words, a marvellous exhibition of the *suaviter in modo* and the *fortiter in re* well mixed; and one can well understand the writer to be an agreeable friend and jolly companion, but a strict disciplinarian:—

Flushing Institute.

DEAR BOYS—Trouble begins Septr. 15.

E. A. FAIRCHILD.

It was said of one of our public schoolmasters that it was a pleasure to be flogged by him. We will take advantage of the present opportunity to remind those who have accepted it as a proverb, and believed it firmly, that the originator of the remark, like the originators of many other observations, never practically put his ideas to the test. Possibly on the same principle it would be a pleasure to have one's property sold off by auction, provided the advertisement were drawn out like that of the Yankee auctioneer from which we select this portion :—

I can sell for eighteen hundred and thirty nine dollars, a palace, a sweet and pensive retirement, on the virgin banks of the Hudson, containing 85 acres. The land is luxuriously divided by the hand of nature and art, into pasture and tillage, into plain and declivity, into the stern abruptness and the dalliance of most tufted meadow. Streams of sparkling gladness (thick with trout) dance through this wilderness of beauty, to the music of the cricket and grasshopper. The evergreen sighs as the evening zephyr flits through its shadowy bosom, and the aspen trembles like the love-splitting heart of a damsel. Fruits of the tropics in golden beauty melt on the bows, and the bees go heavy and sweet from the fields to their garnering hives. The stables are worthy of the steeds of Nimrod or the studs of Achilles, and its henery was built expressly for the birds of paradise; while sombre in the distance, like the cave of a hermit, glimpses are caught of the dog house. Here poets have come and warbled their lays, here sculptors have cut, here painters have robbed the scene of dreamy landscapes, and here the philosopher discovered the stone which made him the alchymist of nature. As the young moon hangs like a cutting of silver from the blue breast of the sky, an angel may be seen each night dancing with golden tiptoes on the greensward. (N.B. This angel goes with the place.)

Even our great Robins in his best form never exceeded this in picturesqueness of description. But our man could stay, and this one had shot his bolt when he got to the finish of the foregoing paragraph. At the commencement of the war against the "Seceshers," a good many of the Northern tradesmen made capital out of it, the following, in a *Tribune* of February 1861, forming a case in point :—

IMPORTANT FROM CHARLESTOWN!

MAJOR ANDERSON TAKEN!

ENTRANCE OBTAINED UNDER A FLAG OF TRUCE!

NEW YORKERS IMPLICATED!

GREAT EXCITEMENT! WHAT WILL THE SOUTHERN CONFEDERACY DO NEXT?

ON the 8th instant, about twelve hours before midnight, under cover of a bright sun, Col. George S. Cooke, of the Charlestown Photographic *Light* Artillery, with a strong force, made his way to Fort

Sumter. On being discovered by the vigilant sentry, he ran up a flag of truce. The gate of the fortress being open, Col. Cooke immediately and heroically penetrated to the presence of Major Anderson, and levelling a double barrelled camera, demanded his unconditional surrender in the name of E. Anthony and the Photographic Community. Seeing that resistance would be in vain, the Major at once surrendered, and was borne in triumph to Charlestown, forwarded to New York, and is now on sale in the shape of Exquisite Card Photographs at 28 cents per copy, by E. Anthony, &c. &c.

"Old McCalla" is or was a character well known in Princetown, Indiana. A few years back, when the following was published, he was nearly ninety years of age, but was still capable of minding his own business :—

WANTED.—Two or three boarders of a decent stripe, such as go to bed at nine o'clock without a pipe or cigar in their mouth. I wish them to rise in time to wash their faces and comb their heads before breakfast. When they put on their boots to draw down their pants over them, and not have them rumpled about their knees, which is a sure sign of a rowdy. When they sit down to rest or warm by the fire, not to put their feet on the mantlepiece or bureau, nor spit in the bread tray. And to pay their board weekly, monthly, or quarterly —as may be agreed upon—with a smile upon their faces, and they will find me as pleasant as an opposum up a persimmon tree.

OLD McCALLA.

Another boarding-house advertisement, which comes from Portland, Oregon, is also characteristic. A correspondent informs us that the Mr Thompson mentioned in it is a hard-working blacksmith, and he and his wife run the concern on the temperance plan :—

THOMPSON'S TWO-BIT HOUSE,

Front St., bet. Main and Madison.

NO DECEPTION THERE!

HI-YOU MUCK-A-MUCK, AND HERE'S YOUR BILL OF FARE:

THREE KINDS OF MEAT FOR DINNER; ALSO FOR Breakfast and Supper. Ham and Eggs every other day, and Fresh Fish, Hot Rolls, and Cake in abundance.

Hurry up; and none of your sneering at CHEAP BOARDING-HOUSES. Now's the time to have the wrinkles taken out of your bellies after the hard winter.

Board and Lodging..........$5 00 | Board..............................$4 00

Six NEW rooms, furnished with beds—the BEST in town—at my Branch House, corner First and Jefferson.

I am ready for the BONE and SINEW of the country.

"Hi-you Muck a-muck," we are also told, is a phrase in the Chinook language for plenty to eat. What the Chinook language is we must leave our readers to discover for themselves. Is it "heathen Chinee" as distinguished from the pure and unadulterated article? We pause for the reply of an expert, and while pausing, think that the following may be contemplated with some degree of interest, for families over here are drifting to the same state of difficulty very fast. A good servant is a jewel to be worn in one's bosom even in London, and so it is nothing wonderful that in Syracuse, U.S., five years back, this should have appeared:—

WANTED—A Good SERVANT GIRL to whom the highest wages will be paid. Having had great difficulty in procuring good help, on account of the misfortune of having seven small children, we will poison, drown, or otherwise make away with four of them on application of a first class servant girl. Apply at the office of this paper.

What a glorious subject this would have been for Leech or Doyle in the palmy days of *Punch*, when wit and humour, and not high art and sober earnest, were considered essentials for the illustration of a comic paper, and when jokes were not regarded as ill-timed on the part of a contributor! Historic painters are now the only humourists, and we do hope one, either English or American, may see this, and avail himself of it. The next is from an Iowa periodical, and will show our impartiality to all states in the Union, no one having received an undue share of attention—that is, beyond its merits. It will, besides, bring us up to comparatively recent dates:—

CAUTION.

WHEREAS, one U. T. S. RICE, a small, insignificant-looking whelp, who wears spectacles, carries a large cane, has a limp in his walk, talks smooth, and lies like Satan, has been obtaining money and credit by representing himself as a partner in the firm of Smart and Parrott, or as agent for us : we hereby caution all persons that we are not responsible for any of his acts. He is in no way connected with us, but is a perfect dead beat in every sense of the word.

"Dead beat" is a comprehensive and transatlantic euphemism for the more expressive thief, scoundrel, swindler, or sharper, any one of which, or all four combined, if he so pleases, the "dead beat" may be; and the subject of the Iowa notice seems a full-fledged and duly-qualified representative of the class.

It is hardly necessary to state that in America quacks and quack medicines abound. The papers are full of the advertisements of these men and their nostrums, and it would be quite easy to fill a very large volume with specimens. So much attention has already been given to the charlatans of Europe that we must perforce content ourselves with a very few specimens from the *répertoires* of their American brethren; but the chief difficulty is not what to select but what to omit. One of the evils which medical impostors in the States pretend to cure is that of drunkenness, and a notice in *Harper's Weekly*, which seems to be the chief organ of this kind of advertisers, runs as follows :—

DRUNKARDS, Stop! G. C. Beers, M.D., 670, Washington Street, Boston, Mass., has a medicine that will cure intemperance. Recommended by Judge Russell. Can be given secretly. Send stamp for circular.

Another vendor of specifics gives in the *New York Sun* this astonishing statement and purely unselfish promise :—

TRIED friends the best of friends. Since the suspension of H. C. Thorpe's advertisements, the number of deaths by consumption is truly astonishing; advertisements will now appear for the benefit of the afflicted.

But this is nothing compared with the marvellous Riga Balsam, about the incomparable virtues of which we have a long advertisement, which, after all sorts of extraordinary statements, ends thus:—

N.B. The trial of the Riga Balsam is this: Take a hew or a ram, drive a nail through its skull, brains and tongue, then pour some of it into the wound, it will directly stop the blood and cure the wound in eight or nine minutes, and the creature will eat as before.

A stoop costs two dollars, and it is sold in smaller portions; at the sale every person gets a direction which describes its surprising virtues and how it is to be used. The glasses, jars and bottles, are sealed up with this seal (A. K. Balsam) to prevent counterfeits.

Ecclesiasticus, chap. xxxiii. ver. 4. The Lord hath created medicines out of the earth, and he that is wise will not abhor them.

Which forcibly reminds us of an equally wonderful specific which was known in Holland about a century ago, if we may believe the *Dutch Mercurius* for January 1772, which states that "on December the 30th, 1771, Mr Tunnestrik experimented in the presence of the Prince Stadholder and sundry professors, by driving an iron spike into a horse's head, and afterwards pulling it out with a pair of pincers. Hereupon he poured certain oils by him invented into the wound, by means of which the horse within six minutes was whole again, and not even a scar remained to be seen." This horse, like the celebrated leg which was cured of its fracture with tar-water and oakum, must have been made of wood. With regard to the Riga Balsam, we might swallow that statement with the assistance, say, of another wonderful American potion, the Plantation Bitters, which, if we are to judge by the following, could help anything down:—

S. T.—1860.—X.

TO be, or not to be, that is the question.
Whether to suffer with mental anguish,
Feverish lips, cracking pains, dyspeptic agonies,
And nameless bodily suffering;
Or whether, with sudden dash,
Seize a bottle of PLANTATION BITTERS,

And, as Gunther swears, be myself a man again.
Gunther said my eyes were sallow,
My visage haggard, my breath tremendous bad,
My disposition troublesome—in fact,
He gently hinted I was fast becoming
Quite a nuisance.
Four bottles now beneath my vest have disappeared:
My food has relish, my appetite is keen,
My step elastic, my mind brilliant, and
Nine pounds avoirdupois is added to my weight.

The formula "S. T.—1860.—X." appears at the top of every advertisement of the bitters, and the first two portions doubtless refer to the name of the inventor and the date of the invention, while *x* may be the unknown quantity which has to be taken before the promises held forth in the advertisement are fulfilled. A good instance of the difference between precept and practice is shown by the annexed, which comes well from a firm in no way disdainful of the uses of advertising:—

S. T.—1860.—X.

SOME of our contemporaries seem to think that the triumph of their cause depended, like the fate of Jericho, upon the amount of noise made. In these days of refinement and luxury, an article of real intrinsic merit is soon appreciated, hence the unbounded and unparalleled success of

PLANTATION BITTERS.

Like the two preceding, this is from *Harper's Weekly*, the price for advertisements in the inner pages of which is said to be 1 dollar 50 cents per line, about five times as much as any of our highest priced papers, for the lines are by no means long for the money. The best customer *Harper's* has, and at the price perhaps the best customer any paper ever had, is Professor Leonidas Hamilton, who puffs himself in the most extraordinary manner, being always well before his beloved public, and now and again having *seven* columns of closely printed matter in *Harper's*, at the exorbitant price just mentioned. This lengthy advertisement is called "A

Timely Warning, and the Reason Why," and is constructed upon truly Yankee principles. It commences:—

HOW sublime, how beautiful the thought that the researches and developments of the Nineteenth Century have added fresh and glorious laurels to the great temple of fame and science! In every department and phase of progressive development the hand of the sage and philosopher is ever busy—ever ready to devise means for the amelioration of human woe and the prolongation of life.

Think you his an enviable position—an existence without stern obstacles and perplexing cares? Nay, far from it; for he plucks the lovely rose in peril of the thorn; he climbs to eminence and renown, and every step he gains is planted on a prostrate foe. He digs the gold and tries it; another and a bolder hand must strike the blow that stamps its worth and gives it currency as genuine.

It must be admitted by every rational mind that the man who contributes the most toward promoting the happiness and welfare of the human race, must of necessity be the most highly esteemed by his fellow-men; acting upon this principle, Prof. R. L. HAMILTON, of New York, has, by patient investigation, and vast experience, solved the uncertain question in relation to the vexed and important subject of Liver Complaints and other chronic diseases.

After a long preamble of this kind the Professor describes the "Symptoms of Liver Complaints," from which by an easy transition he comes to some "Important Facts," informing his "dear reader" that he "has remedies that will strike at the root of them as by magic," for "there is no such word as fail in his treatment." After that, a couple of columns are devoted to enumerate the "Reasons why Dr Hamilton is successful." One of these is—"Because he has investigated every remedy known to science, and, in addition, has new remedies, *of the fields and forests* OF HIS OWN DISCOVERY, and of the greatest possible efficacy and value." He ends this part with the awful words, "The truth must be told if the heavens fall," and a lot of testimonials are produced, each with a sensation heading, and relating the most wonderful effects produced by the Doctor's medicines. Thus one has got "an old lung difficulty;" another has "gained twenty pounds in three months,"—not money unfortunately, but flesh. One of the most curious puffs arising out of these testimonials is the following :—

IS ALL THIS TRUE?

Mr. Samuel L. Furlong, of Muskegan, Mich., in a letter dated April 6, 1868, writes:

"I have cut out SEVENTEEN of the testimonials that were in the *New York Tribune*, and sent them to the persons themselves, with letters of inquiry about them, and also about you, and every one stated that they were true, and recommending your remedies very highly; also giving a history of their cases, which was, indeed, very cheering to a poor man, with a sick wife and six small children to support."

The inconsequence of the conclusion is quite refreshing. What benefit this distressed family could have derived from the perusal of the testimonials we will not presume to say. Thus by an easy climax of sensational headings and cures, we arrive at three final articles, respectively headed, "In his mercy he saves the afflicted!"—"Read, ye afflicted"—and "Appreciate it fully." Then follows the "Conclusion" that it would be useless to cry "humbug," for the above parties have volunteered to give their evidence for the benefit of the suffering and for no other purpose, and the whole ends with a friendly recommendation to "have no hesitancy in writing to the Doctor, and state to him your case in full, and he will deal honestly and promptly with you."

Another very extensive dealer in advertisements, who also uses *Harper's* columns considerably, is the proprietor of the Pain Paint. His works are humorous and entertaining, the following being a fair example :—

MY WIFE HAD AN ULCER
On her Leg
Thirteen years,
Caused by various veins
Extending from her ancle to her knee.
Some places eaten away
To the bone.
I have employed
Over twenty eminent physicians
At vast expense,

But all attempts at cure
Proved utterly abortive
Until I used Wolcott's Pain Paint,
Which the Doctors told me
Was humbug.
But humbug or not
It has done the work complete
In less than one month,
Removing the pain
At first application.
I kept her leg wet
With PAIN PAINT constantly
Till healed.
I wish we had more humbugs as useful
As Dr. Wolcott's PAIN PAINT.
I am well known in this city,
And any person
Can make further inquiry
At 101 West Street, New York,
At the Hanover House
Of which I am proprietor.
And I think I can satisfy
All as to the benefit
Derived by the use of PAIN PAINT.

May 12, 1868. PETER MINCK.

There are many advertisements from Hamilton, Wolcott, and various other "professors" still before us, but with the foregoing we will conclude, and leave the curious to search the American journals for themselves. Those who like to take the trouble will find in them an inexhaustible mine of wealth. The reflection naturally arises in the minds of readers, that the Americans cannot, after all, be such a wonderfully smart nation, to allow an almost countless horde of quacks and impostors to batten on them, and to make large fortunes even in the face of the tremendous sums they have to pay for advertisements.

Extensive as our Colonies are, and numerous and excellent as are the newspapers published in them, the advertisements of the present day may be said with justice to offer no distinctive features whatever. With the exception of the names of streets and towns, the trade and other notices are just the same as appear in the home journals; and even the cries which now and again go up from the Australian papers for missing relatives are paralleled by similar advertisements constantly appearing in our own metropolis. We have, though, two or three quaint old specimens which have been lighted upon at rare intervals, and more because it would be unfair to pass over our extensive dependencies without mention than for any other reason we offer them to the consideration of the reader. The first is nearly eighty years old, and is copied verbatim from a Jamaica paper of the period:—

Kingston, March 7, 1795.

HALF-A-JOE REWARD.

WALKED away, about a Month ago, a Negro Wench, named *Prudence;* she is of the Eboe Country, a yellow Complexion, round chubby Face, goggle or full Eyes, has lost several of her fore Teeth, is short, lively, and active, a great Thief, speaks quick and tolerable good English; is one of the black Parson Lisle's Congregation; she is marked on both Shoulders and the left Cheek R. L.; had a Collar about her Neck, Chain and Lock, as a Punishment for her trying to entice a Man away the second Time; she is capable of very great Deception; she lards almost every Word with "plase God," or some pious Expression, and will thieve at the same Time.

It is likely she will endeavour to pass as free; she formerly belonged to Mary Roberts, and lately to Sarah Osborn; she has been twenty Years in the Town of Kingston, and about fourteen Months in the Country. When she left Kingston she secreted a Quantity of her Clothes with some of her Tribe; if gone there, she will be able to change her Dress. Is well acquainted in Spanish-town, and many other Parts of the Island; she possesses a great Share of the "holy Goggle," that is, throwing up her Eyes, and calling upon everything that is sacred, even when stolen Goods have been found upon her. She lately ran away, and was taken up. Whoever apprehends her a second Time, and lodges her in any Workhouse or Gaol in this Island, shall be entitled to the above Reward, and all reasonable Charges, on Application to Linwood and Nicoll, Merchants, in Kingston; or the Subscriber, at Wakefield, in Cedar Valley, St. George's.

ROBERT LOOSELY.

N.B. All Masters of Vessels are hereby cautioned against carrying her off; and all Persons found harbouring her, will be prosecuted with the utmost Rigour of the Law.

The next is of a considerably later time, being under date 1818, and comes from a different quarter of the globe. It refers to a raffle for women, and was published in a daily paper of Calcutta :—

FEMALES RAFFLED FOR.—Be it known, that Six Fair Pretty Young LADIES, with two sweet and engaging CHILDREN, lately imported from Europe, having roses of health blooming on their cheeks, and joy sparkling in their eyes, possessing amiable tempers and highly accomplished, whom the most indifferent cannot behold without expressions of rapture, are to be raffled for, next door to the British Gallery. Scheme: Twelve Tickets, at 12 rupees each; the highest of the three throws, doubtless, takes the most fascinating, &c. &c.

Modern improvements have, after all, somewhat benefited the world. Who would dream nowadays of such a scheme having been publicly advertised in a British dominion less than sixty years since? And this was not by any means the latest of such speculations either, yet it will be news to many that, even at the date given, such transactions were openly conducted. The next, also from Calcutta, is half-a-dozen years later, and treats of quite another vanity of the owners of the soil :—

NOTICE.—Mr W. M'Cleish begs to state to his friends and the public that he has received by the most recent arrivals the Prettiest Waistcoat Pieces that were ever seen: really it would be worth any gentleman's while even to look at them. It surpasses his weak understanding, how man who is born of a woman and full of trouble, could invent such pretty things.

It strikes him forcibly that the patterns and texture must have been undoubtedly invented by some wise philosopher.

Ladies, although my shop's small, I pray you won't fear,
I turned out my pelisses, the first of the land sure may wear;
If they are not well finished, or the best of trimmings—
I will undertake to eat backs, breasts, sleeves, and linings.

No. 39, Cossitollah, Jan. 4, 1824.

Australia offers us, by means of the *Sydney Gazette* of August 1825, an advertisement worth perusal:—

MRS BROWN respectfully thanks the community of thieves for relieving her from the fatigues and wearisomeness of keeping a chandler's shop, by taking the following goods off her hands; viz. —35 yards of shirting, 12 do. of muslin, 40 do. of calico, and various articles, as the auctioneer terms it, "too many to mention in an advertisement." But the gentlemen in their despatch of business forgot that they had taken along with them an infant's paraphernalia, two dozen of clouts, so elegantly termed by washerwomen. If the professors of felony do not give a dinner to their pals, and convert them into d'oyleys for finger glasses, Mrs Brown will thank them to return them, as they would not be so unmagnanimous and deficient of honour to keep such bagatelles from a poor mother and four children. This is to apprize the receivers of stolen property, that she will sooner or later have the pleasure of seeing their necks stretched, and that they will receive a tight cravat under the gallows by their beloved friend Jack Ketch. As the old saying is "The better the day the better the deed," the fraternity performed their operations on Sunday night last.

17, Philip Street.

Another from the same source, though of somewhat later date, refers to a failing not at all peculiar to the ladies and gentlemen of Sydney, as most owners and collectors of books have doubtless discovered ere now to their cost:—

IT is requested that those Ladies and Gentlemen who have, from time to time, borrowed books from Mr. S. Levy, will return them to the undersigned, who respectfully solicits all books now in possession of persons to whom they do not belong, to comply with the above—a fresh supply may be had. Among the number missing are the Pastor's Fire Side, Tales of my Landlord, Kenilworth, Princess Charlotte, Secret Revenge, Smollett's Works, Ivanhoe, Tales of the Times, Paradise Lost—so are the books until found by B. LEVY.

No. 72, George Street, Sydney.

The solicitation to the books themselves "to comply with the above," is no doubt an Australian figure by which, in order to avoid an obnoxious accusation against the borrowers, the books are supposed to be unwilling to return to the rightful owners. Between forty and fifty years ago it would have been very unpleasant in Australia to imply that any one had a desire to take that which belonged to any one else with a view to its permanent detention.

As we have said, the advertisements of more modern times call for no particular mention, and the papers published in New South Wales and Victoria—excellent journals, some of them capitally illustrated, and all equal to anything at home—contain nothing in their columns of a kind different from what has been already given under some one or other of the various chapter heads of this volume. In Canada the contiguity of the States is now and again apparent in the advertisements; but after the full-flavoured samples of the latter, anything from the Dominion would seem poor indeed.

CHAPTER XX.

ADVERSARIA.

DURING the progress of this book towards completion, we have now and again stumbled across something which would not consistently fit under any of the chapter heads in our plan, nor stand well by itself, and though at first rather puzzled what to do with these trifles, they have in the end accumulated sufficiently to form a chapter of varieties which will fitly conclude, and will doubtless prove neither dull nor uninteresting. In advertising there seems to be always something new springing up, and no sooner do we think we have discovered the last ingenious expedient of the man anxious to display his wares, or to tempt others to display theirs, than another and more novel plan for publicity arrests the attention, and makes its predecessor seem old-fashioned, if not obsolete. At the present moment the plan of an energetic Scotchman is the very latest thing in advertisements. Whether it will be considered a novelty six months hence, or whether it will be considered at all, it would be hard indeed to say, so it will perhaps be enough for us to give the plan to our readers, with the remark that after all the idea is not unlike that of the old newsletters to which reference has been made in an earlier portion of this work. The Scotchman's notion is to substitute advertisements for the intelligence contained in the ancient letters, and thereby reap a rich reward. For sixpence he sells twenty-four sheets of letter-paper, on the outside of each of which is an embossed penny postage-stamp. He fills the two inside pages with sixty advertisements, for which he charges one guinea each, leaving the first page for private correspondence, and the last page, to which the stamp is affixed, for the address. As the stamp will carry an ounce weight, another sheet of plain paper may be enclosed. He guarantees to the advertiser a circulation of five thousand copies. For the advertisements he receives £63, from which he pays five thousand stamps at one penny each—£20, 16s. 8d.—less received for copies sold (twenty-four for sixpence), £5, 4s. 2d.; total, £15, 12s. 6d., leaving the difference, £47, 7s. 6d., to cover the cost of paper and printing. It will be remembered by many that the plan of giving advertisement sheets away has been often tried—notably with metropolitan local newspapers, some of which at first thought to clear the whole of their expenses by means of the charge for notices, &c. It is remarkable, however, that these journals invariably did one of two things. They either got a price fixed on themselves, or died. It is hard to make advertisers believe that it is worth while paying for a notice in a paper which is itself not worth paying for, and no arguments as to increased circulation seem to have any effect.

Parisian advertisements form an item worthy of attention here. Within the past few years a great change has taken place in the system of advertising as known in the capital of France—in fact, as known in all the chief towns of the empire, kingdom, republic — whichever our readers like best or consider the most correct word. Between twenty-five and thirty years ago advertisements were charged at very high rates in the Paris papers, and there were comparatively few of them. The proprietors of journals did not themselves deal with the advertisers, but farmed out their columns at so much a year to advertising establishments or agencies. This was both convenient for the papers and profitable for the agencies. The rates they fixed for advertising in some of the most prominent journals were—*Presse*, one franc per line for each insertion; *Siècle*, one franc fifty centimes per line each insertion for four times, for ten times and upwards one franc per line, special notices three francs per line, editorial items five francs per line; *Nation* and *Débats*, four lines seventy-five centimes per line, advertisements above 150 lines fifty centimes per line, special notices two francs per line, editorial items three francs; *Galignani's Messenger*, seventy-five centimes a line each time, one advertisement above 300 lines fifty centimes a line, editorial items three francs. Other papers were lower, some taking advertisements for from twenty-five to forty centimes, and charging from one franc to two francs a line for editorial items; but their circulation was very limited. What are called broadside advertisements were very frequent in Paris papers; they were very ugly affairs to the eye of an Englishman; set up in sprawling capitals, like a handbill, a single advertisement frequently covering half or the whole of a page of a newspaper. This style of advertisement obtains now, but under different principles. The *Presse* and the *Siècle* used to make more money than any of the other papers by means of advertisements; in the year 1847 the income of the *Presse* for its two advertising pages was 300,000 francs. The advertising of the *Débats* and *Constitutionnel* was also profitable.

Things have very considerably changed since then, and Parisian advertising may fairly be said to have become developed into a flourishing, though at the same time a very unique, system. The remark, "Show me the advertisements of a country, and I will tell you the character of its inhabitants," is not yet current among the choice sayings of great men, yet it or something similar might well be said with regard to modern Parisian notifications. Perhaps in no country so much as in France are public announcements and advertisements so thoroughly characteristic of a people. An important law recently introduced compels all announcements fixed or displayed in public places to bear each a ten-centime stamp, and the Government reserves to itself the right of alone using a perfectly white *affiche.* All posters, playbills, and placards unconnected with State matters must be printed on coloured paper, though a small portion may remain white. The Parisians are proverbially neat in everything but their personal habits; and ugly, gaunt, straggling hoardings like those of London are quite unknown to them. The principal vacant places in front of building ground are usually purchased by one of the principal Sociétés de Publicité. A large frame of wood and canvas is affixed to the hoarding and divided into a number of squares, which are painted a neutral tint. Then in all these squares different announcements are made in gay colours. When completed, the structure resembles the boards of advertisements placed in railway carriages and omnibuses, the scale of course being considerably larger. A well-executed painting of some country seat or park to let frequently figures in these spaces; and few stations are without some well-known and familiar advertisement, the French having like ourselves some firms which make it their business to be on every hoarding and in every paper. A large tailoring and drapery establishment which advertises as follows is perhaps the best known of any:—

MAISON DE LA RUE DE
PONT NEUF
HABILLEMENTS PR HOMMES ET ENFANTS
ON REND L'ARGENT DE TOUT ACHAT QUI À
CESSE DE PLAIRE
**LA MAISON N'EST PAS AU COIN
DU QUAI.**

This advertisement is so well known that recently a *revue* bearing the title "La Maison n'est pas au Coin du Quai" was played at a well-known theatre, and in the recent version of "Orphée aux Enfers" at the Gaîté, the "on rend l'argent" portion is made the peg for a joke by the Monarch of Hell. The following also persistently arrest the attention of the traveller: "Au Bon Diable," "Eau Melisse des Carmes," "Chocolat Ibled," and "Old England British Tailors." The "Piano Quatuor" is also everywhere typified by the picture of a gentleman with hideous long fingers and pointed nails stretching over the strings of four violins.

The theatres usually display their programmes on large columns specially constructed for the purpose, which are fixed about every two hundred yards along the principal Boulevards. As these bills are renewed nearly every day, this department alone must be very remunerative to the Government. No playbills are sold in the theatres, but many of the daily journals publish the programmes of all; and three papers, the *Vert-Vert*, the *Orchestra*, and the *Entr'acte*, are specially printed to serve as bills of the play. One peculiar circumstance connected with theatrical advertisements is worthy of notice. In each of those places of public convenience known to Parisians as "Les Colonnes Rambuteau," some mysterious individual has for years pasted a little piece of paper announcing the drama at the Ambigu Comique and the principal performers therein. Here is an exact copy of the one appearing during the month of June of the present year (1874):—

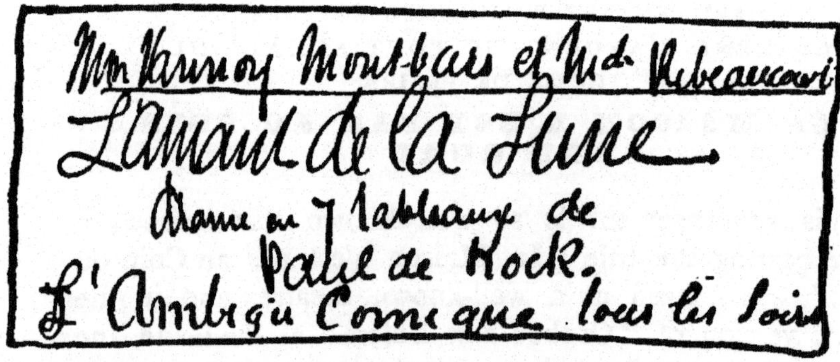

L'amant de la Lune

Drame en 7 tableaux de

Paul de Kock.

L'Ambigu Comique tous les soirs

For years some unknown person has thus maybe gratuitously advertised the house in question, and his identity is one of the mysteries of Paris. Two well-known Parisian journalists, piqued by the eccentricity of the advertisement, lay in wait one whole night and day for the purpose of discovering its author, but their effort was fruitless. While on the subject of these *colonnes*, we may note the fact that their exteriors are covered with advertisements, the most conspicuous among them being the bill of fare of the "Dîner de Rocher," a three-franc ordinary on the Boulevard Montmartre. The interior announcements are not of a nature for publication, and in that respect resemble kindred establishments this side the Channel. Next in importance to the hoardings and "spectacle" columns are the kiosques, in which the newspaper trade of Paris is chiefly carried on. The front is open, with the paper stall before it; but the remaining sides are of coloured glass, and each square contains an advertisement painted or stained upon it, generally in large letters. At night the light in the interior gives the kiosque a very gay and festive appearance. There are various minor methods of attracting public attention practised by the Parisian traders. The managers of the Louvre and Pygmalion, establishments similar to our Shoolbred's and Meeking's, give to each of their customers an air balloon with the name of the establishment from which it is issued painted upon it. Thousands of these are constantly bobbing about along the principal thoroughfares. The tickets given to seat occupiers in the public gardens and parks are beautifully illuminated cards covered with trade announcements. Some of the restaurants give each of their lady-customers a fan in summer, which is prettily ornamented with advertisements. At Duval's famous eating establishments the backs of the bills of fare are sold for a large sum to advertising contractors. It is calculated that this firm issues 30,000 *cartes* a day. Space will not allow us to enumerate the further thousand-and-one plans—some sensible, some silly—which the Parisians adopt for attracting public attention; we therefore pass on to the last and most important medium for advertisements—the Parisian newspapers. In French journals, as in some English, the *réclame*, or editorial puff, is eagerly sought after; and for unblushing effrontery in selling their pens to pushing tradesmen, we must yield the palm to our brother scribes across the water. "They order this matter better in France." Only a short time since M. de Villemessant, the editor of *Le Figaro*, gave a delightful specimen of the art in his own columns. He commenced by relating the history of the Duke of Hamilton and the sheep's wool left on the brambles. Then came a long description of the homes of the Highland shepherds, and their spinning wives. The English word "homespun" being thus introduced, the article wound up by advising *les gentlemen français* to rush to a certain shop in Paris where homespun was sold, and be measured for suits. A few days after the article had been published, its author was sauntering along the Boulevards clad in a homespun suit of the latest cut and pattern.

We present a choice specimen of the *réclame* cut from the pages of the Parisian *gommeux's* favourite journal:—

> *Le Figaro* n'oublie pas que son aïeul était coiffeur, aussi ne dédaigne-t-il pas de parler des chevaliers du démêloir, surtout lorsque ceux-ci se recommandent à l'attention du public par des qualités hors ligne.
>
> Nos lecteurs du quartier de l'Arc-de-Triomphe, y compris les Ternes, l'avenue de l'Impératrice, Neuilly, etc., ne se doutent pas qu'ils possèdent dans leur voisinage, 47, avenue de la Grande-Armée, un expert en fait de coiffures de femmes et d'hommes... Il se nomme Rivals et n'en connait pas (pardon!) pour la dexterité du peigne et la légèreté du rasoir.

Here is another of these exquisite specimens of artistry in puffing. It is from *La Vie Parisienne* of a short time back:—

> — Les voyageurs pour la ligne d'Italie montent en voiture.
>
> — Une minute, sac à papier! je n'ai pas pris mon café.
>
> — Un qui se croit encore au temps des diligence: le chemin de fer n'attend pas.

—N'est-ce que cela, cher? monte dans mon compartiment, et tu n'auras pas à regretter la chicorée du buffet.

Le sifflet fait entendre son son strident. Nous voici partis! Nous avons tiré de son sac de voyage un flacon d'*Essence de café Trablit*. Il me fait un mazagran que je sirote avec autant de délices que si Tortoni l'eût préparé.

En crème, à l'eau, au lait, en grog, l'*Essence de café Trablit* est chose exquise. Recommandée aux voyageuses, dans leur intérêt. 1 fr. 60 le flacon (67, rue Jean-Jacques-Rousseau).

Besides writing up the goods of energetic and aspiring tradesmen, the French journalist is frequently employed by a third or fourth rate actress to write her into notoriety. To do this he carefully avoids any mention of her histrionic abilities; but whenever he gets an opportunity, he describes her dresses, her equipage, her *petits soupers*, and occasionally places in her mouth some clever repartee or daring joke. Once in vogue, a lady of this kind has obtained the object of her ambition, and many a queen of the *demi-monde* owes her success in the realms of guilty splendour to the constant puffing of some hireling scribe. Hireling though he be, the scribe is also an artist, and his work bears an immeasurably favourable comparison with that of his clumsy English rival; for he has rivals in England, and *réclames* are finding their way rapidly into the most pretentious of our papers. Hitherto they have succeeded in deceiving none so much as their writers and those who pay for them; but there is yet hope. Occasionally the French *réclame* mania is worked up into a good joke, as in the following:—

Une maison de blanc portant pour enseigne: *Au bon petit Jésus*, avait pour caissier un affreux gredin qui disparaît un jour avec la grenouille tout entière.

Tous les journaux sont pleins du vol commis au *Bon petit Jésus*.

Le patron court affolé et met la main sur son employé au moment où celui-ci prenait tardivement le chemin de fer. Il lui saute au collet:

— Misérable! tu m'as ruiné!

L'autre répond, sans s'émouvoir:

— Oui, monsieur... mais quelle réclame pour la maison!

Sometimes the advertisement is given in an indirect manner: thus the public read the following in the day's paper:—

Un détail amusant.

Sur le rideau d'annonces des Bouffes on peut lire ce qui suit :

Mesdames, souvenez-vous que les vieilles robes et les ameublements fanés teints par la maison X... sont plus beaux que neufs !

Comme c'est bien en situation !

The next time the reader goes to the theatre the advertisement alluded to catches his eye, and the address is fixed in his memory.

The *réclame* is at present an important feature of French journalism. It generally pays all parties concerned in its manufacture, and its existence is therefore likely to continue for long. The reader has only to pick up *Le Gaulois*, *Le Figaro*, or any of the Parisian lighter papers, and he will be enabled to see for himself to what an extent commerce has infected the Gallic press.

Turning from the *réclames* to the advertisements proper, we find there are five distinct specimens of the latter, so far as style is concerned. Each one of these has its modifications, but the following samples will be found very near the mark. The first will serve a double purpose, as it seems to point out that despite the ridicule cast on English costumes by Parisian satirists, there are not a few who wear them, though they have every opportunity of appearing in the Frenchest of French fashions:—

PANTALONS ANGLAIS

FAITS SUR MESURE: 19 fr 50

OLD ENGLAND

35, *boulevard des Capucines.*

The second specimen is intended for the ladies, who may believe what they like of the statement made about its salutary action, and its adding to the natural beauty :—

La Veloutine

est une poudre de Ris spéciale
préparée au bismuth,
par conséquent
d'une action salutaire sur la peau.
Elle est adhérente et invisible,
aussi donne-t-elle au teint
une fraîcheur et une beauté naturelles.
Ch. FAY, inventeur, 9, rue de la Paix.

Our third refers to something which has been fashionable as long as there has been such a thing as fashion, and which is likely to continue till *la mode* itself has an end :—

MARIAGES
DEMANDEZ LE
TRAIT D'UNION
RÉPERTOIRE COMPLET ET DISCRET DES
DEMANDES ET PROPOSITIONS
DE TOUS PAYS, ADRESSÉES A
M. et à Mme ROULARD, 72, rue de Rivoli.

DOTS DEPUIS 10,000 FR.
Jusqu'aux plus grandes fortunes.
(Timbres pour réponse.)

Our fourth selection refers to a stomachic which is rather fashionable just now :—

Saint Raphaël, vin fortifiant, digestif, Tonique reconstituant, goût excellent, plus efficace, pour les personnes affaiblies, que les ferrugineux, que les quinas. Prescrit dans les fatigues d'estomac, la chlorose, l'anémie, les convalescences. Dose : un demi-verre à bordeaux après les repas.—Principales pharmacies 3 fr. la bouteille.

And our fifth is the following :—

AVIS AUX DAMES

A LA **MAGICIENNE** 129, RUE MONTMARTRE.

La plus grande spécialite pour Dames.
20,000 **Confections** à choisir.

2,000 **Collets cachemire,** ornés soie et guipure, à....... **12**

1,500 **Jacquettes cachemire,** ornées faye et guipure, à..... **15 F.**

800 **Tuniques cachemire,** ornées guipure, valant 60 fr., à **25 F.**

1,000 **Fichus** Marie-Antoinette, ornés passementerie et guip^re **29 F.**

500 **Dolmans** cachemire, tout brodés, garnis guipure, à. **45 F.**

2,500 **Dolmans** fantaisie, brodés toutes nuances, à..... **17 F.**

1,000 **Robes** fantaisie, modèles nouveaux, à......... **39 F.**

Tous les **Costumes** et **Confections** sur mesure au même prix.

Les Magasins sont ouverts les Dimanches et jours de Fêtes.

A LA **MAGICIENNE** 129, RUE MONTMARTRE

An ingenious method of obtaining notoriety, and one which has paid pretty well recently over some theatrical matters in this country, is to fall foul of the official censor. The announcement that "la Censure a interdit 'Palotte' dans les gares" has caused "Palotte," a rather dirty novel, to be an immense success. Why it should be forbidden in the railway stations, and allowed everywhere else, we are not sufficiently behind the scenes to say.

We have now glanced hastily at the leading aspects of French advertising, and after remarking that *Galignani* and the *Gazette des Etrangers* are the great mediums for English and American advertisements in Paris, that a certain American manager who has a theatre in London advertises it and his angular histrionic wonder regularly in the former, and that the principal advertising contractors of Paris have made vast fortunes, we get fairly back to our original remark, that the whole system of advertising in Paris is characteristic of the Parisians—a strange mixture of neatness, effect, frivolity, and childishness. Who shall deny that these four words suit the character of the great mass of the people? The fact that the authorities reserve to themselves the white *affiche* is characteristic to a degree of French Governments, and the savage attack which the French journals made upon the letters of apartments, because their poor little notices "Chambre à louer" were exempted from the ten-centimes tax, was a fair specimen of the frivolous and vexatious spirit which animates the children of *la Grcnde Nation.* For their neatness they are proverbial; and any one walking through the streets of Paris cannot fail to notice the admirable order in which the various stations are kept. No rain-soaked bills peeling off, no mud-plashed announcements of pieces which have been withdrawn for weeks—all is neat and fresh, and corrected to date. The gay colours of the posters, the many-tinted sides of the *kiosques*, the illuminated "spectacle" columns, the gilt-lettered balconies, the quaint gas devices, and the thousand-and-one pretty and ingenious ideas which are pressed into the service of the modern goddess Publicity, are all items in one lovely and harmonious whole, the most beautiful and the best-arranged city of modern times, Paris. We can teach

France many things, probably she can teach us one certainly —which is, that art, even genius, may be successfully applied to such a very small pursuit as that of advertising.

The consideration of *réclames*, which are now regarded as so essentially French, has reminded us, not alone that they were fashionable, though under a humbler name, in this country many, many years ago, as we have already shown, but that they are again coming into fashion. But the "puff-pars" of old England—which may fairly be represented by those which emanated from the establishment of Rowland, the Kalydor man, in his palmy days of advertising —were always clumsy when compared with those *réclames* we have been studying, it being impossible, apparently, to make a British advertiser understand that an advertisement is more valuable in proportion as it looks less like what it really is. The cloven foot always shows forth under the wrapper of fine words; and when we say this, we do not refer to the paragraphs written in odonto or ointment establishments by young men at a pound a week, who are bound to put so many hard words in a line, and keep their productions within the compass of so many lines, whether syntax is agreeable or not; but to the friendly and more able notices which now and again find their way into some daily and weekly papers. The *réclame*, in its best form, is a highly-cultivated flower—an exotic, in fact—and is at present a little over the heads of the advertising public, who like to see plenty for money.

One paragraph which approaches much nearer the true *réclame* than most attempts, we stumbled across the other day. It is an attempt to convey to a wondering world how Perry Davis's Pain Killer came to be used both internally and externally. By it we find that much internal discomfiture had been destroyed by the specific, when one day, in conducting some scientific exploration, its patentee became sadly burned. In his agony he threw the contents of the nearest bottle—which happened to contain Pain Killer—

over the injured parts, and as much to his surprise as satisfaction, he became in a short time perfectly cured. Of a rather more ambitious kind is an attempt made by Messrs Piesse and Lubin in the same direction. It is quite unique, and deserves a place here. At all events we came upon it in a fashionable morning paper, and read some little way before noticing that we were deep in an advertisement:—

On Tuesday evening Countess Wallflower resumed her usual assemblies after the recess, at her residence in the Laboratory of Flowers. Among the members of the diplomatic corps present were the Ambassadors from the principal Gardens of Europe, Asia, Africa, and America, Muskrosa Bey, from the Hanging Garden of Persia, Mdlles. Muskrosabud, Otto Rose, Ambassador from the Balkan and Adrionople Flower Farms, the Countess Hoya Bella, Madame Mignionette, Magnolia Fulgans, the Florida Ambassador, the Countess Flagrant Orchids, the Italian Minister, the Countess Bergamotte, Mdlle. Neroli the Mexican Minister and the Marchioness de Vanille, the Brazilian Minister and the Odorous Opoponax. The general circle comprised, among others, the Princesses Jessamine, Violet, Tuberose, the Viscount Stephanotis, and the Marchioness of May Blossom. Previous to the assembly the Countess and the Right Hon. Sir Scented Stock received at dinner the Duke of Frangipanni and a select party. The company separated by midnight, and rose in the morning more fragrant than ever.

It may be as well to mention here that Messrs Piesse and Lubin claim to be the originators of the enigmatical form of advertising. It was they who started the "Opoponax" mystery, which aroused public curiosity at the time, and has been considerably imitated since. Localities are sometimes used in advertisements as typifying the quality of the articles advertised; Mayfair Sherry is the chief representative of this class, and we suppose that the district is named as evidence of high tone and elegant bottling. Still another kind of advertising is that adopted by Brinsmead, who seems to be a regular champion among pianoforte-makers, and who makes curious little extracts bracketed opposite the names of papers and celebrities that give him testimonials, throughout a long newspaper column, all about his patent check repeater-action gold medal pianofortes. Sir Julius Benedict, the *Examiner*, Brinley Richards, the *Standard*, and Sydney Smith are among many other men and papers quoted. We are not aware who Sydney Smith may be nowadays, but should hardly think the great wit and essayist who died thirty years ago could have known enough about Brinsmead's pianos to enable him to say "their touch is absolute perfection."

Notwithstanding all that has been written and said about the value of newspaper notices as distinguished from advertisements, there is no reasonable room for doubt that a representative of the general advertising class would far sooner see his shop paraded in a pantomime, or hear himself referred to by a low comedian, than be recipient of really valuable attention at the hands of a newspaper writer. There are, of course, exceptions, and these reap the reward their rivals despise. The elder Mathews was a victim to the rather illogical rage for that phase of theatrical advertisement to which we have just referred. Amongst the extraordinary effects of his popularity, were applications made under every kind of pretext, letters being sent to him from all sorts of professors and tradesmen about town. One man offered him snuff for himself and friends for ever, if he would only mention the name and shop of the manufacturer. Another promised him a perpetual polish for his boots upon the same terms. He was solicited to mention every sort of exhibition, and to puff all the new quack medicines. The wines sent to him to taste, though alleged to be of the finest quality, nevertheless required "a bush," which was to be hung out nightly at his "house of entertainment." Patent filters, wigs and waistcoats, boots and boothooks, "ventilating hats" and "bosom friends," all gifts, used to stock Mathews's lumber-room. An advertising dentist one day presented himself, offering to find Mathews's whole family in new teeth, and draw all the old, if the comedian would only in return draw the new patent mineral masticators into notice. In fact, Mathews was so inundated with presents, that his cottage sometimes looked like a bazaar, and his wife had frequently occasion to exercise her ingenuity in contriving how to dispose of the generally useless articles forced upon their acceptance.

Though this was a great many years ago, things remain much the same, and such popular entertainers as Fred Maccabe, and patterers as J. L. Toole, could doubtless sell themselves for large sums in the interests of vocal advertising. Managers invariably avail themselves of the opportunity whenever a chance occurs, as it does now and again in realistic drama, and very frequently in pantomime. Actors are, though, not alone the admiration of the advertiser—they are by no means above making a shrewd bid for popularity themselves by means of the papers. It is not so very long ago that a tragedian, more distinguished in the provinces than in London, and anxious to meet that metropolitan recognition which he felt sure he deserved, gave a small *réckerché* banquet to his early friends at a well-known house near Lincoln's-Inn Fields. Those who were invited must have felt very much like Mr Twemlow used whenever he visited the Veneerings, and those who were in a condition to think when they came away must have felt puzzled to account for the fact that all Mr ——'s early friends had taken to the dramatic-critic, the leader-writer, or the editor line of business—all but one, a kind of literary tradesman, who, however, possibly paid his half for the privilege of being admitted into such splendid society on equal terms, and who had, moreover, made out the list of diners, written the invitations, and maybe provided some of the clean linen. We tell the story as it was told us by two of the invited early friends, who added, that until the night of the dinner they had never seen Mr —— off the stage.

Taking a long stride from London to a Chinese seaport,

we come upon this choice sample of Flowery Land English :—

Chong thie Loong kee.

Most humbly beg leave to acqu : aint the Gentlemen trading to this kort that the above mention : ed chop has been long established dnd is much esteemed for its Black and young Hyson Tea but fearing the foreigners might be cheated by tho : se shumeless persons who forged this chop he therefore take the liberty to pallish these few lines for its remark and trust.

To those who are interested in a peculiarity of advertising unknown in this country, we present the following from the *Berlinische Zeitung* :—

Verlobungen.

Als Verlobte empfehlen sich

Minna Bock,
Fritz Engelhardt.

Berlin, den 13. März 1872.

Which informs us, under the head of Betrothal, that Minna Bock and Fritz Engelhardt beg to announce their betrothal, with compliments. The date is plain. Another announcement in the same paper, and under the same head, is this:—

> Die Verlobung unserer ältesten Tochter **Margarethe** mit dem kaiserlichen Post-Inspektor Herrn Richard **Raab** in Magdeburg beehren wir uns ergebenst anzuzeigen.
>
> Stendal, im März 1872.
>
> Dr. **Goldscheider** nebst Frau.
>
> Margarethe **Goldscheider**,
> Richard **Raab**,
> Verlobte.
> Stendal und Magdeburg.

Which means that Dr Goldscheider and his wife do themselves the honour of most humbly announcing the betrothal of their eldest daughter, Margaret, to Herr Richard Raab, of Magdeburg, Inspector of the Imperial Post. Then follow the signatures of bride and groom, and the whole winds up with the happy conjunction of the two towns, Stendal and Magdeburg.

From the *Journal do Commercio* of Rio de Janeiro, April 4, 1872, we take the following:—

> Fugio da rua da Alfandega n. 297 o preto Mariano, crioulo, estatura regular, rosto compride, pouca barba, com falta de dentes na frente, tem uma fistula debaixo do queixo, costuma trocar o nome, des-confia-se que fosse para os lados de Nitherohy e tem signaes de ser surrado nas costas; quem o apprehender e levar á rua e numero acima ser á gratificado, e protesta-se contra quem o tiver acoutado.

Credulous persons, who believe that with the cessation of the war between the Northern and Southern States of America slavery went right out of existence, except amongst the most barbarous nations, may be astonished to discover that the foregoing, when turned into English, reads thus:—"Ran away from 297 Alfandega Street, the negro Mariano, a half-caste of ordinary stature, long visage, slight beard, has lost some front teeth, and has an ulcer in the lower jaw. He is accustomed to change his name, and is believed to be in the outskirts of Nitherohy. He has marks of flogging on his back. Whoever captures him, and brings him to the above address, will be rewarded, and persons are hereby cautioned against harbouring him."

From the same paper we extract another announcement:—

Antonio Luiz Fernandes da Cunha e sua mulher D. Manoela Pereira Fernandes da Cunha, Leopoldino José da Cunha e sua mulher D. Balbina Alves Pereira da Cunha, convidão ás pessoas de sua amizade para acompanhar o enterro de seu querido filho e neto o innocente Carlos, que ha de sepultarse hoje, ás 10½ horas da manhã, no cemiterio de S. João Baptista, sahindo o corpo da rua da Bella-Vista n. 3, no Rio Comprido.

Which means that Antonio Luiz Fernandez da Cunha and his wifé, Donna Manoela Pereira Fernandes da Cunha, Leopoldino José da Cunha and his wife, Donna Balbina Alves Pereira da Cunha, invite their friends to accompany the funeral of their lamented son and grandson, the innocent Carlos, who will be buried to-day at half-past ten in the morning, in the Cemetery of St John the Baptist. The place of rendezvous concludes the melancholy announcement.

Funeral advertisements seem very popular in Rio, the following being extracted from among a large number of similar announcements in the *Journal do Commercio*:—

✝ D. Joanna da Silva Maia da Conceição e Procopio de Jesus cordialmente agradecem ás pessoas que fizerão o caridoso obsequio de acompanhar os restos mortaes de seu muito prezado esposo e compadre Olegario da Silva ; e de novo rogão ás mesmas pessoas e aos amigos do mesmo finado para assistir à missa de

sentimo dia, que se ha de celebrar, amanhã 5 do corrente, na matriz de Sant'Anna, ás 8 horas; pelo que desde já se confessão summamente gratos.

This is from Donna Joanna da Silva Maia da Conceição and Procopio de Jesus, who cordially thank those friends that performed the charitable office of following to the grave the mortal remains of their very dear husband and godfather, Olegario da Silva. Those and others are again requested to attend the seventh-day mass, which is to be performed on the morrow, in the mother church of St Anna, at eight o'clock, for which attendance the advertisers will be very thankful. There are so many of these notices, all of which are evidently looked forward to with interest, that the reader cannot help thinking a particularly healthy season in Rio would be regarded as quite a public misfortune.

FINIS.

PRINTED BY BALLANTYNE AND COMPANY
EDINBURGH AND LONDON

A List of Books

PUBLISHED BY

CHATTO & WINDUS

74 & 75, PICCADILLY, LONDON, W.

ADVERTISING, A HISTORY OF, from the Earliest Times. Illustrated by Anecdotes, Curious Specimens, and Biographical Notes of Successful Advertisers. By HENRY SAMPSON. Crown 8vo, with Coloured Frontispiece and Illustrations, cloth gilt, 7*s.* 6*d.*

"Amusante histoire de l'annonce dans l'antiquité, c'est-à-dire chez les Grecs et surtout en Italie, où l'on a retrouvé tant de piquants spécimens sur les murailles de Pompéi, puis au moyen âge, au dernier siècle et de nos jours. Un tel livre ne pouvait être bien fait qu'en Angleterre, terre classique des joyeuses excentricités de l'annonce, des loteries et des agences matrimoniales."—*Le Temps* (Paris).

ÆSOP'S FABLES TRANSLATED INTO HUMAN NATURE. By C. H. BENNETT. Crown 4to, 24 Plates beautifully printed in Colours, with descriptive Text, cloth extra, gilt, 6*s.*

"For fun and frolic the new version of Æsop's Fables must bear away the palm. There are twenty-two fables and twenty-two wonderful coloured illustrations; the moral is pointed, the tale adorned. This is not a juvenile book, but there are plenty of grown-up children who like to be amused at Christmas, and indeed at any time of the year; and if this new version of old stories does not amuse them they must be very dull indeed, and their situation one much to be commiserated."—*Morning Post.*

AINSWORTH'S LATIN DICTIONARY. The only Modern Edition which comprises the Complete Work. With numerous Additions, Emendations, and Improvements, by the Rev. B. W. BEATSON and W. ELLIS. Imperial 8vo, cloth extra, 15*s.*

AMUSING POETRY. A Selection from the Best Writers. Edited, with Preface, by SHIRLEY BROOKS. Fcap. 8vo, cloth, gilt edges, 3*s.* 6*d.*

ANACREON. Translated by THOMAS MOORE, and Illustrated by the exquisite Designs of GIRODET. Oblong 8vo, Etruscan gold and blue, 12*s.* 6*d.*

ARTEMUS WARD, COMPLETE.—The Works of CHARLES FARRER BROWNE, better known as ARTEMUS WARD. With fine Portrait, facsimile of Handwriting, &c. Crown 8vo, cloth extra, 7*s.* 6*d.*

AS PRETTY AS SEVEN, and other Popular German Stories. Collected by LUDWIG BECHSTEIN. With Additional Tales by the Brothers GRIMM, and 100 Illustrations by RICHTER. Small 4to, green and gold, 6*s.* 6*d.*; gilt edges, 7*s.* 6*d.*

ASTLE ON WRITING.—THE ORIGIN AND PROGRESS OF WRITING, as well Hieroglyphic as Elementary, Illustrated by Engravings taken from Marbles, Manuscripts, and Charters, Ancient and Modern: also Some Account of the Origin and Progress of Printing. By THOMAS ASTLE, F.R.S., F.A.S., late Keeper of Records in the Tower of London. Royal 4to, half-Roxburghe, with 33 Plates (some Coloured), price £1 15s. A few Large Paper copies, royal folio, half-Roxburghe, the Plates altogether unfolded, price £3 3s.

BACON'S (Francis, Lord) WORKS, both English and Latin, with an Introductory Essay, Biographical and Critical, and copious Indexes. Two Vols., imperial 8vo, with Portrait, cloth extra, £1 4s.

BARDSLEY'S OUR ENGLISH SURNAMES: Their Sources and Significations. By CHARLES WAREING BARDSLEY, M.A. SECOND EDITION, revised throughout, considerably Enlarged, and partially rewritten. Crown 8vo, cloth extra, 9s.

"Mr. Bardsley has faithfully consulted the original mediæval documents and works from which the origin and development of surnames can alone be satisfactorily traced. He has furnished a valuable contribution to the literature of surnames, and we hope to hear more of him in this field."—*Times.*

BAUER AND HOOKER'S GENERA OF FERNS; in which the Characters of each Genus are displayed in a series of magnified dissections and figures, highly finished in colours, after the drawings of FRANCIS BAUER, with letterpress by Sir WILLIAM HOOKER. Imperial 8vo, with 120 beautifully Coloured Plates, half-morocco, gilt, £5 5s.

BEAUTIFUL PICTURES BY BRITISH ARTISTS: A Gathering of Favourites from our Picture Galleries. In Two Series. The FIRST SERIES including Examples by WILKIE, CONSTABLE, TURNER, MULREADY LANDSEER, MACLISE, E. M. WARD, FRITH, Sir JOHN GILBERT, LESLIE, ANSDELL, MARCUS STONE, Sir NOEL PATON, FAED, EYRE CROWE, GAVIN, O'NEIL, and MADOX BROWN. The SECOND containing Pictures by ARMYTAGE, FAED, GOODALL, HEMSLEY, HORSLEY, MARKS, NICHOLLS, Sir NOEL PATON, PICKERSGILL, G. SMITH, MARCUS STONE, SOLOMON, STRAIGHT, E. M. WARD, and WARREN. All engraved on Steel in the highest style of Art. Edited, with Notices of the Artists, by SYDNEY ARMYTAGE, M.A. Price of each Series, imperial 4to, cloth extra, gilt and gilt edges, 21s. *Each Volume is Complete in itself.*

BELL'S (Sir Charles) ANATOMY OF EXPRESSION, as connected with the Fine Arts. Fifth Edition, with an Appendix on the Nervous System by ALEXANDER SHAW. Illustrated with 45 beautiful Engravings. Imp. 8vo, cloth extra, gilt, 16s.

"The artist, the writer of fiction, the dramatist, the man of taste, will receive the present work (which is got up with an elegance worthy of its subject) with gratitude, and peruse it with a lively and increasing interest and delight."—*Christian Remembrancer.*

BINGHAM'S ANTIQUITIES of the CHRISTIAN CHURCH. A New Edition, revised, with copious Index. Two Vols., imperial 8vo, cloth extra, £1 4s.

"A writer who does equal honour to the English clergy and to the English nation, and whose learning is to be equalled only by his moderation and impartiality."—*Quarterly Review.*

BIOGRAPHICAL AND CRITICAL DICTIONARY OF RECENT AND LIVING PAINTERS AND ENGRAVERS, both English and Foreign. By HENRY OTTLEY. Being a Supplementary Volume to "Bryan's Dictionary." Imperial 8vo, cloth extra, 12s.

*** *This is the only work giving an account of the principal living painters of all countries.*

BLAKE'S WORKS.—A Series of Reproductions in Facsimile of the Works of WILLIAM BLAKE, including the "Songs of Innocence and Experience," "The Book of Thel," "America," "The Vision of the Daughters of Albion," "The Marriage of Heaven and Hell," "Europe, a Prophecy," "Jerusalem," "Milton," "Urizen," "The Song of Los," &c. These Works will be issued both coloured and plain. [*In preparation.*

"Blake is a real name, I assure you, and a most extraordinary man he is, if he still be living. He is the Blake whose wild designs accompany a splendid edition of Blair's 'Grave.' He paints in water-colours marvellous strange pictures—visions of his brain—which he asserts he has seen. They have great merit. I must look upon him as one of the most extraordinary persons of the age."—CHARLES LAMB.

BLANCHARD'S (Laman) POEMS. Now first Collected. Edited, with a Life of the Author (including numerous hitherto unpublished Letters from Lord LYTTON, LAMB, DICKENS, ROBERT BROWNING, and others), by BLANCHARD JERROLD. Crown 8vo, cloth extra. [*In preparation.*

BOCCACCIO'S DECAMERON; or, Ten Days' Entertainment. Translated into English, with Introduction by THOMAS WRIGHT, Esq., M.A., F.S.A. With Portrait after RAPHAEL, and STOTHARD'S beautiful Copperplates. Crown 8vo, cloth extra, gilt, 7*s.* 6*d.*

BOLTON'S SONG BIRDS OF GREAT BRITAIN. Illustrated with Figures, the size of Life, of both Male and Female; of their Nests and Eggs, Food, Favourite Plants, Shrubs, Trees, &c. &c. Two Vols. in One, royal 4to, containing 80 beautifully Coloured Plates, half-Roxburghe, £3 13*s.* 6*d.*

BOOKSELLERS, A HISTORY OF. Including the Story of the Rise and Progress of the Great Publishing Houses, in London and the Provinces, and of their greatest Works. By HARRY CURWEN. Crown 8vo, with Frontispiece and numerous Portraits and Illustrations, cloth extra, 7*s.* 6*d.*

"In these days, ten ordinary Histories of Kings and Courtiers were well exchanged against the tenth part of one good History of Booksellers."—THOMAS CARLYLE.

"This stout little book is unquestionably amusing. Ill-starred, indeed, must be the reader who, opening it anywhere, lights upon six consecutive pages within the entire compass of which some good anecdote or smart repartee is not to be found."—*Saturday Review.*

BOUDOIR BALLADS: Vers de Société. By J. ASHBY STERRY. Crown 8vo, cloth extra. [*In preparation.*

BRET HARTE'S CHOICE WORKS in Prose and Poetry. With Introductory Essay by J. M. BELLEW, Portrait of the Author, and 50 Illustrations. Crown 8vo, cloth extra, 7*s.* 6*d.*

BREWSTER'S (Sir David) MARTYRS OF SCIENCE. A New Edition, in small crown 8vo, cloth extra, gilt, with full-page Portraits, 4*s.* 6*d.*

BREWSTER'S (Sir David) MORE WORLDS THAN ONE, the Creed of the Philosopher and the Hope of the Christian. A New Edition, in small crown 8vo, cloth extra, gilt, with full-page Astronomical Plates, 4*s.* 6*d.*

BRIC-À-BRAC HUNTER (The); or, Chapters on Chinamania. By Major H. BYNG HALL. With Photographic Frontispiece. Crown 8vo, cloth, full gilt (from a special and novel design), 10*s.* 6*d.*

BRITISH ESSAYISTS (The): viz., "Spectator," "Tatler," "Guardian," "Rambler," "Adventurer," "Idler," and "Connoisseur." Complete in Three thick Vols., 8vo, with Portrait, cloth extra, £1 7*s.*

BROADSTONE HALL, and other Poems. By W. E. WINDUS. With 40 Illustrations by ALFRED CONCANEN. Crown 8vo, cloth extra, gilt, 5s.

"This little volume of poems is illustrated with such vigour, and shows such a thoroughly practical knowledge of and love for sea-life, that it is quite tonic and refreshing. Maudlin sentimentality is carefully eschewed, and a robust, manly tone of thought gives muscle to the verse and elasticity of mind to the reader."—*Morning Post.*

BROCKEDON'S PASSES OF THE ALPS. Containing 109 fine Engravings by FINDEN, WILLMORE, and others; with Maps of each Pass, and a General Map of the Alps by ARROWSMITH. Two Vols., 4to, half-bound morocco, gilt edges, £3 13s. 6d.

BULWER'S (Lytton) PILGRIMS OF THE RHINE. With Portrait and 27 exquisite Line Engravings on Steel, by GOODALL, WILLMORE, and others; after Drawings by DAVID ROBERTS and MACLISE. Crown 8vo, cloth extra, top edges gilt, 10s. 6d.

BUNYAN'S PILGRIM'S PROGRESS. With 17 beautiful Steel Engravings by STOTHARD, engraved by GOODALL; and numerous Woodcuts. Square 8vo, cloth gilt, 10s. 6d.

BURNET'S HISTORY OF HIS OWN TIME, from the Restoration of Charles II. to the Treaty of Peace at Utrecht. With Historical and Biographical Notes and copious Index. Imp. 8vo, with Portrait, cloth extra, 13s. 6d.

BURNET'S HISTORY OF THE REFORMATION OF THE CHURCH OF ENGLAND. A New Edition, with numerous illustrative Notes and copious Index. Two Vols., imperial 8vo, cloth extra, £1 1s.

BYRON'S (Lord) LETTERS AND JOURNALS. With Notices of his Life. By THOMAS MOORE. A Reprint of the Original Edition, newly revised, complete in a thick volume of 1060 pp., with Twelve full-page Plates. Crown 8vo, cloth extra, gilt, 7s. 6d.

"We have read this book with the greatest pleasure. Considered merely as a composition, it deserves to be classed among the best specimens of English prose which our age has produced. . . . The style is agreeable, clear, and manly, and, when it rises into eloquence, rises without effort or ostentation. Nor is the matter inferior to the manner. It would be difficult to name a book which exhibits more kindness, fairness, and modesty."—MACAULAY, in the *Edinburgh Review.*

CALMET'S BIBLE DICTIONARY. Edited by CHARLES TAYLOR. With the Fragments incorporated and arranged in Alphabetical Order. New Edition. Imperial 8vo, with Maps and Wood Engravings, cloth extra, 10s. 6d.

CANOVA'S WORKS IN SCULPTURE AND MODELLING. 150 Plates exquisitely engraved in Outline by MOSES, and printed on an India tint. With Descriptions by the Countess ALBRIZZI, a Biographical Memoir by CICOGNARA, and Portrait by WORTHINGTON. A New Edition. Demy 4to, cloth extra, gilt, gilt edges, 31s. 6d. [*In the press.*

CARLYLE (Thomas) ON THE CHOICE OF BOOKS. With New Life and Anecdotes. Small post 8vo, brown cloth, 1s. 6d.

CAROLS OF COCKAYNE; Vers de Société descriptive of London Life. By HENRY S. LEIGH. Third Edition. With numerous Illustrations by ALFRED CONCANEN. Crown 8vo, cloth extra, gilt, 5s.

CARTER'S ANCIENT ARCHITECTURE OF ENGLAND. Including the Orders during the British, Roman, Saxon, and Norman Eras; and also under the Reigns of Henry III. and Edward III. Illustrated by 103 large Copperplate Engravings, comprising upwards of Two Thousand Specimens. Edited by JOHN BRITTON. Royal folio, half-morocco extra, £2 8s.

*** *This national work on ancient architecture occupied its author, in drawing, etching, arranging, and publishing, more than twenty years, and he himself declared it to be the result of his studies through life.*

CARTER'S ANCIENT SCULPTURE NOW REMAINING IN ENGLAND, from the Earliest Period to the Reign of Henry VIII.; consisting of Statues, Basso-relievos, Sculptures, &c., Brasses, Monumental Effigies, Paintings on Glass and on Walls; Missal Ornaments; Carvings on Cups, Croziers, Chests, Seals; Ancient Furniture, &c. &c. With Historical and Critical Illustrations by DOUCE, MEYRICK, DAWSON TURNER, and JOHN BRITTON. Royal folio, with 120 large Engravings, many Illuminated, half-bound morocco extra, £8 8*s.*

CATLIN'S ILLUSTRATIONS OF THE MANNERS, CUSTOMS, AND CONDITION OF THE NORTH AMERICAN INDIANS, written during Eight Years of Travel and Adventure among the Wildest and most Remarkable Tribes now existing. Containing 360 Engravings from the Author's original Paintings. Tenth Edition. Two Vols., imperial 8vo, cloth extra, gilt, £1 10*s.*; or with the Plates beautifully Coloured, half-morocco, gilt edges, £8 8*s.*

"One of the most admirable observers of manners who ever lived among the aborigines of America."—HUMBOLDT's *Cosmos.*

CATLIN'S NORTH AMERICAN INDIAN PORTFOLIO. Containing Hunting Scenes, Amusements, Scenery, and Costume of the Indians of the Rocky Mountains and Prairies of America, from Drawings and Notes made by the Author during Eight Years' Travel. A series of 25 magnificent Plates, beautifully coloured in facsimile of the Original Drawings exhibited at the Egyptian Hall. With letterpress descriptions, imperial folio, in handsome portfolio £7 10*s.*

CELEBRATED CLAIMANTS, Ancient and Modern. The History of all the most celebrated Pretenders and Claimants, from PERKIN WARBECK to ARTHUR ORTON. Fcap. 8vo, illustrated boards, 2*s.*

CHAMBERLAINE'S IMITATIONS OF DRAWINGS FROM THE GREAT MASTERS in the Royal Collection. Engraved by BARTOLOZZI and others. 74 fine Plates, mostly tinted; including, in addition, "Ecce Homo," after GUIDO, and the scarce Series of 7 Anatomical Drawings. Imperial folio, half-morocco, gilt edges, £5 5*s.*

CHATTO'S (W. Andrew) HISTORY OF WOOD ENGRAVING, Historical and Practical. A New Edition, with an Additional Chapter. Illustrated by 445 fine Wood Engravings. Imperial 8vo, half-Roxburghe, £2 5*s.*

"This volume is one of the most interesting and valuable of modern times."—*Art Union.*

CHRISTMAS CAROLS AND BALLADS. Selected and Edited by JOSHUA SYLVESTER. Cloth extra, gilt, gilt edges, 3*s.* 6*d.*

CICERO'S FAMILIAR LETTERS, AND LETTERS TO ATTICUS. Translated by MELMOTH and HEBERDEN. With Life of Cicero by MIDDLETON. Royal 8vo, with Portrait, cloth extra, 12*s.*

"Cicero is the type of a perfect letter-writer, never boring you with moral essays out of season, always evincing his mastery over his art by the most careful consideration for your patience and amusement. We should rifle the volumes of antiquity in vain to find a letter-writer who converses on paper so naturally, so engagingly, so much from the heart as Cicero."—*Quarterly Review.*

CLAUDE'S LIBER VERITATIS. A Collection of 303 Prints after the Original Designs of CLAUDE. Engraved by RICHARD EARLOM. With a descriptive Catalogue of each Print, Lists of the Persons for whom, and the Places for which, the original Pictures were first painted, and of the present Possessors of most of them. Three Vols. folio, half-morocco extra, gilt edges, £10 10*s.*

CLAUDE, BEAUTIES OF, containing 24 of his choicest Landscapes, beautifully Engraved on Steel, by BROMLEY, LUPTON, and others. With Biographical Sketch and Portrait. Royal folio, in a portfolio, £1 5*s.*

COLLINS' (Wilkie) NOVELS. New Illustrated Library Editions, price 6s. each, with Frontispiece and several full-page Illustrations in each Volume:—

The Woman in White. Illustrated by Sir JOHN GILBERT and F. A. FRASER.

Antonina; or, The Fall of Rome. Illustrated by Sir JOHN GILBERT and ALFRED CONCANEN.

Basil. Illustrated by Sir JOHN GILBERT and M. F. MAHONEY.

The Dead Secret. Illustrated by Sir JOHN GILBERT and H. FURNISS.

The Queen of Hearts. Illustrated by Sir JOHN GILBERT and ALFRED CONCANEN.

The Moonstone. Illustrated by G. DU MAURIER and F. A. FRASER.

Man and Wife. Illustrated by WILLIAM SMALL.

Hide and Seek; or, The Mystery of Mary Grice. Illustrated by Sir JOHN GILBERT and M. F. MAHONEY.

Poor Miss Finch. Illustrated by GEORGE DU MAURIER and EDWARD HUGHES.

Miss or Mrs.? Illustrated by S. L. FILDES and HENRY WOODS.

The New Magdalen. With Steel-plate Portrait of the Author, and Illustrations by C. S. R.

The Frozen Deep. Illustrated by G. DU MAURIER and M. F. MAHONEY.

My Miscellanies. Illustrated by ALFRED CONCANEN.

THE LAW AND THE LADY, by WILKIE COLLINS, in Three Vols., crown 8vo, 31s. 6d., is now ready at all Libraries and at the Booksellers.

"An exceedingly clever novel, full of admirable writing, abounding in a subtle ingenuity which is a distinct order of genius. . . . . 'The Law and the Lady' will be read with avidity by all who delight in the romances of the greatest master the sensational novel has ever known."—*World.*

"The author exhibits, in Miserrimus Dexter, a portrait which, for originality of conception and skill in depiction, exceeds anything of the kind. The book carries one irresistibly on from the first page to the last."—*John Bull.*

COLMAN'S HUMOROUS WORKS.—Broad Grins, My Nightgown and Slippers, and other Humorous Works, Prose and Poetical, of GEORGE COLMAN. With Life and Anecdotes by G. B. BUCKSTONE, and Frontispiece by HOGARTH. Crown 8vo, cloth extra, gilt, 7s. 6d.

CONDÉ (THE GREAT), and the Period of the Fronde: An Historical Sketch. By WALTER FITZ PATRICK. Second Edition. Two Vols., 8vo, cloth extra, 15s.

CONQUEST OF THE SEA (The). A History of Diving from the Earliest Times. By HENRY SIEBE. Profusely Illustrated. Crown 8vo, cloth extra, gilt, 4s. 6d.

"We have perused this volume, full of quaint information, with delight. Mr. Siebe has bestowed much pains on his work; he writes with enthusiasm and fulness of knowledge."—*Echo.*

"Really interesting alike to youths and to grown-up people."—*Scotsman.*

CONEY'S ENGRAVINGS OF ANCIENT CATHEDRALS, Hôtels de Ville, Town Halls, &c., including some of the finest Examples of Gothic Architecture in France, Holland, Germany, and Italy. 32 large Plates, imperial folio, half-morocco extra, £3 13s. 6d.

CONSTABLE'S GRAPHIC WORKS. Comprising 40 highly finished Mezzotinto Engravings on Steel, by DAVID LUCAS; with desc[illegible] Letterpress by C. R. LESLIE, R.A. Folio, half-morocco, gilt edges, £2 2s.

COTMAN'S ENGRAVINGS OF THE SEPULCHRAL BRASSES IN NORFOLK AND SUFFOLK. With Letterpress Descriptions, an Essay on Sepulchral Memorials by DAWSON TURNER, Notes by Sir SAMUEL MEYRICK, ALBERT WAY, and Sir HARRIS NICOLAS, and copious Index. New Edition, containing 173 Plates, two of them splendidly Illuminated. Two Volsume, small folio, half-morocco extra, £6 6*s*.; Large Paper copies, imperial folio, half-morocco extra, £8 8*s*.

COTMAN'S ETCHINGS OF ARCHITECTURAL REMAINS, chiefly Norman and Gothic, in various Counties in England, but principally in Norfolk, with Descriptive Notices by DAWSON TURNER, and Architectural Observations by THOMAS RICKMAN. Two Vols., imperial folio, containing 240 spirited Etchings, half-morocco, top edges gilt, £8 8*s*.

COTMAN'S LIBER STUDIORUM. A Series of Landscape Studies and Original Compositions for the Use of Art Students, consisting of 48 Etchings, the greater part executed in "soft ground." Imperial folio, half-morocco, £1 11*s*. 6*d*.

COWPER'S POETICAL WORKS. Including his Translation of HOMER. Edited by the Rev. H. F. CARY. With Portrait and 18 Steel Engravings after HARVEY. Royal 8vo, cloth extra, gilt edges, 10*s*. 6*d*.

"I long to know your opinion of Cowper's Translation. The *Odyssey* especially is surely very Homeric. What nobler than the appearance of Phœbus at the beginning of the *Iliad*—lines ending with 'Dread sounding-bounding in the silver bow'?"—CHARLES LAMB, *in a Letter to Coleridge.*

CREASY'S MEMOIRS OF EMINENT ETONIANS; with Notices of the Early History of Eton College. By Sir EDWARD CREASY, Author of "The Fifteen Decisive Battles of the World." A New Edition, with large Additions and Illustrations. Crown 8vo, cloth extra. [*In the press.*

CRUIKSHANK AT HOME. Tales and Sketches by the most Popular Authors. With numerous Illustrations by ROBERT CRUIKSHANK and ROBERT SEYMOUR. Also, CRUIKSHANK'S ODD VOLUME, or Book of Variety, Illustrated by Two Odd Fellows—SEYMOUR and CRUIKSHANK. Four Vols. bound in Two, fcap. 8vo, cloth extra, gilt, 10*s*. 6*d*.

CRUIKSHANK'S COMIC ALMANACK. Complete in Two SERIES: The FIRST from 1835 to 1843; the SECOND from 1844 to 1853. A Gathering of the BEST HUMOUR of THACKERAY, HOOD, MAYHEW, ALBERT SMITH, A'BECKETT, ROBERT BROUGH, &c. With 2000 Woodcuts and Steel Engravings by CRUIKSHANK, HINE, LANDELLS, &c. Crown 8vo, cloth gilt, two very thick volumes, 15*s*.; or, separately, 7*s*. 6*d*. per volume.

CRUIKSHANK'S UNIVERSAL SONGSTER. The largest Collection extant of the best Old English Songs (upwards of 5000). With 8 Engravings on Steel and Wood by GEORGE and R. CRUIKSHANK, and 8 Portraits. Three Vols., 8vo, cloth extra, gilt, 21*s*.

CUSSANS' HANDBOOK OF HERALDRY. With Instructions for Tracing Pedigrees and Deciphering Ancient MSS.; Rules for the Appointment of Liveries, Chapters on Continental and American Heraldry, &c. &c. By JOHN E. CUSSANS. Illustrated with 360 Plates and Woodcuts. Crown 8vo, cloth extra, gilt and emblazoned, 7*s*. 6*d*.

CUSSANS' HISTORY OF HERTFORDSHIRE. A County History, got up in a very superior manner, and ranging with the finest works of its class. By JOHN E. CUSSANS. Illustrated with full-page Plates on Copper and Stone, and a profusion of small Woodcuts. Parts I. to VIII. now ready, 21*s*. each.

**** An entirely new History of this important County, great attention being given to all matters pertaining to Family History.*

CUVIER'S ANIMAL KINGDOM, arranged after its Organization: forming a Natural History of Animals, and an Introduction to Comparative Anatomy. New Edition, with considerable Additions by W. B. CARPENTER and J. O. WESTWOOD. Illustrated by many Hundred Wood Engravings, and numerous Steel Engravings by THOS. LANDSEER, mostly Coloured. Imperial 8vo, cloth extra, 18*s*.

CYCLOPÆDIA OF COSTUME; or, A Dictionary of Dress—Regal, Ecclesiastical, Civil, and Military—from the Earliest Period in England to the reign of George the Third. Including Notices of Contemporaneous Fashions on the Continent, and preceded by a General History of the Costumes of the Principal Countries of Europe. By J. R. PLANCHÉ, Somerset Herald. To be Completed in Twenty-four Parts, quarto, at Five Shillings each, profusely illustrated by Coloured and Plain Plates and Wood Engravings.—A Prospectus will be sent upon application. [*In course of publication.*

"There is no subject connected with dress with which 'Somerset Herald' is not as familiar as ordinary men are with the ordinary themes of everyday life. The gathered knowledge of many years is placed before the world in this his latest work, and when finished, there will exist no work on the subject half so valuable. The numerous illustrations are all effective—for their accuracy the author is responsible; they are well drawn and well engraved, and, while indispensable to a proper comprehension of the text, are satisfactory as works of art."—*Art Journal.*

"These, the first numbers of a Cyclopædia of Ancient and Modern Costume, give promise that the work, when complete, will be one of the most perfect works ever published upon the subject. The illustrations are numerous and excellent, and would, even without the letterpress, render the work an invaluable book of reference for information as to costumes for fancy balls and character quadrilles."—*Standard.*

"Destined, we anticipate, to be the standard English work on dress."—*Builder.*

"Promises to be a very complete work on a subject of the greatest importance to the historian and the archæologist."—*Tablet.*

"Beautifully printed and superbly illustrated."—*Standard*, second notice.

D'ARBLAY'S (Madame) DIARY AND LETTERS. Edited by her Niece, CHARLOTTE BARRETT. A New Edition, in Four Vols., 8vo. Illustrated by numerous fine Portraits engraved on Steel. [*In preparation.*

DIBDIN'S (T. F.) BIBLIOMANIA; or, Book-Madness: A Bibliographical Romance. With numerous Illustrations. A New Edition, with a Supplement, including a Key to the Assumed Characters in the Drama. Demy 8vo, half-Roxburghe, 21*s.*; a few Large Paper copies, half-Roxburghe, the edges altogether uncut, at 42*s.* [*In the press.*

DICKENS' LIFE AND SPEECHES. Royal 16mo, cloth extra, 2*s.* 6*d.*

DISCOUNT TABLES, on a new and simple plan; to facilitate the Discounting of Bills, and the Calculation of Interest on Banking and Current Accounts, &c.; showing, without calculation, the number of days from every day in the year to any other day. By THOMAS READER. Post 8vo, cloth extra, 7*s.*

DON QUIXOTE: A Revised Translation, based upon those of MOTTEUX, JARVIS, and SMOLLETT. With 50 Illustrations by ARMSTRONG and TONY JOHANNOT. Royal 8vo, cloth extra, gilt, 10*s.* 6*d.*

DON QUIXOTE IN SPANISH.—EL INGENIOSO HIDALGO DON QUIJOTE DE LA MANCHA. Nueva Edicion, corregida y revisada. Por MIGUEL DE CERVANTES SAAVEDRA. Complete in One Volume, post 8vo, nearly 700 pages, cloth extra, price 4*s.* 6*d.*

DRURY'S ILLUSTRATIONS of FOREIGN ENTOMOLOGY. Containing, in 150 beautifully Coloured Plates, upwards of 600 Exotic Insects of the East and West Indies, China, New Holland, North and South America, Germany, &c. With important Additions and Scientific Indexes, by J. O. WESTWOOD, F.L.S. Three Vols., 4to, half-morocco extra, £5 5*s.*

DULWICH GALLERY (The): A Series of 50 beautifully Coloured Plates, from the most celebrated Pictures in this Collection, executed by the Custodian, R. COCKBURN, and mounted upon Cardboard, in the manner of Drawings. Imperial folio, in portfolio, £16 16*s.*

DUNLOP'S HISTORY OF FICTION: Being a Critical and Analytical Account of the most celebrated Prose Works of Fiction, from the Earliest Greek Romances to the Novels of the Present Day, with General Index. Third Edition, royal 8vo, cloth extra, 9*s.*

EDGEWORTH'S (Maria) TALES AND NOVELS, Complete. Including "HELEN" (her last work). With 38 highly-finished Steel Engravings after HARVEY and others. Ten Vols., fcap. 8vo, cloth extra, gilt, £1 10*s.*

The Volumes are sold separately at 3s. 6d. each, illustrated, as follows:—

Moral Tales.	**Madame de Fleury, &c.**
Popular Tales.	**Patronage.**
Belinda.	**Comic Dramas, Leonora, &c.**
Castle Rackrent, Irish Bulls, &c.	**Harrington, Bores, &c.**
Fashionable Life.	**Helen.**

"We do not know that Miss Edgeworth in the delineation of manners has, in the whole circle of literature, a rival, except the inimitable authors of Gil Blas and Don Quixote; and the discrimination with which the individuality of her persons is preserved through all the varieties of rank, sex, and nation, gives to her stories a combined charm of truth and novelty, and creates an interest more acute than fiction (if fiction it can be called) ever excited."—*Quarterly Review.*

ELLIS'S (Mrs.) MOTHERS OF GREAT MEN. A New Edition, with Illustrations by VALENTINE BROMLEY. Crown 8vo, cloth gilt, 6*s.*

EMANUEL ON DIAMONDS AND PRECIOUS STONES; Their History, Value, and Properties; with Simple Tests for ascertaining their Reality. By HARRY EMANUEL, F.R.G.S. With numerous Illustrations, Tinted and Plain. A New Edition, crown 8vo, cloth extra, gilt, 6*s.*

ENGLISHMAN'S HOUSE (The): A Practical Guide to all interested in Selecting or Building a House, with full Estimates of Cost, Quantities, &c. By C. J. RICHARDSON. Third Edition. With nearly 600 Illustrations. Crown 8vo, cloth extra, 7*s.* 6*d.*

*** *This book is intended to supply a long-felt want, viz., a plain, non-technical account of every style of house, with the cost and manner of building; it gives every variety, from a workman's cottage to a nobleman's palace.*

FAIRHOLT.—TOBACCO: Its History and Associations; including an Account of the Plant and its Manufacture; with its Modes of Use in all Ages and Countries. By F. W. FAIRHOLT, F.S.A. With coloured Frontispiece and upwards of 100 Illustrations by the Author. Crown 8vo, cloth extra, 6*s.* [*In the press.*

FARADAY'S CHEMICAL HISTORY OF A CANDLE. Lectures delivered to a Juvenile Audience. A New Edition, Edited by W. CROOKES, Esq., F.C.S., &c. Crown 8vo, cloth extra, with numerous Illustrations, 4*s.* 6*d.*

FARADAY'S VARIOUS FORCES OF NATURE. A New Edition, Edited by W. CROOKES, Esq., F.C.S., &c. Crown 8vo, cloth extra, with numerous Illustrations, 4*s.* 6*d.*

FIGUIER'S PRIMITIVE MAN: A Popular Manual of the prevailing Theories of the Descent of Man as promulgated by DARWIN, LYELL, Sir JOHN LUBBOCK, HUXLEY, E. B. TYLOR, and other eminent Ethnologists. Translated from the last French edition, and revised by E. B. T. With 263 Illustrations. Demy 8vo, cloth extra, gilt, 9*s.*

FINISH TO LIFE IN AND OUT OF LONDON; or, The Final Adventures of Tom, Jerry, and Logic. By PIERCE EGAN. Royal 8vo, cloth extra, with spirited Coloured Illustrations by CRUIKSHANK, 21*s.*

FLAGELLATION AND THE FLAGELLANTS.—A History of the Rod in all Countries, from the Earliest Period to the Present Time. By the Rev. W. COOPER, B.A. Third Edition, revised and corrected, with numerous Illustrations. Thick crown 8vo, cloth extra, gilt, 12*s*. 6*d*.

FOX'S BOOK OF MARTYRS: The Acts and Monuments of the Church. Edited by JOHN CUMMING, D.D. With upwards of 1000 Illustrations. Three Vols., imperial 8vo, cloth extra, £2 12*s*. 6*d*.

GELL'S TOPOGRAPHY OF ROME AND ITS VICINITY. A New Edition, revised and enlarged by E. H. BUNBURY. With a large mounted Map of Rome and its Environs (from a careful Trigonometrical Survey). Two Vols., 8vo, cloth extra, 15*s*.

"These volumes are so replete with what is valuable, that were we to employ our entire journal, we could, after all, afford but a meagre indication of their interest and worth. . . . . Learning, applied to the most patient personal research and actual examination of every foot of the interesting classic ground which the inquiry embraces, is the sure recommendation of this very able and standard work."—*Athenæum.*

GELL AND GANDY'S POMPEIANA; or, The Topography, Edifices, and Ornaments of Pompeii. With upwards of 100 Line Engravings by GOODALL, COOKE, HEATH, PYE, &c. Demy 8vo, cloth extra, gilt, 18*s*.

GEMS OF ART: A Collection of 36 Engravings, after Paintings by REMBRANDT, CUYP, REYNOLDS, POUSSIN, MURILLO, TENIERS, CORREGGIO, GAINSBOROUGH, NORTHCOTE, &c., executed in Mezzotint by TURNER, BROMLEY, &c. Folio, in Portfolio, £1 11*s*. 6*d*.

GENIAL SHOWMAN; or, Show Life in the New World. Adventures with Artemus Ward, and the Story of his Life. By E. P. HINGSTON. Third Edition. Crown 8vo, Illustrated by W. BRUNTON, cloth extra, 7*s*. 6*d*.

GIBBON'S ROMAN EMPIRE (The Decline and Fall of the). With Memoir of the Author, and full General Index. Imperial 8vo, with Portrait, cloth extra, 15*s*.

GILBERT'S (W. S.) DRAMATIC WORKS ("A Wicked World," "Charity," "Palace of Truth," "Pygmalion," Sweethearts," &c.). One Vol., crown 8vo, cloth extra. [*In preparation.*

GIL BLAS.—HISTORIA DE GIL BLAS DE SANTILLANA. Por LE SAGE. Traducida al Castellano por el PADRE ISLA. Nueva Edicion, corregida y revisada. Complete in One Vol. Post 8vo, cl. extra, nearly 600 pp., 4*s*. 6*d*.

GILLRAY'S CARICATURES. Printed from the Original Plates, all engraved by Himself between 1779 and 1810; comprising the best Political and Humorous Satires of the Reign of GEORGE THE THIRD, in upwards of 600 highly spirited Engravings. Atlas folio, half-morocco extra, gilt edges, £7 10*s*.—There is also a Volume of the SUPPRESSED PLATES, atlas folio, half-morocco, 31*s*. 6*d*.—Also, a VOLUME OF LETTERPRESS DESCRIPTIONS, comprising a very amusing Political History of the Reign of GEORGE THE THIRD, by THOS. WRIGHT and R. H. EVANS. Demy 8vo, cloth extra, 15*s*.; or half-morocco, £1 1*s*.

GILLRAY, THE CARICATURIST: The Story of his Life and Times, and Anecdotal Descriptions of his Engravings. Edited by THOMAS WRIGHT, Esq., M.A., F.S.A. With 83 full-page Plates, and numerous Wood Engravings. Demy 4to, 600 pages, cloth extra, 31*s*. 6*d*.

"High as the expectations excited by this description [in the Introduction] may be, they will not be disappointed. The most inquisitive or exacting reader will find ready gathered to his hand, without the trouble of reference, almost every scrap of narrative, anecdote, gossip, scandal, or epigram, in poetry or prose, that he can possibly require for the elucidation of the caricatures."—*Quarterly Review.*

GLEIG'S CHELSEA PENSIONERS: Saratoga, the Rivals, and other Stories. By the Rev. G. R. GLEIG, late Chaplain to Her Majesty's Forces. Post 8vo, illustrated boards, 2s.

GOLDEN LIBRARY.

Square 16mo (Tauchnitz size), cloth, extra gilt, price 2s. per Vol.

BYRON'S DON JUAN. Complete in 16 Cantos, with Notes.

CLERICAL ANECDOTES: The Humours and Eccentricities of "the Cloth."

HOLMES'S AUTOCRAT OF THE BREAKFAST TABLE. With an Introduction by GEORGE AUGUSTUS SALA.

HOLMES'S PROFESSOR AT THE BREAKFAST TABLE. With the STORY OF IRIS.

HOOD'S WHIMS AND ODDITIES. Both Series Complete in One Volume, with all the original Illustrations.

IRVING'S (Washington) TALES OF A TRAVELLER.

IRVING'S (Washington) TALES OF THE ALHAMBRA.

JESSE'S (Edward) SCENES AND OCCUPATIONS OF COUNTRY LIFE; with Recollections of Natural History.

LAMB'S ESSAYS OF ELIA. Both Series Complete in One Vol.

LEIGH HUNT'S ESSAYS: A Tale for a Chimney Corner, and other Pieces. With Portrait, and Introduction by EDMUND OLLIER.

MALLORY'S (Sir Thomas) MORT D'ARTHUR: The Stories of King Arthur and of the Knights of the Round Table. Edited by B. M. RANKING.

PASCAL'S PROVINCIAL LETTERS. A New Translation, with Historical Introduction and Notes, by T. M'CRIE, D.D., LL.D.

POPE'S COMPLETE POETICAL WORKS. Reprinted from the Original Editions.

ST. PIERRE'S PAUL AND VIRGINIA AND THE INDIAN COTTAGE. Edited, with Life, by the Rev. E. CLARKE.

SHELLEY'S EARLY POEMS, AND QUEEN MAB, with Essay by LEIGH HUNT.

SHELLEY'S LATER POEMS: Laon and Cythna, &c.

SHELLEY'S POSTHUMOUS POEMS, the SHELLEY PAPERS, &c.

SHELLEY'S PROSE WORKS, including A Refutation of Deism, Zastrozzi, St. Irvyne, &c.

WHITE'S NATURAL HISTORY OF SELBORNE. Edited, with additions, by THOMAS BROWN, F.L.S.

GOLDEN TREASURY OF THOUGHT. An Encyclopædia of Quotations from Writers of all Times and all Countries. Selected and Edited by THEODORE TAYLOR. Crown 8vo, cloth gilt, and gilt edges, 7s. 6d.

GOSPELS (The Holy). Illustrated with upwards of 200 Wood Engravings, after the best Masters, and every page surrounded by ornamental Borders. Handsomely printed, imperial 4to, cloth, full gilt (Grolier style), 10s. 6d.

GRAMMONT (Count) MEMOIRS OF. By ANTHONY HAMILTON. A New Edition, in One Vol., 8vo, with a Biographical Sketch of Count Hamilton, numerous Historical and Illustrative Notes, and 64 Copperplate Portraits by EDWARD SCRIVEN. [*In preparation.*

GREENWOOD'S LOW-LIFE DEEPS. An Account of the Strange Fish to be found there, including the story of "The Man and Dog Fight," as originally published in *The Daily Telegraph*, with much additional and confirmatory evidence; "With a Tally-Man," "A Fallen Star," "The Betting Barber," &c. With Illustrations in tint by ALFRED CONCANEN. Crown 8vo, cloth extra, 7s. 6d. [*In the press.*

GREENWOOD'S WILDS OF LONDON; Descriptive Sketches from Personal Observations and Experience of Remarkable Scenes, People, and Places in London. By JAMES GREENWOOD, the "Lambeth Casual." With 12 Tinted Illustrations by ALFRED CONCANEN. Crown 8vo, cloth extra, gilt, *7s. 6d.*

"Mr. James Greenwood presents himself once more in the character of 'one whose delight it is to do his humble endeavour towards exposing and extirpating social abuses and those hole-and-corner evils which afflict society.'"—*Saturday Review.*

GREVILLE'S CRYPTOGAMIC FLORA. Comprising the Principal Species found in Great Britain, inclusive of all the New Species recently discovered in Scotland. Six Vols., royal 8vo, with 360 beautifully Coloured Plates, half-morocco, gilt, *£7 7s.*; the Plates uncoloured, *£4 14s. 6d.*

"A truly admirable work, which may be honestly designated as so excellent, that nothing can be found to compete with it in the whole range of Indigenous Botany; whether we consider the importance of its critical discussions, the accuracy of the drawings, the minuteness of the analyses, or the unusual care which is evident in the publishing department."—LOUDON.

GRIMM.—GERMAN POPULAR STORIES. Collected by the Brothers GRIMM, and Translated by EDGAR TAYLOR. Edited, with an Introduction, by JOHN RUSKIN. With 22 Illustrations after the inimitable designs of GEORGE CRUIKSHANK. Both Series Complete. Square crown 8vo, *6s. 6d.*; gilt leaves, *7s. 6d.*

"The illustrations of this volume . . . . are of quite sterling and admirable art, of a class precisely parallel in elevation to the character of the tales which they illustrate; and the original etchings, as I have before said in the Appendix to my 'Elements of Drawing,' were unrivalled in masterfulness of touch since Rembrandt (in some qualities of delineation, unrivalled even by him). . . . . To make somewhat enlarged copies of them, looking at them through a magnifying glass, and never putting two lines where Cruikshank has put only one, would be an exercise in decision and severe drawing which would leave afterwards little to be learnt in schools."—*Extract from Introduction by* JOHN RUSKIN.

GULLIVER'S TRAVELS. By JONATHAN SWIFT. With Life of the Author, and numerous Wood Engravings. Demy 8vo, cloth extra, gilt, *5s.*

GUYOT'S EARTH AND MAN; or, Physical Geography in its Relation to the History of Mankind. With Additions by Professors AGASSIZ, PIERCE, and GRAY. With 12 Maps and Engravings on Steel, some Coloured, and a copious Index. A New Edition. Crown 8vo, cloth extra, gilt, *4s. 6d.*

HALL'S (Mrs. S. C.) SKETCHES OF IRISH CHARACTER. With numerous Illustrations on Steel and Wood, by DANIEL MACLISE, Sir JOHN GILBERT, W. HARVEY, and G. CRUIKSHANK. 8vo, cloth extra, gilt, *7s. 6d.*

"The Irish sketches of this lady resemble Miss Mitford's beautiful English Sketches in 'Our Village,' but they are far more vigorous and picturesque and bright."—*Blackwood's Magazine.*

HALL MARKS (BOOK OF); or, Manual of Reference for the Goldsmith and Silversmith. By ALFRED LUTSCHAUNIG. Crown 8vo, with 46 Plates of the Hall-marks of the different Assay Towns of the Kingdom. *7s. 6d.*

HARRIS'S AURELIAN; A Natural History of English Moths and Butterflies, and the Plants on which they feed. A New Edition. Edited, with Additions, by J. O. WESTWOOD. With about 400 exquisitely Coloured Figures of Moths, Butterflies, Caterpillars, &c., and the Plants on which they feed. Small folio, half-morocco extra, gilt edges, *£3 13s. 6d.*

HISTORICAL PORTRAITS; including the Collections of RODD and GRAINGER, RICHARDSON, CAULFIELD, &c. All printed from the Original Plates. Two Vols., large 4to. [*In preparation.*

HEEREN'S HISTORICAL WORKS. Translated from the German by GEORGE BANCROFT, and various Oxford Scholars. Six Vols., 8vo, cloth extra, £1 16*s.*; or, separately, 6*s.* per volume.

*** *The Contents of the Volumes are as follows:*—Vols. 1 and 2. Historical Researches into the Politics, Intercourse, and Trade of the Ancient Nations of Asia; 3. Researches into the Politics, Intercourse, and Trade of the Ancient Nations of Africa, including the Carthaginians, Ethiopians, and Egyptians; 4. History of the Political System of Europe and its Colonies; 5. History of Ancient Greece, with Historical Treatises; 6. A Manual of Ancient History, with special reference to the Constitutions, Commerce, and Colonies of the States of Antiquity.

"Prof. Heeren's Historical Researches stand in the very highest rank among those with which modern Germany has enriched European literature."—*Quarterly Review.*

"We look upon Heeren as having breathed a new life into the dry bones of Ancient History. In countries, the history of which has been too imperfectly known to afford lessons of political wisdom, he has taught us still more interesting lessons—on the social relations of men, and the intercourse of nations in the earlier ages of the world. His work is as learned as a professed commentary on the ancient historians and geographers, and as entertaining as a modern book of travels."—*Edinburgh Review.*

THE ORIGINAL HOGARTH.

HOGARTH'S WORKS. ENGRAVED BY HIMSELF. 153 fine Plates, with elaborate Letterpress Descriptions by JOHN NICHOLS. Atlas folio, half-morocco extra, gilt edges, £7 10*s.*

"I was pleased with the reply of a gentleman who, being asked which book he esteemed most in his library, answered 'Shakespeare'; being asked which he esteemed next best, answered 'Hogarth.'"—CHARLES LAMB.

HOGARTH'S WORKS. With Life and Anecdotal Descriptions of the Pictures, by JOHN IRELAND and JOHN NICHOLS. 160 Engravings, reduced in exact facsimile of the Originals. The whole in Three Series, 8vo, cloth, gilt, 22*s.* 6*d.*; or, separately, 7*s.* 6*d.* per volume.

HOGARTH'S WORKS. Engraved by T. COOK. 84 Plates, atlas folio, half-morocco, £5.

HOGARTH MORALIZED: A Complete Edition of all the most capital and admired Works of WILLIAM HOGARTH, accompanied by concise and comprehensive Explanations of their Moral Tendency, by the late Rev. Dr. TRUSLER; to which are added, an Introductory Essay, and many Original and Selected Notes, by JOHN MAJOR. With 57 Plates and numerous Woodcuts. New Edition, revised, corrected, and enlarged. Demy 8vo, hf.-Roxburghe, 12*s.* 6*d.*

HOGARTH'S FIVE DAYS' FROLIC; or, Peregrinations by Land and Water. Illustrated by Tinted Drawings, made by HOGARTH and SCOTT during the Journey. Demy 4to, cloth extra, gilt, 10*s.* 6*d.*

HOLBEIN'S PORTRAITS OF THE COURT OF HENRY THE EIGHTH. A Series of 84 exquisitely beautiful Tinted Plates, engraved by BARTOLOZZI, COOPER, and others, and printed on Tinted Paper, in imitation of the Original Drawings in the Royal Collection at Windsor. With Historical Letterpress by EDMUND LODGE, Norroy King of Arms. Imperial 4to, half-morocco extra, gilt edges, £5 15*s.* 6*d.*

HOLBEIN'S PORTRAITS OF THE COURT OF HENRY VIII. CHAMBERLAINE'S Imitations of the Original Drawings, mostly engraved by BARTOLOZZI. 92 splendid Portraits (including 8 additional Plates), elaborately tinted in Colours, with Descriptive and Biographical Notes, by EDMUND LODGE, Norroy King of Arms. Atlas fol., half-morocco, gilt edges, £20.—The same, PROOF IMPRESSIONS, uncoloured, half-Roxburghe, £18.

HONE'S SCRAP-BOOKS: The Miscellaneous Collections of WILLIAM HONE, Author of "The Table-Book," "Every-Day Book," and "Year-Book:" being a Supplementary Volume to those works. Now first published. With Notes, Portraits, and numerous Illustrations of curious and eccentric objects. Crown 8vo. [*In preparation.*

HOOD'S (Tom) FROM NOWHERE TO THE NORTH POLE: A Noah's Arkæological Narrative. By TOM HOOD. With 25 Illustrations by W. BRUNTON and E. C. BARNES. Square crown 8vo, in a handsome and specially-designed binding, gilt edges, 6*s.*

"Poor Tom Hood! It is very sad to turn over the droll pages of 'From Nowhere to the North Pole,' and to think that he will never make the young people, for whom, like his famous father, he ever had such a kind, sympathetic heart, laugh or cry any more. This is a birthday story, and no part of it is better than the first chapter, concerning birthdays in general, and Frank's birthday in particular. The amusing letterpress is profusely interspersed with the jingling rhymes which children love and learn so easily. Messrs. Brunton and Barnes do full justice to the writer's meaning, and a pleasanter result of the harmonious co-operation of author and artist could not be desired."—*Times.*

HOOD'S (Tom) HUMOROUS WORKS. Edited, with an Introduction, by his Sister, Mrs. BRODERIP. Crown 8vo, cloth extra, with Portrait, and numerous Illustrations, 6*s.* [*In the press.*

HOOKER'S (Sir William) EXOTIC FLORA. Containing Figures and Descriptions of Rare or otherwise interesting Exotic Plants. With Remarks upon their Generic and Specific Characters, Natural Orders, Culture, &c. Containing 232 large and beautifully Coloured Plates. Three Vols., imperial 8vo, cloth extra, gilt, £6 6*s.*

HOOKER AND GREVILLE'S ICONES FILICUM; or, Figures and Descriptions of Ferns, many of which have been altogether unnoticed by Botanists, or have been incorrectly figured. With 240 beautifully Coloured Plates. Two Vols., folio, half-morocco, gilt, £12 12*s.*

HOPE'S COSTUME OF THE ANCIENTS. Illustrated in upwards of 320 Outline Engravings, containing Representations of Egyptian, Greek, and Roman Habits and Dresses. A New Edition. Two Vols., royal 8vo, with Coloured Frontispiece, cloth extra, £2 5*s.*

HORNE.—ORION. An Epic Poem, in Three Books. By RICHARD HENGIST HORNE. With Photographic Portrait. TENTH EDITION. Crown 8vo, cloth extra, 7*s.*

"Orion will be admitted, by every man of genius, to be one of the noblest, if not the very noblest poetical work of the age. Its defects are trivial and conventional, its beauties intrinsic and supreme."—EDGAR ALLAN POE.

HUGO'S (Victor) LES MISÉRABLES. Complete in Three Parts.—Part I. FANTINE. Illustrated boards, 2*s.*—Part II. COSETTE AND MARIUS. Illustrated boards, 2*s.*—Part III. ST. DENIS AND JEAN VALJEAN. Illustrated boards, 2*s.* 6*d.*

"Its merits do not merely consist in the conception of it as a whole; it abounds, page after page, with details of unequalled beauty."—*Quarterly Review.*

HUGO'S (Victor) BY THE KING'S COMMAND. Complete. English Translation of "L'Homme qui Rit." Post 8vo, illustrated boards, 2*s.* 6*d.*

"The book is great and heroic, tender and strong, full from end to end of divine and passionate love, of holy and ardent pity for men that suffer wrong at the hands of men; full, not less, of lyric loveliness and lyric force, and I for one am content to be simply glad and grateful: content in that simplicity of spirit to accept it as one more benefit at the hands of the supreme singer now living among us the beautiful and lofty life of one loving the race of men he serves, and of them in all time to be beloved."—SWINBURNE.

HUME AND SMOLLETT'S HISTORY OF ENGLAND. With a Memoir of HUME by himself, Chronological Table of Contents, and General Index. Imperial 8vo, with Portraits of the Authors, cloth extra, 15*s.*

HUNT'S (Robert) DROLL STORIES OF OLD CORNWALL; or, POPULAR ROMANCES OF THE WEST OF ENGLAND. With Illustrations by GEORGE CRUIKSHANK. Crown 8vo, cloth extra, gilt, 7*s.* 6*d.*

ITALIAN SCHOOL OF DESIGN (The): 91 beautiful Plates, chiefly Engraved by BARTOLOZZI, after Paintings in the Royal Collection by MICHAEL ANGELO, DOMENICHINO, ANNIBALE CARACCI, and others. Imperial 4to, half-morocco, gilt edges, £2 12*s.* 6*d.*

JARDINE'S (Sir Wm.) NATURALIST'S LIBRARY. 42 vols. Fcap. 8vo, illustrated by over 1200 Coloured Plates, with numerous Portraits and Memoirs of eminent Naturalists, half (imitation) calf, full gilt, top edges gilt, £9 9*s.*; or, separately, cloth extra, 4*s.* 6*d.* per Vol., as follows:—

Vols. 1 to 4. British Birds; 5. Sun Birds: 6 and 7. Humming Birds; 8. Game Birds; 9. Pigeons; 10. Parrots; 11 and 12. Birds of West Africa; 13. Fly Catchers; 14. Pheasants, Peacocks, &c.; 15. Animals—Introduction; 16. Lions and Tigers; 17. British Quadrupeds; 18 and 19. Dogs; 20. Horses; 21 and 22. Ruminating Animals; 23. Elephants, &c.; 24. Marsupialia; 25. Seals, &c.; 26. Whales, &c.; 27. Monkeys; 28. Insects—Introduction; 29. British Butterflies; 30. British Moths, &c.; 31. Foreign Butterflies; 32. Foreign Moths; 33. Beetles; 34. Bees; 35. Fishes—Introduction, and Foreign Fishes; 36 and 37. British Fishes; 38. Perch, &c.; 39 and 40. Fishes of Guiana; 41. Smith's Natural History of Man: 42. Gould's Humming Birds.

JENNINGS' (Hargrave) ONE OF THE THIRTY. With numerous curious Illustrations. Crown 8vo, cloth extra, 10*s.* 6*d.*

JENNINGS' (Hargrave) THE ROSICRUCIANS: Their Rites and Mysteries. With Chapters on the Ancient Fire and Serpent Worshippers, and Explanations of Mystic Symbols in Monuments and Talismans of Primeval Philosophers. Crown 8vo, with 300 Illustrations, 10*s.* 6*d.*

JERROLD'S (Blanchard) CENT. PER CENT. A Story Written on a Bill Stamp. Fcap. 8vo, illustrated boards, 2*s.*

JERROLD'S (Douglas) THE BARBER'S CHAIR, AND THE HEDGEHOG LETTERS. Edited, with an Introduction, by his Son, BLANCHARD JERROLD. Crown 8vo, with Steel-plate Portrait, cloth extra, 7*s.* 6*d.*

"Better fitted than any other of his productions to give an idea of Douglas Jerrold's amazing wit; the 'Barber's Chair' may be presumed to give as near an approach as is possible in print to the wit of Jerrold's conversation."—*Examiner.*

JERROLD'S (Douglas) BROWNRIGG PAPERS, AND MINOR STORIES. Edited by his Son, BLANCHARD JERROLD. Post 8vo, illust. bds, 2*s.*

JOHNSON'S ENGLISH DICTIONARY. Printed verbatim from the Author's Last and most Complete Edition, with all the Examples in full; to which are prefixed a History of the Language and a Grammar of the English Tongue. Imperial 8vo, cloth extra, 15*s.*

JOHNSON'S (Dr. Samuel) WORKS. With Life, by MURPHY. Two thick Vols., 8vo, with Portrait, cloth extra, 15*s.*

JOHNSON'S LIVES OF ENGLISH HIGHWAYMEN, PIRATES, AND ROBBERS. With Additions by WHITEHEAD. Fcap. 8vo, 16 Plates, cloth extra, gilt, 5*s.*

JOSEPHUS (The Works of). Translated by WHISTON. Containing both the "Antiquities of the Jews," and the "Wars of the Jews." Two Vols., 8vo, with 52 Illustrations and Maps, cloth extra, gilt, 14*s.*

KINGSLEY'S (Henry) New Novel, NUMBER SEVENTEEN. In Two Vols., crown 8vo, cloth extra, price 21*s.*, at all Libraries.

KNIGHT'S (H. Gally) ECCLESIASTICAL ARCHITECTURE OF ITALY, from the time of Constantine to the Fifteenth Century, with Introduction and descriptive Text. Complete in Two Series; the FIRST, to the end of the Eleventh Century; the SECOND, from the Twelfth to the Fifteenth Century; containing 81 beautiful Views of Ecclesiastical Buildings in Italy, several of them Illuminated in gold and colours. Imperial folio, half-morocco extra, price £3 13*s.* 6*d.* each Series.

LAMB'S (Charles) COMPLETE WORKS, in Prose and Verse, reprinted from the Original Editions, with many pieces now first included in any Edition, and Notes and Introduction by R. H. SHEPHERD. With Two Portraits and facsimile of a page of the "Essay on Roast Pig." Crown 8vo, cloth extra, gilt, 7*s.* 6*d.*

"A complete edition of Lamb's writings, in prose and verse, has long been wanted, and is now supplied. The editor appears to have taken great pains to bring together Lamb's scattered contributions, and his collection contains a number of pieces which are now reproduced for the first time since their original appearance in various old periodicals."—*Saturday Review.*

LAMB (Mary and Charles) : THEIR POEMS, LETTERS, and REMAINS. With Reminiscences and Notes by W. CAREW HAZLITT. With HANCOCK'S Portrait of the Essayist, Facsimiles of the Title-pages of the rare First Editions of Lamb's and Coleridge's Works, and numerous Illustrations. Crown 8vo, cloth extra, 10*s.* 6*d.*; Large Paper copies, 21*s.*

"Must be consulted by all future biographers of the Lambs."—*Daily News.*

"Very many passages will delight those fond of literary trifles ; hardly any portion will fail in interest for lovers of Charles Lamb and his sister."—*Standard.*

LANDSEER'S (Sir Edwin) ETCHINGS OF CARNIVOROUS ANIMALS. Comprising 38 subjects, chiefly Early Works, etched by his Brother THOMAS or his Father, with Letterpress Descriptions. Roy. 4to, cloth extra, 15*s.*

LEE (General Robert E.) : HIS LIFE AND CAMPAIGNS. By his Nephew, EDWARD LEE CHILDE. With Steel-plate Portrait by JEENS, and a Map. Post 8vo, 9*s.*

"A valuable and well-written contribution to the history of the civil war in the United States."—*Saturday Review.*

"As a clear and compendious survey of a life of the true heroic type, Mr. Childe's volume may well be commended to the English reader."—*Graphic.*

"Though the American War came to a close now almost exactly ten years ago, and though the memory of the doings of many of the men who took part in that disastrous struggle is almost lost, there remains one memory the brilliancy of which is still unclouded. General Robert Lee, the man upon whom for so many months the whole of the Confederate hopes seemed to hang, won for himself the admiration, not only of those who could appreciate military genius, but of those who could understand high honour and that honesty which gives the best charm to manhood. 'The Life of General Lee,' by Mr. Lee Childe, is a work that deserves the most careful attention. Not only does it bring in connection with the early life and training of Robert Lee some things which will help to a better understanding of what his character in manhood was, but it gives, in the fullest and best forms, accounts of the military operations which he conducted. . . . . Mr. Childe has given us a most valuable book ; not the least valuable part of it being the introductory chapter, in which the causes that led to the American Civil War are stated with a fairness and clearness that we have not met with before."—*Scotsman.*

LEMPRIERE'S CLASSICAL DICTIONARY. Miniature Edition. Containing a Full Account of all Proper Names mentioned in Ancient Authors, and much Information respecting the Usages and Habits of the Greeks and Romans, corrected to the present state of knowledge. 18mo, embossed roan, 5*s.*

LIFE IN LONDON; or, The Day and Night Scenes of Jerry Hawthorn and Corinthian Tom. WITH THE WHOLE OF CRUIKSHANK'S VERY DROLL ILLUSTRATIONS, in Colours, after the Originals. Crown 8vo, cloth extra, 7*s.* 6*d.*

LINTON'S (Mrs. E. Lynn) JOSHUA DAVIDSON, CHRISTIAN AND COMMUNIST. SIXTH EDITION, with a New Preface. Small crown 8vo, cloth extra, 4*s.* 6*d.*

"In a short and vigorous preface, Mrs. Linton defends her notion of the logical outcome of Christianity as embodied in this attempt to conceive how Christ would have acted, with whom He would have fraternised, and who would have declined to receive Him, had He appeared in the present generation."—*Examiner.*

LINTON'S (Mrs. E. Lynn) PATRICIA KEMBALL: A Novel. New and Popular Edition. Crown 8vo, cloth extra, gilt, 6*s*.

"A very clever and well-constructed story, original and striking, and interesting all through. . . . A novel abounding in thought and power and interest."—*Times*.

"Perhaps the ablest novel published in London this year (1874) . . . We know of nothing in the novels we have lately read equal to the scene in which Mr. Hamley proposes to Dora . . . We advise our readers to send to the library for the story." —*Athenæum*.

"This novel is distinguished by qualities which entitle it to a place apart from the ordinary fiction of the day; . . . displays genuine humour, as well as keen social observation. . . . . Enough graphic portraiture and witty observation to furnish materials for half a dozen novels of the ordinary kind."—*Saturday Review*.

LONDON.—WILKINSON'S LONDINA ILLUSTRATA; or, Graphic and Historical Illustrations of the most Interesting and Curious Architectural Monuments of the City and Suburbs of London and Westminster (now mostly destroyed). Two Vols., imperial 4to, containing 207 Copperplate Engravings, with historical and descriptive Letterpress, half-bound morocco, top edges gilt, £5 5*s*.

*** *An enumeration of a few of the Plates will give some idea of the scope of the Work:*—St. Bartholomew's Church, Cloisters, and Priory, in 1393; St. Michael's, Cornhill, in 1421; St. Paul's Cathedral and Cross, in 1616 and 1656; St. John's of Jerusalem, Clerkenwell, 1660; Bunyan's Meeting House, in 1687; Guildhall, in 1517; Cheapside and its Cross, in 1547, 1585, and 1641; Cornhill, in 1599; Merchant Taylors' Hall, in 1599; Shakespeare's Globe Theatre, in 1612 and 1647; Alleyne's Bear Garden, in 1614 and 1647; Drury Lane, in 1792 and 1814; Covent Garden, in 1732, 1794, and 1809; Whitehall, in 1638 and 1697; York House, with Inigo Jones's Water Gate, circa 1626; Somerset House, previous to its alteration by Inigo Jones, circa 1600: St James's Palace, 1660; Montagu House (now the British Museum) before 1685, and in 1804.

LONGFELLOW'S PROSE WORKS, Complete. With Portrait and Illustrations by VALENTINE BROMLEY. 800 pages, crown 8vo, cloth gilt, 7*s*. 6*d*.

*** *This is by far the most complete edition ever issued in this country. "Outre-Mer" contains two additional chapters, restored from the first edition; while "The Poets and Poetry of Europe," and the little collection of Sketches entitled "Driftwood," are now first introduced to the English public.*

LONGFELLOW'S POETICAL WORKS. With numerous fine Illustrations. Crown 8vo, cloth extra, gilt, 7*s*. 6*d*. [*In the press*.

LOST BEAUTIES OF THE ENGLISH LANGUAGE. An Appeal to Authors, Poets, Clergymen, and Public Speakers. By CHARLES MACKAY, LL.D. Crown 8vo, cloth extra, 6*s*. 6*d*.

LOTOS LEAVES: Original Stories, Essays, and Poems, by WILKIE COLLINS, MARK TWAIN, WHITELAW REID, JOHN HAY, NOAH BROOKS, JOHN BROUGHAM, P. V. NASBY, ISAAC BROMLEY, and others. Profusely Illustrated by ALFRED FREDERICKS, ARTHUR LUMLEY, JOHN LA FARGE, GILBERT BURLING, GEORGE WHITE, and others. Crown 4to, handsomely bound, cloth extra, gilt and gilt edges, 21*s*.

"A very comely and pleasant volume, produced by general contribution of a literary club in New York, which has some kindly relations with a similar coterie in London. A *livre de luxe*, splendidly illustrated."—*Daily Telegraph*.

MACLISE'S GALLERY OF ILLUSTRIOUS LITERARY CHARACTERS. (THE FAMOUS FRASER PORTRAITS.) With Notes by the late WILLIAM MAGINN, LL.D. Edited, with copious Additional Notes, by WILLIAM BATES, B.A. The volume contains 83 CHARACTERISTIC PORTRAITS, now first issued in a complete form. Demy 4to, cloth gilt and gilt edges, 31*s*. 6*d*.

"One of the most interesting volumes of this year's literature."—*Times*.

"Deserves a place on every drawing-room table, and may not unfitly be removed from the drawing-room to the library."—*Spectator*.

MACQUOID'S THE EVIL EYE, and other Stories. With 8 Illustrations by THOMAS and PERCY MACQUOID. Crown 8vo, cloth extra, price 6*s*. [*In the press.*

MADRE NATURA versus THE MOLOCH OF FASHION. By LUKE LIMNER. With 32 Illustrations by the Author. FOURTH EDITION, revised and enlarged. Crown 8vo, cloth, extra gilt, 2*s*. 6*d*.

"Agreeably written and amusingly illustrated. Common sense and erudition are brought to bear on the subjects discussed in it."—*Lancet.*

MAGNA CHARTA. An exact Facsimile of the Original Document in the British Museum, printed on fine plate paper, nearly 3 feet long by 2 feet wide, with the Arms and Seals of the Barons emblazoned in Gold and Colours. Price 5*s*.

A full Translation, with Notes, printed on a large sheet, price 6*d*.

MANTELL'S PICTORIAL ATLAS OF FOSSIL REMAINS. With Additions and Descriptions. 4to, 74 Coloured Plates, cloth extra, 31*s*. 6*d*.

AUTHOR'S CORRECTED EDITION.

MARK TWAIN'S CHOICE WORKS. Revised and Corrected throughout by the Author. With Life, Portrait, and numerous Illustrations. 700 pages, cloth extra, gilt, 7*s*. 6*d*.

MARK TWAIN'S PLEASURE TRIP on the CONTINENT of EUROPE. Post 8vo, illustrated boards, 2*s*.

MARRYAT'S (Florence) New Novel, OPEN! SESAME! in Three Vols., crown 8vo, 31*s*. 6*d*. At all Libraries and at the Booksellers'.

"A story which arouses and sustains the reader's interest to a higher degree than, perhaps, any of its author's former works. . . . A very excellent story."—*Graphic.*

MARSTON'S (Dr. Westland) DRAMATIC and POETICAL WORKS. Collected Library Edition, in Two Vols., crown 8vo. [*In the press.*

MARSTON'S (Philip Bourke) SONG TIDE, and other Poems. Second Edition. Crown 8vo, cloth extra, 8*s*.

"This is a first work of extraordinary performance and of still more extraordinary promise. The youngest school of English poetry has received an important accession to its ranks in Philip Bourke Marston."—*Examiner.*

MARSTON'S (P. B.) ALL IN ALL: Poems and Sonnets. Crown 8vo, cloth extra, 8*s*.

"Many of these poems are leavened with the leaven of genuine poetical sentiment, and expressed with grace and beauty of language. A tender melancholy, as well as a penetrating pathos, gives character to much of their sentiment, and lends it an irresistible interest to all who can feel."—*Standard.*

MAXWELL'S LIFE OF THE DUKE OF WELLINGTON. Three Vols., 8vo, with numerous highly finished Line and Wood Engravings by Eminent Artists. Cloth extra, gilt, £1 7*s*.

MAYHEW'S LONDON CHARACTERS: Illustrations of the Humour, Pathos, and Peculiarities of London Life. By HENRY MAYHEW, Author of "London Labour and the London Poor," and other Writers. With nearly 100 graphic Illustrations by W. S. GILBERT and others. Cr. 8vo, cl. extra, 6*s*.

"Well fulfils the promise of its title. . . The book is an eminently interesting one, and will probably attract many readers."—*Court Circular.*

MEYRICK'S ENGRAVED ILLUSTRATIONS OF ANCIENT ARMS AND ARMOUR. 154 highly finished Etchings of the Collection at Goodrich Court, Herefordshire, engraved by JOSEPH SKELTON, with Historical and Critical Disquisitions by Sir S. R. MEYRICK. Two Vols., imperial 4to, with Portrait, half-morocco extra, gilt edges, £4 14*s*. 6*d*.

MEYRICK'S PAINTED ILLUSTRATIONS OF ANCIENT ARMS AND ARMOUR: A Critical Inquiry into Ancient Armour as it existed in Europe, but particularly in England, from the Norman Conquest to the Reign of Charles II.; with a Glossary, by Sir S. R. MEYRICK. New and greatly improved Edition, corrected throughout by the Author, with the assistance of ALBERT WAY and others. Illustrated by more than 100 Plates, splendidly Illuminated in gold and silver; also an additional Plate of the Tournament of Locks and Keys. Three Vols., imperial 4to, half-morocco extra, gilt edges, £10 10s.

"While the splendour of the decorations of this work is well calculated to excite curiosity, the novel character of its contents, the very curious extracts from the rare MSS. in which it abounds, and the pleasing manner in which the author's antiquarian researches are prosecuted, will tempt many who take up the book in idleness, to peruse it with care. No previous work can be compared, in point of extent, arrangement, science, or utility, with the one now in question. 1st. It for the first time supplies to our schools of art, correct and ascertained data for costume, in its noblest and most important branch—historical painting. 2nd. It affords a simple, clear, and most conclusive elucidation of a great number of passages in our great dramatic poets—ay, and in the works of those of Greece and Rome—against which commentators and scholiasts have been trying their wits for centuries. 3rd. It throws a flood of light upon the manners, usages, and sports of our ancestors, from the time of the Anglo-Saxons down to the reign of Charles the Second. And lastly, it at once removes a vast number of idle traditions and ingenious fables, which one compiler of history, copying from another, has succeeded in transmitting through the lapse of four or five hundred years.

"It is not often the fortune of a painful student of antiquity to conduct his readers through so splendid a succession of scenes and events as those to which Dr. Meyrick here successively introduces us. But he does it with all the ease and gracefulness of an accomplished *cicerone*. We see the haughty nobles and the impetuous knights—we are present at their arming—assist them to their shields—enter the well-appointed lists with them—and partake the hopes and fears, the perils, honours, and successes of the manly tournaments. Then we are presented to the glorious damsels, all superb and lovely, in 'velours and clothe of golde and dayntie devyces, bothe in pearls and emerawds, sawphires and dymondes,'—and the banquet, with the serving men and bucklers, servitors and trenchers—kings and queens—pageants, &c. &c. We feel as if the age of chivalry had returned in all its glory."—*Edinburgh Review.*

MILLINGEN'S ANCIENT UNEDITED MONUMENTS; comprising Painted Greek Vases, Statues, Busts, Bas-Reliefs, and other Remains of Grecian Art. 62 beautiful Engravings, mostly Coloured, with Letterpress Descriptions. Imperial 4to, half-morocco, £4 14s. 6d.

MILTON'S COMPLETE WORKS, Prose and Poetical. With an Introductory Essay by ROBERT FLETCHER. Imp. 8vo, with Portraits, cl. extra, 15s.

"It is to be regretted that the prose writings of Milton should, in our time, be so little read. As compositions, they deserve the attention of every man who wishes to become acquainted with the full power of the English language. They abound with passages compared with which the finest declamations of Burke sink into insignificance. They are a perfect field of cloth of gold. The style is stiff with gorgeous embroidery. Not even in the earlier books of the 'Paradise Lost' has the great poet ever risen higher than in those parts of his controversial works in which his feelings, excited by conflict, find a vent in bursts of devotional and lyric rapture. It is, to borrow his own majestic language, 'a sevenfold chorus of hallelujahs and harping symphonies.'"—MACAULAY.

MITFORD'S (Mary Russell) COUNTRY STORIES. With 5 Steel-plate Illustrations. Fcap. 8vo, cloth extra, gilt edges, 3s. 6d.

MONTAGU'S (Lady Mary Wortley) LETTERS AND WORKS. Edited by Lord WHARNCLIFFE. With important Additions and Corrections, derived from the Original Manuscripts, and a New Memoir. Two Vols., 8vo, with fine Steel Portraits, cloth extra, 18s.

"I have heard Dr. Johnson say that he never read but one book through from choice in his whole life, and that book was Lady Mary Wortley Montagu's Letters."—BOSWELL.

MONUMENTAL INSCRIPTIONS OF THE WEST INDIES, from the Earliest Date, with Genealogical and Historical Annotations, &c., from Original, Local, and other Sources. Illustrative of the Histories and Genealogies of the Seventeenth Century, the Calendars of State Papers, Peerages, and Baronetages. With Engravings of the Arms of the Principal Families. Chiefly collected on the spot by Capt. J. H. LAWRENCE-ARCHER. Demy 4to, half-Roxburghe, gilt top, 42*s.*

"The coats of arms, wherever they exist, are given both in trick and blazon, and the mechanical execution of the work is entitled to unqualified praise. The volume is indeed a sumptuous one, and must necessarily find a place in the library of every antiquary. . . . . It is not probable that more than once in fifty years an antiquary with the enthusiasm and perseverance of Captain Lawrence-Archer will make his appearance in those regions."—Colonel CHESTER, in *The Academy.*

MOSES' ANTIQUE VASES, Candelabra, Lamps, Tripods, Pateræ, Tazzas, Tombs, Mausoleums, Sepulchral Chambers, Cinerary Urns, Sarcophagi, Cippi, and other Ornaments. 170 Plates, several of which are coloured; with historical and descriptive Letterpress by THOS. HOPE, F.A.S. Small 4to, cloth extra, 18*s.*

MUSES OF MAYFAIR: Vers de Société of the Nineteenth Century. Including Selections from TENNYSON, BROWNING, SWINBURNE, ROSSETTI, JEAN INGELOW, LOCKER, INGOLDSBY, HOOD, LYTTON, C.S.C., LANDOR, AUSTIN DOBSON, HENRY LEIGH, &c. &c. Edited by H. CHOLMONDELEY-PENNELL. Crown 8vo, cloth extra, gilt, gilt edges, 7*s.* 6*d.*

NAPOLEON III., THE MAN OF HIS TIME. From Caricatures. Part I. THE STORY OF THE LIFE OF NAPOLEON III., as told by J. M. HASWELL. Part II. THE SAME STORY, as told by the POPULAR CARICATURES of the past Thirty-five Years. Crown 8vo, with Coloured Frontispiece and over 100 Caricatures, 7*s.* 6*d.*

NATIONAL GALLERY (The). A Selection from its Pictures. By CLAUDE, REMBRANDT, CUYP, Sir DAVID WILKIE, CORREGGIO, GAINSBOROUGH, CANALETTI, VANDYCK, PAUL VERONESE, CARACCI, RUBENS, N. and G. POUSSIN, and other great Masters. Engraved by GEORGE DOO, JOHN BURNETT, WM. FINDEN, JOHN and HENRY LE KEUX, JOHN PYE, WALTER BROMLEY, and others. With descriptive Text. Columbier 4to, cl. extra, full gilt and gilt edges, 42*s.*

NICHOLSON'S FIVE ORDERS of ARCHITECTURE (The Student's Instructor for Drawing and Working the). Demy 8vo, with 41 Plates, cloth extra, 5*s.*

OLD BOOKS—FACSIMILE REPRINTS.

ARMY LISTS OF THE ROUNDHEADS AND CAVALIERS IN THE CIVIL WAR, 1642. SECOND EDITION, Corrected and considerably Enlarged. Edited, with Notes and full Index, by EDWARD PEACOCK, F.S.A. 4to, half-Roxburghe, 7*s.* 6*d.*

D'URFEY'S ("Tom") WIT AND MIRTH; or, PILLS TO PURGE MELANCHOLY. Being a Collection of the best Merry Ballads and Songs, Old and New. Fitted to all Humours, having each their proper Tune for either Voice or Instrument; most of the Songs being new set. London: Printed by W. Pearson, for J. Tonson, at Shakespeare's Head, over against Catherine Street in the Strand, 1719. An exact reprint. In Six Vols., large fcap. 8vo, printed on antique laid paper, antique boards, £3 3*s.*

EARLY NEWS SHEET.—The Russian Invasion of Poland in 1563. (Memorabilis et perinde stupenda de crudeli Moscovitarum Expeditione Narratio, e Germanico in Latinum conversa.) An exact Facsimile of a Contemporary Account, with Introduction, Historical Notes, and full Translation. Large fcap. 8vo, antique paper, half-Roxburghe, 7*s.* 6*d.*

HOGG'S JACOBITE RELICS OF SCOTLAND: The Songs, Airs, and Legends of the Adherents to the House of Stuart. Collected and Illustrated by JAMES HOGG. Two Vols., demy 8vo. ORIGINAL EDITION. Cloth extra, 28*s.*

OLD BOOKS—continued.

ENGLISH ROGUE (The), described in the Life of MERITON LATROON, and other Extravagants, comprehending the most Eminent Cheats of both Sexes. By RICHARD HEAD and FRANCIS KIRKMAN. A Facsimile Reprint of the rare Original Edition (1665-1672), with Frontispiece, Facsimiles of the 12 Copperplates, and Portraits of the Authors. In Four Vols., large fcap. 8vo, printed on antique laid paper, and bound in antique boards, 36*s.*

IRELAND FORGERIES.—Confessions of WILLIAM HENRY IRELAND. Containing the Particulars of his Fabrication of the Shakespeare Manuscripts: together with Anecdotes and Opinions (hitherto unpublished) of many Distinguished Persons in the Literary, Political, and Theatrical World. A Facsimile Reprint from the Original Edition, with several additional Facsimiles. Fcap. 8vo, printed on antique laid paper, and bound in antique boards, 10*s.* 6*d.*; a few Large Paper copies, at 21*s.*

JOE MILLER'S JESTS: The politest Repartees, most elegant Bons-mots, and most pleasing short Stories in the English Language. London: printed by T. Read. 1739. A Facsimile of the Original Edition. 8vo, half-morocco, 9*s.* 6*d.*

LITTLE LONDON DIRECTORY OF 1677. The Oldest Printed List of the Merchants and Bankers of London. Reprinted from the Rare Original, with an Introduction by JOHN CAMDEN HOTTEN. 16mo, binding after the original, 6*s.* 6*d.*

MUSARUM DELICIÆ; or, The Muses' Recreation, 1656; Wit Restored, 1658; and Wit's Recreations, 1640. The whole compared with the Originals. With all the Wood Engravings, Plates, Memoirs, and Notes. A New Edition, in Two Vols., large fcap. 8vo, printed on antique laid paper, and bound in antique boards, 21*s.*

MYSTERY OF THE GOOD OLD CAUSE. Sarcastic Notices of those Members of the Long Parliament that held Places, both Civil and Military, contrary to the Self-denying Ordinance of April 3, 1645; with the Sums of Money and Lands they divided among themselves. Sm. 4to, half-morocco, 7*s.* 6*d.*

RUMP (The); or, An Exact Collection of the Choicest POEMS and SONGS relating to the late Times, and continued by the most eminent Wits; from Anno 1639 to 1661. A Facsimile Reprint of the rare Original Edition (London, 1662), with Frontispiece and Engraved Title-page. In Two Vols., large fcap. 8vo, printed on antique laid paper, and bound in antique boards, 17*s.* 6*d.*

OLD DRAMATISTS.

BEN JONSON'S WORKS. With Notes, Critical and Explanatory, and a Biographical Memoir by WM. GIFFORD. Edited by Col. CUNNINGHAM. Complete in Three Vols., crown 8vo, cloth extra, gilt, with Portrait, 6*s.* each.

CHAPMAN'S (George) COMPLETE WORKS. Now first Collected. In Three Volumes, crown 8vo, cloth extra, with two Frontispieces, price 18*s.*; or, separately, 6*s.* per vol. Vol. I. contains the Plays complete, including the doubtful ones; Vol. II. the Poems and Minor Translations, with an Introductory Essay by ALGERNON CHARLES SWINBURNE; Vol. III. the Translations of the Iliad and Odyssey.

MARLOWE'S WORKS. Including his Translations. Edited, with Notes and Introduction, by Col. CUNNINGHAM. Crown 8vo, cloth extra, gilt, with Portrait, price 6*s.*

MASSINGER'S PLAYS. From the Text of WM. GIFFORD. With the addition of the Tragedy of "Believe as You List." Edited by Col. CUNNINGHAM. Crown 8vo, cloth extra, gilt, with Portrait, price 6*s.*

OLD SHEKARRY'S FOREST AND FIELD: Life and Adventure in Wild Africa. With 8 Illustrations. Crown 8vo, cloth extra, gilt, 6*s.*

OLD SHEKARRY'S WRINKLES; or, Hints to Sportsmen and Travellers upon Dress, Equipment, Armament, and Camp Life. A New Edition, with Illustrations. Small crown 8vo, cloth extra, gilt, 6*s*.

"The book is most comprehensive in its character, nothing necessary to the paraphernalia of the travelling sportsman being omitted, while the hints are given in that plain, unvarnished language which can be easily understood. There are numerous illustrations, and the book has been excellently brought out by the publishers."—*Sportsman*.

ORIGINAL LISTS OF PERSONS OF QUALITY; Emigrants; Religious Exiles; Political Rebels; Serving Men Sold for a Term of Years; Apprentices; Children Stolen; Maidens Pressed; and others who went from Great Britain to the American Plantations, 1600–1700. From MSS. in Her Majesty's Public Record Office. Edited by JOHN CAMDEN HOTTEN. Crown 4to, cloth gilt, 700 pages, 38*s*.; Large Paper copies, half-morocco, 60*s*.

"This volume is an English Family Record, and as such may be commended to English families, and the descendants of English families, wherever they exist."—*Academy*.

O'SHAUGHNESSY'S (Arthur) AN EPIC OF WOMEN, and other Poems. Second Edition. Fcap. 8vo, cloth extra, 6*s*.

O'SHAUGHNESSY'S LAYS OF FRANCE. (Founded on the "Lays of Marie.") Second Edition. Crown 8vo, cloth extra, 10*s*. 6*d*.

O'SHAUGHNESSY'S MUSIC AND MOONLIGHT: Poems and Songs. Fcap. 8vo, cloth extra, 7*s*. 6*d*.

"It is difficult to say which is more exquisite, the technical perfection of structure and melody, or the delicate pathos of thought. Mr. O'Shaughnessy will enrich our literature with some of the very best songs written in our generation."—*Academy*.

OTTLEY'S FACSIMILES OF SCARCE AND CURIOUS PRINTS, by the Early Masters of the Italian, German, and Flemish Schools. 129 Copperplate Engravings, illustrative of the History of Engraving, from the Invention of the Art (the Niellos printed in Silver). Imperial 4to, half-bound morocco, top edges gilt, £6 6*s*.

OUIDA'S NOVELS.—Uniform Edition, crown 8vo, cloth extra, gilt, price 5*s*. each.

Folle Farine.

Idalia. A Romance.

Chandos. A Novel.

Under Two Flags.

Cecil Castlemaine's Gage.

Tricotrin. The Story of a Waif and Stray.

Pascarel. Only a Story.

Held in Bondage; or, Granville de Vigne.

Puck. His Vicissitudes, Adventures, &c.

A Dog of Flanders, and other Stories.

Strathmore; or, Wrought by his Own Hand.

Two Little Wooden Shoes.

PALEY'S COMPLETE WORKS. Containing the Natural Theology, Moral and Political Philosophy, Evidences of Christianity, Horæ Paulinæ, Clergyman's Companion, &c. Demy 8vo, with Portrait, cloth extra, 5*s*.

PARKS OF LONDON: Their History, from the Earliest Period to the Present Time. By JACOB LARWOOD. With numerous Illustrations, Coloured and Plain. Crown 8vo, cloth extra, gilt, 7*s*. 6*d*.

PERCY'S RELIQUES OF ANCIENT ENGLISH POETRY. Consisting of Old Heroic Ballads, Songs, and other Pieces of our Earlier Poets, together with some few of later date, and a copious Glossary. Medium 8vo, with Engraved Title and Frontispiece, cloth extra, gilt, 5*s*.

"The first time I could scrape a few shillings together I bought unto myself a copy of these beloved volumes (*Percy's Reliques*); nor do I believe I ever read a book half so frequently, or with half the enthusiasm."—Sir W. SCOTT.

PLATTNER'S MANUAL OF QUALITATIVE AND QUANTITATIVE ANALYSIS WITH THE BLOWPIPE. From the last German Edition. Revised and enlarged by Prof. TH. RICHTER, Royal Saxon Mining Academy. Edited by T. HUGO COOKESLEY. With numerous Illustrations. Demy 8vo, cloth extra, 21*s.*

"'Plattner's Manual' deservedly stands first among all other works on this subject, and its appearance in English will be hailed by all those who are occupied in the analysis of mineral ores, but who, from ignorance of the German language, have been hitherto unable to study it. It is a work of great practical as well as scientific value."—*Standard.*

"By far the most complete work extant on a subject of growing practical importance and of extreme interest."—*Mining Journal.*

PLUTARCH'S LIVES, Complete. Translated by the LANGHORNES. New Edition, with Medallion Portraits. In Two Vols., 8vo, cloth extra, 10*s.* 6*d.*

POE'S (Edgar Allan) CHOICE PROSE AND POETICAL WORKS. With BAUDELAIRE'S "Essay." 750 pages, crown 8vo, Portrait and Illustrations, cloth extra, 7*s.* 6*d.*

PRACTICAL ASSAYER: A Guide to Miners and Explorers. Giving directions, in the simplest form, for assaying bullion and the baser metals by the cheapest, quickest, and best methods. By OLIVER NORTH. With Tables and Illustrative Woodcuts. Crown 8vo, 7*s.* 6*d.*

PRIVATE BOOK OF USEFUL ALLOYS AND MEMORANDA FOR GOLDSMITHS AND JEWELLERS. By JAMES E. COLLINS, C.E. Royal 16mo, 3*s.* 6*d.*

PROUT, FATHER.—THE FINAL RELIQUES OF FATHER PROUT. Collected and edited, from MSS. supplied by the family of the Rev. FRANCIS MAHONY, by BLANCHARD JERROLD. With Portrait and Facsimiles. [*In the press.*

PUCK ON PEGASUS. By H. CHOLMONDELEY-PENNELL. Profusely illustrated by JOHN LEECH, H. K. BROWNE, Sir NOEL PATON, J. E. MILLAIS, JOHN TENNIEL, RICHARD DOYLE, ELLEN EDWARDS, and other Artists. Seventh Edition, crown 8vo, cloth extra, gilt, price 5*s.*

"The book is clever and amusing, vigorous and healthy."—*Saturday Review.*

PUGIN'S ARCHITECTURAL WORKS.

APOLOGY FOR THE REVIVAL OF CHRISTIAN ARCHITECTURE. With 10 large Etchings. Small 4to, cloth extra, 5*s.*

EXAMPLES OF GOTHIC ARCHITECTURE, selected from Ancient Edifices in England. 225 Engravings by LE KEUX, with descriptive Letterpress by E. J. WILLSON. Three Vols., 4to, cloth extra, £3 13*s.* 6*d.*

FLORIATED ORNAMENTS. 31 Plates in Gold and Colours, royal 4to, half-morocco, tooled back and sides, £1 16*s.*

GOTHIC ORNAMENTS. 90 Plates, by J. D. HARDING and others. Royal 4to, half-bound, £1 16*s.*

ORNAMENTAL TIMBER GABLES. 30 Plates. Royal 4to, cloth extra, 18*s.*

SPECIMENS OF GOTHIC ARCHITECTURE, from Ancient Edifices in England. 114 Outline Plates by LE KEUX and others. With descriptive Letterpress and Glossary by E. J. WILLSON. Two Vols., 4to, cloth extra, £1 16*s.*

TRUE PRINCIPLES OF POINTED OR CHRISTIAN ARCHITECTURE. With 87 Illustrations. Small 4to, cloth extra, 10*s.* 6*d.*

PUNIANA; or, Thoughts Wise and Other-Why's. A New Collection of Riddles, Conundrums, Jokes, Sells, &c. In Two Series, each containing 3000 of the best Riddles, 10,000 most outrageous Puns, and upwards of fifty beautifully-executed Drawings by the Editor, the Hon. HUGH ROWLEY. Price of each Volume, in small 4to, blue and gold, gilt edges, 6*s*. *Each Series Complete in itself.*

"A witty, droll, and most amusing work, profusely and elegantly illustrated."—*Standard.*

PURSUIVANT OF ARMS (The); or, Heraldry founded upon Facts. A Popular Guide to the Science of Heraldry. By J. R. PLANCHÉ, Esq., Somerset Herald. To which are added, Essays on the BADGES OF THE HOUSES OF LANCASTER AND YORK. With Coloured Frontispiece, five full-page Plates, and about 200 Illustrations. Crown 8vo, cloth extra, gilt, 7*s*. 6*d*.

QUEENS AND KINGS, AND OTHER THINGS: A Rare and Choice Collection of Pictures, Poetry, and strange but veritable Histories, designed and written by the Princess HESSE-SCHWARZBOURG. Imprinted in gold and many colours by the Brothers DALZIEL, at their Camden Press. Imperial 4to, cloth gilt and gilt edges, £1 1*s*.

RABELAIS' WORKS. Faithfully translated from the French, with variorum Notes, and numerous Characteristic Illustrations by GUSTAVE DORÉ. Crown 8vo, cloth extra, 700 pages, 7*s*. 6*d*.

READE'S (Winwood) THE OUTCAST. Cr. 8vo, cloth extra, 5*s*.

"He relaxed his mind in his leisure hours by the creation of a new religion."—*Standard.*

"A work of very considerable power, written with great pathos and evident earnestness."—*Athenæum.*

REMARKABLE TRIALS AND NOTORIOUS CHARACTERS. From "Half-Hanged Smith," 1700, to Oxford, who shot at the Queen, 1840. By Captain L. BENSON. With nearly Fifty spirited full-page Engravings by PHIZ. Crown 8vo, cloth extra, gilt, 7*s*. 6*d*.

ROCHEFOUCAULD'S REFLECTIONS & MORAL MAXIMS. With Introductory Essay by SAINTE-BEUVE, and Explanatory Notes. Royal 16mo, cloth extra, 1*s*. 6*d*.

ROLL OF BATTLE ABBEY; or, A List of the Principal Warriors who came over from Normandy with William the Conqueror, and Settled in this Country, A.D. 1066–7. Printed on fine plate paper, nearly three feet by two, with the principal Arms emblazoned in Gold and Colours. Price 5*s*.

ROLL OF CAERLAVEROCK, the Oldest Heraldic Roll; including the Original Anglo-Norman Poem, and an English Translation of the MS. in the British Museum. By THOMAS WRIGHT, M.A. The Arms emblazoned in Gold and Colours. In 4to, very handsomely printed, extra gold cloth, 12*s*.

ROMAN CATHOLICS IN THE COUNTY OF YORK IN 1604 (A LIST OF). Transcribed from the MS. in the Bodleian Library, and Edited, with Notes, by EDWARD PEACOCK, F.S.A. Small 4to, cloth extra, 15*s*.

ROSCOE'S LIFE AND PONTIFICATE OF LEO THE TENTH. Edited by his Son, THOMAS ROSCOE. Two Vols., 8vo, with Portraits and numerous Plates, cloth extra, 18*s*.

*** Also, an Edition in One Vol. 16mo, cloth extra, price 3*s*.

ROSCOE'S LIFE OF LORENZO DE' MEDICI, called "THE MAGNIFICENT." A New and much improved Edition. Edited by his Son, THOMAS ROSCOE. Demy 8vo, with Portraits and numerous Plates, cloth extra, 9*s*.

ROSS'S (C. H.) STORY OF A HONEYMOON. With numerous Illustrations by the Author. Fcap. 8vo, illustrated boards, 2*s*.

ROWLANDSON (Thomas): HIS LIFE AND TIMES; With the History of his Caricatures, and the Key to their Meaning. With very numerous full-page Plates and Wood Engravings. Demy 4to, a thick volume, cloth extra, gilt and gilt edges, 31*s.* 6*d.* [*In preparation.*

SAINT-SIMON (MEMOIRS OF THE DUKE OF), during the Reign of Louis the Fourteenth and the Regency. Translated from the French and Edited by BAYLE ST. JOHN. A New Edition, in Three Vols., 8vo, with numerous Steel-plate Illustrations. [*In preparation.*

SALA (George Augustus) ON COOKERY IN ITS HISTORICAL ASPECT. With very numerous Illustrations by the AUTHOR. Crown 4to, cloth extra, gilt. [*In preparation.*

SEVEN GENERATIONS OF EXECUTIONERS.

SANSON FAMILY, Memoirs of the, compiled from Private Documents in the possession of the Family (1688-1847), by HENRI SANSON. Translated from the French, with an Introduction by CAMILLE BARRÈRE. Two Vols., 8vo, cloth extra. [*In the press.*

*** *Sanson was the hereditary French executioner, who officiated at the decapitation of Louis XVI.*

SCHOLA ITALICA; or, Engravings of the finest Pictures in the Galleries at Rome. Imperial folio, with 40 beautiful Engravings after MICHAEL ANGELO, RAPHAEL, TITIAN, CARACCI, GUIDO, PARMIGIANO, &c., by VOLPATO and others, half-bound morocco extra, £2 12*s.* 6*d.*

SCHOPENHAUER'S THE WORLD AS WILL AND IMAGINATION. Translated by Dr. FRANZ HÜFFER, Author of "Richard Wagner and the Music of the Future." [*In preparation.*

SCOTT'S COMMENTARY ON THE HOLY BIBLE. With the Author's Last Corrections, and beautiful Illustrations and Maps. Three Vols., imperial 8vo, cloth extra, £1 16*s.*

"SECRET OUT" SERIES.

Crown 8vo, cloth extra, profusely Illustrated, price 4*s.* 6*d.* each.

ART OF AMUSING. A Collection of Graceful Arts, Games, Tricks, Puzzles, and Charades. By FRANK BELLEW. 300 Illustrations.

HANKY-PANKY: Very Easy Tricks, Very Difficult Tricks, White Magic, Sleight of Hand. Edited by W. H. CREMER. 200 Illustrations.

MAGICIAN'S OWN BOOK: Performances with Cups and Balls, Eggs, Hats, Handkerchiefs, &c. All from Actual Experience. Edited by W. H. CREMER. 200 Illustrations.

MAGIC NO MYSTERY: Tricks with Cards, Dice, Balls, &c., with fully descriptive Directions. Numerous Illustrations. [*In the press.*

MERRY CIRCLE (The): A Book of New Intellectual Games and Amusements. By CLARA BELLEW. Numerous Illustrations.

SECRET OUT: One Thousand Tricks with Cards, and other Recreations; with entertaining Experiments in Drawing-room or "White Magic." By W. H. CREMER. 300 Engravings.

SEYMOUR'S (Robert) HUMOROUS SKETCHES. 86 Clever and Amusing Caricature Etchings on Steel, with Letterpress Commentary by ALFRED CROWQUILL. A New Edition, with Biographical Notice, and Descriptive List of Plates. Royal 8vo, cloth extra, gilt edges, 15*s.*

SHAKESPEARE.—THE FIRST FOLIO. Mr. WILLIAM SHAKESPEARE'S Comedies, Histories, and Tragedies. Published according to the true Original Copies. Lond., Printed by ISAAC IAGGARD and EDWARD BLOUNT. 1623.—An exact Reproduction of the extremely rare Original, in reduced facsimile by a photographic process—thus ensuring the strictest accuracy in every detail. 8vo, antique binding. [*In the press.*

SHAKESPEARE.—THE LANSDOWNE EDITION. Beautifully printed in red and black, in small but very clear type. Post 8vo, with engraved facsimile of DROESHOUT'S Portrait, cloth extra, gilt, gilt edges, *14s.*; or, illustrated by 37 beautiful Steel Plates, after STOTHARD, cloth extra, gilt, gilt edges, *18s.*

SHAW'S ILLUMINATED WORKS.

ALPHABETS, NUMERALS, AND DEVICES OF THE MIDDLE AGES. Selected from the finest existing Specimens. 4to, 48 Plates (26 Coloured), *£2 2s.*; Large Paper, imperial 4to, the Coloured Plates very highly finished and heightened with Gold, *£4 4s.* [*New Edition preparing.*

ANCIENT FURNITURE, drawn from existing Authorities. With Descriptions by Sir S. R. MEYRICK. 4to, 74 Plates, half-morocco, *£1 11s. 6d.*; or, with some Plates Coloured, 4to, half-morocco, *£2 2s.*; Large Paper copies, imperial 4to, all the Plates extra finished in opaque Colours, half-morocco extra, *£4 14s. 6d.*

DECORATIVE ARTS OF THE MIDDLE AGES. Exhibiting, in 41 Plates and numerous beautiful Woodcuts, choice Specimens of the various kinds of Ancient Enamel, Metal Work, Wood Carvings, Paintings on Stained Glass, Venetian Glass, Initial Illuminations, Embroidery, Fictile Ware, Bookbinding, &c.; with elegant Initial Letters to the various Descriptions. Imperial 8vo, half-morocco extra, *£1 8s.*

DOMESTIC ARCHITECTURE IN ENGLAND during the Reign of QUEEN ELIZABETH, as exemplified in Mr. PALMER'S House at Great Yarmouth. Imperial 4to, 43 Plates of Architectural Ornament, and Portrait, half-morocco, *£1 16s.*; or India Proofs, half-morocco extra, *£2 8s.*

DRESSES AND DECORATIONS OF THE MIDDLE AGES, from the Seventh to the Seventeenth Centuries. 94 Plates, beautifully Coloured, a profusion of Initial Letters, and Examples of Curious Ornament, with Historical Introduction and Descriptive Text. Two Vols., imperial 8vo, half-Roxburghe, *£5 5s.*

ELIZABETHAN ARCHITECTURE (DETAILS OF). With Descriptive Letterpress by T. MOULE. 4to, 60 Plates, half-morocco, *£1 5s.*; Large Paper, imperial 4to, several of the Plates Coloured, half-morocco, *£2 12s. 6d.*

ENCYCLOPÆDIA OF ORNAMENT. Select Examples from the purest and best Specimens of all kinds and all Ages. 4to, 59 Plates, half-morocco, *£1 1s.*; Large Paper copies, imperial 4to, with all the Plates Coloured, half-morocco, *£2 12s. 6d.*

ILLUMINATED ORNAMENTS OF THE MIDDLE AGES, from the Sixth to the Seventeenth Century. Selected from Missals, MSS., and early printed Books. 66 Plates, carefully coloured from the Originals, with Descriptions by Sir F. MADDEN, Keeper of MSS., Brit. Mus. 4to, half-Roxburghe, *£3 13s. 6d.*; Large Paper copies, the Plates finished with opaque Colours and illuminated with Gold, imperial 4to, half-Roxburghe, *£7 7s.*

LUTON CHAPEL: A Series of 20 highly-finished Line Engravings of Gothic Architecture and Ornaments. Imperial folio, India Proofs, half-morocco, *£2 8s.*

ORNAMENTAL METAL WORK: A Series of 50 Copperplates, several Coloured. 4to, half-morocco, *18s.*

SHAW AND BRIDGENS' DESIGNS FOR FURNITURE, with Candelabra and Interior Decoration. 60 Plates, royal 4to, half-morocco, *£1 1s.*; Large Paper, imperial 4to, the Plates Coloured, half-morocco, *£2 8s.*

SHELLEY'S EARLY LIFE. From Original Sources. With Curious Incidents, Letters, and Writings, now First Collected. By D. F. MACCARTHY. Crown 8vo, with Illustrations, cloth extra, *7s. 6d.*

SHERIDAN'S COMPLETE WORKS, with Life and Anecdotes. Including his Dramatic Writings, printed from the Original Editions, his Works in Prose and Poetry, Translations, Speeches, Jokes, Puns, &c.; with a Collection of Sheridaniana. Crown 8vo, cloth extra, gilt, with 10 full-page Tinted Illustrations, 7*s*. 6*d*.

"Whatever Sheridan has done, has been, *par excellence*, always the *best* of its kind. He has written the best comedy (School for Scandal), the *best* drama (the Duenna), the *best* farce (the Critic), and the *best* address (Monologue on Garrick); and, to crown all, delivered the very best oration (the famous Begum Speech) ever conceived or heard in this country."—BYRON.

"The editor has brought together within a manageable compass not only the seven plays by which Sheridan is best known, but a collection also of his poetical pieces which are less familiar to the public, sketches of unfinished dramas, selections from his reported witticisms, and extracts from his principal speeches. To these is prefixed a short but well-written memoir, giving the chief facts in Sheridan's literary and political career; so that with this volume in his hand, the student may consider himself tolerably well furnished with all that is necessary for a general comprehension of the subject of it."—*Pall Mall Gazette.*

SIGNBOARDS: Their History. With Anecdotes of Famous Taverns and Remarkable Characters. By JACOB LARWOOD and JOHN CAMDEN HOTTEN. With nearly 100 Illustrations. SEVENTH EDITION. Crown 8vo, cloth extra, 7*s*. 6*d*.

"Even if we were ever so maliciously inclined, we could not pick out all Messrs. Larwood and Hotten's plums, because the good things are so numerous as to defy the most wholesale depredation."—*The Times.*

SILVESTRE'S UNIVERSAL PALÆOGRAPHY; or, A Collection of Facsimiles of the Writings of every Age. Containing upwards of 300 large and beautifully executed Facsimiles, taken from Missals and other MSS., richly Illuminated in the finest style of art. A New Edition, arranged under the direction of Sir F. MADDEN, Keeper of MSS., Brit. Mus. Two Vols., atlas folio, half-morocco, gilt, £31 10*s*.—Also, a Volume of HISTORICAL AND DESCRIPTIVE LETTERPRESS, by CHAMPOLLION FIGEAC and CHAMPOLLION, Jun. Translated, with Additions, by Sir F. MADDEN. Two Vols., royal 8vo, half-morocco, gilt, £2 8*s*.

"This great work contains upwards of three hundred large and beautifully executed facsimiles of the finest and most interesting MSS. of various ages and nations, illuminated in the highest style of art. The cost of getting up this splendid publication was not far from £20,000."—*Alibone's Dict.*

"The great work on Palæography generally—one of the most sumptuous works of its class ever published."—*Chambers's Encyclopædia.*

SLANG DICTIONARY (The): Etymological, Historical, and Anecdotal. An ENTIRELY NEW EDITION, revised throughout, and considerably Enlarged. Crown 8vo, cloth extra, gilt, 6*s*. 6*d*.

"We are glad to see the Slang Dictionary reprinted and enlarged. From a high scientific point of view this book is not to be despised. Of course it cannot fail to be amusing also. It contains the very vocabulary of unrestrained humour, and oddity, and grotesqueness. In a word, it provides valuable material both for the student of language and the student of human nature."—*Academy.*

"In every way a great improvement on the edition of 1864. Its uses as a dictionary of the very vulgar tongue do not require to be explained."—*Notes and Queries.*

"Compiled with most exacting care, and based on the best authorities."—*Standard.*

SMITH'S HISTORICAL AND LITERARY CURIOSITIES: Containing Facsimiles of Autographs, Scenes of Remarkable Events, Interesting Localities, Old Houses, Portraits, Illuminated and Missal Ornaments, Antiquities, &c. 4to, with 100 Plates (some Illuminated), half-morocco extra, £2 5*s*.

*** *The Autographs are chiefly of a literary character, and include Letters by Coverdale, Sir Christopher Wren, Sir Isaac Newton, Cowley, Pope, Addison, Gray, Milton, Prior, Smollett, Sterne, Locke, Burns, Steele, Hume, Dr. Johnson, Benjamin Franklin, William Penn, &c.*

THIERS' HISTORY OF THE CONSULATE AND EMPIRE OF FRANCE UNDER NAPOLEON. Roy. 8vo, cloth extra, 15*s*.

THIERS' HISTORY OF THE FRENCH REVOLUTION. Roy. 8vo, cloth extra, 15*s*.

"The History of the French Revolution by Thiers is a celebrated and popular book in France—and I believe in Europe. It combines the compactness and unity of the book, the order and arrangement of the journal, the simplicity of the biography, the valuable and minute details of the autobiography, and the enthusiasm, the passion, and the indignation of the pamphlet. There are in many parts of this great book, whole chapters which read as if they had been written with the sword."—JULES JANIN, *in the Athenæum.*

THOMSON'S (James) THE SEASONS, and THE CASTLE OF INDOLENCE. With a Biographical and Critical Introduction by ALLAN CUNNINGHAM, and over 50 fine Illustrations on Steel and Wood. Crown 8vo, cloth extra, gilt, 6*s*. [*In the press.*

THORNBURY.—ON THE SLOPES OF PARNASSUS. By WALTER THORNBURY. Illustrated by J. WHISTLER, JOHN TENNIEL, A. F. SANDYS, W. SMALL, M. J. LAWLESS, J. D. WATSON, G. J. PINWELL, F. WALKER, T. MACQUOID, J. LAWSON, and others. Handsomely printed, crown 4to, cloth extra, gilt and gilt edges, 21*s*. [*In preparation.*

TIMBS' ENGLISH ECCENTRICS and ECCENTRICITIES: Stories of Wealth and Fashion, Delusions, Impostures and Fanatic Missions, Strange Sights and Sporting Scenes, Eccentric Artists, Theatrical Folks, Men of Letters, &c. By JOHN TIMBS, F.S.A. With nearly 50 Illustrations. Crown 8vo, cloth extra, 7*s*. 6*d*.

"The reader who would fain enjoy a harmless laugh in some very odd company might do much worse than take an occasional dip into 'English Eccentrics.' Beaux, preachers, authors, actors, monstrosities of the public shows, and leaders of religious impostures, will meet him here in infinite, almost perplexing, variety. The queer illustrations, from portraits and caricatures of the time, are admirably suited to the letterpress."—*Graphic.*

TIMBS' CLUBS AND CLUB LIFE IN LONDON. With ANECDOTES of its FAMOUS COFFEE HOUSES, HOSTELRIES, and TAVERNS. By JOHN TIMBS, F.S.A. With numerous Illustrations. Crown 8vo, cloth extra, 7*s*. 6*d*.

TOURNEUR'S (Cyril) COLLECTED WORKS, including a hitherto altogether unknown Series of Sonnets. Edited by J. CHURTON COLLINS. Post 8vo, antique boards. [*In preparation.*

TURNER'S (J. M. W.) LIBER FLUVIORUM; or, River Scenery of France. 62 highly-finished Line Engravings by WILLMORE, GOODALL, MILLER, COUSENS, and other distinguished Artists. With descriptive Letterpress by LEITCH RITCHIE, and Memoir by ALARIC A. WATTS. Imperial 8vo, cloth extra, gilt edges, £1 11*s*. 6*d*.

TURNER (J. M. W.) and GIRTIN'S RIVER SCENERY. 20 beautiful Mezzotinto Plates, engraved on Steel by REYNOLDS, BROMLEY, LUPTON, and CHARLES TURNER, principally after the Drawings of J. M. W. TURNER. Small folio, in Portfolio, £1 11*s*. 6*d*.

TURNER'S (J. M. W.) LIFE AND CORRESPONDENCE. Founded upon Letters and Papers furnished by his Friends and Fellow-Academicians. By WALTER THORNBURY. New Edition, entirely rewritten and added to. With numerous Illustrations. Two Vols., 8vo, cloth extra. [*In preparation.*

TURNER GALLERY (The): A Series of Sixty Engravings from the Principal Works of JOSEPH MALLORD WILLIAM TURNER. With a Memoir and Illustrative Text by RALPH NICHOLSON WORNUM, Keeper and Secretary, National Gallery. Handsomely half-bound, India Proofs, royal folio, £10; Large Paper copies, Artists' India Proofs, elephant folio, £20.—A Descriptive Pamphlet will be sent upon application.

VAGABONDIANA; or, Anecdotes of Mendicant Wanderers through the Streets of London; with Portraits of the most Remarkable, drawn from the Life by JOHN THOMAS SMITH, late Keeper of the Prints in the British Museum. With Introduction by FRANCIS DOUCE, and Descriptive Text. With the Woodcuts and the 32 Plates, from the original Coppers. Crown 4to, half-Roxburghe, 12*s.* 6*d.*

VYNER'S NOTITIA VENATICA: A Treatise on Fox-Hunting, the General Management of Hounds, and the Diseases of Dogs; Distemper and Rabies; Kennel Lameness, &c. By ROBERT C. VYNER. Sixth Edition, Enlarged. With spirited Coloured Illustrations by ALKEN. Royal 8vo, cloth extra, 21*s.*

WALPOLE'S (Horace) ANECDOTES OF PAINTING IN ENGLAND. With some Account of the principal English Artists, and incidental Notices of Sculptors, Carvers, Enamellers, Architects, Medallists, Engravers, &c. With Additions by the Rev. JAMES DALLAWAY. New Edition, Revised and Edited, with Additional Notes, by RALPH N. WORNUM, Keeper and Secretary, National Gallery. Three Vols., 8vo, with upwards of 150 Portraits and Plates, cloth extra, £1 7*s.*

WALPOLE'S (Horace) ENTIRE CORRESPONDENCE. Chronologically arranged, with the Prefaces and Notes of CROKER, Lord DOVER, and others; the Notes of all previous Editors, and Additional Notes by PETER CUNNINGHAM. Nine Vols., 8vo, with numerous fine Portraits engraved on Steel, cloth extra, £4 1*s.*

"The charm which lurks in Horace Walpole's Letters is one for which we have no term; and our Gallic neighbours seem to have engrossed both the word and the quality—'elles sont piquantes,' to the highest degree. If you read but a sentence, you feel yourself spell-bound till you have read the volume."—*Quarterly Review.*

WALPOLE'S (Horace) ROYAL AND NOBLE AUTHORS OF ENGLAND, SCOTLAND, AND IRELAND; with Lists of their Works. A New Edition, Annotated, considerably Enlarged, and brought down to the Present Time. Illustrated by nearly 200 Copperplate Portraits. Six Vols., 8vo, cloth extra, £2 14*s.* [*In preparation.*

WALTON AND COTTON, ILLUSTRATED.—THE COMPLETE ANGLER; or, The Contemplative Man's Recreation: Being a Discourse of Rivers, Fish-ponds, Fish and Fishing, written by IZAAK WALTON; and Instructions how to Angle for a Trout or Grayling in a clear Stream, by CHARLES COTTON. With Original Memoirs and Notes by Sir HARRIS NICOLAS, K.C.M.G. With the 61 Plate Illustrations, precisely as in Pickering's two-volume Edition. Complete in One Volume, large crown 8vo, cloth antique, 7*s.* 6*d.*

WARRANT TO EXECUTE CHARLES I. An exact Facsimile of this important Document, with the Fifty-nine Signatures of the Regicides, and corresponding Seals, on paper to imitate the Original, 22 in. by 14 in. Price 2*s.*

WARRANT TO EXECUTE MARY QUEEN OF SCOTS. An exact Facsimile of this important Document, including the Signature of Queen Elizabeth and Facsimile of the Great Seal, on tinted paper, to imitate the Original MS. Price 2*s.*

WATERFORD ROLL (The).—Illuminated Charter-Roll of Waterford, Temp. Richard II. The Illuminations accurately Traced and Coloured for the Work from a Copy carefully made by the late GEORGE V. DU NOYER, Esq., M.R.I.A. Those Charters which have not already appeared in print will be edited by the Rev. JAMES GRAVES, A.B., M.R.I.A. Imperial 4to, cloth extra, gilt, 36*s.* [*Nearly ready.*

WELLS' JOSEPH AND HIS BRETHREN: A Scriptural Drama, and other Poems. By C. O. WELLS. With an Introductory Essay by ALGERNON CHARLES SWINBURNE. Crown 8vo, cloth extra. [*In the press.*

WESTWOOD'S PALÆOGRAPHIA SACRA PICTORIA: being a Series of Illustrations of the Ancient Versions of the Bible, copied from Illuminated Manuscripts, executed between the Fourth and Sixteenth Centuries. Royal 4to, with 50 beautifully Illuminated Plates, half-bound morocco, £3 10*s.*

WILD'S ENGLISH CATHEDRALS. Twelve select examples of the Ecclesiastical Architecture of the Middle Ages; beautifully coloured, after the Original Drawings by CHARLES WILD. Imperial folio, in portfolio, £4 4*s*.

WILD'S FOREIGN CATHEDRALS. Twelve fine plates, imperial folio, coloured, after the Original Drawings, by CHARLES WILD. In portfolio, £4 4*s*.

"These splendid plates are unequalled, whether bound as a volume, treasured in a portfolio, or framed for universal admiration."—*Athenæum*.

WILSON'S AMERICAN ORNITHOLOGY; or, Natural History of the Birds of the United States; with the Continuation by Prince CHARLES LUCIAN BONAPARTE. NEW AND ENLARGED EDITION, completed by the insertion of above One Hundred Birds omitted in the original Work, and Illustrated by valuable Notes, and Life of the Author, by Sir WILLIAM JARDINE. Three Vols., 8vo, with a fine Portrait of WILSON, and 103 Plates, exhibiting nearly four hundred figures of Birds accurately engraved and beautifully coloured, half-bound morocco. [*In the press.*

"The History of American Birds by Alexander Wilson is equal in elegance to the most distinguished of our own splendid works on Ornithology."—CUVIER.

WILSON'S FRENCH-ENGLISH AND ENGLISH-FRENCH DICTIONARY; containing full Explanations, Definitions, Synonyms, Idioms, Proverbs, Terms of Art and Science, and Rules for the Pronunciation of each Language. Compiled from the Dictionaries of the French Academy, BOYER, CHAMBAUD, GARNIER, LAVEAUX, DES CARRIÈRES and FAIN, JOHNSON, and WALKER. Imperial 8vo, 1,323 closely-printed pages, cloth extra, 15*s*.

WONDERFUL CHARACTERS: Memoirs and Anecdotes of Remarkable and Eccentric Persons of every Age and Nation. By HENRY WILSON and JAMES CAULFIELD. Crown 8vo, cloth extra, with 61 full-page Engravings, 7*s*. 6*d*.

WRIGHT'S (Andrew) COURT-HAND RESTORED; or, Student's Assistant in Reading Old Deeds, Charters, Records, &c. Folio, half-morocco, 10*s*. 6*d*.

WRIGHT'S CARICATURE HISTORY of the GEORGES (House of Hanover). With 400 Pictures, Caricatures, Squibs, Broadsides, Window Pictures, &c. By THOMAS WRIGHT, Esq., M.A., F.S.A. Crown 8vo, cloth extra, 7*s*. 6*d*.

"Emphatically one of the liveliest of books, as also one of the most interesting. Has the twofold merit of being at once amusing and edifying."—*Morning Post*.

WRIGHT'S HISTORY OF CARICATURE AND OF THE GROTESQUE IN ART, LITERATURE, SCULPTURE, AND PAINTING, from the Earliest Times to the Present Day. By THOMAS WRIGHT, M.A., F.S.A. Profusely Illustrated by F. W. FAIRHOLT, F.S.A. Large post 8vo, cloth extra, gilt, 7*s*. 6*d*.

"Almost overwhelms us with its infinite research. Mr. Wright dexterously guides the reader to a full survey of our English caricature, from its earliest efforts to the full-blown blossoms of a Rowlandson or a Gillray. The excellent illustrations of Mr. Fairholt add greatly to the value of the volume."—*Graphic*.

"A very amusing and instructive volume."—*Saturday Review*.

XENOPHON'S COMPLETE WORKS. Translated into English. Demy 8vo, with Steel-plate Portrait, a thick volume of 770 pages, 12*s*.

YANKEE DROLLERIES. Edited, with Introduction, by GEORGE AUGUSTUS SALA. In Three Parts, each complete in itself. Crown 8vo, cloth extra, 3*s*. 6*d*. per Vol.

J. OGDEN AND CO., PRINTERS, 172, ST. JOHN STREET, E.C.

DO NOT REMOVE
OR
MUTILATE CARD

CPSIA information can be obtained at www.ICGtesting.com
Printed in the USA
BVOW09s1206270516

449819BV00016B/328/P